TRACTABILITY

Classical computer science textbooks tell us that some problems are "hard". Yet many areas, from machine learning and computer vision, to theorem proving and software verification, have defined their own set of tools for effectively solving complex problems. *Tractability* provides an overview of these different techniques, and of the fundamental concepts and properties used to tame intractability.

This book will help you understand what to do when facing a hard computational problem. Can the problem be modelled by convex, or submodular functions? Will the instances arising in practice be of low treewidth, or exhibit another specific graph structure that makes them easy? Is it acceptable to use scalable, but approximate algorithms? A wide range of approaches is presented through self-contained chapters written by authoritative researchers on each topic. As a reference on a core problem in computer science, this book will appeal to theoreticians and practitioners alike.

LUCAS BORDEAUX is a Senior Research Software Development Engineer at Microsoft Research, where he works on the design and applications of algorithms to solve hard inference problems.

YOUSSEF HAMADI is a Senior Researcher at Microsoft Research. His work involves the practical resolution of large-scale real life problems set at the intersection of Optimization and Artificial Intelligence. His current research considers the design of complex systems based on multiple formalisms fed by different information channels which plan ahead and perform smart decisions. His current focus is on Autonomous Search, Parallel Search, and Propositional Satisfiability, with applications to Environmental Intelligence, Business Intelligence, and Software Verification.

PUSHMEET KOHLI is a Senior Research Scientist in the Machine Learning and Perception group at Microsoft Research. His research interests span the fields of Computer Vision, Machine Learning, Discrete Optimization, Game Theory, and Human-Computer Interaction with the overall aim of "teaching" computers to understand the behaviour and intent of human users, and to correctly interpret (or "see") objects and scenes depicted in colour/depth images or videos. In the context of tractability and optimization, Pushmeet has worked on developing adaptive combinatorial and message passing-based optimization algorithms that exploit the structure of large-scale optimization problems encountered in computer vision and machine learning to achieve improved performance.

TRACTABILITY

Edited by

LUCAS BORDEAUX
Microsoft Research

YOUSSEF HAMADI
Microsoft Research

PUSHMEET KOHLI
Microsoft Research

CAMBRIDGE
UNIVERSITY PRESS

CAMBRIDGE
UNIVERSITY PRESS

University Printing House, Cambridge CB2 8BS, United Kingdom

Cambridge University Press is part of the University of Cambridge.

It furthers the University's mission by disseminating knowledge in the pursuit of
education, learning, and research at the highest international levels of excellence.

www.cambridge.org
Information on this title: www.cambridge.org/9781107025196

© Cambridge University Press 2014

First published 2014

Printed in the United Kingdom by Bell and Bain Ltd

A catalogue record for this publication is available from the British Library

ISBN 978-1-107-02519-6 Hardback

Contents

Contributors

Lucas Bordeaux   *Microsoft Research, 21 Station Rd, Cambridge CB1 2FB, UK.*

lucasb@microsoft.com

Nikolaj Bjørner   *Microsoft Research, One Microsoft Way Redmond, WA 98052, USA.*

nbjorner@microsoft.com

Adnan Darwiche   *Computer Science Department, University of California Los Angeles, Los Angeles CA 90095-1596, USA.*

darwiche@cs.ucla.edu

Lara Dolecek   *Department of Electrical Engineering, University of California Los Angeles, Los Angeles CA 90095-1594, USA.*

dolecek@ee.ucla.edu

Fedor V. Fomin   *Department of Informatics, Universitetet i Bergen, Norway.*

fomin@ii.uib.no

Daniel Golovin   *Google, Inc., Mountain View CA 94043, USA.*

golovin@gmail.com

Georg Gottlob   *Department of Computer Science, University of Oxford, Wolfson Building, Parks Road, Oxford OX1 3QD, UK.*

georg.gottlob@cs.ox.ac.uk

Gianluigi Greco   *Department of Mathematics and Computer Science, Università degli Studi della Calabria, I-87036, Rende(CS), Italy.*

ggreco@mat.unical.it

Youssef Hamadi   *Microsoft Research, 21 Station Rd, Cambridge CB1 2FB, UK.*

youssef@microsoft.com

Peter G. Jeavons   *Department of Computer Science, University of Oxford, Wolfson Building, Parks Road, Oxford OX1 3QD, UK.*

Peter.Jeavons@cs.ox.ac.uk

Tony Jebara   *Department of Computer Science, Columbia University, New York, NY 10027, USA.*
jebara@cs.columbia.edu

Pushmeet Kohli   *Microsoft Research, 21 Station Rd, Cambridge CB1 2FB, UK.*
pkohli@microsoft.com

Vladimir Kolmogorov   *Institute of Science and Technology, Am Campus 1 3400 Klosterneuburg Austria.*
vladimir.kolmogorov@ist.ac.at

Andreas Krause   *Department of Computer Science, Eidgenössische Technische Hochschule Zürich, Universitätstrasse 6, 8092 Zurich, Switzerland.*
krausea@ethz.ch

Ines Lynce   *INESC-ID/IST, Technical University of Lisbon, Rua Alves Redol 9, 1000-029 Lisbon, Portugal.*
ines@sat.inesc-id.pt

Joao Marques-Silva   *CASL/CSI, University College Dublin, Belfield, Dublin 4, Ireland.*
jpms@ucd.ie

Leonardo de Moura   *Microsoft Research, One Microsoft Way Redmond, WA 98052, USA.*
Leonardo@microsoft.com

Saket Saurabh   *Institute of Mathematical Sciences, CIT Campus, Taramani, 600 113 Chennai, India.*
saket@imsc.res.in

Francesco Scarcello   *Department of Computer Science, Modelling, Electronics and Systems Engineering (DIMES), University of Calabria, I-87036, Rende(CS), Italy.*
scarcello@unical.it

Mohit Singh   *Microsoft Research, One Microsoft Way Redmond, WA 98052, USA.*
mohits@microsoft.com

Suvrit Sra   *Max Planck Institute for Intelligent Systems, 72076 Tübingen, Germany.*
suvrit@gmail.com

Kunal Talwar   *Microsoft Research Silicon Valley, 1065 La Avenida Mountain View, CA, 94043, USA.*
kunal@microsoft.com

Stanislav Živný   *Department of Computer Science, University of Oxford, Wolfson Building, Parks Road, Oxford OX1 3QD, UK*
standa@cs.ox.ac.uk

Introduction

Lucas Bordeaux, Youssef Hamadi, Pushmeet Kohli

In mathematics and computer science, optimization is the process of finding the best solution from a set of alternatives that satisfy some constraints. Many applications in allied fields of computer science like machine learning, computer vision, bioinformatics, involve the solution of an optimization problem. For instance, optimization is used to schedule trains and airplanes, allocate the advertisements we see on television or in connection with internet search results, find the optimal placement of sensors to detect and neutralize security threats, or even to make decisions on what is the best way to perform medical surgery on a patient.

Optimization problems are generally hard to solve – their solution may involve exhaustively searching over a set of solutions whose size could increase exponentially with the number of variables whose values we may want to infer. That said, in practice, many of these problems can often be solved with remarkable efficiency. This is usually done by dedicated techniques, developed in each and every application domain, that exploit the "properties" of the problems encountered in practice.

Over the last few decades, researchers working in a number of different disciplines have tried to solve optimization problems that are encountered in their respective fields by exploiting some structure or properties inherent in the problems. In some cases, they have been able to isolate classes of optimization problems that can be solved optimally in time polynomial in the number of variables, while in other cases, they have been able to develop efficient algorithms that can produce solutions that, although not optimal, are good enough. For instance, researchers working on computer vision problems have developed a range of techniques to solve very large scale optimization problems that arise while labelling impage pixels. Similar sets of techniques, tools and fundamental results have been developed by experts in machine learning, operations research, hardware/software verification, and other fields.

The goal of the proposed book is to bring together contributors from these various fields, to reflect on the state-of-the-art techniques for solving combinatorial optimization problems in these fields, and offer a multi-disciplinary understanding of the following question: which properties make hard computational problems solvable ("tractable") in practice?

The coverage of the contributions range from theory to practice, from software verification to computer vision. The researchers and practitioners in these areas work on apparently very different problems, but they are brought together by the common question:

How do we develop efficient algorithms for solving optimization problems?

The contributors to this book answer this question by identifying properties that make certain problems tractable or that allow the use of certain heuristics that can find solutions that are close to the optimal solution. In this introduction we aim to put the theme of tractability in perspective, and to provide a road map of the chapters.

Background

We conceived the book as a follow-up to a successful workshop organized at Microsoft Research, Cambridge, in July 2010[1]. The participants of this workshop were researchers working on solving optimization problems in diverse fields who had made important contributions to the analysis of tractability in their areas. The feedback we received from the participants revealed one main message: everyone was able to learn something new. Despite their extensive expertise, seeing the quest for tractability cast in a different light in a related field opened many opportunities for cross-fertilization and for a more unified view of the fundamentals.

It was this very positive feedback that prompted us to envision this volume, as an up-to-date and in-depth resource, built on multiple points of view coming from several communities.

Optimization Problems

Constraint satisfaction and optimization problems can be formulated in a number of different ways. We consider the following general description of optimization problems that can be described in terms of:

---

[1] http://research.microsoft.com/tractability2010/

- A set of a variables, $X = \{x_1, \ldots, x_n\}$;
- An objective function that is broken down into a number of terms $F = \{f_1, \ldots, f_m\}$, each of which is applied to a subset of variables $x_i \subseteq X$.

Specific problems make this high-level definition concrete by fully specifying:

- The range of the variables;
- The form allowed for the functions f_i;
- The way to aggregate the values of all of these functions.

For instance, the propositional satisfiability (SAT) problem is a special case where the variables range over $\{0, 1\}$, and the functions are Boolean constraints (usually clauses, as described in Chapter 12) that return 1 when satisfied and 0 otherwise. These constraints are aggregated as a sum, which we aim to maximize, which is one of several possible ways to indicate that we want to satisfy all constraints.

In other problems, the variables may range over arbitrary finite sets, or over the real numbers, or they may be logical variables in a language richer than the aforementioned (propositional) SAT framework, for instance the full first-order logic language. The terms in F can take diverse forms and they are usually aggregated into a global objective by summation or product[2].

While the framework described above is extremely abstract and general, it is important to understand its precise boundaries. In these formulations, a user, or domain expert, is required to translate the requirements and costs of the problem at hand into numerical functions, that can in turn be optimized using computational tools. In contrast, there is an important class of "black-box" optimization problems, where an analytical form of the objective function is not available, or cannot be written down mathematically. Instead, the problem is described by means of a black box, to which we can pass candidate solutions one by one, and that returns their quality. Optimizing functions described in such a black-box fashion require a different set of tools that exploit properties of the functions.

There is one important tool surveyed in this book that applies to black-box settings: submodularity. If we know that the function is submodular, then we can optimize it even if it is only available in a black-box form. When we cannot make this assumption, black-box problems fall out of the scope of this collection, because their intractability is due to *information-theoretic* reasons: what makes black-box settings intractable is that in many cases we simply do not know the function until we have queried the value of each

---

[2] Some communities focus by convention on products, which is justified by the observation that summations and products can be interchanged using the identity $\log(a \cdot b) = \log a + \log b$. In this case the graphical models are often referred to as *factor graphs*.

and every of its possible inputs. In contrast, the intractability of the model-based optimization problems we focus on is purely *complexity-theoretic*: the information about the function is all there, yet finding its optimal input may be computationally hard.

Graphical versus Language Properties

An important consequence of the framework previously described, is that there are two types of properties that can make problems tractable:

- *Graphical Properties* are properties of the (hyper-)graph (X, F). Here the functions $f \in F$ are seen purely as hyper-edges, i.e. in terms of what variables they connect, what patterns are found in the layout of these connections. The internal definition of these functions is here ignored. In some problems the graph has for instance a shape that is "tree-like" in a certain, formally-defined sense; in some others it belongs to a specific class such as *perfect* graphs. It is often possible to design algorithms that exploit these properties to solve the optimization problem more efficiently.
- What we call *Language Restrictions* are internal properties of the functions $f \in F$. These functions constitute building blocks, a "language" in which problems are described. If arbitrary functions are allowed, we have a language in which large classes of problems can be expressed, but that is in general intractable. Restricting carefully the types of functions available in this language can in a sense provide a tractability safeguard, preventing the user or modeller from writing down arbitrarily hard problems. The goal here is to find sweet spots: the interesting languages are those that are simple enough to avoid the intractability pitfall, yet expressive enough to capture interesting problems.

Types of Tractability

Graphical properties and language restrictions give rise, in fact, to several types of tractability. The goal is typically to use an algorithm whose runtime, as measured as a function of the input length, can be formally bounded[3]. This bound can be of different types:

Polynomial time guarantees: If the problem exhibits a certain graphical property, or is expressed within certain language restrictions, we can

---

[3] In this book we typically aim to bound the runtime *in the worst case*. One can sometimes refine this bound by analysing, further, the runtime *in expectation*, for certain distributions of problems.

sometimes determine that the time needed to solve it to optimality is bounded by a polynomial of the input length. This represents, in a sense, the ideal case: we have identified a tractable problem.

Controlled combinatorial explosion: In some cases there is no clear polynomial time guarantee, but we can identify a parameter p that is key in estimating problem hardness. This parameter will typically have an intractably high value in the worst case, but lower values in instances met in reality. For instance, problems with n variables might in fact have a "true dimensionality" that is significantly lower than n in the instances we are considering. The complexity is "exponential only" in the reduced dimension, which can be acceptable when this parameter is small enough. We can sometimes, as another example, apply a pre-processing technique that translates the problem into a form for which we know polynomial time algorithms. Such a translation typically blows-up in the worst case and the key parameter here is the size of the output of the pre-processing.

There remain, unfortunately, problems for which we cannot determine any reasonable bound on the runtime. These problems might still be solved in some cases, using the following approaches:

Approximations: Rather than looking for a global optimum to a model that is, after all, only an approximation of reality, it is sometimes acceptable to compute solutions that are only "close enough" to this optimum, or to solve a slightly different model that is tractable, provided that it does not deviate too much from the original model.

Heuristics: While complete algorithms have an exponential runtime in the worst case, the instances for which this worst case provably occurs are often "pathological" or "unnatural" problems: for instance artificially constructed, or completely random, problems that are unlikely to be found in practice. This is therefore a grey area in the resolution of intractable problems: we have an algorithm that has no provable runtime guarantee, and a problem that is not proved, or believed, to be hard. A common practice is to apply the algorithm to the problem and see whether it converges in an acceptable time.

Outline

We have divided the book into five parts:

- Part 1 focusses on fundamental concepts and techniques for graphical structure;

- Part 2 considers fundamental concepts and techniques for language restrictions;
- Part 3 looks at techniques and efficient algorithms for exact or approximate solutions;
- Part 4 focusses on how tractability is approached in different fields in computational sciences;
- Part 5 deals with heuristics.

We start with two chapters on fundamental concepts and techniques related to the two big classes of tractability properties we have mentioned: graphical structure and language restrictions.

Part 1: Graphical Structure

Part 1 starts with a chapter written by Georg Gottlob, Gianluigi Greco, and Francesco Scarcello who show how a number of optimization problems defined over tree (or *hyper-tree*) structures are tractable. Hyper-tree Width, which measures how "tree-like" the graphical model is, is identified as a important parameter for understanding graphical structure.

This is followed by a chapter by Tony Jebara that shows that a variety of hard problems such as graph colouring, maximum clique and maximum stable set are all solvable in polynomial time when the input graph is restricted to be a *perfect graph*.

Part 2: Language Restrictions

Part 2 starts with the chapter by Andreas Krause and Daniel Golovin on submodular function maximization. Submodular functions are a prime example of tractable language: restricting oneself to such functions when modelling a problem offers many tractability guarantees, for instance maximization problems can be approximated with provable bounds using simple and scalable heuristics.

This is followed by a chapter written by Peter G. Jeavons and Stanislav Živný that discusses the family of optimization problems that can be cast as valued constraint satisfaction problems (VCSPs) and provides examples of tractable cases.

Part 2 concludes with a chapter written by Adnan Darwiche which reviews a set of tractable knowledge representation formalisms. A key concept here is that of *Decomposable Negation Normal Forms (DNNF)* for Boolean formulae, a fairly broad class that supersedes, in particular, the widely used

Ordered Binary Decision Diagrams (OBDDs). Formulae that respect this syntactical restriction offer a number of tractability guarantees. This chapter illustrates the notion of tractability as "controlled combinatorial explosion" discussed above: logical formulae can be "compiled" into specific forms such as DNNF: this compilation is in the worst case itself intractable, but turns out to be feasible in interesting cases.

Part 3: Algorithms and their Analysis

Part 3 presents a number of algorithms and techniques that have been proposed to solve optimization problems in different disciplines.

It starts with a chapter from Vladimir Kolmogorov which describes the *tree-reweighted message passing* algorithm that is popularly used for inference of the Maximum a Posteriori (MAP) solutions in probabilistic graphical models.

This is followed by a chapter from Suvrit Sra that provides an overview of the methods used for solving *convex optimization* problems encountered in machine learning. This chapter considers optimization problems that are defined over continuous variables where the property of convexity plays a central role.

We then have a chapter from Mohit Singh and Kunal Talwar that describes techniques that have been developed in the design of *approximation algorithms*. The study of these algorithms is also a broad area in its own right, one that borrows concepts from all other tractability approaches. The chapter gives an overview of the rich possibilities, and also well-understood limitations, of these algorithms.

Part 3 ends with a chapter, written by Fedor V. Fomin and Saket Saurabh, that addresses the topic of kernelization methods for Fixed-Parametrized Complexity. Fixed Parameter Complexity offers a general perspective on the idea, presented above, of identifying key parameters that provide bounds on problem hardness. The chapter focusses specifically on kernelization methods, which provide a systematic study of pre-processing algorithms.

Part 4: Tractability in Some Specific Areas

This part deals with application of optimization algorithms in different application areas and mentions the latest results in the field.

We have a chapter by Pushmeet Kohli that describes the role played by submodular function minimization solvers (and in particular graph cuts), in the field of computer vision, for solving image labelling problems such as image segmentation.

In the final chapter of this part, Lara Dolecek writes about some applications of tractability concepts to coding theory. She shows how some techniques originating from graphical models play a major role in the success of Low Density Parity Codes. Decoding is in this context a seemingly complex task that is in practice handled with surprising efficiency. The author shares recent insights and explanations of this good behaviour.

Part 5: Heuristics

We conclude the book with contributions that explore an open frontier in tractability. Solvers for SAT (Boolean constraints) and for the more general framework of "Satisfiability Modulo Theories" are highly successful in applications such as software verification. These solvers belong to the heuristic category we described before, in that they can in theory consume unreasonable amounts of computational resources in the worst case, but that they turn out to be very efficient in certain classes of applications, for reasons that sometimes defy our current understanding. Like the other contributors, the authors we have invited for these chapters nonetheless succeed in fullfilling two requirements: that of overviewing the state of the art in their repective areas, and that of sharing formalized or personal insights on the causes of tractability.

Part 5 starts off with a chapter from J. Marques-Silva and I. Lynce that gives a high-level overview of the techniques used in popular *SAT solvers*.

This is followed by a chapter from Nikolaj Bjørner and Leonardo de Moura that deals with Modern Satisfiability Modulo Theories (SMT) solvers.

Conclusions

Understanding how to solve an optimization problem is often hard. There is not a well-defined property that singlehandedly determines whether the problem can be efficiently solved. Our current understanding is that there is a toolbox of methods to approach the problems, rather than a comprehensive, unified theory of problem tractability.

For practitioners this is a complicated state of affairs as they face a set of options when dealing with a specific problem, and should try to understand which techniques apply. Often several techniques will work, depending on whether they look at the problem from the viewpoint of graphical structure, of language restriction, or use, say, heuristic approaches. This collection should be a useful resource for such practitioners.

Ultimately, the broad range of viewpoints collected here does more than simply providing practical solutions and answers; it also gives us an overview of the deep questions that are currently open. In many applications such as those presented in the Propositional Satisfiability and Satisfiability Modulo Theory solvers, we have, indeed, a far from full understanding of, or agreement on, the reasons that make problems tractable.

What is it that makes these algorithms work dramatically better on instances found in practice, than on "worst-case" instances or "average-case" ones drawn from certain distributions? Have we explored all the facets of tractability, or can some new approaches emerge within or outside the known broad categories of graphical structure and knowledge restriction? Is there ultimately a unified way of making sense of tractability, or are we dealing with a phenomenon that intrinsically needs multi-faceted answers and solutions? These are some of the questions that are currently open. By overviewing the rich body of results developed across a number of research areas, and by also charting the limits of our current knowledge, we hope that this collection will also be useful to researchers who aim to advance the field.

Acknowledgements

We would like to thank Robert Mateescu, who was a co-organiser of the 2010 workshop and who contributed to early discussions about this book. We would also like to thank the staff at Cambridge University Press who worked hard on this volume: Clare Dennison, Róisín Munnelly and David Tranah.

PART 1

GRAPHICAL STRUCTURE

1

Treewidth and Hypertree Width

Georg Gottlob, Gianluigi Greco, Francesco Scarcello

This chapter covers methods for identifying islands of tractability for NP-hard combinatorial problems by exploiting suitable properties of their graphical structure. Acyclic structures are considered, as well as nearly-acyclic ones identified by means of so-called structural decomposition methods. In particular, the chapter focuses on the tree decomposition method, which is the most powerful decomposition method for graphs, and on the hypertree decomposition method, which is its natural counterpart for hypergraphs. These problem-decomposition methods give rise to corresponding notions of width of an instance, namely, treewidth and hypertree width. It turns out that many NP-hard problems can be solved efficiently over classes of instances of bounded treewidth or hypertree width: deciding whether a solution exists, computing a solution, and even computing an optimal solution (if some cost function over solutions is specified) are all polynomial-time tasks. Example applications include problems from artificial intelligence, databases, game theory, and combinatorial auctions.

Many NP-hard problems in different areas such as AI [42], Database Systems [6, 81], Game theory [45, 31, 20], and Network Design [34], are known to be efficiently solvable when restricted to instances whose underlying structures can be modeled via acyclic graphs or acyclic hypergraphs. For such restricted classes of instances, solutions can usually be computed via dynamic programming. However, as a matter of fact, (graphical) structures arising from real applications are in most relevant cases not properly acyclic. Yet, they are often not very intricate and exhibit some rather limited degree of cyclicity, which suffices to retain most of the nice properties of acyclic instances. Therefore, many efforts have been spent to investigate graph and hypergraph properties that are best suited to identify nearly-acyclic graph/hypergraphs, leading to the definition of a number of so-called *structural decomposition methods*.

In order to apply a decomposition method to a given problem, one first

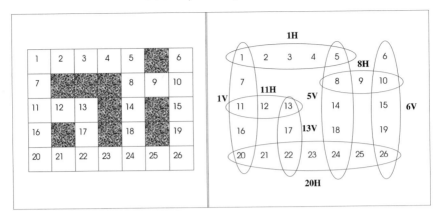

Figure 1.1 A crossword puzzle and its representation as a hypergraph $\mathcal{H}_0$.

needs to describe the structure of the problem through a graph or a hyper-graph. This means that, to each problem instance I, one associates a graph $G(I)$ or a hypergraph $H(I)$. Then, $G(I)$ or $H(I)$ is decomposed into pos-sibly overlapping chunks that have a tree-like (i.e., acyclic) interconnection pattern. The resulting data structure is called a *graph or hypergraph decom-position*. The *width of a decomposition* of a problem instance I corresponds to the size of the largest chunk occurring in the decomposition. The *width of the instance I* is then defined as the minimum width over all decompositions of I.

An overwhelming number of relevant decision or computation problems admit solution algorithms whose runtime is exponential in $O(w)$ where w is the width of the input instance. This means that for classes of bounded width, these problems are solvable in polynomial time. Given that many practical problem instances occurring in real life applications tend to be of low width, decomposition methods are currently among the most effective weapons against NP-hardness.

The structure of many problems is adequately described by graphs. In particular, this is the case when a graph is explicitly part of the problem instance, such as in graph coloring or network problems, or when the prob-lem is about a binary relationship, such as in matching problems, binary constraint networks, or precedence orderings, for example, for major ver-sions of job shop scheduling. For many other problems, however, a graphical representation in terms of hypergraphs is more appropriate. This is usually the case when relations of unbounded arities or families of sets are part of the problem description. For example, in the crossword puzzle depicted on the left of Figure 1.1, empty fields, that are placeholders for letters, are grouped together to form placeholders for words. In general, a word-field consists of several letter-fields. The structure of such a puzzle is thus best described in terms of a hypergraph, as illustrated on the right of Figure 1.1. Examples for other problems whose structure is most adequately described by hypergraphs are general constraint satisfaction problems, conjunctive database queries, and combinatorial auctions, which will all be explained in Section 1.3. Examples where other notions of problem structures (not necessarily graph-based) are more useful for identifying tractable instances are described in other chapters of this book.

This chapter focuses on two relevant decomposition methods for (hyper)graph based structures: the *treewidth*, which is the most powerful decomposition method on graphs, and the *hypertree width*, which is its natural counter-part over hypergraphs. Both methods are specializations of a more general decomposition scheme called *tree projection*, which we will briefly illustrate in Section 1.4.

The rest of this chapter is organized as follows. In Section 1.1 we review the notion of *treewidth*, and in Section 1.2 the notion of *(generalized) hypertree width*, by providing their direct definitions, looking at their connections, and giving pointers to their most recent extensions. A number of applications of such decomposition methods are illustrated. In particular, Section 1.3 discusses tractability results for the *constraint satisfaction (optimization) problem* (CSP), as this is a fundamental framework which is able to express many problems from different fields. Moreover, our current knowledge on the tractability frontier for such problems is illustrated in Section 1.5.

1.1 Treewidth

The concept of treewidth [72], based on tree decompositions of graphs, constitutes a significant success story of Theoretical Computer Science.

There are different possible notions to measure how far a graph is from a tree, that is, to measure its degree of cyclicity or, dually, its tree-likeness (see, e.g., [36]). Among them, the treewidth is provably the most powerful one, in that it is able to extend the nice computational properties of trees to the largest possible classes of graphs, in many applications from different fields.

Definition 1.1 ([72]) A *tree decomposition* of a graph $G = (N, E)$ is a pair $\langle T, \chi \rangle$, where $T = (V, F)$ is a tree, and χ is a labeling function assigning to each vertex $p \in V$ a set of vertices $\chi(p) \subseteq N$, such that the following three conditions are satisfied: (1) for each node b of G, there exists $p \in V$

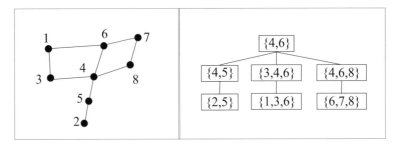

Figure 1.2 A graph G_0 and a tree decomposition for it.

such that $b \in \chi(p)$; (2) for each edge $(b, d) \in E$, there exists $p \in V$ such that $\{b, d\} \subseteq \chi(p)$; and (3) for each node b of G, the set $\{p \in V \mid b \in \chi(p)\}$ induces a connected subtree of T.

The *width* of $\langle T, \chi \rangle$ is the number $\max_{p \in V}(|\chi(p)| - 1)$. The *treewidth* of G, denoted by $tw(G)$, is the minimum width over all its tree decompositions.□

Note that treewidth is a true generalization of graph acyclicity. Indeed, a graph G is acyclic if and only if $tw(G) = 1$.

For example, the graph G_0 reported in Figure 1.2 is cyclic and its treewidth is 2, as it is witnessed by the width-2 tree decomposition depicted in the same figure.

Complexity of Treewidth. To determine the treewidth of a graph G is NP-hard. However, for each fixed natural number k, checking whether $tw(G) \leq k$, and if so, computing a tree decomposition for G of optimal width, is achievable in linear time [8], and was recently shown to be achievable in logarithmic space [26]. Note that the multiplicative constant factor of Bodlaender's linear algorithm [8] is exponential in k. However, there are algorithms that find exact tree decompositions in reasonable time or good upper approximations in many cases of practical relevance—see, for example, [9, 10] and the references therein.

Game-Theoretic Characterization. An alternative definition of treewidth is based on the *robber and cops* game, which is played on a graph $G = (N, E)$ by a robber and a set of cops. The robber stands on a node and can run at great speed along the edges of G; however, she is not permitted to run trough a node that is controlled by a cop. Note that the robber is fast and may see cops that are entering in action. Therefore, while cops move, the robber may run trough those positions that are left by cops or not yet occupied. The goal of the cops is to occupy the vertex on which the robber

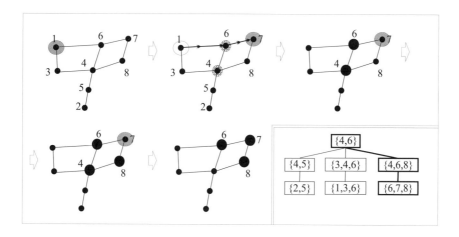

Figure 1.3 The robber and cop game played on the graph G_0 of Figure 1.2.

stands, while the robber tries to avoid her capture. A graph has treewidth bounded by k if and only if $k + 1$ cops can capture the robber [78].

Example 1.2   Consider the robber and cops game played on the graph G_0 of Figure 1.2, and the moves illustrated in Figure 1.3: The robber initially stands on node 1. Then, two cops enter in action by occupying 4 and 6. While these cops are moving, the robber can go to node 7 in a very fast way. Then, another cop comes into play by occupying node 8, thus blocking the robber at node 7. Eventually, the cop that is currently placed at node 4 moves to node 7, and hence captures the robber. Note that the sequence of moves leading to the capture of the robber corresponds to one branch of the tree decomposition of G_0 depicted in Figure 1.2 (and replicated in Figure 1.3, with such branch being evidenced). In fact, the correspondence is not by chance: the depicted width-2 tree decomposition can be seen as encoding a "winning strategy" for 3 cops.   ◁

Note that in the game there is no restriction on the strategy employed by cops to capture the robber. In particular, they are not forced to play *monotonic strategies*, that is, to shrink the robber's escape space in a monotonically decreasing way. However, it was shown in [78] that playing non-monotonic strategies gives no more power to cops. Many results about treewidth are proved simply and elegantly by exploiting the game-theoretic characterization. In particular, the above equivalence between monotonic and non-monotonic capturing strategies turns out to be very useful, because good strategies for the robber may be easily characterized as those strategies that allow the robber to run forever. See [3], for an interesting application of the robber-and-cops game in proofs regarding the power of *k-Consistency* in *constraint satisfaction problems*.

1.1.1 Applications to Decision Problems

Tree decompositions and polynomial algorithms for bounded treewidth are among the most effective weapons to attack NP-hard problems, namely, by recognizing and efficiently solving large classes of tractable problem instances. In particular, the notion of treewidth is at the base of strong meta-theorems such as Courcelle's Theorem [18], which states that any problem expressible in monadic second-order logic (MSO) over structures of bounded treewidth can be solved in linear time. Many problems are easily expressed in terms of MSO, and thus Courcelle's theorem turns out to be a very effective tool for obtaining tractability results.

Finite Structures. The notion of treewidth is easily generalized from graphs to finite structures. A vocabulary τ is a finite set of relation symbols $R_1, \ldots, R_k$ of arities $a_1, \ldots, a_k$, respectively. A relational structure $\mathcal{A}$ over τ consists of a finite domain A and an a_i-ary relation $R_i^{\mathcal{A}} \subseteq A^{a_i}$, for each relation symbol R_i in τ. The *size* of $\mathcal{A}$, denoted by $||\mathcal{A}||$, is the value $||\mathcal{A}|| = |A| + \sum_{j=1}^{k} |R_j| \times a_j$. For further background on finite structures, the interested reader is referred to textbooks on finite model theory (e.g., [44]).

For instance, a graph $G = (N, E)$ can be viewed as a finite structure whose domain is N, and where E is a binary relation encoding its edges.

The *Gaifman graph* of a structure $\mathcal{A}$ is the undirected graph $G(\mathcal{A})$ whose vertices are the elements of the domain of $\mathcal{A}$, and where there is an edge between the elements e and e' if and only if there is a tuple of some relation of $\mathcal{A}$ where e and e' jointly occur. The treewidth of $\mathcal{A}$, denoted by $tw(\mathcal{A})$, is the treewidth of its Gaifman graph, i.e., $tw(\mathcal{A}) = tw(G(\mathcal{A}))$.

MSO. A First Order logic formula is made up of relation symbols, individual variables (usually denoted by lowercase letters), the logical connectives $\vee$, $\wedge$, and $\neg$, and the quantifiers $\exists$ and $\forall$. Monadic Second Order (MSO) enhances the expressiveness of first order logic by allowing the use of set variables (usually denoted by uppercase letters), of the membership relation $\in$, and of the quantifiers $\exists$ and $\forall$ over set variables. In addition, it is often convenient to use symbols like $\subseteq$, $\subset$, $\cap$, $\cup$, and $\rightarrow$ with their usual meaning, as abbreviations. When an MSO formula ϕ is evaluated over a finite structure $\mathcal{A}$, the relation symbols of ϕ are interpreted as the corresponding relations of $\mathcal{A}$ and the variables of ϕ range over the domain A of $\mathcal{A}$. The fact that an MSO formula ϕ holds over $\mathcal{A}$ is denoted by $\mathcal{A} \models \phi$. For a graph G (viewed as a finite structure), this is just meant to state that G satisfies the property expressed by the formula ϕ, as we illustrate below.

Example 1.3   Let $G = (N, E)$ be an undirected graph (interpreted as a finite structure). Then, the fact that G is *3-colorable* can be expressed via the following MSO formula:

$$
\begin{aligned}
\exists R, B, Y, \quad & R \cup B \cup Y = N \ \wedge \\
& R \cap B = \emptyset \ \wedge \ R \cap Y = \emptyset \ \wedge \ B \cap Y = \emptyset \ \wedge \\
& \forall x, \ x \in B \to (\forall y, \{x, y\} \in E \to \neg(y \in B)) \ \wedge \\
& \forall x, \ x \in R \to (\forall y, \{x, y\} \in E \to \neg(y \in R)) \ \wedge \\
& \forall x, \ x \in Y \to (\forall y, \{x, y\} \in E \to \neg(y \in Y))
\end{aligned}
$$

In particular, note that the formula checks whether there exists a partition of the nodes in N into three disjoint sets of nodes R, B, and Y, which respectively correspond to the nodes that are colored red, blue, and yellow. Moreover, the formula checks that for each node, all its adjacent nodes are colored with a different color. ◁

The next theorem relates treewidth to MSO.

Theorem 1.4   *Let ϕ be a fixed MSO sentence, let k be a fixed constant, and let $\mathcal{C}_k$ be a class of finite structures having treewidth bounded by k. Then, for each finite structure $\mathcal{A} \in \mathcal{C}_k$, deciding whether $\mathcal{A} \models \phi$ holds is feasible in linear time [18] and logarithmic space [26] (with respect to $||\mathcal{A}||$).*

From the above theorem and Example 1.3, we can conclude that 3-colorability is a property that can be efficiently checked on classes of graphs having bounded treewidth, while, on arbitrary classes of graphs, the problem is a well-known NP-complete problem.

1.1.2 Applications to Optimization Problems

An important generalization of MSO formulae to *optimization* problems was presented by [2].

Let $\mathcal{A}$ be a finite structure over the domain A, and let w be a list of weights associated with the elements in A, such that $w(v)$ is a rational number for each $v \in A$. The pair $\langle \mathcal{A}, w \rangle$ is hereinafter called a *weighted finite structure*, and its size $||\langle \mathcal{A}, w \rangle||$ is defined as the size of $\mathcal{A}$ plus all the values (numerators and denominators) in w.

Let $\phi(\bar{X})$ be an MSO formula over $\mathcal{A}$, where $\bar{X}$ is the set of free second-order variables (i.e., set variables) occurring in ϕ. For an interpretation $\mathcal{I}$ mapping variables in $\bar{X}$ to subsets of A, we denote by $\phi[\mathcal{I}]$ the MSO formula (without free variables) where each variable $X \in \bar{X}$ is replaced by $\mathcal{I}(X)$.

A *solution* to ϕ over $\langle \mathcal{A}, w \rangle$ is an interpretation $\mathcal{I}$ such that $\mathcal{A} \models \phi[\mathcal{I}]$ holds. The *cost* of $\mathcal{I}$ is the value $\sum_{X \in \bar{X}} \sum_{v \in \mathcal{I}(X)} w(e)$. A solution of minimum cost is said *optimal*.

Example 1.5 Let $G = (N, E)$ be an undirected graph (interpreted as a finite structure). Then, the property that a set X of vertices is a *vertex cover*, i.e., a set such that each edge in E has at least one endpoint incident on it, can be expressed via the *vertexCover*(X) formula (where X is its free variable) defined as follows:

$$X \subseteq N \wedge (\forall x \in N \forall y \in N, \{x, y\} \in E \rightarrow (x \in X) \vee (y \in X))$$

By considering a list w of weights assigning 1 to each vertex in N, we have that an optimal solution to *vertexCover* over $\langle G, w \rangle$ is a minimum-cardinality vertex cover.   ◁

The result below shows that not only the decision problem, but even the associated problem of *computing* a solution of minimum cost is feasible in polynomial time on bounded-treewidth structures.

Theorem 1.6 (simplified from [2]) *Let ϕ be a fixed MSO sentence, let k be a fixed constant, and let $\mathcal{C}_k$ be a class of finite structures having treewidth bounded by k. Then, for each weighted finite structure $\langle \mathcal{A}, w \rangle$ such that $\mathcal{A} \in \mathcal{C}_k$, computing an optimal solution to ϕ over $\langle \mathcal{A}, w \rangle$ is feasible in polynomial time (with respect to $\|\langle \mathcal{A}, w \rangle\|$).*

From the above theorem and Example 1.5, we can immediately conclude that computing a minimum-cardinality vertex cover is feasible in polynomial time on classes of graphs having bounded treewidth whereas, on arbitrary classes of graphs, it is NP-hard.

1.2 Hypertree width

The structure of a computational problem is sometimes better described by a hypergraph rather than by a graph. This is, in particular, the case if local relationships involve many elements together, such as in the case of relational structures with large arities. Therefore, various width-notions for hypergraphs have been defined and studied, and often these are more

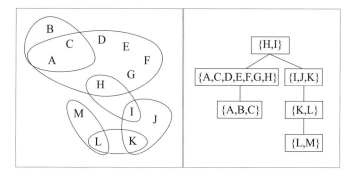

Figure 1.4 A hypergraph $\mathcal{H}_1$ and a join tree $JT(\mathcal{H}_1)$.

effective than simply applying the treewidth on a suitable "binarization" [36, 47].

Width-notions for hypergraphs come as generalizations of *hypergraph acyclicity*, which is recalled next.

A hypergraph $\mathcal{H}$ is *acyclic* iff it has a join tree [6]. A *join tree $JT(\mathcal{H})$* for a hypergraph $\mathcal{H}$ is a tree whose vertices are the hyperedges of $\mathcal{H}$ such that, whenever the same node $X \in V$ occurs in two hyperedges h_1 and h_2 of $\mathcal{H}$, then X occurs in each vertex on the unique path linking h_1 and h_2 in $JT(\mathcal{H})$ (connectedness condition for X). Note that this notion of acyclicity is the most general one known in the literature, coinciding with α-acyclicity according to Fagin [27].

For example, the hypergraph $\mathcal{H}_1$ shown on the left of Figure 1.4 is acyclic as it is witnessed by the join tree $JT(\mathcal{H}_1)$. Instead, the reader can check that the hypergraph $\mathcal{H}_1'$ shown on the left of Figure 1.5, obtained by adding an edge $\{B, M\}$ to $\mathcal{H}_1$, is not acyclic. Indeed, there is no way to build a join tree for it. For instance, the reader may check that every attempt to add a vertex for $\{B, M\}$ to the join tree shown in Figure 1.4 does not satisfy the connectedness condition for B or M. Similarly, it can be seen that the hypergraph $\mathcal{H}_0$ reported on the right of Figure 1.1 is not acyclic, too.

1.2.1 Embedding Hypergraphs in (Hyper)trees

The natural counter-part of the tree decomposition method over hypergraphs is the notion of (generalized) hypertree decomposition [39, 38]. In the following, for a hypergraph $\mathcal{H} = (V, H)$, we denote by $\mathcal{N}(\mathcal{H})$ and $\mathcal{E}(\mathcal{H})$ the sets V and H, respectively. Moreover, its associated *primal graph* is defined over the same set $\mathcal{N}(\mathcal{H})$ of nodes and contains an edge for each pair of nodes included in some hyperedge of $\mathcal{E}(\mathcal{H})$.

A *hypertree for a hypergraph* $\mathcal{H}$ is a triple $\langle T, \chi, \lambda \rangle$, where $T = (N, E)$ is a rooted tree, and χ and λ are labeling functions that associate with each vertex $p \in N$ two sets $\chi(p) \subseteq \mathcal{N}(\mathcal{H})$ and $\lambda(p) \subseteq \mathcal{E}(\mathcal{H})$. The *width* of a hypertree is the cardinality of its largest λ label, i.e., $\max_{p \in N} |\lambda(p)|$.

Hypertree decompositions are similar to tree decompositions, but for the associated notion of width, which is determined by a minimum hyperedge covering of the sets of nodes in the χ labeling.

Definition 1.7 [40] A *generalized hypertree decomposition* of a hypergraph $\mathcal{H}$ is a hypertree $HD = \langle T, \chi, \lambda \rangle$ for $\mathcal{H}$, where $\langle T, \chi \rangle$ is a tree decomposition of the primal graph of $\mathcal{H}$, and λ is a function labeling the vertices of T by sets of hyperedges of $\mathcal{H}$ such that, for each $p \in vertices(T)$, $\chi(p) \subseteq \bigcup_{h \in \lambda(v)} h$. That is, all nodes in the χ labeling are covered by hyperedges in the λ labeling.

A *hypertree decomposition* is a generalized hypertree decomposition that satisfies the following additional condition, called *Descendant Condition* or also *special condition*: $\forall p \in vertices(T), \forall h \in \lambda(p), h \cap \chi(T_p) \subseteq \chi(p)$, where T_p denotes the subtree of T rooted at p, and $\chi(T_p)$ the set of all variables occurring in the χ labeling of this subtree. $\square$

Note that the notions of hypertree width and generalized hypertree width are true generalizations of acyclicity, as the acyclic hypergraphs are precisely those hypergraphs having hypertree width and generalized hypertree width one [40].

Example 1.8   Recall the hypergraph $\mathcal{H}_1'$ shown in Figure 1.5. We have already observed that this hypergraph is not acyclic because it has no join tree. However, the connectedness condition for all nodes may be fulfilled if one may use additional nodes, possibly taken from multiple hyperedges, to label the desired tree. Indeed, this behavior may be observed in the tree decomposition of the primal graph of $\mathcal{H}_1'$ shown in the left part of Figure 1.5.

Note that the width of this decomposition is 7, because the notion of treewidth is based on the number of nodes used in each label. However, this hypergraph is evidently quasi-acyclic. And in fact the hypertree width of $\mathcal{H}_1'$ is at most 2, because all sets of nodes used in the labels may be covered by two hyperedges at most, as witnessed by the hypertree decomposition in the bottom part of Figure 1.5. To complete the picture, we may also conclude that the hypertree width of $\mathcal{H}_1'$ is precisely 2, because the fact that it is cyclic entails $hw(\mathcal{H}_1') > 1$. $\lhd$

At a first glance, a generalized hypertree decomposition may simply be viewed as a clustering of the hyperedges where the classical connectedness

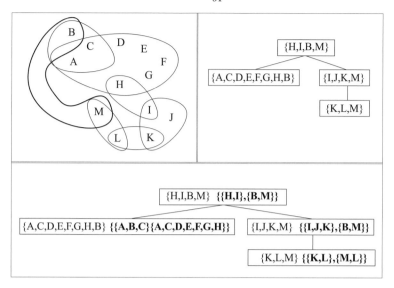

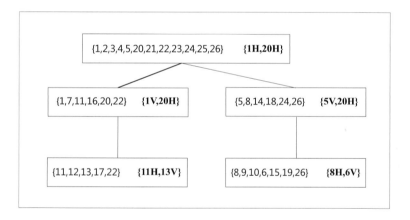

Figure 1.5 A hypergraph $\mathcal{H}'_1$, a tree decomposition for its primal graph, and a width-2 hypertree decomposition for $\mathcal{H}'_1$.

Figure 1.6 A width-2 hypertree decomposition for the hypergraph $\mathcal{H}_0$ reported on the right of Figure 1.1.

condition of join trees holds. However, this is not the case, as it can be seen by looking in more detail at the two labels associated with each vertex p: the set of hyperedges $\lambda(p)$, and the set of *effective* nodes $\chi(p)$, which are subject to the connectedness condition. In particular, all nodes that appear in the hyperedges of $\lambda(p)$ but that are not included in $\chi(p)$ are "ineffective" for v and do not count with respect to the connectedness condition.

Example 1.9 Reconsider the hypergraph $\mathcal{H}_0$ reported on the right of

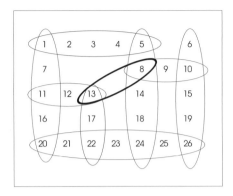

Figure 1.7 The hypergraph $\mathcal{H}_0'$ in Example 1.9.

Figure 1.1 and associated with the crossword puzzle. The hypergraph is not acyclic, and a width-2 hypertree decomposition of it is shown in Figure 1.6, thus witnessing that $hw(\mathcal{H}_0) = 2$. Note, for instance, that the hyperedge $20H$ is used in 3 distinct vertices of the decomposition. In all such occurrences but for that in the root, some of the nodes in $20H$ are "ineffective".

Finally, for a further example, consider the hypergraph $\mathcal{H}_0'$ shown in Figure 1.7, and note that $\mathcal{H}_0'$ is obtained by adding one hyperedge to the hypergraph $\mathcal{H}_0$ shown in Figure 1.1. It can be checked that there exists no width-2 hypertree decomposition of $\mathcal{H}_0'$. In fact, $hw(\mathcal{H}_0') = 3$. ◁

1.2.2 Complexity Issues

Choosing a decomposition tree and suitable χ and λ vertex labelings in order to get a hypertree decomposition below a fixed threshold-width k is not that easy, and it is definitely more difficult than computing a simple tree decomposition.

In fact, it has been shown that generalized hypertree-width is an intractable notion, as deciding whether a hypergraph has generalized hypertree width at most k is an NP-complete problem, for any fixed $k \geq 3$ [41]. It is thus very nice and somehow surprising that dealing with hypertree width is a very easy task. More precisely, for any fixed $k \geq 1$, deciding whether a given hypergraph has hypertree width at most k is in LOGCFL. For the sake of completeness, we recall here that the class LOGCFL consists of all decision problems that are logspace reducible to a context-free language, and that it contains many interesting and natural complete problems, such as evaluating (Boolean) acyclic conjunctive queries [37]. Moreover, the relationship between LOGCFL and other well-known complexity classes can be summarized in the following chain of inclusions:

$$AC^0 \subseteq NC^1 \subseteq L \subseteq NL \subseteq LOGCFL \subseteq AC^1 \subseteq NC^2 \subseteq P,$$

where L denotes logspace, AC^i and NC^i are *logspace-uniform* classes based on the corresponding types of Boolean circuits, NL denotes nondeterministic logspace, and P is polynomial time—for definitions of all these classes, see [57].

Note that, since $LOGCFL \subseteq AC^1 \subseteq NC^2$, deciding whether a given hypergraph has hypertree width at most k is a highly parallelizable problem. Correspondingly, the search problem of computing a k-bounded hypertree decomposition belongs to the functional version of LOGCFL, which is L^{LOGCFL} [39]. However, unlike treewidth for which a linear-time algorithm exists, the problem of deciding whether, for a hypergraph $\mathcal{H}$, $hw(\mathcal{H}) \leq k$ is fixed-parameter intractable (more precisely, W[2]-hard) in the parameter k [33]. Therefore, unless some unlikely collapse occurs in fixed-parameter complexity theory, a bad exponential dependency of the form $O(f_1(n)^{f_2(k)})$ is unavoidable in the running time of sound and complete algorithms. See the chapter by Fomin and Saraubh in this collection, for an introduction to the main concepts in the theory of fixed parameter tractability.

Of course, the notion of hypertree width is less general than the notion of generalized hypertree width. However, it provides a good approximation for generalized hypertree width as, for each hypergraph $\mathcal{H}$, $ghw(\mathcal{H}) \leq hw(\mathcal{H}) \leq 3 \times ghw(\mathcal{H}) + 1$ [1].

1.2.3 Algorithms for Hypertree Computation

Several efforts have been spent in the last few years to define algorithms for hypertree computation. See the Hypertree Decomposition Home Page [75], for available implementations of algorithms for computing hypertree decompositions, and further links to heuristics and other papers on this subject.

Exact approaches. The first proposal in the literature appeared in [39], where an algorithm called k-decomp was presented constructing a ("normalform") hypertree decomposition of minimal width less than or equal to k (if such a decomposition exists). However, k-decomp "runs" on alternating Turing machines using logarithmic workspace, and hence is not designed for real-world applications. A more practical algorithm, named opt-k-decomp, was obtained in [35] by "uprolling" k-decomp in a sequential bottom-up fashion. The algorithm runs in $O(m^{2k}v^2)$ time, where m and v are the number of edges and the number of nodes of the hypergraph, respectively. This algorithm was improved subsequently in [55], where some techniques for limiting redundant computations have been discussed, which actually do not improve the asymptotic worst-case bounds of the original algorithm.

Another approach to the computation of hypertree decompositions was discussed in [80]. Its basic idea is to exploit a backtracking procedure that stops as soon as it discovers a decomposition of width at most k (differently from opt-k-decomp, which implicitly builds a structure from which it is possible to enumerate easily all possible normal-form decompositions of width at most k). The (worst case) time complexity of this approach is $O(v^{3k+3})$.

Heuristics. Most recent research focuses on heuristic approaches for the construction of (generalized) hypertree decompositions of "small" but not necessarily minimal width.

For instance, generalized hypertree decompositions can be constructed starting from tree decompositions, and subsequently covering the variables at each vertex label by a small number of hyperedges. This latter condition can be straightforwardly implemented by set covering (heuristics), so that it is possible to use tree decomposition heuristics for the construction of generalized hypertree decompositions. In particular, *Bucket Elimination* [22] is used in combination with several variable ordering heuristics in [64].

Another technique was discussed in [74], which shows how to use the *branch-decomposition* approach for ordinary graphs [17] for the heuristic construction of generalized hypertree decompositions (based on the fact that every branch decomposition of width k can be transformed into a tree decomposition of width at most $3k/2$).

Reference [60] investigates the idea of computing generalized hypertree decompositions based on the tree decompositions of the primal and of the dual graph.

The use of tabu search for computing (generalized) hypertree decompositions was considered in [66].

More recently, [43] considered a combination of exact and heuristic approaches in the sense that the search space is restricted by a fixed upper bound k, and some heuristics are used to accelerate the search for a generalized hypertree decomposition of width at most k (but not necessarily the minimal one). The resulting algorithm det-k-decomp is based on backtracking, and can also be implemented for parallel executions.

1.2.4 Game-Theoretic Characterizations

Even though the formal definitions of hypertree and generalized hypertree width are quite involved, these notions (similarly to treewidth) have very natural game-theoretic characterizations. Having a game view of graph-theoretic notions not only helps grasping their meaning, but also provides a useful tool for both practical applications and formal results. For instance, game winning-strategies are often related to suitable "normal-form" decompositions. Such decompositions have been used both to speed up the computation of hypertree decompositions and to formally prove that the NP-hard notion of generalized hypertree width is in fact in NP (cf. [32]).

Hypertree Width. *The robber and marshals game* is played by one robber and a number of marshals on a hypergraph. The robber moves on nodes, while marshals move on hyperedges. At each step, any marshal controls an entire hyperedge. During a move of the marshals from the set of hyperedges E to the set of hyperedges E', the robber cannot pass through the nodes in $B = (\cup E) \cap (\cup E')$, where, for a set of hyperedges F, $\cup F$ denotes the union of all hyperedges in F. Intuitively, the vertices in B are those not released by the marshals during their move. The game is won by the marshals if they corner and capture the robber somewhere in the hypergraph, by monotonically shrinking the moving space of the robber. A hypergraph $\mathcal{H}$ has k-bounded hypertree width if, and only if, k marshals win the robber and marshals game on $\mathcal{H}$ [40].

Example 1.10 Consider the robber and marshals game played on the hypergraph $\mathcal{H}_0$ of Figure 1.1, and the moves illustrated in Figure 1.8: the robber initially stands on node 11. Then, two marshals enter in action and block hyperedges $1H$ and $20H$. During the move of the marshals, the robber is fast enough to move on any node of the hypergraph that will not be blocked by them. For instance, the robber might in principle move to node 14. In fact, the robber decides to move to 11 and, hence, (s)he is now confined to the set of nodes $\{7, 11, 12, 13, 16, 17\}$. No matter of the move of the robber, one marshal keeps blocked $20H$ while the other one occupies $1V$. Note that during this move the marshal releases all nodes in $\{2, 3, 4, 5\}$, but still blocks node 1 (which is covered by both $20H$ and $1V$). It follows that the robber cannot escape via node 1, and is now confined to move over $\{12, 13, 17\}$. In fact, no matter of the next move of the robber, the two marshals can now capture the robber by moving on $11H$ and $13V$. Again, note that during this move the "escape doors" of the robber (nodes 11 and 22) remain blocked.

Note that the above described sequence of moves leading to the capture of

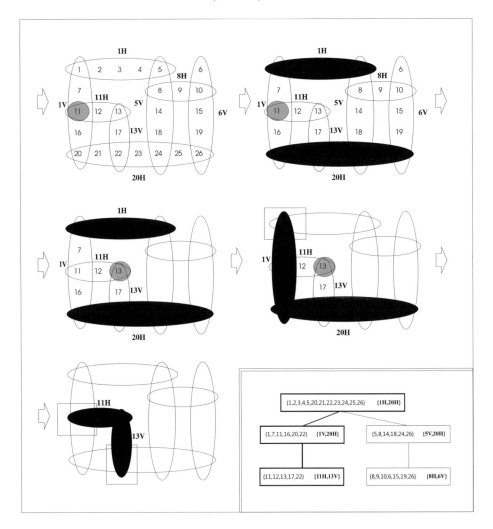

Figure 1.8 The robber and marshal game played on the hypergraph $\mathcal{H}_0$.

the robber corresponds to one branch of the hypertree decomposition of $\mathcal{H}_0$ depicted in Figure 1.1 (and replicated in Figure 1.8, with such branch being evidenced). In fact, the correspondence is not by chance: the depicted width-2 hypertree decomposition can be seen as encoding a "winning strategy" for 2 marshals.   ◁

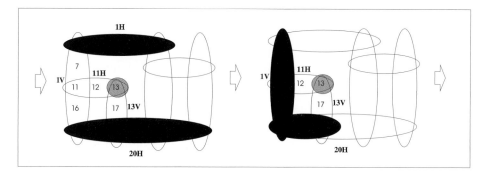

Figure 1.9 A move in the captain and robber game played on the hypergraph $\mathcal{H}_0$ of Figure 1.1.

Generalized Hypertree Width. The *captain and robber game* is played on a hypergraph, by a robber and a captain controlling some squads of cops.[1] The robber stands on a vertex and can run at great speed along the edges; however, (s)he is not permitted to run trough a vertex that is controlled by a cop. Each move of the captain involves one squad of cops, which is encoded as an edge h. The captain may ask *any subset* of cops in the squad h to run in action, as long as they occupy vertices that are currently reachable by the robber, thereby blocking an escape path for the robber. Thus, "second-lines" cops cannot be activated by the captain. The goal of the captain is to place a cop on the vertex occupied by the robber. A hypergraph $\mathcal{H}$ has k-bounded generalized hypertree width if, and only if, a captain controlling k squad of cops wins the captain and robber game on $\mathcal{H}$ [46]. Note that, in contrast with the previous game, in this case the captain is not forced to block entirely a hyperedge with a squad, and (s)he is not required to shrink monotonically the escape-space of the robber. In fact, it turns out that non-monotonic strategies give no more power to the captain [46], similarly to the game characterizing the treewidth.

Example 1.11 In order to understand the main difference between the robber and cops game and the robber and marshals game, consider again the moves depicted in Figure 1.8. In particular, let us focus on the first step where the two marshals occupy $1H$ and $20H$. In the captain and robber game, the same starting configuration may occur as well, because the captain may ask the two squads (associated with hyper edges) $1H$ and $20H$ to enter in action (see Figure 1.9). After this move, either the robber is

---

[1] This game is actually the specialization to generalized hypertree decompositions of the homonymous game played on pairs of hypergraphs that characterizes tree projections [46].

confined to the set of nodes $\{7, 11, 12, 13, 16, 17\}$, or to the set of nodes $\{6, 8, 9, 10, 14, 15, 18, 19\}$, as in the robber and marshals game.

Consider in particular hyperedge $20H$: either nodes 23, 24, 25, 26, or nodes 20, 21, 22, and 23 are no longer reachable by the robber. Hence, they are second-lines and cannot be used by the captain. However, any subset of nodes (cops) potentially useful to actually constrain robber's moves may freely be selected to enter in action. For instance, with the former choice of the robber (say standing on node 13), in the subsequent step the captain may employ the full squad $1V$ and the two cops on nodes 20 and 21 from squad $20H$. In this case the game immediately ends with a final step where the two squads $11H$ and $13V$ enter in action, and the robber cannot move any more.   ◁

1.3 Applications of hypertree width

The notion of (generalized) hypertree width has been exploited profitably in the last few years to single out islands of tractability to a broad spectrum of problems in different application areas. Differently from tree decompositions, there is no theorem à la Courcelle to be used for establishing tractability results for instances having bounded hypertree width via some logic-based encodings. In this case, a useful tool to isolate tractable instances of some given problem is to establish a structure-preserving polynomial-time reduction to some problem for which islands of tractability are already known. In the following, we shall illustrate such a tool for a number of application examples, by focusing on tractable classes of the *constraint satisfaction problem* (CSP), which is able to express in a natural way many problems from different fields.

1.3.1 Application to Constraint Satisfaction

An instance of a *constraint satisfaction problem (CSP)* (also *constraint network*) (e.g., [23]) is a triple $I = (\mathrm{Var}, U, \mathcal{C})$, where Var is a finite set of variables, U is a finite domain of values, and $\mathcal{C} = \{C_1, C_2, \ldots, C_q\}$ is a finite set of constraints. Each constraint C_i is a pair (S_i, r_i), where S_i is a list of variables of length m_i called the *constraint scope*, and r_i is an m_i-ary relation over U, called the *constraint relation*. (The tuples of r_i indicate the allowed combinations of simultaneous values for the variables S_i). A *solution* to a CSP instance is a substitution $\theta : \mathrm{Var} \longrightarrow U$, such that for each $1 \leq i \leq q$, $S_i\theta \in r_i$. The problem of deciding whether a CSP instance has any solution is called *constraint satisfiability*.

Example 1.12 A combinatorial crossword puzzle (see Figure 1.1) is a typical CSP [21, 69]. A set of legal words is associated to each horizontal or vertical array of white boxes delimited by black boxes. A solution to the puzzle is an assignment of a letter to each white box such that to each white array is assigned a word from its set of legal words.

This problem is represented as follows. There is a variable X_i for each white box, and a constraint C for each array D of white boxes. (For simplicity, we just write the index i for variable X_i.) The scope of C is the list of variables corresponding to the white boxes of the sequence D; the relation of C contains the legal words for D. For the example in Figure 1.1, we have

$$
\begin{aligned}
C_{1H} &= ((1,2,3,4,5), r_{1H}), & C_{8H} &= ((8,9,10), r_{8H}), \\
C_{11H} &= ((11,12,13), r_{11H}), & C_{20H} &= ((20,21,22,23,24,25,26), r_{20H}), \\
C_{1V} &= ((1,7,11,16,20), r_{1V}), & C_{5V} &= ((5,8,14,18,24), r_{5V}), \\
C_{6V} &= ((6,10,15,19,26), r_{6V}), & C_{13V} &= ((13,17,22), r_{13V}).
\end{aligned}
$$

Subscripts H and V stand for "Horizontal" and "Vertical," respectively, resembling the usual naming of definitions in crossword puzzles. A possible instance for the relation r_{1H} is $\{\langle h,o,u,s,e\rangle, \langle c,o,i,n,s\rangle, \langle b,l,o,c,k\rangle\}$. ◁

Structural Tractability. The structure of a CSP instance I can be represented by its associated hypergraph $\mathcal{H}(I) = (V, H)$, where $V = \mathrm{Var}$ and $H = \{S \mid (S, r) \in \mathcal{C}\}$. For example, the hypergraph associated with the crossword puzzle formalized above is the one on the left of Figure 1.1.

Constraint satisfiability is in general NP-complete. However, bounded hypertree width of the associated hypergraph is a key for tractability. Formally, we say that a class of instances $\mathcal{C}$ has bounded hypertree width if there exists some natural number k such that $hw(\mathcal{H}(I)) \leq k$, for every $I \in \mathcal{C}$. Observe that a class $\mathcal{C}$ has bounded hypertree width if, and only if, it has bounded generalized hypertree width, after the mentioned constant-approximation relationship between the two notions [1]. We thus speak hereafter only of bounded hypertree width classes. Moreover, it is known that, for any class $\mathcal{C}$, bounded treewidth entails bounded hypertree width, while the converse does not hold in general (unless the maximum size of the constraint scopes in every instance of $\mathcal{C}$ is bounded by a fixed constant).[2]

The following result has been discussed by different authors for different decomposition methods and (hyper)graph representations [24, 59, 14], while the more general version for bounded hypertree width (together with the

---

[2] To be precise, in order to use the notion of treewidth, it should be specified how a non-binary structure is encoded as a graph. However, it has been shown that the above mentioned result holds in fact for all CSP graph-encodings (currently) described in the literature [47, 36].

completeness of the problem for the class LOGCFL) was proven in [39]. Note that the result below is purely structural, as the kind of tuples occurring in the various constraint relations do not play any role.

Theorem 1.13 ([39]) *Constraint satisfiability is feasible in polynomial time over any class $\mathcal{C}$ of bounded hypertree width.*

To establish the result, the idea is to compute a hypertree decomposition $HD = \langle T, \chi, \lambda \rangle$ of hypergraph $\mathcal{H}(I)$ of the given instance I, and then solve constraint satisfiability by traversing HD from the leaves to the root r, by means of a bottom-up procedure. Recall first that each vertex v of T is associated with a set of hyperedges $\lambda(v)$ of $\mathcal{H}(I)$ and, hence, to a set of constraints in I, and define (initially) rel_v as the set of all solutions of the CSP restricted to such constraints, possibly projected over the variables in $\chi(v)$. Note that $|rel_v| \leq C^k$, where k is the hypertree width and C denotes the cardinality of the largest constraint relation. Then, in the bottom-up procedure, at each (non-leaf) vertex v, for each child c of v in T, we filter rel_v by keeping only those substitutions θ_v that coincide with some substitution $\theta_c \in rel_c$ on the variables they have in common. At the end, the given instance I admits a solution if, and only if, rel_r is not empty. By this procedure, I can be evaluated in $O((m-1)C^k \log C)$ where m is the number of vertices of T (which is at most the number of variables, in normal-form decompositions). Note that for $k = 1$, the method above coincides with the well-known algorithm by Yannakakis [81] for the evaluation of acyclic instances.

It is natural to ask whether we can achieve fixed-parameter tractability (FPT) [25] by finding a better algorithm which would allow us to get rid of the constant k in the exponent. Unfortunately, this appears to be very unlikely. In fact, the problem can be shown to be fixed-parameter intractable (more precisely, $W[1]$-hard) in the number of constraints or the number of variables as parameters [68]. The same holds for treewidth.

Strategic Games, Databases. Several problems can be reformulated as CSPs, so that structural tractability follows via Theorem 1.13. A noticeable example comes from the theory of strategic games [67]: Pure Nash equilibria are shown to be computable in polynomial time over compactly specified games (see, e.g., [31, 58, 20]) where the players' interaction is encoded in form of a hypergraph with bounded hypertree width [31]—in general the problem if NP-hard.

For other example, we recall that constraint satisfiability is known to be equivalent to a number of problems in database theory [53, 59], e.g., to the problem of conjunctive query containment [59], or to the problem of evaluating *Boolean conjunctive queries* over a relational database [62]. Therefore, cross fertilization among these different research fields was possible and led to major achievements both in the AI and in the DB communities. However, observe that, even if in principle we are talking about equivalent problems, in practice the instances considered in the applications are very different, and thus one cannot simply take any technique from AI and apply it to DB, or vice-versa. Typical CSP instances are indeed characterized by many constraints with relatively small constraint relations, while typical query-answering tasks involve relatively small queries on large (often huge) databases.

1.3.2 *Application to Enumeration Problems*

We first focus on the tractability of the problem ECSP of enumerating (possibly projected) solutions. In particular, since even easy instances may have an exponential number of solutions, tractability means here having algorithms that compute solutions *with polynomial delay* (WPD): An algorithm M solves WPD a computation problem P if there is a polynomial $p(\cdot)$ such that, for every instance of P of size n, M discovers if there are no solutions in time $O(p(n))$; otherwise, it outputs all solutions in such a way that a new solution is computed within $O(p(n))$ time from the previous one.

We remark that having efficient algorithms for ECSP is important not only in the (obvious) case we are interested in computing all solutions, but also whenever we are interested in solutions having some specific properties that cannot be expressed by standard constraints. For instance, this happens whenever the desired answers are the solutions of a problem beyond NP, hence not expressible as a (standard) CSP instance. Examples are the *Strategic Companies* problem [13], or problems related with *Conformant Planning* and *Conditional Planning* [71], which are all hard for the second level of the polynomial hierarchy. Indeed, in such cases, one typically starts an enumeration (possibly, anytime) algorithm, and for each computed solution checks whether the additional properties are met or not, which may require a completely different algorithm. In the worst case, the complete enumeration of all solutions may be required. Actually, note that in these cases one is usually interested in a (minimal) subset O of variables sufficient to check the additional properties. Moreover, observe that modeling real-world applications through CSP instances typically requires the use of "auxiliary" variables, whose precise values in the solutions are not relevant for the user, and that are (usually) filtered-out from the output. Therefore, computing all combinations of their values occurring in solutions means wasting time, possibly exponential time. Of course, this is irrelevant for computing just one solution, but it is crucial for the enumeration problem.

It was shown that this problem is tractable for classes of instances having bounded treewidth [12]. Actually, such a tractability result has been extended to the more general tree-projection framework [48], which comprise all purely structural decomposition methods. We next recall a specialization to the hypertree width method.

Theorem 1.14 ([48]) *Let C be any class of CSPs having bounded hypertree width. Then, for every $I \in C$ and every set of variables O occurring in I, all the solutions of I projected over O can be enumerated with polynomial delay.*

Analogous positive results hold for the related problem of *counting* the number of solutions. Note that, even for instances with exponentially many solutions, the number of these solutions may well be computed in polynomial time if it is not necessary to actually generate them. Indeed, it has been shown that counting the number of solutions of a CSP is feasible in polynomial time for classes of instances having bounded hypertree width and where the set of output variables O is in fact the full set of variables. The result is also tight on recursively enumerable classes of instances having bounded arity (unless $\mathrm{FPT} = W[1]$) [19]. Moreover, in the general case of classes of instances having bounded hypertree width and with arbitrary sets O of desired variables, the problem is still tractable if either the constraint relations or the constraint scopes have a fixed maximum size [70].

Conjunctive Queries. Note that the above enumeration problem is precisely the classical query answering problem for conjunctive queries over relational databases, which are equivalent to SELECT-PROJECT-JOIN queries. Moreover, counting the number of answers is a basic function in most query languages (just think of the `count` operator in SQL). However, despite the very nice computational properties of structural decomposition methods such as treewidth and hypertree width, they did not have a significant impact on the design of commercial DBMS optimizers, and the interest for these techniques remained only at a theoretical level, until very recently. This is mainly due to two reasons. First, decomposition methods flatten in the hypergraph all the "quantitative" aspects of data, such as selectivity and cardinality of relations, whose knowledge may dramatically speed-up the evaluation time. Second, such methods do not generally take care of the output of the queries, or of aggregate operators. Relevant steps to fill the gap between theory and practice have been made in [77], where the hypertree decomposition method has been extended in order to combine this structural decomposition method with quantitative approaches, and in [29], where methods have been discussed to deal with output variables and aggregate operators. A system prototype implementing these approaches has recently been presented in [28]. The system can be put on top of any existing database management system supporting JDBC technology, by transparently interacting/replacing its standard query optimization module.

1.3.3 Application to Constraint Optimization

Whenever assignments are associated with some cost because of the semantics of the underlying application domain, computing an arbitrary solution might not be enough. For instance, the crossword puzzle in Example 1.12 may admit more than one solution, and expert solvers may be asked to single out the most difficult ones, such as those solutions that minimize the total number of vowels occurring in the used words. For another example, think of database queries, which are often ranked according to user preferences.

In these cases, one is often interested in the *optimization problem* of computing the solution of minimum cost, whose modeling is accounted for in several variants of the basic CSP framework, such as fuzzy, probabilistic, weighted, lexicographic, penalty, valued, and semiring-based CSPs (see [65, 7], Chapter 4 of this book, and the references therein). A thorough analysis of the complexity of constraint optimization under structural restrictions was carried out in [50]. Below, we overview such recent results.

Formal Framework. Let Var be a set of variables and let U be a domain of constants. Let $\succeq$ be a total order over a domain of values $\mathbb{D}$. Then, an *evaluation function* $\mathcal{F}$ over $\mathbb{D}$ and $\succeq$ is a tuple $\langle w, \oplus \rangle$ with $w : \text{Var} \times U \mapsto \mathbb{D}$ and where $\oplus$ is a commutative, associative, and closed binary operator with an identity element over $\mathbb{D}$.

For a substitution $\theta \neq \emptyset$, $\mathcal{F}(\theta)$ is the value $\bigoplus_{X/u \in \theta} w(X, u)$; and, conventionally, $\mathcal{F}(\emptyset)$ is the identity element (with respect to $\oplus$). The evaluation function $\mathcal{F} = \langle w, \oplus \rangle$ is *monotone* if $\mathcal{F}(\theta) \succeq \mathcal{F}(\theta')$ implies that $\mathcal{F}(\theta) \oplus \mathcal{F}(\theta'') \succeq \mathcal{F}(\theta') \oplus \mathcal{F}(\theta'')$, for each triple of substitution $\theta, \theta', \theta''$.

Let $L = [\mathcal{F}_1, \ldots, \mathcal{F}_m]$ be a list of evaluation functions, where each $\mathcal{F}_i$ is defined over a domain $\mathbb{D}_i$ and a total order $\succeq_i$, $\forall i \in \{1, \ldots, m\}$. Then, for any substitution θ, $L(\theta)$ denotes the vector of values $(\mathcal{F}_1(\theta), \ldots, \mathcal{F}_m(\theta)) \in \mathbb{D}_1 \times \cdots \times \mathbb{D}_m$. To compare elements of $\mathbb{D}_1 \times \cdots \times \mathbb{D}_m$, we consider the lexicographical total order $\succeq_{\text{lex}}$, inducing a hierarchy over the preference relations in each domain. Let $\mathbf{x} = (x_1, \ldots, x_m)$ and $\mathbf{y} = (y_1, \ldots, y_m)$ be two vectors with $x_i, y_i \in \mathbb{D}_i$, for each $i \in \{1, \ldots, m\}$. Then, as usual, $\mathbf{x} \succeq_{\text{lex}} \mathbf{y}$, if either $\mathbf{x} = \mathbf{y}$, or there is an index $i \in \{1, \ldots, m\}$ such that $x_i \succ_i y_i$ and $x_j = y_j$ holds, for each $j \in \{1, \ldots, i-1\}$.

Let $L = [\mathcal{F}_1, \ldots, \mathcal{F}_m]$ be a list of evaluation functions. Then, we define $\succeq_L$ as the binary relation such that, for each pair θ_1 and θ_2 of substitutions, $\theta_1 \succeq_L \theta_2$ if, and only if, $L(\theta_1) \succeq_{\text{lex}} L(\theta_2)$. Note that $\succeq_L$ is a preorder, which might be not antisymmetric, as $L(\theta_1) = L(\theta_2)$ does not imply that $\theta_1 = \theta_2$. As the ordering might even not be a partial order at all, it is natural to exploit linearization techniques, as discussed in [11].

Let $\succeq_U$ be an arbitrary total order defined over U. Let $\ell = [X_1, \ldots, X_n]$ be a list including all the variables in *Var*, hereinafter called *linearization*. Then, we define $\succeq_L^\ell$ as the binary relation such that, for each pair θ_1 and θ_2 of substitutions, $\theta_1 \succeq_L^\ell \theta_2$ if, and only if, (i) $\theta_1 = \theta_2$, or (ii) $\theta_1 \succeq_L \theta_2$ and $\theta_2 \not\succeq_L \theta_1$, or (iii) $\theta_1 \succeq_L \theta_2$, $\theta_2 \succeq_L \theta_1$, and there is a variable X_i such that $\theta_1(X_i) \succ_U \theta_2(X_i)$, and $\theta_1(X_j) = \theta_2(X_j)$, for each $j \in \{1, \ldots, i-1\}$. Note that $\succeq_L^\ell$ is a total order, where ties in $\succeq_L$ are resolved according to ℓ and the total order $\succeq_U$ over U. In fact, $\succeq_L^\ell$ is a refinement of $\succeq_L$.

Structural Tractability. An instance $I = (\text{Var}, U, \mathcal{C})$ of a constraint satisfaction problem equipped with a list L of evaluation functions is called a *constraint optimization problem*, and is denoted by I_L. A problem that naturally arises with evaluation functions is the $\text{Min}(I_L, \ell)$ problem of computing the solution θ to I such that there is no solution θ' with $\theta \succ_L^\ell \theta'$ (or recognizing that no solution exists at all). In case of arbitrary evaluation functions, results are bad news about the tractability of Min, even on classes of acyclic instances.

Theorem 1.15 ([50]) Min *is NP-hard for any linearization, even on classes of instances I_L where $\mathcal{H}(I)$ is acyclic.*

However, on monotone functions to be optimized, bounded hypertree width is again a key to ensure tractability. The complexity analysis follows here the usual simple approach of counting 1 each mathematical operation, hence in principle one may compute in polynomial time (operations) values whose size is exponential with respect to the input size. We thus explicitly care about the size of values computed during the execution of algorithms, and look for output polynomial-space algorithms.

Theorem 1.16 ([50]) *On classes of constraint optimization problems I_L where the hypertree width of $\mathcal{H}(I)$ is bounded by some fixed natural number*

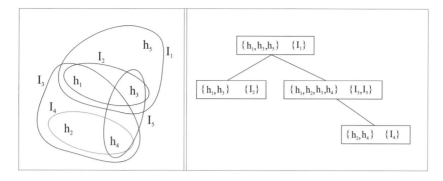

Figure 1.10 A dual hypergraph with a with-2 hypertree decomposition.

and where L is a list of monotone evaluation functions, MIN is feasible in polynomial time and output-polynomial space (for any linearization).

The result is established by modifying the bottom-up procedure illustrated in the section above for constraint satisfiability. The main difference is that, at each (non-leaf) vertex v, for each child c of v in T, one filters rel_v by keeping only the "best" substitutions θ_v, i.e., those on which the solution of minimum cost can be achieved for the CSP obtained by considering the constraints in the subtree rooted at v.

Combinatorial Auctions. The above solution algorithm may be viewed as a generalization to lexicographic optimization of an algorithm discussed in [30] for *combinatorial auctions*, where there is just one function to be optimized.

Combinatorial auctions are well-known mechanisms for resource and task allocation where bidders are allowed to simultaneously bid on combinations of items. Such mechanisms model very well those situations where bidders' valuations of bundles of items are not equal to the sum of their valuations of individual items.

Formally, a *combinatorial auction* is a pair $\langle \mathcal{I}, \mathcal{B} \rangle$, where $\mathcal{I} = \{I_1, \ldots, I_m\}$ is the set of items the auctioneer has to sell, and $\mathcal{B} = \{B_1, \ldots, B_n\}$ is the set of bids from the buyers interested in the items in $\mathcal{I}$. Each bid B_i has the form $\langle item(B_i), pay(B_i) \rangle$, where $pay(B_i)$ is a rational number denoting the price a buyer offers for the items in $item(B_i) \subseteq \mathcal{I}$. An outcome for $\langle \mathcal{I}, \mathcal{B} \rangle$ is a subset $\mathbf{b}$ of $\mathcal{B}$ such that $item(B_i) \cap item(B_j) = \emptyset$, for each pair B_i and B_j of bids in $\mathbf{b}$ with $i \neq j$. Bidder interaction in a combinatorial auction $\langle \mathcal{I}, \mathcal{B} \rangle$ can be represented via its associated *dual hypergraph* [30] $\overline{\mathcal{H}}(\langle \mathcal{I}, \mathcal{B} \rangle)$, whose nodes are the various bids in the auction and hyperedges represent items,

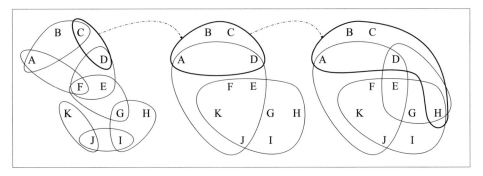

Figure 1.11 A tree projection for the hypergraph $\mathcal{H}_1$ in Figure 1.4 (on the left) with respect to the resource hypergraph reported on the right.

that is, each item $I \in \mathcal{I}$ is associated with a hyperedge consisting of the set of bids that contain I.

For example, the hypergraph in Figure 1.10, on the left, encodes an auction over items $\{I_1, \ldots, I_5\}$ and where bids are on the following bundles of items: $h_1 : \{I_1\}$, $h_2 : \{I_1, I_2, I_3\}$, $h_3 : \{I_1, I_2, I_5\}$, $h_4 : \{I_3, I_4\}$, and $h_5 : \{I_3, I_4, I_5\}$. Note that this hypergraph is not acyclic and its hypertree width 2, as it is witnessed by the decomposition reported in Figure 1.10.

A crucial problem for combinatorial auctions is the *winner determination problem* of determining the outcome $\mathbf{b}^*$ that maximizes the sum of the accepted bid prices (i.e., $\sum_{B_i \in \mathbf{b}^*} pay(B_i)$) over all the possible outcomes. The problem is in general NP-hard [73], while it is tractable on classes of auctions with bounded hypertree-width dual hypergraphs [30].

1.4 Beyond (hyper)tree decompositions

All the known so-called purely-structural decomposition methods, where decompositions are only based on the (hyper)graph structure $\mathcal{H}$ of the given instance, are in fact specializations of the general and abstract framework of *tree projections* [54]. In this view, the goal is to cover the hypergraph $\mathcal{H}$ via an acyclic hypergraph (the tree projection), in a way that each hyperedge is contained in some hyperedge of another given "resource" hypergraph $\mathcal{H}'$ (also known as the acyclic hypergraph sandwich problem). See Figure 1.11, for an example of tree projection.

The existence of a tree projection is often a key to establish tractability results for decision problems [54] and for enumeration ones [48]. Moreover, it guarantees that interesting consistency properties [49] and game-theoretic characterizations [46] hold. According to this unifying view, differences among the various (purely) structural decomposition methods just come in the way the resource hypergraph $\mathcal{H}'$ is defined. In particular, for a fixed natural number k, the treewidth method is obtained by considering as available hyperedges in the resource hypergraph $\mathcal{H}'$ all combinations of k nodes of $\mathcal{H}$; while the generalized hypertree-width method is obtained by considering all combinations of k hyperedges of $\mathcal{H}$. However, note that the notion of tree projection is more general then both treewidth and hypertree width, because the hyperedges of the "resource" hypergraph $\mathcal{H}'$ may model arbitrary subproblems of the given instance whose solutions are easy to compute, or already available from previous computations (for instance, materialized views while answering database queries).

As an example of a different set of useful "resources" (subproblems), we mention a powerful extension of hypertree decompositions, called *fractional* hypertree decompositions [52]. According to this notion, the resources are the width-k fractional covers of hypergraph vertices, instead of the integral covers that characterize hypertree decompositions (where each hyperedge counts 1). It turns out that fractional hypertree-width is strictly more general than the hypertree width, as there exist classes of hypergraphs having bounded fractional hypertree width and unbounded (generalized) hypertree width.

For completeness, we recall the most powerful method known at this time, whose width is determined by suitably covering tree-decomposition bags by using submodular functions. The resulting notion, called submodular width [63], is in its turn strictly more general than fractional hypertree width. However, unlike the previously mentioned methods that guarantee polynomial-time tractability for bounded-width classes, this technique only guarantees that classes of instances having bounded submodular-width are fixed-parameter tractable (and in [63] a tight result is proved for this kind of tractability, see below).

1.5 Tractability frontiers (for CSPs)

Constraint satisfaction is often formalized as a homomorphism problem that takes as input two finite relational structures $\mathcal{A}$ (modeling variables and scopes of the constraints) and $\mathcal{B}$ (modeling the relations associated with constraints), and asks whether there is a homomorphism from $\mathcal{A}$ to $\mathcal{B}$ [59]. We consider problems where $\mathcal{A}$ must be taken from some suitably defined class $\mathbf{A}$ of structures, while $\mathcal{B}$ is any arbitrary structure from the class "$-$" of all finite structures, shortly denoted as $\mathrm{CSP}(\mathbf{A}, -)$. Note that we face the so-called *uniform* homomorphism problem, where both structures are part of the input, i.e., nothing is fixed. For completeness we recall that, instead, in the typical *non-uniform* problem $CSP(-, \mathcal{B})$, $\mathcal{B}$ is a fixed structure (thus, any instance of such a problem just consists of some left-hand structure $\mathcal{A}$).

1.5.1 Decision Problem

Several decomposition methods have been proposed in the last few years, with the aim of discovering further islands of tractability and, ultimately, of charting the tractability frontier for constraint satisfaction. In the bounded-arity case, research has already achieved this ambitious goal.

Theorem 1.17 ([51]) *Assume* FPT $\neq W[1]$. *Then, for any recursively enumerable class of bounded-arity structures* **A**, *CSP*(**A**, $-$) *is solvable in polynomial time if, and only if, the cores of the structures in* **A** *have bounded (hyper)treewidth.*[3]

Note that the latter condition may be equivalently stated as follows: for every $\mathcal{A} \in \mathbf{A}$ there is some $\mathcal{A}'$ homomorphically equivalent to $\mathcal{A}$ and such that its treewidth is below the required fixed threshold. For short, we say that such a class **A** has bounded treewidth modulo homomorphic equivalence.

Things with unbounded-arity classes are, instead, not that clear. Generalized hypertree-width seems the natural counterpart of the tree decomposition method over unbounded-arity classes, and in fact $CSP(\mathbf{A}, -)$ is solvable in polynomial time *if* **A** has bounded hypertree-width modulo homomorphic equivalence [15]. However, it is known that generalized hypertree-width does not characterize all classes of structures where $CSP(\mathbf{A}, -)$ is solvable in polynomial time. Indeed, there are classes of structures having unbounded hypertree width that are tractable, because they have bounded fractional hypertree-width [52]. It seems that tighter results may be obtained by moving from polynomial-time tractability to fixed-parameter tractability (FPT). For any class of hypergraphs $\mathcal{H}$, let $CSP(\mathcal{H})$ denote the class of all homomorphism problem instances $(\mathcal{A}, \mathcal{B})$ where the hypergraph associated with $\mathcal{A}$ belongs to $\mathcal{H}$. Then, under some reasonable technical assumptions, $CSP(\mathcal{H})$ is FPT *if, and only if,* hypergraphs in $\mathcal{H}$ have bounded *submodular* width [63].

It is worthwhile noting that the above mentioned tractability results for classes of instances defined modulo homomorphically equivalence are actually tractability results for the *promise* version of the problem. In fact, unless P = NP, there is no polynomial-time algorithm that may check whether a given instance $\mathcal{A}$ actually belongs to such a class **A**. In particular, it has

---

[3] Recall that, for classes of structures having bounded arity, bounded hypertree width entails bounded treewidth (the converse is always true), so that the two notions are interchangeable for these classes.

been observed by different authors [76, 12] that there are classes of instances having bounded treewidth modulo homomorphically equivalence for which answers computable in polynomial time cannot be trusted. That is, unless P = NP, there is no efficient way to distinguish whether a "yes" answer means that there exists a solution of the problem, or that $\mathcal{A} \notin \mathbf{A}$.

In fact, the tractability frontier for the so-called *search problem* of computing just one solution (whose correctness may be easily checked) is an interesting open problem, which is somehow related to the frontier of the problem of enumerating homomorphisms, discussed next (for more on the relationships between these two problems, see [12]). For completeness, we recall that things are different for the case of non-uniform CSPs, where instead the tractability of the decision problem always entails the tractability of the search problem [16].

1.5.2 Enumeration Problems

Define formally an ECSP instance to be a triple $(\mathcal{A}, \mathcal{B}, O)$, for which we have to compute all solutions (homomorphisms) projected to a set of desired output variables O, denoted by $\mathcal{A}^{\mathcal{B}}[O]$.

In order to identify the (structural) tractability frontier, there are two choices to model the presence of output variables. The first possibility is that output variables are part of the (left-hand) structure. For instance, in [51] an additional "virtual" constraint covering together all possible output variables is added to the input structure. For bounded-arity recursively-enumerable classes of this form, it turns out that the enumeration problem is tractable for a class of instances if, and only if, the class has bounded treewidth modulo homomorphic equivalence. Note that the only possibility to meet this bounded treewidth requirement is having a fixed number of output variables in the class, otherwise the additional virtual constraint will have unbounded arity. Therefore, according to this approach, only instances with a polynomial number of (projected) solutions may be dealt with.

This limitation does not occur in a more recent modeling choice of output-aware structures, where possible output variables are described as those variables X having a domain constraint $dom(X)$, that is, a distinguished unary constraint specifying the domain of this variable. Such variables are said domain restricted. In fact, this choice reflects the classical approach in constraint satisfaction systems, where variables are typically associated with domains, which are heavily exploited by constraint propagation algorithms. Interestingly, for bounded-arity recursively-enumerable classes we get the same kind of statement as above, but now allowing an unbounded number of output variables, and hence the computation of exponentially many solutions, in general.

Theorem 1.18 ([48])   *Let **A** be a class of (left-hand) structures having bounded hypertree-width modulo homomorphic equivalence. Then, **A** has a tractable enumeration problem, i.e., for every $\mathcal{A} \in$ **A**, for every right-hand structure $\mathcal{B}$, and for every set O of domain restricted variables, the ECSP instance $(\mathcal{A}, \mathcal{B}, O)$ is solvable WPD.*

*Furthermore, let **A** be any recursively-enumerable class of structures of bounded arity having a tractable enumeration problem. Then, **A** has bounded (hyper)tree-width modulo homomorphic equivalence (unless* $\mathrm{FPT} = W[1]$*).*

The second possibility to deal with output variables is to leave them completely arbitrary, hence looking for a stronger form of tractability that should hold for any required set O of desired output variables. Intuitively, in this case it is not possible to have tractable instances with intractable substructures. Observe that this latter natural property does not hold if we do not consider projected solutions but we rather look for the enumeration of all (full) solutions, as shown in [12].

The tractability frontier for this case is still an open problem (see, e.g., [51] for a statement of this problem in the context of conjunctive database queries). However, there is a partial answer for the case of bounded-arity classes of structures closed under taking minors. It turns out that, for these classes, the enumeration problem is tractable if, and only if, the whole structures (and not just their cores) have bounded (hyper)treewidth.

Theorem 1.19 ([48])   *Let **A** be any recursively-enumerable class of (left-hand) structures of bounded arity closed under taking minors. Then, for every $\mathcal{A} \in$ **A**, for every right-hand structure $\mathcal{B}$, and for every set O of variables, the ECSP instance $(\mathcal{A}, \mathcal{B}, O)$ is solvable WPD if, and only if, **A** has bounded (hyper)tree-width (unless* $\mathrm{FPT} = W[1]$*).*

A final important observation is that the former results based on homomorphic equivalence, which generalize the results on decision problems to the enumeration problem, suffer of the same practical problem of giving as their output solutions that cannot be trusted, in general (because of the promise). Instead, for the above classes of structures having a bounded-width hypertree decomposition, we are able to compute *certified solutions* with polynomial delay [48], which is what we need in practical applications (think, e.g., of database query answering).

1.5.3 Optimization Problems

The same kind of tight tractability results, based on the existence of a hypertree decomposition of the whole structure, have been found for constraint optimization problems. In particular, besides MIN, we recall the problem of enumerating the best K solutions (TOP-K), and the problem of computing the next solution following one that is given at hand (NEXT). For these problems, good news have been found not only for *monotone* functions, but also for those (possibly) *non-monotone* functions, called *smooth evaluation functions*, which manipulate "small" (in fact, polynomially-bounded) values.

Monotone functions have already been discussed in Section 1.3.3, where we have noticed that the winner determination problem in combinatorial auction can be formulated as a constraint optimization problem over this kind of functions.

For a simple example of a smooth evaluation function, consider a function which counts the number of variables that are mapped to some domain values. This is useful whenever we would like to minimize the variables mapped to some "undesirable" values. Observe that the possible output values of this function are polynomially bounded in the size of the input, because they range from 0 to the number of variables. In fact, it is a smooth *and* monotone function, as it is often the case for functions based on counting.

Finally, as an example of non-monotone smooth evaluation-function, assume for the sake of simplicity to have one "undesirable" value 'a', and consider the following function: take the product of weights associated with variable assignments, where every variable mapped to 'a' is weighed -1, and all the others get 1. That is, we prefer those solutions with an odd number of variables mapped to the "undesirable" value. In general, functions involving multiplications are non-monotone, yet they are smooth if their output values are polynomially bounded (with respect to the input size).

Figure 1.12 provides a picture of the complexity of such optimization problems over classes of instances having bounded hypertree width—there recall from Section 1.3.2 that WPD is the class of all problems that can be solved with polynomial delay. All tractability results are tight on recursively enumerable classes of instances having bounded arity (unless FPT = $W[1]$) [50].

1.6 Conclusion

This chapter describes techniques where graphical structures are profitably exploited to solve efficiently a large number of problem instances. We mentioned only a few possible applications, but we believe the list being not

Problem	**No Restriction**	**Monotone**	**Smooth**
MIN	NP-hard	in P	in P
NEXT	NP-hard	NP-hard	in P
TOP-K	NP-hard	WPD	WPD

Figure 1.12 Summary of complexity results for bounded hypertree-width instances.

exhaustive at all, because such basic (hyper)graph theoretic notions may be actually useful in many different fields, most often outside authors' areas of research. Just to give a rough idea of the wide spectrum of these fields, we recall the connections between the treewidth and the resolution width in propositional proof systems [4] or the applications to natural sciences (e.g., some solutions to structure-sequence alignment problems in bioinformatics exploit the fact that many involved structure graphs, such as almost all existing RNA pseudoknots, have small treewidth [79, 56]).

In fact, it is very common to observe that many instances of real-life problems exhibit a kind of sparse tree-like structure in the large, but have a very dense highly-cyclic structure in local connections. Therefore, it is natural to imagine that in such applications the ability to combine different techniques, possibly based on different notions of "good" structure, will become very important in the near future. For instance, by using the tree projection framework described in Section 1.4, one may arrange in a tree-like structure a number of *dense* subproblems whose solutions are instead computed easily because of completely different properties.

References

[1] I. Adler, G. Gottlob, and M. Grohe. Hypertree-width and related hypergraph invariants. *Eur. J. Comb.*, **28**(8), 2167–2181, 2007.

[2] S. Arnborg, J. Lagergren, and D. Seese. Easy problems for tree-decomposable graphs. *Journal of Algorithms*, **12**(2), 308–340, 1991.

[3] A. Atserias, A.A. Bulatov, and V. Dalmau. On the power of k-consistency, In *Proc. of ICALP'07*, 279–290, 2007.

[4] A. Atserias and V. Dalmau. A combinatorial characterization of resolution width, *Journal of Computer and System Sciences*, **74**(3), 323–334, 2008.

[5] E. Ben-Sasson and A. Wigderson. Short proofs are narrow – resolution made simple. *Journal of the ACM*, **48**(2), 149–169, 2001.

[6] P.A. Bernstein and N. Goodman. The power of natural semijoins. *SIAM Journal on Computing*, **10**(4), 751–771, 1981.

[7] S. Bistarelli, U. Montanari, F. Rossi, T. Schiex, G. Verfaillie, and H. Fargier.

Semiring-based CSPs and valued CSPs: frameworks, properties, and comparison. *Constraints*, **4**(3), 199–240, 1999.

[8] H.L. Bodlaender and F.V. Fomin. A linear-time algorithm for finding tree-decompositions of small treewidth. *SIAM Journal on Computing*, **25**(6), 1305–1317, 1996.

[9] H.L. Bodlaender, F.V. Fomin, A.M.C.A. Koster, D. Kratsch, and D.M. Thilikos. On exact algorithms for treewidth. In *Proc. of ESA'06*, 672–683, 2006.

[10] H.L. Bodlaender and A.M.C.A. Koster. Treewidth computations I. Upper bounds. *Information and Computation*, **208**(3), 259–275, 2010.

[11] R.I. Brafman, F. Rossi, D. Salvagnin, K.B. Venable, and T. Walsh. Finding the next solution in constraint- and preference-based knowledge representation formalisms. In *Proc. of KR'10*, 425–433, 2010.

[12] A. Bulatov, V. Dalmau, M. Grohe, and D. Marx. Enumerating homomorphism. *J. Comput. Syst. Sci.*, **78**(2), 638–650, 2012.

[13] M. Cadoli, T. Eiter, and G. Gottlob. Default logic as a query language. *IEEE Transactions on Knowledge and Data Engineering*, **9**(3), 448–463, 1997.

[14] C. Chekuri and A. Rajaraman. Conjunctive query containment revisited. *Theoretical Computer Science*, **239**(2), 211–229, 2000.

[15] H. Chen and V. Dalmau. Beyond hypertree width: decomposition methods without decompositions. In *Proc. of CP'05*, 167–181, 2005.

[16] D.A. Cohen. Tractable decision for a constraint language implies tractable search. *Constraints*, **9**(3), 219–229, 2004.

[17] W. Cook and P. Seymour. Tour merging via branch-decomposition. *INFORMS Journal on Computing*, **15**(3), 233–248, 2003.

[18] B. Courcelle. Graph rewriting: an algebraic and logic approach. In *Handbook of Theoretical Computer Science, Volume B: Formal Models and Semantics*, MIT Press, 193–242, 1990.

[19] V. Dalmau and P. Jonsson. The complexity of counting homomorphisms seen from the other side. *Theoretical Computer Science*, **329**(1–3), 315–323, 2004.

[20] C. Daskalakis and C.H. Papadimitriou. Computing pure nash equilibria in graphical games via markov random fields. In *Proc. of ACM EC'06*, 91–99, 2006.

[21] R. Dechter. Constraint networks. In *Encyclopedia of Artificial Intelligence*, Volume 1, second edition, Stuart C. Shapiro (ed), 276–285. Wiley, 1992.

[22] R. Dechter. Bucket elimination: a unifying framework for processing hard and soft constraints. In *Proc. of UAI'96*, 211–219, 1996.

[23] R. Dechter. *Constraint Processing*. Morgan Kaufmann, 2003.

[24] R. Dechter and J. Pearl. Tree-clustering schemes for constraint-processing. In *Proc. of AAAI*, 150–154, 1988.

[25] R. Downey and M. Fellows. *Parameterized Complexity*. Springer, 1999.

[26] M. Elberfeld, A. Jakoby, and T. Tantau. Logspace versions of the theorems of Bodlaender and Courcelle. In *Proc. of FOCS'10*, 143–152, 2010.

[27] R. Fagin. Degrees of acyclicity for hypergraphs and relational database schemes. *Journal of ACM*, **30**(3), 514–550, 1983.

[28] L. Ghionna, G. Greco, and F. Scarcello. H-DB: A hybrid quantitative-structural SQL optimizer. In *Proc. of CIKM'11*, 2011.

[29] L. Ghionna, L. Granata, G. Greco, and F. Scarcello. Hypertree decompositions for query optimization. In *Proc. of ICDE '07*, 36–45, 2007.

[30] G. Gottlob and G. Greco. On the complexity of combinatorial auctions: structured item graphs and hypertree decomposition. In *Proc. EC'07*, 152–161, 2007.

[31] G. Gottlob, G. Greco, and F. Scarcello. Pure Nash equilibria: hard and easy games. *Journal of Artificial Intelligence Research*, **24**, 357–406, 2005.

[32] G. Gottlob, G. Greco, Z. Miklós, F. Scarcello, T. Schwentick. Tree projections: game characterization and computational aspects. *Graph Theory, Computational Intelligence and Thought*, LNCS 5420, 217–226, Springer-Verlag, 2009.

[33] G. Gottlob, M. Grohe, N. Musliu, M. Samer, and F. Scarcello. Hypertree decompositions: structure, algorithms, and applications. In *Proc. of WG'05*, 2005.

[34] G. Gottlob and S.T. Lee. A logical approach to multicut problems. *Information Processing Letters*, **103**(4), 136–141, 2007.

[35] G. Gottlob, N. Leone, and F. Scarcello. On tractable queries and constraints. In *Proc. of DEXA'99*, 1–15, 1999.

[36] G. Gottlob, N. Leone, and F. Scarcello. A comparison of structural CSP decomposition methods. *Artificial Intelligence*, **124**(2), 243–282, 2000.

[37] G. Gottlob, N. Leone, and F. Scarcello. The complexity of acyclic conjunctive queries. *Journal of the ACM*, **43**(3), 431–494, 2001.

[38] G. Gottlob, N. Leone, and F. Scarcello. Hypertree decompositions: a survey. In *Proc. of MFCS'01*, 37–57, 2001.

[39] G. Gottlob, N. Leone, and F. Scarcello. Hypertree decompositions and tractable queries. *J. of Computer and System Sciences*, **64**(3), 579–627, 2002.

[40] G. Gottlob, N. Leone, and F. Scarcello. Robbers, marshals, and guards: game-theoretic and logical characterizations of hypertree width. *J. of Computer and System Sciences*, **66**(4), 775–808, 2003.

[41] G. Gottlob, Z. Miklós, and T. Schwentick. Generalized hypertree decompositions: NP-hardness and tractable variants. *Journal of the ACM*, **56**(6), Article 30, 2009.

[42] G. Gottlob, R. Pichler, and F. Wei. Bounded treewidth as a key to tractability of knowledge representation and reasoning. *Artificial Intelligence*, **174**(1), 105–132, 2010.

[43] G. Gottlob and M. Samer. A backtracking-based algorithm for computing hypertree-decompositions. *Journal of Experimental Algorithmics*, **13**, Article 1, 2009.

[44] E. Grädel, P.G. Kolaitis, L. Libkin, M. Marx, J. Spencer, M.Y. Vardi, Y. Venema, S. Weinstein. *Finite Model Theory and its Applications*. Springer, 2007.

[45] G. Greco, E. Malizia, F. Scarcello, and L. Palopoli. On the complexity of core, kernel, and bargaining set. *Artificial Intelligence*, **175**(12–13), 1877–1910, 2011.

[46] G. Greco and F. Scarcello. Tree projections: hypergraph games and minimality. In *Proc. of ICALP'08*, 736–747, 2008.

[47] G. Greco and F. Scarcello. On the power of structural decompositions of graph-based representations of constraint problems. *Artificial Intelligence*, **174**(5–6), 382–409, 2010.

[48] G. Greco and F. Scarcello. Structural tractability of enumerating CSP solutions. *Constraints*, **18**(1), 38–74, 2013.

[49] G. Greco and F. Scarcello. The power of tree projections: local consistency, greedy algorithms, and larger islands of tractability. In *Proc. of PODS'10*, 327–338, 2010. A full version is currently available at CoRR abs/1212.2314 (2012).

[50] G. Greco and F. Scarcello. Structural tractability of constraint optimization. In *Proc. of CP'11*, 340–355, 2011.

[51] M. Grohe. The complexity of homomorphism and constraint satisfaction problems seen from the other side. *Journal of the ACM*, **54**(1), Article 1, 2007.

[52] M. Grohe and D. Marx. Constraint solving via fractional edge covers. In *Proc. of SODA '06*, 289–298, 2006.

[53] M. Gyssens, P.G. Jeavons, and D.A. Cohen. Decomposing constraint satisfaction problems using database techniques. *Journal of Algorithms*, **66**, 57–89, 1994.

[54] N. Goodman and O. Shmueli. The tree projection theorem and relational query processing. *J. of Computer and System Sciences*, **29**(3), 767–786, 1984.

[55] P. Harvey and A. Ghose. Reducing redundancy in the hypertree decomposition scheme. In *Proc. of ICTAI'03*, 474–481, 2003.

[56] Z. Huang, Y. Wu, J. Robertson, L. Feng, R.L. Malmberg, and L. Cai. Fast and accurate search for non-coding RNA pseudoknot structures in genomes. *Bioinformatics*, **24**(20), 2281–2287, 2008.

[57] D.S. Johnson, A catalog of complexity classes. In *Handbook of Theoretical Computer Science, Volume A: Algorithms and Complexity*, MIT Press, 67–161, 1990.

[58] M. Kearns, M. Littman, and S. Singh, S. Graphical models for game theory. In *Proc. of UAI'01*, 253–260, 2001.

[59] P. G. Kolaitis and M. Y. Vardi. Conjunctive-query containment and constraint satisfaction. *Journal of Computer and System Sciences*, **61**(2), 302–332, 2000.

[60] T. Korimort. *Constraint Satisfaction Problems – Heuristic Decomposition*. PhD thesis, Vienna University of Technology, April 2003.

[61] D. Lehmann, R. Müller, and T. Sandholm. The winner determination problem. In *Combinatorial Auctions*, P. Cramton, Y. Shoham, and R. Steinberg (eds). MIT Press, 2006.

[62] D. Maier. *The Theory of Relational Databases*. Computer Science Press, 1986.

[63] D. Marx. Tractable hypergraph properties for constraint satisfaction and conjunctive queries. In *Proc. of STOC'10*, 735–744, 2010.

[64] B. McMahan. Bucket elimination and hypertree decompositions. Implementation report, Institute of Information Systems (DBAI), TU Vienna, 2004.

[65] P. Meseguer, F. Rossi and T. Schiex. Soft constraints. In *Handbook of Constraint Programming*, Elsevier, 2006.

[66] N. Musliu. Tabu search for generalized hypertree decompositions. In *Proc. of MIC'07*, 2007.

[67] J. Nash. Non-cooperative games. *Annals of Mathematics*, **54**(2), 286–295, 1951.

[68] C.H. Papadimitriou and M. Yannakakis. On the complexity of database queries. *Journal of Computer and Systems Sciences*, **58**(3), 407–427, 1999.

[69] J. Pearson and P.G. Jeavons. A survey of tractable constraint satisfaction problems, CSD-TR-97-15, Royal Holloway, Univ. of London, 1997.

[70] R. Pichler and S. Skritek. Tractable counting of the answers to conjunctive queries. *J. Comput. Syst. Sci.*, **79**(6), 984–1001, 2013.

[71] J. Rintanen. Planning and SAT. In *Handbook of Satisfiability*, Frontiers in Artificial Intelligence and Applications, **185**, 483–504, IOS Press, 2009.

[72] N. Robertson and P.D. Seymour. Graph minors. II. Algorithmic aspects of tree width. *Journal of Algorithms*, **7**, 309–322, 1986.

[73] M. H. Rothkopf, A. Pekec, and R. M. Harstad. Computationally manageable combinatorial auctions. *Management Science*, **44**, 1131–1147, 1998.

[74] M. Samer. Hypertree-decomposition via Branch-decomposition. In *Proc. of IJCAI'05*, 1535–1536, 2005.

[75] F. Scarcello. The Hypertree Decompositions HomePage, since 2002. `http://www.dimes.unical.it/scarcello/Hypertrees/` See also the WEB page `http://www.dbai.tuwien.ac.at/proj/hypertree/` mantained by N. Musliu.

[76] F. Scarcello, G. Gottlob, and G. Greco. Uniform constraint satisfaction problems and database theory. In *Complexity of Constraints*, LNCS 5250, 156–195, Springer-Verlag, 2008.

[77] F. Scarcello, G. Greco, and N. Leone. Weighted hypertree decompositions and optimal query plans. *Journal of Computer and System Sciences*, 475–506, 2007.

[78] P.D. Seymour and R. Thomas. Graph searching and a min-max theorem for tree-width. *Journal of Combinatorial Theory, Series B*, **58**, 22–33, 1993.

[79] Y. Song, C. Liu, X. Huang, R.L. Malmberg, Y. Xu, and L. Cai. Efficient Parameterized algorithms for biopolymer structure-sequence slignment. *IEEE/ACM Transactions on Computational Biology and Bioinformatics*, **3**(4), 423–432, 2006.

[80] S. Subbarayan and H. Reif Andersen. Backtracking procedures for hypertree, hyperspread and connected hypertree decomposition of CSPs. In *Proc. of IJCAI'07*, 180–185, 2007.

[81] M. Yannakakis. Algorithms for acyclic database schemes. In *Proc. of VLDB'81*, 82–94, 1981.

2

Perfect Graphs and Graphical Modeling

Tony Jebara

This chapter reduces the inference problem in probabilistic graphical models to an equivalent maximum weight stable set problem on a graph. We discuss methods for recognizing when the latter problem can be solved efficiently by appealing to perfect graph theory. Furthermore, practical solvers based on convex programming and message-passing are presented.

Tractability is the study of computational tasks with the goal of identifying which problem classes are *tractable* or, in other words, *efficiently solvable*. The class of tractable problems is traditionally assumed to be solvable in polynomial time by a *deterministic* Turing machine and is denoted by P. The class contains many natural tasks such as sorting a set of numbers, linear programming (the decision version), determining if a number is prime, and finding a maximum weight matching. Many interesting problems, however, lie in another class that generalizes P and is known as NP: the class of languages decidable in polynomial time on a *non-deterministic* Turing machine. We trivially have that P is a subset of NP (many researchers also believe that it is a strict subset). It is believed that many problems in the class NP are, in the worst case, intractable and do not admit efficient inference. Problems such as maximum stable set, the traveling salesman problem and graph coloring are known to be NP-hard (at least as hard as the hardest problems in NP). It is, therefore, widely suspected that there are no polynomial-time algorithms for NP-hard problems. Rather than stop after labeling a problem class as NP-hard by identifying its worst-case instances, this chapter explores the question: what *instances* of otherwise NP-hard problems still admit efficient inference? The study of perfect graphs [4] helps shed light on this question. It turns out that a variety of hard problems such as graph coloring, maximum clique and maximum stable set are all solvable efficiently in polynomial time when the input graph is restricted to be a perfect graph [16].

Can we extend this promising result to other important problems in applied fields such as data mining and machine learning? This chapter will focus on a central **NP-hard** problem in statistics and machine learning known as the maximum a posteriori (MAP) problem, in other words, *finding the most likely outcome from a set of observations under a given probability distribution.* When can such inference be performed efficiently? Perfect graphs will be a useful tool in carving out what types of MAP estimation problems are tractable.

In the past two decades, the fields of machine learning and statistical inference have increasingly leveraged graph representations and graph-based algorithms in a variety of problem settings. For instance, semi-supervised learning, dimensionality reduction, and unsupervised clustering problems are frequently solved by casting data points as nodes in a graph and then applying graph-theoretic algorithms. Similarly, probabilistic inference problems such as MAP estimation, marginal inference, and so on are solved by casting random variables as nodes in a graphical model and then applying graph algorithms such as message passing, tree approximations and other variants. In many situations, most of the above learning problems are *intractable* and provably **NP-hard** in the worst case [30, 1]. However, when the graph structures are restricted to a subfamily (such as the family of tree-structured graphs), a variety of learning problems may become tractable [27]. Therefore, determining which graphs and graphical models admit efficient inference and which learning problems are solvable in polynomial time is of great importance in machine learning. Following upon previous work [18], this chapter extends the tractability benefits of perfect graphs to statistical inference in graphical models and focuses on the MAP estimation problem as a task of particular interest.

2.1 Berge Graphs and Perfect Graphs

A convenient starting point is the definition of *perfect graphs* according to their pioneer, Claude Berge [4]. Consider the undirected graph $\mathcal{G} = (\mathcal{V}, \mathcal{E})$ with n vertices $\mathcal{V} = \{v_1, v_2, \ldots, v_n\}$ and edges $\mathcal{E} \colon \mathcal{V} \times \mathcal{V} \to \mathbb{B}$. To determine if a graph is perfect, it is necessary to consider its induced subgraphs.

Definition 2.1   A subgraph $\mathcal{H}$ of a graph $\mathcal{G}$ is said to be induced if, for any pair of vertices u and v of $\mathcal{H}$, uv is an edge of $\mathcal{H}$ if and only if uv is an edge of $\mathcal{G}$. In other words, $\mathcal{H}$ is an induced subgraph of $\mathcal{G}$ if it has exactly the edges that appear in $\mathcal{G}$ over the same vertex set. If the vertex set of $\mathcal{H}$ is the subset S of the vertices of $\mathcal{G}$, then $\mathcal{H}$ can be written as $\mathcal{G}[S]$ and is said to be *induced* by S.

Perfect graphs must satisfy the following property involving their induced subgraphs.

Definition 2.2 (PERFECT GRAPH) A graph $\mathcal{G}$ is perfect if and only if each of its induced subgraphs has chromatic number equal to clique number.

Thus, every induced subgraph $\mathcal{H} \subseteq \mathcal{G}$ in any perfect graph has chromatic number[1], $\chi(\mathcal{H})$, equal to its clique number, $\omega(\mathcal{H})$. For all graphs, it is easy to see that the clique number serves as a lower bound on the chromatic number, *i.e.* $\omega(\mathcal{G}) \leq \chi(\mathcal{G})$. For a perfect graph $\mathcal{G}$, this bound is met with equality $(\omega(\mathcal{H}) = \chi(\mathcal{H}))$ for all its induced subgraphs $\mathcal{H} \subseteq \mathcal{G}$. Examples of perfect graphs are shown in Figure 2.1.

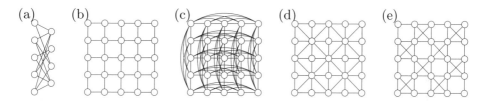

Figure 2.1 Examples of perfect graphs; (a) is bipartite; (b) is a bipartite grid graph; (c) is a Rook's graph; (d) has chromatic number equal to 3; and (e) has chromatic number equal to 4.

Berge also provided two conjectures along with the definition of perfect graphs. The weak perfect graph conjecture was resolved and is now known as the following theorem [25].

Theorem 2.3 (WEAK PERFECT GRAPH THEOREM) *A graph is perfect if and only if its complement is perfect.*

The complement of a graph is defined as follows.

Definition 2.4 (GRAPH COMPLEMENT) The complement $\overline{\mathcal{G}}$ of a graph $\mathcal{G}$ is a graph with the same vertex set[2] as $\mathcal{G}$, where distinct vertices $u, v \in \mathsf{V}(\mathcal{G})$ are adjacent in $\overline{\mathcal{G}}$ if and only if they are not adjacent in $\mathcal{G}$.

So far, it seems that deciding if a graph $\mathcal{G}$ is perfect is a daunting endeavor. One brute force approach is to consider each induced subgraph $\mathcal{H}$ of $\mathcal{G}$ and verify that its coloring number $\chi(\mathcal{H})$ equals its clique number $\omega(\mathcal{H})$. However, Berge also conjectured that perfect graphs are equivalent to another

---

[1] The chromatic number of a graph $\mathcal{G}$, $\chi(\mathcal{G})$, is the minimum number of colors needed to label vertices such that no adjacent vertices have the same color. The clique number of a graph $\mathcal{G}$, $\omega(\mathcal{G})$, is the size of a largest maximal clique (a largest subset of nodes in the graph that are all pairwise adjacent), *i.e.* $\omega(\mathcal{G}) = \max_{\mathbf{c} \in \mathcal{C}} |\mathbf{c}|$ where $\mathcal{C}$ is the set of all maximal-cliques.

[2] We use the notation $\mathsf{V}(\mathcal{G})$ to denote the vertex set $\mathcal{V}$ of a graph $\mathcal{G} = (\mathcal{V}, \mathcal{E})$.

family of graphs defined by forbidding certain induced subgraphs. This family was later named *Berge graphs* [4, 6]. A Berge graph $\mathcal{G}$ is a graph which has no odd holes and has no odd holes in its complement $\overline{\mathcal{G}}$. The notion of a hole in a graph is defined as follows.

Definition 2.5 (HOLE)   A hole of a graph $\mathcal{G}$ is an induced subgraph of $\mathcal{G}$ which is a chordless cycle of length at least 5. An odd (even) hole is a chordless cycle with odd (even) length.

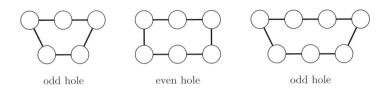

odd hole   even hole   odd hole

Figure 2.2 Various holes or chordless cycles of length 5 or larger.

Therefore, Berge graphs have no holes of length 5, 7, 9 and so on in the graph and the graph's complement. Figure 2.2 depicts a few examples of holes. Intuitively, it is easier to verify if a graph is Berge by checking for holes than it is to verify the chromatic number and clique number of all its induced subgraphs. The strong perfect graph conjecture proposed that a graph is perfect if and only if it is Berge. A formal proof of this conjecture was established recently and it is now known as the strong perfect graph theorem [10].

Theorem 2.6 (STRONG PERFECT GRAPH THEOREM)   *A graph is perfect if and only if it is Berge.*

The proof of the strong perfect graph theorem also establishes that all perfect graphs either are elements of the following basic classes:

- bipartite graphs
- complements of bipartite graphs
- line graphs of bipartite graphs
- complements of line graphs of bipartite graphs
- double split graphs

or admit one of the following structural decompositions:

- a 2-join
- a 2-join in the complement
- an M-join
- a balanced skew partition.

These decompositions are ways of repeatedly breaking up the graph such that eventually, the remaining parts are in one of the basic classes.

Definition 2.7 (LINE GRAPH) The line graph $L(\mathcal{G})$ of a graph $\mathcal{G}$ is a graph which contains a vertex for each edge of $\mathcal{G}$ and where two vertices of $L(\mathcal{G})$ are adjacent if and only if they correspond to two edges of $\mathcal{G}$ with a common end vertex.

The study of perfect graphs involves beautiful combinatorics and is rich with theoretical results. For instance, some important rules have been proposed for adding nodes to perfect graphs while ensuring that perfection is preserved. One example is Lemma 2.8 which is illustrated in Figure 2.3 [25].

Lemma 2.8 (REPLICATION) *Let $\mathcal{G}$ be a perfect graph and let $v \in V(\mathcal{G})$. Define a graph $\mathcal{G}'$ by adding to $\mathcal{G}$ a new vertex v' and joining it to v and all the neighbors of v. Then, $\mathcal{G}'$ is perfect.*

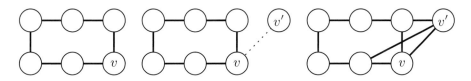

Figure 2.3 Replication. Given an initial perfect graph on the left, a new node can be introduced and attached to any other node v in the perfect graph. If the new node is also adjacent to all the neighbors of v, the resulting graph is also perfect.

Lemma 2.9 (GLUING ON CLIQUES) *A graph $\mathcal{G} = \mathcal{G}_1 \cup \mathcal{G}_2$ is perfect if $\mathcal{G}_1 \cap \mathcal{G}_2$ is a clique and both $\mathcal{G}_1$ and $\mathcal{G}_2$ are perfect graphs.*

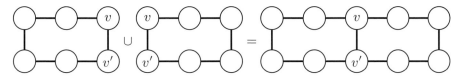

Figure 2.4 Gluing on cliques. The two graphs on the left are perfect graphs. The graph on the right is their union while their intersection is a clique cut-set. Therefore, the rightmost graph must also be perfect.

Another useful property is Lemma 2.9 which is illustrated in Figure 2.4. This property has been generalized into the so-called skew-partition decomposition [5, 10] which is a significantly more powerful tool yet is beyond the scope of this chapter. Perfect graphs have been the subject of much theoretical research. However, they also have fascinating computational properties which will be explored in the following sections.

2.2 Computational Properties of Perfect Graphs

Perfect graphs enjoy very useful computational properties. For instance, it has recently been shown that recognizing if a graph is perfect (or not perfect) only requires polynomial time [9]. Similarly, graph coloring[3], the maximum clique problem[4] and the maximum stable set[5] problem are NP-hard in general yet, remarkably, are solvable in polynomial time for perfect graphs [16]. This chapter will focus on the implications perfect graphs have vis-a-vis two key computational tools in applied machine learning and optimization: linear programming and semidefinite programming.

2.2.1 Integral Linear Programs

Another valuable property is that perfect graphs can be used to construct linear programs which produce solutions that are provably integral. A linear program is an optimization over a vector of variables $\mathbf{x} \in \mathbb{R}^n$ in n-dimensional Euclidean space. A linear program finds the solution of the following constrained optimization problem

$$\max_{\mathbf{x} \in \mathbb{R}^n} \mathbf{f}^\top \mathbf{x} \text{ subject to } \mathbf{A}\mathbf{x} \leq \mathbf{b} \tag{2.1}$$

where $\mathbf{f} \in \mathbb{R}^n$, $\mathbf{A} \in \mathbb{R}^{m \times n}$ and $\mathbf{b} \in \mathbb{R}^m$ are inputs that are specified by the user. It is known that solving such linear programs is in P and algorithms are available that recover the optimal $\mathbf{x}^*$ value in $\mathcal{O}(\sqrt{m}n^3)$ time. This recovered solution $\mathbf{x}^*$ generally contains real values.

In contrast, consider the *binary* linear program

$$\max_{\mathbf{x} \in \mathbb{B}^n} \mathbf{f}^\top \mathbf{x} \text{ s.t. } \mathbf{A}\mathbf{x} \leq \mathbf{b}$$

where the solution vector is forced to be binary, in other words $\mathbf{x} \in \mathbb{B}^n$. This problem is notoriously NP-hard in the worst case and no efficient general solver is available [19].

Interestingly, if we require the constraints matrix $\mathbf{A}$ to have a special form, specifically if it is a *perfect matrix* (see below), then we can further guarantee that the solution $\mathbf{x}^*$ obtained by standard linear programming will only have binary values. Consider the following rearranged form of Equation 2.1 known as a set-packing linear program,

$$\max_{\mathbf{x} \in \mathbb{R}^n, \mathbf{x} \geq \mathbf{0}} \mathbf{f}^\top \mathbf{x} \text{ s.t. } \mathbf{A}\mathbf{x} \leq \mathbf{1}$$

---

[3] To color a graph $\mathcal{G}$ find the smallest set of assignment labels called "colors" such that no two adjacent vertices share the same color.

[4] The maximum clique of a graph $\mathcal{G}$ is a largest subset of nodes in $\mathcal{G}$ that are all pairwise adjacent.

[5] The maximum stable set of a graph $\mathcal{G}$ is a largest set of nodes in $\mathcal{G}$ no two of which are adjacent.

where $\mathbf{0} \in \mathbb{R}^n$ is a vector of all zeros and $\mathbf{1} \in \mathbb{R}^m$ is a vector of all ones. The following theorem shows how standard linear programming can be used to solve certain binary programs [25, 11].

Theorem 2.10 *For every non-negative vector $\mathbf{f} \in \mathbb{R}^n$, the linear program*

$$\max_{\mathbf{x} \in \mathbb{R}^n, \mathbf{x} \geq 0} \mathbf{f}^\top \mathbf{x} \text{ s.t. } \mathbf{A}\mathbf{x} \leq \mathbf{1}$$

recovers a vector $\mathbf{x}^*$ which is integral if and only if the (undominated) rows of $\mathbf{A}$ form the vertex-versus-maximal cliques incidence matrix of some perfect graph.

The constraint matrix $\mathbf{A}$ is obtained from a graph $\mathcal{G}$ according to the following definition.

Definition 2.11 (UNDOMINATED INCIDENCE MATRIX) The undominated incidence matrix of a graph $\mathcal{G}$ with vertices $\{v_1, \ldots, v_n\}$ and maximal cliques $\mathcal{C} = \{\mathbf{c}_1, \ldots, \mathbf{c}_m\}$ is matrix $\mathbf{A} \in \mathbb{B}^{m \times n}$ where $\mathbf{A}_{ij} = 1$ if $v_i \in \mathbf{c}_j$ and $\mathbf{A}_{ij} = 0$ otherwise.

A *perfect matrix* is simply the undominated incidence matrix $\mathbf{A}$ obtained from a graph $\mathcal{G}$ which is perfect. In the following sections, this property will be leveraged for MAP estimation with graphical models.

2.2.2 Lovász Theta Function

The Lovász theta function $\vartheta(\mathcal{G}) \in \mathbb{R}$ accepts as input a graph $\mathcal{G}$ and outputs a non-negative scalar [26, 20]. For any graph, it is computable in polynomial time. Modern solvers can recover $\vartheta(\mathcal{G})$ within a multiplicative approximation factor of $(1 + \epsilon)$ in time $\mathcal{O}(\epsilon^{-2} n^5 \log n)$ using primal-dual methods [8]. The following straightforward semidefinite program recovers the Lovász theta function

$$\vartheta(\mathcal{G}) = \max_{\mathbf{M} \in \mathbb{R}^{n \times n}, \mathbf{M} \succeq 0} \sum_{ij} \mathbf{M}_{ij} \text{ s.t. } \sum_i \mathbf{M}_{ii} = 1, \ \mathbf{M}_{ij} = 0 \ \forall (i,j) \in \mathcal{E}.$$

Remarkably, the Lovász number satisfies the *sandwich* property:

$$\omega(\mathcal{G}) \leq \vartheta(\overline{\mathcal{G}}) \leq \chi(\mathcal{G}). \tag{2.2}$$

Since perfect graphs satisfy $\omega(\mathcal{G}) = \chi(\mathcal{G})$, it is always possible to find the coloring number (or the maximum clique size) efficiently for a perfect graph $\mathcal{G}$ simply by computing the Lovász theta function on its complement. Otherwise, in general, the coloring number can be intractable to compute in the worst case. In the following sections, we shall illustrate how the Lovász theta function can be useful for MAP estimation as well.

2.3 Graphical Models

Great strides have been made by the combinatorics community in the study of perfect graphs. How does this progress advance machine learning and statistical inference? These fields also use graphs to represent problems and use graph-theoretic algorithms to solve them. In machine learning and statistical inference, graphs are extensively used in the study of *graphical models*. A graphical model represents the factorization of a probability density function [32]. This chapter will focus on the factor graph notation for graphical models and use the non-calligraphic font to distinguish these graphs from those discussed in the previous sections. A factor graph is a bipartite graph $G = (V, W, E)$ with *variable* vertices $V = \{1, \ldots, k\}$, *factor* vertices $W = \{1, \ldots, l\}$ and a set of edges E between V and W. In addition, define the universe of discrete random variables $Y = \{y_1, \ldots, y_k\}$ each associated with an element of V and define a set of strictly positive[6] *potential functions* $\Psi = \{\psi_1, \ldots, \psi_l\}$ each associated with an element of W. We will often use the term *factor* and *potential function* interchangeably when re refer to $c \in W$, $\psi_c \in \Psi$ or the arguments of ψ_c. Also, for $j \in V$, each $y_j \in \mathbb{N}$ is a discrete random variable with $|y_j|$ possible configurations[7], in other words $y_j \in \{0, \ldots, (|y_j| - 1)\}$. The factor graph implies that the function $p(Y)$ factorizes as

$$p(y_1, \ldots, y_k) = \frac{1}{Z} \prod_{c \in W} \psi_c(Y_c) \tag{2.3}$$

where Z is the partition function[8] and Y_c is a subset of the random variables that are associated with the neighbors of node c. In other words, $Y_c = \{y_j | j \in \mathsf{Ne}(c)\}$ where $\mathsf{Ne}(c)$ is the set of vertices that are neighbors of the factor c with potential function ψ_c. Thus, each potential $\psi_c : Y_c \to \mathbb{R}^+$ is a function over the corresponding set of random variables Y_c. Note that it is possible to divide each ψ_c function by an arbitrary scalar $\gamma_c > 0$ without changing $p(Y)$ (the partition function Z has to be adjusted accordingly, of course). An example factor graph is shown in Figure 2.5.

---

[6] This article assumes strictly positive potential functions $\psi_c > 0, \forall c$. Note that it is always possible to rewrite $p(Y)$ as an equivalent pairwise Markov random field (MRF) over binary variables [34].

[7] We will abuse notation and take the symbol $|\cdot|$ to mean the largest possible value an integer can achieve as well as use $|\cdot|$ in the traditional sense to indicate the cardinality or size of a set. The meaning of the operator should be clear from the context.

[8] The partition function Z is set such that $\sum_{y_1} \cdots \sum_{y_k} p(y_1, \ldots, y_k) = 1$.

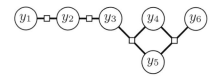

Figure 2.5 An example of a factor graph representing the factorization of a probability distribution $p(y_1, y_2, y_3, y_4, y_5, y_6)$ = $\frac{1}{Z} \psi_{1,2}(y_1, y_2) \psi_{2,3}(y_2, y_3) \psi_{3,4,5}(y_3, y_4, y_5) \psi_{4,5,6}(y_4, y_5, y_6)$. The round nodes represent random variables while square nodes represent potential functions.

A canonical problem that one aims to solve with graphical models is *maximum a posteriori* estimation. Many tasks in image processing, coding, protein folding and more can be cast as MAP estimation which, given a factor graph and potential functions, recovers $\arg\max_Y p(Y)$.

The MAP problem is, in the worst case, NP-hard [30] and may involve exponential work in the storage size of the input graphical model. However, certain types of graphical models do admit exact inference efficiently. For example, MAP estimation in (junction) tree graphical models is efficient [27]. Similarly, graphical models where the potential functions $\psi_1, \ldots, \psi_l$ are submodular also admit efficient MAP estimation [14, 23]. In many situations, the requisite algorithms are implemented using message passing schemes (such as max-product and variants of max-product), linear programming or network-flow solvers [22, 13, 23]. It is also sometimes possible to consider linear programming relaxations or message passing to potentially approximate the MAP solution when exact inference is intractable [13]. However, *how* one goes about building such linear programming relaxations will affect the ultimate effectiveness of linear programming solvers [24]. This chapter will propose a method of compiling the MAP estimation problem into a maximum weight stable set problem (MWSS) which is defined below. The MWSS is also referred to as the maximum weight independent set problem (MWIS). These are hard problems in the worst case but remain tractable if the input graph they are applied to is perfect [15].

2.4 Nand Markov Random Fields

Consider compiling the graphical model G above into another representation which will be referred to as a nand Markov random field (NMRF). A NMRF is a graph $\mathcal{G} = (\mathcal{V}, \mathcal{E})$ with a set of binary variables $\mathcal{X}$ and a set of scalar weights $\mathcal{F}$. For each vertex $v \in \mathcal{V}$, there is one binary variable $x \in \mathcal{X}$ and one scalar weight $f \in \mathcal{F}$ associated with v. More precisely, the set $\mathcal{X}$ (resp.

Algorithm 2.1 COMPILEINTONMRF

Input factor graph $G = (V, W, E)$ with positive $\psi_1(Y_1), \ldots, \psi_l(Y_l)$

Initialize graph $\mathcal{G} = (\mathcal{V}, \mathcal{E})$ as an empty graph, $\mathcal{X} = \{\}$, and $\mathcal{F} = \{\}$
For each factor $c \in W$
    Set γ_c to the smallest value of $\psi_c(Y_c)$
    For each configuration i of the set of variables Y_c
        Add a vertex $v_{c,i}$ to $\mathcal{V}$
        Add a Boolean $x_{c,i} \in \mathbb{B}$ associated with $v_{c,i}$ to $\mathcal{X}$
        Add a weight $f_{c,i} \in \mathbb{R}$ associated with $v_{c,i}$ to $\mathcal{F}$
        Set $f_{c,i} = \log(\psi_c(Y_c = i)/\gamma_c)$
        For each $v_{c',i'} \in \mathcal{V}$ that is incompatible with $v_{c,i}$
            Add an edge between $v_{c,i}$ and $v_{c',i'}$ to $\mathcal{E}$

Output nand Markov random field $\mathcal{G} = (\mathcal{V}, \mathcal{E})$, $\mathcal{X}$, and $\mathcal{F}$

$\mathcal{F}$) contains one Boolean $x_{c,i}$ (resp. non-negative scalar $f_{c,i}$) for each factor $c \in W$ and for each configuration $i \in Y_c$ whenever $\psi_c(Y_c) > 0$. We say that two configurations $x_{c,i}$ and $x_{c',i'}$ are *incompatible* if the configurations i and i' imply different settings of the shared variables in $Y_c \cap Y_{c'}$. The NMRF has edges $\mathcal{E}$ between all pairs of configurations that are *incompatible*. The edges imply incompatibility since at most one node at the base of an edge can be instantiated while ensuring that the graphical model is in a consistent configuration (otherwise, the variables in $Y_c \cap Y_{c'}$ have to be in two configurations simultaneously which is impossible). Thus, each edge represents a nand relationship which we write as $\delta[x_{c,i} + x_{c',i'} \leq 1]$ where $\delta[\cdot] = 1$ if the statement inside the brackets is true and $\delta[\cdot] = 0$ otherwise. Consider Algorithm 2.1 which compiles a graphical model into a NMRF.

Let $n = |\mathcal{V}|$ be the total number of nodes in the NMRF output by Algorithm 2.1. The (unnormalized) probability associated with the NMRF factorizes as follows:

$$\rho(\mathcal{X}) = \prod_{(c,i) \in \mathcal{V}} \exp(f_{c,i} x_{c,i}) \prod_{((c,i),(c',i')) \in \mathcal{E}} (1 - x_{c,i} x_{c',i'}). \qquad (2.4)$$

The nand constraints prevent variables $x_{c,i}$ and $x_{c',i'}$ from both being set to 1 if they share an edge (this drives $\rho(\mathcal{X})$ to zero). We wish to set some of the Boolean entries in $\mathcal{X}$ to 1 to maximize the value of ρ. This is equivalent to maximizing $\sum_{(i,c) \in \mathcal{V}} f_{c,i} x_{c,i}$ while enforcing the nand constraints. This is a *maximum weight stable set* MWSS problem which is a weighted variant of the *maximum stable set* (MSS) problem.

Definition 2.12 (MAXIMUM STABLE SET)   The maximum stable set of a graph $G = (V, E)$ is a largest subset of nodes in G such that no two nodes in the subset are pairwise adjacent.

The MSS problem is merely a MWSS problem where all the weights are constant. Thus, the MWSS strictly generalizes the MSS.

Definition 2.13 (MAXIMUM WEIGHT STABLE SET)   The maximum weight stable set of a graph $G = (V, E)$ with non-negative weights F is a subset of nodes in G with largest total weight such that no two nodes in the subset are pairwise adjacent.

More precisely, to avoid problems in certain special cases, we will be interested in solving a *maximal maximum weight stable set* (MMWSS) problem on the NMRF. This not only maximizes Equation 2.4 but, in the case of ties and in the case where some weights in F are exactly zero, the MMWSS also selects the maximizer which sets the most possible Boolean variables to 1. Thus, the MMWSS strictly generalizes the MWSS.

Definition 2.14 (MAXIMAL MAXIMUM WEIGHT STABLE SET)   The maximal maximum weight stable set of a graph $G = (V, E)$ with non-negative weights F is a maximum weight stable set of G with largest cardinality.

Assume we have recovered the MMWSS of the NMRF $G = (V, E)$ with weights F. This solution can be denoted by $V^* \subseteq V$ or by a set of Booleans X^*. In the Boolean representation X^*, for each $v \in V$, its corresponding Boolean variable $x \in X^*$ is set to 1 if $v \in V^*$ and is set to 0 otherwise. Does the solution recovered by the MMWSS of G coincide with the MAP estimate of $p(Y)$? It is clear that the Booleans in X span a superset (a relaxation) of the set of valid configurations of Y since X can represent inconsistent configurations of Y. In other words, there is a surjective relation between Y and X: each setting of Y can be mapped to a unique corresponding setting in X yet the converse is not true. This leads to an important question: can X^* be used to recover a valid Y^* configuration which coincides with the MAP estimate, in other words $p(Y^*) = \max_Y p(Y)$? Theorem 2.16 shows that X^* indeed produces the MAP estimate. The theorem leverages the following lemma which shows that the MMWSS of G will always produce a unique assignment per factor, in other words, $\sum_i x_{c,i} = 1$ for each $c \in W$.

Lemma 2.15   *The maximal maximum weight stable set X^* of a NMRF graph G satisfies $\sum_i x^*_{c,i} = 1$ for each factor $c \in W$.*

Proof   Setting all the Boolean variables in X to zero produces a value $\rho = 1$

in Equation 2.4. For a non-trivial NMRF, at least one of the weights in $\mathcal{F}$ is strictly positive. Set the Boolean variable that corresponds to this strictly positive weight to 1 while keeping the rest of $\mathcal{X}$ set to zero. This produces a $\rho(\mathcal{X}) > 1$ since $\prod_{((c,i),(c',i'))\in\mathcal{E}}(1 - x_{c,i}x_{c',i'})$ equals 1 if only one Boolean equals 1 in $\mathcal{X}$. Exponentiating a strictly positive weight produces a value $\prod_{(c,i)\in\mathcal{V}}\exp(f_{c,i}x_{c,i})$ that is strictly larger than 1. Therefore, the MMWSS $\mathcal{X}^*$ must achieve $\rho(\mathcal{X}^*) > 1$. Clearly, there can be no incompatible configurations in the MMWSS since $\prod_{((c,i),(c',i'))\in\mathcal{E}}(1 - x^*_{c,i}x^*_{c',i'})$ would go to zero which contradicts the fact that $\rho(\mathcal{X}^*) > 1$. Next note that, for $\mathcal{X}^*$ and for each $c \in W$, one of the following must hold: (i) $\sum_i x^*_{c,i} > 1$, (ii) $\sum_i x^*_{c,i} = 0$ or (iii) $\sum_i x^*_{c,i} = 1$. Since Algorithm 2.1 places edges between disagreeing configurations, the term $\prod_{((c,i),(c',i'))\in\mathcal{E}}(1-x_{c,i}x_{c',i'})$ would go to zero whenever condition (i) is met since two incompatible Boolean variables would have to be simultaneously asserted. Since the MAP estimate achieves $\rho(\mathcal{X}^*) > 1$, condition (i) cannot hold. Consider a factor c where condition (ii) is met. Since there are no incompatibilities in the MMWSS, for any such factor there is always a configuration j that may be selected which agrees with neighboring factors. If the value of $f_{c,j} > 0$, it is possible to preserve compatibility by setting $x_{c,j} = 1$ to strictly increase $\rho(\mathcal{X}^*)$. However, the MMWSS achieves the maximal $\rho(\mathcal{X}^*)$ value possible so the objective cannot be strictly increased. If the value of $f_{c,j} = 0$, the MMWSS will still always set $x_{c,j} = 1$ since this increases the cardinality of the solution. Thus, condition (ii) cannot hold for $\mathcal{X}^*$ either. This leaves condition (iii) as the only valid possibility. Therefore, the MMWSS satisfies $\sum_i x^*_{c,i} = 1$ for all factors $c \in W$.   □

Theorem 2.16   *The MMWSS of a NMRF finds the MAP estimate of Equation 2.3 for a graphical model with strictly positive potential functions.*

Proof   Lemma 2.15 shows that the MAP estimate of Equation 2.4 produces $\sum_i x^*_{c,i} = 1$ for each $c \in W$. So only a single setting, say $x_{c,\hat{\imath}} = 1$, is asserted for each c and the variables Y_c involved in factor c are in a single configuration $Y_c = \hat{\imath}$. Therefore, a consistent setting of the discrete random variables Y^* can be recovered from $\mathcal{X}^*$. Since $\rho(\mathcal{X}^*) \geq \rho(\mathcal{X})$ for all $\mathcal{X}$, since $p(Y) \propto \rho(X)$ for all Y, and since $\mathcal{X}$ is a superset of the configurations of Y, it must be the case that $p(Y^*) \geq p(Y)$ for all Y.   □

Thus, we have shown how to compile any graphical model into a NMRF. The maximal maximum weight stable set of the NMRF can then be found to

---

Algorithm 2.2 FINDMMWSS

Input graph $\mathcal{G} = (\mathcal{V}, \mathcal{E})$ with weights $\mathcal{F}$

Initialize $\mathcal{V}_0 = \{\}$

For each $v \in \mathcal{V}$

   If the weight f associated to v is zero, add v to $\mathcal{V}_0$

Find MWSS on induced subgraph $\mathcal{G}_1 = \mathcal{G}[\mathcal{V} \setminus \mathcal{V}_0]$ and store it in $\hat{\mathcal{V}}_1$

For each $v \in \mathcal{V}_0$

   If v is adjacent to any node in $\hat{\mathcal{V}}_1$ remove v from $\mathcal{V}_0$

Find MSS on induced subgraph $\mathcal{G}_0 = \mathcal{G}[\mathcal{V}_0]$ and store it in $\hat{\mathcal{V}}_0$

Output $\hat{\mathcal{V}}_0 \cup \hat{\mathcal{V}}_1$

---

obtain $\mathcal{X}^*$. Finally, it is straightforward to recover a consistent solution Y^* from $\mathcal{X}^*$. Algorithm 2.2 describes the MMWSS procedure more precisely.

In Algorithm 2.2, it turns out that the maximal maximum weight stable set problem merely requires the solution of a MWSS sub-problem and a MSS sub-problem with some minor book-keeping. The algorithm accepts a graph $\mathcal{G} = (\mathcal{V}, \mathcal{E})$ with weights $\mathcal{F}$ and finds a maximal maximum weight stable set. It does so by first discarding any nodes with zero weight (these are denoted by $\mathcal{V}_0$). It then solves the MWSS on the induced subgraph $\mathcal{G}_1$ over the remaining nodes $\mathcal{V} \setminus \mathcal{V}_0$ (using the corresponding weights in $\mathcal{F}$). Given a MWSS solution $\hat{\mathcal{V}}_1$ on $\mathcal{G}_1$ we can extend the solution to $\mathcal{G}$ by deleting any nodes in $\mathcal{V}_0$ which are adjacent to $\hat{\mathcal{V}}_1$. The remaining nodes in $\mathcal{V}_0$ are then non-adjacent to $\hat{\mathcal{V}}_1$ and another MSS solution $\hat{\mathcal{V}}_0$ can be recovered from the induced subgraph $\mathcal{G}_0 = \mathcal{G}[\mathcal{V}_0]$ separately. The final MMWSS solution is the union of both stable sets, $\hat{\mathcal{V}} = \hat{\mathcal{V}}_0 \cup \hat{\mathcal{V}}_1$. By solving MWSS sub-problems separately on two induced sub-graphs of $\mathcal{G}$ (namely $\mathcal{G}_1$ and $\mathcal{G}_0$), the overall MMWSS problem may potentially remain tractable. As long as $\mathcal{G}_1$ and $\mathcal{G}_0$ are perfect graphs, Algorithm 2.2 is efficient even if the original graph $\mathcal{G}$ itself is a non-perfect graph. Furthermore, since $\mathcal{G}_1$ and $\mathcal{G}_0$ are smaller than $\mathcal{G}$, this approach is also potentially faster even if $\mathcal{G}$ is perfect.

Having shown how to solve the MMWSS problem by solving two MWSS sub-problems (a standard MWSS problem and a MWSS problem with constant weights), we next discuss the implementation of the required MWSS solvers. Further, we ask: what graphical models have easy solutions such that the required MWSS steps of Algorithm 2.2 remain efficient? Hopefully, the MWSS solvers only operate on perfect subgraphs so that they remain efficient.

2.5 Maximum Weight Stable Set

The previous section has shown that MAP estimation with a graphical model reduces to two maximum weight stable set sub-problems. The MWSS problem, however, is NP-hard in the worst case. Fortunately, it can be solved efficiently when the input graph is perfect. Another family of graphs where MWSS can be efficiently solved is the family of claw-free graphs. The MWSS problem takes as input a graph $\mathcal{G} = (\mathcal{V}, \mathcal{E})$ with a set of non-negative weights $\mathcal{F}$ and outputs a subset of nodes with maximal total weight such that no two nodes are adjacent in $\mathcal{G}$. We will show three approaches that solve such a problem when $\mathcal{G}$ is a perfect graph. To solve a maximum stable set (MSS) problem, these three implementations are simply provided with constant weights in $\mathcal{F}$.

2.5.1 Linear Programming

One possibility is using linear programming to solve the MWSS sub-problems in Algorithm 2.2. The linear program is used to estimate $n = |\mathcal{V}|$ variables as follows. First, obtain the vertex-versus-maximal cliques incidence matrix $\mathbf{A} \in \mathbb{B}^{m \times n}$ from graph $\mathcal{G}$ as in Definition 2.11. In general, this requires using an algorithm to find all the cliques $\mathcal{C} = \{\mathbf{c}_1, \ldots, \mathbf{c}_m\}$ in the graph $\mathcal{G}$ [7, 31]. These cliques are then used to construct $\mathbf{A}$. We also rewrite the set of weights $\mathcal{F}$ as a vector $\mathbf{f} \in \mathbb{R}^n$. Then, solve the following linear program

$$\max_{\mathbf{x} \in \mathbb{R}^n, \mathbf{x} \geq 0} \mathbf{f}^{\top} \mathbf{x} \text{ s.t. } \mathbf{A}\mathbf{x} \leq 1 \tag{2.5}$$

to obtain $\mathbf{x}^* \in \mathbb{R}^n$. If the graph $\mathcal{G}$ is perfect, the solution vector $\mathbf{x}^*$ is binary and can be immediately written as a solution over the set of Boolean variables $\mathcal{X}^*$. These, in turn, can easily be used to recover the discrete random variables Y^* in the original graphical model. The runtime of the linear program is $\mathcal{O}(\sqrt{m}n^3)$. The runtime of the clique-finding algorithm is $\mathcal{O}(m)$ however, this component may not be necessary to run each time if the input to the MWSS solver has the same graph topology $\mathcal{G}$ and only the weights $\mathcal{F}$ are allowed to vary. As long as m and n are not too large, such a MWSS solver can be fast in practice.

2.5.2 Message Passing

In situations where n is large, linear programming may be unacceptably slow. Furthermore, in situations where computation needs to be distributed across many devices, linear programming may be impractical as it requires

Algorithm 2.3 SOLVEMWSSVIAMPLP

Input: $\mathcal{G} = (\mathcal{V}, \mathcal{E})$, cliques $\mathcal{C} = \{\mathbf{c}_1, \ldots, \mathbf{c}_m\}$ and weights f_i for $i \in \mathcal{V}$

Initialize $\lambda^0_{i,\mathbf{c}} \in \mathbb{R}^+$ arbitrarily for $i \in \mathcal{V}$ and $\mathbf{c} \in \mathcal{C}$
Until converged do
  Randomly choose $i \in \mathcal{V}$ and $\mathbf{c} \in \mathcal{C}$
  Set $\lambda_{i,\mathbf{c}}^{(t+1)} = \frac{1-|\mathbf{c}|}{|\mathbf{c}|} \sum\limits_{\mathbf{c}' \in \mathcal{C} \backslash \mathbf{c}: i \in \mathbf{c}'} \lambda_{i,\mathbf{c}'}^{(t)} + \frac{1}{|\mathbf{c}|} \frac{f_i}{\sum\limits_{\mathbf{c} \in \mathcal{C}} [i \in \mathbf{c}]}$

  $\qquad\qquad - \frac{1}{|\mathbf{c}|} \max\left[0, \max\limits_{i' \in \mathbf{c} \backslash i}\left[\frac{f_{i'}}{\sum\limits_{\mathbf{c} \in \mathcal{C}} [i' \in \mathbf{c}]} + \sum\limits_{\mathbf{c}' \in \mathcal{C} \backslash \mathbf{c}: i' \in \mathbf{c}'} \lambda_{i',\mathbf{c}'}^{(t)}\right]\right]$

Output: $x_i^* = \sum_{\mathbf{c} \in \mathcal{C}: i \in \mathbf{c}} \lambda_{i,\mathbf{c}}^{(t)}$ for $i \in \mathcal{V}$

centralized storage and computation. An alternative approach is to use message-passing techniques [32] which iteratively send messages between nodes and factors in a graphical model to converge to the MAP estimate. In our case, message-passing will be used to find the MWSS solution in Algorithm 2.2. The most popular message-passing method is the max-product (MP) algorithm [33]. A more convergent variant is the max-product-linear-programming (MPLP) algorithm which solves linear programs in the dual via coordinate descent [13, 18]. The MPLP implementation for solving a MWSS problem is depicted in Algorithm 2.3. Surprisingly, for the MWSS problem, the MPLP algorithm gives the same update rule as the MP algorithm dampened by a factor of $\frac{1-|\mathbf{c}|}{|\mathbf{c}|}$.

The message passing steps underlying Algorithm 2.3 perform coordinate descent in the dual of a linear program. It was later shown that the MPLP algorithm is performing dual coordinate descent in a different linear program rather than the one shown in Equation 2.5. A message passing scheme which repairs this problem was later proposed [12]. It works directly with the dual of the set-packing linear program in Equation 2.5, also known as a covering linear program:

$$\min_{\mathbf{z} \in \mathbb{R}^m, \mathbf{z} \geq \mathbf{0}} \mathbf{1}^\top \mathbf{z} \text{ s.t. } \mathbf{A}^\top \mathbf{z} \geq \mathbf{f}.$$

Coordinate descent in this dual can be implemented as a message-passing scheme with better convergence properties and seems to consistently agree with the output of the set-packing linear program [12]. This improved message-passing solver is known as CD2MP (pairwise coordinate descent message passing) and is summarized in Algorithm 2.4. Given the dual solution, it is straightforward to recover $\mathcal{X}^* = \{x_1^*, \ldots, x_n^*\}$. Recall that, by

---

Algorithm 2.4 SOLVEMWSSVIACD2MP

Input: $\mathcal{G} = (\mathcal{V}, \mathcal{E})$, cliques $\mathcal{C} = \{\mathbf{c}_1, \ldots, \mathbf{c}_m\}$ and weights f_i for $i \in \mathcal{V}$

Initialize $z_j = \max_{i \in \mathbf{c}_j} \frac{f_i}{\sum_{\mathbf{c} \in \mathcal{C}}[i \in \mathbf{c}]}$ for $j \in \{1, \ldots, m\}$

Until converged do

    Randomly choose $a \neq b \in \{1, \ldots, m\}$

    Compute $h_i = \max\left(0, \left(f_i - \sum_{j:i \in \mathbf{c}_j, j \neq a, b} z_j\right)\right)$ for $i \in \mathbf{c}_a \cup \mathbf{c}_b$

    Compute $s_a = \max_{i \in \mathbf{c}_a \setminus \mathbf{c}_b} h_i$

    Compute $s_b = \max_{i \in \mathbf{c}_b \setminus \mathbf{c}_a} h_i$

    Compute $s_{ab} = \max_{i \in \mathbf{c}_a \cap \mathbf{c}_b} h_i$

    Update $z_a = \max\left[s_a, \frac{1}{2}(s_a - s_b + s_{ab})\right]$

    Update $z_b = \max\left[s_b, \frac{1}{2}(s_b - s_a + s_{ab})\right]$

Output: $\mathbf{z}^* = [z_1, \ldots, z_m]^\top$

---

complementary slackness of the dual linear programs, whenever $z_j^* > 0$ the corresponding constraint in the primal is achieved with equality, in other words: $\sum_{i=1}^n \mathbf{A}_{ij} x_i^* = 1$.

2.5.3 Semidefinite Programming

In many cases, the linear programming and message passing methods above may not be practical. This is because the number of maximal cliques m in a graph $\mathcal{G}$ with n vertices can be as large as $3^{n/3}$. Thus, regardless of how quickly one can enumerate the maximal cliques in a graph, the computations underlying linear programming and message passing may still require exponential work in the worst case (even if the input graph is perfect). In those situations, it is best to avoid clique enumeration altogether and instead use the Lovász theta function to directly solve the MWSS problem [35]. Such semidefinite programming methods can require as little as $\tilde{\mathcal{O}}(n^5)$ time and are potentially more efficient than linear programming and message passing methods, particularly if $m \geq \mathcal{O}(n^4)$.

Recall that one may solve the MWSS problem on a weighted graph $\mathcal{G}$ by finding the maximum weight clique in the graph $\overline{\mathcal{G}}$. For perfect graphs, the Lovász theta-function $\vartheta(\overline{\mathcal{G}})$ computes the weight of the maximum clique. Thus, we can recover the size of the maximal stable set via $\vartheta(\mathcal{G})$.

Since we are dealing with weighted graphs (with weights on nodes), however, consider the *weighted* Lovász theta-function which accepts a graph

$\mathcal{G} = (\mathcal{V}, \mathcal{E})$ with weights $\mathcal{F} = \{f_1, \ldots, f_n\}$ where $n = |\mathcal{V}|$ and computes

$$\vartheta_{\mathcal{F}}(\mathcal{G}) = \max_{\mathbf{M} \succeq \mathbf{0}} \sum_{ij} \sqrt{f_i f_j} \mathbf{M}_{ij} \text{ s.t. } \sum_i \mathbf{M}_{ii} = 1, \ \mathbf{M}_{ij} = 0 \, \forall (i, j) \in \mathcal{E}$$

via semidefinite programming. Setting all the weights to 1 gives the usual Lovász theta-function which was introduced earlier. Solving for $\vartheta_{\mathcal{F}}(\mathcal{G})$ on a NMRF with a perfect graph outputs the total weight of the MWSS. Let $\mathbf{M} \in \mathbb{R}^{n \times n}$ be the maximizer of $\vartheta_{\mathcal{F}}(\mathcal{G})$ and let ϑ be the recovered total weight of the MWSS. Under mild conditions, we can recover the solution $\mathcal{X}^*$ from the corresponding vector solution $\mathbf{x}^* = \text{round}(\vartheta \mathbf{M1})$. In other words, we round the matrix multiplied by the all ones vector after scaling by the total weight. While slightly faster semidefinite programs have been proposed [8] that require $\tilde{\mathcal{O}}(n^5)$, even off-the-shelf interior-point solvers return $\mathcal{X}^*$ within $\mathcal{O}(n^6)$. In summary, this method is truly polynomial time for any perfect graph $\mathcal{G}$ even if the graph has an exponential number of cliques. Furthermore, this method is fully polynomial in the input size of the original graphical model G as long Algorithm 2.2 only computes MWSS and MSS sub-problems on perfect graphs. Thus, the semidefinite programming methods underlying the Lovász theta function avoid the clique enumeration problems that plague linear programming and message passing. In this sense, perfect graphs can still provide computational efficiency when the linear programming approaches (despite achieving integral solutions) are inefficient. This is a clear advantage of perfect graphs over traditional linear program integrality and total unimodularity approaches.

The next section enumerates several graphical models that compile into NMRFs that only require solving MWSS problems on perfect graphs. Therefore, the above solution methods (linear programming, message passing and semidefinite programming) are guaranteed to return the necessary MWSS efficiently.

2.6 Tractable Graphical Models

Certain families of graphical models are known to admit efficient MAP estimates. This leads to the natural question: do these graphical models readily compile into NMRFs with perfect graphs? For instance, junction trees and graphical models without cycles can be solved via efficient message passing techniques such as the max-product algorithm [27, 32]. Similarly, graphical models that solve matching and generalized matching problems admit exact inference in cubic time (or better) via the max-product algorithm [2, 17, 29, 3]. Graphical models with arbitrary topologies yet associative (submodular) potentials[9] also admit efficient algorithms via graph-cuts or min-cost network flow methods [14, 23]. We next consider the NMRF representation of these specific MAP problems.

2.6.1 Acyclic Graphical Models

Tree-structured and acyclic graphical models are known to admit both efficient MAP estimation and efficient marginal inference. Recall that we are given as input a graphical model G with discrete random variables $y_1, \ldots, y_k$ with $|y_1|, \ldots, |y_k|$ possible configurations each. A simple acyclic graphical model is a tree with the following factorization

$$p(Y) = \frac{1}{Z} \prod_{i=2}^{k} \psi_i(y_i, pa(y_i))$$

where $pa(y_i)$ is a single node which is a parent of y_i in a directed acyclic graph (DAG) and where y_1 is the root of the tree and has no parent node in the DAG. Consider compiling this graphical model into a NMRF using Algorithm 2.1 as depicted in Figure 2.6.

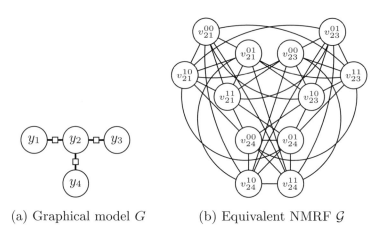

(a) Graphical model G (b) Equivalent NMRF $\mathcal{G}$

Figure 2.6 Compiling a tree structured graphical model G with binary random variables into its NMRF representation $\mathcal{G}$ (therein, subscripts denote the factor the NMRF node corresponds to and superscripts denote the configuration of its corresponding random variables).

Theorem 2.17   *A graphical model with a tree graph G produces a NMRF with a perfect graph $\mathcal{G}$.*

---

[9] In physics, models with associative potentials are also called ferromagnetic.

Proof First consider the simplest case where the input tree graphical model is merely a star. Consider a star graphical model G_a with an internal random variable y and leaf random variables $\{y_1, \ldots, y_p\}$ with $c = 1, \ldots, p$ factors over the pairs of variables $Y_c = \{y, y_c\}$. Compile the graphical model G_a into an NMRF $\mathcal{G}_a$ as follows. Initialize $\mathcal{G}_a = \{\}$ and introduce a NMRF node $v_{c,0+j}$ for each factor Y_c for each of the $j = 0, \ldots, |y| - 1$ configurations of y while fixing the setting $y_c = 0$. Join all these NMRF nodes pairwise if they correspond to different configurations of y. The resulting graph is a complete $|y|$-partite graph which is known to be perfect [5]. To obtain $\mathcal{G}_a$ from the current complete $|y|$-partite graph, sequentially introduce additional nodes $v_{c,i|y|+j}$ for each Y_c for each of the $j = 0, \ldots, |y| - 1$ configurations of y as well as for each of the remaining $i = 1, \ldots, |y_c| - 1$ settings of y_c. Each sequentially introduced node is joined to the corresponding node $v_{c,0+j}$ that is already in $\mathcal{G}_a$ as well as all the neighbors of $v_{c,0+j}$. By the replication procedure in Lemma 2.8, this sequential introduction of additional nodes and edges maintains graph perfection. Once all nodes are added, the resulting graph is precisely the final graph $\mathcal{G}_a$ obtained by compiling a star G_a into NMRF form. Therefore, $\mathcal{G}_a$ is perfect by construction. Next, consider merging two such star-structured graphical models. The first star, G_a, contains the internal random variable y and leaf random variables $\{y_1, \ldots, y_p\}$. The second star, G_b, contains the internal random variable $\tilde{y}$ and leaf random variables $\{\tilde{y}_1, \ldots, \tilde{y}_q\}$. Consider merging these two stars by merging random variable y_1 into node $\tilde{y}$, merging random variable $\tilde{y}_1$ into node y and merging the factor ψ_{y,y_1} and factor $\psi_{\tilde{y},\tilde{y}_1}$ into a single factor $\psi_{y,\tilde{y}}$. The resulting union of two star-shaped graphical models, denoted G_{a+b}, is no longer a star but rather a simple tree-shaped graphical model. The stars G_a and G_b separately give rise to NMRFs $\mathcal{G}_a$ and $\mathcal{G}_b$ which have already been shown to be perfect. The tree G_{a+b} gives rise to a NMRF denoted $\mathcal{G}_{a+b}$. The star shaped graphical models intersect over the factor $\psi_{y,\tilde{y}}$. It is clear, then, that the NMRFs $\mathcal{G}_a$ and $\mathcal{G}_b$ overlap only over the configurations of the factor $\psi_{y,\tilde{y}}$. Thus, $\mathcal{G}_a \cap \mathcal{G}_b$ form a clique cut-set. Furthermore, since $\mathcal{G}_a$ is perfect and $\mathcal{G}_b$ is perfect, Lemma 2.9 ensures that the graph $\mathcal{G}_{a+b}$ is perfect. By induction, incrementally merging star-shaped graphical models with the current tree G_{a+b} can be used to eventually create any arbitrary tree structure in the graph G. Since merging each star preserves the perfection of the compiled NMRF, the final NMRF $\mathcal{G}$ obtained from any tree-structured graphical model G is perfect. $\qquad\square$

Theorem 2.17 can easily be generalized to handle the case where the input graphical model G is not a simple tree as illustrated above but, more generally, any *junction tree* as defined below [32].

Definition 2.18 (JUNCTION TREE)   A graphical model G over the universe of random variables $Y = \{y_1, \ldots, y_k\}$ with factors $1, \ldots, l$ with corresponding potential functions $\psi_1, \ldots, \psi_l$ over subsets of random variables $Y_1, \ldots, Y_l$ is called a *junction tree* if and only if the factors can be made adjacent to each other as nodes in an acyclic graph such that, for any two factors i and j, all factors on the unique path joining i and j contain the variables in the intersection $Y_i \cap Y_j$.

Thus, graph perfection can be used to re-establish that MAP estimation in graphical models without loops is efficient [27].

2.6.2 Associative Graphical Models

In the previous sub-section, the topology of a graphical model was restricted (to tree-structures) in order to guarantee that inference remains efficient for any set of potential functions $\psi_1, \ldots, \psi_l$. Instead of restricting topology while allowing arbitrary choices for potential functions, we may explore restrictions on the potential functions themselves and allow *arbitrary* topology. If all potential functions in the graphical model are associative (or, more generally, submodular), then MAP estimation is known to remain efficient [14, 23]. Such problems frequently arise in computer vision and image processing. Can graph perfection be used to reproduce this efficiency result?

Consider a graphical model over $V = \{1, \ldots, k\}$ nodes with binary variables $Y = \{y_1, \ldots, y_k\}$ where $y_i \in \mathbb{B}$ (the extension beyond binary variables is possible yet outside the scope of this chapter) with pairwise potential functions between all pairs[10] of variables as implied by

$$p(Y) \; = \; \tfrac{1}{Z} \prod_{i \in V} \psi_i(y_i) \prod_{i \neq j} \psi_{ij}(y_i, y_j).$$

The singleton potential functions are specified via two arbitrary scalar values $\psi_i(0), \psi_i(1) \in \mathbb{R}^+$ for all $i \in V$. Meanwhile, the pairwise potential functions (i.e. factors) over a pair of binary variables are specified by four scalar values $\psi_{ij}(0,0), \psi_{ij}(0,1), \psi_{ij}(1,0), \psi_{ij}(1,1) \in \mathbb{R}^+$ for all $i \neq j$. We say that the pairwise potential functions are *associative* (or, more generally, submodular) if their values are restricted to obey the following relation

$$\psi_{ij}(0,0)\psi_{ij}(1,1) \; \geq \; \psi_{ij}(0,1)\psi_{ij}(1,0).$$

---

[10]   To consider an associative graphical model that has sparse connectivity, one may simply assume that the pairwise potentials between some pairs of random variables are chosen to be constant.

If such a property is satisfied for all pairwise potential functions, then the graphical model is associative. Consider compiling such a graphical model into NMRF form. However, before doing so, it will be helpful to rewrite the potential functions as follows

$$\psi_{ij}(y_i, y_j) = \hat{\psi}_{ij}(y_i, y_j)\phi_{ij}(y_i)\eta_{ij}(y_j)$$

where $\phi_{ij}(0) = \psi_{ij}(0,1)$, $\phi_{ij}(1) = \psi_{ij}(1,1)$, $\eta_{ij}(0) = \psi_{ij}(1,0)/\psi_{ij}(1,1)$ and $\eta_{ij}(1) = 1$. Next, consider the following modified pairwise potentials functions

$$\hat{\psi}_{ij}(y_i, y_j) = \begin{cases} \frac{\psi_{ij}(0,0)\psi_{ij}(1,1)}{\psi_{ij}(0,1)\psi_{ij}(1,0)} & \text{if } y_i = y_j = 0 \\ 1 & \text{otherwise.} \end{cases} \qquad (2.6)$$

Rewrite the distribution as follows

$$p(Y) = \frac{1}{Z} \prod_{i \in V} \psi_i(y_i) \prod_{j \neq i} \hat{\psi}_{ij}(y_i, y_j)\phi_{ij}(y_i)\eta_{ij}(y_j).$$

Next, consider the following modified singleton potential functions

$$\hat{\psi}_i(y_i) = \psi_i(y_i) \prod_{j \neq i} \phi_{ij}(y_i)\eta_{ji}(y_i).$$

These modified functions allow us to write the distribution for any associative graphical model as follows

$$p(Y) = \frac{1}{Z} \prod_{i \in V} \hat{\psi}_i(y_i) \prod_{i \neq j} \hat{\psi}_{ij}(y_i, y_j)$$

where the pairwise potential functions are restricted to have the form in Equation 2.6. Apply Algorithm 2.1 to each potential function. Then apply Algorithm 2.2 which obtains a graph $\mathcal{G}_1$ after removing nodes that correspond to $\hat{\psi}_{ij}(0,1)$, $\hat{\psi}_{ij}(1,0)$ and $\hat{\psi}_{ij}(1,1)$ since they all have zero weight (after the logarithm). This leaves a graph where there are two NMRF nodes for each singleton potential $\hat{\psi}_i$ for $i \in V$ and a single node for each pairwise potential $\hat{\psi}_{ij}$ for $i \neq j$. The resulting NMRF has a perfect graph $\mathcal{G}_1$ as shown in the following theorem and as depicted in Figure 2.7.

Theorem 2.19 *A graphical model over binary variables with singleton and associative pairwise potential functions compiles into a MWSS problem on a perfect graph.*

Proof The NMRF graph $\mathcal{G}_1$ from Algorithm 2.2 contains edges between all disagreeing nodes. Therefore, each pair of NMRF nodes v_i^0 and v_i^1 corresponding to the singleton potentials $\hat{\psi}_i$ for $i \in V$ are pairwise adjacent.

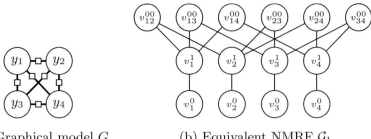

(a) Graphical model G (b) Equivalent NMRF $\mathcal{G}_1$

Figure 2.7 Compiling an associative graphical model G with binary random variables into its NMRF representation $\mathcal{G}_1$ (therein, subscripts denote the factor the NMRF node corresponds to and superscripts denote the configuration of its corresponding random variables).

Each pairwise potential $\hat{\psi}_{ij}$ produces a single NMRF node v_{ij}^{00} which is only adjacent to v_i^1 and v_j^1. Since this set of edges forms a bipartite graph, $\mathcal{G}_1$ is perfect.   □

Due to the perfection of the MWSS sub-problem, Algorithm 2.2 remains efficient. In fact, the required MWSS sub-problem can easily be handled via linear programming which produces an integral solution. The subsequent MSS sub-problem in Algorithm 2.2 is trivial. Finally, given the solution of Algorithm 2.2, say $\mathcal{X}^*$, it is straightforward to deduce the MAP estimate of the random variables Y^*.

It may be the case that a perfect NMRF also emerges if higher-order potentials are used rather than merely associative (pairwise submodular) functions. These potentials give rise to so-called P^n Potts models which are widely used in computer vision [21]. It is sometimes possible that Algorithms 2.1 and 2.2 remain efficient for such graphical models and only require solving MWSS sub-problems on perfect graphs.

2.6.3 Matching Graphical Models

It was recently shown that certain graphical models known as matching (or generalized matching) graphical models also admit efficient MAP estimation [2, 17, 29, 3]. These graphical models are not associative *and* contain many cycles (i.e. are not trees). A matching problem arises, for instance, in a marriage problem, where q males and q females are to be paired together. There is a non-negative scalar score $f_{ij} \geq 0$ between each male i and each female j representing how compatible they are. Our goal is to find the matching where the total score is maximized for the whole population. This problem is known to admit efficient MAP estimation in $\mathcal{O}(q^3)$ via the classic Hungarian marriage algorithm. This maximum weight bipartite matching problem can be written as a graphical model [2, 17] over a set of discrete variables $Y = \{y_1, \ldots, y_q, \tilde{y}_1, \ldots, \tilde{y}_q\}$ as follows:

$$p(Y) = \frac{1}{Z} \prod_{i=1}^{q} \prod_{j=1}^{q} \psi_{ij}(y_i, \tilde{y}_j) \qquad (2.7)$$

where each potential function is defined as

$$\psi_{ij}(y_i, \tilde{y}_j) = \begin{cases} \varepsilon & y_i = j \text{ and } \tilde{y}_j \neq i \\ \varepsilon & y_i \neq j \text{ and } \tilde{y}_j = i \\ \exp(f_{ij}) & y_i = j \text{ and } \tilde{y}_j = i \\ 1 & \text{otherwise.} \end{cases}$$

Here, $1 >> \varepsilon > 0$ is an arbitrarily small positive quantity. Also, take $y_i \in \{1, \ldots, q\}$ to be the partner choice the ith male makes (where $i = 1, \ldots, q$). Also, take $\tilde{y}_j \in \{1, \ldots, q\}$ to be the partner choice the jth female makes (where $j = 1, \ldots, q$). Each ψ_{ij} potential function captures the additional value gained from the marriage of a couple via the entry $\exp(f_{ij})$. The functions also make marriage choices reciprocal (an individual cannot chose someone who has chosen someone else) by returning ε in such situations (for a small enough ε, it is easy to see that reciprocity will be strictly enforced). Clearly, the potential functions are not associative (they are also not submodular). Furthermore, the graphical model has many cycles. Thus, the tractability of this problem falls outside the scope of the two previous sub-sections.

As in the previous section, we shall replace each ψ_{ij} function by factorizing it into a product of another modified pairwise potential $\hat{\psi}_{ij}$ and two singleton potentials ϕ_{ij} and η_{ij}. The intuition lies in finding a modified pairwise potential $\hat{\psi}_{ij} \geq 1$ with as many elements as possible equal to one (in other words, $\hat{\psi}_{ij}$ is log-sparse). Pseudo-code for finding such factorizations automatically is provided in Section 2.9. The result suggests the following factorization which is used to rewrite each potential function in $p(Y)$ as

$$\psi_{ij}(y_i, \tilde{y}_j) = \hat{\psi}_{ij}(y_i, \tilde{y}_j)\phi_{ij}(y_i)\eta_{ij}(\tilde{y}_j)$$

where

$$\hat{\psi}_{ij}(y_i, \tilde{y}_j) = \begin{cases} \exp(f_{ij})/\varepsilon^2 & y_i = j \text{ and } \tilde{y}_j = i \\ 1 & \text{otherwise,} \end{cases}$$

with

$$\phi_{ij}(y_i) = \begin{cases} \varepsilon & y_i = j \\ 1 & \text{otherwise,} \end{cases}$$

and

$$\eta_{ij}(\tilde{y}_j) = \begin{cases} \varepsilon & \tilde{y}_j = i \\ 1 & \text{otherwise.} \end{cases}$$

These potentials are collected to form the following equivalent graphical model involving both singleton and pairwise potential functions

$$p(Y) = \frac{1}{Z} \left(\prod_{i=1}^{q} \prod_{j=1}^{q} \hat{\psi}_{ij}(y_i, \tilde{y}_j) \right) \prod_{i=1}^{q} \hat{\phi}_i(y_i) \prod_{j=1}^{q} \hat{\eta}_j(\tilde{y}_j).$$

where $\hat{\phi}_i(y_i) = \prod_{j=1}^{q} \phi_{ij}(y_i)$ and $\hat{\eta}_j(\tilde{y}_j) = \prod_{i=1}^{q} \eta_{ij}(\tilde{y}_j)$. Remarkably, these final singleton potentials are all constant. Therefore, they can be absorbed into a new normalizer $\hat{Z}$ and the graphical model can be rewritten more succinctly as

$$p(Y) = \frac{1}{\hat{Z}} \prod_{i=1}^{q} \prod_{j=1}^{q} \hat{\psi}_{ij}(y_i, \tilde{y}_j).$$

Consider compiling the above graphical model into a NMRF graph $\mathcal{G}$ via Algorithm 2.1. For each of the q^2 potential functions $\hat{\psi}_{ij}$, $\mathcal{G}$ contains q^2 nodes. Denote the total set of q^4 NMRF nodes in $\mathcal{G}$ by v_{ij}^{kl} where $i, j, k, l \in \{1, \ldots, q\}$. Here, subscripts indicate which potential function the NMRF node comes from and superscripts identify the specific entry of that potential function. More precisely, a left subscript i and a right superscript l means that the ith male chooses the lth female. Similarly, a right subscript j and a left superscript k means that the jth female chooses the kth male. Whenever $k = i$ and $l = j$, the marriage choices are reciprocal and the nodes v_{ij}^{ij} have weight $f_{ij} - 2\log(\varepsilon)$. Denote by $S = \{v_{11}^{11}, \ldots, v_{1q}^{1q}, \ldots, v_{qq}^{qq}\}$ this subset of q^2 nodes with reciprocated marriages. The remaining nodes in $\mathcal{G}$ have weight zero. We then form $\mathcal{G}_1$ via Algorithm 2.2 by removing nodes with zero weight from $\mathcal{G}$. The graph $\mathcal{G}_1$ thus only contains the q^2 nodes in S and the following theorem shows that it is perfect.

Theorem 2.20   *The maximum weight bipartite matching problem compiles into a MWSS problem on a perfect graph.*

Proof   Graph $\mathcal{G}_1$ obtained from the bipartite matching problem contains q^2 nodes v_{ij}^{ij} where $i, j \in \{1, \ldots, q\}$. Pairwise edges exist between v_{ij}^{ij} and v_{ik}^{ik} when $k \neq j$ and between v_{ij}^{ij} and v_{kj}^{kj} when $k \neq i$ since these correspond to

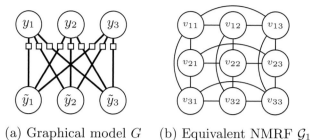

(a) Graphical model G (b) Equivalent NMRF $\mathcal{G}_1$

Figure 2.8 Compiling a bipartite matching graphical model G with binary random variables into its NMRF representation $\mathcal{G}_1$.

incompatible settings of the random variables. It is easy to see that $\mathcal{G}_1$ is a Rook's graph which is the line graph of a (complete) bipartite graph. Since these are basic Berge graphs, $\mathcal{G}_1$ is perfect. □

Since $\mathcal{G}_1$ is perfect, the MWSS sub-problem in Algorithm 2.2 remains efficient. Furthermore, the subsequent MSS sub-problem is trivial. Figure 2.8 depicts the induced subgraph $\mathcal{G}_1$.

Thus, Algorithm 2.2 finds the MAP estimate for graphical models representing bipartite matching problems in polynomial time. In fact, under mild assumptions, certain variants of message passing converge in just $\mathcal{O}(q^2)$ time when applied to the (dense) bipartite matching problem [28]. Perfection can also be used to show when unipartite matching problems achieve integral linear programming relaxations [29, 18]. Informally, this is done by examining the line graph of the unipartite matching graphical model (much like the Rook's graph is the line graph of the bipartite graph in Figure 2.8(a)). If the line graph of the unipartite matching graphical model is a perfect graph, Algorithm 2.2 may potentially involve a MWSS problem over a perfect graph $\mathcal{G}_1$. Thus, the linear programming integrality of matching problems can be explained using graph perfection and the efficiency of MAP estimation for such graphical models is re-confirmed using the tools introduced in this chapter.

2.7 Discussion

Perfect graphs are a useful class of inputs that help outline when otherwise intractable problems admit efficient algorithms. This family of graphs is rich with theoretical and computational properties. Combinatorial problems such as graph coloring, maximum stable set and maximum clique can be efficiently solved when the input is a perfect graph. Off-the-shelf solvers such as linear programming and semidefinite programming are known to provide exact solutions. Similarly, certain canonical problems in machine learning and statistical inference can exploit perfect graph theory and algorithms. This chapter focused on the maximum a posteriori (MAP) estimation problem and showed how it can be compiled into a maximal maximum weight stable set problem on a nand Markov random field. MWSS solution methods such as linear programming, message passing and semidefinite programming can then be brought to bear and remain efficient if the input is a weighted perfect graph. Thus, the tractability benefits of perfect graphs extend into the realm of MAP estimation which otherwise, in the worst case, can be intractable. Furthermore, in cases where MAP estimation was previously known to admit efficient algorithms, it was possible to compile the graphical models into NMRFs with perfect graph topologies that admit efficient MWSS solution. Thus, the perfect graph formalism helps reconfirm previously known efficiency results in graphical modeling. With further work, perfect graphs can potentially help the machine learning and statistics communities discover new families of graphical models that admit efficient MAP estimation.

2.8 Acknowledgments

The author thanks D. Bondatti, K. Choromanski, M. Chudnovsky, M. Danisch, D. Dueck and A. Weller for discussions. This paper is based upon work supported by the National Science Foundation under Grant No. 1117631. Any opinions, findings, and conclusions or recommendations expressed in this material are those of the author and do not necessarily reflect the views of the National Science Foundation.

2.9 Appendix

The Matlab code in Figure 2.9 rewrites a higher-order potential function (over a pair of variables or more) as a product of a log-sparse higher-order potential function (with all elements greater than 1) and singleton potentials. This is accomplished by linear programming to minimize an ℓ_1 norm on the output higher-order potential function. This helps reveal the representation of the graphical model that may lead to a MWSS problem on a perfect graph.

```
function [opsi,singletons] = factorizeClique(psi)
lpsi = log(psi./min(reshape(psi,prod(size(psi)),1)));
spsi = size(lpsi);
N = prod(spsi);
n = sum(spsi);
f = zeros(N+n+1,1);
f(1:(N+n))=1;
lb = -250*ones(N+n+1,1);
lb(1:(N+n))=0;
b = [reshape(lpsi,prod(spsi),1)];
A = zeros(N,N+n+1);
A(1:N,1:N)=eye(N,N);
for i=1:N
  q=ind2subT(spsi,i);
  for j=1:length(spsi)
      A(i,N+sum(spsi(1:(j-1)))+q(j))=1;
  end
end
A(:,end)=1;
ub = 250*ones(N+n,1);
X = linprog(f,[],[],A,b,lb,ub);
opsi = exp(reshape(X(1:N),spsi));
ind = N+1;
for i=1:length(spsi)
  singletons{i} = exp(X(ind:((ind+spsi(i))-1)));
  ind=ind+spsi(i);
end
siz = sz;
nout = length(siz);
siz = double(siz);
```

The above function also uses the following sub-function that simply returns multiple subscripts from a linear index.

```
function [outs] = ind2subT(sz,ndx)
if length(siz)<=nout,
  siz = [siz ones(1,nout-length(siz))];
else
  siz = [siz(1:nout-1) prod(siz(nout:end))];
end
n = length(siz);
k = [1 cumprod(siz(1:end-1))];
outs = zeros(1,nout);
for i = n:-1:1,
  vi = rem(ndx-1, k(i)) + 1;
  vj = (ndx - vi)/k(i) + 1;
  outs(i) = vj;
  ndx = vi;
end
```

Figure 2.9 Matlab code for rewriting a higher-order potential function

References

[1] Aloise, D., Deshpande, A., Hansen, P., and Popat, P. 2009. NP-hardness of Euclidean sum-of-squares clustering. *Machine Learning*, **75**, 245–248.

[2] Bayati, M., Shah, D., and Sharma, M. 2005. Maximum weight matching via max-product belief propagation. In: *IEEE International Symposium on Information Theory, 2005*, 1763–1767.

[3] Bayati, M., Borgs, C., Chayes, J., and Zecchina, R. 2008. On the exactness of the cavity method for weighted b-matchings on arbitrary graphs and its relation to linear programs. *Journal of Statistical Mechanics: Theory and Experiment*, **2008**(06), L06001 (10pp).

[4] Berge, C. 1963. *Six Papers on Graph Theory*. Calcutta: Indian Statistical Institute. Chap. Perfect graphs, pages 1–21.

[5] Berge, C., and Chvátal, V. (eds). 1984. *Topics on Perfect Graphs*. North-Holland, Amsterdam.

[6] Berge, C., and Ramírez-Alfonsín, J.L. 2001. *Perfect Graphs*. Wiley. Chap. Origins and genesis, pages 1–12.

[7] Bron, C., and Kerbosch, J. 1973. Algorithm 457: finding all cliques of an undirected graph. *Communications of the ACM*, **16**(9), 575–577.

[8] Chan, T-H. H., Chang, K.L., and Raman, R. 2009. An SDP primal-dual algorithm for approximating the Lovász-theta function. In: *IEEE International Symposium on Information Theory, 2009*, 2808–2812.

[9] Chudnovsky, M., Cornuéjols, G., Liu, X., Seymour, P., and Vusković, K. 2005. Recognizing Berge graphs. *Combinatorica*, **25**, 143–186.

[10] Chudnovsky, M., Robertson, N., Seymour, P.D., and Thomas, R. 2006. The strong perfect graph theorem. *Ann. Math*, **164**, 51–229.

[11] Chvátal, V. 1975. On certain polytopes associated with graphs. *Journal of Combinatorial Theory, Series B*, **13**, 138–154.

[12] Foulds, J.R., Navaroli, N., Smyth, P., and Ihler, A. 2011. Revisiting MAP estimation, message passing, and perfect graphs. In: *Proceedings of the 14th International Conference on Artificial Intelligence and Statistics*, 278–286.

[13] Globerson, A., and Jaakkola, T. 2007. Fixing max-product: Convergent message passing algorithms for MAP LP-relaxations. In: *Advances in Neural Information Processing Systems* **21**.

[14] Greig, D., Porteous, B., and Seheult, A. 1989. Exact maximum a posteriori estimation for binary images. *J. Royal Statistical Soc., Series B*, **51**(2), 271–279.

[15] Grötschel, M., Lovász, L., and Schrijver, A. 1981. The ellipsoid method and its consequences in combinatorial optimization. *Combinatorica*, **1**, 169–197.

[16] Grötschel, M., Lovász, L., and Schrijver, A. 1988. *Geometric Algorithms and Combinatorial Optimization*. Springer-Verlag. Chap. Stable sets in graphs.

[17] Huang, B., and Jebara, T. 2007. Loopy belief propagation for bipartite maximum weight b-matching. *Journal of Machine Learning Research – Proceedings Track* 2: 195–202 (2007)

[18] Jebara, T. 2009. MAP estimation, message passing, and perfect graphs. In: *UAI '09 Proceedings of the 25th Conference on Uncertainty in Artificial Intelligence*, 258–267.

[19] Karp, R.M. 1972. *Complexity of Computer Computations.* New York: Plenum. Chap. Reducibility Among Combinatorial Problems, pages 85–103.

[20] Knuth, D. 1994. The sandwhich theorem. *Electronic Journal of Combinatorics,* **1**.

[21] Kohli, P., Ladicky, L., and Torr, P. 2009. Robust Higher Order Potentials for Enforcing Label Consistency. *International Journal of Computer Vision,* **82**(3), 302–324.

[22] Kolmogorov, V.N., and Wainwright, M.J. 2005. On the optimality of tree-reweighted max-product message-passing. In: *Proceedings of the 21st Annual Conference on Uncertainty in Artificial Intelligence.*

[23] Kolmogorov, V.N., and Zabih, R. 2004. What energy functions can be minimized via graph cuts? *IEEE Trans. Pattern Analysis and Machine Intelligence,* **26**(2), 147–159.

[24] Komodakis, N., and Paragios, N. 2008. Beyond loose LP-relaxations: Optimizing MRFs by repairing cycles. In: *Proceedings of 10th European Conference on Computer Vision,* LNCS 5304, 806–820.

[25] Lovász, L. 1972. Normal hypergraphs and the weak perfect graph conjecture. *Discrete Math.,* **2**, 253–267.

[26] Lovász, L. 1979. On the Shannon capacity of a graph. *IEEE Transactions on Information Theory,* **25**, 1–7.

[27] Pearl, J. 1988. *Probabilistic Reasoning in Intelligent Systems: Networks of Plausible Inference.* Morgan Kaufmann.

[28] Salez, J., and Shah, D. 2009. Optimality of belief propagation for random assignment problem. In: *Proceedings of the 20th Annual ACM–SIAM Symposium on Discrete Algorithms,* 187–196.

[29] Sanghavi, S., Malioutov, D., and Willsky, A. 2008. Linear programming analysis of loopy belief propagation for weighted matching. In: *Advances in Neural Information Processing Systems* **20**.

[30] Shimony, S.E. 1994. Finding MAPs for belief networks is NP-hard. *Aritifical Intelligence,* **68**(2), 399–410.

[31] Tomita, E., Tanaka, A., and Takahashi, H. 2006. The worst-case time complexity for generating all maximal cliques and computational experiments. *Theoretical Computer Science,* **363**(1), 28–42.

[32] Wainwright, M.J., and Jordan, M.I. 2008. Graphical models, exponential families and variational inference. *Foundations and Trends in Machine Learning,* **1**(1-2), 1–305.

[33] Weiss, Y., and Freeman, W.T. 2001. On the optimality of solutions of the max-product belief-propagation algorithm in arbitrary graphs. *IEEE Transactions on Information Theory,* **47**(2), 736–744.

[34] Yedidia, J.S., Freeman, W.T., and Weiss, Y. 2001. Understanding belief propagation and its generalizations. In: *Exploring Artificial Intelligence in the New Millennium,* 239–269. Morgan Kauffman.

[35] Yildirim, E.A., and Fan-Orzechowski, X. 2006. On extracting maximum stable sets in perfect graphs using Lovász's theta function. *Computational Optimization and Applications,* **33**(2-3), 229–247.

PART 2

LANGUAGE RESTRICTIONS

3

Submodular Function Maximization

Andreas Krause, Daniel Golovin

In this chapter we will introduce submodularity and some of its generalizations, illustrate how it arises in various applications, and discuss algorithms for optimizing submodular functions.

Submodularity[1] is a property of set functions with deep theoretical consequences and far–reaching applications. At first glance it seems very similar to concavity, in other ways it resembles convexity. It appears in a wide variety of applications: in Computer Science it has recently been identified and utilized in domains such as viral marketing [39], information gathering [44], image segmentation [10, 40, 36], document summarization [56], and speeding up satisfiability solvers [73]. Our emphasis in this chapter is on maximization; there are many important results and applications related to minimizing submodular functions that we do not cover[2].

As a concrete running example, we will consider the problem of deploying sensors in a drinking water distribution network (see Figure 3.1) in order to detect contamination. In this domain, we may have a model of how contaminants, accidentally or maliciously introduced into the network, spread over time. Such a model then allows to quantify the benefit $f(A)$ of deploying sensors at a particular set A of locations (junctions or pipes in the network) in terms of the detection performance (such as average time to detection).

---

[1] The study of submodular functions goes back at least to lattice theory [8]. Edmonds [17] first studied submodular functions in context of discrete optimization. See [23] and [67] for an in-depth discussion of submodular functions and their properties. This chapter focuses on modern results on submodular maximization.

[2] There has been extensive research into algorithms for minimizing submodular functions (*cf.*Fujishige [23], Schrijver [67]). Interestingly, unconstrained submodular minimization can be done efficiently, even if f can only be evaluated via a membership oracle (i.e., a black-box subroutine), whereas unconstrained maximization is NP-hard for general (non-monotone) submodular functions, since it includes the maximum cut problem as a special case (via the cut capacity example in Section 3.1.1). There are also efficient online algorithms for submodular minimization in the no-regret framework [35, 37], which complement the results in Section 3.4.

Based on this notion of utility, we then wish to find an optimal subset
$A \subseteq V$ of locations maximizing the utility, $\max_A f(A)$, subject to some constraints (such as bounded cost). This application requires solving a difficult
real-world optimization problem, that can be handled with the techniques
discussed in this chapter (Krause et al. [49] show in detail how submodular
optimization can be applied in this domain.) We will also discuss more complex settings, for example how one can incorporate complex constraints on
the feasible sets A, robustly optimize against adversarially chosen objective
functions f, or adaptively select sensors based on previous observations.

Several algorithms for submodular optimization described in this chapter
are implemented in an open source Matlab toolbox[3] [42].

3.1 Submodular Functions

Submodularity is a property of *set functions*, i.e., functions $f : 2^V \to \mathbb{R}$ that
assign each subset $S \subseteq V$ a value $f(S)$. Hereby V is a finite set, commonly
called the *ground set*. In our example, V may refer to the locations where
sensors can be placed, and $f(S)$ the utility (e.g., detection performance)
obtained when placing sensors at locations S. In the following, we will also
assume that $f(\emptyset) = 0$, i.e., the empty set carries no value. Submodularity has
two equivalent definitions, which we will now describe. The first definition
relies on a notion of discrete derivative, often also called the marginal gain.

Definition 3.1 (Discrete derivative) For a set function $f : 2^V \to \mathbb{R}$, $S \subseteq V$,
and $e \in V$, let $\Delta_f(e \mid S) := f(S \cup \{e\}) - f(S)$ be the *discrete derivative* of
f at S with respect to e.

Where the function f is clear from the context, we drop the subscript and
simply write $\Delta(e \mid S)$.

Definition 3.2 (Submodularity) A function $f : 2^V \to \mathbb{R}$ is *submodular* if
for every $A \subseteq B \subseteq V$ and $e \in V \setminus B$ it holds that

$$\Delta(e \mid A) \geq \Delta(e \mid B).$$

Equivalently, a function $f : 2^V \to \mathbb{R}$ is *submodular* if for every $A, B \subseteq V$,

$$f(A \cap B) + f(A \cup B) \leq f(A) + f(B).$$

For submodular maximization, the intuition provided by the first definition is often helpful: Suppose we interpret $S \subset V$ as a set of actions
which provide some benefit $f(S)$. Then the first definition says that for a

---

[3] The SFO toolbox for submodular optimization is available for download under
http://mloss.org/software/view/201/

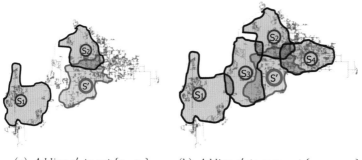

(a) *Adding s' to set $\{s_1, s_2\}$*   (b) *Adding s' to superset $\{s_1, \ldots, s_4\}$*

Figure 3.1 Illustration of the diminishing returns effect in context of placing sensors in a water distribution network to detect contaminations. The blue regions indicate nodes where contamination is detected quickly using the existing sensors S. The red region indicates the additional coverage by adding a new sensor s'. If more sensors are already placed (b), there is more overlap, hence less gain in utility: $\Delta(s' \mid \{s_1, s_2\}) \geq \Delta(s' \mid \{s_1, \ldots, s_4\})$. ©2011 Association for Computing Machinery, Inc. Reprinted from [45] with permission.

submodular function f, after performing a set A of actions, the marginal benefit of any action e does not increase as we perform the actions in $B \setminus A$. Therefore, submodular set functions exhibit a natural diminishing returns property. Figure 3.1 illustrates this effect in our sensor placement application. In this example, the marginal benefit provided by placing a sensor at a fixed location s' given that we deployed sensors at locations s_1, s_2 does not increase as we deploy more sensors (s_3 and s_4).

An important subclass of submodular functions are those which are *monotone*, where enlarging the argument set cannot cause the function to decrease.

Definition 3.3 (Monotonicity) A function $f : 2^V \to \mathbb{R}$ is *monotone* if for every $A \subseteq B \subseteq V$, $f(A) \leq f(B)$.

Note that a function f is monotone iff all its discrete derivatives are non-negative, i.e., iff for every $A \subseteq V$ and $e \in V$ it holds that $\Delta(e \mid A) \geq 0$. Further note that the important subclass of monotone submodular functions can be characterized by requiring that for all $A \subseteq B \subseteq V$ and $e \in V$ it holds that $\Delta(e \mid A) \geq \Delta(e \mid B)$. This is slightly different from Definition 3.2 in that we do not require $e \notin B$.

Typically, and in most of this chapter, we will assume that f is given in terms of a *value oracle*, a black box that computes[4] $f(S)$ on any input set S.

---

[4] In some applications (*cf.*, Kempe et al. [39]), calculating $f(S)$ may itself be difficult. In those cases, we may only be able to approximately evaluate $f(S)$ up to some multiplicative relative error α. Fortunately, most results about maximizing submodular functions are robust against such error (*cf.*, Goundan and Schulz [31], Calinescu et al. [12], Streeter and Golovin [73], Golovin and Krause [27]).

3.1.1 *Examples*

Submodular functions comprise a broad class of functions that arise in several applications. Here are some examples.

Modular functions and generalizations. The simplest example of submodular functions are *modular* functions, those for which the inequalities characterizing submodularity hold with equality, i.e., for all $A, B \subseteq V$ it holds that $f(A) + f(B) = f(A \cup B) + f(A \cap B)$. Such functions are analogous to linear functions, insofar as their discrete derivatives are constant: $\Delta(e \mid B) = \Delta(e \mid A)$ for all A, B and $e \notin A \cup B$. Assuming $f(\emptyset) = 0$, they can always be expressed in the form $f(S) = \sum_{e \in S} w(e)$ for some weight function $w : V \to \mathbb{R}$. Another example is the composition of any monotone modular function $g : 2^V \to \mathbb{R}$ and any concave function $h : \mathbb{R} \to \mathbb{R}$ — for example, $f(S) = \sqrt{|S|}$.

Weighted coverage functions. An important example of a submodular function is the *weighted coverage* of a collection of sets: Fix a set X, a nonnegative modular function $g : 2^X \to \mathbb{R}$, and a collection V of subsets of X. Then for a subcollection $S \subseteq V$, the function

$$f(S) := g\left(\bigcup_{v \in S} v\right) = \sum_{x \in \bigcup_{v \in S} v} w(x),$$

is monotone submodular. Hereby $w : X \to \mathbb{R}$ is the weight function representing g. In our example, X may refer to a set of contamination events, $w(x)$ quantifies the severity of event x, and with each possible sensor location $v \in V$ we associate the subset $v \subseteq X$ of events detected. Perhaps the simplest example is where $g(A) = |A|$ is the cardinality function (which is modular), in which case the problem of maximizing $f(S)$ is the well-known max-cover problem. In fact, $f(S)$ is submodular even for arbitrary *submodular* functions g. It is monotone iff g is monotone.

The rank function of a matroid. Another important class of submodular functions arises in the context of matroids:

Definition 3.4 (Matroid)   A *matroid* is a pair $(V, \mathcal{I})$ such that V is a finite set, and $\mathcal{I} \subseteq 2^V$ is a collection of subsets of V satisfying the following two properties:

- $A \subseteq B \subseteq V$ and $B \in \mathcal{I}$ implies $A \in \mathcal{I}$
- $A, B \in \mathcal{I}$ and $|B| > |A|$ implies $\exists e \in B \setminus A$ such that $A \cup \{e\} \in \mathcal{I}$.

Sets in $\mathcal{I}$ are called *independent*, and matroids generalize the concept of linear independence found in linear algebra. An important function associated with a matroid $(V, \mathcal{I})$, which describes it completely, is its *rank function* $f(S) := \max\{|U| : U \subseteq S, U \in \mathcal{I}\}$. The rank function of any matroid is monotone submodular [9].

Facility location. Suppose we wish to select, out of a set $V = \{1, \ldots, n\}$, some locations to open up facilities in order to serve a collection of m customers. If we open up a facility at location j, then it provides service of value $M_{i,j}$ to customer i, where $M \in \mathbb{R}^{m \times n}$. If each customer chooses the facility with highest value, the total value provided to all customers is modeled by the set function

$$f(S) = \sum_{i=1}^{m} \max_{j \in S} M_{i,j}.$$

Hereby we set $f(\emptyset) = 0$. If $M_{i,j} \geq 0$ for all i, j, then $f(S)$ is monotone submodular [21]. This model is quite general, and captures other applications as well. In our sensor placement example, $M_{i,j}$ could refer to the benefit provided by sensor j in scenario i, quantified, e.g., in terms of the expected reduction in detection time [49].

Entropy. Given a joint probability distribution $P(\mathbf{X})$ over a discrete-valued random vector $\mathbf{X} = [X_1, X_2, \ldots, X_n]$, the function $f(S) = H(\mathbf{X}_S)$ is monotone submodular [22], where H is the Shannon entropy, i.e.,

$$H(\mathbf{X}_S) = -\sum_{\mathbf{x}_S} P(\mathbf{x}_S) \log_2 P(\mathbf{x}_S)$$

where we use the notational convention that $\mathbf{X}_S$ is the random vector consisting of the coordinates of $\mathbf{X}$ indexed by S, and likewise $\mathbf{x}_S$ is the vector consisting of the coordinates of an assignment $\mathbf{x}$ indexed by S. If the random variables are real-valued, with a probability density function f, the differential entropy

$$H(\mathbf{X}_S) = -\int P(\mathbf{x}_S) \log_2 P(\mathbf{x}_S) d\mathbf{x}_S$$

is submodular as well, but not generally monotone.

Mutual information. Given a joint probability distribution $P(\mathbf{X}, \mathbf{Y})$ over two dependent random vectors, $\mathbf{X} = [X_1, X_2, \ldots, X_n]$, $\mathbf{Y} = [Y_1, Y_2, \ldots, Y_m]$, consider the *mutual information*: $f(S) = I(\mathbf{Y}; \mathbf{X}_S) = H(\mathbf{Y}) - H(\mathbf{Y} \mid \mathbf{X}_S)$, which quantifies the expected reduction of uncertainty about $\mathbf{Y}$ upon revelation of $\mathbf{X}_S$. In general, the function f is *not submodular*: Suppose $X_1, X_2 \sim$ Bernoulli(0.5), and $Y = X_1$ XOR X_2. Then $f(\emptyset) = f(\{1\}) = f(\{2\}) = 0$, but $f(\{1,2\}) = 1$, violating submodularity. However, if the variables $\mathbf{X}$ are *conditionally independent* given $\mathbf{Y}$, i.e., for all disjoint sets $A, B \subset V$ if holds that $\mathbf{X}_A \perp \mathbf{X}_B \mid \mathbf{Y}$, then f is monotone submodular [43]. This holds both for discrete and continuous distributions. In our example, we may associate a variable Y_v with the water quality at location $v \in V$, and X_v is a noisy measurement of Y_v that we obtain if we place a sensor at location v. Then $f(S)$ quantifies how much we can reduce our uncertainty about the water quality everywhere when deploying sensors at locations S.

Symmetric mutual information. Let $V = \{1, 2, \ldots, n\}$. Given any joint probability distribution P over a random vector $\mathbf{X} = [X_1, X_2, \ldots, X_n]$, the function $f(S) = I(\mathbf{X}_S; \mathbf{X}_{V \setminus S})$ is submodular. However, f is not monotone in general, since $f(\emptyset) = f(V) = 0$, and unless $X_1, X_2, \ldots, X_n$ are independent, it will be the case that $f(S) > 0$ for some S. This function has been used by Narasimhan et al. [62] for information-theoretic clustering problems, and by Krause et al. [48] for the purpose of sensor placement.

More generally, if $\mathbf{Y} = [Y_1, Y_2, \ldots, Y_m]$ is another random vector, and $\mathbf{X}$ and $\mathbf{Y}$ have joint distribution $P(\mathbf{X}, \mathbf{Y})$ the *conditional mutual information* $I(\mathbf{X}_S; \mathbf{X}_{V \setminus S} \mid \mathbf{Y})$ is submodular (but not monotone). This function arises in the context of structure learning in probabilistic graphical models, as studied by Narasimhan and Bilmes [61].

Cut capacity functions. Fix any undirected graph $G = (V, E)$ with nonnegative edge capacities $c : E \to \mathbb{R}_+$. Let ∂S be the *boundary* of $S \subseteq V$, defined as $\partial S := \{\{u, v\} \in E : |S \cap \{u, v\}| = 1\}$. Then the function $f(S) = \sum_{e \in \partial S} c(e)$ is submodular [67]. The same is true for directed graphs, if we define $\partial S := \{(u, v) \in E : u \in S, v \notin S\}$. Note that f is not generally monotone: In particular, $f(\emptyset) = f(V) = 0$.

3.1.2 Properties of Submodular Functions

Submodular functions have many useful properties. For example, submodularity is preserved under taking nonnegative linear combinations. In other words, if $g_1, \ldots, g_n : 2^V \to \mathbb{R}$ are submodular, and $\alpha_1, \ldots, \alpha_n \geq 0$, then $f(S) := \sum_{i=1}^n \alpha_i g_i(S)$ is submodular as well. This is readily proved using the definition of submodularity based on discrete derivatives. This insight is extremely useful, as it allows to build complex submodular objectives from simpler constituents (*cf.*, Kempe et al. [39], Leskovec et al. [55], Stobbe and Krause [71]). Submodularity is also preserved when we take the *residual*: if $g : 2^V \to \mathbb{R}$ is submodular, and $A, B \subset V$ are any disjoint sets, then the residual $f : 2^A \to \mathbb{R}$ defined via $f(S) := g(S \cup B) - g(B)$ is submodular. Monotone submodular functions remain so under *truncation*: if $g : 2^V \to \mathbb{R}$ is submodular, so is $f(S) := \min\{g(S), c\}$ for any constant c. While truncation preserves submodularity, in general, the minimum and maximum of two submodular functions are not submodular, i.e., for submodular functions f_1 and f_2, the functions $f_{\min}(S) = \min(f_1(S), f_2(S))$ and $f_{\max}(S) = \max(f_1(S), f_2(S))$ are not necessarily submodular.

Interestingly, there are many natural connections between submodular functions and both convex and concave functions. For example, for a function $g : \mathbb{N} \to \mathbb{R}$, the set function $f(S) = g(|S|)$ is submodular if and only if g is concave. In contrast, similar to convex functions, which can be minimized efficiently, (unconstrained) submodular minimization is possible in (strongly) polynomial time (*cf.*, Schrijver [67]). See [58] for a discussion about the relationship between submodular, concave and convex functions.

Submodular set functions can also be extended to continuous functions (defined over the unit cube $[0, 1]^{|V|}$) in several natural ways. See Section 3.3.2 for more details on such extensions.

3.2 Greedy Maximization of Submodular Functions

As argued in Section 3.1.1, submodular functions arise in many applications, and therefore it is natural to study submodular optimization. There is a large amount of work on minimizing submodular functions (*cf.*, Fujishige [23], Schrijver [67]). In this chapter, we will focus on the problem of maximizing submodular functions. That is, we are interested in solving problems of the form

$$\max_{S \subseteq V} f(S) \text{ subject to some constraints on } S. \tag{3.1}$$

The simplest example are *cardinality constraints*, where we require that $|S| \leq k$ for some k. In our example, we may wish to identify the k best locations to place sensors. Unfortunately, even this simple problem is NP-hard, for many classes of submodular functions, such as weighted coverage [19] or mutual information [43]. While there are specialized branch and bound algorithms for maximizing submodular functions [64, 25, 38], ultimately their scalability is limited by the hardness of Problem 3.1. Therefore, in the remaining of this chapter we focus on efficient algorithms with theoretical approximation guarantees.

The greedy algorithm. In the following, we will consider the problem of approximately maximizing monotone submodular functions. A simple approach towards solving Problem 3.1 in the case of cardinality constraints is the *greedy algorithm*, which starts with the empty set S_0, and in iteration i, adds the element maximizing the discrete derivative $\Delta(e \mid S_{i-1})$ (ties broken arbitrarily):

$$S_i = S_{i-1} \cup \{\arg\max_e \Delta(e \mid S_{i-1})\}. \tag{3.2}$$

A celebrated result by Nemhauser et al. [65] proves that the greedy algorithm provides a good approximation to the optimal solution of the NP-hard optimization problem.

Theorem 3.5 (Nemhauser et al. [65])   *Fix a nonnegative monotone submodular function $f : 2^V \to \mathbb{R}_+$ and let $\{S_i\}_{i \geq 0}$ be the greedily selected sets defined in Eq. (3.2). Then for all positive integers k and ℓ,*

$$f(S_\ell) \geq \left(1 - e^{-\ell/k}\right) \max_{S:|S| \leq k} f(S).$$

In particular, for $\ell = k$, $f(S_k) \geq (1 - 1/e) \max_{|S| \leq k} f(S)$.

Proof Nemhauser et al. only discussed the case $\ell = k$, however their very elegant argument easily yields the slight generalization above. It goes as follows. Fix ℓ and k. Let $S^* \in \arg\max \{f(S) : |S| \leq k\}$ be an optimal set of size k (due to monotonicity of f we can assume w.l.o.g. it is of size exactly k), and order the elements of S^* arbitrarily as $\{v_1^*, \ldots, v_k^*\}$. Then we have the following sequence of inequalities for all $i < \ell$, which we explain below.

$$f(S^*) \leq f(S^* \cup S_i) \tag{3.3}$$

$$= f(S_i) + \sum_{j=1}^{k} \Delta\left(v_j^* \mid S_i \cup \{v_1^*, \ldots, v_{j-1}^*\}\right) \tag{3.4}$$

$$\leq f(S_i) + \sum_{v \in S^*} \Delta(v \mid S_i) \tag{3.5}$$

$$\leq f(S_i) + \sum_{v \in S^*} (f(S_{i+1}) - f(S_i)) \tag{3.6}$$

$$\leq f(S_i) + k\left(f(S_{i+1}) - f(S_i)\right) \tag{3.7}$$

Inequality (3.3) follows from monotonicity of f, Eq. (3.4) is a straightforward telescoping sum, the relation (3.5) follows from the submodularity of f, (3.6) holds because S_{i+1} is built greedily from S_i in order to maximize the marginal benefit $\Delta(v \mid S_i)$, and (3.7) merely reflects the fact that $|S^*| \leq k$.

Hence

$$f(S^*) - f(S_i) \leq k \left(f(S_{i+1}) - f(S_i) \right). \tag{3.8}$$

Now define $\delta_i := f(S^*) - f(S_i)$, which allows us to rewrite (3.8) as $\delta_i \leq k \left(\delta_i - \delta_{i+1} \right)$, which can be rearranged to yield

$$\delta_{i+1} \leq \left(1 - \frac{1}{k} \right) \delta_i \tag{3.9}$$

Hence $\delta_\ell \leq \left(1 - \frac{1}{k} \right)^\ell \delta_0$. Next note that $\delta_0 = f(S^*) - f(\emptyset) \leq f(S^*)$ since f is nonnegative by assumption, and by the well-known inequality $1 - x \leq e^{-x}$ for all $x \in \mathbb{R}$ we have

$$\delta_\ell \;\leq\; \left(1 - \frac{1}{k} \right)^\ell \delta_0 \;\leq\; e^{-\ell/k} f(S^*). \tag{3.10}$$

Substituting $\delta_\ell = f(S^*) - f(S_\ell)$ and rearranging then yields the claimed bound of $f(S_\ell) \geq \left(1 - e^{-\ell/k} \right) f(S^*)$. □

The slight generalization allowing $\ell \neq k$ is quite useful. For example, if we let the greedy algorithm pick $5k$ sensors, the approximation ratio (compared to the optimal set of size k) improves from $\approx .63$ to $\approx .99$.

For several classes of submodular functions, this result is the best that can be achieved with any efficient algorithm. In fact, Nemhauser and Wolsey [63] proved that any algorithm that is allowed to only evaluate f at a polynomial number of sets will not be able to obtain an approximation guarantee better than $(1 - 1/e)$. (Subsequently, Vondrák [80] provided more refined results on the best possible approximation factor in terms of a parameter called the *curvature* of f.)

Matroid constraints. Going beyond cardinality constraints, the greedy algorithm is also guaranteed to provide near-optimal solutions for more complex constraints. In our sensing example, in order to preserve energy, each sensor may decide when to activate. The problem of optimizing such a sensing schedule requires maximizing a submodular function subject to a partition matroid constraint [51].

Suppose $(V, \mathcal{I})$ is a matroid, and we wish to solve the problem

$$\max_{S \in \mathcal{I}} f(S),$$

then the greedy algorithm, which starts with S_G and sets

$$S_G \leftarrow S_G \cup \left\{ \underset{e \notin S_G : S_G \cup \{e\} \in \mathcal{I}}{\arg\max} \Delta(e \mid S_G) \right\} \tag{3.11}$$

until there is no more e such that $S_G \cup \{e\} \in \mathcal{I}$ (i.e., there is no element which can be added to create a feasible solution), is guaranteed to produce a solution S_G so that $f(S_G) \geq \frac{1}{2} \max_{S \in \mathcal{I}} f(S)$.

Even more generally, suppose $(V, \mathcal{I}_1), \ldots, (V, \mathcal{I}_p)$ are p matroids, and $\mathcal{I} = \bigcap_i \mathcal{I}_i$. That is, $\mathcal{I}$ consists of all subsets of V that are independent in all p matroids. Even though $(V, \mathcal{I})$ is not generally a matroid anymore, the greedy algorithm (3.11) is guaranteed to produce a solution so that $f(S_G) \geq \frac{1}{p+1} \max_{S \in \mathcal{I}} f(S)$. In fact, this results holds even more generally whenever $(V, \mathcal{I})$ is a *p-extensible system*, a combinatorial notion which generalizes the intersections of p matroids [12].

Min-cost coverage. Instead of maximizing a monotone submodular function subject to constraints, it is also natural to search for minimum cost sets that achieve a given amount q of submodular value. In particular, we may wish to solve

$$S^* = \arg \min_S |S| \text{ s.t. } f(S) \geq q, \tag{3.12}$$

for some quota $0 \leq q \leq f(V)$ of value. In our sensing example, we may wish to deploy as few sensors as possible, while guaranteeing that all possible contamination scenarios are eventually detected.

Wolsey [81] proves the following result about the greedy algorithm:

Theorem 3.6 (Wolsey [81]) *Suppose $f : 2^V \to \mathbb{N}$ is monotone submodular and integer-valued, and let $0 \leq q \leq f(V)$. Let $S_0, S_1, \ldots$ be the sequence of sets picked by the greedy algorithm, and let ℓ be the smallest index such that $f(S_\ell) \geq q$. Then*

$$\ell \leq \left(1 + \ln \max_{v \in V} f(\{v\}) \right) OPT,$$

where $OPT = \min_S |S|$ s.t. $f(S) \geq q$.

In fact, Wolsey proves the special case $q = f(V)$, but the result above immediately follows by applying his result to the submodular function $\min\{f(S), q\}$. Wolsey also proves that the same result holds in the case where the elements of V have non-uniform cost, using a slightly modified greedy algorithm (see also Section 3.3.1).

Speeding up the greedy algorithm through lazy evaluations. In some applications, evaluating the function f can be expensive. In our example, evaluating f may require running computationally costly water quality simulations. In this case, even applying the standard greedy algorithm can be infeasible. Fortunately, submodularity can be exploited algorithmically to implement an accelerated variant of the greedy algorithm, originally proposed by Minoux [59]. In each iteration i, the greedy algorithm must identify the element e with maximum marginal gain $\Delta(e \mid S_{i-1})$, where S_{i-1} is the set of elements selected in the previous iterations. The key insight is that, as a consequence of submodularity of f, the marginal benefits of any fixed element $e \in V$ are monotonically nonincreasing during the iterations of the algorithm, i.e., $\Delta(e \mid S_i) \geq \Delta(e \mid S_j)$ whenever $i \leq j$. Instead of recomputing $\Delta(e \mid S_{i-1})$ for each element $e \in V$ (requiring $O(n)$ computations of f), the accelerated greedy algorithm maintains a list of upper bounds $\rho(e)$ (initialized to ∞) on the marginal gains sorted in decreasing order. In each iteration, the algorithm extracts the maximal element

$$e \in \underset{e':S_{i-1}\cup\{e'\}\in\mathcal{I}}{\arg\max} \; \rho(e')$$

from the ordered list. It then updates the bound $\rho(e) \leftarrow \Delta(e \mid S_{i-1})$. If, after this update, $\rho(e) \geq \rho(e')$ for all $e' \neq e$, then submodularity guarantees that $\Delta(e \mid S_{i-1}) \geq \Delta(e' \mid S_{i-1})$ for all $e' \neq e$, and therefore the greedy algorithm has identified the element of largest marginal gain, without having to compute $\Delta(e' \mid S_{i-1})$ for a potentially large number of elements e'. It sets $S_i \leftarrow S_{i-1} \cup \{e\}$ and repeats until there is no further feasible element which can be added. This idea of using lazy evaluations can lead to orders of magnitude performance speedups, and is useful beyond the greedy algorithm (*cf.*, Leskovec et al. [55]).

3.3 Beyond the Greedy Algorithm: Handling More Complex Constraints

In this section, we will survey some work on submodular optimization beyond the standard greedy algorithm discussed in Section 3.2. Using more complex algorithms allows to handle maximization subject to more complex constraints. We will mostly focus on the case of *monotone* functions, but also mention results about optimizing non-monotone functions.

3.3.1 Knapsack Constraints

Instead of selecting a set of at most k elements, in many applications, the elements $v \in V$ may have non-uniform costs $c(s) \geq 0$, and we may wish to maximize f subject to a budget that the total cost cannot exceed:

$$\max_{S} f(S) \text{ s.t. } \sum_{v \in S} c(v) \leq B.$$

Thus, we would like to maximize $f(S)$ subject to a (w.l.o.g.) nonnegative modular constraint, also called Knapsack constraint (as the problem of maximizing a *modular* f subject to a *modular* constraint c is called the Knapsack problem). Naturally, the standard (uniform cost) greedy algorithm, selecting the next affordable element of maximum marginal gain can perform arbitarily badly, as it ignores cost. It can be easily modified to take cost into account: The cost-benefit greedy algorithm starts with $S_0 = \emptyset$, and iteratively adds

$$S_{i+1} = S_i \cup \left\{ \arg \max_{v \in V \setminus S_i : c(v) \leq B - c(S_i)} \frac{\Delta(e \mid S_i)}{c(v)} \right\}, \tag{3.13}$$

i.e., the element v that maximizes the benefit cost ratio among all elements still affordable with the remaining budget. For the min-cost covering problem Eq. (3.12), Wolsey [81] proves a generalization of Theorem 3.6 for this cost-benefit greedy algorithm. Unfortunately, for the budgeted maximization problem, even though this modified algorithm takes cost into account, it can still perform arbitrarily badly. However, perhaps surprisingly, *at least one* of the greedy solutions – the solution S_{uc} returned by the uniform cost or the one S_{cb} provided by the cost-benefit greedy algorithm cannot perform too badly: it can be shown that $\max\{f(S_{uc}), f(S_{cb})\} \geq (1 - 1/\sqrt{e})OPT$ [55]. In fact, a more computationally complex algorithm, which enumerates all sets S of size 3, and augments them using the cost-benefit greedy algorithm, is known to provide a $1 - 1/e$ approximation [78].

3.3.2 Submodular Maximization using the Multilinear Extension

One important idea, which has seen a number of applications in submodular optimization, is the use of *extensions*. Suppose $f : 2^V \to \mathbb{R}$ is a set function. By identifying sets S with binary vectors e_S (in which the i-th component is 1 if $i \in S$, and 0 otherwise), we can equivalently represent f as a function defined over corners of the unit cube: $\tilde{f} : \{0,1\}^n \to \mathbb{R}$, where $n = |V|$, and $\tilde{f}(e_S) = f(S)$. From this perspective, it is natural to extend $\tilde{f}$ to the entire unit cube $[0,1]^n$. There are several important extensions. The *Lovász extension* [58] extends $\tilde{f}$ to a *convex* function $\hat{f} : [0,1]^n \to \mathbb{R}$, for which (at least some of) its minimizers are attained at a corner of $[0,1]^n$. Minimization of $\hat{f}$ over $[0,1]^n$ is possible using the ellipsoid method, which proved that unconstrained submodular minimization is possible in polynomial time. However, for the purpose of (constrained) submodular *maximization*, a different extension, pioneered by Vondrák [79] has proven to be very useful: The *multilinear extension* of f, $\hat{f} : [0,1]^n \rightarrow \mathbb{R}$ is defined as

$$\hat{f}(\mathbf{x}) = \sum_{S \subseteq V} f(S) \prod_{i \in S} x_i \prod_{j \notin S} (1 - x_j).$$

Thus, $\hat{f}(\mathbf{x})$ is the expected value of f over sets, where each element i is included independently with probability x_i. Several recent algorithms for submodular maximization are built around (approximately) solving the problem

$$\max \hat{f}(\mathbf{x}) \text{ s.t. } \mathbf{x} \in \mathcal{F}$$

over some domain $\mathcal{F} \subseteq [0,1]^n$, and then rounding the continuous solution to obtain a near-optimal set.

The first application of this elegant idea, due to Vondrák [79], is the *continuous greedy algorithm* for maximizing a submodular function subject to matroid constraints. In this application, the feasible set $\mathcal{F}$ is the *matroid polytope*, the convex hull of the independent sets of the underlying matroid. Conceptually, the algorithm traces the continuous particle, parameterized as a function $\mathbf{x} : [0,1] \rightarrow \mathcal{F}$, originating at $\mathbf{x}(0) = \mathbf{0}$, and following the differential equation

$$\dot{\mathbf{x}} = \arg\max_{\mathbf{v} \in \mathcal{F}} \left(\mathbf{v}^T \cdot \nabla \hat{f}(\mathbf{x}) \right).$$

Calinescu et al. [12] prove that for matroid polytopes $\mathcal{F}$, it holds that

$$\hat{f}(\mathbf{x}(1)) \geq (1 - 1/e) \max_{\mathbf{x} \in \mathcal{F}} \hat{f}(\mathbf{x}),$$

thus at time 1, the particle has reached a point which provides a $(1 - 1/e)$ approximation of the optimal value of $\hat{f}$ over $\mathcal{F}$. Calinescu et al. also show how this continuous differential equation can be approximated by a discrete process up to arbitrarily small error. They also show how the continuous solution $\mathbf{y}$ can be efficiently rounded to a feasible discrete solution without loss in objective value, using *pipage rounding* [1]. This result affirmatively closed the long-standing open question of whether the optimal approximation ratio of $(1 - 1/e)$, which the standard greedy algorithm achieves for cardinality constraints, can be achieved for *arbitrary* matroids (for which the standard algorithm only gives a $1/2$ approximation).

However, this general technique of relaxing constrained submodular maximization to a continuous problem, and rounding the obtained solution has proven to be far more general. For example, Kulik et al. [54] have shown how to obtain a $(1 - 1/e - \varepsilon)$ approximation for the problem of maximizing a monotone submodular functions subject to multiple knapsack constraints. Recently, Chekuri et al. [15] have used the multilinear relaxation to obtain a $.38/k$ approximation for maximizing a monotone submodular function subject to k matroid and a constant number of knapsack constraints (as well as an even more general class of other *downward-closed* constraints).

3.3.3 Submodular Optimization over Graphs

Another natural class of constraints arise when solving submodular optimization problems on graphs. Suppose that we identify the elements V as vertices of a (weighted) graph $G = (V, E, w)$ with edges E, and a function w that assigns each edge a nonnegative weight. In this setting, we may wish to maximize a submodular function $f(S)$ defined over the vertices, subject to the constraint that the set S forms a path, or a tree on G of weight at most B. Similarly, we may wish to obtain a tree (path) on G of submodular value q, and with approximately minimal total weight. These problems have natural applications in placing sensors under communication constraints, where the vertices V denote possible locations for sensors, f the informativeness of having sensors at a set of locations, and edges and their weights denote the communication cost between arbitrary pairs of locations [53]. Another application is in planning informative paths for mobile sensors [69]. In these applications, greedy algorithms can be shown to perform arbitrarily poorly.

Calinescu and Zelikovsky [11] develop a polynomial-time algorithm, which, given an integral-valued monotone submodular function f and a quota $0 \leq q \leq f(V)$, and any $\varepsilon > 0$, produce a tree of cost at most $O\left(\frac{1}{\varepsilon} \frac{1}{\ln \ln n} (\ln n)^{2+\varepsilon} \log q\right)$ times the optimal cost. For the related problem of path constraints, Chekuri and Pal [14] develop an algorithm that, given a budget $B > 0$ and nodes $s, t \in V$ produces an s–t path of length at most B (if such exists) of submodular value $\Omega(\frac{OPT}{\log OPT})$. However, the running time of the algorithm is $(n \log B)^{O(\log n)}$, which is only quasi-polynomial in n. Nevertheless, Singh et al. [69] show how this algorithm can be scaled to fairly large problems, and present results on planning informative paths for robotic sensors. For submodular functions that satisfy an additional *locality* property, which arises naturally in spatial monitoring problems, improved algorithms can be obtained, both for tree [47] and path [70] constraints.

3.3.4 *Robust Submodular Optimization*

In our example of placing sensors in a drinking water distribution network, we may wish to protect against malicious contaminations [49]. In this case, there may be a collection of m possible intrusion scenarios (e.g., locations whether contaminants could be introduced), and for each of the scenarios, we use a separate monotone submodular function $f_i(S)$ that quantifies the benefit (e.g., chance of detection) of having sensors at locations S, in scenario i. The problem of optimally placing sensors to protect against an adversary who wants to maximize their chances to go undetected therefore requires to solve

$$S^* = \arg\max_{|S| \le k} \min_i f_i(S), \tag{3.14}$$

where $f_1, \ldots, f_m$ are monotone submodular functions.

Unfortunately, the function $f_{\min}(S) = \min_i f_i(S)$ is not generally submodular. Moreover, the greedy algorithm applied to $f_{\min}$ can perform arbitrarily poorly. In fact, Krause et al. [50] prove that Problem Eq. (3.14) is extremely inapproximable: Unless P=NP, *no* efficient algorithm can provide a solution S such that $f_{\min}(S) \ge \alpha(n)OPT_k$, where $OPT_k = \max_{|S'| \le k} f_{\min}(S')$, for any function α that may even depend on the problem size n (for example, it is not efficiently possible to even recoup an exponentially small fraction of the optimal value). Perhaps surprisingly, given the hardness of the problem, it is possible to provide a different kind of approximation guarantee. Krause et al. [50] develop SATURATE, an algorithm that is guaranteed to efficiently obtain a set S such that $f_{\min}(S) \ge OPT_k$, and $|S| \le (1 + \max_v \ln \sum_i f_i(\{v\}))k$. Thus, it is possible to obtain a set S that provides as much value as the best set of size k, at a cost that is logarithmically larger than k. This logarithmic approximation is optimal under reasonable complexity-theoretic assumptions. Problem 3.14 is much more general. For example, Schulman et al. [68] have recently applied SATURATE in personal robotics in order to plan where to grasp objects.

Instead of committing to a fixed set $S \subseteq V$, in some applications it may be possible to select a probability distribution over sets. For example, when controlling a sensor network in a building to protect against intrusions, we may wish to obtain a randomized sensing strategy that performs as well as possible against an intruder who attempts to evade detection, knowing the randomized strategy. This problem is formalized as

$$p^* = \arg\max_{p:p(S)>0 \Rightarrow |S| \le k} U(p) \text{ where } U(p) = \min_i \mathbb{E}_{S \sim p}[f_i(S)].$$

Thus, we wish to obtain a distribution p^* over feasible sets S, such that our value is maximized in expectation, even under an adversarially chosen objective. Solving this problem optimally is a formidable task, as even representing the optimal distribution may require exponential space. However, Krause et al. [52] show how it is possible, for any $\varepsilon > 0$, to efficiently obtain a distribution $\hat{p}$ over $O(\ln m/\varepsilon^2)$ sets such that $U(\hat{p}) \geq (1 - 1/e)U(p^*) - \varepsilon$.

3.3.5 Nonmonotone Submodular Functions

While most work has focused on maximizing monotone submodular functions, several applications require maximizing *nonmonotone* submodular functions. For example, suppose we have a monotone submodular function f, and a modular cost function c, assigning each element v a cost $c(v)$. In this setting, we may wish to solve the unconstrained problem

$$\max_{S} f(S) - c(S).$$

Here, the function $g(S) = f(S) - c(S)$ is submodular, but nonmonotone. Another example is maximizing the symmetric mutual information $f(S) = I(\mathbf{X}_S; \mathbf{X}_{V \setminus S})$ (*cf.*, §3.1.1). For arbitrary submodular functions f, even verifying whether there exists a set S such that $f(S) > 0$ is NP-hard [18], thus no approximation is possible. However, there have been recent breakthroughs on maximizing arbitrary *nonnegative* submodular functions (i.e., $f(S) \geq 0$ for all sets S).

Feige et al. [18] prove that a local-search algorithm which iteratively adds or removes elements, ensuring that each addition or removal increases the function value by at least a multiplicative factor of $(1 + \frac{\varepsilon}{n^2})$ terminates with a set S such that either S or $V \setminus S$ provides a $(\frac{1}{3} - \frac{\varepsilon}{n})$ approximation to the optimal unconstrained solution. They also prove that a more expensive, randomized local search procedure produces a solution with is a $(\frac{2}{5} - o(1))$ approximation to the optimal value. This is contrasted by their hardness result, proving that no approximation better than $\frac{1}{2}$ is achievable in the value oracle model. Krause and Horvitz [46] present an application of unconstrained submodular maximization to the problem of trading off utility and privacy in online services.

Further improvements have been obtained utilizing the multilinear extension as discussed above. In particular, Gharan and Vondrák [24] show that a simulated annealing algorithm is guaranteed to obtain a 0.41 approximation for unconstrained maximization, and 0.325 approximation for maximization subject to a matroid constraint. Most recently, Chekuri et al. [15] show how the factor 0.325 can also be obtained for a constant number of knapsack constraints, and how a $0.19/k$ approximation is achievable for maximizing any nonnegative submodular function subject to k matroid and a constant number of knapsack constraints.

3.4 Online Maximization of Submodular Functions

In the previous sections, we have assumed that we are given an objective function f that we wish to maximize. In some applications, the objective may not be known in advance. However, if we perform the same task repeatedly while facing objectives $f_1, \ldots, f_T$ drawn from some distribution, we might hope to learn to perform well on average over time. This is the premise behind *no-regret* algorithms, which are widely used in machine learning.

In many interesting applications the (unknown) objective functions f_t are monotone submodular. One example that we discuss below is learning to hybridize different algorithms for a computationally hard problem to generate a meta-algorithm which may outperform all of its constituent algorithms. Other examples include online sensor selection, news recommendation systems, online advertising and others. As we will see below, there are analogues of Theorem 3.5 in this no-regret setting, i.e., it is possible to learn to optimize submodular functions in an online manner.

3.4.1 The No-regret Setting

Suppose we face the problem of repeatedly, over T rounds, choosing an action from a set V. In each round t, after selecting an action $v \in V$, you observe either the reward of every action (in the so-called *full information* feedback model) in that round, or merely the reward of the action you selected (in the so–called *bandit* feedback model). Let $r_t(v)$ denote the reward of action v in round t. Orthogonal to the feedback model, the rewards may be *stochastic*, in which case the reward functions $\{r_t : t = 1, 2, \ldots, T\}$ are drawn from some fixed (but unknown) distribution, or *non-stochastic*, in which case they may be arbitrary (even possibly chosen by an adversary). At first glance it seems impossible to give any interesting performance guarantees for the non-stochastic bandit setting. However, there are many beautiful results in this area based on the notion of minimizing the *regret* against the best action in hindsight (*cf.*, Cesa-Bianchi and Lugosi [13]).

Definition 3.7 (Regret)   The *regret* of action sequence $v_1, \ldots, v_T$ is

$$R_T = \max_{v^*} \sum_{t=1}^{T} r_t(v^*) - \sum_{t=1}^{T} r_t(v_t)$$

and the *average regret* is R_T/T.

There is a large literature on no-regret algorithms, to which we cannot do justice here. However, a key point is that if the reward functions are bounded, e.g., if $r_t(v) \in [0,1]$ for all v and t, then in many settings, such as the case where V is finite, there are randomized algorithms whose expected regret grow as $o(T)$, so that the average regret R_T/T converges to zero as $T \to \infty$. There are algorithms which achieve $O(|V| \log T)$ expected regret for stochastic rewards with bandit feedback [3], $O(\sqrt{T \log |V|})$ for the non-stochastic rewards with full information feedback [20], and $O\left(\sqrt{T|V| \log |V|}\right)$ for the non-stochastic rewards with bandit feedback [4]. This means that in all settings we can converge to the performance of the best action in hindsight.

Now, suppose that instead of choosing an element $v \in V$ in each round you had to choose a set $S \subseteq V$ of bounded cardinality, say, $|S| \leq k$? Naïvely using the algorithms for the single action case ($k = 1$) by treating each feasible set as a distinct action has two major disadvantages. First, the algorithms require time at least linear in the number of feasible sets, namely $\binom{|V|}{k}$. Second, the average regret will shrink very slowly in the bandit feedback model, so that at least $\binom{|V|}{k}$ rounds are required before the regret bounds are meaningful. Unfortunately, for arbitrary reward functions $r_t(S)$, there is not much one can do about this situation. However, if the reward functions $r_t(\cdot)$ are monotone submodular, this structure can be exploited to get regret bounds roughly k times that of the original problem, with the caveat that the regret is against a $(1 - 1/e)$ approximation to the best feasible set in hindsight. We call such a regret measure the $(1 - 1/e)$-regret. Formally, for any $\alpha \geq 0$ the α-regret is defined as follows.

Definition 3.8 (α-Regret)   The α-*regret* of a sequence of sets $S^{(1)}, \ldots, S^{(T)}$ is

$$R_\alpha = \alpha \cdot \max_{S^* \text{ feasible}} \sum_{t=1}^{T} r_t(S^*) - \sum_{t=1}^{T} r_t\left(S^{(t)}\right)$$

and the *average α-regret* is R_α/T.

3.4.2 Submodular Maximization in the No-Regret Setting

Suppose $r_t : 2^V \to [0,1]$ are monotone submodular, with bounded range. (We rescale so that the range is $[0,1]$.) For clarity of exposition, we will focus here on a natural *partially transparent feedback model* defined as follows, but results in other models are available. For an ordered set S, let S_i be the first i elements of S. In the partially transparent feedback model, after selecting ordered set $S^{(t)}$, the marginal benefit of each action is revealed, assuming they were added in order. Formally, we observe $r_t\left(S_i^{(t)}\right) - r_t\left(S_{i-1}^{(t)}\right)$ for each $i = 1, 2, \ldots, k$. In this model, it is possible to obtain results like the following.

Theorem 3.9 (Streeter and Golovin [72]) *There is an efficient algorithm which incurs expected $(1 - 1/e)$-regret at most $O\left(k\sqrt{T|V|\log|V|}\right)$, in the non–stochastic setting with partially transparent feedback.*

Hence it is possible to ensure the expected average $(1 - 1/e)$-regret converges to zero at a rate proportional to $1/\sqrt{T}$, so that asymptotically the algorithm achieves at least $(1 - 1/e)$ of the optimal reward obtained by any fixed set of size k.

One algorithm obtaining the claimed regret bound, called the *online greedy* algorithm, combines the greedy algorithm with no-regret algorithms for the bandit feedback setting in a simple manner: There are k instantiations of such no-regret algorithms $\mathcal{A}_1, \ldots, \mathcal{A}_k$, each with a set of actions V to choose among. In each round t, each $\mathcal{A}_i$ selects an action v_i^t and the set $S^{(t)} = \{v_1^t, \ldots, v_k^t\}$ is selected. For its trouble, $\mathcal{A}_i$ receives reward $r_t\left(S_i^{(t)}\right) - r_t\left(S_{i-1}^{(t)}\right)$, where $S_j^{(t)} = \{v_i^t : i \leq j\}$.

At a very high level, the key reason that the *online greedy* algorithm performs well is that the greedy algorithm is *noise-resistant* in the following sense. Suppose that instead of selecting $S_i = S_{i-1} \cup \{\arg\max_v \Delta(v \mid S_{i-1})\}$ a "noisy" version of the greedy algorithm selects $S_i = S_{i-1} \cup \{v_i\}$ such that $\Delta(v_i \mid S_{i-1}) = \max_v \Delta(v \mid S_{i-1}) - \epsilon_i$ for some $\epsilon_i \geq 0$. Then a relatively straightforward modification of the proof by Nemhauser et al. [65], which may be found in [73], shows that

$$f(S_k) \geq (1 - 1/e) \max_{S:|S|\leq k} f(S) - \sum_{i=1}^{k} \epsilon_i. \tag{3.15}$$

It turns out that the online greedy algorithm can be interpreted as a noisy version of the (standard) greedy algorithm running on a larger instance (which encodes all T instances the online greedy algorithm encounters), where the noise ϵ_i is exactly the regret of $\mathcal{A}_i$. Using known regret bounds for the case of selecting a single action then yields Theorem 3.9. Streeter and Golovin [72] also provide results for other feedback models showing it is possible to obtain expected average $(1 - 1/e)$-regret which converges to zero as $T \to \infty$, up to and including the bandit feedback model in which only the reward of the set selected, namely $r_t\left(S_{i-1}^{(t)}\right)$, is observed at the end of round t (though in this very harsh feedback model the convergence rate on $(1 - 1/e)$-regret is much slower).

3.4.3 Applications of Online Maximization of Submodular Functions

There are several applications that can benefit from the results mentioned in §3.4.2. These include online sensor selection, database query optimization, news recommendation systems, online ad selection, and combining multiple heuristics for computationally hard problems [73, 29, 60, 5, 77, 66, 74]. Here we discuss the problem of combining multiple heuristics in detail.

Combining multiple heuristics online Certain computationally hard problems such as integer programming and boolean satisfiability are ubiquitous in industrial and scientific applications, and a great deal of effort has gone into developing heuristics which solve them as quickly as possible in practice. Typically, there is no single heuristic which outperforms all others on every instance. Rather, heuristics often complement each other, so that there are opportunities for combining them into a meta-heuristic that outperforms its constituent heuristics in practice — in some cases by an order of magnitude or more. Before giving a concrete example where this effect occurs, we must clarify how heuristics are "combined." For this purpose, we use a *task switching schedule*:

Definition 3.10 (Run and Task Switching Schedule) For a heuristic h and $\tau \in \mathbb{R}_+$, a *run* is a pair (h, τ) representing the execution of h until either the problem is solved, or until τ time units have expired, after which execution is terminated. A *task switching schedule* is a sequence of runs, $\{(h_i, \tau_i)\}_{i \geq 0}$, and its *length* is $\sum_{i \geq 0} \tau_i$.

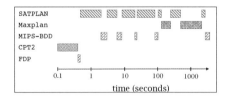

Figure 3.2 Illustration of a task switching schedule over five heuristics output by the online greedy algorithm.

A task switching schedule σ, such as the one illustrated in Figure 3.2, represents a meta-heuristic which performs its constituent runs in order and terminates immediately upon finding a solution. For example, the schedule $(h_1, 1), (h_2, 1)$ will first run h_1 until either the solution is found or one time unit elapses, whichever comes first. If the first run terminates without finding the solution, the schedule next runs h_2 until either the solution is found or one time unit elapses, whichever comes first, and then terminates.

How is it that the best task switching schedule can outperform the best heuristic in it? A simple concrete example of this is for boolean satisfiability (SAT) where there are many randomized heuristics. Any fixed randomized heuristic h defines a family of deterministic heuristics consisting of the h run with random seed r, denoted by h_r, for each possible random seed. Empirically, the running time distribution of h with different seeds on an given SAT instance Φ is commonly heavy tailed. Hence it makes sense to periodically terminate h and restart it with a fresh random seed. In an example given by [75], a particular heuristic solver had about a 20% chance of solving an instance after running for 2 seconds, but also a 20% chance that a run will not terminate after having run for 1000 seconds. Hence restarting the solver every 2 seconds rather than simply running it once until a solution is found reduces the mean time to solution by over an order of magnitude. When multiple solvers with complementary strengths are available, the potential for speedups increases. In experiments, when given access to state–of–the–art solvers entered into various academic competitions, the algorithm we are about to describe generated a meta-solver, which significantly outperformed all of the constituent solvers[5].

Two natural performance measures are *total execution time* to solve a set of instances, and *percent of instances solved* within a fixed time limit. The optimal task switching schedule will often outperform the best heuristic on both measures simultaneously. While there are strong empirical and theoretical results for both performance measures given by [73], for clarity of exposition here we focus on the latter.

Fix an arbitrary computational problem for which we have a finite set of (possibly randomized) heuristics H, and fix a time bound $B \in \mathbb{Z}_+$. We formulate the problem of combining heuristics as a problem of online maximization of submodular functions as follows. Construct a ground set $V = H \times \left\{ \tilde{1}, \tilde{2}, \ldots, \tilde{B} \right\}$ of *potential-runs* in which $(h, \tilde{\tau}) \in V$ represents a random run which is the actual run (h, τ) with probability $1/\tau$ and is $(h, 0)$

---

[5] Empirical evaluations of the online submodular maximization approach to combining heuristics appear in [76] and [73]. Additionally, a solver named MetaProver 1.0 developed based on these ideas competed in the SAT and FNT divisions of the 4th International Joint Conference on Automated Reasoning CADE ATP System Competition (http://www.cs.miami.edu/ tptp/CASC/J4/), where it won both divisions.

(i.e., it does nothing) otherwise. A sequence of instances of our problem arrives online, one per round. In each round t the instance is represented by a monotone submodular function r_t which takes in a set of potential runs as input and gives the probability that at least one of them solves the instance. Formally,

$$r_t(S) := 1 - \prod_{(h,\tilde{\tau}) \in S} \left(1 - \frac{1}{\tau} \mathbb{P}\left[\text{run } (h,\tau) \text{ solves instance } t\right]\right). \quad (3.16)$$

Given a set S of potential runs of size B, we sample a task switching schedule by sampling their actual runs independently for each potential runs. The result is a set of runs R whose total length is B in expectation, and whose probability of solving the tth instance is precisely $r_t(S)$ in expectation. Hence in each round t we can use the online greedy algorithm to select an ordered set of potential runs $S^{(t)}$, from which we can sample a task switching schedule $R^{(t)}$. Executing $R^{(t)}$ allows us to feedback unbiased estimates of the marginal increase in r_t from all of the potential runs, so that we are in the partially transparent feedback model. Hence we can generate a sequence $\{S^{(t)}\}_{t=1}^{T}$ that has vanishing average $(1 - 1/e)$-regret against any fixed set of potential runs. With slightly more work, one can show that the resulting sampled sequence of task switching schedules $\{R^{(t)}\}_{t=1}^{T}$ has vanishing average $(1 - 1/e)$-regret against any fixed task switching schedule of length B.

3.4.4 Online Maximization with Irrevocable Choices: the Submodular Secretaries Problem

In the *no-regret* setting of Section 3.4.1, the choices in any round are not constrained by what one did in previous rounds, and (typically) the goal is to perform well on average. By contrast, in the *competitive* online setting, one is faced with a sequence of irrevocable decisions among options that are revealed over time, and the goal is to do well in hindsight against any set of choices which were feasible given the revealed options. For example, in the *secretary problem*, you must hire exactly one applicant from a pool of applicants (of known size). Each applicant has a score, which is revealed during their interview. The applicants are interviewed in random order, and at the end of each interview you must irrevocably hire or reject the applicant being interviewed. The goal is to find a strategy maximizing the expected score of the hired applicant.

In *submodular secretary* problems, the applicants (denoted by the set V) are also interviewed in random order, and at the end of each interview you must irrevocably hire or reject the applicant being interviewed. However, now you are allowed to hire any subset of applicants in a feasible class $\mathcal{F} \subseteq 2^V$ (e.g., the independent sets of a matroid), and upon hiring a set S of applicants your reward is $f(S)$ for some nonnegative (possibly nonmonotone) submodular function f. Here, the function f is revealed to you during the interview process; after interviewing a set A of applicants, you are granted access to an oracle computing $f(S)$ for any $S \subseteq A$. The goal is to find a strategy maximizing the expected reward of the hired secretaries, measured with respect to f.

Submodular secretary problems generalize several important problems in practice, such as online bipartite matching (for e.g., matching display ads with search engine users) and certain caching problems. Gupta et al. [34] and Bateni et al. [6] provide constant competitive[6] algorithms for the uniform matroid (where $\mathcal{F} = \{S \subseteq V : |S| \leq k\}$ for some k). Gupta et al. also give a $O(\log r)$-competitive algorithm when $\mathcal{F}$ consists of the independent sets of a matroid of rank r, and Bateni et al. give an $O(\ell \log^2 r)$-competitive algorithm when $\mathcal{F}$ is the intersection of the independent sets of ℓ matroids of rank at most r.

3.5 Adaptive Submodularity

In some applications we may wish to *adaptively* select a set, observing and taking into account feedback after selecting any particular element. For example, we may wish to sequentially activate sensors, adaptively taking into account measurements provided by the sensors selected so far when selecting the next sensor[7]. In such adaptive optimization problems, we must optimize over *policies*, i.e., functions from the information we have obtained to the next action. There are many variants of the problem, depending on which modeling assumptions (e.g., about the planning horizon, prior knowledge of the environment, and how the environment is affected by our actions) and goals (e.g., worst-case vs. average case reward) are suitable. Many such problems are notoriously intractable. In this section, we will review the notion of *adaptive submodularity* [27], a recent generalization of submodularity to adaptive optimization, that allows to develop efficient, provably near-optimal policies to an interesting class of adaptive optimization problems.

Example applications that exhibit adaptive submodular structure include

---

[6] In the context of the submodular secretary problem, an algorithm is α-competitive if, in expectation over the random ordering of the interviews, it obtains at least α times the optimal value.

[7] Note that in contrast with the secretary problems of Section 3.4.4, in the adaptive optimization problems of Section 3.5 the information we acquire depends on what action we select.

problems in *active learning*, where we must adaptively select data points to label to maximize the performance of a classifier trained on the selected data points, *machine diagnosis*, where we must adaptively select tests to run on a patient or system to determine the best treatment plan, and certain *adaptive resource deployment* problems, where we irrevocably commit resources over time and may observe the benefits of our previous commitments before making additional commitments.

3.5.1 The Adaptive Submodularity Framework

In order to formalize adaptive optimization, we need to describe the process of how we gather information. We model the state of the world abstractly as a random variable Φ, using ϕ to refer to a concrete value that Φ can take. In our sensing application, Φ may refer to the water quality at all nodes in the network. We presume a Bayesian model, so that we have a prior probability $\mathbb{P}[\phi]$ distribution over Φ[8]. We suppose there is a set of *actions* V we can perform and a set of *outcomes* O we might observe. We interpret the world state ϕ as a function from actions to outcomes of those actions, i.e., $\phi : V \to O$ and $\phi(v)$ is the outcome of performing action v. In our sensing application, $\phi(v)$ may refer to the particular measurement we obtain if we have a sensor at location v, and the world is in state ϕ. We represent the actions we have performed, as well as the outcomes we have observed as a partial function ψ from actions to outcomes. Hereby, the domain of ψ, denoted $\mathrm{dom}(\psi)$, is the set of actions performed up until that point. We call ϕ a *realization* (of the world-state) and ψ a *partial realization*. In our example, ψ may encode water quality measurements obtained at a subset $\mathrm{dom}(\psi)$ of nodes in the network. We assume there is an objective function $f : 2^V \times O^V \to \mathbb{R}_+$ indicating the reward $f(A, \phi)$ obtained from actions A under realization of the world state ϕ. A *policy* π can then be represented as a function from partial realizations ψ to the actions, so that $\pi(\psi)$ is the action taken by π upon observing ψ. See Figure 3.3 for an illustration. If ψ is not in the domain of π, then π terminates upon observing ψ. Finally, define $V(\pi, \phi)$ to be the set of actions played by π under realization ϕ. Informally, two natural optimization problems that arise are to get the most value out of a fixed number of actions, and to get a certain amount of value with as few actions as possible. We formalize these as follows.

---

[8] In general adaptive optimization problems, actions can alter the state of the world, however the framework described in Section 3.5 considers cases where the world state is a fixed sample from the distribution, and does not change in response to our actions.

$$\pi(\emptyset) = a$$
$$\pi(\{(a,0)\}) = b$$
$$\pi(\{(a,1)\}) = c$$
$$\pi(\{(a,0),(b,0)\}) = d$$
$$\pi(\{(a,0),(b,1)\}) = e$$
$$\pi(\{(a,1),(c,1)\}) = d$$

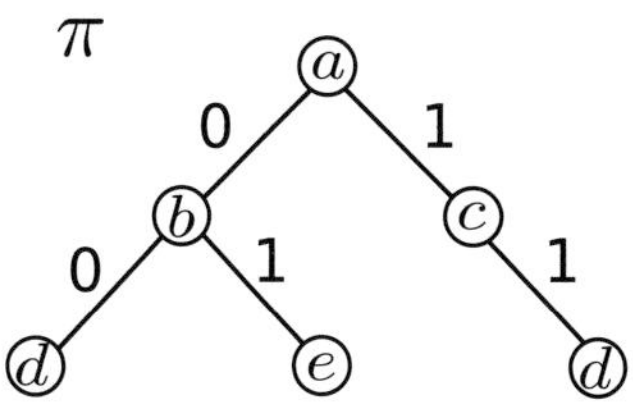

Figure 3.3 A policy and its representation as a decision tree.

Adaptive stochastic maximization. Based on the notation above, the expected reward of a policy π is

$$f_{\mathrm{avg}}(\pi) := \mathbb{E}\left[f(V(\pi,\Phi),\Phi)\right] = \sum_{\phi} \mathbb{P}\left[\phi\right] f(V(\pi,\phi),\phi).$$

The goal of the *Adaptive Stochastic Maximization* problem is to find a policy π^* such that

$$\pi^* \in \arg\max_{\pi} f_{\mathrm{avg}}(\pi) \text{ subject to } |V(\pi,\phi)| \le k \text{ for all } \phi, \qquad (3.17)$$

where k is a budget on how many actions can be played (e.g., we would like to adaptively choose k sensor locations such that the selected sensors provide as much information as possible in expectation).

Adaptive stochastic minimum cost cover. Alternatively, we can specify a quota q of reward that we would like to obtain, and try to find the cheapest policy achieving that quota (e.g., we would like to achieve a certain amount of information, as cheaply as possible in expectation). Formally, we define the average cost $c_{\mathrm{avg}}(\pi)$ of a policy as the expected number of actions it plays, so that $c_{\mathrm{avg}}(\pi) := \mathbb{E}\left[|V(\pi,\Phi)|\right]$. Our goal of this *Adaptive Stochastic Minimum Cost Cover* problem is then to find

$$\pi^* \in \arg\min_{\pi} c_{\mathrm{avg}}(\pi) \text{ such that } f(V(\pi,\phi),\phi) \ge q \text{ for all } \phi, \qquad (3.18)$$

i.e., the policy π^* that minimizes the expected number of items picked such that under all possible realizations, at least reward q is achieved.

Problems (3.17) and (3.18) are intractable in general, even to approximate to a factor of $O(|V|^{1-\epsilon})$, under reasonable complexity-theoretic assumptions. However, if f is satisfies certain conditions, which generalize monotonicity and submodularity, then the classic results bounding the performance of the greedy algorithm generalize. The following definitions are from [27], and presume that in order to observe ψ, all the actions in $\mathrm{dom}(\psi)$ must have already been performed. They rely on a generalization of the discrete derivative $\Delta(v \mid S)$ to the adaptive setting.

Definition 3.11 (Conditional Expected Marginal Benefit) Given a partial realization ψ and an item v, the *conditional expected marginal benefit* of v conditioned on having observed ψ, denoted $\Delta(v \mid \psi)$, is

$$\Delta(v \mid \psi) := \mathbb{E}\left[f(\text{dom}(\psi) \cup \{v\}, \Phi) - f(\text{dom}(\psi), \Phi) \mid \psi\right] \qquad (3.19)$$

where the expectation is taken with respect to $\mathbb{P}[\phi \mid \psi]$.

Definition 3.12 (Adaptive Monotonicity) A function $f : 2^V \times O^V \to \mathbb{R}_+$ is *adaptive monotone* with respect to distribution $\mathbb{P}[\phi]$ if the conditional expected marginal benefit of any item is nonnegative, i.e., for all ψ with $\mathbb{P}[\psi] > 0$ and all $v \in V$ we have

$$\Delta(v \mid \psi) \geq 0. \qquad (3.20)$$

Definition 3.13 (Adaptive Submodularity) A function $f : 2^V \times O^V \to \mathbb{R}_+$ is *adaptive submodular* with respect to distribution $\mathbb{P}[\phi]$ if the conditional expected marginal benefit of any fixed item does not increase as more items are selected and their states are observed. Formally, f is adaptive submodular w.r.t. $\mathbb{P}[\phi]$ if for all ψ and ψ' such that ψ is a subrealization of ψ' (i.e., $\psi \subseteq \psi'$), and for all $v \in V \setminus \text{dom}(\psi')$, we have

$$\Delta(v \mid \psi) \geq \Delta(v \mid \psi'). \qquad (3.21)$$

Adaptive submodularity generalizes the classical notion of submodularity, in the sense that it reduces to submodularity in the case when the world state realization Φ is deterministic. The same is true for adaptive monotonicity. Not surprisingly, there is a natural generalization of the greedy algorithm as well, called the *adaptive greedy algorithm*, which iteratively selects the action maximizing the conditional expected marginal benefit, conditioned on the outcomes of all of its previous actions:

$$
\boxed{
\begin{array}{l}
\text{While not done} \\
\quad \text{Select } v^* \in \arg\max_v \Delta(v \mid \psi); \\
\quad \text{Observe } \phi(v^*); \\
\quad \text{Set } \psi \leftarrow \psi \cup \{(v^*, \phi(v^*))\};
\end{array}
}
\qquad (3.22)
$$

For adaptive stochastic maximization, the algorithm terminates after selecting k actions. For adaptive stochastic minimum cost cover, it stops when it has achieved the quota q of value, i.e., when it has observed ψ such that $f(\text{dom}(\psi), \phi) \geq q$ for all $\psi \subseteq \phi$ (treating ϕ and ψ as relations, i.e., sets of input–output pairs).

Remarkably, it turns out that the adaptive greedy algorithm has performance guarantees that generalize various classic results for the greedy algorithm, for example, Theorem 3.5.

Theorem 3.14 (Golovin and Krause [27]) *Let π_ℓ^{greedy} be the greedy policy implicitly represented by the pseudocode in (3.22), run for ℓ iterations (so that it selects ℓ actions), and let π_k^* be any policy selecting at most k actions for any realization ϕ. Then*

$$f_{avg}(\pi_\ell^{greedy}) \geq \left(1 - e^{-\ell/k}\right) f_{avg}(\pi_k^*) \tag{3.23}$$

where recall $f_{avg}(\pi) := \mathbb{E}\left[f(V(\pi, \Phi), \Phi)\right]$ is the expected reward of π.

Asadpour et al. [2] prove Theorem 3.14 for a special case of stochastic submodular maximization. Golovin and Krause [27] also provide results for the adaptive stochastic min-cost cover problem (3.18) that generalize Theorem 3.6. Furthermore, Golovin and Krause [26] prove generalizations of results for maximizing monotone submodular functions under matroid constraints. Similarly, lazy evaluations (as discussed in §3.2) can still be applied to accelerate the adaptive greedy algorithm.

3.5.2 Example Applications

As mentioned in the beginning of this section, the adaptive submodularity framework has many applications. In some cases, greedily maximizing an adaptive submodular objective is already the algorithm of choice in practice. The framework then immediately provides theoretical justification in the form of approximation guarantees, and allows us to speed up existing algorithms. One example is *active learning* in the noiseless case (*cf.*, Kosaraju et al. [41], Dasgupta [16], Golovin and Krause [27]), in which we must adaptively select data points to be labelled for us (at some cost) until we can infer the labeling of all data points, while attempting to minimize the cost. In some other cases it is possible to frame the problem in the form of optimizing a carefully designed adaptive submodular objective. Given such an objective, the adaptive greedy algorithm may be used with this new objective to obtain a new approximation algorithm for the problem. Recent work on *active learning with noise* [28, 7], where the labels we receive may sometimes be incorrect, falls under this category. Active learning with noise can also be used to tackle *sequential experimental design* problems, in which an algorithm adaptively selects experiments to perform in order to distinguish scientific theories.

Another class of problems where adaptive submodularity is useful is for adaptively committing resources to achieve some goal. For example, in *adaptive sensor placement* one can deploy a set of sensors one by one, and decide where to place the next sensor based on the data obtained from previous sensors. In *adaptive viral marketing*, one must adaptively select people to target with a viral ad campaign – for example, to receive a free subscription to some service – on the premise that some of those targeted will enjoy the service, convince their friends to join, who will in turn convince their friends, and so on. For more information on these applications, see [27]. Golovin et al. [30] consider a *dynamic resource allocation* problem for conservation planning, in which a conservation agency with a fixed annual budget selects additional land parcels to buy each year while attempting to maximize the probability that certain (rare or endangered) species persist in the wild. Liu et al. [57] consider a joint query optimization problem for streaming database systems; their problem is a special case of *stochastic set cover*, as discussed by Golovin and Krause [27].

3.5.3 Worst–Case Adaptive Optimization

Guillory and Bilmes [32, 33] provide a different recent approach to adaptive optimization based on submodularity, tailored to the worst–case scenario in which the outcome of any action is chosen adversarially. In their model there is a set of hypotheses H, actions V with costs $c : V \to \mathbb{R}_+$, and outcomes O, as well as a set of monotone submodular functions $\{f_h : h \in H\}$ of type $2^{V \times O} \to \mathbb{R}_+$, and a threshold $\alpha \in \mathbb{R}_+$. Upon performing action v, an adversary selects outcome $o \in v(h^*)$, where h^* is an adversarially chosen hypothesis. The goal is to adaptively select, as cheaply as possible, actions until the resulting set of action–outcome pairs achieves α reward measured with respect to f_{h^*}. Guillory and Bilmes provide elegant reductions of this problem to a standard min-cost submodular cover problem, including one which, surprisingly, works even in the presence of certain types of adversarially selected noise. This allows them to obtain logarithmic approximations for these problems. They empirically tested their algorithms on a movie recommendation task in which users are asked a sequence of questions in an attempt to recommend movies for them to watch immediately.

3.6 Conclusions

We have reviewed the concept of submodular functions, a natural discrete analogue of convex functions. Focusing on the problem of maximizing submodular functions, we reviewed guarantees about efficient greedy methods, as well as more complex algorithms that can handle complex combinatorial constraints. We discussed extensions of submodular optimization to the online (no-regret and secretary) settings, as well as recent generalizations of submodularity to adaptive (interactive) optimization problems such as active learning.

While much progress was recently made, there are many interesting open problems, such as developing approximation algorithms for handling yet more general classes of constraints. In particular, the online- and adaptive extensions are still rather little explored. Lastly, while we focused on submodular maximization, there is a large literature on submodular minimization, with many open problems, such as the development of efficient methods for large-scale submodular minimization, and approximation algorithms for constrained minimization.

Submodularity is a very powerful concept, and we believe there are many interesting applications of submodular optimization to machine learning, AI and computer science in general yet to be discovered.

References

[1] Ageev, A. A., and Sviridenko, M. I. 2004. Pipage Rounding: a New Method of Constructing Algorithms with Proven Performance Guarantee. *Journal of Combinatorial Optimization*, **8**(3) 307–328.

[2] Asadpour, Arash, Nazerzadeh, Hamid, and Saberi, Amin. 2008. Stochastic Submodular Maximization. Pages 477–489 of: *WINE '08: Proc. of the 4th International Workshop on Internet and Network Economics*. Berlin, Heidelberg: Springer-Verlag.

[3] Auer, Peter, Cesa-Bianchi, Nicolò, and Fischer, Paul. 2002. Finite-time Analysis of the Multiarmed Bandit Problem. *Machine Learning*, **47**(2), 235–256.

[4] Auer, Peter, Bianchi, Nicolò, Freund, Yoav, and Schapire, Robert. 2003. The Nonstochastic Multiarmed Bandit Problem. *SIAM J. Comput.*, **32**(1), 48–77.

[5] Babu, Shivnath, Motwani, Rajeev, Munagala, Kamesh, Nishizawa, Itaru, and Widom, Jennifer. 2004. Adaptive Ordering of Pipelined Stream Filters. Pages 407–418 of: *Proceedings of the 2004 ACM SIGMOD International Conference on Management of Data*.

[6] Bateni, MohammadHossein, Hajiaghayi, MohammadTaghi, and Zadimoghaddam, Morteza. 2010. Submodular Secretary Problem and Extensions. Pages 39–52 of: *Proceedings of the 13th International Conference on Approximation, and 14th International Conference on Randomization, and Combinatorial Optimization: Algorithms and Techniques*. APPROX/RANDOM'10. Berlin, Heidelberg: Springer-Verlag.

[7] Bellala, G., and Scott, C. 2010. *Modified Group Generalized Binary Search with Near-Optimal Performance Guarantees*. Tech. rept. University of Michigan.

[8] Bergmann, G. 1929. Zur Axiomatik der Elementargeometrie. *Monatshefte für Mathematik und Physik*, **36**, 269–284.

[9] Birkhoff, G. 1933. On the Combination of Subalgebras. *Proc. Cambridge Philosophical Society*, **29**, 441–464.

[10] Boykov, Yuri, and Jolly, Marie-Pierre. 2001. Interactive Graph Cuts for Optimal Boundary and Region Segmentation of Objects in N-D Images. Pages 105–112 of: *Proceedings of the 8th International Conference on Computer Vision (ICCV), volume 1*.

[11] Calinescu, G., and Zelikovsky, A. 2005. The Polymatroid Steiner Tree Problems. *Journal of Combinatorial Optimization*, **3**, 281–294.

[12] Calinescu, Gruia, Chekuri, Chandra, Pal, Martin, and Vondrak, Jan. 2011. Maximizing a Submodular Set Function Subject to a Matroid Constraint. *SIAM Journal on Computing* **40**, 1740-1766.

[13] Cesa-Bianchi, Nicolò, and Lugosi, Gábor. 2006. *Prediction, Learning, and Games*. Cambridge University Press.

[14] Chekuri, Chandra, and Pal, Martin. 2005. A Recursive Greedy Algorithm for Walks in Directed Graphs. Pages 245–253 of: *FOCS 2005*.

[15] Chekuri, Chandra, Vondrák, Jan, and Zenklusen, Rico. 2011. Submodular Function Maximization via the Multilinear Relaxation and Contention Resolution Schemes. Pages 783–792 of: *Proceedings of the 43rd ACM Symposium on Theory of Computing (STOC)*.

[16] Dasgupta, Sanjoy. 2004. Analysis of a Greedy Active Learning Strategy. Pages 337–344 of: *Advances in Neural Information Processing Systems* **20**. MIT Press.

[17] Edmonds, Jack. 1970. Submodular Functions, Matroids and Certain Polyhedra. Pages 69–87 of: *Combinatorial Structures and their Applications*. Gordon and Breach, New York.

[18] Feige, U., Mirrokni, V., and Vondrak, J. 2007. Maximizing Non-monotone Submodular Functions. Pages 461–471 of: *FOCS '07*.

[19] Feige, Uriel. 1998. A Threshold of $\ln n$ for Approximating Set Cover. *Journal of the ACM*, **45**(4), 634–652.

[20] Freund, Y, and Schapire, RE. 1999. Adaptive Game Playing Using Multiplicative Weights. *Games and Economic Behavior*, **29**(1-2), 79–103.

[21] Frieze, A. M. 1974. A Cost Function Property for Plant Location Problems. *Mathematical Programming*, **7**, 245–248. 10.1007/BF01585521.

[22] Fujishige, S. 1978. Polymatroidal Dependence Structure of a Set of Random Variables. *Inform. Contr.*, **39**, 55–72.

[23] Fujishige, Satoru. 2005. *Submodular Functions and Optimization*. 2nd edn. Vol. 58. North Holland, Amsterdam: Annals of Discrete Mathematics.

[24] Gharan, Shayan Oveis, and Vondrák, Jan. 2011. Submodular Maximization by Simulated Annealing. Pages 1098–1116 of: *SODA '11: Proceedings of the 22nd Annual ACM–SIAM Symposium on Discrete Algorithms*.

[25] Goldengorin, Boris, Sierksma, Gerard, Tijssen, Gert A., and Tso, Michael. 1999. The Data-Correcting Algorithm for the Minimization of Supermodular Functions. *Management Science*, **45**(11), 1539–1551.

[26] Golovin, Daniel, and Krause, Andreas. 2011a. Adaptive Submodular Optimization under Matroid Constraints. *CoRR*, abs/1101.4450.

[27] Golovin, Daniel, and Krause, Andreas. 2011b. Adaptive Submodularity: Theory and Applications in Active Learning and Stochastic Optimization. *Journal of Artificial Intelligence Research (JAIR)*, **42**, 427–286.

[28] Golovin, Daniel, Krause, Andreas, and Ray, Debajyoti. 2010a. Near-Optimal Bayesian Active Learning with Noisy Observations. Pages 766–774 of: *Advances in Neural Information Processing Systems* **23**.

[29] Golovin, Daniel, Faulkner, Matthew, and Krause, Andreas. 2010b. Online Distributed Sensor Selection. Pages 220–231 of: *Proceedings of the 9th ACM/IEEE International Conference on Information Processing in Sensor Networks (IPSN)*.

[30] Golovin, Daniel, Krause, Andreas, Gardner, Beth, Converse, Sarah J., and Morey, Steve. 2011. Dynamic Resource Allocation in Conservation Planning. In: *AAAI '11: Proceedings of the 25th AAAI Conference on Artificial Intelligence*.

[31] Goundan, Pranava R., and Schulz, Andreas S. 2007. *Revisiting the Greedy Approach to Submodular Set Function Maximization*. Working Paper. Massachusetts Institute of Technology.

[32] Guillory, Andrew, and Bilmes, Jeff. 2010. Interactive Submodular Set Cover. In: *Proceedings of the 27th International Conference on Machine Learning (ICML)*.

[33] Guillory, Andrew, and Bilmes, Jeff A. 2011. Simultaneous Learning and Covering with Adversarial Noise. In: *Proceedings of the 28th International Conference on Machine Learning (ICML)*.

[34] Gupta, Anupam, Roth, Aaron, Schoenebeck, Grant, and Talwar, Kunal. 2010. Constrained Non-monotone Submodular Maximization: Offline and Secretary Algorithms. Pages 246–257 of: *WINE 2010*. LNCS, 6484. Springer.

[35] Hazan, Elad, and Kale, Satyen. 2009. Online Submodular Minimization. Pages 700–708 of: *Advances in Neural Information Processing Systems* **22**.

[36] Jegelka, Stefanie, and Bilmes, Jeff. 2011a. Submodularity Beyond Submodular Energies: Coupling Edges in Graph Cuts. Pages 1897–1904 of: *Proceedings of CVPR 2011*.

[37] Jegelka, Stefanie, and Bilmes, Jeff A. 2011b. Online Submodular Minimization for Combinatorial Structures. In: *Proceedings of the 28th International Conference on Machine Learning (ICML)*.

[38] Kawahara, Yoshinobu, Nagano, Kiyohito, Tsuda, Koji, and Bilmes, Jeff. 2009. Submodularity Cuts and Applications. Pages 916–924 of: *Advances in Neural Information Processing Systems* **22**.

[39] Kempe, David, Kleinberg, Jon, and Tardos, Éva. 2003. Maximizing the Spread of Influence through a Social Network. Pages 137–146 of: *KDD '03: Proceedings of the 9th ACM SIGKDD International Conference on Knowledge Discovery and Data Mining*.

[40] Kohli, Pushmeet, Kumar, Pawan, and Torr, Philip. 2009. $\mathcal{P}^3$ & Beyond: Move Making Algorithms for Solving Higher Order Functions. *IEEE Transactions on Pattern Analysis and Machine Intelligence*, **31**(9), 1645–1656.

[41] Kosaraju, S. Rao, Przytycka, Teresa M., and Borgstrom, Ryan S. 1999. On an Optimal Split Tree Problem. Pages 157–168 of: *Proc. of the 6th International Workshop on Algorithms and Data Structures.* LNCS, 1663. Springer.

[42] Krause, Andreas. 2010. SFO: A Toolbox for Submodular Function Optimization. *Journal of Machine Learning Research*, **11**, 1141–1144.

[43] Krause, A., and Guestrin, C. 2005. Near-optimal Nonmyopic Value of Information in Graphical Models. In: *Proc. of Uncertainty in Artificial Intelligence.* CoRR abs/1207.1394 (2012).

[44] Krause, Andreas, and Guestrin, Carlos. 2007. Near-optimal Observation Selection using Submodular Functions. Pages 1650–1654 of: *AAAI'07: Proceedings of the 22nd National Conference on Artificial intelligence.* AAAI Press.

[45] Krause, A., and Guestrin, C. 2011. Submodularity and its Applications in Optimized Information Gathering. *ACM Transactions on Intelligent Systems and Technology*, **2**(4), Article 32.

[46] Krause, A., and Horvitz, E. 2008. A Utility-Theoretic Approach to Privacy and Personalization. Pages 1181–1188 of: *AAAI '08: Proc. 23rd National Conference on Artificial Intelligence, Volume 2.*

[47] Krause, A., Guestrin, C., Gupta, A., and Kleinberg, J. 2006. Near-optimal Sensor Placements: Maximizing Information while Minimizing Communication Cost. Pages 2–10 of: *IPSN '06: Proceedings of the Fifth International Conference on Information Processing in Sensor Networks.*

[48] Krause, A., Singh, A., and Guestrin, C. 2008a. Near-optimal Sensor Placements in Gaussian Processes: Theory, Efficient Algorithms and Empirical Studies. In: *Journal of Machine Learning Research*, **9**, 235–284.

[49] Krause, Andreas, Leskovec, Jure, Guestrin, Carlos, VanBriesen, Jeanne, and Faloutsos, Christos. 2008b. Efficient Sensor Placement Optimization for Securing Large Water Distribution Networks. *Journal of Water Resources Planning and Management*, **134**(6), 516–526.

[50] Krause, Andreas, McMahan, Brendan, Guestrin, Carlos, and Gupta, Anupam. 2008c. Robust Submodular Observation Selection. *Journal of Machine Learning Research*, **9**, 2761–2801.

[51] Krause, Andreas, Rajagopal, Ram, Gupta, Anupam, and Guestrin, Carlos. 2009. Simultaneous Placement and Scheduling of Sensors. Pages 181–192 of: *IPSN '09: Proc. ACM/IEEE International Conference on Information Processing in Sensor Networks.*

[52] Krause, Andreas, Roper, Alex, and Golovin, Daniel. 2011a. Randomized Sensing in Adversarial Environments. In: *IJCAI '11: Proceedings of the 22nd International Joint Conference on Artificial Intelligence.* To appear.

[53] Krause, Andreas, Guestrin, Carlos, Gupta, Anupam, and Kleinberg, Jon. 2011b. Robust Sensor Placements at Informative and Communication-Effective Locations. *ACM Transactions on Sensor Networks*, **7**(4), Article 31.

[54] Kulik, A., Shachnai, H., and Tamir, T. 2009. Maximizing Submodular Functions Subject to Multiple Linear Constraints. In: *SODA '09: Proceedings of the 20th Annual ACM–SIAM Symposium on Discrete Algorithms.*

[55] Leskovec, Jure, Krause, Andreas, Guestrin, Carlos, Faloutsos, Christos, Van-Briesen, Jeanne, and Glance, Natalie. 2007. Cost-effective Outbreak Detection in Networks. Pages 420–429 of: *KDD '07: Proceedings of the 13th ACM SIGKDD International Conference on Knowledge Discovery and Data Mining*.

[56] Lin, Hui, and Bilmes, Jeff. 2011. A Class of Submodular Functions for Document Summarization. In: *North American chapter of the Association for Computational Linguistics/Human Language Technology Conference (NAACL/HLT-2011)*.

[57] Liu, Zhen, Parthasarathy, Srinivasan, Ranganathan, Anand, and Yang, Hao. 2008. Near-optimal Algorithms for Shared Filter Evaluation in Data Stream Systems. Pages 133–146 of: *SIGMOD '08: Proceedings of the 2008 ACM SIGMOD International Conference on Management of Data*.

[58] Lovasz, L. 1983. Submodular Functions and Convexity. Pages 235–257 of: *Mathematical Programming – State of the Art*, Bachem, A., Korte, B, Grötschel, M. (eds). Springer.

[59] Minoux, M. 1978. Accelerated Greedy Algorithms for Maximizing Submodular Set Functions. Pages 234–243 of: *Optimization Techniques*, LNCIS, **7**.

[60] Munagala, Kamesh, Babu, Shivnath, Motwani, Rajeev, Widom, Jennifer, and Thomas, Eiter. 2005. The Pipelined Set Cover Problem. Pages 83–98 of: *ICDT'05 Proceedings of the 10th International Conference on Database Theory*. LNCS, **3363**.

[61] Narasimhan, Mukund, and Bilmes, Jeff. 2004. PAC-learning Bounded Tree-width Graphical Models. Pages 410–417 of: *UAI '04 Proceedings of the 20th Conference on Uncertainty in Artificial Intelligence*.

[62] Narasimhan, Mukund, Jojic, Nebojsa, and Bilmes, Jeff. 2005. Q-clustering. Pages 979–986 of: *Advances in Neural Information Processing Systems*, **18**.

[63] Nemhauser, G.L., and Wolsey, L.A. 1978. Best Algorithms for Approximating the Maximum of a Submodular Set Function. *Math. Oper. Research*, **3**(3), 177–188.

[64] Nemhauser, G.L., and Wolsey, L.A. 1981. Maximizing Submodular Set Functions: Formulations and Analysis of Algorithms. *Studies on Graphs and Discrete Programming*, volume 11 of *Annals of Discrete Mathematics*.

[65] Nemhauser, George L., Wolsey, Laurence A., and Fisher, Marshall L. 1978. An Analysis of Approximations for Maximizing Submodular Set Functions, I. *Mathematical Programming*, **14**(1), 265–294.

[66] Radlinski, Filip, Kleinberg, Robert, and Joachims, Thorsten. 2008. Learning Diverse Rankings with Multi-Armed Bandits. Pages 784–791 of: *ICML '08 Proceedings of the 25th International Conference on Machine Learning*.

[67] Schrijver, Alexander. 2003. *Combinatorial Optimization: Polyhedra and Efficiency*. Volume B, Part IV, Chapters 39–49. Springer.

[68] Schulman, John D., Goldberg, Ken, and Abbeel, Pieter. 2011. Grasping and Fixturing as Submodular Coverage Problems. In: *ISRR*.

[69] Singh, Amarjeet, Krause, Andreas, Guestrin, Carlos, Kaiser, William J., and Batalin, Maxim A. 2007 (January). Efficient Planning of Informative Paths for Multiple Robots. Pages 2204–2211 of: *IJCAI 2007, Proceedings of the International Joint Conference on Artificial Intelligence*.

[70] Singh, Amarjeet, Krause, Andreas, and Kaiser, William. 2009. Nonmyopic Adaptive Informative Path Planning for Multiple Robots. In: *IJCAI 2009, Proceedings of the International Joint Conference on Artificial Intelligence.*

[71] Stobbe, Peter, and Krause, Andreas. 2010. Efficient Minimization of Decomposable Submodular Functions. Pafes 2208–2216 of: *Advances in Neural Information Processing Systems,* **23**.

[72] Streeter, Matthew, and Golovin, Daniel. 2007. *An Online Algorithm for Maximizing Submodular Functions.* Tech. rept. CMU-CS-07-171. Carnegie Mellon University.

[73] Streeter, Matthew, and Golovin, Daniel. 2008. An Online Algorithm for Maximizing Submodular Functions. Pages 1577–1584 of: *Advances in Neural Information Processing Systems,* **21**.

[74] Streeter, Matthew, Golovin, Daniel, and Smith, Stephen F. 2007a. Combining Multiple Heuristics Online. Pages 1197–1203 of: *AAAI '07: Proceedings of the 22nd AAAI Conference on Artificial Intelligence.*

[75] Streeter, Matthew, Golovin, Daniel, and Smith, Stephen F. 2007b. Restart Schedules for Ensembles of Problem Instances. Pages 1204–1210 of: *AAAI '07: Proceedings of the 22nd AAAI Conference on Artificial Intelligence.*

[76] Streeter, Matthew, Golovin, Daniel, and Smith, Stephen F. 2008. Combining Multiple Constraint Solvers: Results on the CPAI'06 Competition Data. Pages 11–18 of: *Proceedings of the 2nd International CSP Solver Competition.*

[77] Streeter, Matthew, Golovin, Daniel, and Krause, Andreas. 2009. Online Learning of Assignments. Pages 1794–1802 of: *Advances in Neural Information Processing Systems 22.*

[78] Sviridenko, M. 2004. A Note on Maximizing a Submodular Set Function Subject to Knapsack Constraint. *Operations Research Letters,* **32**, 41–43.

[79] Vondrák, Jan. 2008. Optimal Approximation for the Submodular Welfare Problem in the Value Oracle Model. Pages 67–74 of: *STOC '08 Proceedings of the 40th Annual ACM Symposium on Theory of Computing.*

[80] Vondrák, Jan. 2010. Submodularity and Curvature: the Optimal Algorithm. *RIMS Kokyuroku Bessatsu,* **B23**, 253–266.

[81] Wolsey, Laurence A. 1982. An Analysis of the Greedy Algorithm for the Submodular Set Covering Problem. *Combinatorica,* **2**(4), 385–393.

4

Tractable Valued Constraints

Peter G. Jeavons[a] and Stanislav Živný[b]

In this chapter, we will survey recent results on the broad family of optimisation problems that can be cast as valued constraint satisfaction problems (VCSPs). We discuss general methods for analysing the complexity of such problems, and give examples of tractable cases.

4.1 Introduction

Computational problems from many different areas involve finding values for variables that satisfy certain specified restrictions and optimise certain specified criteria.

In this chapter, we will show that it is useful to abstract the general form of such problems to obtain a single generic framework. Bringing all such problems into a common framework draws attention to common aspects that they all share, and allows very general analytical approaches to be developed. We will survey some of these approaches, and the results that have been obtained by using them.

The generic framework we shall use is the *valued constraint satisfaction problem* (VCSP), defined formally in Section 4.3. We will show that many combinatorial optimisation problems can be conveniently expressed in this framework, and we will focus on finding restrictions to the general problem which are sufficient to ensure tractability.

An important and well-studied special case of the VCSP is the constraint satisfaction problem (CSP), which deals with combinatorial search problems which have no optimisation criteria. We give a brief introduction to the CSP in Section 4.2, before defining the more general VCSP framework in

[a] Supported by EPSRC grant EP/G055114/1.
[b] Supported by a Junior Research Fellowship at University College, Oxford.

Section 4.3. Section 4.4 then presents a number of examples of problems that can be seen as special cases of the VCSP.

The remainder of the chapter discusses what happens to the complexity of the valued constraint satisfaction problem when we restrict it in various ways. Section 4.6 considers the important special case of valued constraint problems involving submodular functions. Motivated by this example, we introduce the notion of a *multimorphism*, which can be used to define many other tractable forms of valued constraint, and we use this notion to obtain a complexity classification of all valued constraints over a 2-element domain. In Section 4.7 we present a complexity classification of problems over arbitrary finite domains allowing all unary valued constraints.

Section 4.8 describes the basics of a recently developed general algebraic theory for studying the complexity of different forms of valued constraints. Finally, Section 4.9 concludes with some open problems.

This chapter is self-contained, but we refer the reader to one of the standard textbooks [2, 52, 123] for more detailed background information on the basics of constraint satisfaction. Earlier surveys on the complexity of various forms of restricted constraint satisfaction problems can be found in [27, 25, 100, 47, 79, 85, 118].

4.2 Constraint Satisfaction Problems

In this section, we present the simplest form of constraint satisfaction problem, where there are no optimisation criteria, so all solutions satisfying the specified constraints are considered equally desirable. This form of problem has been widely-studied since the pioneering work of [115], and there are now several textbooks covering this topic [2, 52, 123], as well as a regular international conference devoted to constraint programming.

The basic constraint satisfaction problem (CSP) can be defined in a number of equivalent ways. Here we will present three equivalent standard definitions, each emphasizing different aspects of the problem.

Our first definition is couched in the terminology of predicate logic. Let $\mathbf{B} = (D, R_1, R_2, \ldots)$ be a relational structure, where D is the universe and $R_1, R_2, \ldots$ are relations over D. A first-order formula is called *primitive positive* over $\mathbf{B}$ if it is of the form

$$\exists x_1 \exists x_2 \ldots \exists x_n \ \psi_1 \wedge \cdots \wedge \psi_m$$

where the ψ_i are atomic formulas, i.e., formulas of the form $R(x_{i_1}, \ldots, x_{i_k})$ where R is a relation symbol for a k-ary relation from $\mathbf{B}$.

Definition 4.1 An instance of the constraint satisfaction problem (CSP) is given by a primitive positive sentence, Φ, over a fixed relational structure, **B**. The question is whether Φ is true in **B**.

This logical formulation of constraint satisfaction allows some classical combinatorial problems to be formulated very naturally.

Example 4.2 (Satisfiability) The standard propositional SATISFIABILITY problem for ternary clauses, 3-SAT [66] consists in determining whether it is possible to satisfy a Boolean formula given in CNF as a conjunction of ternary clauses.

This can be viewed as a constraint satisfaction problem by fixing the structure $\mathbf{B}_{3SAT}$ to be $(\{0,1\}, R_1, \dots, R_8)$, where the R_i are the 8 relations definable by a single ternary clause. For example, the clause $x \vee \neg y \vee \neg z$ can be written as $R_1(x, y, z)$, where

$$R_1 = \{\langle 0,0,0\rangle, \langle 0,0,1\rangle, \langle 0,1,0\rangle, \langle 1,0,0\rangle, \langle 1,0,1\rangle, \langle 1,1,0\rangle, \langle 1,1,1\rangle\}.$$

An instance of 3-SAT corresponds to a primitive positive sentence over $\mathbf{B}_{3SAT}$ with a conjunct for each clause.

Example 4.3 (Graph Colouring) The standard k-COLOURABILITY problem [66] consists in determining whether it is possible to assign k colours to the vertices of a given graph so that adjacent vertices are assigned different colours.

This can be viewed as a constraint satisfaction problem by fixing the structure $\mathbf{B}_{kCOL}$ to be $(\{1, \dots, k\}, \neq)$, where $\neq$ is the binary disequality relation on $\{1, \dots, k\}$ given by $\{\langle i, j\rangle \mid i, j \in \{1, \dots, k\}, i \neq j\}$.

An instance of GRAPH k-COLOURING corresponds to a primitive positive sentence over $\mathbf{B}_{kCOL}$ with a conjunct for each edge of the graph.

An important line of research in dealing with constraint satisfaction problems has been the development of programming languages to facilitate the expression of practical problems, and software tools to solve such problems. This approach is known as *constraint programming* [123].

In the field of constraint programming, a constraint satisfaction problem is usually defined in a more operational way, as follows.

Definition 4.4 An instance of the constraint satisfaction problem (CSP) is a triple $\mathcal{P} = \langle V, D, \mathcal{C}\rangle$, where: V is a finite set of *variables*; D is a set of possible *values* that may be assigned to the variables (called the *domain*); $\mathcal{C}$ is a multi-set of *constraints*. Each element of $\mathcal{C}$ is a pair $c = \langle \sigma, R\rangle$ where σ is a tuple of variables called the *scope* of c, and R is a $|\sigma|$-ary *relation* over

D that defines the combinations of assignments to the variables in σ that are allowed by c. An *assignment* for $\mathcal{P}$ is a mapping $s : V \to D$. A *solution* to $\mathcal{P}$ is an assignment which is consistent with all of the constraints.

This formulation focuses attention on the *variables*, the *domain* and the *constraints*; these are the key data structures in a software system for solving constraint satisfaction problems.[1] In this formulation the constraints are often represented by oracles – black-box algorithms for a particular constraint type, known as "propagators" [123], which communicate information with each other during the search for a solution by modifying the domains of the individual variables.

Many real-world problems such as timetabling and scheduling, are captured very naturally in this formulation, as well as classic combinatorial search problems and puzzles [123].

It is easy to translate from this second formulation of the constraint satisfaction problem (Definition 4.4) to our original logical formulation (Definition 4.1). To do this, simply collect together the relations over D that occur in the constraints of $\mathcal{C}$, to give a relational structure $\mathbf{B}$ with universe D. The instance can then be written as a primitive positive sentence over $\mathbf{B}$ with a conjunct $R(\sigma[1], \ldots, \sigma[m])$ for each constraint $\langle \sigma, R \rangle$ of arity m that occurs in $\mathcal{C}$.

In a given CSP instance there may be several constraints with the same constraint relation, but different scopes. If we collect together the scopes associated with a particular constraint relation we get a set of tuples which is itself a relation, but a relation over the set of variables, V. If we do this for each distinct constraint relation occurring in our problem, we obtain a collection of such relations over V, which can be viewed as a relational structure $\mathbf{A}$ with universe V. Note that each relation E in $\mathbf{A}$ corresponds to a relation R in $\mathbf{B}$ of the same arity, and vice versa. This is captured in standard algebraic terminology by saying that the two relational structures, $\mathbf{A}$ and $\mathbf{B}$ are *similar*. Note also that a solution to the original CSP instance is a mapping from V to D that maps any tuple of variables related by a relation E in $\mathbf{A}$ to a tuple of values which are related by the corresponding relation R in $\mathbf{B}$. This is captured in standard algebraic terminology by saying that a solution is a *homomorphism* from $\mathbf{A}$ to $\mathbf{B}$.

These observations gives rise to our third alternative formulation of the CSP, this time in the terminology of algebra.

---

[1] In Definition 4.4, we have assumed that all the variables have the same domain. If this is not the case, we could simply collect together all the possible values occurring in the domains of the individual variables into a single set D.

Definition 4.5   An instance of the constraint satisfaction problem (CSP) is given by a pair of similar relational structures **A** and **B**. The question is whether there exists a homomorphism from **A** to **B**.

This clean algebraic formulation of constraint satisfaction was introduced by [58] (and independently by [84]) and has turned out to be very useful for the analysis of the complexity of different forms of the problem.

Example 4.6 (Graph Homomorphism)   The standard GRAPH HOMOMOR-PHISM problem [78] consists in determining whether it is possible to map the vertices of a given graph G to the vertices of another given graph H so that adjacent vertices of G are mapped to adjacent vertices of H.

This can be viewed as a constraint satisfaction problem by viewing G and H as similar relational structures, each with a single binary relation. A homomorphism between these structures is precisely a mapping with the desired properties.

Example 4.7 (Graph Colouring)   The standard k-COLOURABILITY problem described in Example 4.3 can be viewed as the constraint satisfaction problem which asks whether there is a homomorphism from the given graph G to the structure $\mathbf{B}_{kCOL}$, defined in Example 4.3, which corresponds to a complete graph on k vertices.

This formulation makes it easy to see that the GRAPH k-COLOURABILITY problem is a special case of GRAPH HOMOMORPHISM.

Example 4.8 (Clique)   The standard k-CLIQUE problem [66] consists in determining whether a given graph G has a clique of size k, that is, a set of k vertices which are fully connected. This can be viewed as a constraint satisfaction problem which asks whether there is a homomorphism from the complete graph on k vertices to the given graph G.

This formulation of the problem makes it easy to see that k-CLIQUE is a special case of GRAPH HOMOMORPHISM.

It is clear from the examples above that the general CSP is at least NP-hard. This has prompted many researchers to investigate ways in which restricting the problem can reduce its complexity. We will call a restricted version of the CSP *tractable* if there is a polynomial-time algorithm to determine whether any instance of the restricted problem has a solution.

The algebraic formulation of the CSP, given in Definition 4.5, clearly identifies two separate aspects of the specification of an instance: the *source* structure, **A**, and the *target* structure, **B**.

The source structure, **A**, specifies the tuples referred to in Definition 4.4

as the *scopes* of the constraints. If we restrict the possible source structures that we allow in an instance, then we are restricting the set of variables and the ways in which the constraints may be imposed on those variables. Such restrictions are known as *structural restrictions*, see Chapter 1 of this book.

The target structure, **B**, specifies the relations referred to in Definition 4.4 as *constraint relations*. If we restrict the possible target structures that we allow in an instance, then we are restricting the set of possible values and the types of constraints that may be imposed on those values. Such restrictions are known as *language restrictions*.

Definition 4.9 Given classes of structures, $\mathcal{A}$ and $\mathcal{B}$, we define the problem $\mathrm{CSP}(\mathcal{A}, \mathcal{B})$ to be the class of CSP instances $(\mathbf{A}, \mathbf{B})$, where $\mathbf{A} \in \mathcal{A}$ and $\mathbf{B} \in \mathcal{B}$.

Structural restrictions If $\mathcal{B}$ is the class of all structures, we write $\mathrm{CSP}(\mathcal{A}, -)$ in place of $\mathrm{CSP}(\mathcal{A}, \mathcal{B})$. In this case we impose no restriction on the type of constraint, but some restriction on how the constraints may overlap.

Structural restrictions of this kind have been studied since the pioneering work by [115], who observed that CSPs on trees are solvable in polynomial time. This observation has since been generalised in many different ways [62, 53, 63, 76, 70, 99, 51, 71, 26, 74, 1, 29, 72, 111, 110, 113].

In general, the structural restrictions that ensure tractability are those that enforce a bound on some measure of width in the class of source structures allowed [70]. Complete classifications, identifying all tractable cases, have been obtained for bounded-arity CSPs by [73], and for unbounded-arity CSPs by [112]; see also Section 1.4 of this book for more context.

One example of a constraint satisfaction problem with restricted structure is the k-CLIQUE problem (see Example 4.8), which is tractable for any bounded k, but NP-complete if k is unbounded.

Language restrictions If $\mathcal{A}$ is the class of all structures, we write $\mathrm{CSP}(-, \mathcal{B})$ in place of $\mathrm{CSP}(\mathcal{A}, \mathcal{B})$. In this case we impose no restriction on the way the constraints are placed, but some restriction on the forms of constraints that may be imposed.

Such language restrictions have also been widely studied [86, 88, 58, 20, 18, 19, 50, 23, 6, 4, 5, 107, 7, 81, 22, 14, 21, 3].

One example of a constraint satisfaction problem with a restricted constraint language is the GRAPH k-COLOURABILITY problem, described in Example 4.3, which is tractable when $k \leq 2$, but NP-complete for $k \geq 3$.

Hybrid restrictions Of course it is possible to impose other kinds of restrictions on the CSP, by restricting the possible pairs $(\mathbf{A}, \mathbf{B})$ that are allowed in instances in some other way. Such restrictions are sometimes referred to as *hybrid* restrictions [120], because they involve simultaneous restrictions on both the source structure and the target structure. Hybrid restrictions have been much less widely studied, although some interesting cases have been identified [30, 124, 43, 36, 61].

Related work In this chapter we focus on constraint satisfaction problems over a finite domain, but there has also been considerable work on such problems over infinite domains [12, 13]. The complexity of various forms of the CSP has recently also been studied with respect to fixed-parameter tractability [69, 125, 61].

4.3 Valued Constraint Satisfaction Problems

The standard constraint satisfaction problem, or CSP, described in the previous section, captures only the feasibility aspects of a given problem. Since in practice many problems involve seeking a solution that optimises certain criteria, as well as satisfying certain restrictions, various more general frameworks for so-called *soft* constraint satisfaction have been studied, which allow measures of desirability to be associated with different assignments to the variables [52].

Several very general soft CSP frameworks have been proposed in the literature [126, 10, 123], the two most general being the *semi-ring* CSP and the *valued* CSP.

The main difference between semi-ring CSPs and valued CSPs is that the measures of desirability used in valued CSPs represent costs and have to be totally ordered, whereas the measures used in semi-ring CSPs represent preferences and might be ordered only partially. Hence the semi-ring CSP framework is slightly more general than the valued CSP framework, but the valued CSP framework is sufficiently powerful to model a wide range of optimisation problems [32]. Hence we will simply focus here on the valued CSP framework, which we will now define formally.

For a tuple t, we shall denote by $t[i]$ its i-th component. We shall denote by $\mathbb{Q}_+$ the set of all non-negative[2] rational numbers.[3] We define $\overline{\mathbb{Q}}_+ =$

---

[2] It is standard to define the range of cost functions as non-negative rationals with infinity. However, it is easy to observe that one could define the range to be *all* rationals with infinity. Indeed, any VCSP instance with such cost functions is equivalent to an instance with non-negative costs by adding a suitable constant.

[3] To avoid computational and representational issues, we work with rational numbers rather than

$\mathbb{Q}_+ \cup \{\infty\}$, with the standard addition operation, $+$, extended so that for all $a \in \mathbb{Q}_+$, $a + \infty = \infty$. Members of $\overline{\mathbb{Q}}_+$ are called *costs*.

A function ϕ from D^m to $\overline{\mathbb{Q}}_+$ will be called a *cost function* on D of *arity m*. If the range of ϕ is $\{\alpha, \infty\}$, for some finite $\alpha \in \mathbb{Q}_+$ then ϕ is called *essentially crisp*. If $\alpha = 0$, i.e. the range of ϕ is $\{0, \infty\}$, then ϕ is called *crisp*. If the range of ϕ lies entirely within $\mathbb{Q}_+$, then ϕ is called *finite-valued*. If the range of ϕ includes both nonzero finite costs and infinity, we sometimes emphasise this fact by calling ϕ *general-valued*.

Definition 4.10   An instance of the *valued constraint satisfaction problem*, (VCSP), is a triple $\mathcal{P} = \langle V, D, \mathcal{C} \rangle$ where: V is a finite set of *variables*; D is a set of possible *values* that may be assigned to the variables (called the *domain*); $\mathcal{C}$ is a multi-set of *valued constraints*. Each element of $\mathcal{C}$ is a pair $c = \langle \sigma, \phi \rangle$ where σ is a tuple of variables called the *scope* of c, and ϕ is a $|\sigma|$-ary cost function on D taking values in $\overline{\mathbb{Q}}_+$. An *assignment* for $\mathcal{P}$ is a mapping $s : V \to D$. The cost of an assignment s, denoted $\mathrm{Cost}_{\mathcal{P}}(s)$, is given by the sum of the costs for the restrictions of s onto each constraint scope, that is,

$$\mathrm{Cost}_{\mathcal{P}}(s) \;\overset{\mathrm{def}}{=}\; \sum_{\langle \langle v_1, v_2, \ldots, v_m \rangle, \phi \rangle \in \mathcal{C}} \phi(s(v_1), s(v_2), \ldots, s(v_m)).$$

A *solution* to $\mathcal{P}$ is an assignment with minimum cost, and the question is to find a solution.

Remark   In the original, more general, definition of the VCSP, as given by [11], costs were allowed to lie in any positive totally-ordered monoid, called a valuation structure. However, using costs from $\overline{\mathbb{Q}}_+$ and combining them using standard addition is sufficient for our purposes and standard in operational research. We refer the reader to [38] for details on why the restriction to $\overline{\mathbb{Q}}_+$ is not severe.

There are many alternative frameworks for optimisation problems which can easily be shown to be equivalent to the valued constraint satisfaction problem. These include: Min-Sum Problems, Gibbs energy minimisation, Markov Random Fields (MRF), Conditional Random Fields (CRF) and others [108, 16, 136, 135, 45]. Hence, all of the tractability and intractability results that we derive for the VCSP framework immediately apply to all of these other frameworks as well.

As with the CSP defined in Section 4.2, one can study structural restric-

---

arbitrary real numbers. We note that some of the algorithmic results stated in this chapter have been proved for the reals, but we will state the results only for the special case of the rationals.

tions[4] for the VCSP, and hybrid restrictions for the VCSP (see [40, 41, 42] for recent results on hybrid restrictions).

However, the main focus in this chapter will be on language restrictions for the VCSP. For the remainder of the chapter we will assume that D denotes some fixed finite set D; that is, the size of D is not part of the input. A *valued constraint language* (or simply a *language*) is a set of possible cost functions mapping D^m to $\overline{\mathbb{Q}}_+$. A valued constraint language Γ is called *crisp* (*essentially crisp, finite-valued, general-valued*, respectively) if all cost functions from Γ are crisp (essentially crisp, finite-valued, general-valued, respectively). A language Γ over a two-element domain is called a *Boolean* language.

Definition 4.11 We will denote by $\mathrm{VCSP}(\Gamma)$ the class of all VCSP instances where the cost functions of the valued constraints are all contained in Γ.

A language Γ is called *tractable* if $\mathrm{VCSP}(\Gamma')$ can be solved in polynomial time for every finite subset $\Gamma' \subseteq \Gamma$, and Γ is called *intractable* if $\mathrm{VCSP}(\Gamma)$ is NP-hard for some finite $\Gamma' \subseteq \Gamma$.

Since we are interested in the complexity of languages over fixed finite domains, we can always assume an explicit representation (such as a table of values) for all cost functions from the language.

4.4 Examples of Valued Constraint Languages

We now give some examples of tractable and intractable valued constraint languages that can be used to model a wide variety of discrete combinatorial search and optimisation problems.

Example 4.12 (CSP) The standard constraint satisfaction problem defined in Section 4.2 can be seen as the special case of the VCSP where all cost functions are (essentially) crisp. In other words, the CSP can be seen as $\mathrm{VCSP}(\Gamma_{\mathrm{ecrisp}})$, where Γ_{ecrisp} is the language consisting of all cost functions with range $\{c, \infty\}$, for some fixed finite $c \in \mathbb{Q}_+$.

By the examples given in Section 4.2, the language Γ_{ecrisp} is clearly intractable.

Example 4.13 ((s, t)-Min-Cut) Let $G = \langle V, E \rangle$ be a directed weighted graph such that for every $(u, v) \in E$ there is a weight $w(u, v) \in \overline{\mathbb{Q}}_+$ and let

---

[4] The study of structural restrictions for the VCSP has not led to essentially new results as hardness results for the CSP immediately apply to the (more general) VCSP, and all known tractable structural classes for the CSP (see for example Section 1.3.3 of this book) extend easily to the VCSP, see [8, 52].

$s, t \in V$ be the source and target nodes. Recall that an (s, t)-*cut* C is a subset of vertices V such that $s \in C$ but $t \notin C$. The weight, or the size, of an (s, t)-cut C is defined as $\sum_{(u,v) \in E, u \in C, v \notin C} w(u, v)$. The (s, t)-Min-Cut problem consists in finding a minimum-weight (s, t)-cut in G. We can formulate the search for a minimum-weight (s, t)-cut in G as a VCSP instance as follows.

Let $D = \{0, 1\}$. For any cost $w \in \overline{\mathbb{Q}}_+$, we define

$$\lambda_w(x, y) \stackrel{\text{def}}{=} \begin{cases} w & \text{if } x = 0 \text{ and } y = 1 \\ 0 & \text{if } x = 1 \text{ or } y = 0 \end{cases}.$$

For any value $d \in D$ and cost $c \in \overline{\mathbb{Q}}_+$, we define

$$\mu_c^d(x) \stackrel{\text{def}}{=} \begin{cases} c & \text{if } x = d \\ 0 & \text{if } x \neq d \end{cases}.$$

We denote by Γ_{cut} the set of all cost functions of the form λ_w or μ_c^d, for all $w, c \in \overline{\mathbb{Q}}_+$ and $d \in D$. Any instance of (s, t)-Min-Cut can be formulated in VCSP(Γ_{cut}) as follows:

$$\mathcal{P} = \left\langle V, D, \{\langle \langle u, v \rangle, \lambda_{w(u,v)} \rangle \mid (u, v) \in E\} \cup \{\langle s, \mu_\infty^1 \rangle, \langle t, \mu_\infty^0 \rangle\} \right\rangle.$$

The unary constraints ensure that the source and target nodes take the values 0 and 1, respectively, in any solution. Therefore, a minimum-weight (s, t)-cut in G corresponds to the set of variables assigned the value 0 in some solution to $\mathcal{P}$.

Furthermore, we claim that any instance $\mathcal{P}$ of VCSP(Γ_{cut}) on variables $x_1, \ldots, x_n$ can be solved in $O(n^3)$ time by a reduction to (s, t)-Min-Cut, and then using the standard algorithm [68]. The reduction works as follows: any unary constraint μ_c^0 (respectively μ_c^1) on x_i can be modelled by an edge of weight c from x_i to the target node (respectively, from the source node to the node x_i). Any constraint with cost function $\lambda_w(x_i, x_j)$ is modelled by an edge of weight w from x_i to x_j.

Hence Γ_{cut} is tractable.

Example 4.14 (Max-Cut) Let Γ_{xor} be the language that contains just the single binary cost function $\phi_{\text{xor}} : D^2 \to \overline{\mathbb{Q}}_+$ defined by

$$\phi_{\text{xor}}(x, y) \stackrel{\text{def}}{=} \begin{cases} 1 & \text{if } x = y \\ 0 & \text{if } x \neq y \end{cases}.$$

If $D = \{0, 1\}$, then the problem VCSP(Γ_{xor}) corresponds to the Max-SAT problem for the exclusive-or predicate, which is known to be NP-hard [48].

Therefore, Γ_{xor} is intractable. Moreover, VCSP(Γ_{xor}) is also equivalent to the Max-Cut problem, a well-known NP-complete problem [66].

For $|D| > 2$, VCSP(Γ_{xor}) includes the $|D|$-COLOURING problem, which is also NP-complete.

Example 4.15 (Max-CSP)   An instance of the maximum constraint satisfaction problem (Max-CSP) is an instance of the CSP with the goal to maximise the number of satisfied constraints. In the weighted version, each constraint has a non-negative weight and the goal is to maximise the weighted number of satisfied constraints.

When seeking the optimal solution, maximising the weighted number of satisfied constraints is the same as minimising the weighted number of unsatisfied constraints.[5] Hence for any instance $\mathcal{P}$ of the Max-CSP, we can define a corresponding VCSP instance $\mathcal{P}'$ in which each constraint c of $\mathcal{P}$ with weight w is associated with a cost function over the same scope in $\mathcal{P}'$ which assigns cost 0 to tuples allowed by c, and cost w to tuples disallowed by c.

The complexity of Boolean languages for Max-CSP has been completely classified in [98], see also [48]. First results on languages over arbitrary finite domains appeared in [28]. A complexity classification (with respect to approximability) of languages over three-element domains appeared in [94]. Let Γ_{fix} be the language containing unary cost functions u_d for all $d \in D$, where $u_d(x) = 0$ if $x = d$ and $u_d(x) = 1$ if $x \neq d$. A complexity classification with respect to approximability of all languages including Γ_{fix}, (so-called languages with fixed-value constraints), was obtained in [55].

The last two mentioned results rely heavily on computer search. However, the main results of these papers follow easily from a recent result on conservative VCSPs [103], which we will discuss in Section 4.7.

For recent results on approximability and inapproximability of the Max-CSP, see [122]

A generalisation of the Max-CSP allowing both positive and negative weights has also been considered, and the complexity of all Boolean languages in this framework was classified by [90], later generalised to all languages by [91].

Example 4.16 (Max-Ones)   An instance of the Boolean Max-Ones problem is an instance of the CSP with the goal to maximise the number of variables assigned the value 1. A classification of the complexity of Boolean languages for this problem was obtained by [48]. This result was later generalised to a classification of maximal languages over domains of size up to

---

[5] This statement is not true with respect to approximability, even over Boolean domains [48].

4, and to a classification of languages containing all permutation relations by [96].

Example 4.17 (Min-Cost-Hom)   Given two graphs (directed or undirected) G and H, we denote by $V(G)$ and $V(H)$ the set of vertices of G and H respectively. We denote by $E(G)$ and $E(H)$ the set of edges of G and H respectively. A mapping $f : V(G) \to V(H)$ is a *homomorphism* of G to H if f preserves edges, that is, $(u, v) \in E(G)$ implies $(f(u), f(v)) \in E(H)$.

The homomorphism problem for graphs was described in Example 4.6 as a special case of the CSP. It asks whether an input graph G admits a homomorphism to a fixed graph H. This problem is also known as H-Colouring [77, 78].

For two graphs G and H, define nonnegative rational costs $c_v(u)$, for all $u \in V(G)$ and $v \in V(H)$. The cost of a homomorphism f from G to H can then be defined to be $\sum_{u \in V(G)} c_{f(u)}(u)$. For a fixed H, the Minimum-Cost Homomorphism problem (Min-Cost-Hom) asks for a homomorphism from G to H with minimum cost.

The Min-Cost-Hom problem can be seen as a special case of the VCSP, where all cost functions are either binary crisp functions, or unary finite-valued functions, and each instance has a unary cost function on each variable, and exactly one binary cost function imposed on some pairs of variables.

A complexity classification of Min-Cost-Hom for undirected graphs was obtained in [75]. A complexity classification of Min-Cost-Hom for digraphs follows from results in [129], with generalisations in [130].

Example 4.18 (Max-Sol)   The Maximum Solution problem (Max-Sol) [92] can be seen as a valued constraint satisfaction problem over a domain with positive integer values. It is equivalent to the VCSP over the language consisting of crisp cost functions together with all unary cost functions of the following form: $\mu(d) = wd$ for any domain value d and some fixed $w \in \mathbb{N}$. [95] studied the Max-Sol problem over undirected graphs, that is, for languages containing only a single symmetric binary crisp cost function, and unary functions of the form specified above.[6] Max-Sol has been also studied by [93].

4.5 Expressive Power

In this section, we define and study a notion of *expressibility* for valued constraint languages. This notion has played a key role in the analysis of

---

[6] This problem is a restriction of Min-Cost-Hom for graphs, but a generalisation of both List-Hom for graphs and Max-Ones.

complexity for the CSP and VCSP. Expressibility allows a particular form of problem reduction: if a constraint can be expressed in a given constraint language, then it can be added to the language without changing the computational complexity of the associated class of problems. To indicate its central role we note that the same basic idea of expressibility has been studied under many different names in different fields: implementation [48], pp-definability [25], existential inverse satisfiability [49], structure identification [54] or join and projection operations in relational databases [134]. In the context of the CSP, both upper bounds [87, 89] and lower bounds [137] on the complexity of deciding expressibility have been studied.

Expressibility is also a significant notion in practical constraint programming. As with all computing paradigms, it is desirable for many purposes to have a small language which can be used to describe a large collection of problems. Determining which additional constraints can be expressed by a given constraint language is therefore a central issue in assessing the flexibility and usefulness of a constraint system.

Definition 4.19 For any VCSP instance $\mathcal{P} = \langle V, D, C \rangle$, and any list $L = \langle v_1, \ldots, v_m \rangle$ of variables of $\mathcal{P}$, the *projection* of $\mathcal{P}$ onto L, denoted $\pi_L(\mathcal{P})$, is the m-ary cost function defined as follows:

$$\pi_L(\mathcal{P})(x_1, \ldots, x_m) \stackrel{\text{def}}{=} \min_{\{s:V \to D \; | \; \langle s(v_1), \ldots, s(v_m) \rangle = \langle x_1, \ldots, x_m \rangle\}} \text{Cost}_{\mathcal{P}}(s).$$

We say that a cost function ϕ is *expressible* over a constraint language Γ if there exists a VCSP instance $\mathcal{P} \in \text{VCSP}(\Gamma)$ and a list L of variables of $\mathcal{P}$ such that $\pi_L(\mathcal{P}) = \phi$. We call the pair $\langle \mathcal{P}, L \rangle$ a *gadget* for expressing ϕ over Γ. We define $\langle \Gamma \rangle$ to be the *expressive power* of Γ; that is, the set of all cost functions expressible over Γ.

Example 4.20 Let $\Gamma = \{\phi_{\neq}\}$ be a language over D which consists of a binary crisp cost function, $\phi_{\neq}$, given by

$$\phi_{\neq}(x, y) \stackrel{\text{def}}{=} \begin{cases} \infty & \text{if } x = y \\ 0 & \text{if } x \neq y \end{cases}.$$

Consider an instance $\mathcal{P} = \langle V, D, C \rangle$ of VCSP(Γ), where $n = |D|$, $V = \{x_1, \ldots, x_{n+1}\}$, and

$$C = \{\langle \langle x_i, x_j \rangle, \phi_{\neq} \rangle \mid i \neq j \in \{1, \ldots, n\}\} \cup \{\langle \langle x_i, x_{n+1} \rangle, \phi_{\neq} \rangle \mid i \in \{2, \ldots, n\}\}.$$

An example of this construction for $|D| = 3$ is shown in Figure 4.1.

In order to avoid infinite cost, variables $x_1, \ldots, x_n$ have to be assigned different values. Moreover, the value of the variable x_{n+1} has to be different

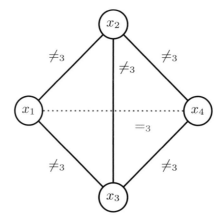

Figure 4.1 Expressing $\phi_=$ over $\Gamma = \{\phi_{\neq}\}$ for $|D| = 3$ (Example 4.20).

from the values of the variables $x_2, \ldots, x_n$. Hence, the only remaining value that can be assigned to the variable x_{n+1} is the value which is assigned to the variable x_1. Therefore, every solution s to $\mathcal{P}$ with minimum total cost (in this case zero) satisfies $s(x_1) = s(x_{n+1})$. Therefore, $\langle \mathcal{P}, \langle x_1, x_{n+1} \rangle \rangle$ is a gadget for expressing the equality cost function, $\phi_=$, given by

$$\phi_=(x, y) \;\overset{\text{def}}{=}\; \begin{cases} 0 & \text{if } x = y \\ \infty & \text{if } x \neq y \end{cases}.$$

In other words, the equality cost function, $\phi_=$, can be expressed using the disequality cost function, $\phi_{\neq}$, that is, $\phi_= \in \langle\!\langle \{\phi_{\neq}\} \rangle\!\rangle$.

The importance of Definition 4.19 is in the following:

Theorem 4.21 ([32])   *For any valued constraint language Γ, Γ is tractable if and only if $\langle\Gamma\rangle$ is tractable.*

Consequently, in order to classify the computational complexity of all valued constraint languages, it is sufficient to consider only those languages which are closed under expressibility.

Example 4.22   By Theorem 4.21 and Example 4.14, in order to show that Γ is an intractable language it is sufficient to show that ϕ_{xor} is expressible over Γ.

Questions related to the expressive power of various valued constraint languages have been studied in [34, 138, 139].

4.6 Submodular Functions and Multimorphisms

In this section, we define submodular functions and multimorphisms. We show how the minimisation problem for submodular functions can be expressed as a particular case of the VCSP, over a language characterised by having a certain binary multimorphism. Moreover, we show several generalisations which give rise to other tractable languages characterised by other kinds of multimorphisms.

Submodular functions For any finite set V, a rational-valued function f defined on subsets of V is called a *set function*.

Definition 4.23 (Submodularity)   A set function $f : 2^V \to \mathbb{Q}_+$ is called *submodular* if for all subsets S and T of V,

$$f(S \cap T) + f(S \cup T) \ \leq \ f(S) + f(T). \tag{4.1}$$

Submodular functions are a key concept in operational research and combinatorial optimisation [117, 116, 133, 128, 64, 104]. Examples include cuts in graphs [67, 121], matroid rank functions [57], set covering problems [59] and entropy functions. Submodular functions are often considered to be a discrete analogue of convex functions [109].

Both minimising and maximising submodular functions, possibly under some additional conditions, have been considered extensively in the literature. Most scenarios use the so-called *oracle value model*: for any set $S \subseteq V$, an algorithm can query an oracle to find the value of $f(S)$.

Submodular function maximisation is easily shown to be NP-hard [128], but good approximation algorithms exist [60]. In contrast, the submodular function minimisation problem can be solved efficiently with only polynomially many oracle calls. Since the first combinatorial[7] polynomial-time algorithms [127, 83] for minimising submodular functions, there have been several improvements in the running times, see [82] for a survey. The time complexity of the fastest known strongly[8] polynomial time algorithm for minimising a submodular function in n variables is $O(n^6 + n^5 L)$, where L is the time required to evaluate the function in n variables [119].

Binary multimorphisms We now define the concept of a binary multimorphism and give several examples.

---

[7] An algorithm is called *combinatorial* if it does not employ the ellipsoid method.
[8] An algorithm is called *strongly polynomial* if the running time does not depend on the maximum value of the function to be minimised.

Definition 4.24 (Binary multimorphisms)   Let $\langle f, g \rangle$ be a pair of operations $f, g : D^2 \to D$. We say that an m-ary cost function $\phi : D^m \to \overline{\mathbb{Q}}_+$ *admits* $\langle f, g \rangle$ as a *multimorphism* if for all $x_1, y_1, \ldots, x_m, y_m \in D$ it holds that

$$\phi(f(x_1, y_1), \ldots, f(x_m, y_m)) + \phi(g(x_1, y_1), \ldots, g(x_m, y_m))$$
$$\leq \phi(x_1, \ldots, x_m) + \phi(y_1, \ldots, y_m). \quad (4.2)$$

If a cost function ϕ admits $\langle f, g \rangle$ as a multimorphism, we also say that ϕ is *improved* by $\langle f, g \rangle$. We say that a language Γ admits $\langle f, g \rangle$ as a multimorphism (or equivalently, that Γ is improved by $\langle f, g \rangle$), if every cost function ϕ from Γ admits $\langle f, g \rangle$ as a multimorphism.

Remark   Using standard vector notation, an m-ary cost function ϕ admits $\langle f, g \rangle$ as a multimorphism if

$$\phi(f(\mathbf{x}, \mathbf{y}) + \phi(g(\mathbf{x}, \mathbf{y})) \leq \phi(\mathbf{x}) + \phi(\mathbf{y})$$

for all $\mathbf{x}, \mathbf{y} \in D^m$, where both f and g are applied coordinate-wise.

Example 4.25 (Submodular cost functions)   Any set function f defined on subsets of $V = \{v_1, \ldots, v_m\}$ can be associated with a cost function $\phi : \{0, 1\}^m \to \overline{\mathbb{Q}}_+$ defined as follows: for each tuple $t \in D^m$, set $\phi(t) = f(T)$, where $T = \{v_i \mid t[i] = 1\}$.

For any tuples s, t over $\{0, 1\}$, if we set $S = \{v_i | s[i] = 1\}$ and $T = \{v_i | t[i] = 1\}$, then $S \cap T = \{v_i \mid \text{Min}(s[i], t[i]) = 1\}$ and $S \cup T = \{v_i \mid \text{Max}(s[i], t[i]) = 1\}$. Here Min is the function returning the minimum of its two arguments and Max is the function returning the maximum of its two arguments. By comparing Definitions 4.24 and 4.23, it can be seen that f is submodular if and only if ϕ admits $\langle \text{Min}, \text{Max} \rangle$ as a multimorphism.

Example 4.26 (Submodular languages)   We denote by Γ_{sub} the set of all cost functions (over some fixed finite totally ordered set D) that admit $\langle \text{Min}, \text{Max} \rangle$ as a multimorphism. Using a polynomial-time strongly combinatorial algorithm for minimising submodular functions, it was shown in [32] that Γ_{sub} is tractable.

However, an instance $\mathcal{P} \in \text{VCSP}(\Gamma_{\text{sub}})$ is a special kind of submodular function minimisation problem, because the objective function is given explicitly by the sum of the cost functions for each individual constraint of $\mathcal{P}$. (Note that submodularity is preserved under addition.) Such functions are also known as locally-defined functions [39] or succinct functions [60]. Hence, one might hope that there is an algorithm for $\text{VCSP}(\Gamma_{\text{sub}})$ with better running time than the general submodular function minimisation algorithms, which work in the oracle-value model and do not assume anything about the structure of the objective function.

In some special cases more efficient algorithms are known. For example, in the case when $D = \{0, 1\}$, the cost functions defined in Example 4.13 are all submodular, so the language Γ_{cut} defined in Example 4.13 is strictly contained in Γ_{sub} for this set D. (Indeed, it is well known that the cut function for any graph is submodular.) Since cut functions can be minimised more efficiently than general submodular functions (see Example 4.13), classes of submodular functions from Γ_{sub} that are expressible over Γ_{cut} have been studied [139, 140]. However, it has been shown in [139, 141] that not all functions from Γ_{sub} are expressible over Γ_{cut}, so this approach cannot be used to obtain a more efficient algorithm for the whole of VCSP(Γ_{sub}).

Other approaches for solving instances from VCSP(Γ_{sub}) include linear programming [39, 44] or submodular flows [101].

Example 4.27 (Max)   Let Γ_{max} be a language, over some totally ordered domain D, which is improved by the pair $\langle \text{Max}, \text{Max} \rangle$, where $\text{Max} : D^2 \to D$ is the binary operation returning the larger of its two arguments. For crisp languages, the tractability of Γ_{max} has been shown in [86]. Using this result, it was shown in [32] that after establishing arc consistency [123] (which might restrict the domains of individual variables), assigning the smallest remaining domain value to all variables will yield an optimal solution. Thus Γ_{max} is tractable.

Example 4.28 (Min)   Let Γ_{min} be a language, over some totally ordered domain D, which is improved by the pair $\langle \text{Min}, \text{Min} \rangle$, where $\text{Min} : D^2 \to D$ is the binary operation returning the smaller of its two arguments. The tractability of Γ_{min} has been shown in [32], using a similar argument to the one in Example 4.27.

Example 4.29 (Bisubmodularity)   For a given finite set V, bisubmodular functions are functions defined on pairs of disjoint subsets of V with a requirement similar to Inequality 4.1 (see [65] for the precise definition). Examples of bisubmodular functions include rank functions of delta-matroids [17, 24]. Bisubmodularity also arises in bicooperative games [9].

A property equivalent to bisubmodularity can be defined on cost functions on the set $D = \{0, 1, 2\}$. We define two binary operations Min_0 and Max_0 as follows:

$$\text{Min}_0(x, y) \overset{\text{def}}{=} \begin{cases} 0 & \text{if } 0 \neq x \neq y \neq 0 \\ \text{Min}(x, y) & \text{otherwise} \end{cases},$$

and

$$\mathrm{Max}_0(x, y) \stackrel{\mathrm{def}}{=} \begin{cases} 0 & \text{if } 0 \neq x \neq y \neq 0 \\ \mathrm{Max}(x, y) & \text{otherwise} \end{cases}.$$

We denote by Γ_{bis} the set of finite-valued cost functions (i.e. with range $\mathbb{Q}_+$) that admit $\langle \mathrm{Min}_0, \mathrm{Max}_0 \rangle$ as a multimorphism. Γ_{bis} can be shown to be tractable using the results of [65, 114].

We remark that the tractability of general-valued languages defined on $D = \{0, 1, 2\}$ and admitting $\langle \mathrm{Min}_0, \mathrm{Max}_0 \rangle$ as a multimorphism remains open. Another open question is the tractability of (even finite-valued) languages defined over D, where $|D| > 3$, and improved by $\langle \mathrm{Min}_0, \mathrm{Max}_0 \rangle$.

Example 4.30 ((Symmetric) tournament pair) A binary operation $f : D^2 \rightarrow D$ is called a *tournament* operation if (i) f is commutative, i.e., $f(x, y) = f(y, x)$ for all $x, y \in D$; and (ii) f is conservative, i.e., $f(x, y) \in \{x, y\}$ for all $x, y \in D$. The *dual* of a tournament operation is the unique tournament operation g satisfying $x \neq y \Rightarrow g(x, y) \neq f(x, y)$.

A *tournament pair* is a pair $\langle f, g \rangle$, where both f and g are tournament operations. A tournament pair $\langle f, g \rangle$ is called *symmetric* if g is the dual of f.

Let Γ be an arbitrary language that admits a symmetric tournament pair multimorphism. It has been shown in [33], by a reduction to the minimisation problem for submodular functions (cf. Example 4.26), that any such Γ is tractable.

Now let Γ be an arbitrary language that admits any tournament pair multimorphism. It has been shown in [33], by a reduction to the symmetric tournament pair case, that any such Γ is also tractable.

Example 4.31 (Tree-submodularity) Now assume that the domain values from D can be arranged into a binary tree T; i.e., a tree where each node has at most two children. Given $a, b \in T$, let P_{ab} denote the unique path in T between a and b of length (=number of edges) $d(a, b)$, and let $P_{ab}[i]$ denote the i-th vertex on P_{ab}, where $0 \leq i \leq d(a, b)$ and $P_{ab}[0] = a$. Let $\langle g_\sqcap, g_\sqcup \rangle$ be two binary operations satisfying $\{g_\sqcap(a, b), g_\sqcup(a, b)\} = \{P_{ab}[\lfloor d/2 \rfloor], P_{ab}[\lceil d/2 \rceil]\}$.

A language admitting $\langle g_\sqcup, g_\sqcap \rangle$ as a multimorphism has been called *strongly tree-submodular*. The tractability of strongly tree-submodular languages was shown in [102].

For $a, b \in T$, let $g_\wedge(a, b)$ be defined as the highest common ancestor of a and b in T; i.e. the unique node on the path P_{ab} that is ancestor of both a and b. We define $g_\vee(a, b)$ as the unique node on the path P_{ab} such that the distance between a and $g_\vee(a,b)$ is the same as the distance between b and $g_\wedge(a,b)$.

A language admitting $\langle g_\wedge, g_\vee \rangle$ as a multimorphism has been called *weakly tree-submodular*, since it has been shown that the property of strong tree-submodularity implies weak tree-submodularity [102]. The tractability of weakly tree-submodular languages on chains[9] and forks[10] has also been shown in [102].

We remark that the tractability of strongly tree-submodular languages defined similarly on general (not necessarily binary) trees remains open. (A special case is a tree on $k + 1$ vertices, where $k > 2$, consisting of a root node with k children. This corresponds precisely to bisubmodular languages on domains of size $k + 1$, cf. Example 4.29.) Moreover, the tractability of weakly tree-submodular languages defined on any trees other than chains and forks remains open.

Example 4.32 (1-defect) Let b and c be two distinct elements of D and let $(D; <)$ be a partial order which relates all pairs of elements except for b and c. We call $\langle f, g \rangle$, where $f, g : D^2 \to D$ are two binary operations, a *1-defect* if f and g are both commutative and satisfy the following conditions:

- If $\{x, y\} \neq \{b, c\}$, then $f(x, y) = \mathrm{Min}(x, y)$ and $g(x, y) = \mathrm{Max}(x, y)$.
- If $\{x, y\} = \{b, c\}$, then $\{f(x, y), g(x, y)\} \cap \{x, y\} = \emptyset$, and $f(x, y) < g(x, y)$.

The tractability of languages that admit a 1-defect multimorphism has recently been shown in [97]. This result generalises the tractability result for weakly tree-submodular languages on chains and forks described in Example 4.31, but is incomparable with the tractability result for strongly tree-submodular languages on binary trees.

General multimorphisms Having seen several examples of binary multimorphisms, we are now ready to define general (not necessarily binary) multimorphisms.

Definition 4.33 (General multimorphisms) Let $\mathbf{g} = \langle g_1, \ldots, g_k \rangle$ be a k-tuple of k-ary operations $g_i : D^k \to D$, $1 \leq i \leq k$. An m-ary cost function $\phi : D^m \to \overline{\mathbb{Q}}_+$ admits $\mathbf{g}$ as a multimorphism if

$$\sum_{i=1}^{k} \phi(g_i(\mathbf{x_1}, \ldots, \mathbf{x_k})) \leq \sum_{i=1}^{k} \phi(\mathbf{x_i}) \tag{4.3}$$

---

[9] A chain is a binary tree in which all nodes except leaves have exactly one child.
[10] A fork is a binary tree in which all nodes except leaves and one special node have exactly one child. The special node has exactly two children.

for all $\mathbf{x}_i \in D^m$, $1 \leq i \leq k$, where all functions g_i, $1 \leq i \leq k$ are applied coordinate-wise.

$$
\begin{array}{cccccc}
\mathbf{x}_1 & \mathbf{x}_1[1] & \mathbf{x}_1[2] & \cdots & \mathbf{x}_1[m] & \phi(\mathbf{x}_1) \\
\mathbf{x}_2 & \mathbf{x}_2[1] & \mathbf{x}_2[2] & \cdots & \mathbf{x}_2[m] & \phi(\mathbf{x}_2) \\
\vdots & & \vdots & & & \vdots \\
\mathbf{x}_k & \mathbf{x}_k[1] & \mathbf{x}_k[2] & \cdots & \mathbf{x}_k[m] & \phi(\mathbf{x}_k)
\end{array}
\xrightarrow{\phi}
\left.\begin{array}{c}\\\\\\\\\end{array}\right\} \sum_{i=1}^{k} \phi(\mathbf{x}_i)
$$

$$
\begin{array}{cccccc}
\mathbf{x}_1' = g_1(\mathbf{x}_1,\ldots,\mathbf{x}_k) & \mathbf{x}_1'[1] & \mathbf{x}_1'[2] & \cdots & \mathbf{x}_1'[m] & \phi(\mathbf{x}_1') \\
\mathbf{x}_2' = g_2(\mathbf{x}_1,\ldots,\mathbf{x}_k) & \mathbf{x}_2'[1] & \mathbf{x}_2'[2] & \cdots & \mathbf{x}_2'[m] & \phi(\mathbf{x}_2') \\
\vdots & & \vdots & & & \vdots \\
\mathbf{x}_k' = g_k(\mathbf{x}_1,\ldots,\mathbf{x}_k) & \mathbf{x}_k'[1] & \mathbf{x}_k'[2] & \cdots & \mathbf{x}_k'[m] & \phi(\mathbf{x}_k')
\end{array}
\xrightarrow{\phi}
\left.\begin{array}{c}\\\\\\\\\end{array}\right\} \sum_{i=1}^{k} \phi(\mathbf{x}_i')
$$

IV

Figure 4.2 Definition of a multimorphism $\mathbf{g} = \langle g_1, \ldots, g_k \rangle$.

Definition 4.33 is illustrated in Figure 4.2, which should be read from left to right. Starting with the m-tuples $\mathbf{x}_1, \ldots, \mathbf{x}_k$, we first apply functions $g_1, \ldots, g_k$ on these tuples coordinate-wise, thus obtaining the m-tuples $\mathbf{x}_1', \ldots, \mathbf{x}_k'$. Inequality 4.3 amounts to comparing the sum of ϕ applied to tuples $\mathbf{x}_1, \ldots, \mathbf{x}_k$ and ϕ applied to tuples $\mathbf{x}_1', \ldots, \mathbf{x}_k'$.

We now give a simple example of a unary multimorphism.

Example 4.34 (*c*-validity)   Given a fixed $c \in D$, we say that language Γ is *c*-valid if for all $\phi \in \Gamma$, $\phi(c, \ldots, c) \leq \phi(\mathbf{x})$ holds for all $\mathbf{x} \in D^m$, where m is the arity of ϕ. It is clear that c-valued languages are tractable as assigning the value c to all variables yields an optimal solution.

It is easy to see that Γ is c-valid if and only if Γ admits $\langle g_c \rangle$ as a multimorphism, where $g_c : D \to D$ is defined as $g_c(x) = c$ for all $x \in D$ (i.e., g_c is the constant function returning the value c).

Example 4.35 (Majority)   A ternary operation $f : D^3 \to D$ is called a majority operation if $f(x,x,y) = f(x,y,x) = f(y,x,x) = x$ for all $x, y \in D$.

Let $\mathbf{g} = \langle g_1, g_2, g_3 \rangle$ be a triple of ternary operations such that g_1, g_2 and g_3 are all majority operations. Let $\phi : D^m \to \overline{\mathbb{Q}}_+$ be an m-ary cost function that admits $\mathbf{g}$ as a multimorphism. It follows from Definition 4.33 that for all $\mathbf{x}, \mathbf{y} \in D^m$, $3\phi(\mathbf{x}) \leq \phi(\mathbf{x}) + \phi(\mathbf{x}) + \phi(\mathbf{y})$ and $3\phi(\mathbf{y}) \leq \phi(\mathbf{y}) + \phi(\mathbf{y}) + \phi(\mathbf{x})$. Therefore, if both $\phi(\mathbf{x})$ and $\phi(\mathbf{y})$ are finite, then we have $\phi(\mathbf{x}) \leq \phi(\mathbf{y})$ and $\phi(\mathbf{y}) \leq \phi(\mathbf{x})$, and hence $\phi(\mathbf{x}) = \phi(\mathbf{y})$. In other words, the range of ϕ is $\{c, \infty\}$, for some finite $c \in \mathbb{Q}_+$, and hence ϕ is essentially crisp.

Let Γ_{Mjty} be the set of cost functions improved by a triple $\mathbf{g} = \langle g_1, g_2, g_3 \rangle$ of ternary majority operations $g_i : D^3 \to D$, $1 \leq i \leq 3$. The tractability of Γ_{Mjty} has been shown by [32], using the earlier result that CSPs closed under a majority polymorphism are tractable [88].

Example 4.36 (Minority)   A ternary operation $f : D^3 \to D$ is called a minority operation if $f(x, x, y) = f(x, y, x) = f(y, x, x) = y$ for all $x, y \in D$. Let Γ_{Mnty} be the set of cost functions improved by a triple $\mathbf{g} = \langle g_1, g_2, g_3 \rangle$ of ternary minority operations $g_i : D^3 \to D$, $1 \le i \le 3$. A similar argument to the one in Example 4.35 shows that the cost functions in Γ_{Mnty} are essentially crisp. The tractability of Γ_{Mnty} has been shown in [32], using the result that CSPs closed under a Mal'tsev polymorphism[11] are tractable [50].

Example 4.37 (Majority & Minority)   Let $\mathbf{g} = \langle g_1, g_2, g_3 \rangle$ be three ternary operations such that g_1 and g_2 are majority operations, and g_3 is a minority operation. Let Γ_{MJN} be an arbitrary language improved by $\mathbf{g}$. The tractability of Γ_{MJN} has been shown in [103], generalising an earlier tractability result for a specific $\mathbf{g}$ of this form from [32].

Having seen several tractable languages characterised by multimorphisms, we are now able to state a dichotomy classification for Boolean languages given in [32].

Theorem 4.38 (Classification of Boolean languages)   *An arbitrary valued constraint language on $D = \{0, 1\}$ is tractable if it admits at least one of the following eight multimorphisms. Otherwise it is intractable.*

1. $\langle g_0 \rangle$ *(i.e., Γ is 0-valid)*,
2. $\langle g_1 \rangle$ *(i.e., Γ is 1-valid)*,
3. $\langle \mathrm{Min}, \mathrm{Min} \rangle$,
4. $\langle \mathrm{Max}, \mathrm{Max} \rangle$,
5. $\langle \mathrm{Min}, \mathrm{Max} \rangle$,
6. $\langle \mathrm{Mjrty}, \mathrm{Mjrty}, \mathrm{Mjrty} \rangle$,
7. $\langle \mathrm{Mnrty}, \mathrm{Mnrty}, \mathrm{Mnrty} \rangle$,
8. $\langle \mathrm{Mjrty}, \mathrm{Mjrty}, \mathrm{Mnrty} \rangle$.

Using results from [103] on conservative languages, as described in the next section, a complete classification of $\{0, 1\}$-valued languages over a domain with at most 4 elements has recently appeared in [97]. It turns out that the only two tractable classes over these domain sizes are those characterised by $\langle \mathrm{Min}, \mathrm{Max} \rangle$ multimorphisms (cf. Example 4.26) and those characterised by 1-defect multimorphisms (cf. Example 4.32).

---

[11] A ternary operation $f : D^3 \to D$ is called Mal'tsev if $f(x, y, y) = f(y, y, x) = x$ for all $x, y \in D$.

4.7 Conservative Valued Constraint Languages

A language Γ is called *conservative* if Γ includes all unary cost functions.[12] In this section, we will survey recent results on the complexity of conservative languages: for further details see [103].

Let Γ be a fixed language on D. Let $P = \{(a, b) \mid a, b \in D, a \neq b\}$. Let $M \subseteq P$ be arbitrary. We denote by $\overline{M}$ the complement of M in P, i.e., $\overline{M} = P \setminus M$.

Let $\langle g_\sqcap, g_\sqcup \rangle$ be two binary operations. We call $\langle g_\sqcap, g_\sqcup \rangle$ a symmetric tournament pair (STP) on M (cf. Example 4.30) if $g_\sqcap$ and $g_\sqcup$ are conservative on D and commutative on M. Let $\langle \mathrm{Mjrty}_1, \mathrm{Mjrty}_2, \mathrm{Mnrty}_3 \rangle$ be three ternary operations. We call $\langle \mathrm{Mjrty}_1, \mathrm{Mjrty}_2, \mathrm{Mnrty}_3 \rangle$ an MJN on $\overline{M}$ if operations $\mathrm{Mjrty}_1, \mathrm{Mjrty}_2, \mathrm{Mnrty}_3$ are conservative and for each triple $\langle a, b, c \rangle \in D^3$ with $\{a, b, c\} = \{x, y\} \in \overline{M}$ operations $\mathrm{Mjrty}_1(a, b, c)$, $\mathrm{Mjrty}_2(a, b, c)$ return the unique majority element among a, b, c (that occurs twice) and $\mathrm{Mnrty}_3(a, b, c)$ returns the remaining minority element.

Given a language Γ, we say that Γ admits *complementary STP and MJN* multimorphisms if there is a set $M \subseteq P$, binary operations $\langle g_\sqcap, g_\sqcup \rangle$ and ternary operations $\langle \mathrm{Mjrty}_1, \mathrm{Mjrty}_2, \mathrm{Mnrty}_3 \rangle$ such that $\langle g_\sqcap, g_\sqcup \rangle$ is an STP on M and $\langle \mathrm{Mjrty}_1, \mathrm{Mjrty}_2, \mathrm{Mnrty}_3 \rangle$ is an MJN on $\overline{M}$, where $\overline{M} = P \setminus M$.

Generalising the tractability results described in Examples 4.30 and 4.37, [103] have shown that languages admitting complementary STP and MJN multimorphisms are tractable. Moreover, for general-valued conservative languages, it has been shown that this class is the *only* tractable case, as the following result from [103] indicates.

Theorem 4.39 (General-valued conservative languages) *A general-valued conservative valued constraint language is tractable if it admits complementary STP and MJN multimorphisms. Otherwise it is intractable.*

In the finite-valued case, the more restricted class from Example 4.30 is the only tractable case, as the following result from [103] indicates.

Theorem 4.40 (Finite-valued conservative languages) *A finite-valued conservative valued constraint language is tractable if it admits a symmetric-tournament pair multimorphism. Otherwise it is intractable.*

These results for conservative languages over arbitrary finite domains are obtained by considering restrictions to all 2-element subdomains, using unary constraints. The possible tractable languages for 2-element domains are already known (see Theorem 4.38) and highly restricted.

---

[12] [103] have shown that this condition is polynomial-time equivalent to the (weaker) requirement that Γ includes all $\{0, 1\}$-valued unary cost functions.

4.8 A General Algebraic Theory of Complexity

One of the three equivalent definitions of the CSP presented in Section 4.2 uses the terminology of algebra (Definition 4.5). This formulation led to the development of an algebraic approach for classifying the complexity of crisp constraint languages, started by [88], which has so far been the most successful technique for precisely identifying the tractable cases [20, 23, 22].

Recently [35] and [37] have presented an extension of this algebraic approach to the more general setting of valued constraint languages.

The basic idea of this extended algebraic theory is to associate with each valued constraint language a set of functions, called *weighted polymorphisms*. These objects are similar to the multimorphisms defined in Section 4.6 (see Example 4.46), but are defined in a slightly more general way. The theory then establishes that there is a one-to-one correspondence between certain sets of weighted polymorphisms and valued constraint languages which are closed under expressibility and scaling. This correspondence simplifies the search for tractable languages to a search for suitable sets of weighted polymorphisms. For example, [46] have used this result to obtain the classification of Boolean valued languages presented in Theorem 4.38 using simple algebraic arguments.

In this section, we will give a brief overview of the main results of this new algebraic theory. We refer the reader to [35] and [37] for full details and proofs.

We first recall some basic terminology from universal algebra [56, 15]. A function $f : D^k \to D$ is called a k-ary *operation* on D. We denote by $\mathbf{O}_D$ the set of all finitary operations on D and by $\mathbf{O}_D^{(k)}$ the k-ary operations in $\mathbf{O}_D$. The k-ary *projections* on D, defined for $i = 1, \ldots, k$, are the operations $e_i^{(k)}$ such that $e_i^{(k)}(a_1, \ldots, a_k) = a_i$. Let $f \in \mathbf{O}_D^{(k)}$ and $g_1, \ldots, g_k \in \mathbf{O}_D^{(l)}$. The *superposition* of f and $g_1, \ldots, g_k$ is the l-ary operation $f[g_1, \ldots, g_k]$ such that $f[g_1, \ldots, g_k](x_1, \ldots, x_l) = f(g_1(x_1, \ldots, x_l), \ldots, g_k(x_1 \ldots, x_l))$.

A set $F \subseteq \mathbf{O}_D$ is called a *clone* of operations if it contains all the projections on D and is closed under superposition. For each $F \subseteq \mathbf{O}_D$ we define $\mathrm{Clone}(F)$ to be the smallest clone containing F. For any clone C, we use $C^{(k)}$ to denote the k-ary terms in C.

Definition 4.41 A *Galois connection* between two sets A and B is a pair $\langle F, G \rangle$ of mappings between the power sets $\mathcal{P}(A)$ and $\mathcal{P}(B)$, $F : \mathcal{P}(A) \to \mathcal{P}(B)$ and $G : \mathcal{P}(B) \to \mathcal{P}(B)$, such that for all $X, X' \subseteq A$ and all $Y, Y' \subseteq B$ the following conditions are satisfied:

1. $X \subseteq G(F(X))$,

2. $Y \subseteq F(G(Y))$,
3. $X \subseteq X' \Rightarrow F(X) \supseteq F(X')$,
4. $Y \subseteq Y' \Rightarrow G(Y) \supseteq G(Y')$.

The algebraic theory of complexity for crisp constraint languages [20, 23] makes use of a standard Galois connection between the set of all relations on a fixed set D and the set of all operations on D [56]. Using this result, [84] showed that there was a one-to-one correspondence between crisp constraint languages over a finite set D which are closed under expressibility and clones of operations on D.

To extend this approach to valued constraint languages, we make the following definitions. We denote by $\mathbf{\Phi}_D$ the set of all cost functions on D taking values in $\overline{\mathbb{Q}}_+$.

Definition 4.42   A valued constraint language $\Gamma \subseteq \mathbf{\Phi}_D$ is called a *weighted relational clone* if it is closed under expressibility, scaling by non-negative rational constants, and addition of rational constants.

We define wRelClone(Γ) to be the smallest weighted relational clone containing Γ.

It follows from Theorem 4.21, and the results of [31], that Γ is tractable if and only if wRelClone(Γ) is tractable.

Definition 4.43   We define a k-ary *weighted operation* on a set D to be a (partial) function $\omega : \mathbf{O}_D^{(k)} \to \mathbb{Q}$ such that $\omega(f) < 0$ only if f is a projection and

$$\sum_{f \in \mathbf{dom}(\omega)} \omega(f) = 0 \, .$$

The *domain* of ω, denoted $\mathbf{dom}(\omega)$, is the subset of $\mathbf{O}_D^{(k)}$ on which ω is defined.

We denote by $\mathbf{W}_D$ the set of all finitary weighted operations on D.

Definition 4.44   Let C be a clone of operations on D. A *weighted clone supported* by C is a set of weighted operations with domain $C^{(k)}$ for some k, which is closed under:

1. **proper translation** Given a k-ary weighted operation $\omega : C^{(k)} \to \mathbb{Q}$ and a list of operations $g_1, \ldots, g_k \in C^{(\ell)}$, we define the *translation* of ω by $g_1, \ldots, g_k$, denoted $\omega[g_1, \ldots, g_k]$, to be the function $\omega' : C^{(\ell)} \to \mathbb{Q}$ satisfying

$$\omega'(f') = \sum_{f \in C^{(k)} : f' = f[g_1,\ldots,g_k]} \omega(f) \, ,$$

for each $f' \in C^{(\ell)}$. A translation is called a *proper translation* if w' is a weighted operation.

2. **addition** Given a pair of k-ary weighted operations $w_1, w_2 : C^{(k)} \to \mathbb{Q}$, we define the *addition* $w_1 + w_2$ to be the weighted operation w' satisfying $w'(f) = w_1(f) + w_2(f)$, for each $f \in C^{(k)}$.

3. **scaling** Given a k-ary weighted operation $w : C^{(k)} \to \mathbb{Q}$ and a rational $\alpha \geq 0$, we define the α-scaling of w, αw, to be the weighted operation w' satisfying $w'(f) = \alpha w(f)$, for each $f \in C^{(k)}$.

For each $W \subseteq \mathbf{W}_D$ we define wClone(W) to be the smallest weighted clone containing W.

Definition 4.45 We say that a weighted operation w of arity k is a *weighted polymorphism* of the cost function ϕ of arity r if, for any $x_1, x_2, \ldots, x_k \in D^r$ such that $\phi(x_i) < \infty$ for $i = 1, \ldots, k$, we have

$$\sum_{f \in \mathbf{dom}(w)} w(f)\phi(f(x_1, x_2, \ldots, x_k)) \leq 0. \tag{4.4}$$

If w is a weighted polymorphism of ϕ we also say ϕ is *improved* by w.

Example 4.46 Consider the class of submodular cost functions from Example 4.25. These are precisely the cost functions satisfying

$$\phi(\mathrm{Min}(x_1, x_2)) + \phi(\mathrm{Max}(x_1, x_2)) - \phi(x) - \phi(y) \leq 0.$$

In other words, the set of submodular functions are defined as the set of cost functions with the 2-ary weighted polymorphism

$$w(f) \overset{\mathrm{def}}{=} \begin{cases} -1 & \text{if } f \in \{e_1^{(2)}, e_2^{(2)}\} \\ +1 & \text{if } f \in \{\mathrm{Min}, \mathrm{Max}\} \end{cases}.$$

Definition 4.47 For any $\Gamma \subseteq \mathbf{\Phi}_D$, we denote by wPol($\Gamma$) the set of all finitary weighted operations on D which are weighted polymorphisms of all cost functions $\phi \in \Gamma$.

Definition 4.48 For any $W \subseteq \mathbf{W}_D$, we denote by Imp(W) the set of all cost functions in $\mathbf{\Phi}_D$ that are improved by all weighted operations $w \in W$.

It follows immediately from Definition 4.41 that, for any set D, the mappings wPol and Imp form a Galois connection between $\mathbf{W}_D$ and $\mathbf{\Phi}_D$. A characterisation of this Galois connection for finite sets D is given by the following theorem from [35]:

Theorem 4.49 (Galois Connection for Valued Constraint Languages)

1. *For any finite sets D and $\Gamma \subseteq \mathbf{\Phi}_D$, $\mathrm{Imp}(\mathrm{wPol}(\Gamma)) = \mathrm{wRelClone}(\Gamma)$.*
2. *For any finite sets D and $W \subseteq \mathbf{W}_D$, $\mathrm{wPol}(\mathrm{Imp}(W)) = \mathrm{wClone}(W)$.*

   Theorem 4.49 is depicted in Figure 4.3. Using the standard properties of Galois connections, it follows that there is a one-to-one correspondence between weighted relational clones on a finite set D and weighted clones on D. Hence, to identify all tractable valued constraint languages on a finite set D it is sufficient to study the possible weighted clones on D. This provides a new approach to the identification of tractable cases, which we hope will prove to be as successful as the algebraic approach has been in the study of crisp constraint languages.

4.9 Conclusions and Open Problems

We have seen in this chapter that the valued constraint satisfaction problem is a powerful general framework that can be used to express many standard combinatorial optimisation problems. The general problem is NP-hard, but there are many special cases that have been shown to be tractable. In particular, by considering restrictions on the cost functions we allow in problem instances, we have identified a range of different sets of cost functions that ensure tractability.

   These restricted sets of cost functions are referred to as valued constraint languages, and we have seen that such languages can sometimes be shown to be tractable, and sometimes be shown to be NP-hard. Some powerful algebraic techniques are now being developed to carry out this classification, as described in Section 4.8, but it is still far from complete.

   In fact, even in the special case of the CSP, discussed in Section 4.2, there is still no complete classification of complexity for the corresponding crisp constraint languages, although many partial results have been obtained over the past 15 years. In particular, it has been shown that the tractable cases fall into two broad groups. The first of these are the problems that can be solved by some form of local consistency [4], and the second are the problems that have a polynomial-sized generating set [81]. These two cases are both characterised by specific algebraic conditions.

   Using the same argument as in Example 4.35, it can be shown that the second condition gives only essentially crisp languages. Hence only the first condition gives rise to interesting tractable valued constraint languages. Local consistency techniques have been generalised to the VCSP, but their power is not fully understood [44].

   Even the classic tractable problem of submodular function minimisation,

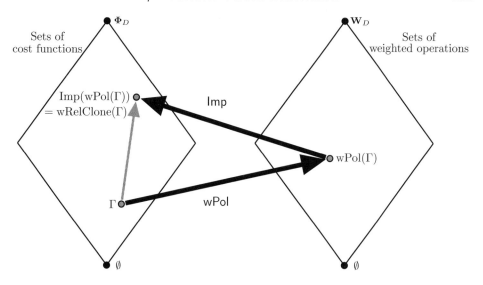

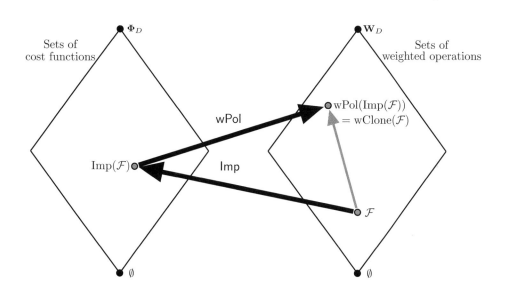

Figure 4.3 Galois connection between $\mathbf{\Phi}_D$ and $\mathbf{W}_D$.

discussed in Section 4.6, is not fully understood. As discussed in Example 4.26, it is currently unknown whether VCSP instances with submodular cost functions can be solved more efficiently than general submodular function minimisation. Moreover, the complexity of submodular function minimisation over a domain D which is partially ordered by a lattice ordering is still unknown for non-distributive lattices. However, it has been shown that there is a pseudo-polynomial-time algorithm for diamonds [106], and several constructions on lattices preserving tractability have been identified [105].

Recently, there has been some significant progress on the complexity of VCSPs.

First, all bisbumodular languages on domains of arbitrary size (cf. Example 4.29), strongly tree-submodular languages on general trees, and weakly tree-submodular languages on general trees (cf. Example 4.31) have been shown tractable [131]. Second, finite-valued languages on domains of size 3 have been classified [80]. Finally, using the concept of weighted polymorphisms described in Section 4.8, *all* finite-valued languages on finite domains of *arbitrary* size have been classified [132].

References

[1] Adler, Isolde, Gottlob, Georg, and Grohe, Martin. 2007. Hypertree width and related hypergraph invariants. *European Journal of Combinatorics*, **28**(8), 2167–2181.

[2] Apt, Krzysztof. 2003. *Principles of Constraint Programming*. Cambridge University Press.

[3] Barto, Libor. 2011. The dichotomy for conservative constraint satisfaction problems revisited. In: *Proceedings of the 26th IEEE Symposium on Logic in Computer Science (LICS'11)*.

[4] Barto, Libor, and Kozik, Marcin. 2009. Constraint satisfaction problems of bounded width. Pages 461–471 of: *Proceedings of the 50th Annual IEEE Symposium on Foundations of Computer Science (FOCS'09)*.

[5] Barto, Libor, Kozik, Marcin, Maróti, Miklós, and Niven, Todd. 2009a. CSP dichotomy for special triads. *Proceedings of the American Mathematical Society*, **137**(9), 2921–2934.

[6] Barto, Libor, Kozik, Marcin, and Niven, Todd. 2009b. The CSP dichotomy holds for digraphs with no sources and no sinks (a positive answer to a conjecture of Bang-Jensen and Hell). *SIAM Journal on Computing*, **38**(5), 1782–1802.

[7] Berman, Joel, Idziak, Pawel, Marković, Petar, McKenzie, Ralph, Valeriote, Matthew, and Willard, Ross. 2010. Varieties with few subalgebras of powers. *Transactions of the American Mathematical Society*, **362**(3), 1445–1473.

[8] Bertelé, Umberto, and Brioshi, Francesco. 1972. *Nonserial Dynamic Programming*. Academic Press.

[9] Bilbao, Jesús M., Fernández, Julio R., Jiménez, Nieves, and López, Jorge J. 2008. Survey of bicooperative games. In: *Pareto Optimality, Game Theory and Equilibria*, Chinchuluun, Altannar, Pardalos, Panos M., Migdalas, Athanasios, and Pitsoulis, Leonidas (eds). Springer.

[10] Bistarelli, Stefano, Montanari, Ugo, and Rossi, Francesca. 1997. Semiring-based constraint satisfaction and optimisation. *Journal of the ACM*, **44**(2), 201–236.

[11] Bistarelli, Stefano, Montanari, Ugo, Rossi, Francesca, Schiex, Thomas, Verfaillie, Gérard, and Fargier, Hélène. 1999. Semiring-based CSPs and valued CSPs: frameworks, properties, and comparison. *Constraints*, **4**(3), 199–240.

[12] Bodirsky, Manuel. 2008. Constraint satisfaction problems with infinite templates. Pages 196–228 of: *Complexity of Constraints*. LNCS, **5250**.

[13] Bodirsky, Manuel, and Kára, Jan. 2010. The complexity of temporal constraint satisfaction problems. *Journal of the ACM*, **57**(2), Article 9.

[14] Bodirsky, Manuel, and Pinsker, Michael. 2011. Schaefer's theorem for graphs. Pages 655–664 of: *Proceedings of the 43rd ACM Symposium on Theory of Computing (STOC'11)*.

[15] Börner, Ferdinand. 2008. Basics of Galois connections. Pages 38–67 of: *Complexity of Constraints*. LNCS, **5250**.

[16] Boros, Endre, and Hammer, Peter L. 2002. Pseudo-Boolean optimization. *Discrete Applied Mathematics*, **123**(1–3), 155–225.

[17] Bouchet, André. 1987. Greedy algorithm and symmetric matroids. *Mathematical Programming*, **38**(1), 147–159.

[18] Bulatov, Andrei. 2006. A dichotomy theorem for constraint satisfaction problems on a 3-element set. *Journal of the ACM*, **53**(1), 66–120.

[19] Bulatov, Andrei, and Dalmau, Víctor. 2006. A Simple Algorithm for Mal'tsev Constraints. *SIAM Journal on Computing*, **36**(1), 16–27.

[20] Bulatov, Andrei, Krokhin, Andrei, and Jeavons, Peter. 2005. Classifying the Complexity of Constraints using Finite Algebras. *SIAM Journal on Computing*, **34**(3), 720–742.

[21] Bulatov, Andrei A. 2011a. Complexity of conservative constraint satisfaction problems. *ACM Transactions on Computational Logic*, **12**(4), 24.

[22] Bulatov, Andrei A. 2011b. On the CSP Dichotomy Conjecture. Pages 331–344 of: *Proceedings of the 6th International Computer Science Symposium in Russia (CSR'11)*. LNCS, **6651**.

[23] Bulatov, Andrei A., and Valeriote, Matthew. 2008. Recent Results on the Algebraic Approach to the CSP. Pages 68–92 of: *Complexity of Constraints*. LNCS **5250**.

[24] Chandrasekaran, Ramaswamy, and Kabadi, Santosh N. 1988. Pseudomatroids. *Discrete Mathematics*, **71**(3), 205–217.

[25] Chen, Hubie. 2006. A rendezvous of logic, complexity, and algebra. *SIGACT News*, **37**(4), 85–114.

[26] Chen, Hubie, and Dalmau, Víctor. 2005. Beyond Hypertree Width: Decomposition Methods Without Decompositions. Pages 167–181 of: *Proceedings of the 11th International Conference on Principles and Practice of Constraint Programming (CP'05)*. LNCS **3709**.

[27] Cohen, David, and Jeavons, Peter. 2006. The complexity of constraint languages. In: *The Handbook of Constraint Programming*, Rossi, F., van Beek, P., and Walsh, T. (eds). Elsevier.

[28] Cohen, David, Cooper, Martin, Jeavons, Peter, and Krokhin, Andrei. 2005. Supermodular functions and the complexity of MAX–CSP. *Discrete Applied Mathematics*, **149**(1–3), 53–72.

[29] Cohen, David, Jeavons, Peter, and Gyssens, Marc. 2008a. A unified theory of structural tractability for constraint satisfaction problems. *Journal of Computer and System Sciences*, **74**(5), 721–743.

[30] Cohen, David A. 2003. A new class of binary CSPs for which arc-constistency is a decision procedure. Pages 807–811 of: *Proceedings of the 9th International Conference on Principles and Practice of Constraint Programming (CP'03)*. LNCS **2833**.

[31] Cohen, David A., Cooper, Martin C., and Jeavons, Peter G. 2006a. An algebraic characterisation of complexity for valued constraints. Pages 107–121 of: *Proceedings of the 12th International Conference on Principles and Practice of Constraint Programming (CP'06)*. LNCS **4204**.

[32] Cohen, David A., Cooper, Martin C., Jeavons, Peter G., and Krokhin, Andrei A. 2006b. The complexity of soft constraint satisfaction. *Artificial Intelligence*, **170**(11), 983–1016.

[33] Cohen, David A., Cooper, Martin C., and Jeavons, Peter G. 2008b. Generalising submodularity and Horn clauses: Tractable optimization problems defined by tournament pair multimorphisms. *Theoretical Computer Science*, **401**(1-3), 36–51.

[34] Cohen, David A., Jeavons, Peter G., and Živný, Stanislav. 2008c. The expressive power of valued constraints: Hierarchies and collapses. *Theoretical Computer Science*, **409**(1), 137–153.

[35] Cohen, David A., Creed, Páidí, Jeavons, Peter G., and Živný, Stanislav. 2011a. An algebraic theory of complexity for valued constraints: Establishing a Galois connection. Pages 231–242 of: *Proceedings of the 36th International Symposium on Mathematical Foundations of Computer Science (MFCS'11)*. LNCS **6907**.

[36] Cohen, David A., Cooper, Martin C., Green, Martin, and Marx, Dániel. 2011b. On guaranteeing polynomially-bounded search tree size. Pages 160–171 of: *Proceedings of the 17th International Conference on Principles and Practice of Constraint Programming (CP'11)*. LNCS **6876**.

[37] Cohen, David A., Cooper, Martin C., Creed, Páidí, Jeavons, Peter G., and Živný, Stanislav. 2013. An algebraic theory of complexity for discrete optimisation, *SIAM Journal on Computing*, to appear.

[38] Cooper, Martin C. 2005. High-order consistency in valued constraint satisfaction. *Constraints*, **10**(3), 283–305.

[39] Cooper, Martin C. 2008. Minimization of locally defined submodular functions by optimal soft arc consistency. *Constraints*, **13**(4), 437–458.

[40] Cooper, Martin C., and Živný, Stanislav. 2011a. Hierarchically nested convex VCSP. Pages 187–194 of: *Proceedings of the 17th International Conference on Principles and Practice of Constraint Programming (CP'11)*. LNCS **6876**.

[41] Cooper, Martin C., and Živný, Stanislav. 2011b. Hybrid tractability of valued constraint problems. *Artificial Intelligence*, **175**(9–10), 1555–1569.

[42] Cooper, Martin C., and Živný, Stanislav. 2011c. Tractable triangles. Pages 195–209 of: *Proceedings of the 17th International Conference on Principles and Practice of Constraint Programming (CP'11)*. LNCS **6876**.

[43] Cooper, Martin C., Jeavons, Peter G., and Salamon, András Z. 2010a. Generalizing constraint satisfaction on trees: Hybrid tractability and variable elimination. *Artificial Intelligence*, **174**(9–10), 570–584.

[44] Cooper, Martin C., de Givry, Simon, Sánchez, Martí, Schiex, Thomas, Zytnicki, Matthias, and Werner, Tomáš. 2010b. Soft arc consistency revisited. *Artificial Intelligence*, **174**(7–8), 449–478.

[45] Crama, Yves, and Hammer, Peter L. 2011. *Boolean Functions – Theory, Algorithms, and Applications*. Cambridge University Press.

[46] Creed, Páidí, and Živný, Stanislav. 2011. On minimal weighted clones. Pages 210–224 of: *Proceedings of the 17th International Conference on Principles and Practice of Constraint Programming (CP'11)*. LNCS **6876**.

[47] Creignou, Nadaia, Kolaitis, Phokion G., and Vollmer, Heribert (eds). 2008a. *Complexity of Constraints: An Overview of Current Research Themes*. LNCS **5250**.

[48] Creignou, Nadia, Khanna, Sanjeev, and Sudan, Madhu. 2001. *Complexity Classification of Boolean Constraint Satisfaction Problems*. SIAM Monographs on Discrete Mathematics and Applications, vol. 7. SIAM.

[49] Creignou, Nadia, Kolaitis, Phokion G., and Zanuttini, Bruno. 2008b. Structure identification of Boolean relations and plain bases for co-clones. *Journal of Computer and System Sciences*, **74**(7), 1103–1115.

[50] Dalmau, Víctor. 2006. Generalized majority–minority operations are tractable. *Logical Methods in Computer Science*, **2**(4).

[51] Dalmau, Víctor, Kolaitis, Phokion G., and Vardi, Moshe Y. 2002. Constraint satisfaction, bounded treewidth, and finite-variable logics. Pages 310–326 of: *Proceedings of the 8th International Conference on Principles and Practice of Constraint Programming (CP'02)*. LNCS **2470**.

[52] Dechter, Rina. 2003. *Constraint Processing*. Morgan Kaufmann.

[53] Dechter, Rina, and Pearl, Judea. 1989. Tree clustering for constraint networks. *Artificial Intelligence*, **38**, 353–366.

[54] Dechter, Rina, and Pearl, Judea. 1992. Structure identification in relational data. *Artificial Intelligence*, **58**, 237–270.

[55] Deineko, Vladimir, Jonsson, Peter, Klasson, Mikael, and Krokhin, Andrei. 2008. The approximability of Max CSP with fixed-value constraints. *Journal of the ACM*, **55**(4), Article 16.

[56] Denecke, Klaus, and Wismath, Shelly L. 2002. *Universal Algebra and Applications in Theoretical Computer Science*. Chapman and Hall/CRC Press.

[57] Edmonds, Jack. 1970. Submodular functions, matroids, and certain polyhedra. Pages 69–87 of: *Combinatorial Structures and their Applications*. Gordon and Breach.

[58] Feder, Tomás, and Vardi, Moshe Y. 1998. The computational structure of monotone monadic SNP and constraint satisfaction: A study through datalog and group theory. *SIAM Journal on Computing*, **28**(1), 57–104.

[59] Feige, Uriel. 1998. A threshold of ln n for approximating set cover. *Journal of the ACM*, **45**(4), 634–652.

[60] Feige, Uriel, Mirrokni, Vahab S., and Vondrák, Jan. 2011. Maximizing non-monotone submodular functions. *SIAM Journal on Computing*, **40**(4), 1133–1153.

[61] Fellows, Michael R., Friedrich, Tobias, Hermelin, Danny, Narodytska, Nina, and Rosamond, Frances A. 2011. Constraint satisfaction problems: convexity makes all different constraints tractable. Pages 522–527 of: *Proceedings of the 22nd International Joint Conference on Artificial Intelligence (IJCAI'11)*.

[62] Freuder, Eugene C. 1985. A sufficient condition for backtrack-bounded search. *Journal of the ACM*, **32**, 755–761.

[63] Freuder, Eugene C. 1990. Complexity of K-tree structured constraint satisfaction problems. Pages 4–9 of: *Proceedings of the 8th National Conference on Artificial Intelligence (AAAI'90)*.

[64] Fujishige, Satoru. 2005. *Submodular Functions and Optimization*. 2nd edn. Annals of Discrete Mathematics, vol. 58. North-Holland.

[65] Fujishige, Satoru, and Iwata, Satoru. 2005. Bisubmodular Function minimization. *SIAM Journal on Discrete Mathematics*, **19**(4), 1065–1073.

[66] Garey, Michael R., and Johnson, David S. 1979. *Computers and Intractability: A Guide to the Theory of NP-Completeness*. W.H. Freeman.

[67] Goemans, Michel X., and Williamson, David P. 1995. Improved approximation algorithms for maximum cut and satisfiability problems using semidefinite programming. *Journal of the ACM*, **42**(6), 1115–1145.

[68] Goldberg, Andrew V., and Tarjan, Rober Endre. 1988. A new approach to the maximum flow problem. *Journal of the ACM*, **35**(4), 921–940.

[69] Gottlob, Georg, and Szeider, Stefan. 2008. Fixed-parameter algorithms for artificial intelligence, constraint satisfaction and database problems. *The Computer Journal*, **51**(3), 303–325.

[70] Gottlob, Georg, Leone, Nicola, and Scarcello, Francesco. 2000. A comparison of structural CSP decomposition methods. *Artificial Intelligence*, **124**(2), 243–282.

[71] Gottlob, Georg, Leone, Nicola, and Scarcello, Francesco. 2002. Hypertree decomposition and tractable queries. *Journal of Computer and System Sciences*, **64**(3), 579–627.

[72] Gottlob, Georg, Miklós, Zoltán, and Schwentick, Thomas. 2009. Generalized hypertree decompositions: NP-hardness and tractable variants. *Journal of the ACM*, **56**(6), Article 30.

[73] Grohe, Martin. 2007. The complexity of homomorphism and constraint satisfaction problems seen from the other side. *Journal of the ACM*, **54**(1), 1–24.

[74] Grohe, Martin, and Marx, Dániel. 2006. Constraint solving via fractional edge covers. Pages 289–298 of: *Proceedings of the 17th Annual ACM–SIAM Symposium on Discrete Algorithms (SODA'06)*.

[75] Gutin, Gregory, Hell, Pavol, Rafiey, Arash, and Yeo, Anders. 2008. A dichotomy for minimum cost graph homomorphisms. *European Journal of Combinatorics*, **29**(4), 900–911.

[76] Gyssens, Marc, Jeavons, Peter G., and Cohen, David A. 1994. Decomposing constraint satisfaction problems using database techniques. *Artificial Intelligence*, **66**(1), 57–89.

[77] Hell, Pavol, and Nešetřil, Jaroslav. 1990. On the complexity of *H*-coloring. *Journal of Combinatorial Theory, Series B*, **48**(1), 92–110.

[78] Hell, Pavol, and Nešetřil, Jaroslav. 2004. *Graphs and Homomorphisms*. Oxford University Press.

[79] Hell, Pavol, and Nešetřil, Jaroslav. 2008. Colouring, constraint satisfaction, and complexity. *Computer Science Review*, **2**(3), 143–163.

[80] Huber, Anna, Krokhin, Andrei, and Powell, Robert. 2013. Skew bisubmodularity and valued CSPs. Pages 1296–1305 of: *Proceedings of the 24th Annual ACM–SIAM Symposium on Discrete Algorithms (SODA'13)*.

[81] Idziak, Pawel M., Markovic, Petar, McKenzie, Ralph, Valeriote, Matthew, and Willard, Ross. 2010. Tractability and learnability arising from algebras with few subpowers. *SIAM Journal on Computing*, **39**(7), 3023–3037.

[82] Iwata, Satoru. 2008. Submodular function minimization. *Mathematical Programming*, **112**(1), 45–64.

[83] Iwata, Satoru, Fleischer, Lisa, and Fujishige, Satoru. 2001. A combinatorial strongly polynomial algorithm for minimizing submodular functions. *Journal of the ACM*, **48**(4), 761–777.

[84] Jeavons, Peter G. 1998. On the algebraic structure of combinatorial problems. *Theoretical Computer Science*, **200**(1-2), 185–204.

[85] Jeavons, Peter G. 2009. Presenting constraints. Pages 1–15 of: *Proceedings of the 18th International Conference on Automated Reasoning with Analytic Tableaux and Related Methods (TABLEAUX'09)*. LNCS **5607**.

[86] Jeavons, Peter G., and Cooper, Martin C. 1995. Tractable constraints on ordered domains. *Artificial Intelligence*, **79**(2), 327–339.

[87] Jeavons, Peter G., Cohen, David A., and Gyssens, Marc. 1996. A test for tractability. Pages 267–281 of: *Proceedings of the 2nd International Conference on Constraint Programming (CP'96), 1996*. LNCS **1118**.

[88] Jeavons, Peter G., Cohen, David A., and Gyssens, Marc. 1997. Closure properties of constraints. *Journal of the ACM*, **44**(4), 527–548.

[89] Jeavons, Peter G., Cohen, David A., and Gyssens, Marc. 1999. How to determine the expressive power of constraints. *Constraints*, **4**(2), 113–131.

[90] Jonsson, Peter. 2000. Boolean constraint satisfaction: complexity results for optimization problems with arbitrary weights. *Theoretical Computer Science*, **244**(1–2), 189–203.

[91] Jonsson, Peter, and Krokhin, Andrei. 2007. Maximum *H*-colourable subdigraphs and constraint optimization with arbitrary weights. *Journal of Computer and System Sciences*, **73**(5), 691–702.

[92] Jonsson, Peter, and Nordh, Gustav. 2008. Introduction to the MAXIMUM SOLUTION Problem. Pages 255–282 of: *Complexity of Constraints*. LNCS **5250**.

[93] Jonsson, Peter, and Thapper, Johan. 2009. Approximability of the Maximum Solution Problem for Certain Families of Algebras. Pages 215–226 of:

Proceedings of the 4th International Computer Science Symposium in Russia (CSR'09). LNCS **5675**.

[94] Jonsson, Peter, Klasson, Mikael, and Krokhin, Andrei. 2006. The approximability of three-valued MAX CSP. *SIAM Journal on Computing,* **35**(6), 1329–1349.

[95] Jonsson, Peter, Nordh, Gustav, and Thapper, Johan. 2007. The maximum solution problem on graphs. Pages 228–239 of: *Proceedings of the 32nd International Symposium on Mathematical Foundations of Computer Science (MFCS'07).* LNCS **4708**.

[96] Jonsson, Peter, Kuivinen, Fredrik, and Nordh, Gustav. 2008. MAX ONES generalized to larger domains. *SIAM Journal on Computing,* **38**(1), 329–365.

[97] Jonsson, Peter, Kuivinen, Fredrik, and Thapper, Johan. 2011. Min CSP on four elements: moving beyond submodularity. Pages 438–453 of: *Proceedings of the 17th International Conference on Principles and Practice of Constraint Programming (CP'11).* LNCS **6876**.

[98] Khanna, Sanjeev, Sudan, Madhu, Trevisan, Luca, and Williamson, David. 2001. The approximability of constraint satisfaction problems. *SIAM Journal on Computing,* **30**(6), 1863–1920.

[99] Kolaitis, Phokion G., and Vardi, Moshe Y. 2000. Conjunctive-query containment and constraint satisfaction. *Journal of Computer and System Sciences,* **61**(2), 302–332.

[100] Kolaitis, Phokion G., and Vardi, Moshe Y. 2007. A logical approach to constraint satisfaction. In: *Finite Model Theory and Its Applications.* Texts in Theoretical Computer Science. An EATCS Series. Springer.

[101] Kolmogorov, Vladimir. 2010. *Minimizing a sum of submodular functions.* Tech. rept. arXiv:1006.1990.

[102] Kolmogorov, Vladimir. 2011. Submodularity on a tree: Unifying $L^\natural$-convex and bisubmodular functions. Pages 400–411 of: *Proceedings of the 36th International Symposium on Mathematical Foundations of Computer Science (MFCS'11).* LNCS **6907**.

[103] Kolmogorov, Vladimir, and Živný, Stanislav. 2013. The complexity of conservative valued CSPs. *Journal of the ACM,* **60**(2), Article 10.

[104] Korte, Bernhard, and Vygen, Jens. 2007. *Combinatorial Optimization.* 4th edn. Algorithms and Combinatorics, vol. 21. Springer.

[105] Krokhin, Andrei, and Larose, Benoit. 2008. Maximizing supermodular functions on product lattices, with application to maximum constraint satisfaction. *SIAM Journal on Discrete Mathematics,* **22**(1), 312–328.

[106] Kuivinen, Fredrik. 2011. On the complexity of submodular function minimisation on diamonds. *Discrete Optimization,* **8**(3), 459–477.

[107] Kun, Gabor, and Szegedy, Mario. 2009. A new line of attack on the dichotomy conjecture. Pages 725–734 of: *Proceedings of the 41st Annual ACM Symposium on Theory of Computing (STOC'09).*

[108] Lauritzen, Steffen L. 1996. *Graphical Models.* Oxford University Press.

[109] Lovász, László. 1983. Submodular functions and convexity. Pages 235–257 of: *Mathematical Programming – The State of the Art,* Bachem, A., Grötschel, M., and Korte, B. (eds). Springer.

[110] Marx, Dániel. 2010a. Approximating fractional hypertree width. *ACM Transactions on Algorithms*, **6**(2), Article 29.

[111] Marx, Dániel. 2010b. Can you beat treewidth? *Theory of Computing*, **6**(1), 85–112.

[112] Marx, Dániel. 2010c. Tractable hypergraph properties for constraint satisfaction and conjunctive queries. Pages 735–744 of: *Proceedings of the 42nd ACM Symposium on Theory of Computing (STOC'10)*.

[113] Marx, Dániel. 2011. Tractable structures for constraint satisfaction with truth tables. *Theory of Computing Systems*, **48**(3), 444–464.

[114] McCormick, S. Thomas, and Fujishige, Satoru. 2010. Strongly polynomial and fully combinatorial algorithms for bisubmodular function minimization. *Mathematical Programming*, **122**(1), 87–120.

[115] Montanari, Ugo. 1974. Networks of constraints: fundamental properties and applications to picture processing. *Information Sciences*, **7**, 95–132.

[116] Narayanan, H. 1997. *Submodular Functions and Electrical Networks*. Amsterdam: North-Holland.

[117] Nemhauser, George L., and Wolsey, Laurence A. 1988. *Integer and Combinatorial Optimization*. John Wiley & Sons.

[118] Nešetřil, Jaroslav, Siggers, Marh H., and Zádori, László. 2010. A combinatorial constraint satisfaction problem dichotomy classification conjecture. *European Journal of Combinatorics*, **31**(1), 280–296.

[119] Orlin, James B. 2009. A faster strongly polynomial time algorithm for submodular function minimization. *Mathematical Programming*, **118**(2), 237–251.

[120] Pearson, Justin K., and Jeavons, Peter G. 1997 (July). *A survey of tractable constraint satisfaction problems*. Tech. rept. CSD-TR-97-15. Royal Holloway, University of London.

[121] Queyranne, Maurice. 1998. Minimising symmetric submodular functions. *Mathematical Programming*, **82**(1–2), 3–12.

[122] Raghavendra, Prasad. 2008. Optimal algorithms and inapproximability results for every CSP? Pages 245–254 of: *Proceedings of the 40th Annual ACM Symposium on Theory of Computing (STOC'08)*.

[123] Rossi, Francesca, van Beek, Peter, and Walsh, Toby (eds). 2006. *The Handbook of Constraint Programming*. Elsevier.

[124] Salamon, András Z., and Jeavons, Peter G. 2008. Perfect constraints are tractable. Pages 524–528 of: *Proceedings of the 14th International Conference on Principles and Practice of Constraint Programming (CP'08)*. LNCS **5202**.

[125] Samer, Marko, and Szeider, Stefan. 2010. Constraint satisfaction with bounded treewidth revisited. *Journal of Computer and System Sciences*, **76**(2), 103–114.

[126] Schiex, Thomas, Fargier, Hélène, and Verfaillie, Gérard. 1995. Valued constraint satisfaction problems: hard and easy problems. In: *Proceedings of the 14th International Joint Conference on Artificial Intelligence (IJCAI'95)*.

[127] Schrijver, Alexander. 2000. A combinatorial algorithm minimizing submodular functions in strongly polynomial time. *Journal of Combinatorial Theory, Series B*, **80**(2), 346–355.

[128] Schrijver, Alexander. 2003. *Combinatorial Optimization: Polyhedra and Efficiency*. Algorithms and Combinatorics, vol. 24. Springer.

[129] Takhanov, Rustem. 2010a. A dichotomy theorem for the general minimum cost homomorphism problem. Pages 657–668 of: *Proceedings of the 27th International Symposium on Theoretical Aspects of Computer Science (STACS'10)*.

[130] Takhanov, Rustem. 2010b. Extensions of the minimum cost homomorphism problem. Pages 328–337 of: *Proceedings of the 16th International Computing and Combinatorics Conference (COCOON'10)*. LNCS **6196**.

[131] Thapper, Johan, and Živný, Stanislav. 2012. The power of linear programming for valued CSPs. Pages 669–678 of: *Proceedings of the 53rd Annual IEEE Symposium on Foundations of Computer Science (FOCS'12)*.

[132] Thapper, Johan, and Živný, Stanislav. 2013. The complexity of finite-valued CSPs. Pages 695–704 of: *Proceedings of the 45th ACM Symposium on the Theory of Computing (STOC'13)*.

[133] Topkis, Donald M. 1998. *Supermodularity and Complementarity*. Princeton University Press.

[134] Ullman, Jeffrey D. 1989. *Principles of Database and Knowledge-Base Systems*. Vol. 1 & 2. Computer Science Press.

[135] Wainwright, Martin J., and Jordan, Michael I. 2008. Graphical models, exponential families, and variational inference. *Foundations and Trends in Machine Learning*, **1**(1–2), 1–305.

[136] Werner, Tomáš. 2007. A linear programming approach to Max-Sum Problem: a review. *IEEE Transactions on Pattern Analysis and Machine Intelligence*, **29**(7), 1165–1179.

[137] Willard, Ross. 2010. Testing expressibility is hard. Pages 9–23 of: *Proceedings of the 16th International Conference on Principles and Practice of Constraint Programming (CP'10)*. LNCS **6308**.

[138] Zanuttini, Bruno, and Živný, Stanislav. 2009. A note on some collapse results of valued constraints. *Information Processing Letters*, **109**(11), 534–538.

[139] Živný, Stanislav. 2009. *The Complexity and Expressive Power of Valued Constraints*. Ph.D. thesis, University of Oxford.

[140] Živný, Stanislav, and Jeavons, Peter G. 2010. Classes of submodular constraints expressible by graph cuts. *Constraints*, **15**(3), 430–452.

[141] Živný, Stanislav, Cohen, David A., and Jeavons, Peter G. 2009. The expressive power of binary submodular functions. *Discrete Applied Mathematics*, **157**(15), 3347–3358.

5

Tractable Knowledge Representation Formalisms

Adnan Darwiche

One approach for dealing with intractability is to utilize representations that permit certain queries of interest to be computable in polytime. Such tractable representations will ultimately be exponential in size for certain problems and they may also not be suitable for direct specification by users. Hence, they are typically generated from other specifications through a process known as knowledge compilation. In this chapter, we review a subset of these tractable representations, known as decomposable negation normal forms (DNNFs), which have proved influential in a number of applications, including formal verification, model-based diagnosis and probabilistic reasoning.

5.1 Introduction

Many areas of computer science have shown a great interest in tractable and canonical representations of propositional knowledge bases (aka, Boolean functions). The ordered binary decision diagram (OBDD) is one such representation that received much attention and proved quite influential in a variety of areas [13]. Within AI, the study of tractable representations has also had a long tradition (e.g., [61, 30, 31, 49, 62, 14, 28, 19, 13, 52, 66, 50]). This area of research, which is also known as *knowledge compilation,* has become more systematic since [28], which showed that many known and useful representations are subsets of negation normal form (NNF) and correspond to imposing specific properties on NNF. The most fundamental of these properties turned out to be *decomposability* and *determinism,* giving rise to the corresponding language of DNNF and its subset, d-DNNF. This chapter is dedicated to DNNF and its subsets, which also include the influential language of OBDDs, and the more recently introduced sentential decision diagrams (SDDs). DNNF and its subsets have found applications in different areas of computer science and artificial intelligence, including formal verification (e.g., [53]), model-based diagnosis (e.g., [3, 33, 63, 64]), planning (e.g., [2, 55, 41, 12]), databases (e.g., [1, 20, 46]), and probabilistic reasoning (e.g., [15, 18, 38]).

Current research on tractable languages and knowledge compilation within AI is focused on two directions. The first direction is the identification of more languages and the study of their properties with respect to both tractability and succinctness. The second direction is the development of compilers that map propositional knowledge bases into tractable representations. It is probably fair to say that the emphasis within the community has been somewhat titled towards the first direction, which is also reflected in the balance of this chapter.

We will start in Section 5.2 with a motivating example, in which we illustrate the approach of knowledge compilation in the context of model-based diagnosis. We then introduce negation normal form in Section 5.3, together with its various subsets, including DNNF and d-DNNF. We follow by introducing the notion of structured decomposability in Section 5.4, which induces new and interesting subsets of DNNF and provides a new dimension for characterizing such subsets. Section 5.5 is dedicated to the notion of $(\mathbf{X}, \mathbf{Y})$-decompositions, which is a recent development that is responsible for semantically characterizing some existing tractable forms and for systematically inducing others. One such example of a newly induced tractable form is discussed in Section 5.6. We then turn to the subject of building compilers in Section 5.7 followed by a discussion on the application of knowledge compilation to probabilistic reasoning in Section 5.8. Section 5.9 concludes.

5.2 A Motivating Example

Consider the device shown in Figure 5.1(a), which is a circuit containing two inverters:

$$\Delta = \left\{ \begin{array}{l} okX \wedge A \Rightarrow \neg B, \\ okX \wedge \neg A \Rightarrow B, \\ okY \wedge B \Rightarrow \neg C, \\ okY \wedge \neg B \Rightarrow C \end{array} \right\}.$$

Here, variables okX and okY denote the health of corresponding inverters (e.g, okX denotes that Inverter X is functioning properly and $\neg okX$ denotes that the inverter is not functioning properly). Moreover, variables A, B and C denote the state of corresponding wires in the circuit (e.g., A denotes that the corresponding wire is high, while $\neg A$ denotes that the wire is low). Suppose now that we observe the input A to be high, the output C to be low, and we are interested in answering diagnostic queries about this behavior.

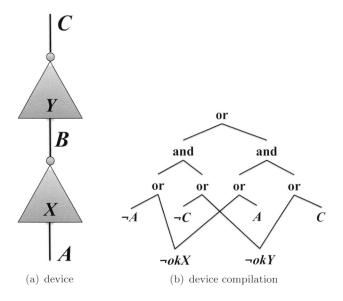

(a) device   (b) device compilation

Figure 5.1 A device and its compilations as DNNF.

For example, is the behavior normal? If not, what are the feasible states of the device? Alternatively, what are the feasible states that include a smallest number of faults? And so on.

The classical approach for dealing with these and similar queries is to invoke specialized algorithms that have been developed for answering diagnostic queries (e.g., [59]). The knowledge compilation approach, however, calls for compiling the device model into some tractable form and then answering diagnostic queries by applying polytime queries and transformations to the compilation. As an example, Figure 5.1(b) depicts a device compilation in decomposable negation normal form (DNNF), which will be discussed in more details later. Moreover, Table 5.1 contains some queries and transformations from [28] that can be applied to the compilation.

A query is an operation that obtains information about a compiled knowledge base (KB). Satisfiability is the classical and simplest example, but there are other more powerful, and more difficult queries, such as: counting the number of satisfying assignments to a KB; finding whether two KBs are equivalent; and testing whether one KB implies another.[1] A transformation is a logical operation that alters the logical content of a KB. For example, one of the more useful transformations is *projection* (also known as *existential quantification* or *forgetting*), which characterizes the knowledge relevant to a particular set of variables in a KB. Given these queries and transformations,

---

[1] Some of these queries can be easily reduced to satisfiability, but that may blow up the KB size.

Notation	Query	Notation	Transformation
CO	consistency check	**CD**	conditioning
VA	validity check	**FO**	forgetting
CE	clausal entailment check	**SFO**	singleton forgetting
IM	implicant check	**∧C**	conjunction
EQ	equivalence check	**∧BC**	bounded conjunction
SE	sentential entailment check	**∨C**	disjunction
CT	model counting	**∨BC**	bounded disjunction
ME	model enumeration	**¬C**	negation

Table 5.1 *Queries and transformations, representing the building blocks for reasoning tasks.*

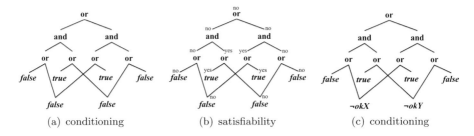

(a) conditioning   (b) satisfiability   (c) conditioning

Figure 5.2 Polytime queries and transformations applied to a device compilation in DNNF (see Figure 5.1). Conditioning amounts to replacing literals by constants. For example, the DNNF in (a) results from conditioning the DNNF in Figure 5.1(b) on the literals $\{A, \neg C, okX, okY\}$. As a result of this conditioning, literal C is replaced by *false* and literal $\neg C$ is replaced by *true*. In (b), satisfiability amounts to sweeping the circuit upwards, while propagating yes/no at each visited node. In (c), the conditioned DNNF is equivalent to $\neg okX \lor \neg okY$.

one can implement a variety of automated reasoning applications, including diagnosis, planning, reliability analysis, probabilistic reasoning, and formal verification. In a way, the use of these *building blocks,* as in Table 5.1, to implement reasoning systems is similar to the use of an SQL engine, which provide a number of primitives—such as join, select, project, etc—to build a database application.[2]

Going back to our diagnostic application, we can check whether the observed behavior is normal (i.e., input A is high and output C is low) by first conditioning the device compilation on literals $\{A, \neg C, okX, okY\}$ as

---

[2] See also the work on QBF (quantified Boolean formula) solvers (e.g., [56, 9, 7, 40, 5, 6]), which provide a related solution to this problem.

in Figure 5.2(a) and then testing the satisfiability of the result as in Figure 5.2(b). The conditioned compilation is not satisfiable in this case, indicating an abnormal device behavior. To determine the feasible states of the device under this observation, we can simply enumerate the models of the conditioned compilation $\Delta \mid A, \neg C$, shown in Figure 5.2(c) and leading to the feasible states $\{okX, \neg okY\}$, $\{\neg okX, okY\}$, and $\{\neg okX, \neg okY\}$. The key observation is that all used queries and transformations have polytime implementations on the used tractable form.

More sophisticated diagnosis applications call for other type of operations, such as *model minimization,* which can be used to find the most likely states of a device given some abnormal behavior (e.g., [3, 33, 63, 64]). Other domains, such as planning and probabilistic reasoning do also require a number of sophisticated operations that go beyond conditioning and satisfiability, as illustrated in [12, 41, 55, 54] (planning) and [18, 60, 44] (probabilistic reasoning). The main point, however, is that if one compiles the given KB to the appropriate tractable form, then all queries and transformations of interest should be computable in polytime. Hence, the only computational investment needed is that of compiling the given knowledge base into a suitable tractable form.

5.3 Negation Normal Form

The goal of knowledge compilation is to identify languages that provide polytime support for different subsets of queries and transformations, and to develop compilers for mapping KBs into such representations. Although different tractable languages have been identified in the literature, we will mostly focus the rest of our discussion on languages that are subsets of negation

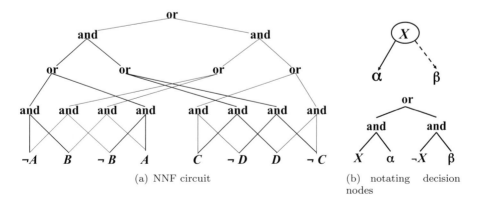

(a) NNF circuit

(b) notating decision nodes

Figure 5.3 NNF circuit and two different notations for decision nodes.

normal form (NNF) [4] and that satisfy the property of decomposability—
leading to decomposable negation normal form (DNNF) [21].

Following [28] and the discussion in [43], we will use circuit representations
of negation normal form. These are circuits with and-gates, or-gates, and
inverters, but where inverters can only appear next to inputs—a property
that is characteristic of negation normal form (NNF): see [4]. Our base
representation is then a directed acyclic graph (DAG), where each internal
node is labeled with a conjunction (*and*, $\land$) or disjunction (*or*, $\lor$), and each
leaf is labeled with a propositional literal or constant (*true/false*, or $1/0$).
We will refer to these DAGs as *NNF circuits* and the set of all such DAGs
as the *NNF language*, or simply *NNF*. Figure 5.3a depicts a propositional
theory represented as an NNF circuit. We will next define some interesting
subsets of the NNF language. For a more comprehensive coverage, however,
we defer the reader to the "knowledge compilation map" in [28].

CNF (conjunctive normal form) can now be defined as the subset of NNF
that satisfies (i) *flatness*: the height of the DAG is at most two; and (ii)
simple-disjunction: any disjunction is over leaf nodes only (i.e., is a clause).
Similarly, DNF (disjunctive normal form) is the subset of NNF that satisfies
flatness and *simple-conjunction*: any conjunction is over leaf nodes only (i.e.,
is a term).

DNNF (decomposable negation normal form) is the set of all NNF circuits
satisfying *decomposability*: conjuncts of any conjunction share no variables.
The next language, d-DNNF, satisfies both decomposability and *determinism*: disjuncts of any disjunction are logically contradictory.[3] The NNF circuit in Figure 5.3(a) is in d-DNNF, while the one in Figure 5.4(a) is in DNNF
but not in d-DNNF as neither of its disjunctions satisfies determinism. The
language of d-DNNF proved quite influential in probabilistic reasoning applications, which is why we dedicate Section 5.8 to this topic.

We now move to the FBDD language. This is the subset of d-DNNF where
the root of every circuit is a *decision* node, which is defined recursively as
either a constant (0 or 1) or a disjunction in the form of Figure 5.3(b)
(bottom)—here, X is a propositional variable and α and β are decision
nodes. Note that an equivalent but more compact drawing of a decision node
as in Figure 5.3(b) (top) is widely used in the formal verification literature,
where FBDDs are equivalently known as BDDs (binary decision diagrams)
that satisfy the *test-once* property: each variable appears at most once on

---

[3] This is sometimes also defined as "disjuncts of any disjunction are mutually exclusive." More
precisely, determinism means that no variable assignment would ever satisfy more than one
child (disjunct) of a disjunction node.

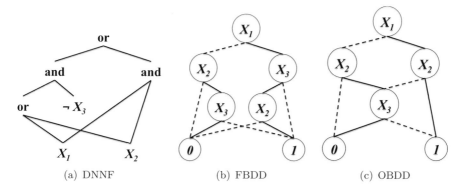

Figure 5.4 Three types of NNF circuits: DNNF, FBDD, and OBDD.

any root-to-sink path [39].[4] Figure 5.4(b) depicts an FBDD using this more compact notation. The OBDD language is the subset of FBDD where all circuits satisfy the *ordering* property: variables appear in the same order on all root-to-sink paths [13]; see Figure 5.4(c) for an example. For a particular variable order $<$, we also write $\text{OBDD}_<$ to denote the corresponding OBDD subset where all circuits use order $<$.

5.3.1 Tractability of NNF Circuits

We now turn to the tractability of languages, which refers to the set of polytime operations they support. As mentioned earlier, one traditionally distinguishes between two types of operations: queries and transformations. The difference between the two is that queries return information about circuits, while transformations modify circuits to generate new ones (in the same language).

Some of the known results from [28] regarding the tractability of languages are summarized in Table 5.2 (queries) and Table 5.3 (transformations). The abbreviations in the first row of Table 5.2 stand for the following eight queries, respectively: *Consistency* (is the formula satisfiable), *Validity* (does the formula evaluate to 1 under all variable assignments), *Clausal Entailment* (does the formula imply a given clause), *Implicant* (is the formula implied by a given term), *Equivalence* (are the two formulas logically equivalent), *Sentential Entailment* (does one formula imply the other), *Model Counting* (how many satisfying assignments does the formula have), *Model Enumeration* (what are the satisfying assignments of the formula). The abbreviations in the first row of Table 5.3 stand for the following eight transformations,

---

[4] FBDDs are also known as *read-once branching programs* [67].

Language	CO	VA	CE	IM	EQ	SE	CT	ME
NNF	o	o	o	o	o	o	o	o
DNNF	√	o	√	o	o	o	o	√
d-DNNF	√	√	√	√	?	o	√	√
BDD	o	o	o	o	o	o	o	o
FBDD	√	√	√	√	?	o	√	√
OBDD	√	√	√	√	√	o	√	√
OBDD$_<$	√	√	√	√	√	√	√	√
DNF	√	o	√	o	o	o	o	√
CNF	o	√	o	√	o	o	o	o

Table 5.2 *Polytime queries supported by a language.* √ *indicates that the language satisfies the property.* o *indicates that the language does not satisfy the property unless P=NP. The presence of ? indicates that we do not know whether the property holds for the language.*

Language	CD	FO	SFO	∧C	∧BC	∨C	∨BC	¬C
NNF	√	o	√	√	√	√	√	√
DNNF	√	√	√	o	o	√	√	o
d-DNNF	√	o	o	o	o	o	o	?
BDD	√	o	√	√	√	√	√	√
FBDD	√	●	o	●	o	●	o	√
OBDD	√	●	√	●	o	●	o	√
OBDD$_<$	√	●	√	●	√	●	√	√
DNF	√	√	√	●	√	√	√	●
CNF	√	o	√	√	√	●	√	●

Table 5.3 *Polytime transformations supported by a language.* √ *indicates that the language satisfies the property.* o *indicates that the language does not satisfy the property unless P=NP.* ● *means the language does not satisfy the property. The presence of ? indicates that we do not know whether the property holds for the language.*

respectively: *Conditioning* (setting a set of variables to constants), *Forgetting* (existentially quantifying a set of variables), *Single-Variable Forgetting* (existentially quantifying a single variable), *Conjunction* (conjoining a set of circuits), *Bounded Conjunction* (conjoining a bounded number of circuits), *Disjunction* (disjoining a set of circuits), *Bounded Disjunction* (disjoining a bounded number of circuits), *Negation* (negating a circuit).

Table 5.2 offers one explanation for the popularity of OBDDs in formal verification where efficient equivalence testing, among other things, is often critical. Although more succinct as discussed below, d-DNNF and FBDD are not known to admit a polynomial-time equivalence test (a polynomial-time probabilistic equivalence test is possible [11, 27]). Note also that although there is no difference between d-DNNF and FBDD to the extent of this table—the question mark on the equivalence test (EQ) could eventually be resolved differently for the two languages.

5.3.2 Succinctness of NNF Circuits

Given a choice of languages in which a KB may be represented, one needs to strike a balance between the size of the representation and the support it provides for the reasoning task at hand, as these two properties of a representation often run counter to each other. The work on knowledge compilation is therefore interested in formally analyzing both the *succinctness* and *tractability* of languages, so that given a required reasoning task, we can choose the most succinct language that supports the set of necessary operations in polynomial time. The following is a classical definition of succinctness:

Definition 5.1 (Succinctness) Let L_1 and L_2 be two subsets of NNF. L_1 is at least as succinct as L_2, denoted $L_1 \leq L_2$, iff there exists a polynomial p such that for every circuit $\alpha \in L_2$, there exists a logically equivalent circuit $\beta \in L_1$ where $|\beta| \leq p(|\alpha|)$. Here, $|\alpha|$ and $|\beta|$ are the sizes of α and β, respectively.

Intuitively, language L_1 is at least as succinct as language L_2 if given any circuit in L_2, there exists a logically equivalent circuit in L_1 whose size does not "blow up." One can also define L_1 to be *strictly more succinct than L_2*, denoted $L_1 < L_2$, if $L_1 \leq L_2$ but $L_2 \not\leq L_1$. It is known, for example, that NNF < DNNF; d-DNNF < FBDD < OBDD; NNF < CNF; and DNNF < DNF [28].

It is worth pointing out that while tractability with respect to the queries generally improves when the language becomes more restrictive (has more conditions imposed), tractability with respect to the transformations may not. DNNF, for example, supports a subset of the queries that are supported by OBDD according to Table 5.2, and is therefore less tractable than OBDD from this point of view. However, when it comes to certain transformations, such as the operation of forgetting (existential quantification), DNNF becomes more tractable than OBDD according to Table 5.3. The key reason for this shift of advantage is that transformations operate on circuits in a given language, and require the result to be in the same language—this requirement can become a burden for the more restrictive language where more conditions need to be satisfied when the result of the transformation is generated.

5.3.3 Extending the Knowledge Compilation Map

Over the last few years, new tractable languages have been introduced and studied in connection to the "knowledge compilation map" [28] that we reviewed in the previous few sections. We will next briefly discuss some of these contributions and then focus our attention again, starting in Section 5.4, on recent developments relating to DNNF and its subsets in particular.

Among the new languages introduced are those obtained by applying *closure principles* to existing languages—that is, extending a particular language by new sentences that result from closure under certain operations. For example, disjunctive closures have been utilized in [35], which proposed closing a language under disjunction, existential quantification and their combination. Moreover, disjunctive closures of several complete languages such as DNF, DNNF, and OBDD have been studied in [35], according to the tractability and succinctness dimensions of [28]. For example, beyond offering some transformations "for free," it was shown that the disjunctive closure of a language is always at least as succinct as, if not strictly more succinct than, the original language. Furthermore, some important queries, such as clausal entailment, have been shown to be preserved by such closures. A further virtue of disjunction closure in particular is that it may complete an otherwise incomplete language.[5] For example, the disjunction closures of well-known incomplete languages have been studied in [36]. This includes the HORN-C fragment (conjunctions of Horn clauses), the Krom fragment (conjunctions of binary clauses) and the affine fragment (conjunctions of XOR clauses). The existential closure of these languages has also been studied in [50].

Another interesting concept that underlies a new class of languages is that of using a tree decomposition of a given representation to improve on the properties of the original representation. This concept was first introduced in [66], which proposed and studied the trees-of-BDDs representation. The proposal was then generalized by [37], leading to the notion of a "trees-of-$\mathcal{L}$" (To$\mathcal{L}$) representation, which allowed one to derive properties of the To$\mathcal{L}$ language based on properties of the underlying language $\mathcal{L}$. This work has

---

[5] Completeness refers to the ability of a language to represent all Boolean functions. For example, CNF is complete, while its Horn subset is not complete (a Horn CNF is one in which every clause is Horn). However any Boolean function can be represented by an existentially quantified Horn CNF with more variables.

Query	DNNF	structured DNNF	d-DNNF	structured d-DNNF	OBDD$_<$
CO	√	√	√	√	√
VA	○	○	√	√	√
CE	√	√	√	√	√
IM	○	○	√	√	√
EQ	○	○	?	√	√
SE	○	○	○	√	√
CT	○	○	√	√	√
ME	√	√	√	√	√

Table 5.4 *Polytime queries supported by a language.* √ *indicates that the language satisfies the property.* ○ *indicates that the language does not satisfy the property unless P=NP. The presence of ? indicates that we do not know whether the property holds for the language.*

also addressed a number of issues that remained open in [66], showing for instance that the trees-of-BDDs language satisfies neither the conditioning transformation, nor the clausal entailment query unless P = NP. It also proved that this language is not comparable in succinctness to CNF, DNF, and DNNF unless the polynomial hierarchy collapses, which explained some of the empirical results reported in [66].

Another dimension for extending the knowledge compilation map formalized in [28] has been to lift some of its findings and basic insights beyond propositional representations. This include, for example, the representation of *Valued Negation Normal Form (VNNF)* introduced by [34]. This normal form aims to represent a more general class of functions that goes beyond Boolean ones, providing generalizations of NNF properties, such as decomposability, determinism, decision, and read-once. Another generalization is AND/OR Multi-Valued Decision Diagrams (AOMDDs) [52]. AOMDDs work with multivalued variables and can be used as a compilation of a number of representations that can be thought of as "weighted graphical models." More recently, the propositional epistemic logic S5 has also been studied from a knowledge compilation perspective [8], yielding an extension of the queries and transformations considered in the classical knowledge compilation map to S5. A first order, yet incomplete, variant of d-DNNF has also been recently proposed in the context of lifted probabilistic inference [32].

Transformation	DNNF	structured DNNF	d-DNNF	structured d-DNNF	OBDD$_<$
CD	√	√	√	√	√
FO	√	√	○	○	●
SFO	√	√	○	?	√
∧C	○	●	○	●	●
∧BC	○	√	○	√	√
∨C	√	√	○	○	●
∨BC	√	√	○	?	√
¬C	○	○	?	?	√

Table 5.5 *Polytime transformations supported by a language. √ indicates that the language satisfies the property. ○ indicates that the language does not satisfy the property unless P=NP. ● means the language does not satisfy the property. The presence of ? indicates that we do not know whether the property holds for the language.*

5.4 Structured Decomposability

We now turn our attention back to propositional DNNF and its subsets, where we discuss the important property of *structured decomposability*. This property has lead to synthesizing new tractable languages and to further explaining the properties of some existing ones.

Structured decomposability was originally introduced in [57], with the goal of identifying additional subsets of DNNF that lend themselves to bottom-up compilation. This type of compilation, which will be discussed in Section 5.7, requires efficient ways of combining compilations using Boolean operators. For example, bottom-up compilation of CNFs requires one to efficiently conjoin compilations; see Section 5.7. As we shall see next, OBDDs already satisfy structured decomposability. However, when the decomposability of DNNF and d-DNNF is structured, the resulting languages are new (called structured DNNF and structured d-DNNF) and support more queries and transformations in polytime as shown in Tables 5.4 and 5.5. Mostly notably, both structured DNNF and structured d-DNNF support a polytime bounded conjoin operation, which is critical for the bottom-up compilation of CNFs.

The basic idea behind structured decomposability is to insist that all decompositions in the DNNF follow a master scheme, specified by a tree structure known as a *vtree*. The vtree is simply a full binary tree whose leaves are in one-to-one correspondence with the given set of Boolean variables. Figure 5.5 depict two vtrees for the same set of variables.

Given an internal node v in a vtree, we will use v^l and v^r to refer to its

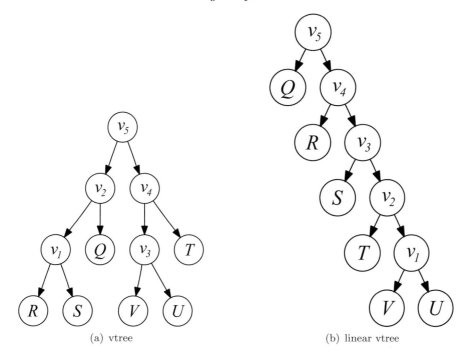

(a) vtree   (b) linear vtree

Figure 5.5 Two vtrees.

left and right children, and use *vars(v)* to denote the set of variables at or below v in the tree. A DNNF is said to be *structured* according to a given vtree if the DNNF respects the vtree according to the following definition.

Definition 5.2 A DNNF respects a vtree iff every and-node has exactly two children N^l and N^r, and we have $vars(N^l) \subseteq vars(v^l)$ and $vars(N^r) \subseteq vars(v^r)$ for some vtree node v.

The DNNF in Figure 5.6(a) and the d-DNNF in Figure 5.6(b) respect the vtree in Figure 5.5(a). The language of structured DNNF (d-DNNF) simply contains all DNNFs (d-DNNFs) that respect a given vtree.[6] Note that a variable ordering corresponds to a *linear vtree* as shown in Figure 5.5(b).[7] Moreover, every OBDD is a DNNF that respects a corresponding linear vtree.

Hence, structured DNNF and structured d-DNNF include OBDD on the one hand, and are included in DNNF and d-DNNF on the other hand. One can provide lower bounds on the size of structured DNNF and structured

---

[6] Some DNNFs do not respect any vtree.

[7] The *pseudo tree* in the context of AOMDD representations [51] can be viewed as a special type of vtree that satisfies certain constraints imposed by the function to be represented [57]. Hence, there may be no AOMDD for a given function that respects a given pseudo tree.

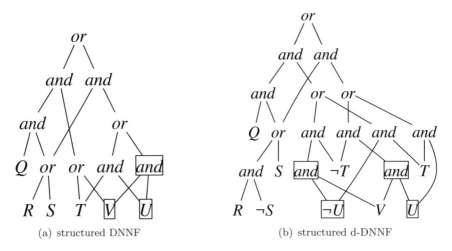

(a) structured DNNF   (b) structured d-DNNF

Figure 5.6 Structured DNNF and structured d-DNNF for the same Boolean function.

d-DNNF, which generalize one of the main lower bounds for OBDDs. This and other interesting recent developments will be discussed later, after we have a chance to introduce the notion of $(\mathbf{X}, \mathbf{Y})$-decompositions.

5.5 $(\mathbf{X}, \mathbf{Y})$-Decompositions of Boolean Functions

Structured decomposability is related to a fundamental notion that was formulated recently, $(\mathbf{X}, \mathbf{Y})$-decompositions [58]. Together, these two developments have provided a new and semantical characterization of several tractable forms, contributing main theoretical and practical insights. For example, these two notions have facilitated the systematic construction of new subsets of DNNF. We will see an example of this in Section 5.6. The discussion of $(\mathbf{X}, \mathbf{Y})$-decompositions, however, requires an additional level of formality and notation that we shall spell out first.

We will use the standard notation for variables and their instantiations. In particular, we use an upper case letter to denote a variable (e.g., X) and a lower case letter to denote its instantiation (e.g., x). Moreover, we use a bold upper case letter to denote a set of variables (e.g., $\mathbf{X}$) and a bold lower case letter to denote their instantiations (e.g., $\mathbf{x}$). A *Boolean function* f over variables $\mathbf{Z}$ maps each instantiation $\mathbf{z}$ to 0 or 1. The *conditioning* of f on instantiation $\mathbf{x}$, written $f|\mathbf{x}$, is a *subfunction* that results from setting variables $\mathbf{X}$ to their values in $\mathbf{x}$. A function f *depends* on variable X iff $f|X \neq f|\neg X$. We write $f(\mathbf{Z})$ to mean that f can only depend on variables in $\mathbf{Z}$. A *trivial* function maps all its inputs to 0 (denoted *false*) or maps them all to 1 (denoted *true*).

In what follows, we will assume that variables $\mathbf{X}$ and $\mathbf{Y}$ form a partition of variables $\mathbf{Z}$ [58].

Definition 5.3 An $(\mathbf{X}, \mathbf{Y})$-decomposition of function $f(\mathbf{Z})$ is a set of pairs $\{(p_1, s_1), \dots, (p_n, s_n)\}$, where p_i are functions that depend only on variables in $\mathbf{X}$, s_i are functions that depend only on variables in $\mathbf{Y}$, and the function f can be expressed as follows:

$$f = (p_1 \wedge s_1) \vee \dots \vee (p_n \wedge s_n).$$

Each conjunct $p_i \wedge s_i$ is called an <u>element</u> of the decomposition and n is called the <u>size</u> of the decomposition.

Intuitively, an $(\mathbf{X}, \mathbf{Y})$-decomposition allows one to express a function in terms of smaller functions, that depend only on variables in $\mathbf{X}$ or variables in $\mathbf{Y}$. One can define several types of $(\mathbf{X}, \mathbf{Y})$-decompositions, which lead to a new characterization of structured DNNF, structured d-DNNF and OBDDs. This new characterization has two main implications. First, it leads to an interesting lower bound on the size of these representations, which can be viewed as a generalization of the influential Seiling and Wegner bound on OBDDs [65]. Second, the new characterization provides a semantical and systematic way for inducing new tractable languages, by simply defining new types of $(\mathbf{X}, \mathbf{Y})$-decompositions. In fact, we will in the next section define a new tractable representation, the *sentential decision diagram (SDD)*, by simply defining a new type of $(\mathbf{X}, \mathbf{Y})$-decomposition; see Figure 5.7.

Let us now consider some examples of $(\mathbf{X}, \mathbf{Y})$-decompositions and their types. Consider the Boolean function $f = (X_1 \wedge Y_1) \vee (X_2 \wedge Y_2) \vee (X_2 \wedge Y_3)$ and let $\mathbf{X} = \{X_1, X_2\}$ and $\mathbf{Y} = \{Y_1, Y_2, Y_3\}$. The following are two decompositions of this function, where each row in a table corresponds to an element of the associated decomposition:

i	$p_i(\mathbf{X})$	$s_i(\mathbf{Y})$
1	X_1	Y_1
2	X_2	$Y_2 \vee Y_3$

i	$p_i(\mathbf{X})$	$s_i(\mathbf{Y})$
1	X_1	Y_1
2	$\neg X_1 \wedge X_2$	$Y_2 \vee Y_3$
3	$X_1 \wedge X_2$	$\neg Y_1 \wedge (Y_2 \vee Y_3)$

The decomposition to the right is called a *deterministic decomposition* since its elements are mutually exclusive. The decomposition to the left is not deterministic as it does not satisfy this property. Note that if elements

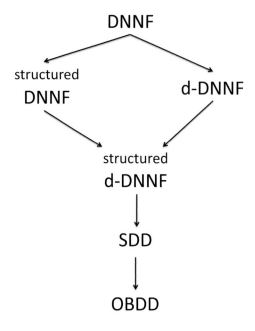

Figure 5.7 DNNF and some of its subsets.

$p_i \wedge s_i$ and $p_j \wedge s_j$ are mutually exclusive, then either p_i and p_j are mutually exclusive, or s_i and s_j are mutually exclusive. When mutual exclusiveness is always on the p_i components, or always on the s_i components, the decomposition is said to be *strongly deterministic*. Interestingly enough, different subsets of DNNF induce different types of decompositions. This has implications on both the characterization of these subsets and on their sizes as well, as shown by the following theorem [58].

Theorem 5.4 *Suppose we are given a DNNF for function $f(\mathbf{Z})$ and the DNNF respects a given vtree, which has a node with variables $\mathbf{X}$. Let $\mathbf{Y} = \mathbf{Z} \setminus \mathbf{X}$. The DNNF must have at least k nodes, where k is the size of a smallest $(\mathbf{X}, \mathbf{Y})$-decomposition of function $f(\mathbf{Z})$. The theorem also holds for d-DNNF and deterministic decompositions. It also holds for OBDDs and strongly deterministic decompositions.*

There is a more specific version of this theorem, reported in [58], which shows how one can extract $(\mathbf{X}, \mathbf{Y})$-decompositions with the appropriate properties from the structured DNNF, structured d-DNNF or OBDD. We will not delve into such details here, but will simply provide some examples. Consider the DNNF in Figure 5.6(a) which respects the vtree in Figure 5.5(a). Consider vtree node v_3 which has variables $\mathbf{X} = \{U, V\}$ and, hence, $\mathbf{Y} = \{R, S, T, Q\}$. This DNNF induces the following (non-deterministic) decomposition, whose first three elements correspond to the boxed nodes in Figure 5.6(a):[8]

i	$p_i(\mathbf{X})$	$s_i(\mathbf{Y})$
1	$V \wedge U$	$R \vee S$
2	U	$T \wedge (R \vee S)$
3	V	$Q \wedge (R \vee S)$
4	$true$	$Q \wedge T \wedge (R \vee S)$

That is, the function represented by the DNNF in Figure 5.6(a) is equivalent to $p_1 \wedge s_1 \vee \ldots \vee p_4 \wedge s_4$, where p_i and s_i are defined in the table above.

Consider now the d-DNNF in Figure 5.6(b) and the same vtree node v_3 in Figure 5.5(a). This d-DNNF induces the following deterministic decomposition, whose elements correspond to boxed nodes in the d-DNNF:

i	$p_i(\mathbf{X})$	$s_i(\mathbf{Y})$
1	$\neg U \wedge V$	$\neg T \wedge Q \wedge (S \vee (R \wedge \neg S))$
2	$V \wedge U$	$\neg T \wedge (S \vee (R \wedge \neg S))$
3	U	$T \wedge (S \vee (R \wedge \neg S))$
4	$\neg U$	$T \wedge Q \wedge (S \vee (R \wedge \neg S))$

Finally, consider the OBDD in Figure 5.8(a). This OBDD respects the linear vtree in Figure 5.5(a). Consider vtree node v_1 which has variables $\mathbf{X} = \{U, V\}$ and, hence, $\mathbf{Y} = \{R, S, T, Q\}$. The OBDD induces the following decomposition of the function represented by the OBDD.

---

[8] Each boxed node represents one s_i. Functions p_i are obtained from considering paths to the boxed nodes as discussed in [58].

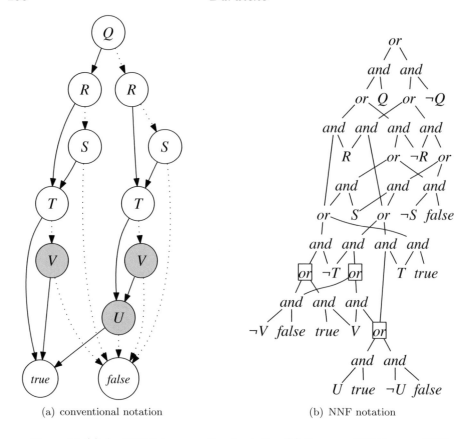

(a) conventional notation   (b) NNF notation

Figure 5.8 (a) An OBDD in conventional notation (b) the same OBDD as an NNF circuit.

i	$p_i(\mathbf{X})$	$s_i(\mathbf{Y})$
1	$V \wedge U$	$\neg T \wedge (R \vee (S \wedge \neg R)) \wedge \neg Q$
2	V	$\neg T \wedge (R \vee (S \wedge \neg R)) \wedge Q$
3	U	$T \wedge (R \vee (S \wedge \neg R)) \wedge \neg Q$
4	$true$	$T \wedge (R \vee (S \wedge \neg R)) \wedge Q$

If we carefully examine this decomposition, we find that it is not just deterministic, but also strongly deterministic. In particular, not only does every pair of elements contradict each other, but the contradiction can be established by considering only the $\mathbf{Y}$ component of each element. Hence, this is an example of a strongly deterministic decomposition. The elements of a decomposition that is strongly deterministic on $\mathbf{Y}$ directly encodes all consistent sub-functions of the form $f|\mathbf{y}$, where f is the function represented by the decomposition. This observation was used in [58] to show that the lower bound of Theorem 5.4 is indeed a generalization of the lower bound given by Seiling and Wegner in [65] since OBDDs always induce strongly deterministic decompositions [58].

5.6 Sentential Decision Diagrams

We now illustrate a major implication of structured decomposability and $(\mathbf{X}, \mathbf{Y})$-decompositions: Their ability to facilitate the induction of new tractable forms. In particular, we will next discuss one of the latest discoveries in knowledge compilation, *sentential decision diagrams (SDDs)* [26], which result from using structured decomposability with a new type of $(\mathbf{X}, \mathbf{Y})$-decompositions.

SDDs are a subset of structured d-DNNF and a superset of OBDDs; see Figure 5.7. The interest in SDDs stems from their canonicity and polytime support for combination under Boolean operators, and from their strict inclusion of OBDDs (which are popular for exactly these reasons). SDDs are based on a new type of $(\mathbf{X}, \mathbf{Y})$-decompositions, known as $(\mathbf{X}, \mathbf{Y})$-partitions. We first define this decomposition and then follow by introducing SDDs.

Consider an $(\mathbf{X}, \mathbf{Y})$-decomposition $\{(p_1, s_1), \ldots, (p_n, s_n)\}$ of function $f(\mathbf{Z})$ and suppose that the decomposition is strongly deterministic on $\mathbf{X}$. This basically means that p_i and p_j are mutually exclusive for each $i \neq j$. The decomposition is called an $(\mathbf{X}, \mathbf{Y})$-partition of function f if the functions $p_1, \ldots, p_n$ form a partition. That is, in addition to $p_i \wedge p_j = \textit{false}$ for $i \neq j$, we must also have $p_i \neq \textit{false}$ for each i, and $p_1 \vee \ldots \vee p_n = \textit{true}$. In this case, the functions p_i are called *primes* and the functions s_i are called *subs*. Moreover, an $(\mathbf{X}, \mathbf{Y})$-partition is said to be *compressed* iff its subs are distinct ($s_i \neq s_j$ for $i \neq j$).

Consider decompositions $\{(A, B), (\neg A, \textit{false})\}$ and $\{(A, B)\}$ of function $f = A \wedge B$. The first is an (A, B)-partition. The second is not. Decompositions $\{(\textit{true}, B)\}$ and $\{(A, B), (\neg A, B)\}$ are both (A, B)-partitions of function $f = B$. The first is compressed. The second is not since its subs are not distinct. A decomposition can be compressed by repeated replacement of elements (p, s) and (q, s) with $(p \vee q, s)$.

The following property of partitioned decompositions is responsible for many properties of SDDs.

Theorem 5.5   *Let $\circ$ be a Boolean operator and let $\{(p_1, s_1), \ldots, (p_n, s_n)\}$*

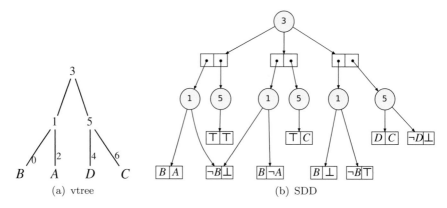

(a) vtree   (b) SDD

Figure 5.9 A vtree and a corresponding compressed SDD for function $f = (A \wedge B) \vee (B \wedge C) \vee (C \wedge D)$.

and $\{(q_1, r_1), \ldots, (q_m, r_m)\}$ *be* $(\mathbf{X}, \mathbf{Y})$-*partitions of* $f(\mathbf{X}, \mathbf{Y})$ *and* $g(\mathbf{X}, \mathbf{Y})$. *Then* $\{(p_i \wedge q_j, s_i \circ r_j) \mid p_i \wedge q_j \neq false\}$ *is an* $(\mathbf{X}, \mathbf{Y})$-*partition of* $f \circ g$.

According to Theorem 5.5, the $(\mathbf{X}, \mathbf{Y})$-partition of $f \circ g$ has size $O(nm)$, where n and m are the sizes of $(\mathbf{X}, \mathbf{Y})$-partitions for f and g. This is why SDDs can be combined using any Boolean operator in polytime. For an example, consider functions $f = A \vee C$ and $g = B \vee C$ and the corresponding $(\{A, B\}, \{C\})$-partitions $\{(A, true), (\neg A, C)\}$ and $\{(B, true), (\neg B, C)\}$. Theorem 5.5 gives $\{(A \wedge B, true), (A \wedge \neg B, true), (\neg A \wedge B, true), (\neg A \wedge \neg B, C)\}$ as an $(\{A, B\}, \{C\})$-partition for function $f \vee g$. This is not compressed since its subs are not distinct. We compress it by simply disjoining the primes of equal subs, leading to $\{(A \vee B, true), (\neg A \wedge \neg B, C)\}$.

SDDs can be made canonical due to the following result.

Theorem 5.6 *A function* $f(\mathbf{X}, \mathbf{Y})$ *has exactly one compressed* $(\mathbf{X}, \mathbf{Y})$-*partition.*

A canonical SDD representation for a Boolean function is obtained by recursively decomposing the function using compressed $(\mathbf{X}, \mathbf{Y})$-partitions and according to a given vtree.[9] Figure 5.9 depicts a vtree for variables A, B, C and D and a corresponding compressed SDD for the function $f = (A \wedge B) \vee (B \wedge C) \vee (C \wedge D)$.

We will now show how one can construct a canonical SDD representation of function f in Figure 5.9 using the vtree in the same figure. We start at the root of the vtree, $v = 3$. The *left* subtree contains variables $\mathbf{X} = \{A, B\}$ and

---

[9] The vtree was originally introduced in [57], but without making a distinction between left and right children of a node. For SDDs, the distinction is quite important however.

the *right* subtree contains $\mathbf{Y} = \{C, D\}$. Hence, we start by computing the unique compressed $(\mathbf{X}, \mathbf{Y})$-partition of function f, $\{(p_1, s_1), (p_2, s_2), (p_3, s_3)\}$, where

i	p_i	s_i
1	$A \wedge B$	*true*
2	$\neg A \wedge B$	C
3	$\neg B$	$C \wedge D$

This decomposition is depicted by the root node of Figure 5.9(b). That is, the decomposition is represented by a circle with outgoing edges pointing to its elements (numbers in circles identify vtree nodes). An element is represented by a paired box, where the left box represents the prime and the right box represents the sub. Each prime is decomposed recursively using the left child of the vtree root, $v^l = 1$, and each sub is also decomposed recursively, but using the right child of the vtree root, $v^r = 5$. This decomposition process continues until we reach Boolean functions that are over single variables (vtree leaves). There are exactly four different Boolean functions over a single variable X: X, $\neg X$, *true* and *false*. These are represented using *terminal* SDDs: literals, $\top$ for function *true*, or $\bot$ for function *false*. The constructed SDD is not only compressed, but also normalized.[10]

If one adjusts for notation, by replacing circle-nodes with or-nodes, and paired-boxes with and-nodes, one obtains a structured d-DNNF [57]. The SDD has stronger properties, however, since its decompositions are not only deterministic, or strongly deterministic, but also partitioned. Hence, SDDs form a strict subset of structured d-DNNFs, which result from using decompositions with stronger properties. What is interesting, however, is that using $(\mathbf{X}, \mathbf{Y})$-partitions in SDDs (instead of deterministic $(\mathbf{X}, \mathbf{Y})$-decompositions in structured d-DNNF) allows SDDs to be combined in polytime using any Boolean operator including conjoin, disjoin and negate.[11] On the other hand, structured d-DNNF currently support only a polytime conjoin.

SDDs are also a strict superset of OBDDs. The latter are obtained by using *right-linear vtrees* in which every left child is a leaf. Figure 5.10 depicts a right-linear vtree, a corresponding SDD, and the OBDD it represents once one adjusts for notation. Using a right-linear vtree forces $\mathbf{X}$-decompositions to be such that $\mathbf{X}$ is always a singleton. In this case, the $(\mathbf{X}, \mathbf{Y})$-partition

---

[10] There are other variations on SDDs, which are also canonical yet not normalized. See [26] for details.

[11] The polytime operations defined in [26] do not guarantee compression of the output though.

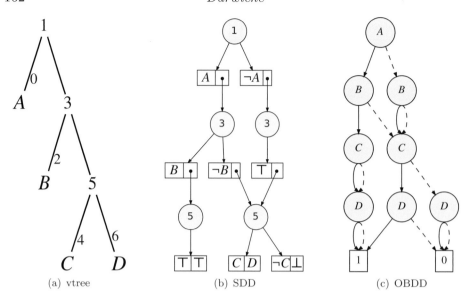

(a) vtree   (b) SDD   (c) OBDD

Figure 5.10 A vtree, SDD and OBBD for function $f = (A \wedge B) \vee (C \wedge D)$.

of a function f is binary and has the form $\{(X, f|X), (\neg X, f|\neg X)\}$. This is known as a Shannon decomposition of function f and this type of decompositions is known to characterize OBDDs. SDDs use arbitrary vtrees, however, leading to $(\mathbf{X}, \mathbf{Y})$-partitions in which $\mathbf{X}$ is a set of variables instead of being a singleton. Hence, the decompositions of an SDD are not necessarily binary. This explains the name, *sentential decision diagrams*, in contrast to *binary decision diagrams,* since the branching in SDDs is accomplished by evaluating sentential primes instead of evaluating binary primes (i.e., literals).[12]

5.7 The Process of Compilation

We now turn our attention to the process of compiling knowledge bases (KBs) into various subsets of DNNFs.

Compiling KBs is typically done using either a top-down or a bottom-up approach. A bottom-up approach implies an ability to perform transformations efficiently on compilations. For example, to compile a CNF, one needs to conjoin compilations that correspond to CNF clauses. The compilation

---

[12] More precisely, when using right-linear vtrees, the resulting SDDs correspond to what is known as *quasi-reduced OBDDs*. A quasi-reduced OBDD is a minimal-size OBDD that mentions every variable in its variable order in all paths from root to leaf (e.g., Figure 5.10(c)). Quasi-reduced OBDDs are also canonical, and are at most a factor $n+1$ larger than the corresponding reduced OBDD [67].

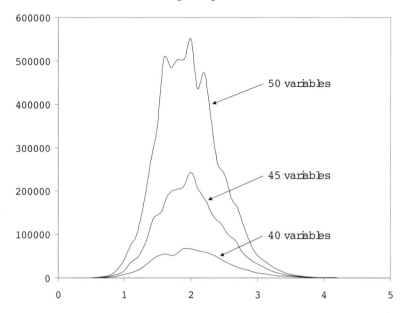

Figure 5.11 OBDD sizes of random 3-CNFs as a function of the clauses-to-variables ratio of the CNFs [42].

of KBs into OBDDs is traditionally done using a bottom-up approach, since two OBDDs can be efficiently combined using any Boolean operator (see Table 5.2). The main advantage of bottom-up compilation is that it usually works for any representation of the input KB. For example, to compile a DNF, one needs to first compile each term in the DNF, and then disjoin the compilations of such terms. Since two OBDDs can be disjoined efficiently, compiling DNFs into OBDDs lends itself well to bottom-up compilation. Another advantage of bottom-up compilation is that it can be done incrementally. This is critical for applications in which the whole KB may not be available initially, but is built up incrementally. Certain formal verification and planning applications have this property, making bottom-up compilation the only viable option. The main disadvantage of bottom-up compilation, however, is that it may yield some very large intermediate compilations, thus preventing it from compiling certain KBs whose intermediate compilations may be too large to allow the process to finish.[13]

---

[13] Figure 5.11 from [42] illustrates this problem in the context of compiling CNFs into OBDDs. This figure shows the size of OBDD compilations for randomly generated 3-CNFs, with varying clauses-to-variables ratios. Suppose for example that our goal is to compile a CNF whose clauses-to-variables ratio is around 3. In a bottom-up compilation of this CNF, one has to compile a subset of clauses that correspond to a CNF whose clauses-to-variables ratio is around 2. As this figure shows, such intermediate CNFs have much larger OBDDs than ones with ratio 3. One must therefore incur the time and space penalty associated with compiling such intermediate CNFs before one is able to compile the original CNF.

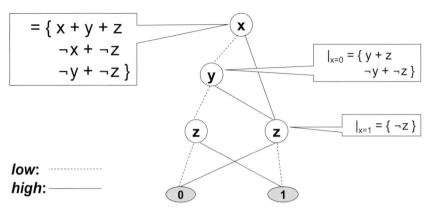

Figure 5.12 A CNF and its OBDD [42].

The alternative to bottom-up compilation is top-down compilation. In this approach, one operates on the full KB at once, recursively compiling conditionings of the KB and then combing the resulting compilations into a compilation for the original KB. This is best illustrated in the context of compiling CNFs into OBDDs as shown in Figure 5.12 from [42]. The figure depicts an OBDD compilation for a given CNF, showing a correspondence between nodes in the OBDD and conditionings of the CNF. For example, the root of the OBDD corresponds to the input CNF. One child of the root corresponds to conditioning the CNF on the negative literal $\neg X$, while another child corresponds to conditioning the CNF on the positive literal X. Top-down compilation will recursively compile each of these conditionings of the original CNF and then combines the result into an OBDD for the original CNF. Top-down compilation depends critically on the use of caching schemes, which attempt to ensure that equivalent conditionings of the CNF are not compiled redundantly. This is done by caching the results of finished compilations and checking the cache before attempting new compilations. For example, a specific caching scheme is detailed in [42], allowing one to compile CNFs into OBDDs in time and space that are exponential only in the *pathwidth* of given CNF.

Top-down compilation has also been to compile CNFs into more general subsets of DNNF. For example, a top-down algorithm is given in [24] for compiling CNFs into deterministic DNNF. The proposed method uses its own caching scheme and employs techniques for identifying independent components in conditioned CNFs, so they are compiled independently. A more general treatment is given in [43], showing how different subsets of DNNF, including OBDDs, FBDDs, and deterministic DNNF, can be compiled using top-down algorithms that are variations on the DPLL procedure used by satisfiability solvers. In particular, it is shown in this work that one can systematically build top-down compilers by keeping a *trace* of DPPL and variants.

Top-down compilation tends to require less space than bottom-up compilation as it does not suffer from the problem of intermediate compilations discussed earlier. This mode of compilation can also easily benefit from the vast set of techniques developed in the satisfiability literature [10], which can be used to simplify, decompose and cache conditioned CNFs before their compilation is attempted. The main disadvantage of top-down compilation is that it requires the original KB to be fully available before compilation can start. Moreover, all existing top-down compilation methods that have been explored assumes input KBs in CNF form. A good discussion on the relative merits of top-down versus bottom-up compilation can be found in [42], in the context of compiling CNFs to OBDDs.

5.8 Knowledge Compilation in Probabilistic Reasoning

This section is dedicated to the use of knowledge compilation in probabilistic reasoning, which turned out to be quite influential and currently underlies state-of-the-art methods for exact probabilistic inference (e.g., [18, 16]). The d-DNNF language is at the center of this usage since the polytime operations it supports are sufficient to efficiently implement probabilistic reasoning. Recall that d-DNNF is the language of NNF circuits that satisfy decomposability and determinism; see Figure 5.13. As it turns out, probabilistic reasoning can be reduced to weighted model counting and the latter can be implemented in polytime on NNF circuits that satisfy decomposability and determinism [60, 17].

As an illustration of this technique, consider the Bayesian network in Figure 5.14(a).[14] There are a variety of algorithms available for performing exact inference in such networks, including variable elimination [68, 29], the jointree algorithm [45, 48] and recursive conditioning [22], which have running time complexities that are generally exponential in the network's

---

[14] A *Bayesian network* (see, e.g., [25]) is an example of a *probabilistic graphical model* (see, e.g., [47]). A Bayesian network is a compact representation of a probability distribution and has two components. The first is a directed acyclic graph (DAG) in which nodes corresponds to variables of interest. The second component is a set of conditional probability tables (CPTs), one CPT for each node in the DAG. The CPT for node X with parents $\mathbf{U}$ specifies a conditional distribution for variable X given each instantiation $\mathbf{u}$ of its parents $\mathbf{U}$. Each CPT entry, typically denoted by $\theta_{x|\mathbf{u}}$, is called a *network parameter* and represents the probability of $X = x$ given $\mathbf{U} = \mathbf{u}$, that is, $\theta_{x|\mathbf{u}} = Pr(X = x | \mathbf{U} = \mathbf{u})$. In the Bayesian network of Figure 5.14(a), the CPT for variable A would have two parameters θ_A and $\theta_{\neg A}$. Moreover, the CPT for variable B would have four parameters $\theta_{B|A}$, $\theta_{B|\neg A}$, $\theta_{\neg B|A}$ and $\theta_{\neg B|\neg A}$.

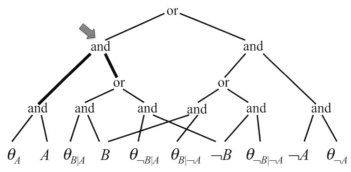

(a) **Decomposability:** Conjuncts do not share variables

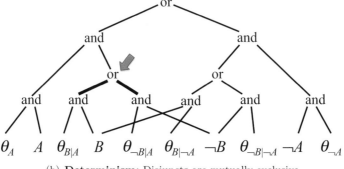

(b) **Determinism:** Disjuncts are mutually exclusive

Figure 5.13 Decomposability and determinism of an NNF circuit.

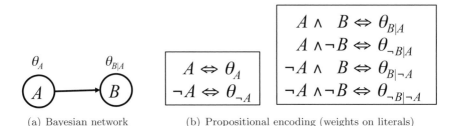

(a) Bayesian network   (b) Propositional encoding (weights on literals)

Figure 5.14 A Bayesian network and a propositional encoding. The weight of each literal $\theta_{\cdot|\cdot}$ equals the value of its corresponding parameter in the network. Each other literal (positive and negative) has weight 1.

treewidth (see, e.g., [25]). Consider now the knowledge base Δ in Figure 5.14. This knowledge base "encodes" the Bayesian network in the following sense. For any event α, the weighted model count of $\Delta \wedge \alpha$ equals the probability of event α. Hence, probabilistic inference on the Bayesian network can now be reduced to weighted model counting on the knowledge base Δ, which is equivalent to the d-DNNF in Figure 5.13. As such, probabilistic reasoning is now reduced to weighted model counting on this d-DNNF, which can be performed in time linear in its size (given its decomposability and determinism). This means that the only computational work needed for probabilistic reasoning is an ability to enforce decomposability and determinism on KBs that are expressed in CNF (Bayesian networks can be easily encoded as CNFs [23, 60, 17, 25]).[15]

The key advantage of the described approach is that it exploits local structure (i.e., the structure of parameters that quantify the network) in addition to the global structure (i.e., network topology). Given the current state of the art in exact probabilistic inference, any method that does not exploit local structure would have to be exponential in treewidth and is therefore not feasible on networks that are topologically too connected; see [18, 17] for some empirical results.

The above approach to exact inference based on knowledge compilation also applies equally to different probabilistic representations, such as Bayesian networks, Markov networks, and factor graphs. The only difference between all these representations is that each requires its own "encoding" into a propositional knowledge base. Hence, to apply this approach practically to a new probabilistic representation, all one needs to do is provide an "encoder" of that representation into an appropriate propositional knowledge base. For example, recently, the approach has been applied to reasoning with probabilistic logic programs using appropriate CNF encodings [38]. It has also been applied to lifted probabilistic inference, using a first order variant of d-DNNF [32].

The approach described in this section is supported by a publicly available software system known as ACE.[16] This system is based on two components: An encoder of Bayesian networks into CNFs, and a compiler called C2D which converts CNFs into d-DNNFs.[17] More recently, a new open-source compiler, called DSHARP, was released which can be one-to-two orders of magnitude more efficient than C2D on some benchmarks.[18]

5.9 Conclusion

As mentioned in the introduction, current research on tractable languages and knowledge compilation within AI has been mostly focused on two direc-

---

[15] In the encoding of Figure 5.14(b), Boolean variables are introduced for each network parameter. In general, variables in a Bayesian network do not have to be binary. Boolean encodings of these networks can still be developed in such a case (see [25] for a review of such encodings).

[16] The ACE system is available at `http://reasoning.cs.ucla.edu/ace/`

[17] The C2D compiler is available at `http://reasoning.cs.ucla.edu/c2d/`

[18] The DSHARP system is available at `http://www.haz.ca/research/dsharp/`

tions. The first is the identification of more languages and the study of their properties with respect to both tractability and succinctness. The second direction is the development of compilers that map propositional knowledge bases into tractable representations. It is our assessment that the emphasis within the community has been somewhat titled towards the first direction, while more work is needed to support the development of knowledge compilers. This objective can be strongly served by encouraging the practice of developing open source compilers. Experience has shown that developing scalable compilers typically requires a significant engineering effort, and can sometimes correspond to several years of investment. Open source compilers can help in making these investments available for the broader community to capitalize on. This can significantly speed up progress as it can encourage a larger portion of the research and development communities to join the effort of building compilers. This practice has indeed proved very effective in enabling the substantial progress made in other communities, such as the SAT community. Another bottleneck in this regard has been the lack of compilers that target multiple subsets of DNNF at once. For example, while one finds compilers for OBDDs and others for d-DNNFs, there are no publicly available compilers that incrementally enforce various properties on NNFs to systematically yield compilers of corresponding languages. The work in [43] provides some theoretical and practical foundations for building such compilers. We also believe that the recent notions of structured decomposability and $(\mathbf{X}, \mathbf{Y})$-decompositions provide another theoretical and practical step in this direction since these notions narrow the gap between various properties of NNFs and the computational techniques needed to enforce them systematically by compilers.

References

[1] Arvelo, Yolifé, Bonet, Blai, and Vidal, Maria-Esther. 2006. Compilation of Query-Rewriting Problems into Tractable Fragments of Propositional Logic. Pages 225–230 of: *AAAI06: Proceedings of the 21st National Conference on Artificial Intelligence.*

[2] Barrett, Anthony. 2004. From Hybrid Systems to Universal Plans via Domain Compilation. Pages 44–51 of: *Proceedings of the 14th International Conference on Automated Planning and Scheduling (ICAPS).*

[3] Barrett, Anthony. 2005. Model Compilation for Real-Time Planning and Diagnosis with Feedback. Pages 1195–1200 of: *IJCAI05: Proceedings of the 19th International Joint Conference on Artificial Intelligence.*

[4] Barwise, Jon (ed). 1977. *Handbook of Mathematical Logic.* North-Holland.

[5] Benedetti, M. 2006. Abstract Branching for Quantified Formulas. Pages 16–21 of: *AAAI06: Proc. of 21st National Conference on Artificial Intelligence.*

[6] Benedetti, M., Lallouet, A., and Vautard, J. 2007. QCSP made Practical by Virtue of Restricted Quantification. Pages 38–43 of: *IJCAI07: Proc. of 10th International Joint Conference on Artificial Intelligence.*

[7] Benedetti, Marco. 2005. sKizzo: A Suite to Evaluate and Certify QBFs. Pages 369–376 of: *CADE'20: Proceedings of the 20th International Conference on Automated Deduction*, LNCS, **3632**.

[8] Bienvenu, Meghyn, Fargier, Hélène, and Marquis, Pierre. 2010. Knowledge Compilation in the Modal Logic S5. Pages 261–266 of: *AAAI10: Proceedings of the 24th National Conference on Artificial Intelligence.*

[9] Biere, Armin. 2004. Resolve and Expand. Pages 59–70 of: *Proceedings of SAT'04*, LNCS bf 3542.

[10] Biere, Armin, Heule, Marijn J. H., van Maaren, Hans, and Walsh, Toby (eds). 2009. *Handbook of Satisfiability*. Frontiers in Artificial Intelligence and Applications, vol. 185. IOS Press.

[11] Blum, Manuel, Chandra, Ashok K., and Wegman, Mark N. 1980. Equivalence of Free Boolean Graphs Can Be Decided Probabilistically in Polynomial Time. *Information Processing Letters*, **10**(2), 80–82.

[12] Bonet, Blai, and Geffner, Hector. 2006. Heuristics for Planning with Penalties and Rewards Using Compiled Knowledge. Pages 452–462 of: *KR'06: Proceedings of the 10th International Conference on Principles of Knowledge Representation and Reasoning.*

[13] Bryant, Randal E. 1986. Graph-Based Algorithms for Boolean Function Manipulation. *IEEE Transactions on Computers*, **35**(8), 677–691.

[14] Cadoli, Marco, and Donini, Francesco M. 1997. A survey on knowledge compilation. *AI Communications*, **10**, 137–150.

[15] Chavira, Mark, and Darwiche, Adnan. 2005. Compiling Bayesian Networks with Local Structure. Pages 1306–1312 of: *Proceedings of the 19th International Joint Conference on Artificial Intelligence (IJCAI).*

[16] Chavira, Mark, and Darwiche, Adnan. 2007. Compiling Bayesian Networks Using Variable Elimination. Pages 2443–2449 of: *Proceedings of the 20th International Joint Conference on Artificial Intelligence (IJCAI).*

[17] Chavira, Mark, and Darwiche, Adnan. 2008. On Probabilistic Inference by Weighted Model Counting. *Artificial Intelligence*, **172**(6–7), 772–799.

[18] Chavira, Mark, Darwiche, Adnan, and Jaeger, Manfred. May 2006. Compiling Relational Bayesian Networks for Exact Inference. *International Journal of Approximate Reasoning*, **42**(1–2), 4–20.

[19] Coste-Marquis, Sylvie, Berre, Daniel Le, Letombe, Florian, and Marquis, Pierre. 2005. Propositional Fragments for Knowledge Compilation and Quantified Boolean Formulae. Pages 288–293 of: *AAAI05: Proceedings of the 20th National Conference on Artificial Intelligence.*

[20] Dalvi, Nilesh, Schnaitter, Karl, and Suciu, Dan. 2010. Computing Query Probability with Incidence Algebras. Pages 203–214 of: *Proceedings of ACM SIG-MOD/PODS Conference.*

[21] Darwiche, Adnan. 2001a. Decomposable Negation Normal Form. *Journal of the ACM*, **48**(4), 608–647.

[22] Darwiche, Adnan. 2001b. Recursive Conditioning. *Artificial Intelligence*, **126**(1-2), 5–41.

[23] Darwiche, Adnan. 2002. A Logical Approach to Factoring Belief Networks. Pages 409–420 of: *KR'02: Proceedings of 8th International Conference on Principles and Knowledge Representation and Reasoning*.

[24] Darwiche, Adnan. 2004. New Advances in Compiling CNF into Decomposable Negation Normal Form. Pages 328–332 of: *ECAI 2004: Proceedings of the 16th European Conference on Artificial Intelligence*, IOS Press.

[25] Darwiche, Adnan. 2009. *Modeling and Reasoning with Bayesian Networks*. Cambridge University Press.

[26] Darwiche, Adnan. 2011. SDD: A New Canonical Representation of Propositional Knowledge Bases. Pages 819–826 of: *22nd International Joint Conference on Artificial Intelligence (IJCAI)*.

[27] Darwiche, Adnan, and Huang, Jinbo. 2002. *Testing Equivalence Probabilistically*. Tech. Rep. D-123. Computer Science Department, UCLA.

[28] Darwiche, Adnan, and Marquis, Pierre. 2002. A Knowledge Compilation Map. *Journal of Artificial Intelligence Research*, **17**, 229–264.

[29] Dechter, Rina. 1996. Bucket Elimination: A Unifying Framework for Probabilistic Inference. *Artificial Intelligence*, **113**(1–2), 41–85.

[30] del Val, Alvaro. 1994. Tractable Databases: How to Make Propositional Unit Resolution Complete Through Compilation. Pages 551–561 of: *KR'94: Proceedings of the Fourth International Conference on Principles of Knowledge Representation and Reasoning*.

[31] del Val, Alvaro. 1995. An Analysis of Approximate Knowledge Compilation. Pages 830–836 of: *Proceedings of the 14th International Joint Conference on Artificial Intelligence (IJCAI)*.

[32] den Broeck, Guy Van, Taghipour, Nima, Meert, Wannes, Davis, Jesse, and Raedt, Luc De. 2011. Lifted Probabilistic Inference by First-Order Knowledge Compilation. Pages 2178–2185 of: *Proceedings of the 26th International Joint Conference on Artificial Intelligence (IJCAI)*.

[33] Elliott, Paul, and Williams, Brian. 2006. DNNF-based Belief State Estimation. In: *AAAI06: Proceedings of the 21st National Conference on Artificial Intelligence*.

[34] Fargier, Hélène, and Marquis, Pierre. 2007. On Valued Negation Normal Form Formulas. Pages 360–365 of: *Proceedings of the 20th International Joint Conference on Artifical intelligence (IJCAI)*.

[35] Fargier, Hélène, and Marquis, Pierre. 2008a. Extending the Knowledge Compilation Map: Closure Principles. Pages 50–54 of: *ECAI 2008: Proceedings of the 18th European Conference on Artificial Intelligence*, IOS Press.

[36] Fargier, Hélène, and Marquis, Pierre. 2008b. Extending the Knowledge Compilation Map: Krom, Horn, Affine and Beyond. Pages 442–447 of: *AAAI08: Proceedings of the 23rd National Conference on Artificial Intelligence*.

[37] Fargier, Hélène, and Marquis, Pierre. 2009. Knowledge Compilation Properties of Trees-of-BDDs, Revisited. Pages 772–777 of: *IJCAI'09: Proceedings of the 21st International Joint Conference on Artifical Intelligence*, Morgan Kauffman.

[38] Fierens, Daan, den Broeck, Guy Van, Thon, Ingo, Gutmann, Bernd, and Raedt, Luc De. 2011. Inference in Probabilistic Logic Programs using Weighted CNFs. Pages 211–220 of: *UAI-11: Proceedings of the 27th Annual Conference on Uncertainty in Artificial Intelligence.*

[39] Gergov, J., and Meinel, C. 1994. Efficient Analysis and Manipulation of OBDDs Can Be Extended to FBDDs. *IEEE Transactions on Computers*, **43**(10), 1197–1209.

[40] Giunchiglia, Enrico, Narizzano, Massimo, and Tacchella, Armando. 2006. Quantifier Structure in Search Based Procedures for QBFs. Pages 812–817 of: *DATE '06: Proceedings of the Conference on Design, Automation and Test in Europe.*

[41] Huang, Jinbo. 2006. Combining Knowledge Compilation and Search for Conformant Probabilistic Planning. Pages 253–262 of: *Proceedings of the 16th International Conference on Automated Planning and Scheduling (ICAPS).*

[42] Huang, Jinbo, and Darwiche, Adnan. 2005. Using DPLL for Efficient OBDD Construction. Pages 157–172 of: *SAT 2004, Proceedings of the 7th International Conference on Theory and Applications of Satisfiability Testing, Revised Selected Papers.* LNCS, **3542**.

[43] Huang, Jinbo, and Darwiche, Adnan. 2007. The Language of Search. *Journal of Artificial Intelligence Research*, **29**, 191–219.

[44] Huang, Jinbo, Chavira, Mark, and Darwiche, Adnan. 2006. Solving MAP Exactly by Searching on Compiled Arithmetic Circuits. Pages 143–148 of: *AAAI06: Proceedings of the 21st National Conference on Artificial Intelligence.*

[45] Jensen, F. V., Lauritzen, S.L., and Olesen, K.G. 1990. Bayesian Updating in Recursive Graphical Models by Local Computation. *Computational Statistics Quarterly*, **4**, 269–282.

[46] Jha, Abhay, and Suciu, Dan. 2011. Knowledge Compilation Meets Database Theory: Compiling Queries to Decision Diagrams. Pages 162–173 of: *ICDT'11: Proceedings of the 14th International Conference on Database Theory.*

[47] Koller, Daphne, and Friedman, Nir. 2009. *Probabilistic Graphical Models: Principles and Techniques.* MIT Press.

[48] Lauritzen, S.L., and Spiegelhalter, D.J. 1988. Local Computations with Probabilities on Graphical Structures and their Application to Expert Systems. *Journal of Royal Statistical Society, B*, **50**(2), 157–224.

[49] Marquis, Pierre. 1995. Knowledge Compilation Using Theory Prime Implicates. Pages 837–843 of: *Proceedings of the 14th International Joint Conference on Artificial Intelligence (IJCAI).*

[50] Marquis, Pierre. 2011. Existential Closures for Knowledge Compilation. Pages 996–1001 of: *Proceedings of the 22nd International Joint Conference on Artificial Intelligence (IJCAI).*

[51] Mateescu, Robert, and Dechter, Rina. 2006. Compiling Constraint Networks into AND/OR Multi-valued Decision Diagrams (AOMDDs). Pages 329–343 of: *CP 2006: Principles and Practice of Constraint Programming*, LNCS, **4204**.

[52] Mateescu, Robert, Dechter, Rina, and Marinescu, Radu. 2008. AND/OR Multi-Valued Decision Diagrams (AOMDDs) for Graphical Models. *J. Artif. Intell. Res. (JAIR)*, **33**, 465–519.

[53] McMillan, K.L. 1993. *Symbolic Model Checking*. Kluwer Academic Publishers.

[54] Palacios, Héctor, and Geffner, Hector. 2005. Mapping Conformant Planning into SAT Through Compilation and Projection. Pages 311–320 of: *Current Topics in Artificial Intelligence*, LNCS, **4177**.

[55] Palacios, Hector, Bonet, Blai, Darwiche, Adnan, and Geffner, Hector. 2005. Pruning Conformant Plans by Counting Models on Compiled d-DNNF Representations. Pages 141–150 of: *Proceedings of the 15th International Conference on Automated Planning and Scheduling (ICAPS)*.

[56] Papadimitriou, Christos H. 1994. *Computational Complexity*. Addison-Wesley, Reading, Mass.

[57] Pipatsrisawat, Knot, and Darwiche, Adnan. 2008. New Compilation Languages Based on Structured Decomposability. Pages 517–522 of: *AAAI'08 Proceedings of the 23rd National Conference on Artificial Intelligence*, Volume 1.

[58] Pipatsrisawat, Knot, and Darwiche, Adnan. 2010. A Lower Bound on the Size of Decomposable Negation Normal Form. Pages 345–350 of: *AAAI10: Proceedings of the 24th National Conference on Artificial Intelligence*.

[59] Reiter, Raymond. 1987. A Theory of Diagnosis from First Principles. *Artificial Intelligence*, **32**(1), 57–95.

[60] Sang, Tian, Beame, Paul, and Kautz, Henry. 2005. Solving Bayesian Networks by Weighted Model Counting. Pages 475–482 of: *AAAI05: Proceedings of the 20th National Conference on Artificial Intelligence*, Volume 1.

[61] Selman, Bart, and Kautz, Henry. 1991. Knowledge Compilation Using Horn Approximation. Pages 904–909 of: *AAAI91: Proceedings of the 9th National Conference on Artificial Intelligence*, Volume 2.

[62] Selman, Bart, and Kautz, Henry. 1996. Knowledge Compilation and Theory Approximation. *Journal of the ACM*, **43**(2), 193–224.

[63] Siddiqi, Sajjad, and Huang, Jinbo. 2007. Hierarchical Diagnosis of Multiple Faults. Pages 581–586 of: *Proceedings of the 20th International Joint Conference on Artificial Intelligence (IJCAI)*.

[64] Siddiqi, Sajjad Ahmed. 2011. Computing Minimum-Cardinality Diagnoses by Model Relaxation. Pages 1087–1092 of: *Proceedings of the 22nd International Joint Conference on Artificial Intelligence (IJCAI)*.

[65] Sieling, Detlef, and Wegener, Ingo. 1993. NC-Algorithms for Operations on Binary Decision Diagrams. *Parallel Processing Letters*, **3**, 3–12.

[66] Subbarayan, Sathiamoorthy, Bordeaux, Lucas, and Hamadi, Youssef. 2007. Knowledge Compilation Properties of Tree-of-BDDs. Pages 502–507 of: *AAAI07: Proceedings of the 22nd National Conference on Artificial Intelligence*.

[67] Wegener, Ingo. 2000. *Branching Programs and Binary Decision Diagrams: Theory and Applications*. SIAM.

[68] Zhang, Nevin Lianwen, and Poole, David. 1996. Exploiting Causal Independence in Bayesian Network Inference. *Journal of Artificial Intelligence Research*, **5**, 301–328.

PART 3

ALGORITHMS AND THEIR ANALYSIS

6

Tree-Reweighted Message Passing

Vladimir Kolmogorov

This chapter is devoted the problem of minimizing a function of discrete variables with unary and pairwise terms. The problem is NP-hard in general, but for some applications good results can be obtained with a certain Linear Programming (LP) relaxation of the problem. We focus on message passing algorithms that approximately solve this LP; they can tackle very large instances that occur in computer vision and other areas. In particular, we describe the Sequential Tree-Reweighted Message Passing (TRW-S) algorithm that shows good performance in practice. We also analyze properties of its fixed points and relate it to other message passing algorithms.

6.1 Introduction

This chapter is devoted to the problem of minimizing functions of the form

$$f(\boldsymbol{x} \mid \theta) = \sum_{u \in \mathcal{V}} \theta_u(x_u) + \sum_{(u,v) \in \mathcal{E}} \theta_{uv}(x_u, x_v) \qquad (6.1)$$

Here $(\mathcal{V}, \mathcal{E})$ is an undirected graph, $\theta_u(\cdot)$ and $\theta_{uv}(\cdot, \cdot)$ are unary and pairwise cost functions (sometimes called *potentials*), and x_u, for each node $u \in V$, is a discrete variable that takes values in a finite set $\mathcal{X}_u$. The value $x_u \in \mathcal{X}_u$ is called the *label* of node u, and the vector $\boldsymbol{x} = \{x_u \mid u \in V\}$ is called a *labelling*. The set of all labellings will be denoted by $\mathcal{X} = \otimes_{u \in V} \mathcal{X}_u$.

The problem above occurs in many fields of science and engineering. One prominent example is low-level computer vision. It is concerned with the following task: given an observed image corrupted by noise, infer some hidden properties for each pixel u, i.e. assign a value x_u from the set of possible labels $\mathcal{X}_u$ (which is usually the same for all pixels). The set $\mathcal{X}_u$ can be binary (e.g. $\mathcal{X}_u = \{background, foreground\}$ in a binary image segmentation problem) or multi-label (e.g. $\mathcal{X}_u = \{grass, sky, building, \ldots\}$ in object recognition, or $\mathcal{X}_u$ can be the set of discretized disparity values in the stereo matching problem).

Energy minimization has proved to be one of the most successful approaches for tackling such tasks. It can be motivated in a probabilistic framework: minimizing function (6.1) corresponds to computing a *maximum a posteriori* (MAP) labelling in a *Markov Random Field* [8] or a *Conditional Random Field* [22]. In computer vision applications $(\mathcal{V}, \mathcal{E})$ is often a regular grid graph with a 4- or 8-connected neighborhood system. We refer to [39] for a further discussion of the energy minimization approach in computer vision and computer graphics. Other application areas of this approach include statistical physics, signal processing, image processing, medical imaging and tomography, geophysics and remote sensing, circuit layout design, communication and coding theory, distributed estimation in sensor networks, and bioinformatics (see e.g. references in [12]).

Tree-reweighted message passing In general, minimizing the function $f(\cdot \mid \theta)$ is an NP-hard problem, so researchers have focused on approximate minimization algorithms. One prominent approach is to solve the following linear programming (LP) relaxation of the problem:

$$
\min \quad \sum_{u \in \mathcal{V}, i \in \mathcal{X}_u} \theta_u(i) x_{u;i} + \sum_{(u,v) \in \mathcal{E}, (i,j) \in \mathcal{X}_u \times \mathcal{X}_v} \theta_{uv}(i,j) x_{uv;ij} \tag{6.2a}
$$

$$
\text{subject to} \quad \sum_{j \in \mathcal{X}_v} x_{uv;ij} = x_{u;i} \quad \forall (u,v) \in E, i \in \mathcal{X}_u \tag{6.2b}
$$

$$
\sum_{i \in \mathcal{X}_u} x_{uv;ij} = x_{v;j} \quad \forall (u,v) \in E, j \in \mathcal{X}_v \tag{6.2c}
$$

$$
x_{uv;ij} \geq 0 \quad \forall (u,v) \in E, (i,j) \in \mathcal{X}_u \times \mathcal{X}_v \tag{6.2d}
$$

This LP has a polynomial number of variables and constraints, so in theory it can be solved in polynomial time. However, generic LP solvers cannot always tackle the typical instances with millions of variables that occur in practice [45]. Therefore, a lot of research has gone into designing specialized algorithms for solving relaxation (6.2). This chapter describes one such approach—*tree-reweighted message passing*, or *TRW* [42], and its *sequential* version called *TRW-S* [14]. TRW techniques are frequently used for MAP-MRF inference, and performed well in recent studies [45, 39].

To derive TRW algorithms, we will first formulate a lower bound on the function (6.1) by decomposing it into tree-structured functions. TRW algorithms will then try to find a decomposition that maximizes this lower

bound. This maximization problem can be viewed as dual to the minimization problem (6.2): their optimal values coincide.

Unfortunately, TRW algorithms are not guaranteed to find the optimal
bound: they may get stuck in a suboptimal point (although in practice this
is not always a problem). Fixed points of TRW can be characterized by the
weak tree agreement condition (WTA) described in section 6.4.2. Section 6.7
will describe a few related approaches that have the same stopping condition.

Outline The chapter is organized as follows. In section 6.2 we introduce
some basic notations, such as the formulation of the lower bound via convex
combination of trees. Then in section 6.3 we describe a generic form of the
TRW-S algorithm, and analyze its behaviour in section 6.4. We recommend
using a special case of the algorithm, namely TRW-S with *monotonic chains*,
described in section 6.5. A reader who wants to implement this technique
can skip sections 6.2 and 6.3 and go directly to section 6.6, which gives a
summary of the algorithm. Finally, we discuss a few related approaches in
section 6.7 and give conclusions in section 6.8.

6.2 Preliminaries

First, let us introduce some notation. Function $f(\boldsymbol{x} \,|\, \theta)$ is specified by unary
terms $\theta_u(i)$ and pairwise terms $\theta_{uv}(i, j)$. We will denote these terms as $\theta_{u;i}$
and $\theta_{uv;ij}$ respectively, so that θ can be viewed as a vector $\theta = \{\theta_\alpha \,|\, \alpha \in \mathcal{I}\} \in \mathbb{R}^d$ where the index set $\mathcal{I}$ is

$$\mathcal{I} = \{(u; i)\} \cup \{(uv; ij)\}.$$

Note that $(uv; ij) \equiv (vu; ji)$, so $\theta_{uv;ij}$ and $\theta_{vu;ji}$ are the same element. We
will use the notation θ_u to denote a vector of size $|\mathcal{X}_u|$ and θ_{uv} to denote
a vector of size $|\mathcal{X}_u \times \mathcal{X}_v|$. We define $\Phi(\theta) = \min_{\boldsymbol{x} \in \mathcal{X}} f(\boldsymbol{x} \,|\, \theta)$ to be the
minimum of the function defined by the parameter vector θ.

The following definition will play a central role in this chapter.

Definition 6.1 (Reparameterization)   If two parameter vectors θ and $\bar{\theta}$
define the same function (i.e. $f(\boldsymbol{x} \,|\, \theta) = f(\boldsymbol{x} \,|\, \bar{\theta})$ for all $\boldsymbol{x} \in \mathcal{X}$) then θ is
called a *reparameterization* of $\bar{\theta}$. We will write this as $\theta \equiv \bar{\theta}$.

Note that the condition $\theta \equiv \bar{\theta}$ does not necessarily imply that $\theta = \bar{\theta}$.
Indeed, consider a vector $m = \{m_{uv;j}\}$ with components $m_{uv;j} \in \mathbb{R}$ for each
directed edge $(u \to v) \in \mathcal{E}$ and label $j \in \mathcal{X}_v$.[1] (The subvector $m_{uv} \in \mathbb{R}^{|\mathcal{X}_v|}$

---

[1] Here and below we overload the notation slightly: we write $(u \to v) \in \mathcal{E}$ to denote a *directed*
edge of $(\mathcal{V}, \mathcal{E})$. In general, we always assume that condition $(u, v) \in \mathcal{E}$ implies $(v, u) \notin \mathcal{E}$ and
$(u \to v), (v \to u) \in \mathcal{E}$.

will be called a *message* from u to v.) It is easy to check that any such vector defines a reparameterization $\theta = \bar{\theta}[m]$ of the vector $\bar{\theta}$ as follows:

$$
\begin{aligned}
\theta_{u;i} &= \bar{\theta}_u + \sum_{(v \to u) \in \mathcal{E}} m_{vu;i} \\
\theta_{uv;ij} &= \bar{\theta}_{uv;ij} - m_{uv;j} - m_{vu;i}
\end{aligned}
\tag{6.3}
$$

In fact, any reparameterization θ of the vector $\bar{\theta}$ can be expressed via messages (assuming that the graph $(\mathcal{V}, \mathcal{E})$ is connected), i.e. $\theta \equiv \bar{\theta}$ implies that that $\theta = \bar{\theta}[m]$ for some message vector m; see [14, 44].[2]

The algorithms described in this chapter can be naturally viewed in terms of reparameterization. These algorithms start with the original parameter vector (which we will denote as $\bar{\theta}$) and apply iteratively certain reparameterization operations to $\bar{\theta}$. The goal of these operations is to maximize a lower bound on $\Phi(\bar{\theta}) = \min_{\boldsymbol{x}} f(\boldsymbol{x} \mid \bar{\theta})$; this lower bound is defined in the next section.

6.2.1 Lower Bound via Convex Combination of Trees

In this section we describe the lower bound on function (6.1) proposed in [41]. Let $\boldsymbol{\theta} = \{\theta^T \in \mathbb{R}^d \mid T \in \mathcal{T}\}$ be a collection of vectors indexed by a finite set $\mathcal{T}$ and ρ be a probability distribution on $\mathcal{T}$ (so that $\rho^T \geq 0$ for all T and $\sum_{T \in \mathcal{T}} \rho^T = 1$). Suppose that $\boldsymbol{\theta}$ is a *ρ-reparameterization of $\bar{\theta}$*, i.e.

$$
\bar{\theta} \equiv \sum_{T \in \mathcal{T}} \rho^T \theta^T.
\tag{6.4}
$$

The function $\Phi(\cdot)$ is concave, so by Jensen's inequality we have

$$
\sum_{T \in \mathcal{T}} \rho^T \Phi(\theta^T) \leq \Phi(\sum_{T \in \mathcal{T}} \rho^T \theta^T) = \Phi(\bar{\theta}).
\tag{6.5}
$$

Thus, the expression $\mathcal{L}(\boldsymbol{\theta}) \triangleq \sum_T \rho^T \Phi(\theta^T)$ is a lower bound on the function.

In general, this bound may not be very useful since computing it may be as hard as minimizing the function $f(\boldsymbol{x} \mid \bar{\theta})$. However, if the vectors θ^T correspond to tree-structured graphs then the values $\Phi(\theta^T)$ can be computed very efficiently (see next section). We will thus assume that each $T \in \mathcal{T}$ is a tree $T = (\mathcal{V}^T, \mathcal{E}^T)$ with $\mathcal{V}^T \subseteq \mathcal{V}$, $\mathcal{E}^T \subseteq \mathcal{E}$. The vector θ^T must respect the structure of T, i.e. it must belong to the set

$$
\Omega^T = \{\theta^T \in \mathbb{R}^d \mid \theta^T_\alpha = 0 \quad \forall \alpha \in \mathcal{I} - \mathcal{I}^T\}
$$

---

[2] If $(\mathcal{V}, \mathcal{E})$ is not connected, then θ can be expressed via messages up to a *constant parameter vector*, i.e. $\theta = \bar{\theta}[m] + c$ where $c_{u;i} = const_u$ and $c_{uv;ij} = const_{uv}$.

where $\mathcal{I}^T \subseteq \mathcal{I}$ is the set of indexes corresponding to T:

$$\mathcal{I}^T = \{(u;i) \mid u \in \mathcal{V}^T\} \cup \{(uv;ij) \mid (u,v) \in \mathcal{E}^T\}.$$

The goal will now be to find a vector $\boldsymbol{\theta} = \{\theta^T \in \Omega^T \mid T \in \mathcal{T}\}$ which is a ρ-reparameterization of $\bar{\theta}$ and gives the tightest possible bound (6.5). In other words, we will be interested in solving the following maximization problem:

$$\max \qquad \mathcal{L}(\boldsymbol{\theta}) = \sum_{T \in \mathcal{T}} \rho^T \Phi(\theta^T) \tag{6.6a}$$

$$\text{subject to} \quad \theta^T \in \Omega^T \qquad \forall T \in \mathcal{T} \tag{6.6b}$$

$$\sum_{T \in \mathcal{T}} \rho^T \theta^T \equiv \bar{\theta}. \tag{6.6c}$$

As shown in [41], see also [14], this maximization problem is dual to the LP relaxation (6.2):

Theorem 6.2 *Suppose that each edge $(u, v) \in \mathcal{E}$ is covered by a tree with non-zero probability, i.e. $(u, v) \in \mathcal{E}^T$ for some $T \in \mathcal{T}$ with $\rho^T > 0$. Then the optimal value of the maximization problem (6.6) coincides with the optimal value of the LP relaxation (6.2) for the function $f(\boldsymbol{x} \mid \bar{\theta})$.*

An interesting consequence of this theorem is that the optimal value of problem (6.6) does not depend on the choice of trees and their probabilities (as long as each edge is covered with non-zero probability).

6.2.2 Max-Product Belief Propagation

The bound described above requires the computation of $\Phi(\theta)$ where the vector θ corresponds to a tree-structured graph $T = (\mathcal{V}^T, \mathcal{E}^T)$. To perform this computation, we will use *max-product belief propagation* (BP) introduced in [24]. This technique is reviewed below.

The basic operation of BP is *passing a message* from node u to node v for a directed edge $(u \to v) \in \mathcal{E}^T$. To pass a message, we first compute

$$m_{uv;j} = \min_{i \in \mathcal{X}_u} \{\theta_{u;i} + \theta_{uv;ij}\} \qquad \forall j \in \mathcal{X}_v \tag{6.7a}$$

and then update vectors θ_v and θ_{uv} as follows[3]:

$$\begin{aligned} \theta_{v;j} &:= \theta_{v;j} + m_{uv;j} \\ \theta_{uv;j} &:= \theta_{uv;ij} - m_{uv;j} \end{aligned} \qquad \forall j \in \mathcal{X}_v. \qquad (6.7\text{b})$$

We will say that a directed edge $(u \to v)$ has a *valid message* if the values $m_{uv;j}$ computed in (6.7a) satisfy $m_{uv;j} = const_{uv}$ where $const_{uv}$ does not depend on j. In that case passing a message from u to v does not change θ_v and θ_{uv} (or changes them by a constant). We say that vector θ is in **normal form** if all edges have valid messages.

The BP algorithm keeps passing messages for edges in some order until convergence, i.e. until all edges have valid messages. If the graph contains loops then in general convergence is not guaranteed. However, for tree-structured graphs only two passes are needed to convert θ to a normal form: inward (sending messages from leaves to a root) and outward (sending messages from the root to leaves). Note that any node can serve as a root.

Min-marginals Let us define functions $\Phi_{s;j}, \Phi_{st;jk} : \mathbb{R}^d \to \mathbb{R}$ that give information about the minimum values of function f under different constraints:

$$\begin{aligned} \Phi_{u;i}(\theta) &= \min_{\boldsymbol{x} \in \mathcal{X}, x_u=i} \quad f(\boldsymbol{x} \mid \theta) \\ \Phi_{uv;ij}(\theta) &= \min_{\boldsymbol{x} \in \mathcal{X}, x_u=i, x_v=j} \ f(\boldsymbol{x} \mid \theta). \end{aligned}$$

The values $\Phi_{u;i}(\theta)$ and $\Phi_{uv;ij}(\theta)$ are called *min-marginals* for node u and edge (u, v), respectively. There is a close connection between BP and min-marginals, as the following proposition shows.

Proposition 6.3 ([41]) Suppose that vector θ corresponds to a tree-structured function. If θ is in a normal form then $\theta_{u;i}$ and $\theta_{uv;ij}$ give min-marginals for function $f(\cdot \mid \theta)$:

$$\Phi_{u;i}(\theta) = \theta_{u;i} + const_u \qquad (6.8\text{a})$$

$$\Phi_{uv;ij}(\theta) = \{\theta_{u;i} + \theta_{uv;ij} + \theta_{v;j}\} + const_{uv} \qquad . \qquad (6.8\text{b})$$

---

[3] Note, this description differs from the standard definition of BP: see [24]. The standard version maintains vector θ and messages $m = \{m_{uv} \mid (u \to v) \in \mathcal{E}\}$. The vector θ is not modified; instead, messages m are updated according to

$$m_{uv;j} := \min_{i \in \mathcal{X}_u} \{(\theta_{u;i} + \sum_{(w \to u) \in \mathcal{E}^T, w \neq v} m_{wu;i}) + \theta_{uv;ij}\}.$$

It can be seen [41] that the two versions are equivalent under transformations (6.3).

---

0. Initialize $\boldsymbol{\theta} = \{\theta^T \mid T \in \mathcal{T}\}$ so that $\theta^T \in \Omega^T$ for all $T \in \mathcal{T}$ and $\sum_T \rho^T \theta^T \equiv \bar{\theta}$.

1. Select some order for nodes and edges in $\mathcal{V} \cup \mathcal{E}$. For each element $\omega \in \mathcal{V} \cup \mathcal{E}$ find all trees $\mathcal{T}_\omega \subseteq \mathcal{T}$ containing ω. If there is more than one tree, then do the following:

   (a) For all trees $T \in \mathcal{T}_\omega$ reparameterize θ^T such that the values $\theta^T_{u;i}$ (if $\omega = u$ is a node) or $\theta^T_{u;i} + \theta^T_{uv;ij} + \theta^T_{v;j}$ (if $\omega = (u,v)$ is an edge) give correct min-marginals for the tree T as in formulas (6.8).

   (b) "Averaging" operation:

   If $\omega = u$ is a node in $\mathcal{V}$ then

   - Compute $\tilde{\theta}_u = \frac{1}{\rho_u} \sum_{T \in \mathcal{T}_u} \rho^T \theta^T_u$
   - Set $\theta^T_u := \tilde{\theta}_u$ for trees $T \in \mathcal{T}_u$.

   If $\omega = (u,v)$ is an edge in $\mathcal{E}$ then

   - Compute $\tilde{\nu}_{uv;ij} = \frac{1}{\rho_{uv}} \sum_{T \in \mathcal{T}_{uv}} \rho^T (\theta^T_{u;i} + \theta^T_{uv;ij} + \theta^T_{v;j})$
   - Set θ^T_u, θ^T_{uv}, θ^T_v for trees $T \in \mathcal{T}_{uv}$ so that $\theta^T_{u;i} + \theta^T_{uv;ij} + \theta^T_{v;j} = \tilde{\nu}_{uv;ij}$.

2. Check whether a stopping criterion is satisfied; if yes, terminate, otherwise go to step 1.

Figure 6.1 **Sequential tree-reweighted algorithm (TRW-S).** $\rho_u = \sum_{T \in \mathcal{T}_u} \rho^T$ is the node appearance probability, i.e. the probability that a tree chosen randomly under ρ contains node u. Similarly, $\rho_{uv} = \sum_{T \in \mathcal{T}_{uv}} \rho^T$ is the edge appearance probability.

6.3 Sequential Tree-Reweighted Message Passing (TRW-S)

In the previous section we formulated a lower bound on the function $f(\boldsymbol{x} \mid \bar{\theta})$ via a convex combination of trees, and formulated the maximization problem (6.6). Next, we present the TRW-S algorithm that attempts to solve this maximization problem. TRW-S maintains a vector $\boldsymbol{\theta} = \{\theta^T \mid T \in \mathcal{T}\}$ that satisfies all constraints (6.6), i.e. we always have $\theta^T \in \Omega^T$ for all $T \in \mathcal{T}$ and $\sum_T \rho^T \theta \equiv \bar{\theta}$. The main property of TRW-S will be a monotonic behaviour of the lower bound $\mathcal{L}(\boldsymbol{\theta})$: each step of the algorithm does not decrease this bound.

The algorithm is shown in Fig. 6.1. It iterates between two steps: (a) reparameterizing vectors θ^T and (b) averaging element $\omega \in \mathcal{V} \cup \mathcal{E}$. The goal of the reparameterization step is to make sure that the algorithm satisfies the *min-marginal property*:

- *At the start of the averaging operation for the element ω, the components of vectors θ^T corresponding to ω should give correct min-marginals for the trees $T \in \mathcal{T}_\omega$ (eqn. (6.8)).*

As we will see later, this property will ensure that the averaging operation does not decrease the lower bound.

Reparameterization step 1(a) can be implemented in many different ways.

One possibility is to convert the vectors θ^T to normal forms by running the ordinary max-product BP. However, this would be very expensive if the trees are large. A more efficient technique is discussed in section 6.5.

Remark 1 Tree-reweighted message passing algorithms were first introduced in [42], where the algorithms also perform tree reparameterizations and node/edge averaging operations, but in a different order[4]. The algorithms of [42] do not satisfy the min-marginal property; as a result, they may sometimes decrease the lower bound, which may lead to an oscillatory behaviour. The sequential version (TRW-S) with monotonicity guarantees was proposed in [14]. According to experiments in [14], TRW-S outperforms algorithms of [42] in practice.

6.4 Analysis of the Algorithm

In this section we discuss properties of TRW-S. First, we establish in section 6.4.1 that the lower bound never goes down. Then in section 6.4.2 we introduce the *weak tree agreement* condition (WTA), and show in section 6.4.3 that WTA characterizes the stopping criterion of TRW-S.

6.4.1 Monotonicity of the Lower Bound

Proposition 6.4 Every step of TRW-S does not decrease $\mathcal{L}(\boldsymbol{\theta})$.

Proof By construction, step 1(a) performs a reparameterization of the vectors θ^T; such an operation does not change the values $\Phi(\theta^T)$ and thus $\mathcal{L}(\boldsymbol{\theta})$. Let us consider the averaging operation 1(b) for element $\omega \in \mathcal{V} \cup \mathcal{E}$. For simplicity, we only consider the case when $\omega = u \in \mathcal{V}$ is a node (the case when $\omega = (u, v)$ is an edge is analogous). We write $\boldsymbol{\theta}$ and $\tilde{\boldsymbol{\theta}}$ for the vectors before and after the averaging operation for node u, respectively.

By the min-marginal property we have

$$\Phi_{u;i}(\theta^T) = \theta^T_{u;i} + c \qquad \forall i \in \mathcal{X}_u \tag{6.9}$$

where c is some constant. We claim that

$$\Phi_{u;i}(\tilde{\theta}^T) = \tilde{\theta}^T_{u;i} + c \qquad \forall i \in \mathcal{X}_u. \tag{6.10}$$

Indeed, let $\boldsymbol{x} \in \arg\min\{f(\boldsymbol{x} \,|\, \theta^T) \,|\, \boldsymbol{x} \in \mathcal{X}, x_u = i\}$ be an optimal labelling for

---

[4] [42] proposed two algorithms, which we refer to as TRW-T and TRW-E. The former iterates between two phases: (a) running max-product BP for *all* trees, and (b) performing averaging operation for *all* nodes and edges. TRW-E is similar, except that in phase (a) it performs one parallel message update operation for all trees.

function $f(\boldsymbol{x}|\theta^T)$ under the constraint $x_u = i$. The node-averaging operation does not change components θ_α^T for $\alpha \in \mathcal{I} - \{u; i | i \in \mathcal{X}_u\}$, therefore $\boldsymbol{x}$ remains an optimal labelling for the function $f(\boldsymbol{x}|\tilde{\theta}^T)$ under the constraint $x_u = i$. Thus,

$$\Phi_{u;i}(\tilde{\theta}^T) = f(\boldsymbol{x}|\tilde{\theta}^T) = f(\boldsymbol{x}|\theta^T) - \theta_{u;i}^T + \tilde{\theta}_{u;i}^T$$
$$= \Phi_{u;i}(\theta^T) - \theta_{u;i}^T + \tilde{\theta}_{u;i}^T = c + \tilde{\theta}_{u;i}^T$$

as claimed.

We can now write

$$\mathcal{L}(\tilde{\boldsymbol{\theta}}) \overset{(1)}{=} \sum_T \rho^T \min_i [\tilde{\theta}_{u;i}^T + c] \overset{(2)}{=} \min_i \sum_T \rho^T [\tilde{\theta}_{u;i}^T + c]$$

$$\overset{(3)}{=} \min_i \sum_T \rho^T [\theta_{u;i}^T + c] \geq \sum_T \rho^T \min_i [\theta_{u;i}^T + c] \overset{(4)}{=} \mathcal{L}(\boldsymbol{\theta})$$

where (1) and (4) follow from the definition of $\mathcal{L}(\cdot)$ and equations (6.9) and (6.10), equality (2) follows from the fact that $\tilde{\theta}_u^T = \tilde{\theta}_u^{T'}$ for $T, T' \in \mathcal{T}_u$, and equality (3) follows from the definition of the node-averaging operation. $\square$

6.4.2 Weak Tree Agreement

The algorithm in Fig. 6.1 does not specify what the stopping criterion is. In this section we address this issue by giving the *weak tree agreement* condition (WTA). Later we will show that it characterizes local maxima of the algorithm with respect to the function $\mathcal{L}$. More precisely, we will prove that the algorithm has a subsequence converging to a vector satisfying the WTA condition. Moreover, if a vector satisfies this condition, then the algorithm will not make any progress, i.e. it will not increase the function $\mathcal{L}$.

Let $\mathrm{OPT}(\theta^T) = \arg \min\{f(\boldsymbol{x}|\theta^T) | \boldsymbol{x} \in \mathcal{X}\}$ be the set of optimal labellings for the parameter θ^T. We define the WTA condition as follows.

Definition 6.5 A vector $\boldsymbol{\theta} = \{\theta^T\}$ is said to satisfy the *weak tree agreement* condition if there exists a collection of sets $\mathbb{S} = \{\mathbb{S}^T \,|\, \mathbb{S}^T \neq \varnothing, \mathbb{S}^T \subseteq \mathrm{OPT}(\theta) \,\forall T \in \mathcal{T}\}$ that satisfies the following two conditions:

(a) If node u is contained in trees T and T' then for every labelling $\boldsymbol{x} \in \mathbb{S}^T$ there exists a labelling $\boldsymbol{x}' \in \mathbb{S}^{T'}$ which agrees with $\boldsymbol{x}$ on node u, i.e. $x_u = x_u'$.

(b) If edge (u, v) is contained in trees T and T' then for every labelling $\boldsymbol{x} \in \mathbb{S}^T$ there exists a labelling $\boldsymbol{x}' \in \mathbb{S}^{T'}$ which agrees with $\boldsymbol{x}$ on nodes u and v, i.e. $x_u = x_u'$, $x_v = x_v'$.

A vector $\boldsymbol{\theta}$ is also said to satisfy the *strong tree agreement* condition if it admits a collection of sets $\mathbb{S}$ with the properties above such that $|\mathbb{S}^T| = 1$ for all $T \in \mathcal{T}$.

Clearly, if $\boldsymbol{\theta}$ satisfies the strong tree agreement with the collection of sets $\mathbb{S}$ then there exists the unique labelling $\boldsymbol{x} \in \mathcal{X}$ such that $x_u^T = x_u$ for all $u \in \mathcal{V}$, $T \in \mathcal{T}_u$ and $\boldsymbol{x}^T \in \mathbb{S}^T$. Furthermore, this labelling is a minimizer of function $f(\boldsymbol{x} \mid \bar{\theta})$ where $\bar{\theta} = \sum_T \rho^T \theta^T$: see [42]. It should be mentioned, however, that determining whether strong tree agreement holds (and computing the corresponding set $\mathbb{S}$ and labelling $\boldsymbol{x}$) is in general an NP-hard problem[5].

Note that the WTA condition is different from the *fixed point* condition of TRW algorithms. The latter means that any step of the algorithm does not change vector $\boldsymbol{\theta}$. This in turn implies that all vectors θ^T are in a normal form and $\theta_\omega^T = \theta_\omega^{T'}$ for every element $\omega \in \mathcal{V} \cup \mathcal{E}$ and for every pair of trees $T, T' \in \mathcal{T}_\omega$. It is easy to see that every fixed point of TRW satisfies the WTA condition, but not the other way around.

6.4.3 Convergence Properties

We are now ready to present convergence results for the TRW-S algorithm (proofs can be found in [14]). First, we establish that the WTA condition is indeed the stopping criterion for TRW-S.

Theorem 6.6   (a) *If the vector $\boldsymbol{\theta}$ does not satisfy the WTA condition then after a finite number of iterations the function $\mathcal{L}$ will increase.*

(b) *If the vector $\boldsymbol{\theta}$ satisfies the WTA condition with a collection $\mathbb{S} = \{\mathbb{S}^T\}$ then after any number of steps it will still satisfy WTA with the same collection $\mathbb{S}$. The function $\mathcal{L}$ will not change.*

As an immediate consequence of part (a) we get the following result:

Corollary   *If a vector $\boldsymbol{\theta}$ maximizes problem (6.6) then $\boldsymbol{\theta}$ satisfies the WTA condition.*

Unfortunately, the converse is not necessarily true; counterexamples can be found in [14] and [44].

Finally, we give the convergence theorem.

---

[5] This can be shown, for example, by casting the graph 3-colouring problem, which is NP-hard, as a minimization problem with the function $f(\boldsymbol{x} \mid \bar{\theta}) = \sum_{(i,j)\in\mathcal{E}}[x_i \neq x_j]$ where $[\cdot]$ is 1 if its argument is true and 0 otherwise. We can select $\theta^T = \{\theta^T\}$ such that $\theta_{u;i}^T = 0$ for all nodes and $\theta_{uv;ij}^T = c_{uv}^T \cdot [i \neq j]$, $c_{uv}^T > 0$ for all edges $(u,v) \in \mathcal{E}^T$. Clearly, a 3-colouring exists iff $\boldsymbol{\theta}$ satisfies the strong tree agreement condition.

Theorem 6.7   *Let* $\{\boldsymbol{\theta}^{(t)}\}_i$ *be an infinite sequence of vectors obtained by applying step 1 of TRW-S algorithm.*

(i) *There exists a bounded sequence* $\{\widetilde{\boldsymbol{\theta}}^{(t)}\}_t$ *which is a reparameterization of the input sequence, i.e.* $(\widetilde{\boldsymbol{\theta}}^t)^T \equiv (\boldsymbol{\theta}^t)^T$ *for all* $T \in \mathcal{T}$.

(ii) *Any such bounded sequence* $\{\widetilde{\boldsymbol{\theta}}^{(t)}\}_t$ *has a subsequence* $\{\widetilde{\boldsymbol{\theta}}^{(t(m))}\}_m$ *such that:*

(a) *it converges to some vector* $\boldsymbol{\theta}^*$ *with* $(\boldsymbol{\theta}^*)^T \in \Omega^T$ *and* $\sum_T (\boldsymbol{\theta}^*)^T \equiv \bar{\theta}$;

(b) *the sequence* $\{\mathcal{L}(\widetilde{\boldsymbol{\theta}}^{(t)})\}_t$ *converges to* $\mathcal{L}(\boldsymbol{\theta}^*)$;

(c) *the vector* $\boldsymbol{\theta}^*$ *satisfies the WTA condition.*

Note that since the algorithm does not specify exactly how we reparameterize the vectors $\boldsymbol{\theta}^{(t)}$, the sequence $\{\boldsymbol{\theta}^{(t)}\}_t$ may be unbounded, in which case it would not have a converging subsequence. For this reason we repameterized $\{\boldsymbol{\theta}^{(t)}\}_t$ into a bounded sequence $\{\widetilde{\boldsymbol{\theta}}^{(t)}\}_t$. Clearly, such a reparameterization does not affect the lower bound $\mathcal{L}$.

6.5 TRW-S with Monotonic Chains

In this section we focus on step 1(a) – the reparameterization of vector θ^T. Recall that its goal is to make sure that the algorithm satisfies the min-marginal property.

For simplicity, consider the case when $\omega = u$ is a node. In general, a complete inward pass of the ordinary max-product BP is needed for trees $T \in \mathcal{T}_u$ – sending messages from leaves to node u which we treat as a root[6]. However, this would make the algorithm very inefficient if the trees were large. Fortunately, a complete inward pass is not always necessary.

The key idea is that the averaging operation does not invalidate certain messages in trees T, as proposition 6.8 below shows. In other words, if a message was valid before the operation, then it remains valid after the operation[7]. Therefore, we can "reuse" some of the messages passed in previous steps, i.e. not pass them again.

Proposition 6.8   The averaging operation for element $\omega \in \mathcal{V} \cup \mathcal{E}$ does not invalidate messages in trees $T \in \mathcal{T}_\omega$ oriented *towards* ω.

---

[6] Note that the outward pass (sending messages from the root to leaves) is not needed. It would convert vector θ^T to a normal form but would not affect components $\theta_{u;i}^T$.

[7] Recall that the algorithm is message-free. As discussed in section 6.2.2, the phrase "message is valid for directed edge $(u \to v)$ in tree T" means that sending a message from u to v does not change the vectors θ_v and θ_{uv} (or changes them by a constant).

0. Initialize $\boldsymbol{\theta} = \{\theta^T\}$ so that $\theta^T \in \Omega^T$ for all $T \in \mathcal{T}$ and $\sum_T \rho^T \theta^T \equiv \bar{\theta}$.
1. For nodes $u \in \mathcal{V}$ do the following operations in the order of increasing $\pi(u)$:

   (a) Perform the averaging operation for node u.
   (b) For every edge $(u \to v) \in \mathcal{E}$ with $\pi(v) > \pi(u)$ do the following:

      - if $\mathcal{T}_{uv}$ contains more than one chain then perform the averaging operation for edge (u, v) so that vectors θ_u^T do not change.
      - for chains in $\mathcal{T}_{uv}$ pass a message from u to v.

2. Reverse the ordering: set $\pi(u) := |\mathcal{V}| + 1 - i(u)$.
3. Check whether a stopping criterion is satisfied; if yes, terminate, otherwise go to step 1.

Figure 6.2 **TRW-S algorithm for a graph with monotonic chains.** *For a description of node- and edge-averaging operations see Fig. 6.1.*

Proof Consider an edge $(u \to v)$ oriented towards w in tree T. The averaging operation can affect only the endpoint vector θ_v^T. Thus, components θ_u^T and θ_{uv}^T and values $m_{uv;j}$ in equation (6.7a) are not changed, and so the validity of message for the edge $(u \to v)$ is preserved. □

To exploit this property fully, we need to choose trees and the order of averaging operations in a particular way. Specifically, we require trees to be chains which are *monotonic* with respect to some ordering on the graph:

Definition 6.9 The graph $\mathcal{G}$ and chains $T \in \mathcal{T}$ are said to be *monotonic* if there exists an ordering of nodes $\pi : \mathcal{V} \to \{1, 2, \ldots, |\mathcal{V}|\}$ such that each chain T satisfies the following property: if $u_1^T, \ldots, u_{n(T)}^T$ are the consecutive nodes in the chain, then the sequence $\pi(u_1^T), \ldots, \pi(u_{n(T)}^T)$ is monotonic.

As an example, we could choose $\mathcal{T}$ to be the set of edges; it is easy to see that they are monotonic for any ordering of nodes. However, it might be advantageous to choose longer trees since the information might propagate faster through the graph.

The algorithm for a graph with monotonic chains is shown in Fig. 6.2. Its properties are summarized by the following lemma (its proof is given in [14]).

Lemma 6.10 *Starting with the second pass, the following properties hold during step 1 for node u:*

(a) *Consider node v with $\pi(v) < \pi(u)$. For each edge $(v, w) \in \mathcal{E}$ with $\pi(v) < \pi(w)$, messages $(v \to w)$ in trees $T \in \mathcal{T}_{vw}$ are valid. This property also holds for node $v = u$ in the end of step 1(b).*

(b) *Consider node v with $\pi(v) > \pi(u)$. For each edge $(v, w) \in \mathcal{E}$ with $\pi(v) <$*

$\pi(w)$, *messages* $(w \to v)$ *in trees* $T \in \mathcal{T}_{vw}$ *are valid. This property also holds for node* $v = u$ *at the start and at the end of step* 1(a).

In addition, property (a) *holds during the first pass of the algorithm.*

The lemma implies that starting with the second pass, all messages in trees $T \in \mathcal{T}_\omega$ oriented towards element $\omega \in \mathcal{V} \cup \mathcal{E}$ are valid at the start of the averaging operation for element ω. Therefore, passing messages from leaves to ω would not change the parameters θ^T (except for constants), so the algorithm satisfies the min-marginal property. Note that this property may not hold during the first pass of the algorithm; however, we can treat this pass as a part of initialization. Then the algorithm in Fig. 6.2 becomes a special case of the algorithm in Fig. 6.1.

Efficient implementation The algorithm in Fig. 6.2 requires $O(|\mathcal{T}_u| \cdot |\mathcal{X}_u|)$ extra storage for node u and $O(|\mathcal{T}_{uv}| \cdot |\mathcal{X}_u| \cdot |\mathcal{X}_v|)$ storage for edge (u, v). We now show how to reduce it to $O(|\mathcal{X}_u|)$ and $O(|\mathcal{X}_u| + |\mathcal{X}_v|)$ per edge (u, v), respectively.[8]

First, it can be seen that the algorithm maintains equalities $\theta^T_{uv} = \theta^{T'}_{uv}$ for $T, T' \in \mathcal{T}_{uv}$ (assuming that they hold after initialization). Second, in step 1(b) the averaging operation for edge (u, v) can be performed by simply averaging components θ^T_v for chains $T \in \mathcal{T}_{uv}$. This follows from the fact that before this operation we have $\theta^T_u = \theta^{T'}_u$, $\theta^T_{uv} = \theta^{T'}_{uv}$ for chains $T, T' \in \mathcal{T}_{uv}$ (the first equality is ensured by step 1(a)).

With these observations we can now describe an efficient implementation. Instead of storing all parameters $\boldsymbol{\theta} = \{\theta^T\}$, we will maintain only a *cumulative* parameter vector $\bar{\theta} = \sum_T \rho^T \theta^T$. This cumulative vector will be stored implicitly via messages $m_{uv} = \{m_{uv;j} \mid j \in \mathcal{X}_v\}$ for directed edges $(u \to v) \in \mathcal{E}^T$ according to the following formulas:

$$\hat{\theta}_u = \bar{\theta}_u + \sum_{(v \to u) \in \mathcal{E}^T} m_{vu}$$
$$\hat{\theta}_{uv;ij} = \bar{\theta}_{uv;ij} - m_{uv;j} - m_{vu;i}.$$

Node- and edge-averaging operations do not affect the cumulative vector $\hat{\theta}$ (and thus messages m_{uv}), so we only need to consider the message passing operation from u to v in step 1(b). At this point we have $\theta^T_u = \theta^{T'}_u$ for

---

[8] We assume that the storage required for the vectors $\bar{\theta}_{uv}$ is negligible. This holds for many energy functions used in practice, e.g. for functions with Potts terms.

---

0. Set all messages to zero.

1. Set $\Phi_{bound} = 0$.

  For nodes $u \in \mathcal{V}$ do the following operations in the order of increasing $\pi(u)$:

  - Compute $\widehat{\theta}_u = \bar{\theta}_u + \sum_{(w,u) \in \mathcal{E}} m_{wu}$. Normalize the vector $\widehat{\theta}_u$ as follows:

  $$\delta := \min_i \widehat{\theta}_{u;i} \qquad \widehat{\theta}_{u;i} := \widehat{\theta}_{u;i} - \delta \qquad \Phi_{bound} := \Phi_{bound} + \delta$$

  - For every edge $(u, v) \in \mathcal{E}$ with $i(u) < i(v)$ update and normalize message m_{uv} as follows:

  $$m_{uv;j} := \min_i \left\{ (\gamma_{uv}\widehat{\theta}_{u;i} - m_{vu;i}) + \bar{\theta}_{uv;ij} \right\}$$

  $$\delta := \min_j m_{uv;j} \quad m_{uv;j} := m_{uv;j} - \delta \quad \Phi_{bound} := \Phi_{bound} + \delta$$

2. Reverse the ordering: set $\pi(u) := |\mathcal{V}| + 1 - \pi(u)$.

3. Check whether a stopping criterion is satisfied; if yes, terminate, otherwise go to step 1.

Figure 6.3 Efficient implementation of the algorithm in Fig. 6.2 using messages. For a description of ordering $\pi(\cdot)$ and coefficients γ_{uv}, see section 6.6. At the end of step 1 value Φ_{bound} gives a lower bound on the function $f(\boldsymbol{x} \mid \bar{\theta})$. This value cannot decrease with time.

$T, T' \in \mathcal{T}_u$ and $\theta_{uv}^T = \theta_{uv}^{T'}$ for $T, T' \in \mathcal{T}_{uv}$, and therefore we get

$$\theta_u^T \quad = \quad \frac{1}{\sum_{T \in \mathcal{T}_u} \rho^T} \, \widehat{\theta}_u \quad = \quad \frac{1}{\rho_u}(\bar{\theta}_u + \sum_{(v \to u) \in \mathcal{E}^T} m_{vu})$$

$$\theta_{uv;ij}^T \quad = \quad \frac{1}{\sum_{T \in \mathcal{T}_{uv}} \rho^T} \, \widehat{\theta}_{uv;ij} \quad = \quad \frac{1}{\rho_{uv}}(\bar{\theta}_{uv;ij} - m_{uv;j} - m_{vu;i}).$$

With these equations we can calculate how the cumulative vector $\widehat{\theta}$ and message m_{uv} change in step 1(b). This results in the algorithm shown in Fig. 6.3. (We have introduced the notation $\gamma_{uv} = \rho_{uv}/\rho_u$ for a directed edge $(u \to v) \in \mathcal{E}$.)[9]

6.6 Summary of the TRW-S Algorithm

In previous sections we described several versions of TRW-S algorithm. For a practical implementation we recommend using the technique in Fig. 6.3. We now summarize various algorithmic details.

  The input to the algorithm is an objective function specified by parameter vector $\bar{\theta}$. The method works by passing messages; for each directed edge

---

[9] It was claimed in [14] that the algorithm in Fig. 6.2 maintains equalities $\theta_w^T = \theta_w^{T'}$ $(T, T' \in \mathcal{T}_w)$ for all nodes w. This claim was incorrect: sending a message from u to v may violate this equality for node v. The equality is only guaranteed to hold for nodes w with $\pi(w) \leq \pi(u)$, and in particular for node $w = u$, which is used in the argument above.

$(u \rightarrow v) \in \mathcal{E}$ there is message m_{uv} which is a vector with $|\mathcal{X}_v|$ components. Before running the algorithm we need to make the following choices:

- Select an ordering of nodes $\pi(\cdot)$ (i.e. a mapping of nodes in $\mathcal{V}$ onto the set $\{1, 2, \dots, |\mathcal{V}|\}$).
- Select chains $T \in \mathcal{T}$ which are monotonic with respect to $\pi(\cdot)$ (see definition 6.9). Each edge must be covered by at least one chain.
- Choose probability distribution ρ over chains $T \in \mathcal{T}$ such that $\rho^T > 0$, $\sum_T \rho^T = 1$.

These choices define coefficients γ_{uv} in Fig. 6.3 in the following way: $\gamma_{uv} = \rho_{uv}/\rho_u$ where ρ_{uv} and ρ_u are edge and node appearance probabilities, respectively. In other words, γ_{uv} is the probability that a tree chosen randomly under ρ contains edge (u, v) *given* that it contains u.

It can be seen that the algorithm in Fig. 6.3 requires half as much memory compared to traditional BP. Indeed, the latter needs to store messages in both directions for each edge, while we can store only messages oriented *towards* the current node u (or, more precisely, messages that are valid according to lemma 6.10). The reverse messages are not needed since we update them before they are used. The same space in memory can be used for storing either message m_{uv} or m_{vu}. The exact moment when m_{vu} gets replaced with m_{uv} is when edge (u, v) is processed during step 1 for node u. This observation can also be applied to traditional BP with the same schedule of passing messages – we just need to set $\gamma_{uv} = 1$.

Note that for many important choices of terms $\bar{\theta}_{uv}$ the message update in step 1 can be done very efficiently in time $|\mathcal{X}_v|$ using distance transforms [7]. Then the complexity of one pass of our algorithm is $O(|\mathcal{E}| \cdot K)$ where $K = \max_u |\mathcal{X}_u|$.

We conclude this section with the discussion of various implementational details.

Choice of node ordering and monotonic chains Automatic selection of node ordering for an arbitrary graph is an interesting open question, which is not addressed in this chapter. Intuitively, good ordering should allow long monotonic chains. The code in [15] implements a certain heuristic, but it can clearly be improved upon.

Given an ordering, we can construct monotonic chains in a greedy manner as follows. Let us select a monotonic chain such that it is not possible to extend it, i.e. for the first node u there are no edges (w, u) with $i(w) < i(u)$, and for the last node v there are no edges (v, w) with $i(w) > i(v)$. After that we remove corresponding edges from the graph and repeat the procedure until no edges are left. Thus, we ensure that each edge is covered by exactly one tree. All trees are assigned a uniform probability.

Although this method can produce different sets of trees depending on what chains we choose, the behaviour of the TRW-S algorithm is specified uniquely (assuming that the order of nodes is fixed). Indeed, the algorithm depends only on coefficients $\gamma_{uv} = \rho_{uv}/\rho_u$ for edges $(u \rightarrow v)$. It can be seen that the number of trees containing the node u is

$$n_u = \max \{ |(w, u) \in \mathcal{E} : i(w) < i(u)| , |(u, w) \in \mathcal{E} : i(w) > i(u)| \}$$

Therefore, we have $\gamma_{uv} = 1/n_u$.

Stopping criterion A conservative way for checking whether the WTA condition has been achieved follows from definition 6.5: keep adding optimal labellings to the set $\mathbb{S}^T$ until either $\mathbb{S} = \{\mathbb{S}^T\}$ satisfies conditions (a,b) of definition 6.5 or no more labellings can be added. This, however, may be expensive. As a practical alternative, we suggest the following heuristic criterion inspired by theorem 6.6(a): stop if the value of the lower bound Φ_{bound} has not increased (within some precision) during, say, the last 10 iterations. It is worth noting that even if WTA has been achieved and the lower bound no longer changes, the messages may still keep changing as may the configuration x computed from the messages.

One could also imagine other stopping criteria, e.g. fixing the number of iterations. Different criteria will lead to different tradeoffs between speed and accuracy.

Choosing a solution An important question is how to construct a solution x given a reparameterization $\widehat{\theta} = \sum_T \rho^T \theta^T$. A possible approach is to choose a label x_u for node u that minimizes $\widehat{\theta}_u(x_u)$. However, it can often be the case that the minimum is not unique within the precision of floating point numbers. This is not suprising. Indeed, if all nodes have a unique minimum then we have found the optimal solution, as shown in [42]. In general we cannot expect this since minimizing function (6.1) is NP-hard.

Thus, it is essential to understand how to treat nodes with multiple minima. In the code [15] we used the following technique. We assign labels to nodes in some order $\pi(u)$ (which in fact was the same as in the TRW-S algorithm). For each node u we choose a label x_u that minimizes $\widehat{\theta}_u(x_u) + \sum_{\pi(w)<\pi(u)} \widehat{\theta}_{wu}(x_w, x_u)$ where the sum is over edges $(w, u) \in \mathcal{E}$. In terms of messages, this is equivalent to minimizing

$$\bar{\theta}_u(x_u) + \sum_{i(w)<i(u)} \bar{\theta}_{wu}(x_w, x_u) + \sum_{i(v)>i(u)} m_{vu;x_u}.$$

This scheme alleviates the problem of multiple minima, but does not solve it completely. Many nodes may still be assigned essentially at random (more precisely, the solution is determined by numerical errors)[10].

6.7 Related Approaches

Due to its importance, the problem of solving the LP relaxation (6.2) continues to be a very active research topic. In this section we review a few recent developments in this area. We will focus on techniques characterized by the same stopping criterion as TRW algorithms, namely the WTA condition. As discussed in section 6.4.3, such techniques are not guarananteed to solve the LP relaxation – they may get stuck in a suboptimal point.

6.7.1 WTA-based Techniques

As with TRW algorithms, the approaches discussed in this section also try to maximize a lower bound on the function f. However, this lower bound is defined slightly differently:

$$\max \quad \mathcal{L}^\star(\theta) = \sum_{u \in \mathcal{V}} \min_{i \in \mathcal{X}_u} \theta_{u;i} + \sum_{(u,v) \in \mathcal{E}} \min_{i \in \mathcal{X}_u, j \in \mathcal{X}_v} \theta_{uv;ij} \quad (6.11a)$$

$$\text{subject to} \quad \theta \equiv \bar{\theta}. \quad (6.11b)$$

This formulation was proposed in [29]. It can be seen that $\mathcal{L}^\star(\theta) \leq \Phi(\theta) = \Phi(\bar{\theta})$, so $\mathcal{L}^\star(\theta)$ is indeed a lower bound on the function. Furthermore, the optimal value of (6.11) coincides with the optimal value of the bound (6.6), and thus of the relaxation (6.2).[11] The analogue of the WTA condition for the formulation (6.11) is known as *virtual arc consistency* [6]:

Definition 6.11 A vector θ is said to be *virtual arc-consistent* (VAC) if there exist non-empty sets $\mathbb{S}_u \subseteq \arg\min\{\theta_{u;i} \mid i \in \mathcal{X}_u\}$ for nodes $u \in \mathcal{V}$ and $\mathbb{S}_{uv} \subseteq \arg\min\{\theta_{uv;ij} \mid (i,j) \in \mathcal{X}_u \times \mathcal{X}_v\}$ for edges $(u,v) \in \mathcal{E}$ such that

$$\begin{matrix} \{i \in \mathcal{X}_u \mid \exists (i,j) \in \mathbb{S}_{uv}\} = \mathbb{S}_u \\ \{j \in \mathcal{X}_v \mid \exists (i,j) \in \mathbb{S}_{uv}\} = \mathbb{S}_v \end{matrix} \quad \forall (u,v) \in \mathcal{E}. \quad (6.12)$$

---

[10] This technique can be motivated by the following observation: if a reparameterization satisfies the WTA condition and the set of nodes with multiple minima consists of disjoint chains which are monotonic with respect to the ordering used, then the procedure will find a global minimum (see [23]).

[11] This can shown, for example, by considering the formulation (6.6) where the set of trees is chosen as the set of nodes and edges of the input graph: $\mathcal{T} = \mathcal{V} \cup \mathcal{E}$. Tree probabilities are chosen to be uniform: $\rho^T = const$ for all $T \in \mathcal{T}$. Define a mapping from solutions $\boldsymbol{\theta} = \{\theta^T\}$ of problem (6.6) to solutions θ of problem (6.11) as follows: $\theta_u = \rho^u \theta_u^u$, $\theta_{uv;ij} = \rho^{uv}(\theta_{u;i}^{uv} + \theta_{uv;ij}^{uv} + \theta_{v;j}^{uv})$. Clearly, this mapping is surjective, and preserves the value of the lower bound: $\mathcal{L}^\star(\theta) = \mathcal{L}(\boldsymbol{\theta})$.

The VAC condition inspired one of the early techniques for solving (6.11) – the **Augmenting DAG** algorithm: see[29, 21, 44]. Given the current reparameterization θ, the algorithm tries to find a proof that θ is virtual arc consistent by running the *arc consistency* algorithm. A failure to do so gives a sequence of reparameterization operations that strictly increases the lower bound. A detailed description of the algorithm and computational experiments can be bound in [44].

Equalization-based approaches Some algorithms try to find a reparameterization $\theta = \bar{\theta}[m]$ (see equation (6.3)) using a (block-)coordinate ascent scheme: at step t they take a subset of directed edges $\mathcal{E}^t$ and update messages $\{m_{uv} \mid (u \rightarrow v) \in \mathcal{E}^t\}$ to maximize the lower bound $\mathcal{L}^\star(\bar{\theta}[m])$ while fixing m_{uv} for $(u \rightarrow v) \notin \mathcal{E}^t$. In general, this maximization problem has multiple solutions m; among these solutions, the algorithms select m so that the vector $\theta = \bar{\theta}[m]$ satisfies certain "equalization" conditions for all edges $(u \rightarrow v) \in \mathcal{E}^t$. Two conditions have been considered in the literature:

$$\theta_{v;j} = \min_{i \in \mathcal{X}_u} \theta_{uv;ij} \qquad\qquad \forall j \in \mathcal{X}_v \qquad\qquad (6.13a)$$

$$\theta_{v;j} = \min_{i \in \mathcal{X}_u} [\theta_{uv;ij} + \theta_{u;i}] \qquad \forall j \in \mathcal{X}_v. \qquad (6.13b)$$

Condition (6.13a) is used by the following algorithms:

- **Max-sum diffusion algorithm (MSD)** of Kovalevski and Koval (approx. 1975); see [44]. It equalizes a single directed edge, i.e. $\mathcal{E}^t = \{(u \rightarrow v)\}$. ([44] also mentions that the algorithm can be adapted to the set $\mathcal{E}^t = \{(u \rightarrow v) \mid u \in \mathcal{N}(v)\}$ where $\mathcal{N}(v) = \{u \in \mathcal{V} \mid (u, v) \in \mathcal{E}\}$ is the set of neighbours of v.)
- **MSD++** ([37]). It performs a block-coordinate ascent over $\mathcal{E}^t = \{(u \rightarrow v), (v \rightarrow u)\}$ for a fixed edge $(u, v) \in \mathcal{E}$.

Condition (6.13b) is used by *Message-Passing Linear Programming (MPLP)* algorithms:

- **MPLP with edge-based updates**, or just **MPLP** (see [9], also [37] for an alternative presentation). Similar to MSD++, it uses $\mathcal{E}^t = \{(u \rightarrow v), (v \rightarrow u)\}$ for a fixed edge $(u, v) \in \mathcal{E}$. As shown in [37], MPLP outperforms MSD++, which suggests that equalization condition (6.13b) is preferable over (6.13a), i.e. it leads to faster convergence.
- **MPLP with node-based updates** [9, 37]. This uses $\mathcal{E}^t = \{(u \rightarrow v), (v \rightarrow u) \mid u \in \mathcal{N}(v)\}$ for a fixed node $v \in \mathcal{V}$. (Some equations in [9] contained a mistake which was corrected in [37]).

In all above cases the optimal update for m can be found in a closed form. Using techniques from [14] it is not difficult to show that the algorithms above have a convergence guarantee similar to that of TRW-S (theorem 6.7).

We also mention that an alternative convergence theorem for the MSD algorithm was given in [30]: it is proved that the quantity $\epsilon(\theta)$ goes to zero, where $\epsilon(\theta)$ is the minimum value of $\epsilon \geq 0$ for which θ satisfies the ϵ-*VAC condition*. The latter condition is defined similarly to the standard VAC, but instead of requiring $\mathbb{S}_u \subseteq \arg\min_i \theta_{u;i}$ one only needs $\theta_i \leq \min_{i'} \theta_{u;i'} + \epsilon$ for all $i \in \mathbb{S}_u$, and similarly for $\mathbb{S}_{uv}$. It is also conjectured in [44] that the MSD algorithm converges to a fixed point θ that satisfies the equalization condition (6.13a) for all edges $(u \to v) \in \mathcal{E}$, but this has not been proven yet.

Tree-block coordinate ascent A natural question is whether the block-coordinate ascent scheme is possible for larger sets $\mathcal{E}^t$. The case when $\mathcal{E}^t = \{(u \to v), (v \to u) \mid (u, v) \in \mathcal{E}^T\}$ corresponds to a tree $(\mathcal{V}^T, \mathcal{E}^T)$ in the input graph was considered in [36]. Two update schemes for maximizing the lower bound $\mathcal{L}^\star(\bar{\theta}[m])$ were proposed. Note, these update schemes do not enforce equalization conditions (6.13) for edges $(u \to v) \in \mathcal{E}^t$; it appears that in this case there is no closed-form solution for enforcing (6.13).

An appealing feature of the tree-block coordinate ascent approach is that trees $(\mathcal{V}^T, \mathcal{E}^T)$ can be chosen dynamically during the algorithm, using e.g. maximum spanning tree computations. Such a dynamic scheme was explored in [40]; on some instances it performed better than TRW-S with monotonic chains, and on others TRW-S was faster.

Remark 2 It is not difficult to see that TRW-S also performs a block-coordinate ascent on the function $\mathcal{L}(\boldsymbol{\theta})$. For example, the averaging step 1(b) for node $u \in \mathcal{V}$ fixes all components of $\boldsymbol{\theta}$ except for $\{\theta_{u;i}^T \mid T \in \mathcal{T}_u, i \in \mathcal{X}_u\}$ and updates parameters so that the objective $\mathcal{L}(\boldsymbol{\theta})$ is maximized and the ρ-reparameterization condition $\sum_T \rho^T \theta^T \equiv \bar{\theta}$ is preserved. The reparameterization step 1(a) for tree T fixes all components of $\boldsymbol{\theta}$ except for θ^T and performs a similar update. (Such update cannot change the value of the objective $\mathcal{L}(\boldsymbol{\theta})$.) Note, in general the maximum of $\mathcal{L}(\boldsymbol{\theta})$ is attained by many different vectors, as with the algorithms above, TRW-S chooses a very specific solution among them.

6.7.2 Properties of WTA

As we saw above, the WTA condition (or the related VAC condition) plays a prominent role in the study of LP relaxation (6.2): it provides a stopping criterion for many proposed algorithms. It is thus important to understand the theoretical properties of WTA/VAC conditions.

Recall that any vector $\boldsymbol{\theta}^*$ that maximizes the function $\mathcal{L}(\cdot)$ in problem (6.6) satisfies the WTA condition (corollary 6.4.3). Similarly, any maximizer θ^* of function $\mathcal{L}^\star(\cdot)$ in problem (6.11) satisfies the VAC condition. Unfortunately, the reverse is not true, i.e. the algorithms discussed above may get stuck in suboptimal points [14, 44]. This should not be surprising: a coordinate ascent for a function that is convex but not strictly convex does not always converge to an optimal solution.

Nevertheless, for some special classes of functions $f(\cdot \,|\, \bar{\theta})$ the WTA/VAC condition does correspond to an optimal solution of the LP relaxation. We discuss two such classes: (permuted) submodular functions and functions of binary variables. Below we always assume that the vectors $\boldsymbol{\theta}$ and θ satisfy the constraints of problems (6.6) and (6.11), respectively.

Submodular functions Suppose that $\mathcal{X}_u = \{1, \ldots, K_u\}$ for each node $u \in \mathcal{V}$. (Recall that $\mathcal{X}_u$ is the domain for variable x_u: $x_u \in \mathcal{X}_u$.) For labels $x_u, y_u \in \mathcal{X}_u$ write $x_u \wedge y_u = \min\{x_u, y_u\}$, $x_u \vee y_u = \max\{x_u, y_u\}$. The function $f(\cdot \,|\, \bar{\theta})$ is called *submodular*[12] if

$$f(\boldsymbol{x} \wedge \boldsymbol{y} \,|\, \bar{\theta}) + f(\boldsymbol{x} \wedge \boldsymbol{y} \,|\, \bar{\theta}) \leq f(\boldsymbol{x} \,|\, \bar{\theta}) + f(\boldsymbol{y} \,|\, \bar{\theta}) \qquad \forall \boldsymbol{x}, \boldsymbol{y} \in \mathcal{X}$$

where operations $\wedge$ and $\vee$ are applied component-wise.

Theorem 6.12 ([31, 44]) *Suppose that the function $f(\cdot|\bar{\theta})$ is submodular. If θ satisifes the VAC condition then θ is an optimal solution of problem (6.11), and furthermore $\mathcal{L}^\star(\theta) = \min_{\boldsymbol{x}} f(\boldsymbol{x} \,|\, \bar{\theta})$.*

Permuted submodularity It can be shown that operations $\wedge, \vee : \mathcal{X}_u \times \mathcal{X}_u \to \mathcal{X}_u$ (and thus the definition of submodularity) depend on the ordering of labels in $\mathcal{X}_u$. Schlesinger [28] considered the following problem: given a function $f(\cdot \,|\, \bar{\theta})$, decide whether there exists orderings of domains $\mathcal{X}_u$ for which f is submodular. It was shown that this problem can be solved in polynomial time, assuming that all costs are finite-valued. (When infinite costs are allowed, the tractability of this problem remains an open question.)

---

[12] For more on submodular functions see Chapters 3 and 10.

Functions f for which such orderings exists were called *permuted submodular*. Clearly, theorem 6.12 applies to permuted submodular functions as well.

Functions of binary variables Now suppose that each variable x_u can take only two labels: $\mathcal{X}_u = \{0, 1\}$. Then we have

Theorem 6.13 ([17]) *If a vector $\boldsymbol{\theta}$ satisfies the WTA condition then it is an optimal solution of problem (6.6), and thus $\mathcal{L}(\boldsymbol{\theta})$ is equal to the optimal value of LP relaxation (6.2).*

Thus, studying the WTA (or VAC) condition in the case $|\mathcal{X}_u| = 2$ is equivalent to studying the LP relaxation (6.2). It turns out that in this special case the relaxation has many interesting properties:

- It can be solved efficiently by computing a maximum flow in a specially constructed graph proposed in [4]. According to the experiments in [14], this is significantly faster than TRW-S.
- The vertices of the polytope defined by constraints of problem (6.2) are half-integral: $x_{u;i}, x_{uv;ij} \in \{0, \frac{1}{2}, 1\}$. Therefore, relaxation (6.2) has a half-integral optimal solution.
- The relaxation has the *persistency*, or *partial optimality* property that is, if $\{\hat{x}_{u;i}, \hat{x}_{uv;ij}\}$ is a half-integral optimal solution then there exists an optimal solution $\boldsymbol{x}^* \in \arg\min f(\boldsymbol{x}|\bar{\theta})$ of the original minimization problem such that $\hat{x}_{u;i} = 1$ implies $x_u^* = i$.

We refer to [3, 16] for a further review of these properties. Note, the persistency property for an equivalent LP formulation was first proved in [10]. In [17] this property was formulated in the context of the WTA condition.

Per-instance guarantees For general functions $f(\cdot|\bar{\theta})$ the properties described above are not guaranteed to hold. However, sometimes we can still get some guarantees for individual instances. Consider a vector θ satisfying the VAC condition with sets $\{\mathbb{S}_u, \mathbb{S}_{uv}\}$. The following theorem is a variation of the result given in [43]:

Theorem 6.14 *Let $\mathcal{U} = \{u \in \mathcal{V} \mid |\mathbb{S}_u| = 1\}$ be the set of nodes in $\mathcal{V}$ without ties, and let $\overline{\mathcal{U}} = \mathcal{V} \setminus \mathcal{U}$.*

(a) Suppose that each "boundary" edge $(u, v) \in \mathcal{E}$ with $u \in \mathcal{U}, v \in \overline{\mathcal{U}}$ satisfies

$$\theta_{uv;x_u x_v} = \min_{i \in \mathcal{X}_u} \theta_{uv;i x_v} \qquad \forall x_v \in \mathcal{X}_v. \tag{6.14}$$

Then partial optimality holds: there exists minimizer x of $f(\cdot|\theta)$ with $x_u \in \mathbb{S}_u$ for all $u \in \mathcal{U}$.

(b) *Let $\bar{x}$ is a labelling of $\overline{\mathcal{U}}$ which minimizes the function*

$$\bar{f}(\bar{x} \mid \theta) = \sum_{v \in \overline{U}} \left[\theta_{v;\bar{x}_v} + \sum_{\substack{(u,v) \in \mathcal{E} \\ u \in \mathcal{U}}} \min_{i \in \mathcal{X}_u} \theta_{uv;i\bar{x}_v} \right] + \sum_{\substack{(u,v) \in \mathcal{E} \\ u,v \in \overline{U}}} \theta_{uv;\bar{x}_u\bar{x}_v}. \qquad (6.15)$$

Suppose that condition (6.14) holds for $x_v = \bar{x}_v$. Then labelling x with $x_u \in \mathbb{S}_u$ ($u \in \mathcal{U}$) and $x_v = \bar{x}_v$ ($v \in \overline{\mathcal{U}}$) is a minimizer of $f(\cdot \mid \theta)$.

Proof Clearly, part (a) follows from part (b), so it suffices to prove the latter. We will denote labellings of $\mathcal{V}$ by $(z, \bar{z})$ where $z, \bar{z}$ are labellings of $\mathcal{U}, \overline{\mathcal{U}}$ respectively. For brevity, we will write $f(\cdot \mid \theta)$, $\bar{f}(\cdot \mid \theta)$ as simply $f(\cdot)$ and $\bar{f}(\cdot)$. We need to show that $(x, \bar{x})$ is a minimizer of $f(\cdot)$, where $x_u \in \mathbb{S}_u$ for $u \in \mathcal{U}$. Let us represent function f as $f(z, \bar{z}) = f^1(z) + f^{12}(z, \bar{z}) + f^2(\bar{z})$ where the first term contains unary and pairwise terms inside $\mathcal{U}$, the second term contains pairwise terms between $\mathcal{U}$ and $\overline{\mathcal{U}}$, and the last term contains unary and pairwise terms inside $\overline{\mathcal{U}}$. For an arbitrary labelling $(y, \bar{y})$ we can write

$$f(y, \bar{y}) = f^1(y) + f^{12}(y, \bar{y}) + f^2(\bar{y}) \geq f^1(y) + \bar{f}(\bar{y})$$
$$\geq f^1(x) + \bar{f}(\bar{x}) = f^1(x) + f^{12}(x, \bar{x}) + f^2(\bar{x}) = f(x, \bar{x}).$$

$\square$

Note that (6.14) is guaranteed to hold for all $x_v \in \mathbb{S}_v$ (since we have $(x_u, x_v) \in \mathbb{S}_{uv}$ from condition (6.12) and the fact $\mathbb{S}_u = \{x_u\}$). Therefore, condition (6.14) always holds when $|\mathcal{X}_u| = 2$ for nodes $u \in \mathcal{V}$, so theorem 6.14 can be viewed as a generalization of the persistency property described earlier.

Condition (a) in the theorem is stronger than condition (b), however it is much easier to check. We refer to [43] for computational experiments that use a slightly different version of these conditions. These experiments use a *junction tree* algorithm for computing a labelling of $\overline{\mathcal{U}}$.

6.7.3 Beyond WTA

There is a vast amount of literature devoted to the problem of minimizing functions of the form (6.1); message-passing techniques described above represent only a small fraction of possible approaches. Reviewing this body of work is outside the scope of this chapter; here we mention just a few papers.

One direction of research has been developing algorithms that are guaranteed to converge to an optimal solution of the LP relaxation (6.2). Examples include subgradient ascent techniques ([38, 32, 20, 11]), proximal projections ([25]), and Nesterov schemes ([13, 27]).

For difficult problems the LP relaxation (6.2) may not be very tight, and so applying TRW algorithms is unlikely to give good results. Tighter LP relaxations based on adding short cycles have been proposed in [35, 18, 1]. Alternative ways to tighten the relaxation can be found in [34, 33, 26, 46]; some of the approaches are applicable to binary problems only ($|\mathcal{X}_u| = 2$). Yet another direction of research has been incorporating lower bounds on the function into branch-and-bound or $A^\star$ search algorithms [6, 2].

Finally, we mention that there is a large body of work devoted to minimizing functions f with a special structure. Many proposed techniques are based on the *maximum flow* algorithm. A well-known example is the *alpha-expansion* algorithm ([5]) applicable when pairwise terms $\bar{\theta}_{uv}$ form a *metric*. (A faster version of this algorithm was developed in [19].)

6.8 Conclusions and Discussion

In this chapter we described several algorithms that try to solve the LP relaxation (6.2) by maximizing a lower bound on function $f(\cdot)$. Essentially, they perform a specialized (block-)coordinate ascent on the objective function $\mathcal{L}(\cdot)$ or $\mathcal{L}^\star(\cdot)$. An important limitation of these techniques is that they may get stuck in a suboptimal point characterized by the weak tree agreement condition (WTA). This fact should not be surprising: a coordinate ascent for a function that is convex but not strictly convex does not always converge to an optimal solution.

Despite this limitation, WTA-based techniques have proved to have a good performance in practice. For example, [39] studied inference problems that arise from several vision applications, and found TRW-S with monotonic chains to be among the top performing techniques. In another study ([45]) a particular version of TRW (parallel updates with damping) was shown to signficantly outperform LP solvers from the commercial CPLEX v0.9 package on the *stereo* and *side chain prediction* problems. In fact, TRW often produced a global minimum of function (6.1), sometimes with the help of the *junction tree algorithm* used in a post-processing step (which however took negligible time).

Several open questions in the context of TRW-S remain. At the moment it is only known that TRW-S has a limit point $\boldsymbol{\theta}^*$ that satisfies the WTA condition (under the boundedness assumption – see theorem 6.7); can one prove that TRW-S actually converges to a fixed point? If yes, what is the rate of convergence? On the practical side, how should one choose the ordering of nodes for TRW-S with monotonic chains to maximize the rate of convergence?

Acknowledgments I thank Thomas Schoenemann for proof-reading the manuscript, and spotting the bug described in the footnote on page 188.

References

[1] Batra, Dhruv, Nowozin, Sebastian, and Kohli, Pushmeet. 2011. Tighter Relaxations for MAP-MRF Inference: A Local Primal-Dual Gap based Separation Algorithm. *JMLR Workshop and Conference Proceedings*, **15**, 146–154.

[2] Bergtholdt, M., Kappes, J., Schmidt, S., and Schnörr, C. 2010. A Study of Parts-Based Object Class Detection Using Complete Graphs. *IJCV*, **87**(1–2), 93–117.

[3] Boros, E., and Hammer, P.L. 2002. Pseudo-boolean Optimization. *Discrete Applied Mathematics*, **123**(1-3), 155–225.

[4] Boros, E., Hammer, P. L., and Sun, X. 1991. *Network flows and minimization of quadratic pseudo-Boolean functions*. Tech. rep. RRR 17-1991. RUTCOR.

[5] Boykov, Y., Veksler, O., and Zabih, R. 2001. Fast Approximate Energy Minimization via Graph Cuts. *PAMI*, **23**(11), 1222–1239.

[6] Cooper, M.C., de Givry, S., Sánchez, M., Schiex, T., and Zytnicki, M. 2008. Virtual Arc Consistency for Weighted CSP. Pages 253–258 of: *AAAI'08: Proceedings of the 23rd National Conference on Artificial Intelligence*, Volume 1.

[7] Felzenszwalb, P.F., and Huttenlocher, D.P. 2004. Efficient Belief Propagation for Early Vision. Pages 261–268 of: *Proceedings of the 2004 IEEE Computer Society Conference on Computer Vision and Pattern Recognition*, Volume 1.

[8] Geman, S., and Geman, D. 1984. Stochastic Relaxation, Gibbs Distributions, and the Bayesian Restoration of Images. *PAMI*, **6**, 721–741.

[9] Globerson, Amir, and Jaakkola, Tommi. 2007. Fixing Max-Product: Convergent Message Passing Algorithms for MAP LP-Relaxations. Poster at: *NIPS 2007*.

[10] Hammer, P.L., Hansen, P., and Simeone, B. 1984. Roof Duality, Complementation and Persistency in Quadratic 0–1 Optimization. *Math. Programming*, **28**, 121–155.

[11] Jancsary, J., Matz, G., and Trost, H. 2010. An Incremental Subgradient Algorithm for MAP Estimation in Graphical Models. In: *NIPS 2010 Workshop on Optimization for Machine Learning*.

[12] Johnson, Jason K. 2008. *Convex Relaxation Methods for Graphical Models: Lagrangian and Maximum Entropy Approaches*. Ph.D. thesis, MIT.

[13] Jojic, V., Gould, S., and Koller, D. 2010. Accelerated Dual Decomposition for MAP Inference. In: *Proceedings of the 27th International Conference on Machine Learning*.

[14] Kolmogorov, V. 2006. Convergent Tree-Reweighted Messages Passing. *PAMI*, **28**(10), 1568–1583.

[15] Kolmogorov, V. 2009. `http://research.microsoft.com/en-us/downloads/dad6c31e-2c04-471f-b724-ded18bf70fe3/`.

[16] Kolmogorov, V., and Rother, C. 2007. Minimizing Non-submodular Functions with Graph Cuts – a review. *PAMI*, **29**(7), 1274–1279.

[17] Kolmogorov, V., and Wainwright, M. 2005. On the Optimality of Tree-reweighted Max-product Message Passing. In: *Proceedings of 21st Conference on Uncertainty and Artificial Intelligence*.

[18] Komodakis, N., and Paragios, N. 2008. Beyond Loose LP-relaxations: Optimizing MRFs by Repairing Cycles. Pages 806–820 of: *ECCV 2008: Proceedings of the 10th European Conference on Computer Vision*, LNCS **5304**.

[19] Komodakis, N., Tziritas, G., and Paragios, N. 2007a. Fast, Approximately Optimal Solutions for Single and Dynamic MRFs Pages 1–8 of: *CVPR '07: Proceedings of the IEEE Conference on Computer Vision and Pattern Recognition*.

[20] Komodakis, N., Paragios, N., and Tziritas, G. 2007b. MRF Optimization via Dual Decomposition: Message-Passing Revisited. Pages 1–8 of: *ICCV 2007: Proceedings of the IEEE 11th International Conference on Computer Vision*.

[21] Koval, V.K., and Schlesinger, M.I. 1976. Two-dimensional Programming in Image Analysis Problems. *Automatics and Telemechanics*, **2**, 149–168. In Russian.

[22] Lafferty, J., McCallum, A., and Pereira, F. 2001. Conditional Random Fields: Probabilistic Models for Segmenting and Labelling Sequence Data. Pages 282–289 of: *ICML '01: Proceedings of the 18th International Conference on Machine Learning*, Morgan Kauffman.

[23] Meltzer, T., Yanover, C., and Weiss, Y. 2005. Globally Optimal Solutions for Energy Minimization in Stereo Vision using Reweighted Belief Propagation. Pages 428–435 of: *ICCV '05: Proceedings of the Tenth IEEE International Conference on Computer Vision*, Volume 1.

[24] Pearl, J. 1988. *Probabilistic Reasoning in Intelligent Systems: Networks of Plausible Inference*. Morgan Kaufmann.

[25] Ravikumar, P., Agarwal, A., and Wainwright, M.J. 2010. Message-passing for Graph-structured Linear Programs: Proximal Projections, Convergence, and Rounding Schemes. *JMLR*, **11**, 1043–1080.

[26] Reddi, Sashank Jakkam, Sarawagi, Sunita, and Vishwanathan, Sundar. 2010. MAP estimation in Binary MRFs via Bipartite Multi-cuts. Pages 955–963 of: *Advances in Neural Information Processing Systems*, **23**.

[27] Savchynskyy, B., Kappes, J. H., Schmidt, S., and Schnörr, C. 2011. A Study of Nesterov's Scheme for Lagrangian Decomposition and MAP Labeling. Pages 1817–1823 of: *CVPR 2011: IEEE Conference on Computer Vision and Pattern Recognition*.

[28] Schlesinger, D. 2007. Exact Solution of Permuted Submodular MinSum Problems. Pages 28–38 of: *Energy Minimization Methods in Computer Vision and Pattern Recognition*, LNCS **4679**.

[29] Schlesinger, M.I. 1976. Syntactic Analysis of Two-dimensional Visual Signals in Noisy Conditions. *Kibernetika*, **4**, 113–130. In Russian.

[30] Schlesinger, M.I., and Antoniuk, K.V. 2011. Diffusion Algorithms and Structural Recognition Optimization Problems. *Cybernetics and Systems Analysis*, **47**(2), 175–192.

[31] Schlesinger, M.I., and Flach, B. 2000. Some Solvable Subclasses of Structural Recognition Problems. In: *Czech Patt. Recog. Workshop*.

[32] Schlesinger, M.I., and Giginyak, V.V. 2007. Solution to Structural Recognition (MAX,+)-problems by their Equivalent Transformations. *Control Systems and Computers*, (1), 3–15; (2), 3–18.

[33] Schraudolph, N.N. 2010. Polynomial-Time Exact Inference in NP-Hard Binary MRFs via Reweighted Perfect Matching. *JMLR, Workshop and Conference Proceedings*, **9**, 717–724.

[34] Sontag, D., and Jaakkola, T. 2007. New Outer Bounds on the Marginal Polytope. Pages 1393–1400 of: *Advances in Neural Information Processing Systems* **20**.

[35] Sontag, D., Meltzer, T., Globerson, A., Weiss, Y., and Jaakkola, T. 2008. Tightening LP Relaxations for MAP using Message Passing. Pages 503–510 of: *Proceedings of the International Conference on Uncertainty in Artificial Intelligence*.

[36] Sontag, David, and Jaakkola, Tommi. 2009. Tree Block Coordinate Descent for MAP in Graphical Models. Pages 544–551 of: *JMLR Workshop and Conference Proceedings*, **5**, 544–551.

[37] Sontag, David, Globerson, Amir, and Jaakkola, Tommi. 2011. Introduction to Dual Decomposition for Inference. In: *Optimization for Machine Learning*, Sra, Suvrit, Nowozin, Sebastian, and Wright, Stephen J. (eds). MIT Press.

[38] Storvik, Geir, and Dahl, Geir. 2000. Lagrangian-Based Methods for Finding MAP. *IEEE Trans. on Image Processing*, **9**(3), 469–479.

[39] Szeliski, R., Zabih, R., Scharstein, D., Veskler, O., Kolmogorov, V., Agarwala, A., Tappen, M., and Rother, C. 2008. A Comparative Study of Energy Minimization Methods for Markov Random Fields with Smoothness-Based Priors. *PAMI*, **30**(6), 1068–1080.

[40] Tarlow, D., Batra, D., Kohli, P., and Kolmogorov, V. 2011. Dynamic Tree Block Coordinate Ascent. Pages 113–120 of: *ICML 2011: Proceedings of the 28th International Conference on Machine Learning*.

[41] Wainwright, M. J., Jaakkola, T. S., and Willsky, A. S. 2004. Tree consistency and bounds on the performance of the max-product algorithm and its generalizations. *Statistics and Computing*, **14**(2), 143–166.

[42] Wainwright, M. J., Jaakkola, T. S., and Willsky, A. S. 2005. MAP estimation via agreement on (hyper)trees: Message-passing and linear-programming approaches. *IEEE Transactions on Information Theory*, **51**(11), 3697–3717.

[43] Weiss, Y., Yanover, C., and Meltzer, T. 2007. MAP Estimation, Linear Programming and Belief Propagation with Convex Free Energies. Pages 416–425 of: *Proceedings of the International Conference on Uncertainty in Artificial Intelligence*.

[44] Werner, T. 2007. A Linear Programming Approach to Max-sum Problem: A Review. *PAMI*, **29**(7), 1165–1179.

[45] Yanover, Chen, Meltzer, Talya, and Weiss, Yair. 2006. Linear Programming Relaxations and Belief Propagation – an Empirical Study. *JMLR*, **7**, 1887–1907.

[46] Yarkony, J., Morshed, R., Ihler, A., and Fowlkes, C. 2011. Tightening MRF Relaxations with Planar Subproblems. Pages 770–777 of: *Proceedings of the International Conference on Uncertainty in Artificial Intelligence*.

7

Tractable Optimization in Machine Learning

Suvrit Sra[a]

Machine learning and data analysis have driven explosive growth in interest in the methods of large-scale optimization. Many commonly used techniques such as stochastic-gradients date back several decades, but owing to their practical success they have gained great importance in machine learning. Before interior point methods totally dominated the field of optimization, first-order methods had already been studied and theoretically analyzed in substantial detail. But interest in these techniques skyrocketed after the prolific rise of applications in machine learning, signal processing, etc. This chapter is a brief introduction to this vast and flourishing area of large-scale optimization.

7.1 Introduction

Machine Learning (ML) broadly encompasses a variety of adaptive, autonomous, and intelligent tasks where one must "learn" to predict from observations and feedback. Throughout its evolution, ML has drawn heavily and successfully on optimization algorithms; this relation to optimization is not surprising as "learning" and "adapting" ultimately involve problems where some quality function must be optimized.

But the interaction between ML and optimization is now undergoing rapid change. The increased size, complexity, and variety of ML problems, not only prompts a refinement of existing optimization techniques, but also spurs development of new methods tuned to the specific needs of ML applications.[1]

In particular, ML applications must usually cope with large-scale data, which forces us to prefer "simpler," perhaps less accurate but more scalable algorithms. Such methods can also crunch through more data, and may actually be better suited for learning – for a more precise characterization

[a] Part of this work completed while the author was visiting the EE Department at the University of Washington, Seattle.
[1] This viewpoint is not limited to ML; other domains that deal with large-scale data (e.g., bioinformatics, astroinformatics, signal processing) face similar concerns.

see [11]. The use of possibly less accurate methods is also grounded in pragmatic concerns: modeling limitations, observational noise, uncertainty, and computational errors are pervasive in real data. Hence, trusting more than a few digits of numerical accuracy would be unrealistic. From an engineering perspective, simpler algorithms translate into more reliable software that is easier to implement, debug, and deploy.

Before we get carried away by these benefits, we must recall a sobering statement of Nesterov [39]: *"in general, optimization problems are unsolvable."* In other words, obtaining globally optimal solutions is in general intractable. Fortunately, nature makes a generous exception for *convex optimization*, which is not only tractable [35] but also widely applicable [12].

We therefore limit our attention to convex optimization, particularly focusing on algorithms that are simple, scalable, and amenable to theoretical analysis that characterizes their tractability.

It is inevitable that an overview such as this has to be superficial. Nevertheless, we hope that it still provides a quick entry into large-scale convex optimization for newcomers, while offering pointers to literature that more experienced readers may find useful.

7.2 Background

A generic convex optimization problem may be written as

$$\min \quad \phi(\boldsymbol{x}) \quad \text{subject to } \boldsymbol{x} \in \mathcal{X}, \tag{7.1}$$

where $\phi : \mathbb{R}^n \to \mathbb{R}$ is a proper convex function, also called the *cost* or *objective function*, and $\mathcal{X}$ is a nonempty, compact convex set, also called the *constraint* or *feasible set*. In this chapter, we talk less about casting ML problems into the form (7.1); we focus more on algorithms for solving important instances of (7.1).

Example 7.1 (NNLS) Suppose we wish to estimate a nonnegative signal (e.g., frequency, probability, intensity) from a noisy measurement; for simplicity, assume that the measurement process is linear. Let the measurement be given by vector $\boldsymbol{b} \in \mathbb{R}^m$, and the linear process be encoded by a matrix $\boldsymbol{A} \in \mathbb{R}^{m \times n}$. We wish to estimate an underlying nonnegative signal $\boldsymbol{x}$ that satisfies $\boldsymbol{b} \approx \boldsymbol{A}\boldsymbol{x}$. Assuming the noise to be additive and Gaussian, we may estimate $\boldsymbol{x}$ by solving the *nonnegative least-squares* (NNLS) problem:

$$\min_{\boldsymbol{x}} \quad \|\boldsymbol{A}\boldsymbol{x} - \boldsymbol{b}\|^2, \quad \text{s.t.} \quad \boldsymbol{x} \geq 0, \tag{7.2}$$

which is essentially (since its solution is bounded) of the form (7.1).

To avoid triviality, assume that (7.1) has a solution: that is, there exists a point $\boldsymbol{x}^* \in \mathcal{X}$ for which $\phi(\boldsymbol{x}^*) \leq \phi(\boldsymbol{x})$ for all $\boldsymbol{x} \in \mathcal{X}$ (compactly, $\phi^* \leq \phi$). Ideally, the goal of an optimization algorithm is to compute $\boldsymbol{x}^*$, but

Figure 7.1 Noiseless and noisy first-order oracles. The noisy oracle returns values perturbed by mean-zero bounded variance noise. More generally, these oracles may receive / use any of their previous inputs or outputs when creating an output for the current $\boldsymbol{x}$.

almost always it is impossible to compute an *exact* $\boldsymbol{x}^*$ in finite time. Thus, we speak of "ϵ-accuracy," a term whose meaning may vary. Consider for instance, an *unconstrained* version of (7.1) where $\mathcal{X} = \mathbb{R}^n$. For differentiable ϕ, the condition $\nabla\phi(\boldsymbol{x}^*) = 0$ is necessary and sufficient for $\boldsymbol{x}^*$ to be a global minimizer. So an ϵ-accurate solution could be a point $\bar{\boldsymbol{x}}$, for which $\|\nabla\phi(\bar{\boldsymbol{x}})\| \le \epsilon$ (we use $\|\boldsymbol{x}\| := \sqrt{\sum_i x_i^2}$). Alternatively, we may seek a point $\bar{\boldsymbol{x}}$ for which $\|\bar{\boldsymbol{x}} - \boldsymbol{x}^*\| \le \epsilon$, or maybe just $\phi(\bar{\boldsymbol{x}}) - \phi(\boldsymbol{x}^*) \le \epsilon$.

Intuitively, the tighter the accuracy ϵ, the harder it will be to compute an ϵ-accurate solution. Can this notion be made precise? Are there algorithms that can actually compute such solutions? These questions lie at the heart of the complexity theory of convex optimization, as pioneered by Yudin and Nemirovskii [69]; see also [35, 46]. For a nice historical account see [63].

7.2.1 Information-Based Complexity

Observe that since we are working over the reals, the usual Turing machine-based complexity analysis does not apply. It is more convenient to perform *information-based* complexity analysis using an *oracle model* of computation. More specifically, we consider algorithms that optimize (7.1) iteratively; at each iteration the algorithm queries a *first-order oracle*[2] using its current guess $\boldsymbol{x}$; the oracle responds by outputting the pair $(\phi(\boldsymbol{x}), \phi'(\boldsymbol{x}))$ – here ϕ' denotes the gradient $\nabla\phi$ for differentiable ϕ, or a subgradient from the sub-differential[3] $\partial\phi(\boldsymbol{x})$, otherwise. We also speak of a *noisy first-order oracle*, which does not output ϕ and ϕ' exactly but rather their unbiased estimates.

We measure complexity of an algorithm by the number of queries that it makes for computing an ϵ-accuracy solution. If this number is at most a polynomial (in $1/\epsilon$), then the problem is called *tractable*. Different tractable problems have different lower-complexity bounds on the number of queries that must be made; and an algorithm that achieves this lower bound (for all problems in its class) is called *optimal*.

---

[2] We may also speak of zeroth, second-order, or other types of oracles, but for brevity we omit these from our discussion.

[3] Please refer to [53] for this and other key ideas of convex analysis.

This chapter describes some fundamental tractable and optimal algorithms; we divide our presentation into two parts: (i) smooth (at least once differentiable), and (ii) nonsmooth (but continuous) convex optimization. We discuss both noise-free and noisy oracles while highlighting both classical and modern results. Some concrete examples are interspersed to make our presentation clearer.

7.3 Smooth Convex Optimization

We begin with an instructive setup: unconstrained, smooth convex optimization for the class of *Lipschitz continuous* functions.

Definition 7.2 (Lipschitz continuity)   Let $\phi : \mathbb{R}^n \to \mathbb{R}$ be k times continuously differentiable on $\mathcal{X} \subseteq \mathbb{R}^n$. If the kth derivative $\phi^{(k)}$ satisfies

$$\|\phi^{(k)}(\boldsymbol{x}) - \phi^{(k)}(\boldsymbol{y})\| \le L\|\boldsymbol{x} - \boldsymbol{y}\|, \quad \forall\, \boldsymbol{x}, \boldsymbol{y} \in \mathcal{X}, \tag{7.3}$$

for some constant L, then ϕ is said to have a *Lipschitz continuous kth derivative*, and we denote this by writing $\phi \in C_L^k(\mathcal{X})$.

Example 7.3   Some familiar functions satisfying (7.3) are (verify!):
- *Linear:* $\langle \boldsymbol{a}, \boldsymbol{x} \rangle + c$ lies in $C_{\|\boldsymbol{a}\|}^0(\mathbb{R}^n)$ and also belongs to $C_0^1(\mathbb{R}^n)$
- *Hinge loss:* $\max(0, 1 - x)$ lies in $C_1^0(\mathbb{R})$;
- *Logistic loss:* $\log(1 + e^x)$ lies in $C_2^1(\mathbb{R})$;
- *Quadratic loss:* $\frac{1}{2}\boldsymbol{x}^{\mathsf{T}}\boldsymbol{A}\boldsymbol{x}$ lies in $C_{\|\boldsymbol{A}\|}^1(\mathbb{R}^n)$; here $\|A\|$ is the operator 2-norm.

Note that the *Log-loss:* $\phi(x) = -\log x \notin C_L^1(\mathbb{R}_{++})$ for any finite L.

Among Lipschitz continuous functions, the class $C_L^1(\mathcal{X})$ of functions with Lipschitz continuous gradients is of great importance. Most of the above examples lie in this class; and several differentiable (not necessarily convex) optimization problems encountered in machine learning and related areas feature C_L^1 functions. One reason why this class enjoys such importance is the following important lemma.

Lemma 7.4 (Descent lemma)   *Let $\phi \in C_L^1(\mathcal{X})$. Then, it follows that*

$$|\phi(\boldsymbol{x}) - \phi(\boldsymbol{y}) - \langle \nabla\phi(\boldsymbol{y}), \boldsymbol{x} - \boldsymbol{y} \rangle| \le \tfrac{1}{2}L\|\boldsymbol{x} - \boldsymbol{y}\|^2, \quad \forall\, \boldsymbol{x}, \boldsymbol{y} \in \mathcal{X}. \tag{7.4}$$

Proof   Since f is differentiable, it has the Taylor expansion

$$\phi(\boldsymbol{x}) = \phi(\boldsymbol{y}) + \int_0^1 \langle \nabla\phi(\boldsymbol{y} + t(\boldsymbol{x} - \boldsymbol{y})), \boldsymbol{x} - \boldsymbol{y} \rangle dt$$
$$= \phi(\boldsymbol{y}) + \langle \nabla\phi(\boldsymbol{y}), \boldsymbol{x} - \boldsymbol{y} \rangle + \int_0^1 \langle \nabla\phi(\boldsymbol{y} + t(\boldsymbol{x} - \boldsymbol{y})) - \nabla\phi(\boldsymbol{y}), \boldsymbol{x} - \boldsymbol{y} \rangle dt.$$

Rearranging, taking absolute values, invoking the triangle and Cauchy–Schwarz inequalities, along with Definition (7.3), we ultimately obtain

$$|\phi(\boldsymbol{x}) - \phi(\boldsymbol{y}) - \langle \nabla\phi(\boldsymbol{y}), \boldsymbol{x} - \boldsymbol{y}\rangle| \leq L\|\boldsymbol{x} - \boldsymbol{y}\|^2 \int_0^1 t\,dt = \tfrac{1}{2}L\|\boldsymbol{x} - \boldsymbol{y}\|^2. \quad \square$$

Let us now look at optimization methods for convex $C_L^1(\mathcal{X})$ functions.

7.3.1 Gradient Based Methods

For solving (7.1), perhaps the simplest general purpose algorithm is *gradient-projection*, summarized in (7.5) below.

$$
\begin{array}{|l|}
\hline
\text{Initialize } \boldsymbol{x}_0 \in \mathbb{R}^n \\
\text{For } k \geq 0 \text{ iterate:} \\
\quad\quad \text{Select a suitable stepsize } \alpha_k > 0 \\
\quad\quad \boldsymbol{x}_{k+1} = P_{\mathcal{X}}(\boldsymbol{x}_k - \alpha_k \nabla\phi(\boldsymbol{x}_k)). \\
\hline
\end{array}
\qquad (7.5)
$$

Iteration (7.5) consists of three key components: (i) the gradient $\nabla\phi$; (ii) the stepsize $\alpha_k > 0$; and (iii) the *projection operator*

$$P_{\mathcal{X}}(\boldsymbol{y}) := \operatorname*{argmin}_{\boldsymbol{x}\in\mathcal{X}} \tfrac{1}{2}\|\boldsymbol{x} - \boldsymbol{y}\|_2^2. \qquad (7.6)$$

As per our assumption, the gradient $\nabla\phi$ is obtained from an oracle. The stepsize α_k can be set using various well-known strategies [8, 39], so we do not discuss it further. Finally, it is important to note that unless $\mathcal{X}$ is "simple", applying the projection operator (7.6) can be as difficult as solving the overall problem itself.

Therefore, for simplicity we first analyze iteration (7.5) for the *unconstrained* case $\mathcal{X} = \mathbb{R}^n$, for which $P_{\mathcal{X}} \equiv \mathrm{Id}$. Here, we answer two key questions: (i) what is an *upper bound* on the number of oracle calls (iterations) needed by (7.5) to obtain an ϵ-accuracy solution; and (ii) how far is this upper bound from the *lower bound* on oracle calls?

Theorem 7.5 (Upper bound) *Let ϕ be a convex, $C_L^1(\mathbb{R}^n)$ function. Let $\alpha_k = 1/L$ and let $\boldsymbol{x}^*$ be an optimal solution to (7.1). Define the "diameter" $D := \|\boldsymbol{x}_0 - \boldsymbol{x}^*\|$. Then the iterates $\{\boldsymbol{x}_k\}$ of (7.5) satisfy*

$$\phi(\boldsymbol{x}_k) - \phi(\boldsymbol{x}^*) \leq \frac{2LD^2}{k+4}. \qquad (7.7)$$

Proof We follow [39, Theorem 2.1.14], and present the details as they are instructive. Define the residue $r_k = \|\boldsymbol{x}_k - \boldsymbol{x}^*\|$, let $\boldsymbol{g}_k \equiv \nabla\phi(\boldsymbol{x}_k)$, and $\boldsymbol{g}^* = \nabla\phi(\boldsymbol{x}^*)$. Recall now the optimality condition

$$\langle \boldsymbol{g}_k - \boldsymbol{g}^*, \boldsymbol{x}_k - \boldsymbol{x}^*\rangle \geq 0 \qquad \text{for all } \boldsymbol{x}_k.$$

This, together with the constant stepsize $\alpha_k = 1/L$, implies that

$$r_{k+1}^2 = \|\boldsymbol{x}_k - \boldsymbol{x}^* - \alpha_k \boldsymbol{g}_k\|^2 \quad \leq \quad r_k^2 - \tfrac{1}{L}\|\boldsymbol{g}_k\|^2,$$

and in particular that, $r_k \leq r_0 = D$. Now let $\Delta_k := \phi(\boldsymbol{x}_k) - \phi(\boldsymbol{x}^*)$, and use convexity of ϕ and the Cauchy–Schwarz inequality to obtain

$$\Delta_k \leq \langle \boldsymbol{g}_k, \boldsymbol{x}_k - \boldsymbol{x}^* \rangle \leq \|\boldsymbol{g}_k\|\|\boldsymbol{x}_k - \boldsymbol{x}^*\| = \|\boldsymbol{g}_k\| r_k \leq \|\boldsymbol{g}_k\| D. \tag{7.8}$$

Invoke Lemma 7.4 with $\boldsymbol{x} = \boldsymbol{x}_{k+1}$ and $\boldsymbol{y} = \boldsymbol{x}_k$, to now see that

$$\phi(\boldsymbol{x}_{k+1}) \leq \phi(\boldsymbol{x}_k) + \langle \boldsymbol{g}_k, \boldsymbol{x}_{k+1} - \boldsymbol{x}_k \rangle + \tfrac{1}{2} L \|\boldsymbol{x}_{k+1} - \boldsymbol{x}_k\|^2.$$

Then use $\boldsymbol{x}_{k+1}$ from iteration (7.5) with $\alpha_k = 1/L$ to obtain

$$\phi(\boldsymbol{x}_{k+1}) \leq \phi(\boldsymbol{x}_k) - \tfrac{1}{2L}\|\boldsymbol{g}_k\|^2,$$

which implies the inequality $\Delta_{k+1} \leq \Delta_k - (1/2L)\|\boldsymbol{g}_k\|^2$. From inequality (7.8) and Lemma 7.4 we further obtain the bound

$$\Delta_{k+1} \leq \Delta_k - \Delta_k^2/(2LD^2) = \Delta_k(1 - \beta),$$

for some $\beta \in (0,1)$. Take reciprocals and note that $(1 - \beta)^{-1} \leq 1 + \beta$, which yields $\frac{1}{\Delta_{k+1}} \geq \frac{1+\beta}{\Delta_k} = \frac{1}{\Delta_k} + \frac{1}{2LD^2}$. Summing this over k we obtain

$$\frac{1}{\Delta_{k+1}} \geq \frac{1}{\Delta_0} + \frac{k+1}{2LD^2},$$

which upon rearranging yields

$$\phi(\boldsymbol{x}_k) - \phi(\boldsymbol{x}^*) \leq \frac{2LD^2\Delta_0}{2LD^2 + k\Delta_0} \leq \frac{2LD^2}{k+4}. \tag{7.9}$$

The final inequality follows because $\Delta_0 \leq \tfrac{1}{2}LD^2$ (Lemma 7.4) and because the second-last term in (7.9) is an increasing function of Δ_0. $\square$

Corollary 7.6 *The gradient method (7.5) requires $O(1/\epsilon)$ iterations (calls to the oracle) to obtain a solution of ϵ-accuracy.*

Proof From Theorem 7.5 it follows that if $k + 4 \geq \frac{2LD^2}{\epsilon}$, then $\phi(\boldsymbol{x}_k) - \phi(\boldsymbol{x}^*) \leq \epsilon$; thus, $O(1/\epsilon)$ iterations yield a solution of ϵ-accuracy. $\square$

Let us now state a lower-bound on the number of oracle calls. In particular, this bound applies to methods that generate the kth iterate $\boldsymbol{x}_k$ by linearly combining the information obtained from the oracle up to step $k-1$. These methods generate iterates that satisfy

$$\boldsymbol{x}_k \in \boldsymbol{x}_0 + \mathrm{Lin}(\nabla\phi(\boldsymbol{x}_0), \ldots, \nabla\phi(\boldsymbol{x}_{k-1})). \tag{7.10}$$

Theorem 7.7 (Lower bound)   *Using the same notation as in Theorem 7.5, and assuming that $1 \leq k \leq \frac{1}{2}(n-1)$, there exists a convex function $\phi \in C_L^1$, such that any method that generates a sequence $\{\boldsymbol{x}_k\}$ satisfying (7.10), must also satisfy*

$$\phi(\boldsymbol{x}_k) - \phi(\boldsymbol{x}^*) \geq \frac{3LD^2}{32(k+1)^2}. \tag{7.11}$$

Proof   See [39, Section 2.1.2]. $\square$

Both the upper and lower accuracy bounds show (slow) sublinear convergence. So a natural question is if there is a subclass of C_L^1 functions for which we can obtain faster convergence rates? It turns out that for the subclass of *strongly convex* functions, we do have better rates.

Definition 7.8 (Strong convexity)   A function $\phi : \mathcal{X} \subset \mathbb{R}^n \to \mathbb{R}$ is said to be *strongly convex* with parameter $\mu > 0$, denoted $\phi \in S_{L,\mu}^1(\mathcal{X})$, if

$$\phi(\boldsymbol{x}) \geq \phi(\boldsymbol{y}) + \langle \nabla\phi(\boldsymbol{y}), \boldsymbol{x} - \boldsymbol{y} \rangle + \tfrac{1}{2}\mu\|\boldsymbol{x} - \boldsymbol{y}\|^2, \quad \forall \boldsymbol{x}, \boldsymbol{y} \in \mathcal{X}. \tag{7.12}$$

For such functions we have the following upper and lower bounds.

Theorem 7.9 (SC upper-bound)   *Let $\phi \in S_{L,\mu}^1(\mathbb{R}^n)$, and set $\alpha_k = 2/(L+\mu)$. Then, the iteration (7.5) generates a sequence $\{\boldsymbol{x}_k\}$ such that*

$$\phi(\boldsymbol{x}_k) - \phi(\boldsymbol{x}^*) \leq \frac{L}{2}\left(\frac{\kappa-1}{\kappa+1}\right)^{2k} D^2, \tag{7.13}$$

where $\kappa = L/\mu$ denotes the "condition number" of ϕ.

Theorem 7.10 (SC lower-bound)   *There exists an infinitely differentiable $S_{\mu,\mu\kappa}^1$ function such that any first-order method that generates $\{\boldsymbol{x}_k\}$ satisfying (7.10) must also satisfy*

$$\phi(\boldsymbol{x}_k) - \phi(\boldsymbol{x}^*) \geq \frac{\mu}{2}\left(\frac{\sqrt{\kappa}-1}{\sqrt{\kappa}+1}\right)^{2k} D^2. \tag{7.14}$$

For proofs of these theorems, refer to [39, Section 2.1.4].

Comparing the upper-bounds (7.7) and (7.13) with the lower-bounds (7.11) and (7.14), respectively, we see that gradient-descent is far from optimal. In a breakthrough paper Nesterov [36] introduced a new *optimal gradient method* whose upper complexity bound matches (up to constants) the above lower bound. While the derivation of the optimal method and its analysis lie outside the scope of this chapter, some intuitive insight may be obtained by recalling the *heavy-ball method* [48]. For a fixed $\gamma > 0$, this method performs the iteration

$$\boldsymbol{x}_{k+1} = \boldsymbol{x}_k - \alpha_k \nabla \phi(\boldsymbol{x}_k) + \gamma(\boldsymbol{x}_k - \boldsymbol{x}_{k-1}). \tag{7.15}$$

Let ϕ be an $S_{L,\mu}^2$ function. Set $\alpha_k = \frac{4}{\mu} \frac{1}{(1+\sqrt{\kappa})^2}$ and $\gamma = (\frac{\sqrt{\kappa}-1}{\sqrt{\kappa}+1})^2$; then, some algebra reveals that the "multistep" iteration (7.15) satisfies

$$\|\boldsymbol{x}_k - \boldsymbol{x}^*\|^2 \le \left(\frac{\sqrt{\kappa}-1}{\sqrt{\kappa}+1}\right)^{2k} D^2.$$

Notice that this matches the optimal rate (7.14) (up to constants).

Thus, we might expect a multistep iteration to be effective also for $C_L^1(\mathbb{R}^n)$ functions. Nesterov's optimal method is such an iteration, though with a key difference: it uses iteration dependent values of γ. Here's how.

Let $\boldsymbol{y}_0 = \boldsymbol{x}_0$, $\alpha_0 \ge 1/\sqrt{\kappa}$
For $k \ge 0$ iterate:

$$\begin{aligned}
\boldsymbol{x}_{k+1} &= \boldsymbol{y}_k - \tfrac{1}{L}\nabla\phi(\boldsymbol{y}_k) \\
\alpha_{k+1} &= \tfrac{1}{2\kappa} - \tfrac{\alpha_k^2}{2} + \sqrt{\alpha_k^2 + \left(\tfrac{1}{2\kappa} - \tfrac{\alpha_k^2}{2}\right)^2}
\end{aligned} \tag{7.16a}$$

$$\begin{aligned}
\gamma_k &= \tfrac{\alpha_k(1-\alpha_k)}{\alpha_k^2 + \alpha_{k+1}} \\
\boldsymbol{y}_{k+1} &= \boldsymbol{x}_{k+1} + \gamma_k(\boldsymbol{x}_{k+1} - \boldsymbol{x}_k).
\end{aligned} \tag{7.16b}$$

The similarity of iteration (7.16b) to (7.15) is unmistakable. Theorem 7.11 characterizes the optimality of the above method.

Theorem 7.11 *Let $\{\boldsymbol{x}_k\}$ be generated by (7.16) with $\alpha_0 = \hat{\alpha} + \sqrt{1+\hat{\alpha}^2}$, where $\hat{\alpha} = -1/2 + 1/(2\kappa)$. Then, we have the upper bound:*

$$\phi(\boldsymbol{x}_k) - \phi(\boldsymbol{x}^*) \le \frac{3}{2} L D^2 \times \min\left\{\left(\frac{\sqrt{\kappa}-1}{\sqrt{\kappa}}\right)^k, \frac{4}{(k+2)^2}\right\}. \tag{7.17}$$

Proof Use $\gamma_0 = L$ in [39, Theorem 2.2.3] along with the inequality (follows from Lemma 7.4) that $\phi(\boldsymbol{x}_0) - \phi(\boldsymbol{x}^*) \le \frac{1}{2} L D^2$. $\qquad\square$

Comparing (7.17) with the lower bound (7.11) one sees that for general $C_L^1(\mathbb{R}^n)$ convex functions, method (7.16) is optimal to within constant factors. For the strongly convex case, the lower bound (7.14) implies that if $\phi(\boldsymbol{x}_k) - \phi(\boldsymbol{x}^*) \le \epsilon$, then $2k \log\left(1 + \frac{2}{\sqrt{\kappa}-1}\right) \ge \log\left(\frac{\mu D^2}{2\epsilon}\right)$, whereby

$$k \ge \frac{\sqrt{\kappa}-1}{4}\left(\log(\tfrac{1}{\epsilon} + \log\tfrac{\mu D^2}{2})\right)$$

iterations are needed to obtain an ϵ-accuracy solution. Since $\phi(\boldsymbol{x}_k) - \phi(\boldsymbol{x}^*) \leq (3/2)LD^2(1 - 1/\sqrt{\kappa})^k$, using the inequality $-\log(1 - 1/\sqrt{\kappa}) < 1/\sqrt{\kappa}$ for $\kappa > 1$, we conclude that $k \leq \sqrt{\kappa}(\log \frac{1}{\epsilon} + \log \frac{3LD^2}{2})$ iterations suffice to obtain an ϵ-accurate solution. Thus, the complexity bound (7.17) is within constant factors of the lower bound (7.14).

Digression: A faster method?

A curious multistep algorithm is the nonmonotonic gradient descent of Barzilai and Borwein [5] (BB). Here one first computes the differences $\boldsymbol{s}_k = \boldsymbol{x}_k - \boldsymbol{x}_{k-1}$, $\boldsymbol{y}_k = \nabla\phi(\boldsymbol{x}_k) - \nabla\phi(\boldsymbol{x}_{k-1})$, and then iterates (7.5) using the stepsize

$$\alpha_k = \langle \boldsymbol{s}^k, \boldsymbol{y}^k \rangle / \|\boldsymbol{y}^k\|^2, \quad \text{or} \quad \alpha_k = \|\boldsymbol{s}^k\|^2 / \langle \boldsymbol{s}^k, \boldsymbol{y}^k \rangle. \tag{7.18}$$

These stepsizes may be viewed as scalar approximations to the Hessian or its inverse; this approximation of the curvature explains to some extent the impressive empirical speedups enjoyed by BB gradient-descent (see Fig. 7.2).

Constrained problems

We can accommodate "simple" constraints into the above gradient based methods without changing their upper complexity bounds. In particular, say $\boldsymbol{x}$ lies in $\mathcal{X}$ which is "simple" so that the *orthogonal projection* (7.6) can be computed *exactly*. The upper and lower bounds stated in Theorems 7.5 and 7.9 extend easily to this *constrained* problem. Nesterov's optimal method (7.16) too, extends easily if we use the projected update $\boldsymbol{x}_{k+1} = P_{\mathcal{X}}(\boldsymbol{y}_k - \frac{1}{L}\nabla\phi(\boldsymbol{y}_k))$. However, if the constraint set is not simple then additional work is needed as the projection $P_{\mathcal{X}}$ cannot be computed exactly anymore – see for example the recent work of Schmidt et al. [56] which provides a good discussion on handling the case with inexact projections (and more).

7.4 Nonsmooth Convex Optimization

After our brief discussion of smooth convex optimization we now turn to a class of problems pervasive in machine learning: *nonsmooth convex optimization*. More specifically, we consider optimizing convex functions that are Lipschitz continuous over a compact set containing the solution.

Example 7.12 (Hinge loss SVM) Let $\{(\boldsymbol{x}_i, y_i) : 1 \leq i \leq m\}$ be labeled training examples, where $\boldsymbol{x}_i \in \mathbb{R}^n$ are feature vectors and $y_i \in \{\pm 1\}$ their labels. One way of classifying an unlabeled point $\boldsymbol{x}$ is to assign to it the label $\mathrm{sgn}(\boldsymbol{w}^T \boldsymbol{x} + b)$, where $\boldsymbol{w} \in \mathbb{R}^n$ is a weight vector that must be learned and $b \in \mathbb{R}$ is a "bias" term. A fundamental choice for computing $\boldsymbol{w}$ and b is the *Hinge loss Support Vector Machine (SVM)*, which involves solving the nonsmooth problem:

$$\min_{\boldsymbol{w},b} \; \phi(\boldsymbol{w}, b) := \tfrac{1}{2}\|\boldsymbol{w}\|_2^2 + C \sum_{i=1}^{m} \max(0, 1 - y_i(\boldsymbol{w}^T \boldsymbol{x}_i + b)), \tag{7.19}$$

where $C > 0$ is a tradeoff parameter. The hinge loss terms in (7.19) are easily seen

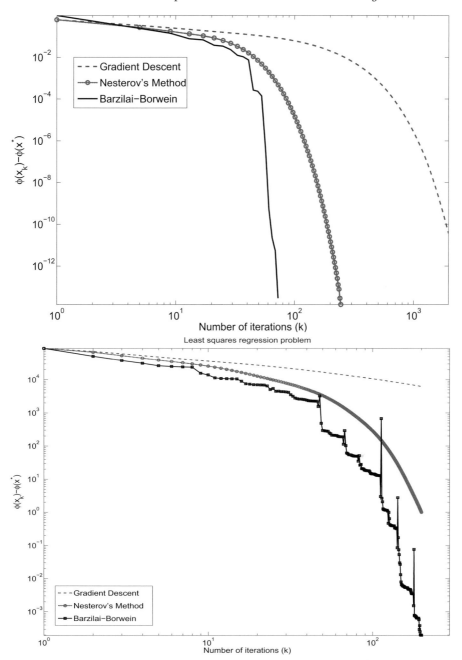

Figure 7.2 Gradient-descent (7.5), Nesterov's method (7.16), and gradient-descent with Barzilai–Borwein (BB) stepsizes (7.18). In the upper plot we minimize $\phi(\boldsymbol{x}) = 0.5\|\boldsymbol{D}^{\mathrm{T}}\boldsymbol{x} - \boldsymbol{b}\|^2$, with $\boldsymbol{D}$ being an $(n-1) \times n$ matrix having -1s on its diagonal and 1s on the first superdiagonal. We used $n = 50$. The vector $\boldsymbol{b}$ is set to $\mathbf{2}$ (all twos). Here, $L = \lambda_{\max}(\boldsymbol{D}\boldsymbol{D}^{\mathrm{T}}) \approx 4$, and $\mu = \lambda_{\min}(\boldsymbol{D}\boldsymbol{D}^{\mathrm{T}}) \approx 1/(0.1n^2 + 0.6n)$ (so $\boldsymbol{D}$ is very ill-conditioned). The stepsize $\alpha_k = 1/L$ is used for (7.5). The superiority of Nesterov's optimal method over gradient descent is evident; surprisingly, the BB method performs even better. The lower plot runs a least squares problem similar to the upper plot, but this time on the UCI Year–Prediction dataset [22]. Specifically, we solve $\min_{\boldsymbol{w}} \|\boldsymbol{X}\boldsymbol{w} - \boldsymbol{y}\|^2$ on a $463{,}715 \times 90$ data matrix $\boldsymbol{X}$ (normalized to have unit columns); here $L/\mu \approx 933$.

to be Lipschitz continuous and convex. Assuming that the optimal w^* lies in a ball of radius D, we see that $2D$ suffices as a Lipschitz constant for the (convex) regularizer $\|w\|_2^2$. Thus, $\phi(w, b)$ is Lipschitz continuous and convex.

7.4.1 Basic Theory

We start our discussion of nonsmooth convex optimization by recalling an extremely important concept from convex analysis.

Definition 7.13 (Subdifferential)   Let ϕ be convex. For any $y \in \operatorname{dom} \phi$ the *subdifferential* of ϕ at y, written $\partial\phi(y)$, is defined to be the set

$$\partial\phi(y) := \{g \mid \phi(x) \geq \phi(y) + \langle g, x - y \rangle \ \forall x \in \operatorname{dom} \phi\}. \qquad (7.20)$$

The subdifferential generalizes the concept of a gradient: if ϕ is differentiable, then the subdifferential is a singleton $\partial\phi(y) = \{\nabla\phi(y)\}$. Akin to gradients, subdifferentials also help characterize optimality. Indeed, using (7.20) an easy exercise shows that for a given point x^*,

$$\phi(x^*) \leq \phi(x) \quad \text{for all } x, \quad \text{if and only if } 0 \in \partial\phi(x^*). \qquad (7.21)$$

Given these properties of the subdifferential, we may hope to generalize iteration (7.5) to accommodate nondifferentiable convex functions. A fairly natural choice is to introduce the (projected) *subgradient method*

$$x_{k+1} = P_{\mathcal{X}}(x_k - \alpha_k g_k), \quad k = 0, 1, \ldots, \qquad (7.22)$$

where, instead of the gradient, we use an arbitrary *subgradient* $g_k \in \partial\phi(x_k)$; α_k is a suitable stepsize. Although similar in form to (7.5), iteration (7.22) differs crucially: unlike the (negative) gradient, an arbitrary subgradient *does not* provide a direction of descent. This limitation forces us to use stepsizes that are less flexible than for gradient-descent, and also contributes to making (7.22) converge slowly.

Example 7.14 (Nesterov [43])   Let $\phi(x) = |x|$, for $x \in \mathbb{R}$. The subgradient method (7.22) is $x_{k+1} = x_k - \alpha_k g_k$, where $g_k \in \partial|x_k|$. If $x_0 = 1$ and $\alpha_k = \frac{1}{\sqrt{k+1}} + \frac{1}{\sqrt{k+2}}$ (this stepsize is known to be optimal [43]), then $|x_k| = \frac{1}{\sqrt{k+1}}$, so that $O(1/\epsilon^2)$ iterations are needed to obtain ϵ-accuracy.

The dismal behavior shown in Example 7.14 is typical for the subgradient method which exhibits $O(1/\sqrt{k})$ convergence. One may wonder: *Can we do better than the subgradient method?* The answer is, unfortunately, *No*. Theorem 7.15 asserts this claim formally.

Theorem 7.15 (Nesterov [39])   *Assume that the solution x^* lies in a Euclidean ball of radius $D > 0$ around a given initial point x_0, denoted $\mathcal{B}$. There* exists a function ϕ in $C_L^0(\mathcal{B})$ *(with $L > 0$), such that for $0 \le k \le n-1$, the inequality*

$$\phi(\boldsymbol{x}_k) - \phi(\boldsymbol{x}^*) \ge \frac{LD}{2(1+\sqrt{k+1})}, \tag{7.23}$$

holds for any algorithm that generates $\boldsymbol{x}_k$ by linearly combining the previous iterates and subgradients (cf. (7.10)).

Compared with the C_L^1 convex case, the situation for the nonsmooth case looks much worse. Nesterov [38, 41] showed how to circumvent the $O(1/\sqrt{k})$ barrier of (7.23) by making a simple (in hindsight) but far-reaching observation: *we don't always work with black boxes but explicitly know the problem structure, which can be exploited to obtain faster algorithms.* Let us now describe the key consequences of this observation.

7.4.2 Smooth Minimization of Nonsmooth Functions

Intuitively, if we could replace a nonsmooth problem with a "good enough" smooth approximation, we could approximately solve the nonsmooth problem faster. This idea may be expected to work because on a compact set, a Lipschitz continuous convex function can be approximated to any uniform accuracy $\epsilon > 0$ by a C_L^1 convex function. If L is of the order $O(1/\epsilon)$, then an optimal method that requires $O(\sqrt{L/\epsilon})$ iterations could yield a nonsmooth optimization method that converges as $O(1/\epsilon)$, thereby breaking the $O(1/\sqrt{k})$ barrier (which corresponds to $O(1/\epsilon^2)$).

Nesterov [41] builds on this intuition to consider nonsmooth functions $\phi(\boldsymbol{x})$ that possess an *explicit max-structure*; that is,

$$\phi(\boldsymbol{x}) = \hat{\phi}(\boldsymbol{x}) + \max_{\boldsymbol{z} \in \mathcal{Z} \subseteq \mathbb{R}^m} \{\langle \boldsymbol{A}\boldsymbol{x}, \, \boldsymbol{z} \rangle - \hat{\phi}(\boldsymbol{z})\}, \tag{7.24}$$

where $\hat{\phi}$ is convex and lies in $C_{L(\hat{\phi})}^1(\mathcal{X})$; $\hat{\phi}(\boldsymbol{z})$ is continuous and convex on $\mathcal{Z}$, and $\boldsymbol{A} \in \mathbb{R}^{m \times n}$. For such ϕ, he then introduces a smoothness parameter $\mu > 0$, and defines the *smooth approximation:*[4]

$$\phi_\mu(\boldsymbol{x}) := \hat{\phi}(\boldsymbol{x}) + \max_{\boldsymbol{z} \in \mathcal{Z}} \{\langle \boldsymbol{A}\boldsymbol{x}, \, \boldsymbol{z} \rangle - \hat{\phi}(\boldsymbol{z}) - \tfrac{1}{2}\mu\|\boldsymbol{z}\|^2\}. \tag{7.25}$$

The "max" term in (7.25) has a unique solution (since $\hat{\phi}$ is continuous, $\|\boldsymbol{z}\|^2$ is strongly convex and $\mathcal{Z}$ is compact), say $\boldsymbol{z}_\mu(\boldsymbol{x})$. From standard results [e.g., 54, Theorem 2.26] it follows that

$$\nabla\phi_\mu(\boldsymbol{x}) = \nabla\hat{\phi}(\boldsymbol{x}) + \boldsymbol{A}^T \boldsymbol{z}_\mu(\boldsymbol{x}), \tag{7.26}$$

---

[4] This approximation is essentially the negative *Moreau envelope* of $\hat{\phi}$.

with a Lipschitz constant given by

$$L(\phi_\mu) := L(\hat{\phi}) + \tfrac{1}{\mu}\|A\|^2. \tag{7.27}$$

Depending on the set $\mathcal{Z}$, instead of $\|z\|^2$, a different "prox-function" might be more appropriate – we omit discussion for simplicity and refer the reader to [27, 41]. Instead, we directly present Nesterov's smoothing algorithm.

For $k \geq 0$ iterate:

$$\begin{aligned}
&y_k = P_\mathcal{X}(x_k - \tfrac{1}{L(\phi_\mu)}\nabla\phi_\mu(x_k)) \\
&z_k = \operatorname{argmin}_{x \in \mathcal{X}} \tfrac{1}{2}L(\phi_\mu)\|x\|^2 + \sum_{i=0}^{k}\tfrac{i+1}{2}\langle\nabla\phi_\mu(x_i), x\rangle \qquad (7.28) \\
&x_{k+1} = \tfrac{2}{k+3}z_k + \tfrac{k+1}{k+3}y_k
\end{aligned}$$

To describe the complexity of iteration (7.28), we need the (primal and dual) diameters $D_\mathcal{X} := \max_{x \in \mathcal{X}}\|x\|$ and $D_\mathcal{Z} := \max_{z \in \mathcal{Z}}\|z\|$. Nesterov [41, Theorem 3] shows that upon setting $\mu = \frac{2\|A\|}{N+1}\frac{D_\mathcal{X}}{D_\mathcal{Z}}$, after N iterations of (7.28), the vector y_N solves (7.24) to an accuracy upper-bounded by

$$\frac{4\|A\|}{N+1}D_\mathcal{X}D_\mathcal{Z} + \frac{4L(\hat{\phi})D_\mathcal{X}^2}{(N+1)^2}. \tag{7.29}$$

And what's more, it can be shown that (modulo constant factors) this bound is unimprovable [27].

An instructive example where algorithm (7.28) applies is shown as Example 7.16 below.

Example 7.16 (Least absolute deviations)   A regression task that is more robust (perchance less stable) than least-squares is least absolute deviations (LAD) [49]. Here, we minimize the ℓ_1-norm cost $\phi(x) = \|Ax - b\|_1$. Unlike least-squares, LAD does not have an analytic solution, so it has attracted several iterative approaches; we are unaware if Nesterov's smoothing technique has been so far applied to it.

Since the cost ϕ is separable, on noting $|x_i| = \max_{|z_i| \leq 1} z_i x_i$, we obtain

$$\phi(x) = \max_{\|z\|_\infty \leq 1}\{\langle Ax - b, z\rangle\}, \qquad \text{(notice: } \hat{\phi} = 0\text{)},$$

so that $\phi_\mu(x) := \max_{\|z\|_\infty \leq 1}\{\langle Ax - b, z\rangle - \tfrac{1}{2}\mu\|z\|^2\}$. Hence, $z_\mu(x)$ can be computed simply by projecting the scaled residual $\mu^{-1}(Ax - b)$ onto the ball $\|z\|_\infty \leq 1$. Notice that $\|z\| \leq \sqrt{n}\|z\|_\infty \leq \sqrt{n} =: D_\mathcal{Z}$. Some linear algebra shows that we can essentially restrict x to lie in a Euclidean ball with diameter $D_\mathcal{X} < \infty$. Thus, we can invoke (7.28) to solve LAD.

For more sophisticated examples, see [68], who apply the smoothing technique to *metric learning*, and [59], who apply the smoothing technique to approximately minimize a subclass of decomposable submodular functions.

Excessive Gap Technique

Scheme (7.28) has a disadvantage: to set the smoothing parameter μ, the number of steps must be known in advance. Nesterov [40] overcomes this disadvantage by assuming slightly more structure, for which he develops a new *excessive-gap technique* (EGT). This leads to $O(1/k)$ rate for problems with max-structure, and a faster $O(1/k^2)$ rate for strongly convex objectives. We summarize the key ideas below.

First, some convex analysis shows that the (Fenchel) *dual* to (7.24) is

$$g(z) := -\hat{\phi}(z) + \min_{x \in \mathcal{X}}\{\langle Ax,\, z\rangle + \hat{\phi}(x)\}. \tag{7.30}$$

For this dual, we let $\nu > 0$ and introduce the smooth approximation

$$g_\nu(z) := -\hat{\phi}(z) + \min_{x \in \mathcal{X}}\{\langle Ax,\, z\rangle + \hat{\phi}(x) + \tfrac{1}{2}\nu\|x\|^2\}. \tag{7.31}$$

We require the gradient of (7.31), which is simply given by

$$\nabla g_\nu(z) = -\nabla\hat{\phi}(z) + A x_\nu(z),$$

where $x_\nu(z)$ denotes the unique solution to the "min" in (7.31). One may quickly verify that the gradient ∇g_ν is Lipschitz with the constant

$$L(g_\nu) := L(\hat{\phi}) + \tfrac{1}{\nu}\|A\|^2.$$

Observe that *weak-duality* implies that $g(z) \le \phi(x)$ for all pairs $(x, z) \in \mathcal{X} \times \mathcal{Z}$, while *strong-duality* mandates $\min_{x \in \mathcal{X}} \phi(x) = \max_{z \in \mathcal{Z}} g(z)$. Thus, for a given pair (x, z) we may compute the *duality gap* $\phi(x) - g(z)$, but what about the "smoothed" gap $\phi_\mu(x) - g_\nu(z)$? This gap can be positive or negative (as any of the inequalities $g \le \phi$, $\phi_\mu \le \phi$, or $g \le g_\nu$ can hold), so it is useful to consider the *excessive gap condition*:

$$\phi_\mu(\bar{x}) \le g_\nu(\bar{z}) \quad \text{for a pair} \quad (\bar{x}, \bar{z}) \in \mathcal{X} \times \mathcal{Z}. \tag{7.32}$$

Condition (7.32) lies at the heart of the EGT. To see why, observe that

$$\phi(x) - \mu D_{\mathcal{Z}}^2 \le \phi_\mu(x) \quad \text{and} \quad g(z) + \nu D_{\mathcal{X}}^2 \ge g_\nu(z). \tag{7.33}$$

Thus, for a primal-dual pair $(\bar{x}, \bar{z})$ that satisfies the excessive gap condition (7.32), the corresponding duality gap is bounded by

$$\phi(\bar{x}) - g(\bar{z}) \le \mu D_{\mathcal{Z}}^2 + \nu D_{\mathcal{X}}^2. \tag{7.34}$$

In other words, the duality gap is bounded by a function linear in μ and ν. So, if both of these parameters shrink to zero, the duality gap will also shrink to zero, at least as fast.

The aim of Nesterov's EGT is, therefore, to generate a sequence $\{(\bar{x}_k, \bar{z}_k)\}$ of primal-dual iterates that satisfy condition (7.32), and to simultaneously choose scalar sequences $\{\mu_k\}$ and $\{\nu_k\}$ that tend to zero at the desired rate. For example, when $L(\hat{\phi}) = L(\hat{\phi}) = 0$, then Nesterov [40, Iteration (6.8)] shows how to generate such sequences, and to thereby obtain the desired $O(1/k)$ upper-bound

$$\phi(\bar{x}_k) - g(\bar{z}_k) \leq \frac{4\|A\|}{k+1} D_X D_Z. \tag{7.35}$$

If, in addition, the function $\hat{\phi}$ in (7.24) is σ-strongly-convex, then an even faster rate of convergence is possible; specifically, we have that

$$\phi(\bar{x}_k) - g(\bar{z}_k) \leq \frac{4D_Z(L(\hat{\phi}) + \sigma^{-1}\|A\|^2)}{(k+1)(k+2)}. \tag{7.36}$$

A point worth noting about (7.36) is that in contrast to (7.35), the rate does not depend on D_X, so in principle, the set X need not be bounded.

Example 7.17 (Structured prediction)   In [70] the authors apply the EGT (with non-Euclidean prox-functions) to maximum-margin Markov networks, by minimizing the regularized "hinge loss":

$$\phi(w) := \frac{\gamma}{2}\|w\|^2 + \frac{1}{m}\sum_{i=1}^{m} \max_{y \in \mathcal{Y}} \phi_i(y, w; z_i),$$

where $z_i = (x_i, y_i)$ are labeled data, $\mathcal{Y}$ the labels space, and ϕ_i are loss functions. Observe that the same idea also applies to the hinge loss SVM of Example 7.12 and other regularized prediction problems.

Example 7.18 (Large-scale Linear Programming)   Chen and Burer [14] apply the EGT (with some modifications) to solve large-scale instances of the following linear programming problem

$$\min_{x,y} \quad c^T x + d^T y$$
$$x, y \geq 0.$$

The authors also show applications to some machine learning problems.

Note. The smoothing ideas can be generalized to problems whose objective function ϕ admits the *saddle-point* representation

$$\phi(x) := \max_{z \in \mathcal{Z}} \quad \Phi(x, z), \tag{7.37}$$

where Φ has a Lipschitz continuous gradient on $X \times \mathcal{Z}$. Instead of Nesterov's smoothing algorithms, we can also solve (7.37) by using the Mirror-Prox algorithm [33] that yields a $O(1/k)$ rate.

7.4.3 Composite Objective Minimization

We just saw how exploitation of structure can be used to circumvent lower bounds and improve convergence rates substantially. Can this idea be taken even further? It turns out that for certain problems, it indeed can. Assume that the objective can be written as

$$\phi(x) := \ell(x) + r(x), \tag{7.38}$$

where $\ell \in C_L^1$ and r is a continuous convex regularizer. Objective (7.38) is called *composite* as it is a mix of smooth and nonsmooth terms.[5]

Composite objectives enjoy great importance in machine learning, largely because of their flexibility and wide applicability. The smooth part measures quality of the estimation, while the nonsmooth part encourages the solution to satisfy certain desirable structural properties such as sparsity. We note in passing that one can alternatively view the loss $\ell(x)$ as a negative log-likelihood term and the regularizer $r(x)$ as a prior, though we do not pursue such connections further.

Example 7.19   Let $\ell(x) = \frac{1}{2}\|Ax - b\|^2$ denote a generic quadratic loss; we list some corresponding choices for the regularizer $r(x)$ below.

- *Lasso* [62] uses $r(x) = \lambda\|x\|_1$, primarily to effect feature selection. The ℓ_1-norm is known to prefer sparse solutions (i.e., solutions with many zeros), which effectively selects columns of matrix A that play a dominant role in explaining the observation vector b. The ℓ_1-norm also enjoys great popularity in the field of compressed sensing, where it is formally used as a proxy for the cardinality function [4].
- *Fused lasso* [61] combines the ℓ_1-norm on the vector x with an ℓ_1-norm on the "discrete gradient" of x, i.e., it uses $r(x) = \lambda\|x\|_1 + \sum_{i=1}^{n-1} |x_{i+1} - x_i|$. This combination elicits not only sparse vectors x, but also enforces their gradients to be sparse – thus, a few large changes will be preferred to several small changes in adjacent components of x. This idea proves useful in applications such as change detection and feature selection [61].
- *Total variation.* Suppose the variable x is a matrix in $\mathbb{R}^{n \times n}$. The classical total-variation regularizer used for image denoising is [55]:

$$r(x) = \sum_{1 \le i,j < n} \|(\nabla x)_{i,j}\|_2, \quad \text{where } (\nabla x)_{i,j} = \begin{bmatrix} x_{i+1,j} - x_{i,j} \\ x_{i,j+1} - x_{i,j} \end{bmatrix}.$$

  However, we warn the reader that this choice of $r(x)$ does not fully fit with the theory that we will describe next, though it can be accommodated using the "inexact" methods proposed in [56].
- *Mixed-norm regression.* Assume that x is split into potentially overlapping "groups" of subvectors $x_1, \ldots, x_G$. Instead of selecting features individually, as

---

[5] This formulation is complementary to (7.24) where the max-term may be viewed as a nonsmooth loss and $\hat{\phi}$ as a regularizer.

is done in Lasso, we could now select features groupwise, e.g., using

$$r(\boldsymbol{x}) := \left(\sum\nolimits_{i=1}^{G} \|\boldsymbol{x}_i\|_q^p \right)^{1/p}.$$

We refer the reader to [3] for a more detailed development.

Let us now see how to solve (7.38). Nesterov [42] showed how to minimize ϕ at a rate limited by only the smooth part of the objective as long as r is *simple*; that is, the following operator is assumed to be computable exactly.[6]

Definition 7.20 (Proximity operator) Let $r : \mathcal{X} \subseteq \mathbb{R}^n \to \mathbb{R}$ be lower semicontinuous and convex. The *proximity operator* for r, indexed by scalar $\eta > 0$, is the following nonlinear map:

$$\operatorname{prox}_\eta^r : \quad \boldsymbol{y} \mapsto \operatorname{argmin}_{\boldsymbol{x} \in \mathcal{X}} \left(r(\boldsymbol{x}) + \tfrac{1}{2\eta} \|\boldsymbol{x} - \boldsymbol{y}\|^2 \right). \tag{7.39}$$

Operator (7.39) generalizes the projection operator (*cf.* (7.6)): if $r(\boldsymbol{x})$ is the indicator function of set $\mathcal{X}$, then $\operatorname{prox}_\eta^r \equiv P_{\mathcal{X}}$. It also enjoys several other nice properties – see [15] for a survey.

In analogy to iteration (7.5) where the projection operator $P_{\mathcal{X}}$ handles constraints, we may wonder similarly whether $\operatorname{prox}_\eta^r$ allows us to handle the nonsmooth term $r(\boldsymbol{x})$ if we simply iterate

$$\boldsymbol{x}_{k+1} = \operatorname{prox}_{\eta_k}^r (\boldsymbol{x}_k - \alpha_k \nabla \ell(\boldsymbol{x}_k)), \quad k = 0, 1, \ldots. \tag{7.40}$$

It turns out that this is indeed possible. Iteration (7.40) is the so-called *forward backward splitting* [e.g., 16] method, which converges at the rate $O(1/k)$; this matches the rate achieved by the smoothing methods of the previous section. Extending the analogy to gradient-projection, it is fitting to ask whether this $O(1/k)$ rate can be improved.

No surprise, such an improved version was developed by Nesterov [42]; also by Beck and Teboulle [6]. These improved methods achieve the optimal rate $O(1/k^2)$; if in addition ℓ is strongly convex, this rate improves to (optimal) linear [42]. We summarize Beck and Teboulle's method FISTA, which incidentally is almost implicit (modulo the prox-operator) in Nesterov's optimal method (7.16).

---

[6] Large parts of the theory also carry over to inexact proximity operators, see [56] for a nice account.

Choose $\boldsymbol{x}_0 \in \mathbb{R}^n$; $\boldsymbol{y}_0 = \boldsymbol{x}_0$; and $\alpha_0 = 1$
For $k \geq 0$ iterate:

$$
\begin{aligned}
\boldsymbol{x}_{k+1} &= \operatorname{prox}^r_{1/L}(\boldsymbol{y}_k - \tfrac{1}{L}\nabla\ell(\boldsymbol{y}_k)) \\
\alpha_{k+1} &= (1 + \sqrt{4\alpha_k^2 + 1})/2 \\
\boldsymbol{y}_{k+1} &= \boldsymbol{x}_{k+1} + \tfrac{\alpha_k - 1}{\alpha_{k+1}}(\boldsymbol{x}_{k+1} - \boldsymbol{x}_k)
\end{aligned}
\qquad (7.41)
$$

From (7.41) it is clear that the computing $\boldsymbol{x}_{k+1}$ is the hard part. Thus, a lot of attention has been paid to efficient computation of proximity operators. Discussing this computation would take us beyond the scope of this chapter; we refer the interested reader to [57, 32]; also see the useful survey by [47].

Another digression: a faster method?

We saw that among gradient-based methods, the nonmonotonic method of Barzilai and Borwein [5] can empirically outperforms gradient descent and Nesterov's optimal method (Fig. 7.2). Do we have a similarly strong method for the composite objective case? There are at least two such methods: SpaRSA [67] and TRIP [29]. The latter is based on a non-smooth trust-region strategy that builds quadratic approximations to its objective function by using BB-formulae, and then uses proximity operators to handle the nonsmooth part; the trust-region strategy ensures convergence. Empirically, TRIP seems to yield impressive performance – see Figs. 7.3 and 7.4.

7.5 Stochastic Optimization

So far we assumed access to a noiseless oracle. It is more realistic to consider *noisy oracles*, where one does not have access to exact objective function or gradient values, but rather to their noisy estimates (usually zero mean, bounded variance noise is assumed).

This setup is fundamental to machine learning and has attracted enormous interest in the community. Therefore, it is impossible to survey this topic here, and we refer the reader to the tutorial [58] that expostulates the connection between stochastic optimization and machine learning; see also [11] and [23] for background and algorithms. We limit our attention to the very recent work of Ghadimi and Lan [23], because of its generality and algorithmic simplicity.

In this section too, we are interested in computing

$$
\phi^* := \min_{\boldsymbol{x} \in \mathcal{X}}\big(\phi(\boldsymbol{x}) := f(\boldsymbol{x}) + r(\boldsymbol{x})\big), \qquad (7.42)
$$

where $\mathcal{X} \subseteq \mathbb{R}^n$ is a compact convex set and $r(\boldsymbol{x})$ is a 'simple' convex function

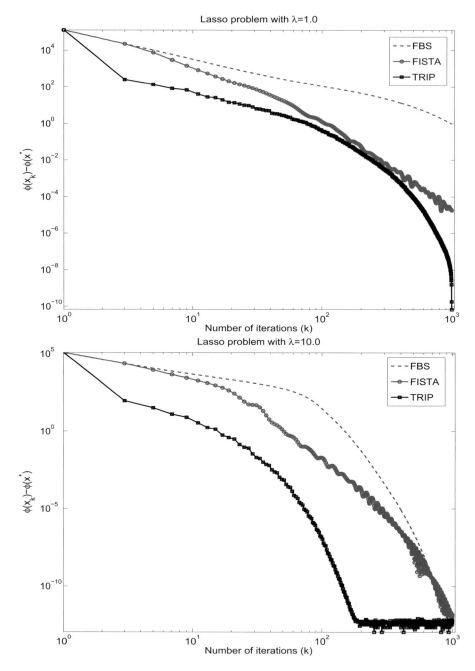

Figure 7.3 Lasso problem that solves $\min \frac{1}{2}\|\boldsymbol{D}^T\boldsymbol{x} - \boldsymbol{b}\|^2 + \lambda\|\boldsymbol{x}\|_1$, where $\boldsymbol{D}$ is as in Fig. 7.2 with $n = 500$. Upper plot shows a run with $\lambda = 1$, which leads to $\approx 7\%$ sparsity; lower plot shows run with $\lambda = 10$, which leads to $\approx 41\%$ sparsity. As sparsity increases, FBS performs similar to FISTA. Surprisingly, the TRIP method of Kim et al. [29], which combines Barzilai–Borwein stepsizes with proximity operators, outperforms both, more so for higher sparsity.

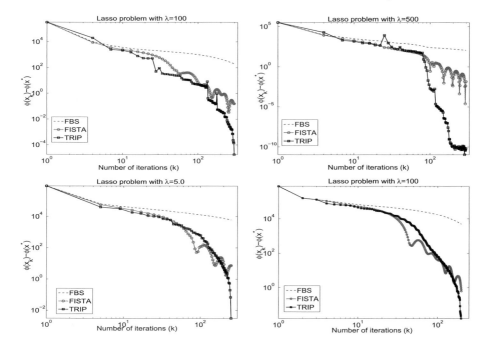

Figure 7.4 Lasso problem on two UCI datasets. Top row: Abalone dataset (4177×8); bottom row: Year Prediction dataset (463715×90) [22]. Both FISTA and TRIP outperform FBS, and TRIP seems to yield higher accuracy solutions. Note that we used datasets with more rows than columns to make it easy to compute the optimal L and μ parameters needed by FISTA and FBS.

as before. We assume that $f : \mathcal{X} \to \mathbb{R}$ is convex and satisfies

$$\tfrac{1}{2}\mu\|\boldsymbol{y}-\boldsymbol{x}\|^2 \le f(\boldsymbol{y}) - f(\boldsymbol{x}) - \langle f'(\boldsymbol{x}), \, \boldsymbol{y}-\boldsymbol{x} \rangle$$
$$\le \tfrac{1}{2}L\|\boldsymbol{y}-\boldsymbol{x}\|^2 + M\|\boldsymbol{y}-\boldsymbol{x}\|, \quad \text{for all } \boldsymbol{x}, \boldsymbol{y} \in \mathcal{X}, \quad (7.43)$$

but that it is *not* known exactly. Specifically, assume that f (and f') are available to us via a stochastic oracle, which on receiving $\boldsymbol{x}_k$ as input, returns the noisy estimates ($\{\xi_k\}$ is a sequence of i.i.d. noise variables):

$$F(\boldsymbol{x}_k, \xi_k) \in \mathbb{R}, \quad \text{and} \quad G(\boldsymbol{x}_k, \xi_k) \in \mathbb{R}^n. \quad (7.44)$$

Further, it is assumed that the estimates (7.44) satisfy

$$\mathbb{E}[F(\boldsymbol{x}, \xi_k)] = f(\boldsymbol{x}), \quad \mathbb{E}[G(\boldsymbol{x}, \xi_k)] = f'(\boldsymbol{x}) \in \partial f(\boldsymbol{x}), \quad (7.45)$$

and that the variance of the (sub)gradient estimates is bounded, so that

$$\mathbb{E}[\|G(\boldsymbol{x}, \xi_k) - f'(\boldsymbol{x})\|^2] \le \sigma^2 \quad \text{for } k \ge 1. \quad (7.46)$$

The above setup is parameterized by the tuple (L, M, μ, σ), different choices of which cover different scenarios. For example, $\sigma = 0$ reduces to the zero-noise, non-stochastic case. If $f \in S_{L,\mu}^1$, then $M = 0$, while if $f \in C_{L(f)}^0$, then (7.43) holds with $L = 0$, $\mu = 0$, and $M = 2L(f)$. Ghadimi and Lan [23] present a general algorithm for solving the (L, M, μ, σ) setup; a simplified version of which is presented below.

Let $\boldsymbol{x}_0 \in \mathcal{X}$; $\boldsymbol{z}_0 = \boldsymbol{x}_0$; and $\gamma \geq 0$ be provided.
For $k \geq 1$ iterate:

$$\alpha_k = \frac{2}{k+1}; \quad \gamma_k = \frac{4L}{k(k+1)} + \frac{2\gamma}{\sqrt{k}}; \quad \tau_k = \frac{(1-\alpha_k)(\mu+\gamma_k)}{\gamma_k + (1-\alpha_k^2)\mu}$$

$$\boldsymbol{y}_k = \tau_k \boldsymbol{z}_{k-1} + (1 - \tau_k)\boldsymbol{x}_{k-1}$$

Invoke stochastic oracle to compute $\boldsymbol{g}_k = G(\boldsymbol{y}_k, \xi_k)$

$$
\begin{aligned}
\hat{\boldsymbol{x}}_k &= \alpha_k \mu \boldsymbol{y}_k + ((1-\alpha_k)\mu + \gamma_k)\boldsymbol{x}_{k-1} - \alpha_k \boldsymbol{g}_k \\
\boldsymbol{x}_k &= \text{prox}_{\alpha_k/(\gamma_k+\mu)}^r (\hat{\boldsymbol{x}}_k/(\mu + \gamma_k)) \\
\boldsymbol{z}_k &= \alpha_k \boldsymbol{x}_k + (1 - \alpha_k)\boldsymbol{z}_{k-1};
\end{aligned}
\tag{7.47}
$$

The above algorithm enjoys the following complexity results.

Theorem 7.21 (Ghadimi and Lan [23]) *Let $\{\boldsymbol{z}_k\}_{k \geq 1}$ be generated by (7.47) and let $D := \sup_{\boldsymbol{x} \in \mathcal{X}} \|\boldsymbol{x} - \boldsymbol{x}^*\|$, where $\phi(\boldsymbol{x}^*) = \phi^*$. If we set $\gamma \approx 1.94\sqrt{M^2 + \sigma^2}/D$, then for the case with $\mu = 0$ we have*

$$\mathbb{E}[\phi(\boldsymbol{z}_k) - \phi^*] \leq \frac{2LD^2}{k(k+1)} + \frac{34D\sqrt{M^2 + \sigma^2}}{5\sqrt{k}}. \tag{7.48}$$

For $\mu > 0$ we can set $\gamma = 0$; then we have

$$\mathbb{E}[\phi(\boldsymbol{z}_k) - \phi^*] \leq \frac{2LD^2}{k(k+1)} + \frac{8(M^2 + \sigma^2)}{\mu(k+1)}. \tag{7.49}$$

We omit the proof as it is very tedious. It is worth noting that in the absence of strong convexity (i.e., $\mu = 0$), the result (7.48) is optimal to within constants. For strongly convex optimization, the result (7.49) is optimal in the slower $O(1/k)$ term, but suboptimal in the faster term. Specifically, it is known [35] that to find a point $\bar{\boldsymbol{x}} \in \mathcal{X}$ such that $\mathbb{E}[\phi(\bar{\boldsymbol{x}}) - \phi^*] \leq \epsilon$, the number of calls to the stochastic oracle cannot be smaller than

$$C\left(\sqrt{\frac{L}{\mu}} \log\left(\frac{LD^2}{\epsilon}\right) + \frac{(M+\sigma)^2}{\mu\epsilon}\right),$$

where D is as defined in Theorem 7.21, and C is an absolute constant.

Ghadimi and Lan [23] also develop a multistage version of (7.47) that achieves the above cited lower bound, though at the cost of a more complicated algorithm; large-deviation results that show bounds in terms of probability (rather than expected values) are also presented.

7.5.1 Other Closely Related Algorithms

We conclude this section by mentioning two other setups algorithmically related to stochastic optimization: (i) online convex optimization; and (ii) incremental (sub)gradient and proximal methods. For an accessible account of the former please see [25], while for a survey treatment of the latter see [9].

In the stochastic setup we assume the "samples" ξ_i to be i.i.d. In contrast, in online optimization, we receive samples that need not follow any distribution and may even be chosen adversarially. In general, at each step an online algorithm selects a point, say $\boldsymbol{x}_k \in \mathcal{X}$ (from a fixed set $\mathcal{X}$). Then, the adversary reveals its cost function $f_k : \mathcal{X} \to \mathbb{R}$ (assumed to be convex), and the online algorithm incurs a cost $f_k(\boldsymbol{x}_k)$. Since the online method selects $\boldsymbol{x}_k$ before seeing the cost, its decision might be suboptimal. So, the method suffers *regret*, which measures departure from the best (in hindsight) decision:

$$R_K := \sum_{k=1}^{K} f_k(\boldsymbol{x}_k) - \min_{\boldsymbol{x} \in \mathcal{X}} \sum_{k=1}^{K} f_k(\boldsymbol{x}). \tag{7.50}$$

In online optimization, we are interested in obtaining algorithms for which the average regret R_K/K is sublinear, so that as the number of rounds $K \to \infty$, the algorithm converges to the optimal answer. When the functions f_k are Lipschitz continuous but do not have any additional structure, regret $O(\sqrt{k})$ is the best attainable, and can be attained for example by the regularized follow-the-leader method [25]. Assuming more structure, such as strong-convexity, logarithmic regret $O(\log k)$ can be attained – recent work of [26] indicates that this might be the best possible.

A strong resemblance to the online setup is borne by *incremental algorithms*. The key difference here is that the components of the objective function are *fixed in advance*. Here too, the objective function is decomposable and we solve

$$\min_{\boldsymbol{x} \in \mathcal{X}} \quad \phi(\boldsymbol{x}) := \sum_{i=1}^{m} f_k(\boldsymbol{x}), \tag{7.51}$$

where each $f_k : \mathcal{X} \to \mathbb{R}$ is convex. If we apply the projected (sub)gradient method to (7.51) we obtain the iteration

$$\boldsymbol{x}_{k+1} = P_{\mathcal{X}}\left(\boldsymbol{x}_k - \alpha_k \sum_{i=1}^{m} f_k'(\boldsymbol{x}_k)\right), \quad f_k'(\boldsymbol{x}) \in \partial f_k(\boldsymbol{x}). \tag{7.52}$$

However, if the number of components m in (7.51) is very large, it can be impractical to compute the entire (sub)gradient at each iteration. Instead, we could use *incremental (sub)gradients* and simply iterate as

$$\boldsymbol{x}_{k+1} = P_{\mathcal{X}}\left(\boldsymbol{x}_k - \alpha_k f'_{i(k)}(\boldsymbol{x}_k)\right), \tag{7.53}$$

where $i(k) \in [1..m]$ is a suitably chosen index. (If $i(k)$ is picked uniformly at random, then (7.53) is essentially a stochastic subgradient method.) Numerical experience suggests that these methods can be much faster when one is far away from convergence, but become increasingly inferior close to convergence [9]. These methods can also be shown to require $O(1/\epsilon^2)$ cycles (through all the m components) to converge to an ϵ-accuracy solution, though the constants in the big-Oh are much worse for a deterministic choice of $i(k)$ than for a randomized one.

7.6 Summary

In this chapter we surveyed some fundamental algorithms and complexity results in large-scale convex optimization. Given the great importance of this class of optimization problems, especially for applications in data intensive areas such as machine learning, we could not cover all works that deserve a mention. In the notes we offer pointers to additional interesting material; we apologize in advance to the authors whose work has escaped our summary and will be grateful if they or the reader would alert us to such an omission.

7.6.1 Notes

Complexity. The complexity bounds discussed in this chapter draw on the seminal work of Nemirovsky and Yudin [35]. However, we followed Nesterov's (2004) gentler exposition for greater accessibility. The lower bounds proved by [35] invoke 'resisting oracles' (adversarial), which can require very ingenious construction. More recently, Raginsky and Rakhlin [50] presented a simpler technique based on relating optimization to statistical hypothesis testing, which also yields several of the lower bounds for convex optimization.

Despite the acceleration achieved by the methods that exploiting problem structure to circumvent the black box assumption, these lower-bounds and subgradient methods remain important as ever. This is so because often the problem structure is too complex or too opaque to be exploited; and in such circumstances, subgradient schemes can still be employed – see [44] for more discussion.

Smooth convex optimization. As mentioned in Theorem 7.7, for sufficiently large problem dimension, the number of iterations of any first-order method cannot be better than $O(\sqrt{LD^2/\epsilon})$. This result was first shown by Nemirovsky and Yudin [35], who also provided a nearly optimal method that achieved this lower-bound up to logarithmic factors. Nesterov's breakthrough work [36] provided the first provably optimal method. Later, Nesterov [37, 41] presented two more optimal methods. Other variations on Nesterov's optimal methods have also been considered; for a nice summary and simplified explanation of such methods, we refer the reader to Tseng's (2008) manuscript.

Nonsmooth optimization. As hinted by Theorem 7.15, the number of iterations of any first-order method cannot be smaller than $O(L^2D^2/\epsilon^2)$. The simple subgradient method attains this bound (up to constant factors). Nemirovsky and Yudin [35] presented the *mirror-descent* procedure that may be much more effective than ordinary subgradient method (which is merely mirror descent in a Euclidean setup) when dealing with non-Euclidean setups: the key idea is to use a different (non quadratic) 'prox-function' based on Bregman divergences. Nesterov [40] also allows using Bregman divergence based prox-functions.

In general, mirror-descent has been shown to be a workhorse in fact for optimally tackling all convex optimization settings, including strongly convex, smooth, stochastic, and online; moreover, its analysis can be simpler than that of Nesterov's optimal methods – we refer the reader to [27, 28].

Stochastic optimization. Here the optimization problem may be written as one of minimizing an expected loss $\phi(\boldsymbol{x}) := \mathbb{E}[\Phi(\boldsymbol{x}, \xi)]$. The random variable ξ models parameter variation and uncertainty, and its value is not known; only its distribution is assumed to be available. The goal of stochastic programming is to find an $\boldsymbol{x}$ that minimizes ϕ on average, or with high probability. The expectation involves a multidimensional integral, so closed-form expressions for ϕ are almost never available. Instead, one has to resort to Monte-Carlo sampling, leading to the *sample average approximation* (SAA) and *stochastic approximation* (SA) methods. The SA method dates back to the classic paper of Robbins and Monro [52]. Since then stochastic methods have exploded in interest; see [35], [30], [34], [20] and references therein.

It was believed that the SAA approach is superior to SA, but Nemirovski et al. [34] derived a mirror-descent version of SA that exhibits an unimprovable rate of convergence $O((M+\sigma)/\sqrt{k})$; see also [44]. We remark in passing that in classic SA, the objective function ϕ is assumed to be smooth (C_L^2)

and strongly convex, and only recently, interest in nonsmooth stochastic setups has surged – see also [10].

Algorithms. Figures 7.2 and 7.3 indicate that other first-order algorithms not discussed in this chapter can also be very competitive. Some noteworthy ones among these are: (i) alternating direction method of multipliers (ADMM) – see the recent survey treatment by [13], who also advocate ADMM as a practical method for distributed and parallel optimization; (ii) coordinate descent methods [66, 45]; (iii) trust-region methods for composite minimization [29]; (iv) interior point methods specialized to machine learning problems [24, 1] (though generally not scalable, unless the Hessian has special structure or is very sparse); (v) bundle and cutting plane methods [60]; (vi) specialized primal-dual methods [21]; (vii) level-set methods for composite optimization [31]; (viii) dual augmented Lagrangian methods [64]; (ix) Nesterov style methods with optimal rates despite inexact proximity operators [56].

Other setups. We mention some important setups missing in this chapter: (i) bandit optimization [2]; (ii) nonconvex stochastic optimization [10, 20]; (iii) variational inequalities [33]; (iv) robust optimization [7]; (v) derivative free minimization [18]; (vi) trust-region methods [17]; (vii) distributed and parallel optimization [9, 71, 19, 51].

Acknowledgments

I am grateful to Jeff Bilmes for hosting me at the University of Washington, Seattle, during my unforeseen visit in July 2011; large-parts of this chapter were written during that time.

References

[1] Andersen, M.S., Dahl, J., Liu, Z., and Vandenberghe, L. 2011. Interior-point methods for large-scale cone programming. In: *Optimization for Machine Learning*, Sra, S., Nowozin, S., and Wright, S.J. (eds). MIT Press.

[2] Audibert, J.-Y., and Munos, R. 2011. *Introduction to Bandits: Algorithms and Theory*. ICML 2011 Tutorial.

[3] Bach, F., Jenatton, R., Mairal, J., and Obozinski, G. 2011. Convex optimization with sparsity-inducing norms. In: *Optimization for Machine Learning*, Sra, S., Nowozin, S., and Wright, S.J. (eds). MIT Press.

[4] Baraniuk, R. 2007. Compressive sensing. *IEEE Signal Processing Magazine*, **24**(4), 118–121.

[5] Barzilai, J., and Borwein, J. M. 1988. Two-point step size gradient methods. *IMA J. Num. Analy.*, **8**(1), 141–148.

[6] Beck, A., and Teboulle, M. 2009. A fast iterative shrinkage-thresholding algorithm for linear inverse problems. *SIAM J. Imaging Sciences*, **2**(1), 183–202.

[7] Ben-Tal, A., El Ghaoui, L., and Nemirovski, A. 2009. *Robust Optimization*. Princeton University Press.

[8] Bertsekas, D. P. 1999. *Nonlinear Programming*. Second edition. Athena Scientific.

[9] Bertsekas, D. P. 2010. *Incremental gradient, subgradient, and proximal methods for convex optimization: a survey*. Tech. rep. LIDS-P-2848. MIT.

[10] Bertsekas, D. P., and Tsitsiklis, J. N. 2000. Gradient convergence in gradient methods with errors. *SIAM J. on Optimization*, **10**(3), 627–642.

[11] Bottou, L., and Bousquet, O. 2011. The tradeoffs of large-scale learning. In: *Optimization for Machine Learning*, Sra, S., Nowozin, S., and Wright, S.J. (eds). MIT Press.

[12] Boyd, S., and Vandenberghe, L. 2004. *Convex Optimization*. Cambridge University Press.

[13] Boyd, S., Parikh, N., Chu, E., Peleato, B., and Eckstein, J. 2011. Distributed optimization and statistical learning via the alternating direction method of multipliers. Pages 1–124 of: *Foundations and Trends in Machine Learning*, volume 3, Jordan, Michael (ed). NOW.

[14] Chen, J., and Burer, S. 2011. A first-order smoothing technique for a class of large-scale linear programs. *Argonne National Labs Preprint*.

[15] Combettes, P.L., and Pesquet, J.-C. 2010. Proximal splitting methods in signal processing. *arXiv:0912.3522v4*, May.

[16] Combettes, P.L., and Wajs, V.R. 2005. Signal recovery by proximal forward-backward splitting. *Multiscale Modeling and Simulation*, **4**(4), 1168–1200.

[17] Conn, A.R., Gould, N.I.M., and Toint, P.L. 2000. *Trust-Region Methods*. SIAM.

[18] Conn, A.R., Scheinberg, K., and Vicente, L.N. 2009. *Introduction to Derivative-Free Optimization*. SIAM.

[19] Duchi, J., Agarwal, A., and Wainwright, M. 2011. Dual averaging for distributed optimization: convergence analysis and network scaling. *IEEE Transactions on Automatic Control*. **57**(3), 592–606.

[20] Ermoliev, Y. 1981. *Stochastic quasigradient methods and their applications in systems optimization*. Tech. rep. WP-81-2. International Institute for Applied Systems Analysis.

[21] Esser, E., Zhang, X., and Chan, T. F. 2010. A general framework for a class of first order primal–dual algorithms for convex optimization in imaging science. *SIAM J. Imaging Sciences*, **3**(4), 1015–1046.

[22] Frank, A., and Asuncion, A. 2010. *UCI Machine Learning Repository*.

[23] Ghadimi, S., and Lan, G. 2012. Optimal stochastic approximation algorithms for strongly convex stochastic composite optimization. *SIAM J. Optimization*. **22**(4), 1469–1492.

[24] Gondzio, J. 2011. Interior point methods in machine learning. In: *Optimization for Machine Learning*, Sra, S., Nowozin, S., and Wright, S.J. (eds). MIT Press.

[25] Hazan, E. 2011. The convex optimization approach to regret minimization. In: *Optimization for Machine Learning*, Sra, S., Nowozin, S., and Wright, S.J. (eds). MIT Press.

[26] Hazan, E., and Kale, S. 2011. Beyond the regret minimization barrier: an optimal algorithm for stochastic strongly-convex optimization. *Journal of Machine Learning Research Proceedings Track* **19**, 421–436.

[27] Juditsky, A., and Nemirovski, A. 2011a. First-order methods for nonsmooth convex large-scale optimization, I: General purpose methods. In: *Optimization for Machine Learning*, Sra, S., Nowozin, S., and Wright, S.J. (eds). MIT Press.

[28] Juditsky, A., and Nemirovski, A. 2011b. First-Order methods for nonsmooth convex large-scale optimization, II: Utilizing problem's structure. In: *Optimization for Machine Learning*, Sra, S., Nowozin, S., and Wright, S.J. (eds). MIT Press.

[29] Kim, D., Sra, S., and Dhillon, I. S. 2010. A scalable trust-region algorithm with application to mixed-norm regression. In: *ICML-10: Proceedings of the 27th International Conference on Machine Learning*.

[30] Kushner, H. J., and Yin, G. G. 2003. *Stochastic Approximation and Recursive Algorithms and Applications*. Springer.

[31] Lan, G. 2011. Level methods uniformly optimal for composite and structured nonsmooth convex optimization. *Mathematical Programming* (submitted).

[32] Liu, J., Ji, S., and Ye, J. 2009. *SLEP: Sparse Learning with Efficient Projections*. Arizona State University, `http://www.public.asu.edu/~jye02/Software/SLEP`.

[33] Nemirovski, A. 2004. Prox-method with rate of convergence $O(1/t)$ for variational inequalities with Lipschitz continuous monotone operators and smooth convex–concave saddle point problems. *SIAM J. on Optimization*, **15**, 229–251.

[34] Nemirovski, A., Juditsky, A., Lan, G., and Shapiro, A. 2009. Robust stochastic approximation approach to stochastic programming. *SIAM Journal on Optimization*, **19**(4), 1574–1609.

[35] Nemirovsky, A. S., and Yudin, D. B. 1983. *Problem Complexity and Method Efficiency in Optimization*. Wiley-Interscience. Translated by: E. R. Dawson.

[36] Nesterov, Yu. 1983. A method for solving a convex programming problem with rate of convergence $O(1/k^2)$. *Soviet Math. Dokady*, **27**(2), 372–376.

[37] Nesterov, Yu. 1988. On an approach to the construction of optimal methods of minimization of smooth convex functions. *Ekonom. i. Mat. Metody*, **24**, 509–517.

[38] Nesterov, Yu. 2003. *Smooth minimization of non-smooth functions*. Tech. rep. 2003/12. Université Catholique de Louvain, Center for Operations Research and Econometrics (CORE).

[39] Nesterov, Yu. 2004. *Introductory Lectures on Convex Optimization: A Basic Course*. Springer.

[40] Nesterov, Yu. 2005a. Excessive gap technique in nonsmooth convex minimization. *SIAM Journal on Optimization*, **16**(1), 235–249.

[41] Nesterov, Yu. 2005b. Smooth minimization of nonsmooth functions. *Math. Program., Series A*, **103**, 127–152.

[42] Nesterov, Yu. 2007. *Gradient methods for minimizing composite objective function.* Tech. rep. 2007/76. Université Catholique de Louvain, Center for Operations Research and Econometrics (CORE).

[43] Nesterov, Yu. 2008. How to advance in structural convex optimization. *OPTIMA, MPS Newsletter*, **78**, 2–5.

[44] Nesterov, Yu. 2009. Primal-dual subgradient methods for convex problems. *Mathematical Programming*, **120**, 221–259.

[45] Nesterov, Yu. 2010. *Efficiency of coordinate descent methods on huge-scale optimization problems.* Tech. rep. 2010/2. Université Catholique de Louvain, Center for Operations Research and Econometrics (CORE).

[46] Nesterov, Yu., and Nemirovski, A. 1994. *Interior Point Polynomial Algorithms in Convex Programming.* SIAM.

[47] Patriksson, M. 2005 (Oct.). *A survey on a classic core problem in operations research.* Tech. rep. 2005:33. Chalmers University of Technology and Göteborg University.

[48] Polyak, B.T. 1987. *Introduction to Optimization.* Optimization Software Inc.

[49] Portnoy, Stephen, and Koenker, Roger. 1997. The Gaussian hare and the Laplacian tortoise: computability of squared-error versus absolute-error estimators. *Statistical Science*, **12**(4), 279–300.

[50] Raginsky, M., and Rakhlin, A. 2011. Information-based complexity, feedback and dynamics in convex programming. *IEEE Transactions on Information Theory*, **57**(10), 7036–7056.

[51] Recht, Benjamin, Re, Christopher, Wright, Stephen, and Niu, Feng. 2011. Hogwild: a lock-free approach to parallelizing stochastic gradient descent. Pages 693–701 of: *Advances in Neural Information Processing Systems* **24**, Shawe-Taylor, J., Zemel, R.S., Bartlett, P., Pereira, F.C.N., and Weinberger, K.Q. (eds).

[52] Robbins, H., and Monro, S. 1951. A stochastic approximation method. *Annals of Mathematical Statistics*, **22**(3), 400–407.

[53] Rockafellar, R.T. 1970. *Convex Analysis.* Princeton University Press.

[54] Rockafellar, R.T., and Wets, R.J.-B. 1998. *Variational Analysis.* Springer.

[55] Rudin, Leonid I., Osher, Stanley, and Fatemi, Emad. 1992. Nonlinear total variation based noise removal algorithms. *Physica D*, **60**, 259–268.

[56] Schmidt, M., Roux, N. Le, and Bach, F. 2011. Convergence rates of inexact proximal-gradient methods for convex optimization. In: *Advances in Neural Information Processing Systems (NIPS)*.

[57] Sra, S., Nowozin, S., and Wright, S.J. (eds). 2011. *Optimization for Machine Learning.* MIT Press.

[58] Srebro, N., and Tewari, A. 2010. *Stochastic Optimization for Machine Learning.* ICML 2010 Tutorial.

[59] Stobbe, P., and Krause, A. 2010. Efficient minimization of decomposable submodular functions. In: *Advances in Neural Information Processing Systems (NIPS)*.

[60] Teo, C. H., Vishwanthan, S.V.N., Smola, A.J., and Le, Q.V. 2010. Bundle methods for regularized risk minimization. *J. Machine Learning Research*, **11**, 311–365.

[61] Tibshirani, R., Saunders, M., Rosset, S., Zhu, J., and Knight, K. 2005. Sparsity and smoothness via the fused lasso. *J. Royal Stat. Soc. Series B*, **67**(1), 91–108.

[62] Tibshirani, Robert. 1996. Regression shrinkage and selection via the lasso. *J. R. Statist. Soc.*, **58**(1), 267–288.

[63] Tikhomirov, V.M. 1996. The evolution of methods of convex optimization. *American Mathematical Monthly*, **103**(1), 65–71.

[64] Tomioka, R., Suzuki, T., and Sugiyama, M. 2011. Super-linear convergence of dual augmented Lagrangian algorithm for sparsity regularized estimation. *J. Machine Learning Research*, **12**, 1537–1586.

[65] Tseng, P. 2008. On accelerated gradient methods for convex–concave minimization. `https://www.math.washington.edu/ tseng/papers/apgm.pdf`.

[66] Tseng, P., and Yun, S. 2009. A block-coordinate gradient descent method for linearly constrained nonsmooth separable optimization. *J. Optim. Theory Appl.*, **140**, 513–535.

[67] Wright, S. J., Nowak, R. D., and Figueiredo, M. A. T. 2009. Sparse reconstruction by separable approximation. *IEEE Trans. Sig. Proc.*, **57**(7), 2479–2493.

[68] Ying, Yiming, Huang, Kaizhu, and Campbell, Colin. 2009. Sparse metric learning via smooth optimization. Pages 2214–2222 of: *Advances in Neural Information Processing Systems* **22**, Bengio, Y., Schuurmans, D., Lafferty, J., Williams, C.K.I., and Culotta, A. (eds).

[69] Yudin, D.B., and Nemirovskii, A.S. 1976. Informational complexity and effective methods of solution for convex extremal problems. *Ekonomika i Matematicheski Metody*, **12**, 357–369.

[70] Zhang, X., Saha, A., and Vishwanathan, S. V. N. 2011. Accelerated training of max–margin Markov networks with kernels. Pages 292–307 of: *Algorithmic Learning Theory*, LNCS **6925**.

[71] Zinkevich, M., Weimer, M., Smola, A., and Li, L. 2010. Parallelized stochastic gradient descent. Pages 2595–2603 of: *Advances in Neural Information Processing Systems* **23**, Lafferty, J., Williams, C.K.I., Shawe-Taylor, J., Zemel, R.S., and Culotta, A. (eds).

8

Approximation Algorithms

Mohit Singh, Kunal Talwar

Optimization problems are often hard to solve precisely. However solutions that are only *nearly optimal* are often good enough in practical applications. Approximation algorithms can find such solutions efficiently for many interesting problems. Profound theoretical results additionally help us understand what problems are approximable. This chapter gives an overview of existing approximation techniques, along five broad categories: greedy algorithms, linear and semi-definite programming relaxations, metric embeddings and special techniques. It concludes with an overview of the main inapproximability results.

8.1 Introduction

NP-hard optimization problems are ubiquitous, and unless P=NP, we cannot expect algorithms that find *optimal* solutions on *all* instances in *polynomial* time. This intractability thus forces us to relax one of the three above mentioned constraints. Approximation algorithms relax the optimality constraint, and aim to do so by as small an amount as possible. We shall concern ourselves with discrete optimization problems, where the goal is to find amongst the set of *feasible* solutions, the one that minimizes (or maximizes) the value of the *objective function*. Usually, the space of feasible solutions is defined implicitly, e.g. the set of cuts in a graph on n vertices. The objective function associates with each feasible solution a real value; this usually has a succinct representation as well, e.g. the number of edges in the cut. We measure the performance of an approximation algorithm on a given instance by the ratio of the value of the solution output by the algorithm, to that of the optimal solution. The approximation ratio of the algorithm is the worst-case value of this ratio, taken over all possible inputs. Thus an approximation algorithm is measured by its worst case performance guarantee.

This apparently pessimistic viewpoint frees us from making any assumptions about the distribution of the inputs that we see. Attempting to prove worst-case guarantees forces us to understand well the structure of the problem and this understanding is often vital in the design of heuristics. For example, knowing the kind of instances on which one algorithm performs poorly often motivates the design of better algorithms. Moreover an approximation algorithm by definition comes with a certificate of near-optimality, which provides us with both an upper and a lower bound on the value of the optimum, even though the actual value of the optimum is NP-hard to compute! These bounds can be useful subroutines for heuristics such as branch-and-bound. Moreover, the best possible approximation ratio for a problem, often called its *approximability*, gives a finer distinction about the hardness of the problems than plain vanilla NP-hardness. Indeed some problems such as the knapsack problem have polynomial time approximation schemes (PTASes): for any fixed constant $\epsilon > 0$, one can get a $(1 + \epsilon)$-approximation algorithm in polynomial time depending on ϵ. For others, such as the maximum coverage problem, the approximability is some constant: we can design a constant factor approximation, and can prove that it cannot be improved unless $P = NP$. Yet others such as the set cover problem and the maximum clique problem, have approximation ratios that must get worse as the instance size increases. In this chapter, we will encounter problems with varying degrees of hardness illustrating this distinction.

In this chapter, we survey some of the beautiful techniques that have been developed in the design of approximation algorithms. We have chosen to concentrate on, and organize this survey around, general techniques for attacking optimization problems, rather than on specific practical problems. We will illustrate these techniques on simple and often abstract optimization problems to present the ideas clearly; they however extend to a large variety of problems. These problems have been chosen to ease the exposition, and may not necessarily be the most practically useful ones where these techniques apply. For the purposes of this chapter, polynomial running time will be the proxy for computational efficiency and we do not discuss approaches to get faster runtimes. Some of the theorems in this chapter are presented without proofs. Additionally, several important related topics such as smoothed analysis, stochastic optimization, streaming algorithms, sublinear algorithms, online algorithms, mechanism design, etc. are not covered for lack of space. We refer the reader to a recent textbook such as [55, 53] on the topic for a more complete treatment of the subject.

This chapter is organized as follows. We start with simple combinatorial algorithmic techniques such as greedy and local search in Section 8.2. Linear

Programming is one of the most widely used tools in approximation algorithms, and is described in Section 8.3. Section 8.4 studies the more powerful technique of semidefinite programming. Section 8.5 discusses structural properties of the inputs that often make problems easier. Some of these are exploited in Section 8.6 which discusses the use of metric embeddings in approximation algorithms. We conclude with Section 8.7 that discusses tools used to prove the impossibility (under standard complexity-theoretic assumptions) of designing good approximation algorithms for several problems.

8.2 Combinatorial Algorithms

In this section, we describe some of the simplest and oldest techniques in the design of (exact and) approximation algorithms. Below we give examples of greedy and local search based algorithms. Dynamic programming is another combinatorial tool that will be illustrated in Section 8.5.

8.2.1 Greedy Algorithm

Greedy algorithms informally refer to a class of algorithms that make a sequence of irreversible decisions using a certain criteria where each of the decisions is locally optimal. A classical example of an exact greedy algorithm is Kruskal's algorithm (see e.g. Chapter 23 [18]) for the minimum spanning tree problem that repeatedly picks the cheapest edge that connects two different components in the graph of currently picked edges. For the minimum spanning tree problem, this algorithm returns an exact optimum solution.

For many NP-hard optimization problems, greedy algorithms give nontrivial approximation guarantees and are easy to implement. In this section, we shall illustrate this using the example of the set cover problem [34, 44].

Set Cover
Input: A universe $U = [n]$, a collection $S_1, \ldots, S_m \subseteq U$, cost $c_j \in \Re_+$ for $j \in [m]$.
Output: A subset $C \subseteq [m]$ such that $\cup_{j \in C} S_j = U$.
Objective: Minimize the cost $c(C) = \sum_{j \in C} c_j$.

The greedy algorithm iteratively picks a set that costs the least relative to the number of uncovered elements that it covers. It stops when all elements are covered. Formally the algorithm is given in Figure 8.1.

The following theorem proves the approximation guarantee of the algorithm.

1. Let $C \leftarrow \emptyset$, $R_0 \leftarrow U$, $t \leftarrow 0$.
2. While $R_t \neq \emptyset$ do
   (a) $t \leftarrow t + 1$.
   (b) Let j_t be such that S_{j_t} minimizes $c(S_j)/|R_{t-1} \cap S_j|$.
   (c) $R_t \leftarrow R_{t-1} \setminus S_{j_t}$, $C \leftarrow C \cup \{j_t\}$.
3. Return C.

Figure 8.1 Greedy Algorithm for Set Cover

Theorem 8.1   *The Greedy algorithm returns a set cover of cost at most H_n times the optimal.*

Proof   Let OPT denote the optimal solution. In iteration t, when R_{t-1} is the set of uncovered elements, the sets in OPT cover the R_{t-1} remaining elements at cost $c(OPT)$. Thus there must be a set in OPT whose cost-to-benefit ratio is at most $c(OPT)/|R_{t-1}|$. Thus the cost-to-benefit ratio for the set S_{j_t} picked by the Greedy algorithm is no larger. Thus

$$c(C) = \sum_t c(S_{j_t}) = \sum_t |R_{t-1} \cap S_{j_t}| \cdot \frac{c(S_{j_t})}{|R_{t-1} \cap S_{j_t}|}$$

$$\leq \sum_t |R_{t-1} \cap S_{j_t}| \frac{c(OPT)}{|R_{t-1}|} \leq c(OPT) \cdot \sum_i \frac{1}{i}$$

$$= H_n \cdot c(OPT). \qquad \square$$

Surprisingly, as we discuss in Section 8.7, this $H_n \approx \ln n$ approximation guarantee of the simple greedy algorithm for the set cover problem cannot be improved unless $P = NP$. Greedy algorithms tend be versatile and achieve good performance on many variants and generalizations of the set cover problem. For example, in the *max coverage problem*, we are also given an integer k and the goal is to pick k sets from the collection $S_1, \ldots, S_m$ such that the union of the k chosen sets is maximized. A natural greedy algorithm, which in each step picks the set covering the largest number of uncovered elements, gives a $(1 - \frac{1}{e}) \approx 0.63$-approximation. Similar greedy algorithms continue to perform well for the significantly general problem of maximizing a *submodular function* subject to cardinality k constraint [48] or even subject to a matroid constraint [54]. Also see Chapter 3 for applications and more details on algorithms for submodular function optimization.

8.2.2 *Local Search*

Local search is a metaheuristic where in each step we try to find a better solution in certain well-defined neighborhood of the current solution. Consider
any minimization problem π and let $\mathcal{F}$ denote the set of all feasible solutions
and $cost : \mathcal{F} \to \Re_+$ denote the objective function. We define a neighborhood
set for each solution in $\mathcal{F}$ given by $\mathcal{N} : \mathcal{F} \to 2^{\mathcal{F}}$. A short description of the
local search heuristic is given in Figure 8.2. Local search for maximization
problems is analogously defined.

---

1. Initialize F to be an arbitrary solution from $\mathcal{F}$.
2. While there exists a $F' \in \mathcal{N}(F)$ such that $\text{cost}(F') < \text{cost}(F)$

   Do $F \leftarrow F'$.

3. Return F

Figure 8.2 Local Search Heuristic

Since the final solution returned by the local search algorithm cannot be
improved by any local improving steps, we call it a *locally optimal* solution
(with respect to the neigborhood function). The neighborhood function $\mathcal{N}$
is the most crucial aspect of defining a local search heuristic. Informally ex-
panding the neighborhood improves the quality of locally optimal solutions.
On the other hand, the search for an improving move in a larger neighborhood usually takes longer. We will show an example of this tradeoff in this
section. Local search has been a popular heuristic for optimization problems,
the most famous example being the 1-exchange heuristic given by [42] for
the traveling salesman problem. Here, we show two examples of local search
algorithms for the maximum cut problem and the k-median problem.

Maximum Cut
Input: A graph $G = (V, E)$.
Output: A bipartition of vertices (U, U^c).
Objective: Maximize the number of cut edges $|E(U, U^c)| = |\{(u, v) : u \in U, v \in U^c\}|$.

Here $E(S, T) = \{\{u, v\} \in E : u \in S, v \in T\}$ denotes the set of edges
between sets of vertices S and T. The local search algorithm is a simple
algorithm and given in Figure 8.3. Here we define the neighborhood of a
solution (U, U^c) to be all other solutions (W, W^c) such that U and W differ
by at most one vertex. Thus each iteration can be implemented by evaluating
a total of at most $|V|$ different solutions.

Lemma 8.2 *For any locally optimal solution, (U, U^c), $E(U, U^c) \geq \frac{|E|}{2}$.*

---

1. Initialize U to be an arbitrary set of V.
2. While there exists an improving step do
   (a) If there exists $u \in U$ such that $E(u, U) > E(u, U^c)$ then $U \leftarrow U \setminus \{u\}$.
   (b) If there exists $u \in U^c$ such that $E(u, U^c) > E(u, U)$ then $U \leftarrow U \cup \{u\}$.
3. Return (U, U^c).

Figure 8.3 Local Search Algorithm for Max-Cut

Proof Let (U, U^c) be the solution returned by the algorithm. Then, for each $u \in U$ we have $E(u, U^c) \geq E(u, U)$ and for each $u \in U^c$, we have $E(u, U) \geq E(u, U^c)$. Thus,

$$2|E(U, U^c)|$$
$$= \sum_{u \in U} E(u, U^c) + \sum_{u \in U^c} E(u, U)$$
$$\geq \frac{1}{2} \left(\sum_{u \in U} E(u, U^c) + \sum_{u \in U} E(u, U) + \sum_{u \in U^c} E(u, U) + \sum_{u \in U^c} E(u, U^c) \right)$$
$$\geq |E| \geq OPT$$

where OPT denotes the size of the optimal solution. $\qquad \square$

The above lemma already implies that the local search algorithm is a $\frac{1}{2}$-approximation. Also observe that each iteration increases the size of the cut by at least 1, so that the algorithm terminates in polynomial time.

Theorem 8.3 *The local search algorithm is a $\frac{1}{2}$-approximation algorithm for the max-cut problem.*

We will see later in Section 8.4 that semi-definite programming can yield better algorithms for the maxcut problem.

Local search has also been successfully applied to many facility location problems [8]. We next discuss one variant of the problem that also illustrates two important aspects of local search algorithms.

k-median Problem
Input: A set of facilities F, clients C, an integer $k \geq 1$ and a distance metric $d : C \cup F \times C \cup F \rightarrow \Re_+$.
Output: A subset of facilities $S \subseteq F$ such that $|S| \leq k$
Objective: Minimize $c(S) = \sum_{i \in C} \min\{d(i, f) : f \in S\}$.

In Figure 8.4, we give a local search algorithm for the k-median problem.

Here a neighborhood of a solution $S \subseteq F$ is the set of all solutions which can be obtained by swapping one facility for another.

---

1. Initialize S to be an arbitrary subset of F of size k.
2. While there exists an improving step do

   (Swap) If there exists $f \in S$ and $f' \in F \setminus S$ such that $c(S \cup \{f'\} \setminus \{f\}) < c(S)$ then $S \leftarrow S \cup \{f'\} \setminus \{f\}$.

3. Return S.

Figure 8.4 Local Search Algorithm for k-median Location

We state without proof the following lemma due to [8].

Lemma 8.4 *Let S be any locally optimal solution returned by the local search algorithm for the k-median problemm. Then $c(S) \le 5c(S^*)$ where S^* is an optimal solution.*

Unfortunately, the above lemma does not directly imply a 5-approximation for the problem since the local search algorithm is not guaranteed to run in polynomial time, a typical problem with many local search algorithms. A standard fix is to modify the algorithm and implement an improving step only if the value of the objective function reduces by a multiplicative factor of $(1 + \epsilon)$ for some fixed constant $\epsilon > 0$. We call a solution returned by the modified local search algorithm a *pseudo-locally* optimal solution. The following lemma can be analogously proved.

Lemma 8.5 *Let S be any pseudo-locally optimal solution returned by the local search algorithm for the facility location problem. Then $c(S) \le 5(1 + \epsilon)c(S^*)$ where S^* is an optimal solution.*

The fact that each step of the algorithm gives a multiplicative improvement in the cost ensures that the running time is polynomial in the input size.

Theorem 8.6 *For any fixed $\epsilon > 0$, the pseudo-local search algorithm for the k-median problem runs in polynomial time and returns a solution S such that $c(S) \le (5 + \epsilon) \cdot c(S^*)$ where S^* is an optimal solution.*

The k-median problem also illustrates another attractive feature of local search algorithms. Consider a modified local search algorithm where we increase the neighborhood of any solution and check for improvements by swapping every subset of p facilities, for some fixed integer $p \ge 1$. Since the number of possible swaps is bounded by n^p, each improving step can be implemented in polynomial time. The following result, also proved in [8], shows that the larger the value of p, the better is the locally optimal solution.

Lemma 8.7   *Let S be a locally optimal solution returned by the local search algorithm for k-median problem which checks for any improving solution by swapping p facilities. Then $c(S) \leq (3 + \frac{2}{p})c(S^*)$ where S^* is the optimal solution.*

8.3 Linear Programming Based Algorithms

Mathematical programming and in particular, linear programming has been a crucial ingredient in the design of approximation algorithms for many problems. We refer the reader to introductory text on linear programming [17, 46] and assume basic familiarity with linear programming. The following is a standard recipe in the design of approximation algorithms. First, the optimization problem is modeled as an integer linear program where the constraints and the objective function are linear but variables can be restricted to integer values. The second step is to relax the integrality condition on the variable and allow the variables to take values in a certain interval to obtain a linear program. The last part of the recipe is to convert the fractional solution in to an integral solution which corresponds to feasible solution of the problem.

The first step is usually rather simple for a large class of optimization problems; nevertheless often we add a family of constraints that may be redundant for the integer program itself, but tighten the linear programming relaxation. Since the integer program exactly models the problem, it is NP-hard to optimize, and hence the second step is important. A seminal result of [35] shows that linear programs can be solved in polynomial time. Thus, in polynomial time, we obtain a *fractional* solution to the linear programming relaxation. Many different techniques have been developed for the last part of the recipe, the rounding algorithm. These includes randomized rounding [51], using linear algebraic properties of optimum fractional solution [41, 32, 39], interpreting linear programming solutions as metrics (see Section 8.6), and deterministic rounding (see Chapter 4 in [55]). The optimal solution to the linear programming relaxation is (for a minimization problem) always no larger than the integer optimum. It is usually a proxy for the optimum value: we prove the approximation guarantee by comparing the cost of the rounded integral solution to the cost of the fractional one. In this section, we will illustrate randomized rounding for the set cover problem and show that it achieves the same guarantee as the greedy algorithm.

Another class of algorithms based on linear programming are primal-dual algorithms. These algorithms do not solve the linear program but are guided by duality of linear programming. They construct a feasible solution to the

$$IP_{SC}: \quad \min \sum_{i=1}^{m} c_i x_i$$
$$\text{s.t.}$$
$$\forall e \in E, \; \sum_{i:e \in S_i} x_i \geq 1$$
$$\forall 1 \leq i \leq m, \quad x_i \quad \in \{0,1\}$$

$$LP_{SC}: \quad \min \sum_{i=1}^{m} c_i x_i$$
$$\text{s.t.}$$
$$\forall e \in E, \; \sum_{i:e \in S_i} x_i \geq 1$$
$$\forall 1 \leq i \leq m, \quad x_i \quad \geq 0$$

Figure 8.5 Integer Program

Figure 8.6 Linear Program

problem alongside a feasible solution to the dual linear program which guarantees the quality of the returned solution. Since solving of linear programs is avoided, primal-dual algorithms are usually faster in running time. We will illustrate a primal-dual algorithm for the set cover problem and discuss the method in some detail.

8.3.1 Randomized Rounding

In this section, we demonstrate one of the simplest yet surprisingly effective rounding procedure for linear programs, as applied to the set cover problem. The first step is to formulate an integer program for the set cover problem. To do this, we introduce a binary decision variable x_i for each set S_i, $1 \leq i \leq m$. The setting of value 1 to the variable x_i denotes that S_i is included in the solution and $x_i = 0$ denotes that S_i is not included in the solution. The integer program is given in Figure 8.5. There is one constraint for each element $e \in E$ indicating that one must pick at least one set containing e. It is easy to verify that the feasible solutions to the integer program exactly correspond to the feasible solutions of the set cover problem. We relax the integrality constraints to get a linear programming relaxation as given in Figure 8.6. Solving the linear programming relaxation gives us a *fractional* solution x^* such that cost $(x^*) \leq OPT$ where OPT is the cost of the optimal solution.

The solution x^* is fractional and may take arbitrary values in the interval $[0, 1]$, we aim to obtain an integral solution whose cost can be related to the cost of x^*. Since $x_i^* = 1$ corresponds to the set S_i being picked and $x_i^* = 0$ corresponds to it not being picked, a natural choice is to interpret an arbitrary $x_i^* \in (0, 1)$ to be the probability with which the linear program suggests that we pick set S_i in the final solution. Thus we obtain a natural randomized rounding algorithm for the set cover problem given in Figure 8.7. To ensure feasibility of the solution, we repeat $O(\log n)$ times.

We now prove the performance of the randomized rounding algorithm.

---

1. Solve LP_{SC} to get the optimal fractional solution x^*. Initialize $\mathcal{I} \leftarrow \emptyset$.
2. For $4 \log n$ independent rounds do
    Include set S_i in $\mathcal{I}$ with probability x_i^* for each $1 \leq i \leq m$.
3. For every element e in E which is not covered by some set in $\mathcal{I}$, include the cheapest set containing e in $\mathcal{I}$.
4. Return $\mathcal{I}$.

Figure 8.7 Randomized Rounding Algorithm for Set Cover

Theorem 8.8 *Randomized Rounding algorithm returns a solution $\mathcal{I}$ such that $E(\text{cost}(\mathcal{I})) = O(\log n) \cdot OPT$ where OPT is the cost of the optimal solution.*

Proof It is easy to check that the algorithm runs in polynomial time and returns a feasible solution. We now argue that its expected cost is $O(\log n)OPT$. Consider any element $e \in E$. The probability that the element is not covered by a set included in one iteration of Step 2 is at most

$$\prod_{i: e \in S_i} (1 - x_i^*) \leq \prod_{i: e \in S_i} e^{-x_i^*} = e^{\sum_{i: e \in S_i} -x_i^*} \leq \frac{1}{e}$$

where the first inequality follows from the fact that $1 - x \leq e^{-x}$ for any x and the last inequality follows from the feasibility of solution x^* to LP_{SC}. Since the coin tosses in the $4 \log n$ iterations are independent, the probability that e is not covered by any set in $\mathcal{I}$ after the $4 \log n$ iterations in Step 2 is at most $(\frac{1}{e})^{4 \log n} \leq \frac{1}{n^2}$. On the other hand, the expected cost of the sets included in any single iteration of Step 2 is at most

$$\sum_{i=1}^{m} c(S_i) \cdot Pr[S_i \text{ is included in } \mathcal{I}] = \sum_{i=1}^{m} c(S_i) \cdot x_i^* = OPT_{LP} \leq OPT$$

Thus the expected cost of the sets included in $4 \log n$ iterations is at most $4 \log n \cdot OPT$. In the unlikely event that e is left uncovered in $4 \log n$ iterations, the set included to cover e costs at most OPT. Thus the expected total cost of sets included in Step 3 is at most $\frac{1}{n^2} n \cdot OPT \leq OPT$. Thus the total expected cost of the solution is $O(\log n)OPT$ as claimed. □

We remark that this, and other randomized algorithms presented in this chapter can be *derandomized* to get deterministic algorithms with the same performance guarantee.

$$LP_{SC}: \quad \min \sum_{i=1}^{m} c_i x_i \qquad\qquad DLP_{SC}: \quad \max \sum_{e \in E} y_e$$
$$\text{s.t.} \qquad\qquad\qquad\qquad\qquad \text{s.t.}$$
$$\forall e \in E \ \sum_{i:e \in S_i} x_i \geq 1 \qquad \forall 1 \leq i \leq m \ \sum_{e:e \in S_i} y_e \leq c_i$$
$$\forall 1 \leq i \leq m \qquad x_i \quad \geq 0 \qquad\qquad \forall e \in e \quad y_e \quad \geq 0$$

Figure 8.8 Linear Program   Figure 8.9 Dual Linear Program

8.3.2 Primal Dual Algorithms

Primal-dual is a general algorithmic paradigm which has proved successful for many combinatorial optimization problems. Its roots lie in exact algorithms for minimum cost matchings in bipartite graphs [21, 38] and as an algorithm to solve general linear programs [19]. It has been a very powerful technique to obtain exact algorithms for polynomial time solvable problems including min-cost flows and matchings. Here we will illustrate its successful export to the design of approximation algorithms which involves certain new ideas over the basic method. Apart from being a generic algorithmic paradigm, primal-dual algorithms are often faster than linear programming rounding algorithms since they use linear programs to guide the algorithm design but do not actually need an LP solver as a subroutine.

Linear programming duality plays a crucial role in the design and analysis of primal-dual algorithms and we shall review it briefly here. We refer the reader to [17] for basic facts about duality. We will illustrate the primal dual method on the set cover problem defined in Section 8.2.1. A linear program for the set cover problem, and its dual linear program DLP_{SC} are given in Figure 8.8 and Figure 8.9.

The following theorem states the strong and weak duality of linear programming as applied to the above linear program. It is easy to verify that both LP_{SC} and DLP_{SC} are feasible, so that strong duality holds.

Theorem 8.9   *For every feasible solutions x of LP_{SC} and y of DLP_{SC} we must have $OPT \geq \sum_i c_i x_i \geq \sum_{e \in E} y_e$ where OPT is the optimal integral solution to the set cover problem. Moreover, there exists optimal solutions x^* and y^* to LP_{SC} and $Dual_{SC}$, respectively, which satisfy the following conditions.*

1. *(Strong Duality) $\sum_{i=1}^{m} c_i x_i^* = \sum_{e \in E} y_e^*$.*
2. *(Primal complementary slackness) If $x_i^* > 0$ then $\sum_{e:e \in S_i} y_e^* = c_i$.*
3. *(Dual Complementary slackness) If $y_e^* > 0$ then $\sum_{i:e \in S_i} x_i^* = 1$.*

The guiding principle of primal dual algorithms is to start with an infeasible primal *integral* solution $\hat{x} = 0$ and a feasible dual solution $\hat{y} = 0$. As the algorithm progresses, we maintain the primal complementary slackness conditions but relax the dual complementary conditions; however we maintain an integral primal. This is in contrast to the traditional primal-dual algorithms for exact optimization where both the complementary slackness conditions are maintained. In each iteration, we either improve upon the feasibility of the primal solution or increase the objective of the dual solution. The algorithm is given in Figure 8.10.

---

1. Start with an infeasible primal solution $\hat{x} = 0$ and feasible dual $\hat{y} = 0$.
2. While x remains infeasible
   (a) Choose an e' such that $\hat{x}$ violates the constraint corresponding to e', (i.e. $\sum_{i:e' \in S_i} \hat{x}_i \not\geq 1$).
   (b) Increase $\hat{y}_{e'}$ to the maximum value ensuring that $\hat{y}$ remains feasible, i.e., until there exists a set S_i containing e' such that $\sum_{e \in S_i} \hat{y}_e = c_i$.
   (c) Update $\hat{x}_i = 1$.
3. Let $\mathcal{C} = \{S_i : \hat{x}_i = 1\}$. Return $\mathcal{C}$.

Figure 8.10 Primal Dual Algorithm

Observe that the primal complementary conditions are satisfied since we set $\hat{x}_i = 1$ only if $\sum_{e \in S_i} y_i = c_i$. The dual complementary slackness conditions are violated, but as we show next, bounding the extent of the violation allows us to bound the approximation factor of the algorithm.

Theorem 8.10 *The primal-dual algorithm for set cover problem is a ρ-approximation where $\rho = \max_{e \in E} |\{S_i : e \in S_i\}|$.*

Proof We have

$$\text{cost}(\mathcal{C}) = \sum_{i=1}^{n} c_i \cdot \hat{x}_i = \sum_{i=1}^{n} (\sum_{e \in S_i} \hat{y}_e) \hat{x}_i$$

$$= \sum_{e \in E} \hat{y}_e (\sum_{i:e \in S_i} \hat{x}_i) \leq \rho \sum_{e \in E} \hat{y}_e \leq \rho \cdot OPT$$

where the first equality follows from primal complementary slackness conditions. Since each $\hat{x}_i$ is at most 1, the sum $\sum_{i:e \in S_i} \hat{x}_i$ is at most ρ. In other words, the dual complementary slackness conditions hold up a factor of ρ. Finally an application of weak duality completes the proof. □

The above algorithm implies a 2-approximation for the *vertex cover problem*. In the vertex cover problem, we are given a graph $G = (V, E)$ with costs $c : V \rightarrow \Re_+$ on the vertices and the goal is to select a subset W of vertices of minimum cost such that for every $\{u, v\} \in E$, $\{u, v\} \cap W \neq \emptyset$. A simple reduction to set cover problem is given by setting $U = E$ and defining a set $S_v = \{\{u, v\} \in E : u \in V\}$ for each vertex $v \in V$ of cost c_v. Any set cover solution exactly corresponds to a vertex cover solution of the same cost and the set cover instance has $\rho = \max_{e \in E} |\{S_v : e \in S_v\}| = 2$. Thus the primal-dual algorithm is a 2-approximation for the vertex cover problem.

The primal dual method lends itself to simple modifications, for example, increasing multiple dual variables at once for some well chosen set of violated constraints instead of a single constraint as done in Step 2(b), or pruning the final solution to a *minimal feasible* solution at the end. Thus for example, a modified primal dual algorithm gives an $\ln n$ approximation to set cover. Such techniques have been very successful for network design problems like Steiner forest problem [1, 27] and more generally, survivable network design problem. Recently, primal-dual algorithms have found applications in design of online algorithms [15] where data is not known completely in advance and is slowly revealed to the algorithm.

8.4 Semi-Definite Programming Based Algorithms

A n by n matrix X is positive semi-definite if for all vectors $z \in \Re^n$, we have $z^T X z \geq 0$. A semi-definite program is a generalization of a linear program where the objective function and constraints are linear, as in a linear program, but there is an additional constraint that a matrix consisting of variables is positive semi-definite. A typical semi-definite program is given in Figure 8.11. Here X is a $n \times n$ matrix of variables, C, A^k for $1 \leq k \leq m$ are $n \times n$ matrices of scalars. Here for matrices A and B, the inner product $A \cdot B$ is defined as $\sum_{i,j} a_{ij} b_{ij}$. Using Cholesky decomposition, a semi-definite program can be shown to be equivalent to a vector program as given in Figure 8.12. Thus we effectively have a linear program, where the variables are required to representable as dot products of vector variables. This geometric restriction tightens the relaxation and gives us the additional structure to design better approximation algorithms. The vector program is much easier to work with for combinatorial optimization problems and we will use this formulation here. We refer the reader to the survey by [26] and lecture notes by [45] for an introduction to semi-definite programming and its applications in combinatorial optimization.

$$SDP_1: \quad \min \ C \cdot X$$
$$\text{s.t.}$$
$$\forall 1 \le k \le m \ \ A^k \cdot X \ge b_k$$
$$X \succeq 0$$

$$SDP_2: \quad \min \ \sum_{i,j} c_{ij} \mathbf{v_i} \cdot \mathbf{v_j}$$
$$\text{s.t.}$$
$$\forall 1 \le k \le m, \ \sum_{i,j} A_{ij}^k \mathbf{v_i} \cdot \mathbf{v_j} \ge b_k$$
$$\forall 1 \le i \le n, \qquad \mathbf{v_i} \qquad \in R^n$$

Figure 8.11 Semi-Definite Program

Figure 8.12 Vector Program

$$SDP_{MC}: \quad \max \sum_{\{i,j\} \in E} \frac{w_{ij}}{2} \cdot (1 - \mathbf{v_i} \cdot \mathbf{v_j})$$
$$\text{s.t.}$$
$$\forall i \in V, \qquad \mathbf{v_i} \cdot \mathbf{v_i} = \mathbf{1}$$
$$\forall i \in V, \qquad \mathbf{v_i} \in \mathbf{R^n}$$

Figure 8.13 Vector Program for Maximum Cut

While semi-definite programs (SDP) are more general than linear programs, they are still convex programs and are polynomial time solvable [30]. For certain optimization problems, semi-definite programs give better relaxations and lead to improved approximation algorithms. Starting with the seminal work of [28] on approximation algorithms for the maximum cut problem, SDP's have had a strong influence in development of approximation algorithms. Currently, the best algorithms for sparsest cut [7] (see Section 8.6) and many classes of constraint satisfaction problems [52] are achieved via rounding their semi-definite relaxations. Here, we will illustrate the use of semi-definite programming by describing the aforementioned algorithm of [28] for the maximum cut problem.

We first formulate a vector programming relaxation for the maximum cut problem. The relaxation is given in Figure 8.13. There is a variable vector $\mathbf{v_i}$ for each vertex $i \in G$. The constraints imply that each of these vectors is a unit vector. We first argue that this vector program is a relaxation for the maximum cut problem. Let (U, U^c) be the optimal maximum cut solution. We set $\mathbf{v_i} = (+1, 0, 0, \ldots, 0)$ for each $i \in U$ and $\mathbf{v_i} = (-1, 0, 0, \ldots, 0)$ for each $i \notin U$. It is easily verified that this solution satisfies all the constraints and its SDP objective value is exactly $\sum_{e \in E(U, U^c)} w_e$.

Figure 8.14 gives a simple randomized rounding algorithm for the problem. The algorithm picks a random hyperplane whose normal vector is given by vector $\mathbf{r}$ in the algorithm and includes all vertices i in U which lie on one side of the hyperplane. We prove the following Lemma.

1. Solve SDP_{MC} to get the optimal vector solution $\mathbf{v}^*$.
2. Sample a unit vector $\mathbf{r}$ uniformly at random.
3. For each vertex $i \in V$

    If $\mathbf{v}_i^* \cdot \mathbf{r} \geq \mathbf{0}$, then $U \leftarrow U \cup \{i\}$.
4. Return (U, U^c).

Figure 8.14 Randomized Rounding Algorithm for Maximum Cut

Lemma 8.11 *For any pair of vertices $i, j \in V$, the probability that vertices i and j are separated by cut (U, U^c) is exactly $\frac{\cos^{-1}(\mathbf{v}_i^* \cdot \mathbf{v}_j^*)}{\pi}$.*

Proof The vectors $\mathbf{v}_i^*$ and $\mathbf{v}_j^*$ span a two dimensional plane, and the projection $\tilde{\mathbf{r}}$ of $\mathbf{r}$ onto this plane is a uniformly random two-dimensional vector. Vertex i falls in U if $\mathbf{v}_i^* \cdot \tilde{\mathbf{r}} \geq 0$, which happens when $\tilde{\mathbf{r}}$ makes an angle smaller than $\frac{\pi}{2}$ with $\mathbf{v}_i^*$. From Figure 8.15, it is easy to see that the edge (i, j) is cut by the rounding algorithm if $\tilde{\mathbf{r}}$ lies in the shaded region, which happens with probability $2\theta/2\pi$ where θ is the angle between $\mathbf{v}_i^*$ and $\mathbf{v}_j^*$. The claim follows. $\qquad\square$

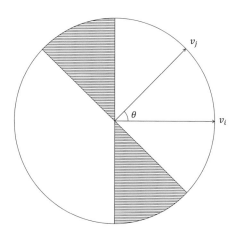

Figure 8.15 Maximum cut rounding

The following Lemma follows from simple calculus.

Lemma 8.12 *For any $\alpha \in [-1, 1]$, we have*

$$\frac{\cos^{-1}\alpha}{\pi} \geq 0.878 \cdot \frac{1-\alpha}{2}.$$

We are now ready to prove the performance guarantee of the algorithm.

Theorem 8.13 *Randomized rounding algorithm for the maximum cut problem outputs a solution of expected value at least 0.878 times the SDP optimum value.*

Proof Let $x_{ij}^* = \frac{1-\mathbf{v}_i^* \cdot \mathbf{v}_j^*}{2}$ and let X_{ij} be the 0-1 random variable that is 1 if vertices i and j are separated by the cut (U, U^c) and 0 otherwise. Thus the value ALG of the cut (U, U^c) is given by $\sum_{(i,j)\in E} w_{ij} X_{ij}$. Moreover, the SDP objective function value can be written as $SDP = \sum_{ij} w_{ij} x_{ij}^*$. By Lemmas 8.11 and 8.12, for every $(i,j) \in E$, we have

$$\mathbf{E}[X_{ij}] = \frac{\cos^{-1}(\mathbf{v}_i^* \cdot \mathbf{v}_j^*)}{\pi} \geq 0.878 \cdot \frac{1 - \mathbf{v}_i^* \cdot \mathbf{v}_j^*}{2} = 0.878 \cdot x_{ij}^*.$$

By linearity of expectation, we conclude that

$$\mathbf{E}[ALG] = \sum_{(i,j)\in E} w_{ij} \mathbf{E}[X_{ij}]$$

$$\geq \sum_{(i,j)\in E} w_{ij}(0.878 \cdot x_{ij}^*)$$

$$= 0.878 \cdot SDP. \qquad \square$$

The algorithm can be derandomized to get a deterministic algorithm with the same performance guarantee.

8.5 Algorithms for Special Instances

For special subclasses of instances, several hard optimization problems are easier to solve. These can be of interest if instances seen in practice belong to the subclass (e.g. planar or Euclidean), or if the general case be reduced to the special case with some slack. For example, several graph problems can be solved in polynomial time on trees. Planar graphs have special structural properties that make it easier to solve certain problems. Indeed many problems such as independent set, vertex cover, and the traveling salesman problem that are hard to approximate in general, have polynomial time approximation schemes for planar graphs [11, 29]. Similarly, problems such as the traveling salesman problem that involve a metric as an input are easier on Euclidean metrics [3, 47].

In this section, we give an example of an NP-hard graph problem that is easy to solve on trees; this also illustrates the use of dynamic programming in the design of exact and approximation algorithms. We study the minimum bisection problem, where given a graph G, we want to find the minimum cut that breaks the graph into two pieces of equal size. We will see in Section 8.6

how this result for trees actually leads to a good approximation algorithm for all instances.

Minimum Bisection Problem

Input: A graph $G = (V, E)$ with cost function $c : E \to \Re_+$.

Output: A partition (S, S^c) of V such that $|S| = \lfloor \frac{|V|}{2} \rfloor$.

Objective: Minimize the cut size $c(S, S^c) = \sum_{(u,v) \in E : u \in S, v \in S^c} c(u, v)$.

The problem is NP-hard [25]. Here we study the special case when G is a tree and give a polynomial time algorithm for it. In fact we will consider a slight variant that we call binary tree leaf partition as it is a simpler setting to illustrate the ideas. The problem on arbitrary trees can be reduced to this problem by a simple transformation.

Binary Tree Leaf Partition Problem

Input: A binary tree $T = (V, E)$ with cost function $c : E \to \Re_+$ and with $L \subseteq V$ as its set of leaves. An integer $k \leq |L|$.

Output: A partition (S, S^c) of V such that $|S \cap L| = k$.

Objective: Minimize the cut size $c(S, S^c)$.

Let T be rooted at a root r. For an internal node v, let $T(v)$ denote the subtree rooted at v and $L(v)$ denote $L(v) = L \cap T(v)$ to be the set of leaves in $T(v)$. Let $n_v = |L(v)|$. We shall compute (using dynamic programming) for each v and each $j \leq n_v$, an optimal solution $(S_{v,j}, S^c_{v,j})$ to the Binary Tree Leaf Partition problem on $T(v)$ such that $v \in S_{v,j}$. Denote by $c_{v,j}$ its cost $c(S_{v,j}, S^c_{v,j})$. We compute these solutions bottom up. For a node v and an integer j, suppose we already have solutions for its children v_1 and v_2 and for all integers $k \leq n$. Let n_1 and n_2 denote $|L(v_1)|$ and $|L(v_2)|$ respectively. The best solution such that both v_1 and v_2 are in $S_{v,j}$ is easy to compute. Indeed by picking an i minimizing $c_{v_1,i} + c_{v_2,j-i}$, we get such a solution as $\{v\} \cup S_{v_1,i} \cup S_{v_2,j-i}$. Similarly, the best solution with $v_1 \in S_{n,j}, v_2 \notin S_{v,j}$ corresponds to the i minimizing $c(v, v_2) + c_{v_1,i} + c_{v_2,n_2-j+i}$, as the edge (v, v_2) is cut in this case. Here we then set $S_{n,j}$ to $\{v\} \cup S_{v_1,i} \cup (T(v_2) \setminus S_{v_2,n_2-j+i})$. The case when $v_1 \notin S_{v,j}$ and $v_2 \in S_{v,j}$ is similar. Finally, the best $S_{v,j}$ not containing either of v_1, v_2 corresponds to the i that minimizes $c(v, v_1) + c(v, v_2) + c_{v_1,n_1-i} + c_{v_2,n_2-j+i}$, and sets $S_{v,j}$ to $\{v\} \cup (T(v_1) \setminus S_{v_1,n_1-i}) \cup (T(v_2) \setminus S_{v_2,n_2-j+i})$. These four candidate solutions can be computed in time $O(n_1 + n_2)$ given the solutions for v_1 and v_2 and the cheapest amongst these four defines $S_{v,j}$ and $c_{v,j}$. Thus each $S_{n,j}$ can be computed in $O(n)$ time, and since there are only $O(n^2)$ possible (n, j) pairs, we get an $O(n^3)$ time dynamic programming algorithm. The better of the cuts $S_{r,\lfloor \frac{n}{2} \rfloor}$ and $S_{r,\lceil \frac{n}{2} \rceil}$ then gives us the optimal bisection.

Similar dynamic programming based algorithms are possible for other problems of interest on trees. Many of these results can be extended to graphs with bounded *treewidth* (defined in Chapter 1).

8.6 Metric Embeddings

A metric[1] is a symmetric distance function $d : V \times V \to \Re_+$ that satisfies $d(u, u) = 0$, and the triangle inequality $d(u, v) \le d(u, w) + d(v, w)$ for all $u, v, w \in V$. For any graph $G = (V, E)$ with non-negative lengths on edges, the shortest path distance function is a metric. Metrics often arise as part of the input to a combinatorial optimization problem, for example, the distances between the cities in the traveling salesman problem. Additionally, metrics can often arise from the natural convex relaxation of an optimization problem, as in the sparsest cut problem studied below.

An embedding is a representation of the points of one metric in another, usually more structured, metric such that distances between points are approximately preserved. Formally a function $f : (V, d) \to (X, d')$ is an embedding with distortion α if

$$d(u, v) \le d'(f(u), f(v)) \le \alpha d(u, v) \quad \forall u, v \in V.$$

The paradigm of metric embedding has turned out be very successful in approximation algorithms. A common approach is to start from a metric d, that arises from the input to the problem or its convex relaxation, and embed it into a *simpler* metric d'. The algorithm then solves the problem on the simpler metric d' and the distortion α of the embedding naturally affects the approximation factor of the algorithm. We will illustrate this paradigm by two examples below.

8.6.1 Approximating Sparsest Cut

We study the following graph partitioning problems.

Sparsest Cut (Uniform)
Input: A graph $G = (V, E)$.
Output: A partitioning (S, S^c) of V.
Objective: Minimize the *sparsity* $\frac{|E(S,S^c)|}{|S|\cdot|S^c|}$.

The above is a special case of the general sparsest cut problem.

---
[1] Technically, this is a semimetric since we allow $d(u, v) = 0$ for $u \ne v$. We shall ignore this distinction in this survey.

Sparsest Cut (General)
Input: A graph $G = (V, E)$, a demand graph $H = (V, E_H)$.
Output: A partitioning (S, S^c) of V.
Objective: Minimize the *sparsity* $\frac{|E(S,S^c)|}{|E_H(S,S^c)|}$.

Building up on the work of [40], the following algorithm was given by [43] and [9]. We first write a linear programming relaxation of the sparsest cut problem, where the constraint "d is a metric" is shorthand for the set of linear constraints defining a metric. There are $O(n^3)$ such constraints, and the linear program below can be solved in polynomial time.

$$\text{Minimize} \quad \sum_{(u,v)\in E} d(u, v)$$

$$\text{subject to:}$$

$$\sum_{(s,t)\in E_H} d(s,t) = 1$$

$$d \text{ is a metric}$$

Figure 8.16 Linear Program for Sparsest Cut

For a cut (S, S^c) we can define a *cut metric*

$$d_S(u, v) = \begin{cases} 1 & \text{if } |\{u, v\} \cap S| = 1 \\ 0 & \text{otherwise} \end{cases}$$

The fact that this is a relaxation of the sparsest cut problem can be seen by observing that $\frac{1}{|E_H(S,S^c)|} \cdot d_S(\cdot, \cdot)$ is a feasible solution to the linear program, for any cut S and the objective function of the linear program is exactly the sparsity of the cut S.

Let d denote the metric in an optimal solution to the above linear relaxation. Thus

$$OPT \geq \frac{\sum_{(u,v)\in E} d(u, v)}{\sum_{(s,t)\in E_H} d(s,t)}$$

A celebrated result of [14] states that for any n-point metric (V, d) there is an embedding f into Euclidean space $(\Re^k, \|\cdot\|_2)$ with distortion $O(\log n)$, for some k; here $\|\cdot\|_p$ denotes the l_p norm $\|x - y\|_p = \sqrt[p]{\sum_i (x_i - y_i)^p}$ for any $p \geq 1$. Observe that $\|\cdot\|_2$ is the usual Euclidian distance. It can be easily shown that the above result also implies an embedding into $(\Re^k, |\cdot|_1)$. [43] showed that that such an embedding can be computed efficiently.

This implies that there is a function $f : V \to \Re^k$ for some $k \geq 1$ such that for all $u, v \in V$, $d(u, v) \leq |f(u) - f(v)|_1 \leq O(\log n)d(u, v)$. Since ℓ_1 is equivalent to linear combination of cut metrics (see e.g. [20]), we can find a family of $O(n^2)$ cuts (S_j, S_j^c) and positive coefficients λ_j such that

$$d(u, v) \leq \sum_j \lambda_j d_{S_j}(u, v) \leq O(\log n) \cdot d(u, v) \quad \forall u, v \in V.$$

The rounding algorithm finds such cuts (S_j, S_j^c) and picks the best cut amongst these.

$$\min_j \frac{\sum_{(u,v)\in E} d_{S_j}(u, v)}{\sum_{(s,t)\in E_H} d_{S_j}(s, t)} \leq \frac{\sum_j \lambda_j (\sum_{(u,v)\in E} d_{S_j}(u, v))}{\sum_j \lambda_j (\sum_{(s,t)\in E_H} d_{S_j}(s, t))}$$

$$= \frac{\sum_{(u,v)\in E} \sum_j \lambda_j d_{S_j}(u, v)}{\sum_{(s,t)\in E_H} \sum_j \lambda_j d_{S_j}(s, t)}$$

$$\leq \frac{\sum_{(u,v)\in E} O(\log n)d(u, v)}{\sum_{(s,t)\in E_H} d(s, t)}$$

$$\leq O(\log n) \cdot OPT.$$

Thus this gives an $O(\log n)$ approximation to the sparsest cut problem. This can be improved to $O(\log |E_H|)$ by slightly modifying Bourgain's construction. We refer the reader to [55] for details.

Using semidefinite programming, this result can be further improved. An SDP relaxation can be used to optimize over ℓ_2^2 metrics: these are metrics such that $d(u, v) = \|f(u) - f(v)\|_2^2$ for some mapping $f : V \to \Re^n$. [7] gave a rounding algorithm that gives an approximation guarantee of $O(\sqrt{\log n})$ for the uniform sparsest cut. Using this result, [6] (see also [16]) showed that ℓ_2^2 metrics embed into ℓ_1 with distortion $\tilde{O}(\sqrt{\log n})$. This implies an $\tilde{O}(\sqrt{\log n})$-approximation algorithm for the general sparsest cut problem since SDP constraints can capture ℓ_2^2 metrics in the same spirit as linear constraints can capture arbitrary metrics.

8.6.2 Probabilistic Embeddings into Trees

In the example in the previous subsection, the embedding simplified the structure of the metric to make it amenable to a relatively simple algorithm. In this section, we describe a different embedding result that is useful in many settings.

Given a weighted graph $G = (V, E)$ with weights $w : E \to \Re_+$, the shortest path metric $d_G : V \times V \to \Re_+$ is defined by setting $d_G(u, v)$ to be shortest path distance between u and v in the weighted graph G. A tree metric is a shortest path metric when G is a tree. [2] and [12, 13] defined the notion of probabilistic embeddings into tree metrics. Improving on their results, the following result was shown by [22].

Theorem 8.14 *For any n-point metric space (V, d), there is a distribution $\mathcal{D}$ over tree metrics T_i on V such that*

- *For all T in the support of $\mathcal{D}$, $T(u, v) \geq d(u, v), \forall u, v \in V$, and*
- $\mathbf{E}_{T \sim \mathcal{D}} T(u, v) \leq O(\log n) d(u, v), \forall u, v \in V.$

For several optimization problems that are easy to solve on tree metrics, this result enables us to get logarithmic approximation to the problem in the general case. We describe here an application due to [10]. Consider the buy-at-bulk network design problem where we are given a graph with edge lengths and k source-sink pairs. The goal is to route one unit of flow between each demand pair, so as to minimize the total cost, where the the cost of routing f pairs through an edge e is $l_e c(f_e)$ for a cost function c obeying economies of scale.

Buy-at-Bulk Network Design
Input: A graph $G = (V, E)$ with lengths l_e on edges, source-sink pairs (s_i, t_i) for $i = 1, \ldots, k$ and a non-decreasing concave cost function $c : \Re_+ \to \Re_+$ where $c(0) = 0$.
Output: An s_i-t_i path P_i for each $i = 1, \ldots, k$.
Objective: Minimize the total cost $\sum_e l_e c(f_e)$ where $f_e = |\{i : e \in P_i\}|$.

When the graph G is a tree, there is a unique simple path for each demand pair, and hence the problem is easy to solve. Our algorithm is as follows: we sample a tree T from the distribution $\mathcal{D}$ defined by using the above result on the shortest path metric of (G, l_e). We compute the optimal solution on T and let P_i^T denote the tree path between s_i and t_i. For each tree edge (x, y) consider the shortest path P_{xy} in G between x and y. The path P_i is the defined by replacing each edge (x, y) in P_i^T by the corresponding path P_{xy}.

We now analyze the cost of this algorithm. We do so in two steps. First we argue that the optimal solution on the instance defined on the tree T has expected cost at most $O(\log n)$ times the (unknown) optimal solution to the original instance. Indeed let P_i^* be the s_i-t_i path in OPT. For every edge (u, v) in G, there is a path P_{uv} in T between u and v. Moreover by the second property of the tree embedding $\mathbf{E}_{T \sim \mathcal{D}} \sum_{e' \in P_{uv}} l_{e'} \leq O(\log n) \cdot l_{uv}$. The simple tree path P_i^T between s_i and t_i is no longer than the (potentially non-simple) path formed by concatenating the paths P_{uv} for $(u, v) \in P_i^*$. Thus

$$\text{Cost of Tree solution} = \sum_{e' \in T} l_{e'} c(|i : e' \in P_i^T|)$$

$$\leq \sum_{e' \in T} l_{e'} c(\cup_{(u,v):e' \in P_{uv}} |i : (u, v) \in P_i^*|)$$

$$\leq \sum_{e' \in T} \sum_{(u,v) \in E : e' \in P_{uv}} l_{e'} c(|i : (u, v) \in P_i^*|) \quad \text{(by concavity of } c)$$

$$= \sum_{(u,v) \in E} c(|i : (u, v) \in P_i^*|) \sum_{e' \in T : e' \in P_{uv}} l_{e'}$$

The expected value of $\sum_{e' \in T : e' \in P_{uv}} l_{e'}$ is bounded by $O(\log n) l_{(u,v)}$, and hence by linearity of expectation, the expected cost of the tree solution is at most $O(\log n) \sum_{(u,v) \in E} l_{(u,v)} c(|i : (u, v) \in P_i^*|)$. Thus we have established that the expected cost of the tree solution is no more than $O(\log n) \cdot OPT$.

We also need to argue that the cost of the routing P_i defined by the algorithm is no more than the routing P_i^T on the tree instance. This follows from an argument very similar to the one above, except that we use the first property in Theorem 8.14 which holds deterministically for every tree T in the support of $\mathcal{D}$. We omit the details and refer the reader to [55]. Thus we can conclude that

Theorem 8.15   *There is a randomized $O(\log n)$-approximation to the buy-at-bulk network design problem.*

While the distance preserving embeddings are useful for problems involving distances (or where distances arise from a solution to a convex relaxation), many problems involve capacities on edges. For such problems, the capacity preserving embeddings of [49, 50] play an analogous role. These embeddings into distributions over capacitated trees allow translating algorithms on trees to approximation algorithms on general graphs at an $O(\log n)$ loss. For example, using the algorithm on trees from Section 8.5, one can get an $O(\log n)$ approximation to graph bisection using these techniques. The reader is referred to [50] for further details.

8.7 Hardness of Approximation

Certain problems such as the knapsack problem have approximation schemes where for every fixed $\epsilon > 0$ there is a $(1+\epsilon)$-approximation algorithm, which is essentially the best we can expect for an NP-hard optimization problem unless P = NP. For the set cover problem, we showed a $\ln n$-approximation algorithm and it is natural to ask: Can we do better? Hardness of approximation results play the same role for approximation algorithms that NP-hardness results play for exact algorithms: they allow us to understand the limits of polynomial time computation as far as worst-case guarantees go.

In some cases, a hardness of approximation result fall out of the NP-hardness result. For example for the bin packing problem, the NP-hardness reduction shows that it is NP-hard to determine if the given set of items can be packed into k bins, for a certain parameter k. Since the objective function is an integer, this rules out an approximation ratio better than $\frac{k+1}{k}$ unless P=NP. Indeed for the bin packing problem, a reduction from the partition problem can be used to show hardness of determining if $OPT = 2$, thus showing a factor $\frac{3}{2}$-hardness for the problem [25]. Similar results can be shown for other problems such as coloring and minimum makespan scheduling on unrelated machines. An extreme example is the traveling salesman problem with arbitrary distances where the NP-hardness of Hamiltonian path implies that it is NP-hard to approximate the TSP better than any polynomial factor [25].

For some problems, hardness of approximation results can be obtained with a little more work. Consider for example the following problem

Maximum Edge Disjoint Paths Problem (EDP)

Input: A directed graph $G = (V, E)$, k source-sink pairs $(s_1, t_1), \ldots, (s_k, t_k)$.
Output: A subset $R \subseteq [k]$ and for each $i \in R$, an (s_i, t_i) path P_i such that no two P_i intersect.
Objective: Maximize the size $|R|$.

For the EDP, a classical NP hardness result [24] shows that even with two source-sink pairs, it is NP hard to decide whether they can be simultaneously routed. This factor of two hardness can be boosted. Let $(G, (s_1, t_1), (s_2, t_2))$ be an instance of EDP. Consider the graph H in Figure 8.17 where we have N source-sink pairs such that every s_i-t_i path intersects every s_j-t_j path for $i \neq j$. Moreover, the canonical s_i-t_i paths (shown in the figure) have the property that every edge lies on at most one canonical path, except for the diagonal edges that lie on exactly two paths. We can then construct a graph H_G where each of these diagonal edges where two paths intersect is replaced by a copy of the graph G, with the two paths attached to (s_1, t_1) and (s_2, t_2) respectively. Observe that if the optimum of the instance on G is 1, then at most one of the paths can be routed so that the copy of G is equivalent to a single edge. Thus H_G is equivalent to H in this case and the optimum is 1. On the other hand, if both pairs of demands can be routed in G, then both

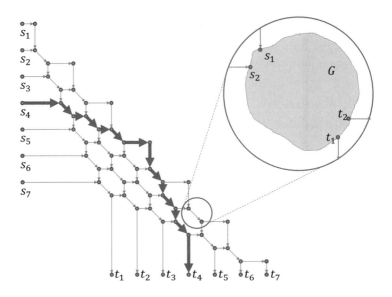

Figure 8.17 The graph H for $N = 7$, with the canonical path for s_4 highlighted. H_G is formed by replacing each of the diagonal edges by a copy of G, as shown above.

the paths going through the a copy of G can be routed on disjoint paths. It is then easy to see that all pairs of demands in H can be routed on edge disjoint paths. Thus the case $OPT = N$ and the case $OPT = 1$ are hard to distinguish. Choosing N carefully, we get an $\Omega(n^{\frac{1}{2}-\epsilon})$ hardness for any $\epsilon > 0$.

Unfortunately, such direct reductions are known for very few problems. A much more general tool is the PCP Theorem [4, 5] which allows us to prove stronger and more robust hardness results for a larger class of optimization problem. This result states that all languages in NP admit *probabilistically checkable proofs*: for every yes instance, one can write down a polynomially sized proof such that a verifier can inspect a constant number of bits of the proof and always accepts a valid proof. Moreover, every invalid proof is rejected with constant probability. Formally,

Theorem 8.16 (PCP Theorem [4, 5])   *Let L be any language in NP. Then there is an absolute constant k, and a polynomial-time probabilistic algorithm V (a* verifier*) such that:*

Efficiency *Given an input string $x \in \{0,1\}^n$, and given random access to a string $\pi \in \{0,1\}^{n^{O(1)}}$ (a proof), the verifier V uses $O(\log n)$ bits*

of randomness to pick k locations of π to query. Given the contents of these locations and x, V outputs accept *or* reject.

Completeness *Given an input $x \in L$, there exists a proof π such that V always accepts on x and π.*

Soundness *Given an input $x \notin L$, for any π, the probability (taken over randomness of V) that V accepts x and π is at most $\frac{1}{2}$.*

This surprising result can be used to prove hardness of approximation results. Indeed as stated, it implies the existence of a k-ary boolean function f, and for every string $x \in \{0,1\}^n$, a polynomial sized collection of k tuples of variables $y_1, \ldots, y_{n^c}$ such that:

- If $x \in L$, then there is an assignment to the variables such that f evaluates to 1 on *all* of the k-tuples in the collection.
- If $x \notin L$, then for any assignment to the variables, f evaluates to 0 on at least half of the k tuples in the collection.

Recall that for an NP-hard language L, it is NP-hard to distinguish between the case $x \in L$ from the case $x \notin L$. If we had, say, a polynomial time $\frac{2}{3}$-approximation to the problem of maximizing the number of tuples in a collection that satisfy f, then we would be able to use that algorithm to distinguish between these two cases in polynomial time, thus showing that P=NP. Thus the above result rules out such an approximation. In fact it shows that the (potentially contrived) problem of maximizing the number of tuples satisfying f is NP-hard to approximate better than a factor of two! Armed with this hardness of approximation result, several others can be proven by reductions, or by designing probabilistically checkable proofs tailored for the problem at hand. We state below some such results for problems studied in this survey.

Theorem 8.17 ([31]) *For any $\epsilon > 0$, there is no $(\frac{7}{8} + \epsilon)$-approximation to the MAX3SAT problem, unless P=NP.*

Theorem 8.18 ([23]) *For any $\epsilon > 0$, there is no $(1-\epsilon) \ln n$-approximation to set cover unless NP has $n^{O(\log \log n)}$ time deterministic algorithms.*

Theorem 8.19 ([33]) *For any $\epsilon > 0$, There is no $(1+\frac{2}{e}-\epsilon)$-approximation to k-median unless NP has $n^{O(\log \log n)}$ time deterministic algorithms.*

Theorem 8.20 ([31]) *There is no 0.941-approximation to MAXCUT unless P=NP.*

While the PCP theorem has led to tight hardness of approximation results for several problems, there are those for which large gaps remain. The

sparsest cut problem is one such problem where the best known approximation algorithm gives an $O(\sqrt{\log n})$-approximation, while we cannot rule out
even a PTAS. Similarly for the MAXCUT problem, there is a gap between
the upper bound in Theorem 8.13 and the lower bound in Theorem 8.20.
In recent years, optimal hardness of approximation results have been shown
for several problem such as MAXCUT and vertex cover, if one assumes the
Unique Games Conjecture of [37]. We refer the reader to a survey [36] for
additional details.

References

[1] Agrawal, Ajit, Klein, Philip N., and Ravi, R. 1991. When Trees Collide: An
    Approximation Algorithm for the Generalized Steiner Problem on Networks.
    Pages 134–144 of: *STOC '91: Proceedings of the 23rd Annual ACM Symposium
    on Theory of Computing.*

[2] Alon, Noga, Karp, Richard M., Peleg, David, and West, Douglas. 1995. A
    Graph-Theoretic Game and its Application to the k-server Problem. *SIAM J.
    Comput.*, **24**(1), 78–100.

[3] Arora, Sanjeev. 1998. Polynomial Time Approximation Schemes for Euclidean
    Traveling Salesman and other Geometric Problems. *Journal of ACM*, **45**(5),
    753–782.

[4] Arora, Sanjeev, and Safra, Shmuel. 1992. Probabilistic Checking of Proofs; A
    New Characterization of NP. *J. ACM*, **45**(1), 70–122.

[5] Arora, Sanjeev, Lund, Carsten, Motwani, Rajeev, Sudan, Madhu, and Szegedy,
    Mario. 1992. Proof Verification and Hardness of Approximation Problems. *J.
    ACM*, **45**(3), 501–555.

[6] Arora, Sanjeev, Lee, James R., and Naor, Assaf. 2007. Fréchet Embeddings of
    Negative Type Metrics. *Discrete & Computational Geometry*, **38**(4), 726–739.

[7] Arora, Sanjeev, Rao, Satish, and Vazirani, Umesh V. 2009. Expander flows,
    geometric embeddings and graph partitioning. *J. ACM*, **56**(2), Article 5.

[8] Arya, Vijay, Garg, Naveen, Khandekar, Rohit, Meyerson, Adam, Munagala,
    Kamesh, and Pandit, Vinayaka. 2004. Local Search Heuristics for k-Median
    and Facility Location Problems. *SIAM J. Comput.*, **33**(3), 544–562.

[9] Aumann, Yonatan, and Rabani, Yuval. 1998. An (log) Approximate Min-Cut
    Max-Flow Theorem and Approximation Algorithm. *SIAM J. Comput.*, **27**(1),
    291–301.

[10] Awerbuch, Baruch, and Azar, Yossi. 1997. Buy-at-Bulk Network Design. Pages
    542–547 of: *Proceedings of the 38th Annual IEEE Symposium on Foundations
    of Computer Science.*

[11] Baker, Brenda S. 1994. Approximation Algorithms for NP-Complete Problems
    on Planar Graphs. *J. ACM*, **41**(1), 153–180.

[12] Bartal, Yair. 1996. Probabilistic Approximations of Metric Spaces and Its
    Algorithmic Applications. Pages 184–193 of: *Proceedings of the 37th Annual
    Symposium on Foundations of Computer Science.*

[13] Bartal, Yair. 1998. On Approximating Arbitrary Metrics by Tree Metrics. Pages 161–168 of: *Proceedings of the 30th Annual ACM Symposium on Theory of Computing.*

[14] Bourgain, J. 1985. On Lipschitz Embedding of Finite Metric Spaces in Hilbert Space. *Israel Journal of Mathematics*, **52**, 46–52.

[15] Buchbinder, Niv, and Naor, Joseph. 2009. The Design of Competitive Online Algorithms via a Primal-Dual Approach. *Foundations and Trends in Theoretical Computer Science*, **3**(2-3), 93–263.

[16] Chawla, Shuchi, Gupta, Anupam, and Räcke, Harald. 2008. Embeddings of Negative-type Metrics and an Improved Approximation to Generalized Sparsest Cut. *ACM Transactions on Algorithms*, **4**(2), Article 22.

[17] Chvátal, Vasek. 1983. *Linear Programming.* W. H. Freeman.

[18] Cormen, Thomas H., Leiserson, Charles E., Rivest, Ronald L., and Stein, Clifford. 2001. *Introduction to Algorithms.* Second ed. MIT Press and McGraw-Hill.

[19] Dantzig, G.B., Ford, L.R., and Fulkerson, D.R. 1956. *A Primal–Dual Algorithm for Linear Programs.* Pages 171–181 of: *Linear Inequalities and Related Systems*, Kuhn, H.W. and Tucker, A.W. (eds). Princeton University Press.

[20] Deza, M.M., and Laurent, M. 1997. *Geometry of Cuts and Metrics.* Springer-Verlag.

[21] Egerváry, Jenö. 1931. Matrixok kombinatorius tulajdonságairól (in Hungarian: On Combinatorial Properties of Matrices). *Matematikaiés Fizikai Lapok*, **38**, 16–28.

[22] Fakcharoenphol, Jittat, Rao, Satish, and Talwar, Kunal. 2004. A Tight Bound on Approximating Arbitrary Metrics by Tree Metrics. *J. Comput. Syst. Sci.*, **69**(3), 485–497.

[23] Feige, Uriel. 1998. A Threshold of ln for Approximating Set Cover. *J. ACM*, **45**(4), 634–652.

[24] Fortune, S., Hopcroft, J., and Wyllie, J. 1980. The Directed Subgraph Homeomorphism Problem. *Theoretical Computer Science*, **10**, 111–121.

[25] Garey, M. R., and Johnson, David S. 1979. *Computers and Intractability: A Guide to the Theory of NP-Completeness.* W. H. Freeman.

[26] Goemans, Michel X. 1997. Semidefinite Programming in Combinatorial Optimization. *Math. Program.*, **79**, 143–161.

[27] Goemans, Michel X., and Williamson, David P. 1995. A General Approximation Technique for Constrained Forest Problems. *SIAM Journal on Computing*, **24**, 296–317.

[28] Goemans, Michel X., and Williamson, David P. 1995. Improved Approximation Algorithms for Maximum Cut and Satisfiability Problems Using Semidefinite Programming. *J. ACM*, **42**(6), 1115–1145.

[29] Grigni, Michelangelo, Koutsoupias, Elias, and Papadimitriou, Christos H. 1995. An Approximation Scheme for Planar Graph TSP. Pages 640–645 of: *FOCS '95: Proceedings of the 36th Annual Symposium on Foundations of Computer Science.*

[30] Grötschel, Martin, Lovász, László, and Schrijver, Alexander. 1981. The Ellipsoid Method and its Consequences in Combinatorial Optimization. *Combinatorica*, **1**(2), 169–197.

[31] Håstad, Johan. 2001. Some Optimal Inapproximability Results. *J. ACM*, **48**(4), 798–859.

[32] Jain, Kamal. 2001. A Factor 2 Approximation Algorithm for the Generalized Steiner Network Problem. *Combinatorica*, **21**, 39–60.

[33] Jain, Kamal, Mahdian, Mohammad, and Saberi, Amin. 2002. A New Greedy Approach for Facility Location Problems. Pages 731–740 of: *STOC '02: Proceedings of the 34th Annual ACM Symposium on Theory of Computing*.

[34] Johnson, David S. 1974. Approximation Algorithms for Combinatorial Problems. *J. Comput. Syst. Sci.*, **9**, 256–278.

[35] Khachiyan, L G. 1979. A Polynomial Algorithm in Linear Programming. *Soviet Mathematics Doklady*, **20**(1), 191–194.

[36] Khot, S. 2010. On the Unique Games Conjecture. Pages 99–121 of: *CCC 2010. IEEE 25th Annual Conference on Computational Complexity*.

[37] Khot, Subhash. 2002. On the Power of Unique 2-prover 1-round Games. Pages 767–775 of: *STOC '02: Proceedings of the 34th Annual ACM Symposium on Theory of Computing*.

[38] Kuhn, H. W. 1955. The Hungarian Method for the Assignment Problem. *Naval Research Logistic Quarterly*, **2**, 83–97.

[39] Lau, Lap Chi, Ravi, R., and Singh, Mohit. 2011. *Iterative Methods in Combinatorial Optimization*. Cambridge Texts in Applied Mathematics. Cambridge University Press.

[40] Leighton, Frank Thomson, and Rao, Satish. 1988. An Approximate Max-Flow Min-Cut Theorem for Uniform Multicommodity Flow Problems with Applications to Approximation Algorithms. Pages 422–431 of: *FOCS '88: Proceedings of the 29th Annual Symposium on Foundations of Computer Science*.

[41] Lenstra, Jan Karel, Shmoys, David B., and Tardos, Éva. 1990. Approximation Algorithms for Scheduling Unrelated Parallel Machines. *Math. Program.*, **46**, 259–271.

[42] Lin, S., and Kernighan, B.W. 1973. An Effective Heuristic Algorithm for the Traveling-Salesman Problem. *Operations Research*, **21**(2), 498–516.

[43] Linial, Nathan, London, Eran, and Rabinovich, Yuri. 1995. The Geometry of Graphs and Some of its Algorithmic Applications. *Combinatorica*, **15**(2), 215–245.

[44] Lovász, L. 1975. On the Ratio of Optimal Integral and Fractional Covers. *Discrete Mathematics*, **13**, 383–390.

[45] Lovasz, L. 1995. *Semidefinite Optimization* (lecture notes).

[46] Matoušek, Jiří, and Gärtner, Bernd. 2006. *Understanding and Using Linear Programming*. Springer.

[47] Mitchell, Joseph S. B. 1999. Guillotine Subdivisions Approximate Polygonal Subdivisions: A Simple Polynomial-Time Approximation Scheme for Geometric TSP, k-MST, and Related Problems. *SIAM Journal of Computing*, **28**(4), 1298–1309.

[48] Nemhauser, G. L., Wolsey, L. A., and Fisher, M. L. 1978. An Analysis of Approximations for Maximizing Submodular Set Functions: I. *Mathematical Programming*, **14**, 265–294.

[49] Räcke, Harald. 2002. Minimizing Congestion in General Networks. Pages 43–52 of: *FOCS '02: Proceedings of the 43rd Annual IEEE Symposium on Foundations of Computer Science*.

[50] Räcke, Harald. 2008. Optimal Hierarchical Decompositions for Congestion Minimization in Networks. Pages 255–264 of: *STOC '08: Proceedings of the 40th Annual ACM Symposium on Theory of Computing*.

[51] Raghavan, Prabhakar, and Thompson, Clark D. 1987. Randomized Rounding: a Technique for Provably Good Algorithms and Algorithmic Proofs. *Combinatorica*, **7**, 365–374.

[52] Raghavendra, Prasad. 2008. Optimal Algorithms and Inapproximability Results for every CSP? Pages 245–254 of: *STOC '08: Proceedings of the 40th Annual ACM Symposium on Theory of Computing*.

[53] Vazirani, Vijay V. 2001. *Approximation Algorithms*. Springer.

[54] Vondrák, Jan. 2008. Optimal Approximation for the Submodular Welfare Problem in the Value Oracle Model. Pages 67–74 of: *STOC '08: Proceedings of the 40th Annual ACM Symposium on Theory of Computing*.

[55] Williamson, David P., and Shmoys, David B. 2011. *The Design of Approximation Algorithms*. Cambridge University Press.

9

Kernelization Methods for Fixed-Parameter Tractability

Fedor V. Fomin and Saket Saurabh

Preprocessing or data reduction means reducing a problem to something simpler by solving an easy part of the input. This type of algorithm is used in almost every application. In spite of wide practical applications of preprocessing, a systematic theoretical study of such algorithms remains elusive. The framework of parameterized complexity can be used as an approach to analysing preprocessing algorithms. In this framework, the algorithms have, in the addition to the input, an extra parameter that is likely to be small. This has resulted in a study of preprocessing algorithms that reduce the size of the input to a pure function of the parameter (independent of the input size). Such types of preprocessing algorithms are called kernelization algorithms. In this survey we give an overview of some classical and new techniques in the design of such algorithms.

9.1 Introduction

Preprocessing (data reduction or kernelization) as a strategy for coping with hard problems is used in many situations. The history of this approach can be traced back to the 1950s [34], where truth functions were simplified using reduction rules. A natural question arises: how can we measure the quality of preprocessing rules proposed for a specific problem? For a long time the mathematical analysis of polynomial time preprocessing algorithms was neglected. The basic reason for this oversight was the following impossibility result: if, starting with an instance I of an NP-hard problem, we could compute in polynomial time an instance I' equivalent to I and with $|I'| < |I|$, then it would follow that P=NP, thereby contradicting classical complexity assumptions. The situation changed drastically with advent of parameterized complexity [14]. Combining tools from parameterized complexity and classical complexity it became possible to derive upper and lower bounds on the sizes of reduced instances, or so called *kernels*. The importance of preprocessing and the mathematical challenges it poses is beautifully expressed in the following quote from Fellows [16]:

It has become clear, however, that far from being trivial and uninteresting, pre-processing has unexpected practical power for real world input distributions, and is mathematically a much deeper subject than has generally been understood.

Historically, the study of kernelization is rooted in parameterized complexity but it quickly became apparent that the challenges of kernelization tractability are deeply linked to classical polynomial time tractability. In classical computational complexity originated from 1970s, we distinguish between tractable and intractable computational problems. This theory classifies computational problems according to the time or space required to solve them, as a function of the size of the input. We can solve tractable problems by efficient algorithms, i.e. algorithms running in time polynomial of the input size, and this is the world of polynomial time computations. We also believe that we cannot solve intractable problems efficiently. Ignoring the structural information about the input, and defining intractability according to only the input size, can make some problems appear harder than they are. Parameterized complexity tries to address this issue and measures complexity in terms of the input size but also of additional parameters. In parameterized complexity the notion of efficiency, as polynomial time computability, is refined by the notion of fixed parameter tractability. The running time of a fixed parameter tractable algorithm is polynomial in the size of the input but can be exponential in terms of the parameters. A surprisingly large number of intractable problems have been shown to exhibit fixed parameter tractable algorithms.

Kernelization algorithms are polynomial time algorithms that reduce parameterized problems to equivalent problems while the size of the reduced problem is estimated by some function of the parameter. Thus kernelization can be seen as a refinement of the notion of the classical polynomial time tractability from a parameterized perspective. The development of kernelization algorithms demonstrates the importance of the second (and maybe even other) measures and indicates that polynomial time computation is much more powerful than was thought before.

In this survey we discuss both some of the classical and the more recent algorithmic techniques for obtaining kernels. We do not try to give a comprehensive overview of all significant results in the area—doing this would require at least a book. We refer the reader to the surveys of Fellows [16] and Guo and Niedermeier [16, 22] for further reading on kernelization algorithms. We also do not discuss here techniques for deriving lower bounds on the sizes of the kernels. The reader can consult the fairly comprehensive survey of Misra et al. [31] on kernelization intractability.

Examples of kernelization In parameterized complexity each problem instance comes with a parameter k. As a warm-up, let us consider the following parameterized examples. Our first example is about vertex cover. A set of vertices S in a graph is a vertex cover if every edge of the graph contains at least one vertex from S. In the parameterized version of vertex cover, which we call p-VERTEX COVER, using the prefix $p-$ to emphasise that this is the parameterized problem, the parameter is integer k and we ask if the given graph has a vertex cover of size k. A second problem, p-LONGEST PATH, asks if a given graph contains a path of length at least k. And finally, p-DOMINATING SET is the problem of deciding if a given graph has a dominating set of size k, i.e. a set of vertices such that every vertex of the input graph is either in this set or is adjacent to some vertex from the set.

The parameterized problem is said to admit a *kernel* if there is an algorithm that reduces the input instance down to an instance with size bounded by some function $h(k)$ of k only, while preserving the answer. The running time of this algorithm should be polynomial in the input size, and the degree of this polynomial should be independent of the parameter k. Such an algorithm is called a *kernelization* algorithm. If the function $h(k)$ is polynomial in k, then we say that the problem admits a polynomial kernel.

In our examples, p-VERTEX COVER admits a polynomial kernel—there is a polynomial time algorithm that for any instance (G, k) of the problem outputs a new instance (G', k') such that G' has at most $2k$ vertices and G has a vertex cover of size at most k if and only if G' has a vertex cover of size at most k' [10]. The second example, p-LONGEST PATH, admits a kernel but the bounding function $h(k)$ is exponential. It is possible to show that under some assumptions from complexity theory, the problem does not admit a polynomial kernel [5]. The problem does not admit a polynomial kernel even when the input graph G is planar. Finally, p-DOMINATING SET admits no kernel unless FPT=W[2], i.e. there is a collapse of several levels in the parameterized complexity hierarchy [14]. However, on planar graphs, p-DOMINATING SET admits a kernel with the function $h(k) = \mathcal{O}(k)$, i.e. a linear kernel.

9.2 Basic Definitions

Here we mainly follow the notation of the book by Flum and Grohe [18]. We describe decision problems as languages over a finite alphabet Σ.

Definition 9.1 Let Σ be a finite alphabet.

(1) A *parameterization* of Σ^* is a polynomial time computable mapping $\kappa : \Sigma^* \to \mathbb{N}$.

(2) A *parameterized problem* (over Σ) is a pair (Q, κ) consisting of a set $Q \subseteq \Sigma^*$ of strings over Σ and a parameterization κ of Σ^*.

For a parameterized problem (Q, κ) over an alphabet Σ, we call the strings $x \in \Sigma^*$ the *instances* of Q or (Q, κ) and the number of $\kappa(x)$ the corresponding *parameters*. We usually represent a parameterized problem in the form

Instance:	$x \in \Sigma^*$.
Parameter:	$\kappa(x)$.
Problem:	Decide whether $x \in Q$.

Very often the parameter is also a part of the instance. For example, consider the following parameterized version of the minimum feedback vertex set problem, where the instance consists of a graph G and a positive integer k, and we have to decide whether G has a feedback vertex set, i.e. a set of vertices whose removal destroys all cycles in the graph, of k elements.

p-FEEDBACK VERTEX SET	
Instance:	A graph G, and a non-negative integer k.
Parameter:	k.
Problem:	Decide whether G has a feedback vertex set with at most k elements.

In this problem the instance is the string (G, k) and $\kappa(G, k) = k$. When the parameterization κ is defined as $\kappa(x, k) = k$, the parameterized problem can be defined as subsets of $\Sigma^* \times \mathbb{N}$. Here the parameter is the second component of the instance. In this survey we use both notations for parameterized problems.

While the parameterization $\kappa(x, k) = k$ is the most natural and classical, there can be many other ways to parameterize. For example, we could take a classical parameterization of the minimum vertex cover problem:

---

p-VERTEX COVER
> *Instance:* A graph $G = (V, E)$, and a non-negative integer k.
> *Parameter:* k.
> *Problem:* Decide whether G has a vertex cover of size at most k.

But since in every graph the minimum size of a vertex cover is always at least the minimum size of a feedback vertex set, the following parameterization can be interesting as well:

---

p-VERTEX COVER BY FVS
> *Instance:* A graph G, a feedback vertex set F of size k, and non-negative integer ℓ.
> *Parameter:* k.
> *Problem:* Decide whether G has a vertex cover of size at most ℓ.

The notion of kernelization is intimately linked with the notion of fixed-parameter tractability. Fixed-parameter tractable algorithms are a class of exact algorithms where the exponential blowup in the running time is restricted to a small parameter associated with the input size. That is, the running time of such an algorithm on an input of size n is of the form $\mathcal{O}\left(f\left(k\right)n^c\right)$, where k is a parameter that is typically small compared to n, $f\left(k\right)$ is a (typically super-polynomial) function of k that does not involve n, and c is a constant. Formally,

Definition 9.2 A parameterized problem (Q, κ) is *fixed-parameter tractable* if there exists an algorithm that decides in $f\left(\kappa(x)\right) \cdot n^{\mathcal{O}(1)}$ time whether $x \in Q$, where $n := |x|$ and f is a computable function that does not depend on n. The algorithm is called a *fixed-parameter algorithm* for the problem. The complexity class containing all fixed parameter tractable problems is called FPT.

There is also a hierarchy of intractable parameterized problem classes above FPT, the main ones are:

$$\text{FPT} \subseteq M[1] \subseteq W[1] \subseteq M[2] \subseteq W[2] \subseteq \cdots \subseteq W[P] \subseteq XP$$

The principal analogue of the classical intractability class NP is $W[1]$, which is a strong analogue, because a fundamental problem complete for $W[1]$ is the k-STEP HALTING PROBLEM FOR NONDETERMINISTIC TURING MACHINES (with unlimited nondeterminism and alphabet size) — this completeness result provides an analogue of Cook's Theorem in classical complexity. A convenient source of $W[1]$-hardness reductions is provided by the result that p-CLIQUE is complete for $W[1]$. Other highlights of the theory include that p-DOMINATING SET is, by contrast, complete for $W[2]$. Another highlight is that FPT $= M[1]$ if and only if the *Exponential Time Hypothesis* fails [18]. The classical reference on Parameterized Complexity is the book of Downey and Fellows [14]. For more updated material we refer to books of Flum and Grohe [18] and Niedermeier [32].

The notion of *kernelization* is formally defined as follows.

Definition 9.3 Let (Q, κ) be a parameterized problem over a finite alphabet Σ. A *kernelization algorithm*, or in short, a *kernelization*, for (Q, κ) is an algorithm that for any given $x \in \Sigma^*$ outputs in time polynomial in $|x| + \kappa(x)$ a string $x' \in \Sigma^*$ such that

$$(x \in Q \iff x' \in Q) \text{ and } |x'|, |\kappa(x')| \leq h(\kappa(x)),$$

where h is an arbitrary computable function. If K is a kernelization of (Q, κ), then for every instance x of Q the result of running K on input x is called the *kernel* of x (under K). The function h is referred to as the *size* of the kernel. If h is a polynomial function then we say the kernel is polynomial.

We often say that a problem (Q, κ) admits a kernel of size h, meaning that every instance of Q has a kernel of size h. We also often say that (Q, κ) admits a kernel with property Π, meaning that every instance of Q has a kernel with property Π. For example, by saying p-VERTEX COVER admits a kernel with $\mathcal{O}(k)$ vertices and $\mathcal{O}(k^2)$ edges, we mean that there is a kernelization algorithm K such that, for every instance (G, k) of the problem, there is a kernel with $\mathcal{O}(k)$ vertices and $\mathcal{O}(k^2)$ edges.

It is easy to see that if a decidable problem admits kernelization for some function f, then the problem is FPT—for every instance of the problem we run the polynomial time kernelization algorithm and then use the decision algorithm to identify if the reduced instance is valid. Since the size of the kernel is bounded by some function of the parameter, the running time of the decision algorithm depends only on the parameter. Interestingly, the converse also holds, that is, if a problem is FPT then it admits a kernelization. The proof of this fact is quite simple, and we present it here.

Lemma 9.4 (Folklore, [18, 32]) *If a parameterized problem (Q, κ) is FPT then it admits kernelization.*

Proof Suppose there is an algorithm deciding if $x \in Q$ in time $f(\kappa(x))|x|^c$ time for some function f and constant c. If $|x| \geq f(\kappa(x))$, then we run the decision algorithm on the instance in time $f(\kappa(x))|x|^c \leq |x|^{c+1}$. If the decision algorithm outputs YES, the kernelization algorithm outputs a constant size YES instance, and if the decision algorithm outputs NO, the kernelization algorithm outputs a constant size NO instance. On the other hand, if $|x| < f(\kappa(x))$, then the kernelization algorithm outputs x. This yields a kernel of size $f(\kappa(x))$ for the problem. □

Lemma 9.4 shows that kernelization can be seen as an alternative definition of fixed-parameter tractable problems. However, we are interested in kernels that are as small as possible, and a kernel obtained using Lemma 9.4 has a size that depends on the running time of the best known FPT algorithm for the problem. The question is: can we do better? The answer is that quite often we can. In fact, for many problems we can do so with polynomial kernels. In this chapter we survey some of the known techniques for showing that problems admit polynomial kernels.

We conclude this section with some definitions from graph theory. Let $G = (V, E)$ be a graph. For a vertex v in G, we write $N_G(v)$ to denote the set of v's neighbours in G, and we write $\deg_G(v)$ to denote the *degree* of v, that is, the number of v's neighbours in G. If it is clear from the context which graph is meant, we write $N(v)$ and $\deg(v)$, respectively, for brevity. A graph $G' = (V', E')$ is a *subgraph* of G if $V' \subseteq V$ and $E' \subseteq E$. The subgraph G' is called an *induced subgraph* of G if $E' = \{\{u, v\} \in E \mid u, v \in V'\}$; in this case, G' is also called the subgraph *induced by V'* and denoted by $G[V']$. A vertex v *dominates* a vertex u if $u \in N(v)$.

9.3 Classical Techniques

In this section we give several examples of techniques for obtaining kernels. Some of them are almost trivial and some of them are more involved. We start with the parameterized version of MAX3SAT. Our other examples in this section include a polynomial kernel for d-HITTING SET using the *Sunflower Lemma*, a kernel for VERTEX COVER using *crown decomposition* and an exponential kernel for (EDGE) CLIQUE COVER.

Max-3-Sat An r-CNF formula $F = c_1 \wedge \cdots \wedge c_m$ on a variable set $V(F)$ is a Boolean formula where each clause is of size exactly r and each clause is a disjunction of literals. In the optimization version of the problem the task is to find a truth assignment satisfying the maximum number of clauses. The parameterized version of the problem is the following.

---

p-MAX-r-SAT
> *Instance:* A r-CNF formula F, and a non-negative integer k.
> *Parameter:* k
> *Problem:* Decide whether F has a truth assignment satisfying
> at least k clauses.

Let (F, k) be an instance of p-MAX-3-SAT, i.e. the case of $r = 3$, and let m be the number of clauses in F and n the number of variables. It is well known that in any Boolean CNF formula, there is an assignment that satisfies at least half of the clauses (given any assignment that does not satisfy half the clauses, its bitwise complement will). So if the parameter k is less than $m/2$, then there is always an assignment to the variables that satisfies at least k of the clauses. In this case, we reduce the instance to the trivial instance with one clause and the parameter $k = 1$, which is always a YES instance. Otherwise, $m \leq 2k$, and so $n \leq 6k$, and (F, k) itself is the kernel of polynomial size.

*p-d-**Hitting Set*** Our next example is a kernelization for

---

p-d-HITTING SET
> *Instance:* A family $\mathcal{F}$ of sets, each of
> cardinality d, over a universe $\mathcal{U}$, and a positive integer k
> *Parameter:* k
> *Problem:* Decide whether there is a subset $U \subseteq \mathcal{U}$ of size
> at most k such that U contains at least one
> element from each set in $\mathcal{F}$.

Our kernelization algorithm is based on the following widely used Sunflower Lemma. We first define the terminology used in the statement of the lemma. A *sunflower* with k *petals* and a *core* Y is a collection of sets $S_1, S_2, \ldots, S_k$ such that $S_i \cap S_j = Y$ for all $i \neq j$; the sets $S_i \setminus Y$ are petals and we require none of them to be empty. Note that a family of pairwise disjoint sets is a sunflower (with an empty core). We need the following classical result of Erdős and Rado [15], see also [18].

Lemma 9.5 [**Sunflower Lemma**] *Let $\mathcal{F}$ be a family of sets, each of cardinality d, over a universe $\mathcal{U}$. If $|\mathcal{F}| > d!(k-1)^d$ then $\mathcal{F}$ contains a sunflower with k petals and such a sunflower can be computed in time polynomial in the size of $\mathcal{F}$ and $\mathcal{U}$.*

Now we are ready to prove the following theorem about kernelization for p-d-HITTING SET

Theorem 9.6 *d-*HITTING SET *admits a kernel with* $\mathcal{O}(k^d \cdot d!)$ *sets and* $\mathcal{O}(k^d \cdot d! \cdot d)$ *elements.*

Proof Crucially, note that if $\mathcal{F}$ contains a sunflower $S = \{S_1, \cdots, S_{k+1}\}$ of cardinality $k + 1$ then every hitting set H of $\mathcal{F}$ of cardinality k must intersect with the core Y of the sunflower S. Indeed, if H does not intersect C, it should intersect each of the $k + 1$ disjoint petals $S_i \setminus C$. Therefore if we let $\mathcal{F}' = \mathcal{F} \setminus (S \cup Y)$, then the instances $(\mathcal{U}, \mathcal{F}, k)$ and $(\mathcal{U}, \mathcal{F}', k)$ are equivalent.

Now we apply the Sunflower Lemma for all $d' \in \{1, \ldots, d\}$ on collections of sets with d' elements by repeatedly replacing sunflowers of size at least $k + 1$ with their cores until the number of sets for any fixed $d' \in \{1, \ldots, d\}$ is at most $O(k^{d'} d'!)$. We also remove elements which do not belong to any set. Summing over all d', we obtain that the new family of sets $\mathcal{F}'$ contains $\mathcal{O}(k^d \cdot d!)$ sets. Every set contains at most d elements, and thus the number of elements in the kernel is $\mathcal{O}(k^d \cdot d! \cdot d)$. $\square$

Crown Decomposition: Vertex Cover Crown decomposition is a general kernelization technique that can be used to obtain kernels for many problems. The technique is based on the classical matching theorems of Kőnig and Hall [25, 29].

Definition 9.7 A crown decomposition of a graph G is a partitioning of $V(G)$ as C, H and R, where C and H are nonempty and the partition satisfies the following properties:

1. C is an independent set,
2. There are no edges between vertices of C and R, i.e. H separates C and R;
3. Let E' be the set of edges between vertices of C and H; then E' contains a matching of size $|H|$.

The set C can be seen as a crown placed on the head H of the remaining part R of the royal body. Fig. 9.1 provides an example of a crown decomposition. Note that the fact that E' contains a matching of size $|H|$ implies that there is a matching of H into C, i.e. a matching in the bipartite subgraph $G' = (C \cup H, E')$ saturating all the vertices of H.

We demonstrate the application of crown decompositions on a kernelization for p-VERTEX COVER. We can model p-VERTEX COVER as p-2-HITTING SET with universe $\mathcal{U} = V$ and $\mathcal{F} = \{\{u, v\} \mid uv \in E\}$ and hence using Theorem 9.6 we can obtain a kernel with $\mathcal{O}(k^2)$ and $\mathcal{O}(k^2)$ vertices. Here we give a kernel with at most $3k$ vertices.

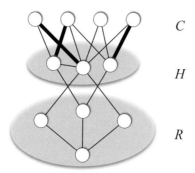

Figure 9.1 Example of a crown decomposition. Set C is an independent set, H separates C and R, and H has a matching into C.

Given a crown decomposition (C, H, R) of G, one can reduce the instance (G, k) of p-VERTEX COVER by making use of the following rule.

Crown Rule for Vertex Cover: Construct a new instance of the problem (G', k') by removing $H \cup C$ from G and reducing k by $|H|$. In other words, $G' = G[R]$ and $k' = k - |H|$.

The the Crown Rule is sound follows from the following lemma.

Lemma 9.8 *Let (C, H, R) be a crown decomposition of a graph G. Then G has a vertex cover of size k if and only if $G' = G[R]$ has a vertex cover of size $k' = k - |H|$.*

Proof Let S be a vertex cover of G of size k. By the properties of crown decomposition, there is a matching H into C. This matching is of size $|H|$ and it saturates every vertex of H. Thus $|S \cap (H \cup C)| \geq |H|$, as each vertex cover must pick at least one vertex from each of the matching edge. Hence the number of vertices in S covering the edges not incident to $H \cup C$ is at most $k - |H|$.

For the other direction, if S' is a vertex cover of size $k - |H|$ in G', it follows that $S' \cup H$ is a vertex cover of size k for G. $\square$

Next we show how Crown Rule can be used to obtain a kernel with $3k$ vertices.

Theorem 9.9 *p-VERTEX COVER admits a kernel with at most $3k$ vertices.*

Proof Given an input graph G and a positive integer k, we proceed as follows. We first find a maximal matching M of G. Let $V(M)$ be the set of endpoints of edges in M. Now if $|V(M)| > 2k$, we answer NO and stop as every vertex cover must contain at least one vertex from each of the matching edges and hence has size greater than k.

Let us assume that $|V(M)| \leq 2k$. Because M is a maximal matching, the remaining set $I = V(G) \setminus V(M)$ is an independent set. By Kőnig's Theorem, the minimum size of a vertex cover of a bipartite graph $G_{I,V(M)}$ formed by edges of G between $V(M)$ and I is equal to the maximum size of the matching. Thus we can compute a minimum-sized vertex cover of X of this bipartite graph in polynomial time. If $|X| > k$, we again answer NO. So we assume that $|X| \leq k$. If no vertex of X is in $V(M)$, then every vertex of I should be in X (we assume here that graph G has no isolated vertices). But then $|I| \leq k$, and G has at most $3k$ vertices.

So we assume that $X \cap N(I) \neq \emptyset$, but in this case we are able to obtain a crown decomposition (C, H, R) as follows. We put $H = X \cap V(M)$ and $C = I \setminus X$. Obviously, C is an independent set. Because X is a vertex cover $G_{I,V(M)}$, every vertex of C can be adjacent only to vertices of H. By Kőnig's Theorem, $G_{I,V(M)}$ contains a matching of size $|X|$. Every edge of this matching contains has exactly one endpoint in X, and thus the edges of this matching with endpoints in H form a matching of H into C.

Given a crown decomposition (C, H, R), we apply the Crown Rule and obtain a smaller instance for a vertex cover with graph $G' = G[R]$ and parameter $k' = k - |H|$. Now we repeat the above procedure with this reduced instance until we either get a NO answer, or reach a kernel with $3k$ vertices. □

The bound obtained on the kernel for p-VERTEX COVER in Theorem 9.9 can be further improved to $2k$ with a more sophisticated use of crown decomposition. An alternative method for obtaining a $2k$ size kernel is through a Linear Programming formulation of p-VERTEX COVER. See [18] and [32] for further details on a Linear Programming based kernelization of p-VERTEX COVER.

Clique Cover Unfortunately, not all known problem kernels can be shown to have polynomial size. Here, we present some data reduction results with exponential-size kernels. Clearly, it is a pressing challenge to find out whether these bounds can be improved to polynomial ones.

Here is an example:

---

p-EDGE CLIQUE COVER
    Instance: A graph $G = (V, E)$, and a non-negative integer k.
  Parameter: k
    Problem: Decide whether edges of G can be covered
                 by at most k cliques.

We use $N(v)$ to denote the neighbourhood of vertex v in G, namely, $N(v) := \{u \mid uv \in E\}$. The *closed* neighbourhood of vertex v, denoted by $N[v]$, is $N(v) \cup \{v\}$.

We formulate data reduction rules for a generalized version of p-EDGE CLIQUE COVER, in which already some edges may be marked as "covered". Then, the question is to find a clique cover of size k that covers all uncovered edges. We apply the following data reduction rules from [21]:

Rule 1 Remove isolated vertices and vertices that are only adjacent to covered edges.

Rule 2 If there is an edge uv whose endpoints have exactly the same closed neighbourhood (that is, $N[u] = N[v]$), then mark all edges incident to u as covered. To reconstruct a solution for the non-reduced instance, add u to every clique containing v.

Theorem 9.10 ([21]) p-EDGE CLIQUE COVER *admits a kernel with at most 2^k vertices.*

Proof   Let $G = (V, E)$ be a graph that has a clique cover $C_1, \ldots, C_k$ and such that none of two rules can be applied to G. We claim that G has at most 2^k vertices. To exhibit a contradiction, let us assume that G has more than 2^k vertices. We assign to each vertex $v \in V$ a binary vector b_v of length k where bit i, $1 \leq i \leq k$, is set to 1 if and only if v is contained in clique C_i. Since there are only 2^k possible vectors, there must be $u \neq v \in V$ with $b_u = b_v$. If b_u and b_v are zero vectors, the first rule applies; otherwise, u and v are contained in the same cliques. This means that u and v are adjacent and share the same neighbourhood, and thus the second rule applies. Hence, if G has more than 2^k vertices, at least one of the reduction rules can be applied to it, which contradicts the initial assumption.   □

9.4 Recent Upper Bound Machinery

9.4.1 Protrusion Based Replacement

In this part we discuss the kernelization of different classes of sparse graphs. An important result in the area of kernelization by Alber et al. [1] is a linear sized kernel for the p-DOMINATING SET problem on planar graphs. This work triggered an explosion of papers on kernelization, and in particular on kernelization of problems on planar and different classes of sparse graphs. Combining the ideas of Alber et al. with *problem specific* data reduction rules, linear kernels were obtained for a variety of parameterized problems on planar graphs including p-CONNECTED VERTEX COVER, p-INDUCED MATCHING and p-FEEDBACK VERTEX SET. In 2009 Bodlaender et al. [4] obtained meta kernelization algorithms that eliminated the need for the design of problem specific reduction rules by providing an automated process that generates them. They show that all problems that have a "distance property" and are expressible in a certain kind of logic or "behave like a regular language" admit a polynomial kernel on graphs of bounded genus. In what follows we give a short description of these meta theorems.

Informal Description. The notion of "protrusions and finite integer index" is central to recent meta kernelization theorems. In the context of problems on graphs, there are three central ideas that form the undercurrent of all protrusion-based reduction rules:

- describing an equivalence that classifies all instances of a problem in an useful manner,
- the ability to easily identify, given a problem, whether the said equivalence has finite index,
- given an instance of a problem, finding large subgraphs that "can be replaced" with smaller subgraphs that are equivalent to the original.

One of the aspects of this development that requires some ingenuity is coming up with the right definition for describing the circumstances in which a subgraph may be replaced. This is captured by the notion of a protrusion. In general, an *r-protrusion* in a graph G is simply a subgraph H such that the number of vertices in H that have neighbours in $G \setminus H$ is at most r and the treewidth of H is at most r. (We refer to Chapter 1 by Gottlob, Greco and Scarcello for the definition of treewidth.) The *size* of the protrusion is the number of vertices in it, that is, $|V(H)|$. The vertices in H that have neighbours in $G \setminus H$ comprise the *boundary* of H. Informally, H may be thought of as a part of the graph that is separated from the "rest of the graph" by a small-sized separator, and everything about H may be understood in terms of the graph induced by H itself and the limited interaction it has with $G \setminus H$ via its boundary vertices. If the size of the protrusion is large, we may want to replace it with another graph X that is much smaller but whose behaviour with respect to $G \setminus H$ is identical to H in the context of the problem that we are studying. Specifically, we would like that the solution to the problem in question does not change after we have made the replacement (or changes in a controlled manner that can be tracked as we make these replacements). This motivates us to define an equivalence that captures the essence of what we hope to do in terms of the replacement. We would like to declare H equivalent to X if the size of the solution of G and $(G \setminus H) \cup^* X$ is exactly the same, where $\cup^*$ is some notion of replacement that we have not defined precisely yet. Notice, however, that a natural notion of replacement would leave the boundary vertices intact and perform a cut-and-paste on the rest of H. This is precisely what the protrusion-based reduction rules do. Combined with some combinatorial properties of graphs this results in polynomial and, in most cases linear, kernels for variety of problems.

Overview of Meta Kernelization Results. Given a graph $G = (V, E)$, we define $\mathbf{B}_G^r(S)$ to be the set of all vertices of G whose distance from some vertex in S is at most r. Let $\mathcal{G}$ be the family of planar graphs and let the integer $k > 0$ be a parameter. We say that a parameterized problem $\Pi \subseteq \mathcal{G} \times \mathbb{N}$ is *compact* if there exist an integer r such that for all $(G = (V, E), k) \in \Pi$, there is a set $S \subseteq V$ such that $|S| \leq r \cdot k$, $\mathbf{B}_G^r(S) = V$ and $k \leq |V|^r$. Similarly, Π is *quasi-compact* if there exists an integer r such that for every $(G, k) \in \Pi$, there is a set $S \subseteq V$ such that $|S| \leq r \cdot k$, $\mathbf{tw}(G \setminus \mathbf{B}_G^r(S)) \leq r$ and $k \leq |V|^r$ where $\mathbf{tw}(G)$ denotes the treewidth of G. Notice that if a problem is compact then it is also quasi-compact. For ease of presentation the definitions of *compact* and *quasi-compact* are more restrictive here than in [4].

The following theorem from [4] yields linear kernels for a variety of problems on planar graphs. To this end they utilise the notion of *finite integer index*. This term first appeared in the work by Bodlaender and van Antwerpen-de Fluiter [8] and is similar to the notion of *finite state*. We first define the notion of t-boundaried graphs and the gluing operation. A *t-boundaried graph* is a graph $G = (V, E)$ with t distinguished vertices, uniquely labelled from 1 to t. The set $\partial(G)$ of labelled vertices is called the *boundary* of G. The vertices in $\partial(G)$ are referred to as *boundary vertices* or *terminals*. Let G_1 and G_2 be two t-boundaried graphs. By $G_1 \oplus G_2$ we denote the t-boundaried graph obtained by taking the disjoint union of G_1 and G_2 and identifying each vertex of $\partial(G_1)$ with the vertex of $\partial(G_2)$ with the same label; that is, we *glue* them together on the boundaries. In $G_1 \oplus G_2$ there is an edge between two labelled vertices if there is an edge between them in G_1 or in G_2. For a parameterized problem, Π on graphs in $\mathcal{G}$ and two *t*-boundaried graphs G_1 and G_2, we say that $G_1 \equiv_\Pi G_2$ if there exists a constant c such that for all *t*-boundaried graphs G_3 and for all k we have $G_1 \oplus G_3 \in \mathcal{G}$ if and only if $G_2 \oplus G_3 \in \mathcal{G}$ and $(G_1 \oplus G_3, k) \in \Pi$ if and only if $(G_2 \oplus G_3, k + c) \in \Pi$. Note that for every t, the relation $\equiv_\Pi$ on *t*-boundaried graphs is an equivalence relation. A problem Π has *finite integer index* (FII) if and only if for every t, $\equiv_\Pi$ is of finite index that is, has a finite number of equivalence classes. Compact problems that have FII include DOMINATING SET and CONNECTED VERTEX COVER while FEEDBACK VERTEX SET has FII and is quasi-compact but not compact. We are now in position to state the theorem.

Theorem 9.11 *Let* $\Pi \subseteq \mathcal{G} \times \mathbb{N}$ *be quasi-compact and has* FII. *Then* Π *admits a linear kernel.*

Outline of the Proof. We give an outline of the main ideas used to prove Theorem 9.11. For a problem Π and an instance $(G = (V, E), k)$ the kernelization algorithm repeatedly identifies a part of the graph to reduce and replaces this part by smaller equivalent part. Since each such step decreases the number of vertices in the graph the process stops after at most $|V|$ iterations. In particular, the algorithm identifies a *constant-size separator* S that cuts off a *large* chunk of the graph of *constant treewidth*. This chunk is then considered as a $|S|$-boundaried graph $G' = (V', E')$ with boundary S. Let G^* be the other side of the separator; that is $G' \oplus G^* = G$. Since Π has FII there exists a finite set $\mathcal{S}$ of $|S|$-boundaried graphs such that $\mathcal{S} \subseteq \mathcal{G}$, and for any $|S|$-boundaried graph G_1 there exists a $G_2 \in \mathcal{S}$ such that $G_2 \equiv_\Pi G_1$. The definition of "large chunk" is that G' should be larger than the largest graph in $\mathcal{S}$. Hence we can find a $|S|$-boundaried graph $G_2 \in \mathcal{S}$ and a constant c such that $(G, k) = (G' \oplus G^*, k) \in \Pi$ if and only if $(G_2 \oplus G^*, k - c) \in \Pi$. The reduction is just to change (G, k) into $(G_2 \oplus G^*, k - c)$. Given G' we can identify G_2 in time linear in $|V'|$ by using the fact that G' has constant treewidth and that all graphs in $\mathcal{S}$ have constant size.

We now proceed to analyze the size of any reduced yes-instance of Π. We show that if Π is compact (not quasi-compact), then the size of a reduced yes-instance (G, k) must be at most $O(k)$. Since $(G = (V, E), k) \in \Pi$ and Π is compact, there is an $O(k)$-sized set $S' \subseteq V$ such that $\mathbf{B}_G^r(S') = V$ for some constant r depending only on Π. One can show that if such a set S' exists there must exist another $O(k)$-sized set S such that the connected components of $G[V \setminus S]$ can be grouped into $O(k)$ chunks as described in the previous paragraph. If any of these chunks has more vertices than the largest graph in $\mathcal{S}$ we could have performed the reduction. This implies that any reduced yes-instance has size at most ck for some fixed constant c. Hence if a reduced instance is larger than ck the kernelization algorithm returns NO.

Finally to prove Theorem 9.11 even when Π is quasi-compact, the authors of [4] show that the set of reduced instances of a quasi-compact problem is in fact compact. Observe that it is the set of reduced instances that becomes compact and *not* Π itself. The main idea is that if $G = (V, E)$ has a set $S \subseteq V$ such that the treewidth of $G[V \setminus \mathbf{B}_G^r(S)]$ is constant, and that there exists a vertex v which is far away from S, then we can find a large subgraph to reduce.

The parameterized versions of many fundamental optimization problems have finite integer index. Such problems include DOMINATING SET, r-DOM-INATING SET,VERTEX COVER, CONNECTED r-DOMINATING SET, CON-NECTED VERTEX COVER, MINIMUM MAXIMAL MATCHING, CONNECTED DOMINATING SET, FEEDBACK VERTEX SET, CYCLE DOMINATION, EDGE DOMINATING SET, CLIQUE TRANSVERSAL, INDEPENDENT SET, r-SCATT-ERED SET, MIN LEAF SPANNING TREE, INDUCED MATCHING, TRIANGLE PACKING, CYCLE PACKING, MAXIMUM FULL-DEGREE SPANNING TREE, and many others [4, 13].

There are problems such as INDEPENDENT DOMINATING SET, LONGEST PATH, LONGEST CYCLE, MAXIMUM CUT, MINIMUM COVERING BY CLIQUES, INDEPENDENT DOMINATING SET, and MINIMUM LEAF OUT-BRANCHING and various edge-packing problems which are known not to have FII: see [13]. It was shown in [4] that compact problems expressible in an extension of Monadic Second-Order Logic, namely Counting Monadic Second-Order Logic, have polynomial kernels on planar graphs. This implies polynomial kernels for INDEPENDENT DOMINATING SET, MINIMUM LEAF OUT-BRANCHING, and some edge-packing problems on planar graphs. The results from [4] hold not only for planar graphs but for graphs of bounded genus. It was shown in [19] that if instead of quasi-compactness, we request another combinatorial property of bidimensionality with certain separabil-ity properties, then an analogue of Theorem 9.11 can be obtained for much more general graph classes, like graphs excluding some fixed (apex) graph as a minor.

9.4.2 Algebraic and Probabilistic Methods

In Section 9.3, we gave a kernel for p-MAX-3-SAT. Let us discuss in more details kernelization for p-MAX-r-SAT.

Observe that the expected number of clauses satisfied by a random truth assignment that sets each variable of F to one or zero is equal to

$$\mu_F = (1 - 2^{-r})m$$

and thus there is always an assignment satisfying at least μ_F clauses. This implies that at least $m/2$ clauses are always satisfied and hence this parameterization of MAX-r-SAT always has a polynomial kernel because of the following argument. If $k \le m/2$ then the answer is yes else we have that $m \le 2k$ and hence $n \le 2kr$. Thus given a r-CNF formula F, the more meaningful question is whether there exists a truth assignment for F satisfying at least $\mu_F + k$ clauses. We refer to this version of the MAX-r-SAT problem as to p-AG-MAX-r-SAT; that is, the problem where the parameterization is beyond the guaranteed lower bound on the solution.

---

p-AG-MAX-r-SAT
>   *Instance:*   A r-CNF formula F, and a non-negative integer k.
> *Parameter:* k
>   *Problem:*   Decide whether F has a truth assignment satisfying
>   at least $\mu_F + k$ clauses.

The parameterized study of problems above a guaranteed lower bound was initiated by Mahajan and Raman [30]. They showed that several above-guarantee versions of MAX-CUT and MAX-SAT are FPT and provided a number of open problems around parameterizations beyond guaranteed lower and upper bounds. In a breakthrough paper Gutin et al [23] developed a probabilistic approach to problems parameterized above or below tight bounds. Alon et al. [2] combined this approach with methods from algebraic combinatorics and Fourier analysis to obtain FPT algorithm for parameterized MAX-r-SAT beyond the guaranteed lower bound. Other significant results in this direction include quadratic kernels for ternary permutation constraint satisfaction problems parameterized above average and results around system of linear equations modulo 2; [12, 24]. In what follows we outline the method and then illustrate it using an example.

Informal Description of the Method. We give a brief description of the probabilistic method with respect to a given problem Π parameterized above a tight lower bound or below a tight upper bound. We first apply some reductions rules to reduce Π to its special case Π'. Then we introduce a random variable X such that the answer to Π is YESif and only if X takes, with positive probability, a value greater or equal to the parameter k. Now using some probabilistic inequalities on X, we derive upper bounds on the size of NO-instances of Π' in terms of a function of the parameter k. If the size of a given instance exceeds this bound, then we know the answer is YES; otherwise, we produce a problem kernel.

Probabilistic Inequalities. A random variable is *discrete* if its distribution function has a finite or countable number of positive increases. A random variable X is a *symmetric* if $-X$ has the same distribution function as X. If X is discrete, then X is symmetric if and only if $\text{Prob}(X = a) = \text{Prob}(X = -a)$ for each real a. Let X be a symmetric variable for which the first moment $\mathbb{E}(X)$ exists. Then $\mathbb{E}(X) = \mathbb{E}(-X) = -\mathbb{E}(X)$ and, thus, $\mathbb{E}(X) = 0$. The following is easy to prove [23].

Lemma 9.12 *If X is a symmetric random variable and $\mathbb{E}(X^2) < \infty$, then*

$$\text{Prob}(\, X \geq \sqrt{\mathbb{E}(X^2)}\,) > 0.$$

Unfortunately, we often have that X is not symmetric, but Lemma 9.13 provides an inequality that can be used in many such cases. This lemma was proved by Alon et al. [3]; a weaker version was obtained by Håstad and Venkatesh [26].

Lemma 9.13 *Let X be a random variable and suppose that its first, second and fourth moments satisfy $\mathbb{E}(X) = 0$, $\mathbb{E}(X^2) = \sigma^2 > 0$ and $\mathbb{E}(X^4) \leq b\sigma^4$, respectively. Then $\text{Prob}(\, X > \frac{\sigma}{4\sqrt{b}}\,) \geq \frac{1}{4^{4/3}b}$.*

Since it is often rather nontrivial to evaluate $\mathbb{E}(X^4)$ in order to check whether $\mathbb{E}(X^4) \leq b\sigma^4$ holds, one can sometimes use the following extension of Khinchin's Inequality by Bourgain [9].

Lemma 9.14 *Let $f = f(x_1, \ldots, x_n)$ be a polynomial of degree r in n variables $x_1, \ldots, x_n$ with domain $\{-1, 1\}$. Define a random variable X by choosing a vector $(\epsilon_1, \ldots, \epsilon_n) \in \{-1, 1\}^n$ uniformly at random and setting $X = f(\epsilon_1, \ldots, \epsilon_n)$. Then, for every $p \geq 2$, there is a constant c_p such that*

$$(\mathbb{E}(|X|^p))^{1/p} \leq (c_p)^r (\mathbb{E}(X^2))^{1/2}.$$

In particular, $c_4 \leq 2^{3/2}$.

An Illustration. Consider the following problem: given a digraph $D = (V, A)$ and a positive integer k, does there exist an acyclic subdigraph of D with at least k arcs? It is easy to prove that this parameterized problem has a linear kernel. Observe that D always has an acyclic subdigraph with at least $|A|/2$ arcs. Indeed, consider a bijection $\alpha : V \rightarrow \{1, \ldots, |V|\}$ and the following subdigraphs of D: $(V, \{\, xy \in A : \alpha(x) < \alpha(y)\,\})$ and $(V, \{\, xy \in A : \alpha(x) > \alpha(y)\,\})$. Both subdigraphs are acyclic and at least one of them has at least $|A|/2$ arcs. Thus the input D itself is a kernel with $2k$ arcs and at most $4k$ vertices. Thus a more natural interesting parameterization is the following: decide whether $D = (V, A)$ contains an acyclic subdigraph with at least $|A|/2 + k$ arcs. We choose $|A|/2 + k$ because $|A|/2$ is a *tight lower bound* on the size of a largest acyclic subdigraph. Indeed, the size of a largest acyclic subdigraph of a symmetric digraph $D = (V, A)$ is precisely $|A|/2$. A digraph $D = (V, A)$ is *symmetric* if $xy \in A$ implies $yx \in A$. More precisely, we study the following problem.

---

p-LINEAR ORDERING ABOVE TIGHT LOWER BOUND (LOALB)

> *Instance:*   A digraph D with each arc ij with integer positive weight w_{ij}, and a positive integer k.
>
> *Parameter:* k
>
> *Problem:*   Decide whether is an acyclic subdigraph of D of weight at least $W/2 + k$, where $W = \sum_{ij \in A} w_{ij}$.

Consider the following reduction rule:

Reduction Rule 1   Assume D has a directed 2-cycle iji; if $w_{ij} = w_{ji}$ delete the cycle, if $w_{ij} > w_{ji}$ delete the arc ji and replace w_{ij} by $w_{ij} - w_{ji}$, and if $w_{ji} > w_{ij}$ delete the arc ij and replace w_{ji} by $w_{ji} - w_{ij}$.

It is easy to check that the answer to LOALB for a digraph D is YES if and only if the answer to LOALB is YES for a digraph obtained from D using the reduction rule as long as possible.

Let $D = (V, A)$ be an oriented graph, let $n = |V|$ and $W = \sum_{ij \in A} w_{ij}$. Consider a random bijection: $\alpha : V \rightarrow \{1, \ldots, n\}$ and a random variable $X(\alpha) = \frac{1}{2} \sum_{ij \in A} \epsilon_{ij}(\alpha)$, where $\epsilon_{ij}(\alpha) = w_{ij}$ if $\alpha(i) < \alpha(j)$ and $\epsilon_{ij}(\alpha) = -w_{ij}$, otherwise. It is easy to see that $X(\alpha) = \sum \{ w_{ij} : ij \in A, \alpha(i) < \alpha(j) \} - W/2$. Thus, the answer to LOALB is YES if and only if there is a bijection $\alpha : V \rightarrow \{1, \ldots, n\}$ such that $X(\alpha) \geq k$. Since $\mathbb{E}(\epsilon_{ij}) = 0$, we have $\mathbb{E}(X) = 0$. Let $W^{(2)} = \sum_{ij \in A} w_{ij}^2$. Then one can prove the following.

Lemma 9.15 ([23]) $\mathbb{E}(X^2) \geq W^{(2)}/12$.

Using Lemma 9.15 we can now prove the main result of this section.

Theorem 9.16 ([23])   *The problem LOALB admits a kernel with $O(k^2)$ arcs.*

Proof   Let H be a digraph. We know that the answer to LOALB for H is YES if and only if the answer to LOALB is YES for a digraph D obtained from H using Reduction Rule 1 as long as possible. Observe that D is an oriented graph. Let $\mathcal{B}$ be the set of bijections from V to $\{1, \ldots, n\}$. Observe that $f : \mathcal{B} \to \mathcal{B}$ such that $f(\alpha(v)) = |V| + 1 - \alpha(v)$ for each $\alpha \in \mathcal{B}$ is a bijection. Note that $X(f(\alpha)) = -X(\alpha)$ for each $\alpha \in \mathcal{B}$. Therefore, $\text{Prob}(X = a) = \text{Prob}(X = -a)$ for each real a and thus X is symmetric. Hence, by Lemmas 9.12 and 9.15, we have $\text{Prob}(X \geq \sqrt{W^{(2)}/12}) > 0$. Therefore, if $\sqrt{W^{(2)}/12} \geq k$, there is a bijection $\alpha : V \to \{1, \dots, n\}$ such that $X(\alpha) \geq k$ and, thus, the answer to LOALB (for both D and H) is YES. Otherwise, $|A| \leq W^{(2)} < 12 \cdot k^2$. □

9.5 Conclusion

In this chapter we have given several examples of how parameterized complexity and kernelization allow us to analyze different preprocessing algorithms.

In parameterized complexity there there are many reasonable ways to "parameterize a problem". For example, for a graph optimization problem a parameter could be the solution size, a parameter measuring the structure of the graph (such as treewidth or pathwidth), the distance of the graph to some polynomially solvable subclasses (for an example deleting at most k vertices to transform a graph into an interval graph). Other parameters can be obtained by analyzing the hardness proof, or analyzing the data or the dimension. We refer to the survey of Niedermeier [33] for a more detailed exposition of this. Bodlaender and Jansen [27] parameterized VERTEX COVER by the size of a feedback vertex set. This parameterization is interesting because the minimum size of a feedback vertex is always at most the size of the vertex cover number. It was shown in [27] that this parameterized problem admits a cubic kernel. See [6, 7, 27, 28] for other studies of kernelization for parameterizing one problem by the solution to another problem. Parameterizing a graph optimization problem by another graph optimization problem such as vertex cover number, max-leaf number has been studied before from the algorithmic perspective [17] but so far there are very few results from the view point of kernelization complexity.

Developing rigorous mathematical theories that explain the behaviour of practical algorithms and heuristics has become an increasingly important challenge in Theory of Computing for the 21st century [11]:

While theoretical work on models of computation and methods for analyzing algorithms has had enormous payoff, we are not done. In many situations, simple algorithms do well. We don't understand why! It is apparent that worst-case analysis does not provide useful insights on the performance of algorithms and heuristics and our models of computation need to be further developed and refined.

We believe that a kernelization approach based on

(i) identifying parameters that guarantee the tractability, and
(ii) verifying that these parameters are low in instances that occur in practice,

can not only shed light on the mystery of heuristics by providing rigorous mathematical tools for analyzing their behaviour, but can also be a new source of efficient algorithms for handling computational intractability.

References

[1] Jochen Alber, Michael R. Fellows, and Rolf Niedermeier. 2004. Polynomial-time data reduction for dominating set. *Journal of the ACM*, **51**(3), 363–384.

[2] Noga Alon, Gregory Gutin, Eun Jung Kim, Stefan Szeider, and Anders Yeo. 2010. Solving MAX-r-SAT above a tight lower bound. Pages 511–517 of: *SODA 2010: Proceedings of the 21st Annual ACM-SIAM Symposium on Discrete Algorithms*.

[3] Noga Alon, Gregory Gutin, and Michael Krivelevich. 2004. Algorithms with large domination ratio. *J. Algorithms*, **50**(1), 118–131.

[4] H. Bodlaender, F.V. Fomin, D. Lokshtanov, E. Penninkx, S. Saurabh, and D.M. Thilikos. 2009. (Meta) kernelization. Pages 629–638 of: *FOCS 2009; Proceedings of the 50th Annual IEEE Symposium on Foundations of Computer Science*.

[5] Hans L. Bodlaender, Rodney G. Downey, Michael R. Fellows, and Danny Hermelin. 2009. On problems without polynomial kernels. *J. Comput. Syst. Sci.*, **75**(8), 423–434.

[6] Hans L. Bodlaender, Bart M.P. Jansen, and Stefan Kratsch. 2011. Cross-composition: A new technique for kernelization lower bounds. In *STACS 2011: Proceedings of the 28th International Symposium on Theoretical Aspects of Computer Science*, LIPIcs, **9**, 165–176.

[7] Hans L. Bodlaender, Bart M. P. Jansen, and Stefan Kratsch. 2011. Preprocessing for treewidth: A combinatorial analysis through kernelization. Pages 437–448 of: *ICALP 2011: Proceedings of the 38th International Colloquium on Automata, Languages and Programming*, LNCS **6755**.

[8] Hans L. Bodlaender and Babette van Antwerpen-de Fluiter. 2001. Reduction algorithms for graphs of small treewidth. *Inf. Comput.*, **167**(2), 86–119.

[9] J. Bourgain. 1980. Walsh subspaces of l^p-product space. *Séminaire d'analyse fonctionnelle, Ecole Polytechnique*, Exp. No. 4A, 9.

[10] Jianer Chen, Iyad A. Kanj, and Weijia Jia. 2001. Vertex cover: further observations and further improvements. *Journal of Algorithms*, **41**(2), 280–301.

[11] Anne Condon, Herbert Edelsbrunner, E. Allen Emerson, Lance Fortnow, Stuart Haber, Richard Karp, Daniel Leivant, Richard Lipton, Nancy Lynch, Ian Parberry, Christos Papadimitriou, Michael Rabin, Arnold Rosenberg, James S. Royer, John Savage, Alan L. Selman, Carl Smith, Eva Tardos and Jeffrey

Scott Vitter. 1999. Challenges for the theory of computing: Report for an NSF-sponsored workshop on research in theoretical computer science. Available at `http://www.cs.buffalo.edu/selman/report/`.

[12] Robert Crowston, Gregory Gutin, Mark Jones, Eun Jung Kim, and Imre Z. Ruzsa. Systems of linear equations over $\mathbb{F}_2$ and problems parameterized above average. 2010. Pages 164–175 of: *SWAT 2010: Proceedings of the 12th Scandinavian Symposium and Workshops on Algorithm Theory)*, LNCS **6139**.

[13] Babette de Fluiter. 1997 *Algorithms for Graphs of Small Treewidth*. PhD thesis, Utrecht University.

[14] R. G. Downey and M. R. Fellows. 1999. *Parameterized Complexity*. Springer.

[15] P. Erdős and R. Rado. 1960. Intersection theorems for systems of sets. *J. London Math. Soc.*, **35**, 85–90.

[16] Michael R. Fellows. The lost continent of polynomial time: Preprocessing and kernelization. 2006. Pages 276–277 of: *IWPEC 2006: Proceedings of the 2nd International Workshop on Parameterized and Exact Computation*, LNCS **4169**.

[17] Michael R. Fellows, Daniel Lokshtanov, Neeldhara Misra, Matthias Mnich, Frances A. Rosamond, and Saket Saurabh. 2009. The complexity ecology of parameters: An illustration using bounded max leaf number. *Theory Comput. Syst.*, **45**(4), 822–848.

[18] Jörg Flum and Martin Grohe. 2006. *Parameterized Complexity Theory*. Texts in Theoretical Computer Science. Springer.

[19] F.V. Fomin, D. Lokshtanov, S. Saurabh, and D. M. Thilikos. 2010. Bidimensionality and kernels. Pages 503–510 of: *SODA 2010: Proceedings of the 21st Annual ACM-SIAM Symposium on Discrete Algorithms*.

[20] Fedor V. Fomin, Daniel Lokshtanov, Neeldhara Misra, Geevarghese Philip, and Saket Saurabh. 2011. Hitting forbidden minors: Approximation and kernelization. *STACS 2011: Proceedings of the 28th International Symposium on Theoretical Aspects of Computer Science. LIPIcs*, **9**, 189–200.

[21] Jens Gramm, Jiong Guo, Falk Hüffner, and Rolf Niedermeier. 2008. Data reduction and exact algorithms for clique cover. *ACM Journal of Experimental Algorithmics*, **13**, Article 2.

[22] Jiong Guo and Rolf Niedermeier. 2007. Invitation to data reduction and problem kernelization. *SIGACT News*, **38**(1), 31–45.

[23] Gregory Gutin, Eun Jung Kim, Stefan Szeider, and Anders Yeo. 2011. A probabilistic approach to problems parameterized above or below tight bounds. *J. Comput. Syst. Sci.*, **77**(2), 422–429.

[24] Gregory Gutin, Leo van Iersel, Matthias Mnich, and Anders Yeo. 2010. All ternary permutation constraint satisfaction problems parameterized above average have kernels with quadratic numbers of variables. Pages 326–337 of: *ESA 2010: Proceedings of the 18th Annual European Symposium on Algorithms*, LNCS **6346**.

[25] Philip Hall. 1935 On representatives of subsets. *J. London Math. Soc.*, **10**, 26–30.

[26] Johan Håstad and Srinivasan Venkatesh. 2002. On the advantage over a random assignment. Pages pages 43–52 of: *STOC 2002: Proceedings of the 34th Annual ACM Symposium on Theory of Computing.*

[27] Bart M.P. Jansen and Hans L. Bodlaender. 2011. Vertex cover kernelization revisited: Upper and lower bounds for a refined parameter. *STACS 2011: Proceedings of the 28th International Symposium on Theoretical Aspects of Computer Science. LIPIcs,* **9**, 177–188.

[28] Bart M.P. Jansen and Stefan Kratsch. 2011. Data reduction for graph coloring problems. Pages 90–101 of: *FCT 2011: Fundamentals of Computation Theory,* LNCS **6914**.

[29] Dénes Kőnig. 1916. Über Graphen und ihre Anwendung auf Determinantentheorie und Mengenlehre. *Math. Ann.,* **77**(4), 453–465.

[30] Meena Mahajan and Venkatesh Raman. 1999. Parameterizing above guaranteed values: Maxsat and maxcut. *J. Algorithms,* **31**(2), 335–354.

[31] Neeldhara Misra, Venkatesh Raman, and Saket Saurabh. 2011. Lower bounds on kernelization. *Discrete Optim.,* **8**(1), 110–128.

[32] Rolf Niedermeier. 2006. *Invitation to Fixed-parameter Algorithms,* Oxford Lecture Series in Mathematics and its Applications, volume 31. Oxford University Press.

[33] Rolf Niedermeier. 2010. Reflections on multivariate algorithmics and problem parameterization. *STACS 2010: Proceedings of the 27th International Symposium on Theoretical Aspects of Computer Science. LIPIcs,* **5**, 17–32.

[34] W.V. Quine. 1952. The problem of simplifying truth functions. *Amer. Math. Monthly,* **59**, 521–531.

[35] Stéphan Thomassé. 2010. A $4k^2$ kernel for feedback vertex set. *ACM Transactions on Algorithms,* **6**(2).

PART 4

TRACTABILITY IN SOME SPECIFIC AREAS

10

Efficient Submodular Function Minimization for Computer Vision

Pushmeet Kohli

Markov Random Fields have been successfully applied to many computer vision problems such as image segmentation, 3D reconstruction, and stereo. The problem of estimating the Maximum a Posteriori (MAP) solution of models such as Markov Random Fields (MRF) can be formulated as a function minimization problem. This has made function minimization an indispensable tool in computer vision. The problem of minimizing a function of discrete variables is, in general, NP-hard. However, functions belonging to certain classes of functions, such as submodular functions, can be minimized in polynomial time. In this chapter, we discuss examples of popular models used in computer vision for which the MAP inference problem results in a tractable function minimization problem. We also discuss how algorithms used in computer vision overcome challenges introduced by the scale and form of function minimization problems encountered in computer vision.

10.1 Labeling Problems in Computer Vision

Many problems in computer vision and scene understanding can be formulated in terms of finding the most probable values of certain hidden or unobserved variables. These variables encode some property of the scene and can be continuous or discrete. These problems are commonly referred to as *labelling problems* as they involve assigning a label to the hidden variables. Labelling problems occur in many forms, from lattice based problems of dense stereo and image segmentation discussed in [6, 40] to the use of pictorial structures for object recognition as done by [10]. Some examples of problems which can be formulated in this manner are shown in Figure 10.1.

One of the major advances in computer vision in the past few years has been the use of efficient deterministic algorithms for solving discrete labelling problems. In particular, efficient graph cut based minimization algorithms have been extremely successful in solving many low level vision problems. These methods work by inferring the maximum a posteriori (MAP) solutions

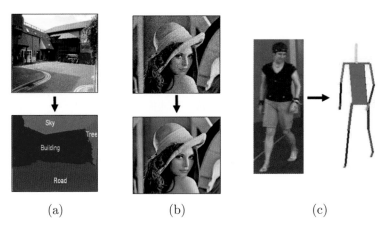

(a)   (b)   (c)

Figure 10.1 *Some labelling problems in computer vision. (a) Object segmentation and recognition: Given any image, we want to find out which object each pixel in the image belongs to. There is one discrete random variable for each pixel in the image which can take any value from a set $\mathcal{L}$ of object labels. For instance, we can use the set of objects: {road, building, tree, sky}. (b) Image denoising: Given a noisy image of the scene, we want to infer the true colour of each pixel in the image. The problem is formulated in a manner similar to object segmentation. Again we use one discrete random variable per pixel which can take any value in RGB space. (c) Human pose estimation: Given an image, we want to infer the pose of the human visible in it. The problem is formulated using a vector of continuous pose variables which encode the orientation and different joint angles of the human.*

of conditional and Markov random fields which are generally used to model these problems.

10.2 Markov and Conditional Random Fields

Random fields provide an elegant probabilistic framework to formulate labelling problems. They are able to model complex interactions between random variables in a simple and precise manner. The power of this representation lies in the fact that the probability distribution over different labellings of the random variables factorizes, and thus allows efficient inference of the most probable solution.

Consider a discrete random field $\mathbf{X}$ defined over a lattice $\mathcal{V} = \{1, 2, \ldots, n\}$ with a neighbourhood system $\mathcal{N}$. Each random variable $X_i \in \mathbf{X}$ is associated with a lattice point $i \in \mathcal{V}$ and takes a value from the label set $\mathcal{L} = \{l_1, l_2, \ldots, l_k\}$. The neighbourhood system $\mathcal{N}$ of the random field is defined by the sets $\mathcal{N}_i, \forall i \in \mathcal{V}$, where $\mathcal{N}_i$ denotes the set of all neighbours of the variable X_i. A clique c is a set of random variables X_c which directly depend on each other. Any possible assignment of labels to the random variables is called a *labelling* or *configuration*. It is denoted by the vector $\mathbf{x}$, and takes values from the set $\mathbf{L} = \mathcal{L}^n$.

A random field is said to be a Markov random field (MRF) with respect to a neighbourhood system $\mathcal{N} = \{\mathcal{N}_v | v \in \mathcal{V}\}$ if and only if it satisfies the positivity property: $\Pr(\mathbf{x}) > 0 \; \forall \mathbf{x} \in \mathcal{X}^n$, and the Markovian property:

$$\Pr(x_v | \{x_u : u \in \mathcal{V} - \{v\}\}) = \Pr(x_v | \{x_u : u \in \mathcal{N}_v\}) \qquad \forall v \in \mathcal{V}. \qquad (10.1)$$

Here we refer to $\Pr(X = \mathbf{x})$ by $\Pr(\mathbf{x})$ and $\Pr(X_i = x_i)$ by $\Pr(x_i)$. The pairwise MRF commonly used to model image labelling problems is shown in Figure 10.2.

A conditional random field (CRF) may be viewed as an MRF globally conditioned on the data. The conditional distribution $\Pr(\mathbf{x}|\mathbf{D})$ over the labellings of the CRF is a *Gibbs* distribution and can be written in the form:

$$\Pr(\mathbf{x}|\mathbf{D}) = \frac{1}{Z} \exp(-\sum_{c \in \mathcal{C}} \psi_c(\mathbf{x}_c)), \qquad (10.2)$$

where Z is a normalizing constant known as the partition function, and $\mathcal{C}$ is the set of all cliques. The term $\psi_c(\mathbf{x}_c)$ is known as the potential function of the clique c where $\mathbf{x}_c = \{x_i, i \in c\}$ is the vector encoding the labelling of the variables constituting the clique. The corresponding Gibbs energy is given by

$$E(\mathbf{x}) = -\log \Pr(\mathbf{x}|\mathbf{D}) - \log Z = \sum_{c \in \mathcal{C}} \psi_c(\mathbf{x}_c) \qquad (10.3)$$

The most probable or maximum a posteriori (MAP) labelling $\mathbf{x}^*$ of the random field is defined as

$$\mathbf{x}^* = \arg \max_{\mathbf{x} \in \mathbf{L}} \Pr(\mathbf{x}|\mathbf{D}). \qquad (10.4)$$

and can be found by minimizing the energy function E. This equivalence to MAP inference has made discrete energy minimization extremely important for problems which are solved using probabilistic methods.

10.2.1 CRFs for Image Segmentation

The image segmentation problem is commonly formulated using the CRF model where the vertex set $\mathcal{V}$ corresponds to the set of all image pixels, $\mathcal{N}$ is a neighbourhood defined on this set[1], the set $\mathcal{L}$ consists of the labels representing the different image segments (which in our case are 'foreground'

---

[1] In this work, we have used the standard 8-neighbourhood i.e., each pixel is connected to the 8 pixels surrounding it.

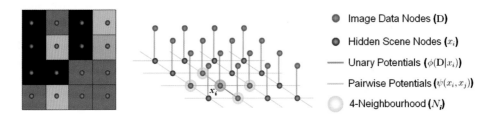

Figure 10.2 *The pairwise MRF commonly used to model image labelling problems. The random field contains a hidden node corresponding to each pixel in the image. The MRF shown in the figure has a 4-neighbourhood, i.e. each node representing the random variables is connected to 4 neighbouring nodes.*

and 'background'), and the value x_v denotes the labelling of the pixel v of the image. Every configuration $\mathbf{x}$ of such a CRF defines a segmentation. The image segmentation problem can thus be solved by finding the least energy configuration of the CRF.

The energy function characterizing the CRFs used for image segmentation can be written as a sum of likelihood ($\phi(\mathbf{D}|x_i)$) and prior ($\psi(x_i, x_j)$) terms as:

$$\Psi_1(\mathbf{x}) = \sum_{i \in \mathcal{V}} \left(\phi(\mathbf{D}|x_i) + \sum_{j \in \mathcal{N}_i} \psi(x_i, x_j) \right) + \text{const.} \qquad (10.5)$$

The term $\phi(\mathbf{D}|x_i)$ in the CRF energy is the data log likelihood which imposes individual penalties for assigning any label $k \in \mathcal{L}$ to pixel i. If we only take the appearance model into consideration, the likelihood is given by

$$\phi(\mathbf{D}|x_i) = -\log \Pr(i \in \mathcal{S}_k | \mathcal{H}_k) \qquad \text{if } x_i = k, \qquad (10.6)$$

where $\mathcal{H}_k$ is the RGB (or for grey scale images, the intensity value) distribution for the segment[2] $\mathcal{S}_k$ denoted by label $k \in \mathcal{L}$. The probability of a pixel belonging to a particular segment i.e. $\Pr(i \in \mathcal{S}_k | \mathcal{H}_k)$ is proportional to the likelihood $\Pr(I_i | \mathcal{H}_k)$, where I_i is the colour intensity of the pixel i. The likelihood $\Pr(I_i | \mathcal{H}_k)$ is generally computed from the colour histogram of the pixels belonging to the segment $\mathcal{S}_k$.

The prior $\psi(x_i, x_j)$ terms takes the form of a Ising or Potts model:

$$\psi(x_i, x_j) = \begin{cases} K_{ij} & \text{if } x_i \neq x_j, \\ 0 & \text{if } x_i = x_j. \end{cases} \qquad (10.7)$$

---

[2] In our problem, we have only 2 segments i.e., the foreground and the background.

The CRF used by [2, 4] to model the image segmentation problem also contains a contrast term that favors pixels with similar colours having the same label. This term is incorporated in the energy function by increasing the cost within the Potts model (for two neighbouring variables being different) in proportion to the similarity in intensities of their corresponding pixels. In our experiments, we use the function:

$$\gamma(i, j) = \lambda \exp \left(\frac{-g^2(i, j)}{2\sigma^2} \right) \frac{1}{\text{dist}(i, j)}, \tag{10.8}$$

where $g^2(i, j)$ measures the difference in the RGB values of pixels i and j and $\text{dist}(i, j)$ gives the spatial distance between i and j. This is a likelihood term (not prior) as it is based on the data, and hence has to be added separately from the smoothness prior. The energy function of the CRF now becomes

$$\Psi_2(\mathbf{x}) = \sum_{i \in \mathcal{V}} \left(\phi(\mathbf{D}|x_i) + \sum_{j \in \mathcal{N}_i} (\phi(\mathbf{D}|x_i, x_j) + \psi(x_i, x_j)) \right) \tag{10.9}$$

The contrast term of the energy function has the form

$$\phi(\mathbf{D}|x_i, x_j) = \begin{cases} \gamma(i, j) & \text{if } x_i \neq x_j \\ 0 & \text{if } x_i = x_j. \end{cases} \tag{10.10}$$

By adding this term to the energy, we have diverged from the strict definition of an MRF. The resulting energy function now characterizes a Conditional Random Field [31]. The pairwise MRF commonly used to model image labelling problems is shown in Figure 10.2.

10.2.2 Higher-Order Potentials for Enforcing Label Consistency

A common method for solving various image labeling problems like object segmentation, stereo and single view reconstruction is to formulate them using image segments (called super-pixels in [34]) obtained from unsupervised segmentation algorithms. Researchers working with these methods have made the observation that all pixels constituting the segments often have the same label, that is they might belong to the same object or might have the same depth.

Standard super-pixel based methods use label consistency in super-pixels as a hard constraint. Kohli et al. [22] proposed a higher-order CRF model for image labeling that used label consistency in super-pixels as a *soft constraint*. This was done by using higher-order potentials defined on the image segments generated using unsupervised segmentation algorithms. Specifically, they extend the standard pairwise CRF model often used for object segmentation by incorporating higher-order potentials defined on sets or regions of pixels. In particular, they use the unary and pairwise potentials from TextonBoost, which is the method proposed in [38]. The Gibbs energy of the higher-order CRF of [22] can be written as:

$$E(\mathbf{x}) = \sum_{i \in \mathcal{V}} \psi_i(x_i) + \sum_{(i,j) \in \mathcal{E}} \psi_{ij}(x_i, x_j) + \sum_{c \in \mathcal{S}} \psi_c(\mathbf{x}_c), \qquad (10.11)$$

where $\mathcal{E}$ represents the set of all edges in a 4- or 8-connecting neighbourhood system, $\mathcal{S}$ refers to a set of image segments (or super-pixels), and ψ_c are higher-order *label consistency potentials* defined on them.

In the formulation of [22], the set $\mathcal{S}$ consisted of all segments of multiple segmentations of an image obtained using an unsupervised image segmentation algorithm such as mean-shift from [8]. The labels constituting the label set $\mathcal{L}$ of the CRF represent the different objects. Every possible assignment of the random variables $\mathbf{x}$ (or configuration of the CRF) defines a segmentation.

The label consistency potential used by [22] is a higher-order generalization of the smoothness prior used in [4]. It favors all pixels belonging to a segment to take the same label. It takes the form of the P^n Potts model proposed by [21] and is formally defined as:

$$\psi_c(\mathbf{x}_c) = \begin{cases} 0 & \text{if} \quad x_i = l_k, \forall i \in c, \\ \theta_1 |c|^{\theta_\alpha} & \text{otherwise.} \end{cases} \qquad (10.12)$$

where $|c|$ is the cardinality[3] of the pixel set c, and θ_1 and θ_α are parameters of the model. The expression $\theta_1 |c|^{\theta_\alpha}$ gives the label inconsistency cost, i.e. the cost added to the energy of a labeling in which different labels have been assigned to the pixels constituting the segment. Figure 10.3(left) visualizes a P^n Potts potential.

The P^n Potts model enforces label consistency rigidly. For instance, if all but one of the pixels in a super-pixel take the same label then the same cost is incurred as if they were all to take different labels. Due to this high cost, the potential might not be able to deal with inaccurate super-pixels or resolve conflicts between overlapping regions of pixels. Kohli et al. [22] resolved this problem by using the *Robust* higher-order potentials defined as:

$$\psi_c(\mathbf{x}_c) = \begin{cases} N_i(\mathbf{x}_c) \frac{1}{Q} \gamma_{\max} & \text{if } N_i(\mathbf{x}_c) \le Q \\ \gamma_{\max} & \text{otherwise.} \end{cases} \qquad (10.13)$$

where $N_i(\mathbf{x}_c)$ denotes the number of variables in the clique c not taking the

---

[3] For the problem of [22] this is the number of pixels constituting super-pixel c.

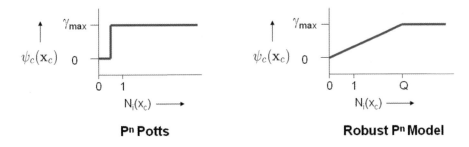

Figure 10.3 *Behavior of the rigid P^n Potts potential (left) and the Robust P^n model potential (right). The figure shows how the cost enforced by the two higher-order potentials changes with the number of variables in the clique not taking the dominant label i.e. $N_i(\mathbf{x}_c) = \min_k(|c| - n_k(\mathbf{x}_c))$, where $n_k(.)$ returns the number of variables x_i in $\mathbf{x}_c$ that take the label k. Q is the truncation parameter used in the definition of the higher-order potential (see equation 10.13).*

dominant label i.e. $N_i(\mathbf{x}_c) = \min_k(|c| - n_k(\mathbf{x}_c))$, $\gamma_{max} = |c|^{\theta_\alpha}(\theta_1 + \theta_2 G(c))$ where $G(c)$ is the measure of the quality of the super-pixel c, and Q is the truncation parameter which controls the rigidity of the higher-order clique potential. Figure 10.3(right) visualizes a robust P^n Potts potential.

Unlike the standard P^n Potts model, this robust potential function gives rise to a cost that is a linear truncated function of the number of inconsistent variables (see Figure 10.3). This enables the robust potential to allow some variables in the clique to take different labels. Figure 10.4 shows results for different models.

10.3 Minimizing Energy Functions for MAP Inference

The computation of the most probable solution (see equation 10.4) under the models proposed in earlier sections can be performed by minimizing the corresponding energy function. In this chapter, we will limit our attention to models defined over discrete variables[4]. Although minimizing a function defined over discrete variables is NP-hard in general, there exist families of energy functions for which this could be done in polynomial time. Submodular set functions constitute one such well studied family.

10.4 Submodular Functions

Submodular set functions are encountered in many areas of research. They are particularly useful in combinatorial optimization, probability and geometry (see [12, 32]). Many optimization problems relating to submodular

---

[4] These are widely used in computer vision.

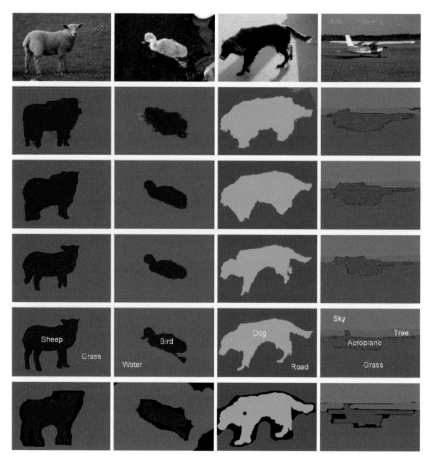

Figure 10.4 *Some qualitative results. Please view in colour. First Row: Original Image. Second Row: Unary likelihood labeling from the TextonBoost method of [38]. Third Row: Result obtained using a pairwise contrast preserving smoothness potential as described in [38]. Fourth Row: Result obtained using the P^n Potts model potential proposed in [21]. Fifth Row: Results using the Robust P^n model potential (10.13) with truncation parameter $Q = 0.1|c|$, where $|c|$ is equal to the size of the super-pixel over which the Robust P^n higher-order potential is defined. Sixth Row: Hand labeled segmentations. The ground truth segmentation are not perfect and many pixels (marked black) are unlabelled. Observe that the Robust P^n model gives best results. For instance, the leg of the sheep and bird have been accurately labeled which was missing in the other results.*

functions can be solved efficiently. In some respects they are similar to convex/concave functions encountered in continuous optimization.

Consider the set $N = \{1, 2, \ldots, n\}$. A set function $f_s : 2^N \to \mathbb{R}$ is said to be submodular if and only if for all subsets $A, B \subseteq N$ the function satisfies:

$$f_s(A) + f_s(B) \geq f_s(A \cup B) + f_s(A \cap B). \qquad (10.14)$$

Every set function $f_s : 2^N \rightarrow \mathbb{R}$ can be written in terms of a function of binary variables $f_b : \{0, 1\}^n \rightarrow \mathbb{R}$. For each element i in set N, a corresponding binary variable $X_i \in \{0, 1\}$ is needed for this representation. Any subset G of the set N can be represented by a labelling of the binary variables. For instance, if an element i is in the subset G then the corresponding binary variables X_i will take value 1. This will be made clearer by the following example.

Example 10.1 Consider a set function f_s defined over the set $N = \{1, 2\}$. As the set N contains 2 elements, the corresponding function (f_b) of binary variables takes two binary variables X_1 and X_2 as arguments. Under the above defined encoding scheme, the subset $G = \{2\}$ will be represented by the labelling $(X_1, X_2) = (0, 1)$. Similarly, the empty subset $G = \emptyset$ will result in the labeling: $(X_1, X_2) = (0, 0)$. The submodularity condition (10.14) for two particular subsets $A = \{1\}$ and $B = \{2\}$ of G is:

$$f_s(\{1\}) + f_s(\{2\}) \geq f_s(\{1, 2\}) + f_s(\emptyset). \tag{10.15}$$

This condition for the equivalent binary function f_b becomes:

$$f_b(1, 0) + f_b(0, 1) \geq f_b(1, 1) + f_b(0, 0). \tag{10.16}$$

We will now extend the definition of submodularity to functions of binary variables. For this however, we will first need to define the concept of a projection of a function.

Definition 10.2 A projection of a function $f : \mathcal{L}^n \rightarrow \mathbb{R}$ on s variables is a function $f^p : \mathcal{L}^s \rightarrow \mathbb{R}$ which is obtained by fixing the values of $n - s$ arguments of $f(\cdot)$. Here p refers to the set of variables whose values have been fixed.

Example 10.3 The function $f^{\{x_1=0\}}(x_2, \ldots, x_n) = f(0, x_2, \ldots, x_n)$ is a projection of the function $f(x_1, x_2, \ldots, x_n)$.

Definition 10.4 A function of one binary variable is always submodular. A function $f(x_1, x_2)$ of two binary variables $\{x_1, x_2\}$ is submodular if and only if:

$$f(0, 1) + f(1, 0) \geq f(0, 0) + f(1, 1) \tag{10.17}$$

A function $f : \mathcal{L}^n \rightarrow R$ is submodular if and only if all its projections on 2 variables are submodular [3, 27].

The definition of submodularity can also be extended to functions of multi-valued variables (referred to as multi-label functions). However, this requires the existence of an ordering over the labels that each variable can take.

Definition 10.5 Let $\mathcal{L}$ be a completely ordered set of labels where the label l_{i+1} is above label l_i. A second-order multi-label function $f : \mathcal{L}^2 \rightarrow R$ is submodular if

$$f(l_1, l_2) - f(l_1 + 1, l_2) - f(l_1, l_2 + 1) + f(l_1 + 1, l_2 + 1) \leq 0. \qquad (10.18)$$

10.4.1 Minimizing Submodular Functions

The first strongly polynomial time algorithms for minimizing submodular functions were proposed independently by [17] and [37]. These algorithms had high runtime complexity. Although recent work has been partly successful in reducing the complexity of algorithms for general submodular function minimization, they are still quite computationally expensive and cannot be used to minimize large problems. For instance, a recently proposed algorithm in [33] for general submodular function minimization has complexity $O(n^5 Q + n^6)$ where Q is the time taken to evaluate the function. This characteristic renders these algorithms impractical for most computer vision problems which involve large number of random variables.

Certain submodular functions can be minimized by solving an st-mincut problem (see [3] for a detailed discussion). Specifically, all submodular functions of binary variables of order at most 3 can be minimized in this manner. Researchers have shown that certain higher-order functions can be transformed into submodular functions of order 2, and thus can also be minimized using graph cuts (see [3, 11, 21, 22, 27, 48]). The same transformation technique can be used to minimize some functions of multi-valued variables as discussed by [15] and [36].

10.5 Graph Cuts for MAP Inference

Graph cuts have been extensively used in computer vision to compute the maximum a posteriori (MAP) solutions for various discrete pixel labelling problems such as image restoration, segmentation, voxel occupancy and stereo (see [40]). Greig et al. [14] were one of the first to use graph cuts in computer vision. They showed that if the pairwise potentials of a two-label *pairwise* MRF were defined as an Ising model, then its exact MAP solution can be obtained in polynomial time by solving a st-mincut problem.

One of the primary reasons behind the growing popularity of graph cuts is the availability of efficient algorithms for computing the maximum flow (max-flow) in graphs of arbitrary topology (see [1, 5]). These algorithms have low polynomial runtime complexity, and enable fast computation of the minimum cost st-cut (st-mincut) problem. This in turn allows for the computation of globally optimal solutions for important classes of energy functions which are encountered in many vision problems. Even in problems where they do not guarantee globally optimal solutions, these algorithms can be used to find solutions which are strong local minima of the energy as shown by [6, 28, 21, 41]. These solutions for certain problems have been shown to be better than the ones obtained using other inference methods [40].

10.5.1 *Energy minimization and st-Mincut*

The procedure for energy minimization using graph cuts comprises of building a graph in which each st-cut defines a configuration $\mathbf{x}$. The cost of an st-cut is equal to the energy $E(\mathbf{x}|\theta)$ of its corresponding configuration $\mathbf{x}$. Finding the minimum cost st-cut in this graph thus provides us with the configuration having the least energy. Algorithms for finding the st-mincut require that all edges in the graph have non-negative weights. This condition results in a restriction on the class of energy functions that can be solved in this manner. For instance, binary second-order functions can be minimized by solving a st-mincut problem only if they are submodular [27]. Boros and Hammer [3], Kolmogorov and Zabih [27] describe the procedure to construct graphs for minimizing pseudo-boolean functions of order at most 3. The graph constructions for functions of multi-valued variables were given by [15] and [36].

We now explain the graph construction for minimizing energies involving binary random variables. We use the notation of [26] and write a second-order function as:

$$E(\mathbf{x}|\theta) = \theta_{\text{const}} + \sum_{v \in V, i \in \mathcal{L}} \theta_{v;i} \delta_i(x_v) + \sum_{(u,v) \in E, (j,k) \in \mathcal{L}^2} \theta_{uv;jk} \delta_j(x_u) \delta_k(x_v),$$

(10.19)

where $\theta_{v;i}$ is the cost for assigning label i to latent variable x_v, $\theta_{uv;ij}$ is the cost for assigning labels i and j to the latent variables x_u and x_v respectively. Further, each $\delta_j(x_v)$ is an indicator function, which is defined as:

$$\delta_j(x_v) = \begin{cases} 1 & \text{if } x_v = j, \\ 0 & \text{otherwise.} \end{cases}$$

Pseudo-boolean functions can be written as:

$$E(\mathbf{x}|\theta) = \theta_{\text{const}} + \sum_{v \in V} (\theta_{v;1} x_v + \theta_{v;0} \bar{x}_v)$$

$$+ \sum_{(u,v) \in E} (\theta_{st;11} x_u x_v + \theta_{st;01} \bar{x}_u x_v + \theta_{st;10} x_u \bar{x}_v + \theta_{st;00} \bar{x}_u \bar{x}_v).$$

The individual unary and pairwise terms of the energy function are represented by weighted edges in the graph. Multiple edges between the same

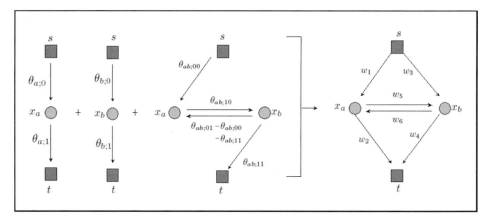

Figure 10.5 *Energy minimization using graph cuts. The figure shows how individual unary and pairwise terms of an energy function taking two binary variables are represented and combined in the graph. Multiple edges between the same nodes are merged into a single edge by adding their weights. For instance, the cost w_1 of the edge (s, x_a) in the final graph is equal to: $w_1 = \theta_{a;0} + \theta_{ab;00}$. The cost of a st-cut in the final graph is equal to the energy $E(\mathbf{x})$ of the configuration $\mathbf{x}$ the cut induces. The minimum cost st-cut induces the least energy configuration $\mathbf{x}$ for the energy function.*

nodes are merged into a single edge by adding their weights. The graph construction for a two-variable energy function is shown in Figure 10.5. The constant term θ_{const} of the energy does not depend on $\mathbf{x}$ and thus is not considered in the energy minimization procedure. The st-mincut in this graph provides us with the minimum solution $\mathbf{x}^*$. The cost of this cut corresponds to the energy of the solution $E(\mathbf{x}^*|\theta)$. The labelling of a latent variable depends on the terminal it is disconnected from by the minimum cut. In our notation, if the node is disconnected from the source, we assign it the label zero and one otherwise.

10.5.2 Minimizing Higher-order Energy functions

Any higher-order function can be converted to a pairwise one, by introducing additional auxiliary random variables (see [3, 25]). This enables the use of conventional inference algorithms such as Belief Propagation, Tree Reweighted message passing, and Graph cuts for such models. However, as discussed in [16, 29, 35], this approach suffers from the problem of combinatorial explosion. Specifically, a naive transformation can result in an exponential number of auxiliary variables (in the size of the corresponding clique) even for higher-order potentials with special structure.

In order to avoid the undesirable scenario presented by the naive transformation, researchers have recently started focusing on higher-order potentials that afford efficient algorithms (see [22, 21, 45, 46, 47]). Most of the efforts in this direction have been towards identifying useful families of higher-order potentials and designing algorithms specific to them. While this approach has led to improved results, its long term impact on the field is limited by the restrictions placed on the form of the potentials. To address this issue, some recent works such as [25, 30, 9, 16, 29, 35] have attempted to characterize the higher-order potentials that are amenable to optimization. These works have successfully been able to exploit the *sparsity* of potentials and provide a convenient parameterization of tractable potentials.

Transforming Higher-order Pseudo-boolean Functions The problem of transforming a general submodular higher-order function to a second-order one has been well studied. It has been known that all submodular functions of order 3 can be transformed to one of order 2, and thus can be solved using graph cuts (see [3] and [27]). Freedman and Drineas [11] showed how certain submodular higher-order functions can be transformed to submodular second-order functions. However, their method, in the worst case, needed to add an exponential number of auxiliary binary variables to make the energy function second-order.

The special structure of certain higher-order potential functions allows them to be transformed to a pairwise model more efficiently. For instance, the special form of the Robust P^n model (10.13) allows it to be transformed to a pairwise function with the addition of only two binary variables per higher-order potential. More formally, Kohli *et al.* [22] showed that higher-order pseudo-boolean functions of the form:

$$f(\mathbf{x}_c) = \min \left(\theta_0 + \sum_{i \in c} w_i^0 (1 - x_i), \theta_1 + \sum_{i \in c} w_i^1 x_i, \theta_{\max} \right) \qquad (10.20)$$

can be transformed to submodular quadratic pseudo-boolean functions, and hence can be minimized using graph cuts. Here, $x_i \in \{0, 1\}$ are binary random variables, c is a clique of random variables, $\mathbf{x}_c \in \{0, 1\}^{|c|}$ denotes the labelling of the variables involved in the clique, and $w_i^0 \geq 0$, $w_i^1 \geq 0$, θ_0, θ_1, $\theta_{\max}$ are parameters of the potential satisfying the constraints $\theta_{\max} \geq \theta_0, \theta_1$, and

$$\left(\left(\theta_{\max} \leq \theta_0 + \sum_{i \in c} w_i^0 (1 - x_i) \right) \vee \left(\theta_{\max} \leq \theta_1 + \sum_{i \in c} w_i^1 x_i \right) \right) = 1 \quad \forall \mathbf{x} \in \{0, 1\}^{|c|}$$

$$(10.21)$$

where $\vee$ is a boolean OR operator. The transformation to a quadratic pseudo-boolean function requires the addition of only two binary auxiliary variables making it computationally efficient.

Theorem 10.6 *The higher-order pseudo-boolean function:*

$$f(\mathbf{x}_c) = \min\left(\theta_0 + \sum_{i\in c} w_i^0(1 - x_i), \theta_1 + \sum_{i\in c} w_i^1 x_i, \theta_{\max}\right) \qquad (10.22)$$

can be transformed to the submodular quadratic pseudo-boolean function:

$$f(\mathbf{x}_c) = \min_{m_0, m_1}\left(r_0(1-m_0)+m_0\sum_{i\in c} w_i^0(1-x_i)+r_1 m_1+(1-m_1)\sum_{i\in c} w_i^1 x_i - K\right) \qquad (10.23)$$

by the addition of binary auxiliary variables m_0 and m_1. Here, $r_0 = \theta_{\max} - \theta_0$, $r_1 = \theta_{\max} - \theta_1$ and $K = \theta_{\max} - \theta_0 - \theta_1$.

For a proof see [24].

Multiple higher-order potentials of the form (10.20) can be summed together to obtain higher-order potentials of the more general form

$$f(\mathbf{x}_c) = F_c\left(\sum_{i\in c} x_i\right) \qquad (10.24)$$

where $F_c : \mathbb{R} \to \mathbb{R}$ is any concave function. However, if the function F_c is convex then this transformation scheme does not apply. [25] have shown how the minimization of energy function containing higher-order potentials of the form (10.24) with convex functions F_c can be transformed to a compact max-min problem. However, this problem is computationally hard and does not lend itself to conventional maxflow based algorithms.

10.6 Minimizing Non-Submodular Functions

There are number of labelling problems whose solution involves minimization of non-submodular functions. These problems have generally been formulated as integer programming problems that are tackled by solving a linear programming (LP) relaxation (as in [7], [43], [44] and [28]). The linear programs which arise in computer vision problems contain many variables and are thus computationally expensive to solve using the general methods mentioned above. A number of algorithms have been developed (refer to [26, 28, 43, 44]) which attempt to solve the LP relaxation by exploiting the special structure of the problem. In particular, researchers have proposed a number of message passing algorithms which are able to approximately solve large LP problems extremely efficiently (see [26, 43]). It has also been shown that certain LP relaxations (such as the roof-dual relaxation (see [3]) and its extension to multi-label problems proposed in [23]) can be efficiently solved by minimizing a quadratic pseudo-boolean function using graph cuts.

Move making algorithms are another family of methods that have proved to be successful for minimizing non-submodular functions of discrete (but not binary) variables. These method are iterative algorithms that *move* from one labeling to the other while ensuring that the energy of the labeling never increases. The move space (that is, the search space for the new labeling) is restricted to be a subset of the original search space that can be explored efficiently. Generally a move algorithm with a bigger move space has a higher chance of reaching a good solution. This observation has been formalized by [19] who give bounds on the error of a particular move making algorithm. [6] showed that for many classes of energy functions, graph cuts allow the computation of the optimal move in a move space whose size is exponential in the number of variables in the original function minimization problem. These move algorithms have been used to find solutions which are strong local minima of the energy (as shown in [6, 28, 21, 41]). In [40] it is empirically demonstrated that these solutions for certain problems have been shown to be better than the ones obtained using other inference methods.

10.7 Discussion

In this chapter we reviewed how submodular functions encountered in the formulation of image labeling problems are minimized by solving an equivalent st-mincut problem. We will conclude now by discussing work on making these algorithms more efficient.

The graphs encountered in the solution of computer vision problems are typically sparse in their connectivity structure and are mostly grid based. This sparse structure results in st-mincut problems that are easier to solve. Some maxflow algorithms have been developed to exploit this property to reduce running times by [13, 5].

In many real world applications, multiple similar instances of a problem need to be solved sequentially e.g. performing image segmentation on the frames of a video. The data (image) in this problem changes from one time instance to the next. Given the solution to an instance of the problem, the question arises as to whether this solution can help in solving other similar instances. This question has been addressed by a number of researchers such as [20] and [18] who have shown that the minimization algorithm could be speeded up by reusing the solution of the maximum flow or the solution of the st-mincut from the previous iteration.

References

[1] Ahuja, R.K., Magnanti, T.L., and Orlin, J.B. 1993. *Network Flows*. Prentice Hall.

[2] Blake, A., Rother, C., Brown, M., Perez, P., and Torr, P.H.S. 2004. Interactive Image Segmentation Using an Adaptive GMMRF Model. Pages 428–441 of: *ECCV 2004: Proceedings of the 8th European Conference on Computer Vision*, LNCS, **3021**.

[3] Boros, E., and Hammer, P.L. 2002. Pseudo-Boolean Optimization. *Discrete Applied Mathematics*, **123**(1-3), 155–225.

[4] Boykov, Y., and Jolly, M. P. 2001. Interactive Graph Cuts for Optimal Boundary and Region Segmentation of Objects in N-D Images. Pages I: 105–112 of: *ICCV 2001. Proceedings of the 8th IEEE International Conference on Computer Vision*, Volume 1.

[5] Boykov, Y., and Kolmogorov, V. 2004. An Experimental Comparison of Min-Cut/Max-Flow Algorithms for Energy Minimization in Vision. *IEEE Trans. Pattern Anal. Mach. Intell.*, **26**(9), 1124–1137.

[6] Boykov, Y., Veksler, O., and Zabih, R. 2001. Fast Approximate Energy Minimization via Graph Cuts. *IEEE Trans. Pattern Anal. Mach. Intell.*, **23**(11), 1222–1239.

[7] Chekuri, C., Khanna, S., Naor, J., and Zosin, L. 2005. A Linear Programming Formulation and Approximation Algorithms for the Metric Labeling Problem. *SIAM Journal of Discrete Mathematics*, **18**(3), 608–625.

[8] Comaniciu, D., and Meer, P. 2002. Mean Shift: A Robust Approach Toward Feature Space Analysis. *IEEE Trans. Pattern Anal. Mach. Intell.*, **24**(5), 603–619.

[9] Delong, Andrew, Osokin, Anton, Isack, Hossam N., and Boykov, Yuri. 2010. Fast Approximate Energy Minimization with Label Costs. *International Journal of Computer Vision*, **96**,(1), 1–27.

[10] Felzenszwalb, P.F., and Huttenlocher, D.P. 2000. Efficient Matching of Pictorial Structures. Pages 2066–2073 of: *IEEE Conference on Computer Vision and Pattern Recognition*.

[11] Freedman, D., and Drineas, P. 2005. Energy Minimization via Graph Cuts: Settling What is Possible. Pages 939–946 of: *CVPR 2000: IEEE Conference on Computer Vision and Pattern Recognition*, Volume 2.

[12] Fujishige, S. 1991. *Submodular Functions and Optimization*. Amsterdam: North-Holland.

[13] Goldberg, Andrew V., Hed, Sagi, Kaplan, Haim, Tarjan, Robert Endre, and Werneck, Renato Fonseca F. 2011. Maximum Flows by Incremental Breadth-First Search. In: *ESA'11: Proceedings of the 19th European Conference on Algorithms*, LNCS, **6942**.

[14] Greig, D., Porteous, B., and Seheult, A. 1989. Exact Maximum a Posteriori Estimation for Binary Images. *J. Roy. Statist. Soc., Series B*, **51**(2), 271–279.

[15] Ishikawa, H. 2003. Exact Optimization for Markov Random Fields with Convex Priors. *IEEE Trans. Pattern Anal. Mach. Intell.*, **25**, 1333–1336.

[16] Ishikawa, Hiroshi. 2009. Higher-order Clique Reduction in Binary Graph Cut.

Pages 2993–3000 of: *CVPR 2009: Proceedings of the IEEE Conference on Computer Vision and Pattern Recognition*.

[17] Iwata, S., Fleischer, L., and Fujishige, S. 2001. A combinatorial strongly polynomial algorithm for minimizing submodular functions. *J. ACM*, **48**(4), 761–777.

[18] Juan, Olivier, and Boykov, Yuri. 2006. Active Graph Cuts. In: *CVPR 2006: Proceedings of the IEEE Cobference on Computer Vision and Pattern Recognition*, Volume 1.

[19] Jung, Kyomin, Kohli, Pushmeet, and Shah, Devavrat. 2009. Local Rules for Global MAP: When Do They Work ? Pages 871–879 of: *Advances in Neural Information Processing Systems* **22**.

[20] Kohli, P., and Torr, P. H. S. 2005. Efficiently Solving Dynamic Markov Random Fields using Graph Cuts. Pages 922–929 of: *ICCV 2005: Proceedings of the 10th IEEE International Conference on Computer Vision*, Volume 2.

[21] Kohli, P., Kumar, M.P., and Torr, P.H.S. 2007. P^3 and Beyond: Solving Energies with Higher Order Cliques. Pages 1–8 of: *CVPR 2007: Proceedings of the IEEE Conference on Computer Vision and Pattern Recognition*.

[22] Kohli, P., Ladicky, L., and Torr, P.H.S. 2008a. Robust Higher-order Potentials for Enforcing Label Consistency. Pages 1–8 of: *CVPR 2008: Proceedings of the IEEE Conference on Computer Vision and Pattern Recognition*.

[23] Kohli, Pushmeet, Shekhovtsov, Alexander, Rother, Carsten, Kolmogorov, Vladimir, and Torr, Philip H. S. 2008b. On Partial Optimality in Multi-label MRFs. Pages 480-487 of: *ICML '08: Proceedings of the 25th International Conference on Machine Learning*.

[24] Kohli, Pushmeet, Ladicky, Lubor, and Torr, Philip H. S. 2009. Robust Higher Order Potentials for Enforcing Label Consistency. *IJCV*, **82**)(3), 302–324.

[25] Kohli, Pushmeet, and Kumar, M. Pawan. 2010. Energy minimization for linear envelope MRFs. Pages 1863–1870 of: *CVPR 2008: Proceedings of the IEEE Conference on Computer Vision and Pattern Recognition*.

[26] Kolmogorov, V. 2006. Convergent Tree-Reweighted Message Passing for Energy Minimization. *IEEE Trans. Pattern Anal. Mach. Intell.*, **28**(10), 1568–1583.

[27] Kolmogorov, V., and Zabih, R. 2004. What Energy Functions Can Be Minimized via Graph Cuts?. *IEEE Trans. Pattern Anal. Mach. Intell.*, **26**(2), 147–159.

[28] Komodakis, N., and Tziritas, G. 2005. A New Framework for Approximate Labeling via Graph Cuts. Pages 1018–1025 of: *ICCV 2005: Proceedings of the 10th IEEE International Conference on Computer Vision*, Volume 2.

[29] Komodakis, Nikos, and Paragios, Nikos. 2009. Beyond Pairwise Energies: Efficient Optimization for Higher-Order MRFs. Pages 2985–2992 of: *CVPR 2009: Proceedings of the IEEE Conference on Computer Vision and Pattern Recognition*.

[30] Ladicky, Lubor, Russell, Christopher, Kohli, Pushmeet, and Torr, Philip H.S. 2010. Graph Cut Based Inference with Co-occurrence Statistics. Pages 239–253 of: *ECCV 2010: Proceedings of the 11th European Conference on Computer Vision*, LNCS **6315**..

[31] Lafferty, J., McCallum, A., and Pereira, F. 2001. Conditional Random Fields: Probabilistic models for segmenting and labelling sequence data. Pages 282–289 of: *ICML '01: Proceedings of the 18th International Conference on Machine Learning*, Morgan Kauffman.

[32] Lovasz, L. 1983. Submodular Functions and Convexity. Pages 235–257 of: *Mathematical Programming – State of the Art*, Bachem, A., Korte, B, Grötschel, M. (eds). Springer.

[33] Orlin, J.B. 2007. A Faster Strongly Polynomial Time Algorithm for Submodular Function Minimization. *Mathematical Programming*, **118**(2), 237–251.

[34] Ren, X., and Malik, J. 2003. Learning a Classification Model for Segmentation. Pages 10–17 of: *ICCV 2003: Proceedings of the 9th IEEE International Conference on Computer Vision*, Volume 1.

[35] Rother, Carsten, Kohli, Pushmeet, Feng, Wei, and Jia, Jiaya. 2009. Minimizing Sparse Higher Order Energy Functions of Discrete Variables. Pages 1382–1389 of: *CVPR 2009: Proceedings of the IEEE Conference on Computer Vision and Pattern Recognition*.

[36] Schlesinger, D., and Flach, B. 2006 (April). *Transforming an Arbitrary Min-Sum Problem into a Binary One*. Tech. rep. TUD-FI06-01. Dresden University of Technology.

[37] Schrijver, A. 2000. A Combinatorial Algorithm Minimizing Submodular Functions in Strongly Polynomial Time. *J. Comb. Theory, Ser. B*, **80**(2), 346–355.

[38] Shotton, J., Winn, J.M., Rother, C., and Criminisi, A. 2006. *TextonBoost*: Joint Appearance, Shape and Context Modeling for Multi-class Object Recognition and Segmentation. Pages 1–15 of: *ECCV 2006: Proceedings of the 9th European Conference on Computer Vision, Part 1*, LNCS **3951**.

[39] Snow, D., Viola, P., and Zabih, R. 2000. Exact Voxel Occupancy with Graph Cuts. Pages 345–352 of: *CVPR 200: Proceedings of the IEEE Conference on Computer Vision and Pattern Recognition*, Volume 1.

[40] Szeliski, R., Zabih, R., Scharstein, D., Veksler, O., Kolmogorov, V., Agarwala, A., Tappen, M. F., and Rother, C. 2008. A Comparative Study of Energy Minimization Methods for Markov Random Fields. *IEEE Transactions on Pattern Analysis and Machine Intelligence*, **30**(6), 1068–1080.

[41] Veksler, O. 2007. Graph Cut Based Optimization for MRFs with Truncated Convex Priors. Pages 1–8 of: *CVPR 2007: Proceedings of the IEEE Conference on Computer Vision and Pattern Recognition*.

[42] Vogiatzis, G., Torr, P.H.S., and Cipolla, R. 2005. Multi-View Stereo via Volumetric Graph-Cuts. Pages 391–398 of: *CVPR 2005: Proceedings of the IEEE Conference on Computer Vision and Pattern Recognition*, Volume 2.

[43] Wainwright, M.J., Jaakkola, T., and Willsky, A.S. 2005. MAP Estimation via Agreement on Trees: Message-passing and Linear Programming. *IEEE Transactions on Information Theory*, **51**(11), 3697–3717.

[44] Werner, T. 2005. *A Linear Programming Approach to Max-sum Problem: A Review*. Research Rep. CTU–CMP–2005–25. Center for Machine Perception, Czech Technical University.

[45] Werner, T. 2009. High-arity Interactions, Polyhedral Relaxations, and Cutting Plane Algorithm for Soft Constraint Optimisation (MAP-MRF). Pages 1–8

of: *CVPR 2008: Proceedings of the IEEE Conference on Computer Vision and Pattern Recognition.*

[46] Woodford, O.J., Torr, P.H.S., Reid, I.D., and Fitzgibbon, A.W. 2008. Global Stereo Reconstruction under Second Order Smoothness Priors. Pages 1–8 of: *CVPR 2008: Proceedings of the IEEE Conference on Computer Vision and Pattern Recognition.*

[47] Woodford, Oliver, Rother, Carsten, and Kolmogorov, Vladimir. 2009. A Global Perspective on MAP Inference for Low-Level Vision. Pages 2319–2326 of: *ICCV 2008: Proceedings of the 12th International Conference on Computer Vision.*

[48] Zivny, Stanislav, Cohen, David A., and Jeavons, Peter G. 2009. The Expressive Power of Binary Submodular Functions. Pages 744–757 of: *Mathematical Foundations of Computer Science 2009*, LNCS **5734**.

11

Towards Practical Graph-Based, Iteratively Decoded Channel Codes: Insights through Absorbing Sets

Lara Dolecek

This chapter discusses recent advances in modern coding theory, in particular the use of popular graph-based codes and their low complexity decoding algorithms. We describe absorbing sets as the key object for characterizing the performance of iteratively-decoded graph-based codes and we propose several directions for future investigation in this thriving discipline.

Chapter Overview

Every engineered communication system, ranging from satellite communications to hard disk drives to Ethernet must operate under noisy conditions. The key to reliable communication and storage is to add an appropriate amount of redundancy to make the system reliable. The field of channel coding is concerned with constructing channel codes and their decoding algorithms: controlled redundancy is introduced into a message prior to its transmission over a noisy channel (the encoding step), and this redundancy is removed from the received noisy string to unveil the intended message (the decoding step). The encoded message is referred to as the codeword. The collection of all codewords is a channel code. Assuming all the messages have the same length, and all the codewords have the same length, the ratio of message length to codeword length is the code rate. To make coding systems implementable in practice, channel codes must provide the best possible protection to noise while their decoding algorithms must be of acceptable complexity.

There is a clear tension with this dual goal: if a channel code protects a fairly long encoded message with relatively few but carefully derived redundancy bits (necessary for high performance), the optimal, maximum likelihood decoding algorithm has exponential complexity. Such algorithms quickly become intractable for practical purposes. If the channel code adds many redundant bits to a short message, the optimal maximum likelihood decoding can be made practical. However, with too much redundancy, the encoding scheme becomes bandwidth inefficient, and too far from the optimal minimum redundancy.

Conventional coding theory has adopted the latter approach: starting with simple Hamming codes correcting only error, the coding theoretic arsenal has expanded to include ubiquitous BCH and Reed-Solomon codes. These algebraic coding solutions come equipped with reasonably practical encoding and decoding algorithms and the *worst-case performance guarantee*. For the prescribed message length and the prescribed amount of redundancy, the worst-case performance guarantee tells us what is the highest number of errors that can be introduced during noisy transmission such that (with the aid of the decoding algorithm) the original encoded sequence can be unambiguously derived from the noisy string. To make decoding algorithms implementable, conventional algebraic codes feature a lot of structure. However, while the hard constraints on the worst-case performance are met and practical decoding algorithms are possible, code structure also upper bounds the code performance. While conventional algebraic codes notoriously fall short of meeting the optimal minimum redundancy, for decades it was strongly believed that these are the best solutions that the coding theory can offer.

Modern coding theory (see e.g., [28]), primarily focuses on the *average, ensemble-wide code performance* of graph-based channel codes decoded using message passing decoding (iterative decoding) algorithms. The average performance approach (rather than the worst-case performance analysis) is also more in the spirit of Shannon's channel coding theorem [31]. Shannon proved the fundamental limit on the rate of reliable communication using the random coding argument: instead of analyzing one single code instance, he computed the average performance, averaged over all possible codes of prescribed rates, and demonstrated that on average such coding systems are reliable as long as the code rate is below the so-called channel capacity.

Codes defined on sparse bipartite graphs, also known as *low-density parity-check (LDPC) codes*, were invented by Gallager in his ground-breaking thesis in 1963 [11], but were regrettably forgotten until the turn of the century. With their graphical representation, LDPC codes are well-suited for low-complexity iterative decoding algorithms. A central contribution in modern coding theory is on the performance of LDPC codes: via the elegant theory of density evolution, a result in [27] demonstrated that for very long codeword lengths, LDPC codes *on average* have excellent performance, and can achieve that performance with (at least in principle) low-complexity iterative decoding algorithms.

Due to these encouraging asymptotic results, LDPC codes were over the
recent years quickly adopted in many practical applications. While the performance analysis of LDPC codes in the limit of very long codeword lengths
permits one to ignore cycles in the graphical representation of the code, when
the length of the encoded message is finite (as must be the case in practice),
the presence of cycles cannot be neglected. In fact, it is well known that
message passing decoding algorithms on graphs with cycles are suboptimal.
Cycles significantly complicate the analysis and can undermine LDPC code
performance. What is more, in practice one would not implement an entire
collection of codes to evaluate their average performance. Instead, one seeks
a particular code with desired properties.

With no universally applicable analytical tool to capture the performance
of a practical LDPC code, the go-to approach is to run lengthy Monte Carlo
simulations. As the number of possible choices for a channel code rapidly
multiplies even for modest code parameters, pure simulation-based approach
quickly becomes intractable.

At first glance, it appears that for achieving excellent performance of a
practical channel code, we have no choice but to succumb to a computationally intensive (if not impossible) task, either in the code selection or in
the decoder implementation, or even both. As we shall see, with a careful
combinatorial analysis and elimination of certain simple graphical structures
we refer to as absorbing sets, we can successfully exploit low complexity of
message passing decoding algorithms, while reducing the perimeter search
for good graph-based codes. Absorbing sets can be viewed as equivalents of
codewords when an iterative decoder (suboptimal but practical) is used in
place of the maximum likelihood decoder (optimal but impractical).

The LDPC code design problem under message passing decoding is a very
active research area, and the universal analysis tools are still being developed. Nonetheless, the methods outlined in this chapter provide a practical
approach to code design, an approach that to a large extent obviates intractable problems in code design and decoder implementation. In a way,
the discussed framework finds a sweet spot between the worst-case performance guarantee from the conventional coding theory and the graph-based,
iteratively decoded channel codes at the core of the modern coding theory
to offer a range of solutions that meet the reliability demands of emerging
communication and storage systems.

We start off with a quick summary of the necessary background in channel
coding in Section 11.1. In Section 11.2, we then turn our attention to LDPC
codes and the simplest message passing decoder: the majority bit-flipping
decoding. Section 11.3 discusses an illustrative example that captures a rep-

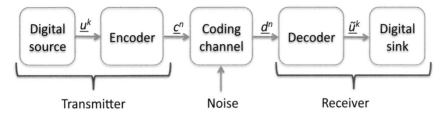

Figure 11.1 A mathematical model of a coding system. A digital message m of length k bits is encoded into a codeword c of length n bits. The received string d of length n bits is decoded to produce the estimate of the original message.

resentative decoding error caused by a small detrimental configuration, a so-called absorbing set. Absorbing sets are defined and further discussed in Section 11.4. The main differences between the maximum likelihood decoding and the message passing decoding are encapsulated in Section 11.5. We then provide several strategies for improved design of practical LDPC coding systems in Section 11.6. Concluding remarks and suggestions for future investigation are provided in Section 11.7.

11.1 Coding-Theoretic Preliminaries

A coding system. All practical communication and storage systems have to operate under noisy conditions. A channel coding system introduces a suitably designed redundancy into the transmitted message to make the transmission reliable. A coded system, as shown in Figure 11.1, can be viewed as consisting of the following sequential blocks: (a) a digital source, (b) an encoder, (c) a noisy coding channel, (d) a decoder, and (e) a digital sink, [19]. In digital communication, the transmission takes place over space between physically separated transmitter and receiver. In data storage, the physical medium is fixed and the transmission takes place over time. Both digital communication systems and storage systems can be conveniently cast in terms of the same mathematical model shown in Figure 11.1.

A *digital source* produces a binary source message $\underline{u}^k$ of length k, taken from the set of all 2^k binary messages of length k bits. The *encoder* adds the redundancy into the source message prior to the transmission over the noisy channel and sends the coded message $\underline{c}^n$ of blocklength n $(n > k)$. The encoding rules are specified by the channel code. The *rate* of encoding is $R = k/n$.

The receiver sees string $\underline{d}^n$, of length n, that is a corrupted version of $\underline{c}^n$. The *decoder* uses the redundancy introduced prior to transmission to overcome the channel noise and to produce the estimate $\tilde{u}^k$ of length k of the original message u^k. The estimate is captured by the *digital sink*.

Let us assume that the channel affects the input sequence bit-wise equi-probably. Two popular channel models embody this behavior: a channel that flips bits with certain probability is called the binary symmetric channel (BSC). A channel that erases bits is called the binary erasure channel (BEC). Of particular interest in our forthcoming discussion is the BSC channel since it serves as a useful proxy for for ubiquitous but more complicated channels with Gaussian noise.

When the estimate $\tilde{u}^k$ provided by the decoder is different than the transmitted message u^k, a decoding error occurs. If there are no decoding errors, the coding system successfully operates, and the transmission is reliable.

Channel capacity. Shannon capacity [31] provides the theoretical limit on the maximum rate of reliable transmission (assuming that the blocklength n tends to infinity and that the decoding error is vanishingly small). In particular, the capacity CAP of a noisy channel with input X and output Y that probabilistically depends on X, is given by

$$CAP = \sup_{p_X} I(X;Y), \tag{11.1}$$

where $I(X;Y)$ denotes the mutual information between X and Y, and p_X ranges over all input distributions of the channel input X.

Shannon's capacity proof, while deeply fundamental, is non-constructive in the sense that it does not provide the actual encoding map nor does it offer practical decoding schemes, but rather it states the limit on the best achievable performance. The proof is about the average performance: if the average of all possible codes has vanishingly small probability of the decoding error, there must exist at least one code that offers reliable transmission. Codes that get close rate-wise to the Shannon capacity limit (11.1) are *capacity-achieving*.

To bring this capacity result into a practical realm, we need to have a principled approach to code design.

A linear binary channel code and the parity check matrix. The most common way to encode a source message is to divide it into blocks of equal size. A *binary channel code C* parameterized by n and k is defined as a mapping of the set of all binary messages of length k into the set of binary codewords of length n, with $n > k$. A *linear* binary channel code of dimension k can be represented by a full-rank $n - k$ by n *parity check* *matrix* H whose row space is the null space of the code C. That is, the rows of the parity check matrix are the parity check equations for the code C. It is sometimes convenient to have redundant parity checks to preserve certain structure; we shall see an example later.

Several interrelated issues must be addressed when one designs a coding system. A code needs to be simple both to encode and to decode while providing the best possible performance. Let's consider the following code construction idea.

The repetition code. The simplest way to add redundancy into the input message is to repeat each bit a certain number of times. Say if we repeat each of the k bits in the input message r times, then the coded message consists of $k \times r$ bits. Such a code is called a *repetition* code. The decoder is easy: it simply looks at the contiguous bits in the r-bit intervals and applies the majority rule to estimate the transmitted bit. However, this approach is very bandwidth inefficient, since the rate of the code is only $1/r$. Clearly, repetition codes are in general not capacity-achieving.

An example of a coding system with $k = 2, n = 6$, and $r = 3$ is shown in (11.2).

$$
\begin{array}{ccccccccc}
\underline{u}^2 & \rightarrow & \underline{c}^6 & \rightarrow & channel & \rightarrow & \underline{d}^6 & \rightarrow & \underline{\tilde{u}}^2 \\
01 & \rightarrow & 000111 & \rightarrow & channel & \rightarrow & 001110 & \rightarrow & 01.
\end{array}
\tag{11.2}
$$

The parity check matrix for this coding system is

$$
H = \begin{bmatrix}
1 & 1 & 0 & 0 & 0 & 0 \\
1 & 0 & 1 & 0 & 0 & 0 \\
0 & 0 & 0 & 1 & 0 & 1 \\
0 & 0 & 0 & 0 & 1 & 1
\end{bmatrix}.
\tag{11.3}
$$

Since we seek to construct useful codes that tolerate maximal noise introduced during transmission, the codewords should be far apart (in a suitable sense) from each other in order to minimize the decoding error, while also achieving the desired rate of transmission. For example, for the repetition code, the separation between codewords is in multiples of r, and the decoding error occurs when in a contiguous r-bit interval associated with the same input bit, more than $r/2$ bits get altered during the transmission.

Maximum likelihood (ML) decoding. The goal of the receiver is to, upon seeing a length-n corrupted sequence, determine the most likely transmitted codeword. This is a classical Maximum a Posteriori (MAP) problem already discussed in previous chapters. Further adopting a common assumption that all codewords are equiprobable, the inference problem amounts to computing the maximum likelihood (ML) codeword. A quick exercise is to show that for the repetition code, majority decoding based on r-bit intervals is ML.

In principle, the decoder needs to compare the received string with each of the possible transmitted codewords and declare as the estimate the one that is (in certain sense) closest to the received string. Unfortunately, even for modest code lengths of n being say around 100 bits, and moderate code rates of say 0.5, the ML decoding quickly becomes prohibitively expensive since there are 2^{50} (this is more than a quadrillion!) possible transmitted codewords. In general, there are $2^k = 2^{nR}$ codewords, so, clearly, for practical applications, such as emerging storage systems, where the code length is in thousands and the code rate is above 0.8, ML decoding is out of question.

Minimum code distance and Hamming weight. Let us suppose for a moment that the ML decoding is doable. How should we then construct a channel code? Recall that we want the codewords to be sufficiently far apart from each other so that the decoding can still be successful even under large transmission noise. Under the ML decoding, the decoding error occurs when a codeword that is not a transmitted codeword is declared as the decoded codeword. This error is called *mis-correction*, and occurs when the noise introduced during transmission pushes the string into the decoding region associated with a non-transmitted codeword.

Minimum code distance represents the minimum pairwise separation between the codewords under the Hamming metric. For linear binary codes, it can be easily verified that the *minimum code distance* is the smallest Hamming weight of a non-zero codeword, where the *Hamming weight* of a binary string is the number of its '1's. Under ML decoding, it is therefore prudent to maximize the minimum code distance so that the probability of mis-correction is minimized. In fact, the minimum code distance is the key performance parameter in the conventional coding theoretic sense.

It is not hard to see that for a linear code, the collection of pairwise distances from a chosen codeword to all other codewords is independent of the chosen codeword. It thus suffices to consider a transmission of the all-zeros codeword when evaluating the code performance.

For a more fine-grained performance evaluation, one is interested in establishing the code *weight enumerator polynomial* that captures the number of codewords of a particular Hamming weight.

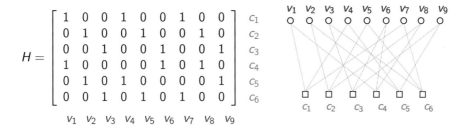

$$H = \begin{bmatrix} 1 & 0 & 0 & 1 & 0 & 0 & 1 & 0 & 0 \\ 0 & 1 & 0 & 0 & 1 & 0 & 0 & 1 & 0 \\ 0 & 0 & 1 & 0 & 0 & 1 & 0 & 0 & 1 \\ 1 & 0 & 0 & 0 & 0 & 1 & 0 & 1 & 0 \\ 0 & 1 & 0 & 1 & 0 & 0 & 0 & 0 & 1 \\ 0 & 0 & 1 & 0 & 1 & 0 & 1 & 0 & 0 \end{bmatrix}$$

Figure 11.2 A parity check matrix and the accompanying bipartite graph.

11.2 LDPC Codes and Bit-Flipping Decoding

With their graphical representation, LDPC codes are well-suited for low-complexity iterative decoding algorithms wherein the messages are being locally exchanged between neighboring check nodes and variable nodes.

The parity check matrix of an LDPC code can be conveniently represented by a *bipartite graph* $G = G(V, F, E)$, where the set V contains n variable nodes, the set F contains m check nodes, and the set E is comprised of the edges connecting variable nodes and check nodes. For LDPC codes, the parity check matrix is sparse, in the sense that a small subset of the variable nodes participates in any given check. See Figure 11.2 for illustration. The left panel shows the parity check matrix H of an LDPC code, and the right panel shows the associated bipartite graph G. The parity check matrix and the bipartite graph offer the equivalent representations of this code; the parity check matrix is simply the adjacency matrix of the graph.

Suppose that in a given LDPC code each of n variable nodes has degree d_v and each of m check nodes has degree d_c. When all check nodes have the same degree and all the variable nodes have the same degree, the LDPC code is said to be *regular*. In Figure 11.2, for example, we have a code consisting of 9 variable nodes each of degree 2 and 6 check nodes each of degree 3. In this example, one of the rows of H is redundant (it is a linear combination of other rows) so the actual rate of this code is $4/9$.

Each parity check c_j, $1 \leq j \leq m$, ensures that $\sum_{i \in \mathcal{N}(c_j)} x_i \equiv 0 \pmod 2$, where $\mathcal{N}(c_j)$ is the set of d_c variable nodes that are the neighbors of c_j, and where x_i is the $0 - 1$ bit value of the variable node v_i, $1 \leq i \leq n$. If this equation holds, the check is *satisfied*. If the equation does not hold, the check is *unsatisfied*. Note that the n-bit sequence is a codeword if and only if all checks are satisfied.

Majority bit flipping. Let us consider a simple *majority bit flipping algorithm* and let us also assume a transmission over a BSC. The following list describes the consecutive steps of a canonical algorithm.

Initialization The variable nodes are initialized by the channel outputs, valued as 0 or 1.

V-to-C messages Each variable node sends its current value (0 or 1) to each neighboring check node. This constitutes the variable-to-check messages.

C updates Upon receiving the incoming v-to-c messages from all of its neighboring variable nodes, each check computes the modulo 2 sum of the incoming messages. If all checks are satisfied, the current values of the variable nodes constitute a codeword. The algorithm can terminate at this point since a codeword is decoded.

C-to-V updates If not all check nodes are satisfied, each check node sends a message to each of its neighboring variable nodes. For a given neighboring variable node v_i, the check c_j (of degree d_c) computes the modulo 2 sum of the other $d_c - 1$ values it received from all of its other neighbors. If the computed value is the same as the v-to-c message v_i has most recently sent to c_j, the node c_j sends the message STAY to v_i. If the computed value is the opposite of the v-to-c message, the node c_j sends the message FLIP to v_i.

V updates Upon receiving the messages from all of its d_v neighboring check nodes, each variable node updates its value: it flips the current value if the majority of the incoming messages are FLIPs, otherwise it maintains its current value. The next iteration starts with the v-to-c messages described above, and the process continues.

It is well-known that message passing algorithms are exact on cycle-free graphs. The bipartite graph of an LDPC code inevitably contains cycles. Since the decoding algorithm is not guaranteed to achieve the all-checks-satisfied state, the maximum number of iterations is typically specified. If the algorithm does not terminate by the time the maximum number of iterations is reached, the algorithm outputs the configuration reached at the end of last iteration.

Note that in the systems where the noise is continuous, such as in popular Additive White Gaussian Noise (AWGN) channels, it is more appropriate to exchange likelihood ratios, instead of single bits. Such iterative decoding algorithms are known under the names that include sum-product, min-sum, normalized min-sum, an so on.

While the majority bit-flipping decoding is fairly elementary, it does serve as a useful proxy for the more sophisticated likelihood-ratio based iterative decoding algorithms. This is particularly true in the high signal-to-noise (SNR) regime where the decoding error needs to be extremely small, as it constitutes the operating region of many emerging communication and storage applications.

Finite-length code performance and the error-floor. Iterative decoding of LDPC codes offers a low-complexity alternative to the ML decoding, and works exceptionally well in the asymptotic setting, when the code length n tends to infinity. In this setting one may assume that a graph neighborhood of a given node is sufficiently cycle-free so that the exchanged messages act independently. Density evolution [27] is a beautiful theory that demonstrates concentration of messages during iterative decoding, and proves that LDPC codes can have capacity-approaching performance.

However, in practical systems, codes must necessarily be of finite length. In this regime, the cycle-free assumption quickly fails. It is well recognized that the mathematical suboptimality of iterative decoders can cause performance degradation in the finite length regime. This degradation is manifested as a so-called *error-floor* [26] wherein the decoder fails to continue to correct transmission errors even as the channel conditions improve. In practical systems, this is a particularly problematic issue since the power margins are very thin. The unforeseen performance degradation can have dire consequences for the manufacturers and vendors. Since a message passing algorithm is suboptimal when many short cycles are present, a popular approach is to eliminate very short cycles to prevent performance degradation [33, 32]. Another popular technique (in part due to the legacy of the conventional coding theory) is to characterize an LDPC code viz. its minimum code distance. As we shall see shortly, an intricate overlap of relatively short cycles can significantly affect the performance of iteratively decoded LDPC codes even when the shortest cycles are designed to be strictly larger than 4. Resulting decoding errors in fact trump the mis-correction errors, deeming the minimum code distance no longer the primary code parameter.

Code performance evaluation via Monte Carlo simulation. While the iterative decoding algorithms empirically perform quite well, the exact analysis becomes fairly difficult even beyond the first iteration [29] since the cycles in the bipartite graph of the code create message dependencies. As a result, the de facto way of evaluating LDPC code performance is the Monte Carlo method. Using Monte Carlo simulations, for the given channel parameter, one generates noise sequences at random and computes the number of times the decoder fails to decode correctly. This fraction then serves as a performance estimate of the code at the prescribed channel quality.

While the Monte Carlo approach is now ubiquitous, it suffers two major problems. First, as the target decoding error decreases, the number of necessary simulation runs grows in proportion. For example, for the target decoding error rate of 10^{-10}, one needs to run at least 10^{12} simulations for statistical significance[1]. On a standard computer, this may take weeks of simulation time. With the on-going push to even higher levels of reliability, the Monte Carlo simulations quickly become futile. Second, Monte Carlo approach, while simple to implement, is notoriously opaque. Since it merely outputs the count of decoding errors, it gives no insight into the causes of the error floor, nor it predicts the onset of this performance degradation. In fact, under Monte Carlo, if only a single code parameter is changed, the simulations must start anew with each code choice, thus further burdening an already costly performance evaluation.

We now take a closer look at the performance of LDPC codes decoded using the bit-flipping decoder, and investigate the reasons behind the troublesome error floor. The developed theory will then be used as the driver for a systematic code design that not only challenges the conventional minimum code distance approach, but also offers substantial computational savings over the Monte Carlo approach.

11.3 Bit Flipping in Practice: a Caveat LDPC Example

Suppose the code described by the bipartite graph shown in Figure 11.3 is used for transmission. This code has 25 variable nodes and 15 check nodes. The minimum code distance is 6.[2]

Let us assume without loss of generality that the all-zero codeword was transmitted. Let us suppose that four bits marked in color are flipped during the transmission.

We now follow the steps of the majority bit-flipping decoder to see how the estimates of the bit values evolve iteration-wise.

Initialization First, the variable nodes are initialized with the 0/1 channel output values, indicated in Figure 11.3.

---

[1] Modern storage technologies demand the target error rate of 10^{-15} and below.

[2] To see this, suppose that variable nodes in positions $5, 6, 7, 11, 15$ and 17 when counted left to right in the figure have value '1' and that all other variable nodes have value '0'. It is not hard to see that the modulo 2 sum is zero at each check node. Therefore, the associated configuration is a codeword of Hamming weight 6. By exhaustive elimination, one can show that a codeword of Hamming weight less than 6 does not exist.

Channel Outputs

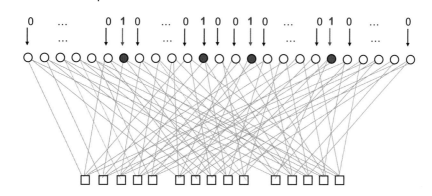

Figure 11.3 A bipartite LDPC graph and a noise realization.

V-to-C messages The variable-to-check messages are sent to all the check nodes indicating the initial values of the variable nodes.

C update Since some of the bit values are incorrect, some of the check nodes are not satisfied. In particular, the two unsatisfied checks are marked in color in Figure 11.4.

C-to-V update Since not all check nodes are satisfied, all check nodes compute the modulo 2 sums for each of the incident variable nodes. The check nodes send their STAY/FLIP signals to the neighboring check nodes, depending on whether this computation and the incident v-to-c message agree or not. A subset of STAY/FLIP messages is shown in Figure 11.5.

V update Now, quite interestingly, none of the bit values changes its value, despite the presence of unsatisfied checks. Four of twenty five variable nodes are highlighted in Figure 11.5: all the majorities are STAYs. It is straightforward to verify that the majorities of the remaining variable nodes are also STAYs.

V-to-C messages and onwards On the next iteration, all the variable nodes again send their original, unaltered values to the neighboring check nodes. In return, the check nodes send the exact same FLIP or STAY messages as in the preceding iteration. It is easy to see that this process repeats verbatim iteration after iteration.

This example illustrates a possibility of having a fixed-point of the bit-flipping decoder that is not a codeword. This string has weight 4, and results in 2 unsatisfied checks. More alarmingly, the weight of this string, 4 in our example, is strictly less than the minimum code distance of 6!

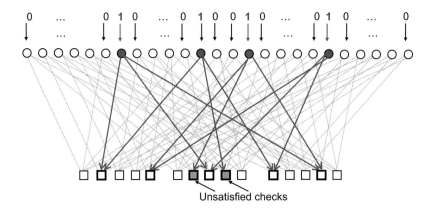

Figure 11.4 An illustration of V-to-C messages and C updates.

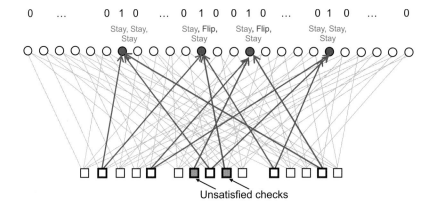

Figure 11.5 An illustration of C-to-V messages.

The example now motivates us to introduce combinatorial definitions that describe decoding errors of the majority bit-flipping decoder.

11.4 Absorbing Sets

For a variable node subset $V_{as} \subset V$, analogous to G, let $G_{as} = (V_{as}, F_{as}, E_{as})$ be the bipartite graph consisting of V_{as}, their neighboring check nodes given by $F_{as} \subset F$, and the edge set E_{as}, $E_{as} \subset E$, connecting nodes in V_{as} and F_{as}.

Let $o(V_{as}) \subset F_{as}$ be the neighbors of V_{as} with odd degree in G_{as} and $e(V_{as}) \subset F_{as}$ be the neighbors of V_{as} with even degree in G_{as}.

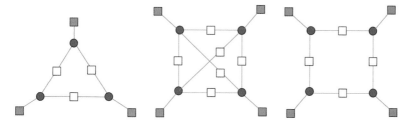

Figure 11.6 Examples of small absorbing sets. Left: $(3,3)$ absorbing set. Center: $(4,4)$ absorbing set. Right: $(4,4)$ absorbing set. Unsatisfied checks are marked in color. Note that each variable node has strictly more satisfied than unsatisfied checks. The leftmost and the rightmost panel correspond to $d_v = 3$, and the middle panel corresponds to $d_v = 4$.

Definition 11.1 ((Fully) Absorbing Set) [8] An (a, b) absorbing set is a set $V_{as} \subset V$ with $|V_{as}| = a$ and $|o(V_{as})| = b$, where each node in V_{as} has strictly fewer neighbors in $o(V_{as})$ than in $e(V_{as})$. Moreover, if each variable node in $V \backslash V_{as}$ has strictly fewer neighbors in $o(V_{as})$ than in $F \backslash o(V_{as})$, an (a, b) absorbing set is called an (a, b) *fully* absorbing set.

An important property of fully absorbing sets is that they are stable under bit-flipping decoding in which the bit values of variable nodes are flipped if a majority of their neighboring check nodes are not satisfied.

Consider the four green colored variable nodes in Figure 11.5 as the set V_1. Then, the graph $G_1 = (V_1, F_1, E_1)$ is the subgraph of G, induced by V_1. The set $o(V_1)$ consists of the two check nodes marked in yellow and the set $e(V_1)$ consists of the five check nodes with highlighted edges: each node in $o(V_1)$ is connected to V_1 once, and each node in $e(V_1)$ is connected to V_1 twice. The edge set E_1 consists of green colored edges. The two outermost variable nodes in V_1 each have all three edges to $e(V_1)$, whereas the two innermost variable nodes in V_1 each have two edges to $e(V_1)$ and one edge to $o(V_1)$. Therefore, all four nodes in V_1 have more edges to $e(V_1)$ than to $o(V_1)$. Since $|o(V_1)| = 2$, the set V_1 is a $(4, 2)$ absorbing set. It is not hard to see that all variable nodes in $V \backslash V_1$ have more edges to $F \backslash o(V_1)$ than to $o(V_1)$. Therefore, this absorbing set is also a fully absorbing set.

Additional examples of small absorbing sets are provided in Figure 11.6.

We now state the main properties of absorbing sets and their relationship with the codewords.

Remark Note that a codeword is always an absorbing set. For a codeword, all checks are satisfied by definition so all the messages sent from check nodes will be STAYs, and as a result no variable node will change its value under the bit flipping decoding in subsequent iterations. As the example above shows, there can exist a fixed point of the algorithm that is not a codeword. Therefore, the collection of absorbing sets subsumes the collection of codewords.

The following observation is analogous to the assumption regarding the transmission of the all-zeros codeword we established earlier for the maximum likelihood decoding.

Remark Consider an LDPC code C of length n bits and let $G = (V, F, E)$ denote the associated bipartite graph. Let V_1, $V_1 \subset V$, describe an (a, b) fully absorbing set. Suppose that the binary string $\mathbf{s}$ of length n has support specified by the variable nodes in an (a, b) fully absorbing set in G. That is, the entries in $\mathbf{s}$ are '1's in the positions that correspond to the a variable nodes of the absorbing set, and all other entries in $\mathbf{s}$ are '0's. Let $\mathbf{c}$ be a codeword in C and let V_2, $V_2 \subset V$, be specified by the non-zero entries in $\mathbf{c}$. By definition, the set $o(V_2)$ is empty.

Construct a string $\mathbf{y}$ such that $\mathbf{y} = \mathbf{c} + \mathbf{s}$ mod 2 and let V_3, $V_3 \subset V$, be specified by the non-zero entries in $\mathbf{y}$. Since $o(V_2)$ is empty, $o(V_3) = o(V_1)$. Therefore, the allocation of satisfied and unsatisfied checks does not change with the addition of a codeword.

Hence, without loss of generality, one may assume that the all-zeros codeword was transmitted and consider absorbing set errors caused by noise introduced during such transmissions.

Related non-codeword structures. It is worth noting that other combinatorial non-codeword objects also play an important role in characterizing relevant non-codewords. A *stopping set* is a subset V_{ss} of V with the property that each check node that is a neighbor of a bit node in V_{ss} is connected at least twice to the set of bit nodes in V_{ss} [6]. Stopping sets are of central importance in the analysis of iterative decoding algorithms over the binary erasure channels (BECs).

Recall that in a BEC transmission, a bit node is either "erased" (wherein the 0/1 bit becomes "e") or is received correctly. Iterative decoding algorithm successively resolves erasures: for a given check node if only one neighboring variable node is "e", the erasure can be uniquely resolved based on the values of other incident variable nodes. The decoding algorithm successfully terminates when all the erasures are resolved. If the erasures induce a stopping set configuration, the neighboring check nodes cannot resolve them since the values of their other incident variable nodes cannot uniquely simultaneously resolve more than one incident erasure. In this case, the algorithm fails.

The behavior of the stopping sets is in general very well understood [24]. Since the nature of transmission error is more intricate to describe under BSC and other similar channels, than under BEC (note that in the latter case it is always known whether the bit is corrupted or not, whereas in the former case this is not known), stopping set analysis cannot be directly applied to the additive noise channels such as BSC, that are of primary significance in practical high-reliability applications. Clearly, since stopping sets and absorbing sets impose different constraints on the subgraph, a stopping set need not be an absorbing set and vice versa.

Two early landmark papers in the modern coding literature already discussed non-codeword decoding errors under additive-noise channels. Consider an LDPC code C defined by the parity check matrix H. *Near-codewords* were introduced in [20] as follows: a near-codeword (a, b) is simply a binary string $\mathbf{y}$ that has Hamming weight a, such that the syndrome $\mathbf{z} = \mathbf{y}H^T$ has Hamming weight b. A binary string that is a codeword of C produces a syndrome of Hamming weight zero. Therefore, near-codewords of interest are binary strings that are "almost like" codewords in the sense that the induced syndrome has Hamming weight "almost" zero.

A *trapping set*, as defined by Richardson in his pivotal work on error floors [26], is a union of all bits not eventually decoded correctly. While this definition is operational, subsequent works have used the same trapping set terminology to denote a subgraph of the variable node set that has Hamming weight a and that has b unsatisfied checks [2]. This popular usage effectively equates the support of a near-codeword to the trapping set.

Absorbing sets can be viewed as special cases of trapping sets that are stable under bit flipping operations. That is, an absorbing set is always the support of near-codeword/trapping set but a near-codeword/trapping set need not produce an absorbing set. Consider the configuration in Figure 11.7. The configuration has $a = 3$ variable nodes and $b = 9$ unsatisfied checks, and is thus a $(3, 9)$ trapping set. However, this configuration is not an absorbing set since each variable node has more unsatisfied than satisfied checks (3 vs. 2). In fact, this configuration is not stable under the bit-flipping algorithm described earlier.

Even though the class of trapping sets is less restrictive than the the class of absorbing sets, and may in fact include unstable points, results on the trapping set spectrum can still provide useful characterization of the average code performance, especially for small node degrees [1, 15].

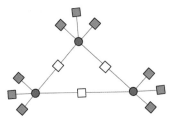

Figure 11.7 A configuration that is a trapping set but not an absorbing set.

A graph-theoretic lower bound. We also recall a result from [7] regarding the smallest absorbing sets. Let g denote the girth of the code, that is, the length of the shortest cycle in the associated bipartite graph.

Theorem 11.2 *For a regular (d_c, d_v) LDPC code with $g \geq 6$, for the smallest (a^*, b^*) absorbing sets, a^* is no less than $1 + \sum_{i=0}^{l} t(t-1)^i$ for $g \equiv 2$ modulo 4, and no less than $1 + \sum_{i=0}^{l-1} t(t-1)^i + (t-1)^l$ for g a multiple of 4, where $t = \lceil \frac{d_v+1}{2} \rceil$ and $l = \lfloor \frac{g}{4} \rfloor - 1$. The quantity b^* is no less than $a^* \cdot \lfloor \frac{d_v-1}{2} \rfloor$.*

Note that for $g = 6$ and $d_v = 3$, the theorem says that the smallest absorbing sets are $(3, 3)$ absorbing sets; for $g = 6$ and $d_v = 4$ the smallest absorbing sets are $(4, 4)$ absorbing sets, and for $g = 8$ and $d_v = 3$ the smallest absorbing sets are $(4, 4)$ absorbing sets. These configurations are precisely as shown in Figure 11.6.

11.5 Rethinking the Minimum Distance

It is particularly problematic when an absorbing set configuration has the weight less than the minimum code distance, since it suggests that the code performance can be affected by low-weight non-codewords. Our earlier example shows exactly that scenario. Therefore, in contrast to conventional coding theory that assumes ML decoding (optimal albeit intractable) and associated minimum distance as the most relevant metric, under iterative decoding (suboptimal but implementable) one must *depart from the conventional approach to code design and investigate relevant non-codeword fixed points.*

The relevant landscapes are illustrated in Figure 11.8. On the left is the partition of the n-dimensional space under the ML decoding into Voronoi regions associated with different codewords. Here the regions have regular geometric shapes. On the right is a sketch of the partition of the n-dimensional

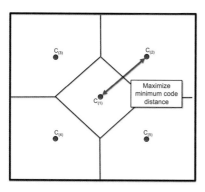 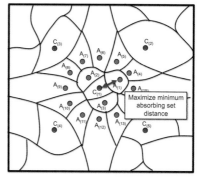

Figure 11.8 An illustration of the relevant sequence landscape under (a) ML decoding (b) message passing decoding. Red circles denote codewords and blue circles denote non-codeword absorbing sets.

space under the iterative decoding. The regions are less regular and, in addition to codewords, a new class of objects acts as attractors for the decoding algorithm. In this case, one ought to focus on the distance to nearest absorbing sets, not nearest codewords.

As a generalization of the weight enumerator polynomial that counts the number of codewords of each possible weight, we let the *absorbing spectrum* denote the number of (a, b) absorbing sets across the range of parameters a and b.

11.6 Design Strategies for Practical LDPC Coding Systems

Now that we have identified the key objects of interest, we present strategies for improved design of practical iteratively-decoded graph-based codes.

These strategies can be divided into two groups: decoder-based approaches and encoder-based approaches. Decoder-based approaches implicitly assume that the code is predetermined and use the knowledge of absorbing set/trapping sets to control the evolution of messages during the iterative decoding. Encoder-based approaches are concerned with code construction that possesses good absorbing set properties.

Alarmingly, an LDPC code (of code length $n = 2048$ and the rate above 0.9) already adopted in the Ethernet standard has a dominant class of absorbing sets: the smallest absorbing sets are $(8, 8)$ [30] whereas empirical results revealed that the minimum code distance is 14. For this code, the $(8, 8)$ absorbing sets are the main culprit of the error floor and the performance degradation in the high-reliability region. In practice, decoder-centric solutions must now be employed to overcome this code weakness [39]. Successful heuristics are based on a careful re-weighting of certain messages to prevent the absorbing set errors [37], backtracking out of an absorbing set to recover from such an error [12], and suitable quantization of messages over iterations based on the knowledge of absorbing/trapping sets [25]. Such practical decoders can recover the error floor performance loss.

The encoder approach, when possible, is arguably more fundamental: once a good code is identified, its practical performance can be seamlessly improved with decoder-based solutions whereas the standalone decoding improvements are always limited by the quality of the code chosen in the first place. However, constructing a good LDPC code that has desirable structure *and* attractive absorbing set properties is far from easy. In fact, an exhaustive enumeration of error prone subgraphs in an arbitrary LDPC code is known to be NP-hard [21].

Recently proposed algorithms use the structure of erroneous configurations to efficiently enumerate small and dominant absorbing sets [16, 13, 40] of a given LDPC code. These algorithms can be particularly useful when a quick characterization of a given code and its fixed parameters is needed.

A good LDPC code can be designed from scratch by ensuring that no small absorbing sets/trapping sets appear, such as in the recent works in [23, 22] for $d_v = 3$ codes. In this greedy approach, parity check constraints are sequentially added to the parity check matrix while ensuring that the current collection of parity constraints does not induce a detrimental configuration in the bipartite graph of the code. Another good way to improve the absorbing/trapping sets of a code is by sufficiently enlarging and then suitably modifying its bipartite graph, as proposed in [17]. Disadvantages of such greedy approaches is that they offer a single-point solution and the resultant code may lack structure needed for compact implementation.

Another approach is to systematically modify an entire LDPC *code family* such that the structure is preserved while provably eliminating dominant absorbing sets. This approach was developed in [34, 35, 36] for a family of circulant-based LDPC codes.

Circulant-based LDPC codes constitute a class of (d_v, d_c) regular LDPC codes with a parity check matrix H built out of a two-dimensional array circulants, as shown in (11.4). Each circulant matrix $M_{i,j}$ is some cyclic shift of the $d_c \times d_c$ identity matrix

$$H = \begin{bmatrix} M_{1,1} & M_{1,2} & \cdots & M_{1,d_c} \\ M_{2,1} & M_{2,2} & \cdots & M_{2,d_c} \\ \cdots & \cdots & \cdots & \cdots \\ M_{d_v,1} & M_{d_v,2} & \cdots & M_{d_v,d_c} \end{bmatrix}. \tag{11.4}$$

Circulant-based LDPC codes are particularly attractive from the practical standpoint since they enable high-throughout hardware implementations of compact designs [38]. Several well-known constructions [9, 32, 10] fall into the class of separable circulant-based LDPC codes.

As first shown in [8] for $d_v \leq 4$ using combinatorial techniques, when $M_{i,j}$ is the ij-th shift of the identity matrix (precisely corresponding to popular, so-called array-based codes, with girth 6, [9]), the smallest absorbing sets are strictly smaller than the minimum code distance. Carefully designed mapping rules $(i,j) \rightarrow M_{i,j}$ pick constituent submatrices such that smallest absorbing sets are provably prevented. Results in [34, 35, 36] demonstrate at least an order of magnitude improvement using such combinatorial manipulations while maintaining code structure, girth and minimum distance.

We note that the presence of detrimental small absorbing sets/trapping sets is far from being specific to circulant constructions. In fact, it was shown in [18] that permutation-based LDPC codes constructed based on Steiner triple systems [3] also have small trapping sets that are smaller than the minimum code distance. It is expected that a combinatorial analysis that ensures no small absorbing sets are present would also offer improved code constructions within this code family. It would be interesting to extend such an approach to a more general code family.

11.7 Concluding Remarks and Future Outlook

The objective of this chapter was to present recent developments in modern coding theory, with an emphasis on practical graph-based LDPC codes and their message passing decoding algorithms. While message passing algorithms are an excellent choice for replacing intractable ML decoding, several issues need to be considered when analyzing and designing coding systems. In particular, we showed that the conventional, ML-based design metric, the minimum code distance, is not sufficient when the codes are decoded using iterative procedures. In fact, not even the standalone girth condition is sufficient. Rather, one ought to consider the presence of detrimental substructures (e.g., absorbing sets and stopping sets) for code evaluation. For a popular code family based on circulant composition on a sparse graph, we showed that a new combinatorial analysis fully characterizes dominant absorbing sets. Moreover, the analysis suggests strategies for a provable improvement of the absorbing spectrum and, in turn, the overall code performance.

Given the timeliness and the importance of a proper channel code design, there are several directions worth pursuing. We thus conclude with a number of interesting questions for future research:

- Density evolution method demonstrated that LDPC codes with irregular degrees offer performance advantage over regular codes in the asymptotic regime [4]. While efficient search algorithms are available for a single code instance, it would be valuable to provide a family-wide characterization of the absorbing spectrum when the family is of a finite length and has mildly irregular degree distribution.
- Our discussion exclusively focused on binary constructions. Empirical evidence suggests that non-binary LDPC codes where code is symbol-based, rather than bit-based, can outperform their non-binary counterparts [5]. Characterizing and analyzing absorbing sets and other important subgraphs can be particularly important in establishing the promise of non-binary LDPC codes.
- A graph cover conveniently captures the fact that under message passing, and also under relaxed linear programming decoding, the code constraints are locally satisfied. Pseudocodewords are objects in the graph cover of the code that compete with the codewords to be decoder's final output [14]. It is interesting to further explore the connections among various graphical objects of interest, as such results can give insights into unified code performance under seemingly different decoding algorithms.
- Our exposition assumed a BSC channel as a representative of channel models that affect the transmitted sequence on a per bit basis. It is also interesting to define and further investigate relevant combinatorial structures when the coding channel has memory.

Acknowledgement The work is supported in part by a grant from UC Discovery–Western Digital, funding support from ASTC consortium and NSF CAREER grant CCF-1150212.

References

[1] Abu-Surra, S., Divsalar, D., and Ryan, W.E. 2011. Enumerators for protograph-based ensembles of LDPC and generalized LDPC codes. *IEEE Trans. on Info. Theory*, **57**(2), 858–886.

[2] Chilappagari, S.K., Sankaranarayanan, S., and Vasic, B. 2006. Error floors of LDPC codes on the binary symmetric channel. Pages 1089–1094 of: *ICC '06: Proceedings of the IEEE International Conference on Communications*, Vol. 3.

[3] Colbourn, C.J. and Rosa, A. 1999. *Triple Systems*. Oxford University Press.

[4] Chung, S.Y., Forney, G.D., Urbanke, R., and Richardson, T.J. 2001. On the design of low-density parity-check codes within 0.0045dB of the Shannon limit. *IEEE Communications Letters*, **5**(2), 58–60.

[5] Davey, M.C. and MacKay, D.J.C. 1998. Low density parity check codes over GF(q). *IEEE Communications Letters*, **2**(6), 165–167.

[6] Di, C., Proietti, D., Telatar, I.E., Richardson, T.J., and Urbanke, R.L. 2002. Finite length analysis of low-density parity-check codes on the binary erasure channel. *IEEE Trans. on Information Theory*, **48**(6), 157–1579.

[7] Dolecek, L. 2010. On absorbing sets of structured sparse graph codes. Pages 1–5 of: *ITA 2010: Proceedings of the Information Theory and Applications Workshop.*

[8] Dolecek, L., Zhang, Z., Wainwright, M.J., Anantharam, V., and Nikolic, B. 2010. Analysis of absorbing sets and fully absorbing sets of array-based LDPC codes. *IEEE Trans. on Information Theory*, **56**(1), 6261–6268.

[9] Fan, J. L. 2000. Array codes as low-density parity-check codes. Pages 195–203 of: *Constrained Coding and Soft Iterative Decoding*, Springer International Series in Engineering and Computer Science, **621**.

[10] Fossorier, M.P.C. 2004. Quasi-cyclic low-density parity-check codes from circulant permutation matrices. *IEEE Trans. on Information Theory*, **58**(8), 1788–1793.

[11] Gallager, R. 1963. *Low-Density Parity-Check Codes*, MIT Press.

[12] Kang, J., Huang, Q., Lin, S., and Abdel-Ghaffar, K. 2011. An iterative decoding algorithm with backtracking to lower the error-floors of LDPC Codes. *IEEE Trans. on Communications*, **59**(1), 64–73.

[13] Karimi, M., and Banihashemi, A.H. 2011. An efficient algorithm for finding dominant trapping sets of irregular LDPC codes. Pages 1091–1095 of: *ISIT 2011: Proceedings of the IEEE International Symposium on Information Theory.*

[14] Koetter, R. and Vontobel, P. 2003. Graph-covers and iterative decoding of finite length codes. Pages 75–81 of: *Proceedings of the 3rd IEEE International Symposium on Turbo Codes and Related Topics.*

[15] Koller, C., Graell i Amat, A., Kliewer, J., and Costello, D.J. 2009. Trapping set enumerators for repeat multiple accumulate code ensembles. Pages 1819–1823 of: *ISIT 2009: Proceedings of the IEEE International Symposium on Information Theory.*

[16] Kyung, G.B., and Wang, C.C. 2010. Exhaustive search for small fully absorbing sets and the corresponding low error-floor decoder. Pages 739–743 of: *ISIT 2010: Proceedings of the IEEE International Symposium on Information Theory.*

[17] Ivkovic, M., Chilappagari, S.K., and Vasic, B. 2008. Eliminating trapping sets in low-density parity-check codes by using Tanner graph covers. *IEEE Trans. on Information Theory*, **54**(8), 3763–3768.

[18] Laender, S., Milenkovic, O., and Huber, J.B. 2010. Characterization of small trapping sets in LDPC codes from Steiner triple systems. Pages 93–97 of: *ISTC 2010: Proceedings of the 6th International Symposium on Turbo Codes and Iterative Information Processing.*

[19] Lin, S., and Costello, D.J. 2004. *Error Control Coding*, 2nd ed., Prentice Hall.

[20] MacKay, D.J.C., and Postol, M. 2003. Weaknesses of Margulis and Ramanujan–Margulis low-density parity-check codes. *Electronic Notes in Theoretical Computer Science,* **74**, 1–8.

[21] McGregor, A., and Milenkovic, O. 2010. On the hardness of approximating stopping and trapping sets. *IEEE Trans. on Information Theory,* **56**(4), 1640–1650.

[22] Nguyen, D.V., Leslie, M., and Vasic, B. 2010. Short column-weight-three LDPC codes without small trapping sets. Pages 172–179 of: *Proceedings of the 48th Annual Allerton Conference on Communication, Computing and Control.*

[23] Nguyen, D. V., Vasic, B., Marcellin, M., and Chilappagari, S.K. 2010. Structured LDPC codes from permutation matrices free of small trapping sets. Pages 1–5 of: *ITW 2010: Proceedings of the IEEE Information Theory Workshop.*

[24] Orlitsky, A., Viswananthan, K., and Zhang, J. 2005. Stopping set distribution of LDPC code ensembles. *IEEE Trans. on Information Theory,* **51**(3), 929–953.

[25] Planjery, S.K., Declercq, D., and Vasic, B. 2010. Multilevel decoders surpassing belief propagation on the binary symmetric channel. Pages 769–773 of: *ISIT 2010: Proceedings of the IEEE International Symposium on Information Theory.*

[26] Richardson, T.J. 2003. Error floors of LDPC codes. Pages 1426–1435 of: *Proceedings of the 41st Annual Allerton Conference on Communication, Computing and Control.*

[27] Richardson, T.J., and Urbanke, R. 2001. The capacity of low-density parity-check codes under message-passing decoding. *IEEE Trans. on Information Theory,* **47**(2), 599–618.

[28] Richardson, T.J., and Urbanke, R. 2008. *Modern Coding Theory.* Cambridge University Press.

[29] Sankaranarayanan, S., Chilappagari, S.K., Radhakrishnan, R., and Vasic, B. 2006. Failures of the Gallager B decoder: Analysis and applications. In: *Proceedings of the Information Theory and its Applications Workshop, UCSD.*

[30] Schlegel, C., and Zhang, S. 2010. On the dynamics of the error floor behavior in (regular) LDPC codes. *IEEE Trans. on Information Theory,* **56**(7), 3248–3264.

[31] Shannon, C.E. 1948. A mathematical theory of communication. *J. of Bell System Tech.,* **27**, 379–423 and 623–656.

[32] Tanner, R.M., Sridhara, D., Sridharan, A., Fuja, T.E., and Costello, D.J. 2004. LDPC block and convolutional codes based on circulant matrices. *IEEE Trans. on Information Theory,* **50**(12), 2966–2984.

[33] Vasic, B. and Milenkovic, O. 2004. Combinatorial constructions of low-density parity-check codes for iterative decoding. *IEEE Trans. on Information Theory,* **50**(6), 1156–1176.

[34] Wang, J., Dolecek, L., and Wesel, R.D. 2011. Controlling LDPC absorbing sets via the null space of the cycle consistency matrix. Pages 1–6 of: *ICC 2011: Proceedings of the IEEE International Conference on Communications.*

[35] Wang, J., Dolecek, L., Zhang, Z., and Wesel, R.D. 2011. Absorbing set spectrum approach for practical code design. Pages 2726–2730 of: *ISIT 2011: Proceedings of the IEEE International Symposium on Information Theory.*

[36] Wang, J., Dolecek, L., and Wesel, R.D. 2013. The cycle consistency matrix approach to absorbing sets in separable circulant-based LDPC codes. *IEEE Transactions on Information Theory*, **59**(4), 2293–2314.

[37] Zhang, Z., Dolecek, L., Nikolic, B., Anantharam, and V., Wainwright, M.J., 2008. Lowering LDPC error floors by postprocessing. Pages 1–6 of: *GLOBE-COM 2008: Proceedings of the IEEE Global Telecommunications Conference.*

[38] Zhang, Z., Dolecek, L., Nikolic, B., Anantharam, V., and Wainwright, M.J. 2009. Design of LDPC decoders for improved low error rate performance: quantization and algorithm choices. *IEEE Trans. on Communications*, **57**(11), 3258–3268.

[39] Zhang, Z., Anantharam, V., Wainwright, M., and Nikolic, B. 2010. An efficient 10GBASE-T Ethernet LDPC decoder design with low error floors. *IEEE Journal of Solid-State Circuits*, **45**(4), 843–855.

[40] Zhang, X., and Siegel, P.H. 2011. Efficient algorithms to find all small error-prone substructures in LDPC codes. Pages 1–6 of: *Proc. IEEE Globecom.*

PART 5

HEURISTICS

12

SAT Solvers

Joao Marques-Silva and Ines Lynce

Boolean Satisfiability (SAT) can be considered a success story of Computer Science. Since the mid-90s, SAT has evolved from a decision problem with theoretical interest, to a problem with key practical benefits, finding a wide range of practical applications. From the early 60s until the mid 90s, existing SAT solvers were able to solve small instances with few tens of variables and hundreds of clauses. In contrast, modern SAT solvers are able to solve practical instances with hundreds of thousands of variables and millions of clauses. This chapter describes the techniques that are implemented in SAT solvers aiming to explain why SAT solvers work (so well) in practice. These techniques range from efficient search techniques to dedicated data structures, among others. Whereas some techniques are commonly implemented in modern SAT solvers, some others are more specific in the sense that only some instances benefit from its implementation. Furthermore, a tentative glimpse of the future is presented.

12.1 Introduction

Boolean Satisfiability (SAT) is an *NP-complete* decision problem [14]. SAT was the first problem to be shown NP-complete. There are *no* known polynomial time algorithms for SAT. Moreover, it is believed that any algorithm that solves SAT is exponential in the number of variables, in the worst-case.

Although SAT is in theory an NP-complete problem, in practice it can be seen as a success story of Computer Science. There have been remarkable improvements since the mid 90s, namely clause learning and unique implication points (UIPs) [43], search restarts [15, 26], lazy data structures [48], adaptive branching heuristics [48], clause minimization [59] and preprocessing [18]. The impact of such improvements is clearly visible in the extensive practical applications: hardware model checking, software model checking, termination analysis of term-rewrite systems, test pattern generation (testing of software and hardware), model finding, symbolic trajectory evaluation, planning, knowledge representation, games (n-queens, sudoku, etc.), haplotype inference, pedigree checking, equivalence checking, delay computation, fault diagnosis, digital filter design, noise analysis, cryptanalysis, inversion attacks on hash functions, graph coloring, traveling salesperson and van der Waerden numbers, just to name a few.

Besides being used in practical applications, SAT solvers are also used as a core engine for other solvers, such as pseudo-Boolean (PB), maximum satisfiability (MaxSAT), quantified Boolean formulas (QBF), counting SAT (#SAT), answer set programming (ASP), satisfiability modulo theories (SMT), multi-valued logics (MVL) and constraint satisfaction problems (CSP). SAT solvers have also been integrated into theorem provers such as HOL and Isabelle.

This chapter provides a brief overview of SAT research, covering the (recent) past, the present and provides (a tentative) glimpse of the (near) future. Our main goal is to provide the reader an overview of the most important features which are implemented in modern SAT solvers. We will restrict our document to SAT solvers which are dedicated to solving practical problems.

The chapter is organised as follows. After introducing preliminaries, section 12.2 describes the most significant contributions to the SAT field in the recent past. The next section covers what can be considered the present of SAT research, and overviews state of the art SAT solvers. Section 12.4 outlines tentative research directions for the near future. Finally, section 12.5 concludes the paper.

12.2 Preliminaries

A Boolean formula φ is defined over a set of n propositional variables $x_1, \ldots, x_n$, using the standard propositional connectives $\neg$, $\wedge$, $\vee$, $\rightarrow$, $\leftrightarrow$, and parenthesis. The domain of propositional variables is $\{0, 1\}$ corresponding to truth values *false* and *true*, respectively. For example, $\varphi = ((\neg x_1 \wedge x_2) \vee x_3) \wedge (\neg x_2 \vee x_3)$ is a Boolean formula.

A Boolean formula φ in conjunctive normal form (CNF) is a conjunction ($\wedge$) of *clauses*, where a clause is a disjunctions ($\vee$) of *literals* and a literal is a variable x or its complement $\neg x$. For example, $\varphi(x_1, x_2, x_3) = (\neg x_1 \vee x_2) \wedge (\neg x_2 \vee x_3)$ is a Boolean formula in CNF. One can encode *any* Boolean formula into CNF [61].

The Boolean satisfiability (SAT) problem is to decide whether there is an assignment to the variables $x_1, \ldots, x_n$ such that $\varphi(x_1, \ldots, x_n) = 1$, or prove that no such assignment exists. In case affirmative the formula is then said to be *satisfiable* (an the assignment is said to be a *solution*); otherwise it is *unsatisfiable*.

Propositional variables can be assigned value 0 or 1. In some contexts variables may be *unassigned*. Given a variable x that is assigned truth value ν, the corresponding positive literal x is assigned value ν and the corresponding negative literal $\neg x$ is assigned value $1 - \nu$. A clause is *satisfied* if at least one of its literals is assigned value 1. A clause is *unsatisfied* if all of its literals are assigned value 0. Unsatisfied clauses originate *conflicts*. A clause is *unit* if it contains one single unassigned literal and all other literals are assigned value 0. A formula is *satisfied* if *all* of its clauses are satisfied. A formula is *unsatisfied* if *at least one* of its clauses is unsatisfied.

A literal is *pure* if it only occurs as a positive literal or as a negative literal in a CNF formula. For example, given the CNF formula $\varphi = (\neg x_1 \lor x_2) \land (x_3 \lor \neg x_2) \land (x_4 \lor \neg x_5) \land (x_5 \lor \neg x_4)$, x_1 and x_3 are pure literals. According to the pure literal rule, clauses containing pure literals can be removed from the formula (i.e. just assign pure literals to the values that satisfy the clauses). For this example, the resulting formula becomes $\varphi = (x_4 \lor \neg x_5) \land (x_5 \lor \neg x_4)$. Although the pure literal rule has been a reference technique until the mid 90s, it is nowadays seldom used.

The unit clause rule [16] states that, given a unit clause, its only unassigned literal *must* be assigned value 1 for the clause to be satisfied. For example, given the assignments $x_1 = 0$ and $x_2 = 1$ and the (unit) clause $(x_1 \lor \neg x_2 \lor \neg x_3)$, x_3 *must* be assigned value 0.

Unit propagation is the name given to the iterated application of the unit clause rule. For example, consider the formula $(x_1 \lor \neg x_2 \lor \neg x_3) \land (\neg x_1 \lor \neg x_3 \lor x_4) \land (\neg x_1 \lor \neg x_2 \lor \neg x_4)$ and the assignments $x_2 = 1$ and $x_3 = 1$. As a result of applying the unit clause rule to the first clause, variable x_1 is assigned value 1. Consequently, the second clause $(\neg x_1 \lor \neg x_3 \lor x_4)$ becomes unit, implying the assignment $x_4 = 1$. Note that unit propagation can *satisfy* clauses but can also *unsatisfy* clauses, thus originating *conflicts*. In the example given above, the last clause $(\neg x_1 \lor \neg x_2 \lor \neg x_4)$ becomes unsatisfied after making all the assignments.

The resolution rule [53] states that if a formula φ contains clauses $(x \lor \alpha)$ and $(\neg x \lor \beta)$, where α and β correspond to a disjunction of literals, then infer resolvent clause $(\alpha \lor \beta)$, i.e. $\text{RES}(x \lor \alpha, \neg x \lor \beta) = (\alpha \lor \beta)$.

Resolution forms the basis of a complete algorithm for SAT [16] which is illustrated in Algorithm 12.1. Unit propagation and the pure literal rules are iteratively applied to formula φ. Applying these simplification techniques may lead to identifying the formula as unsatisfiable (if a conflict is reached during unit propagation) or satisfiable (if all clauses are satisfied). Moreover,

---

Algorithm 12.1 DP resolution-based algorithm

Input : Boolean CNF Formula φ
Output: SATISFIABLE or UNSATISFIABLE
begin
    while *TRUE* **do**
        if *ApplyUnitPropagation*(φ) $==CONFLICT$ **then**
            return UNSATISFIABLE
        ApplyPureLiteralRule(φ)   **if** *AllClausesSatisfied*(φ) **then**
            return SATISFIABLE
        $x =SelectVariable$(φ)   *EliminateVariable*(φ, x)
end

---

in each iteration one variable x is selected and eliminated through resolution. Resolution is applied to all pairs of clauses containing x and $\neg x$. At the end, all clauses containing x and $\neg x$ are removed from φ and the resolvents are added to φ.

In 1960, M. Davis and H. Putnam proposed what was called the Davis-Putnam (DP) algorithm [16], where resolution is used to eliminate one variable at each step and both the pure literal rule and unit propagation are applied.

The original algorithm was inefficient. In 1962, M. Davis, G. Logemann and D. Loveland proposed an alternative algorithm [17], where instead of eliminating variables, the algorithm would split on a given variable at each step. The pure literal rule and unit propagation were also applied. The 1962 algorithm is actually an implementation of backtrack search. Over the years, this algorithm became known as the DPLL (sometimes DLL) algorithm.

The DPLL algorithm is a standard backtrack search algorithm which is illustrated in Algorithm 12.2. At each iteration, the search tree is characterised by a depth level d. In order to better understand how modern SAT solvers are built, each iteration of the algorithm is considered to have three main steps: (1) *Decide*, (2) *Deduce* and (3) *Diagnose*. In the decision step, a (decision) variable is assigned a value. If all variables are assigned, implying that no more decisions can be made, then the formula is satisfiable (and the current set of assignments is a solution). In the deduction step, unit propagation and the pure literal rule are applied. Applying unit propagation may result in reaching a conflict. In this case, the diagnosis step takes place. Diagnosing a conflict results in identifying to which level β the search must backtrack to, i.e. to the most recent level where the value of the decision variable has not yet been toggled. If the search cannot backtrack further, i.e.

Algorithm 12.2 DPLL-based backtrack search algorithm

Input : Boolean CNF Formula φ
Output: SATISFIABLE or UNSATISFIABLE
begin

$\quad d \leftarrow 0$ **while** $Decide(\varphi, d) == DECISION$ **do**

$\qquad$ **if** $Deduce(\varphi, d) == CONFLICT$ **then**

$\qquad\quad \beta = Diagnose(\varphi, d)$ **if** $\beta == -1$ **then**

$\qquad\qquad$ $\lfloor$ **return** UNSATISFIABLE

$\qquad\quad$ **else**

$\qquad\qquad$ $\lfloor$ Backtrack(φ, β) $\quad d = \beta$

$\qquad$ **else**

$\qquad\quad \lfloor d = d + 1$

$\quad \lfloor$ **return** SATISFIABLE

end

$\beta == -1$, which means that all decision variable values have been toggled, then the formula is unsatisfiable.

Consider formula $\varphi = (x_1 \vee \neg x_2 \vee x_4) \wedge (x_1 \vee \neg x_2 \vee x_5) \wedge (\neg x_2 \vee \neg x_4 \vee \neg x_5) \wedge (x_1 \vee x_2 \vee x_3 \vee x_4) \wedge (x_1 \vee x_2 \vee x_3 \vee \neg x_4) \wedge (x_1 \vee x_2 \vee \neg x_3 \vee x_5) \wedge (x_1 \vee x_2 \vee \neg x_3 \vee \neg x_5)$ to which is applied the DPLL algorithm with the sequence of variable assignments x_1, x_2 and x_3. For simplicity, let us assume that the pure literal rule is not applied.

Figure 12.1 illustrates the search tree for this example. Each node represents a decision to assign a variable and each branch a decision to assign a value to that variable. A branch represented by a dashed line corresponds to value 0 and by a solid line corresponds to value 1. The first conflict arises after assigning $x_1 = 0$ and $x_2 = 1$. These assignments imply $x_4 = 1$ and $x_5 = 1$ by applying unit propagation to the first and second clauses, respectively, which make the third clause $(\neg x_2 \vee \neg x_4 \vee \neg x_5)$ unsatisfied. The algorithm proceeds with backtracking and toggling the value of variable x_2 to value 0. None of the clauses in φ becomes unit and therefore unit propagation is not applied. Assigning $x_3 = 0$ implies assigning $x_4 = 0$ as a result of applying unit propagation to the fourth clause $(x_1 \vee x_2 \vee x_3 \vee x_4)$, thus making the fifth clause $(x_1 \vee x_2 \vee x_3 \vee \neg x_4)$ unsatisfied. Backtracking and assigning $x_3 = 1$ implies assigning $x_5 = 1$ through the penultimate clause $(x_1 \vee x_2 \vee \neg x_3 \vee x_5)$ thus unsatisfying the last clause $(x_1 \vee x_2 \vee \neg x_3 \vee \neg x_5)$. Finally, a solution is found with assignments $x_1 = 1$ and $x_2 = 0$. Observe that all clauses either have literal x_1 or $\neg x_2$.

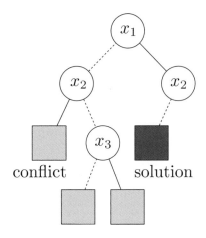

Figure 12.1 Example of DPLL algorithm

12.3 The Present

The last years have seen SAT evolving to become a well established community. The SAT field has now a yearly conference on theory and applications and a biannual competition where solvers are evaluated on solving different problem instances. This leap is in part due to the successful use of SAT on solving practical applications. In a first phase, SAT has replaced the existing technology. Nowadays, SAT is considered as a technology to be worth trying when solving an NP-hard problem.

Modern SAT solvers, most often called Conflict-Driven Clause Learning (CDCL) solvers, are characterized by a few basic techniques which are essential to efficiently solve real world problem instances.

12.3.1 Conflict-Driven Clause Learning (CDCL)

Conflict-Driven Clause Learning (CDCL) SAT solvers are based on the DPLL algorithm [17], and therefore are able to prove both satisfiability and unsatisfiability. Still, the DPLL algorithm *per se* is not competitive enough to justify the wide spread use of SAT.

The first significant shift to be introduced in the DPLL algorithm was the exploitation of conflicts. Clause learning consists in learning a new clause for each conflict occurred during backtrack search to explain and prevent the repetition of the same conflict later in the search [43]. Of course the same set of decisions will not take place again in the future and so the clauses to be learnt result from analysing the structure of the implications which resulted in a conflict. These implications are represented using a direct acyclic graph and the identification of unique implication points (UIPs) is critical to guarantee that the most useful clauses are learnt. UIPs correspond to dominators in the graph, i.e. nodes which belong to any path starting in a given decision variable and ending in a conflict.

Consider formula $\varphi = (x_1 \lor x_2) \land (\neg x_2 \lor x_3 \lor x_4) \land (\neg x_2 \lor x_5) \land (\neg x_4 \lor \neg x_5 \lor x_6) \land \ldots$. Assume that the following decisions have been made: $x_3 = 0$ and $x_6 = 0$. Now assign $x_1 = 0$ and imply assignments $x_2 = x_4 = x_5 = 1$. As a result, a conflict is reached: clause $(\neg x_4 \lor \neg x_5 \lor x_6)$ is unsatisfied. This means that the assignments $x_3 = x_6 = x_1 = 0$ make the formula unsatisfiable. In other words, we must have $x_1 = 1 \lor x_3 = 1 \lor x_6 = 1$ for the formula to be satisfied. This information is represented by a new clause $(x_1 \lor x_3 \lor x_6)$ to be added to the formula.

Observe that learned clauses, as expected, are unsatisfied when they are created. Hence, for the search to proceed, after learning a new clause the search should backtrack to one of the causes of the conflict. In this case, the new clause implies to flip the value of the assignment to variable x_1. In some cases, as will be illustrated next, clause learning further allows to backtrack non-chronologically [43] as opposed to backtracking chronologically to the most recent yet not flipped decision assignment.

Consider formula $\varphi = (x_1 \lor x_2) \land (\neg x_2 \lor x_3 \lor x_4) \land (\neg x_2 \lor x_5) \land (\neg x_4 \lor \neg x_5 \lor x_6) \land (\neg x_1 \lor x_7) \land (\neg x_7 \lor x_2) \land (\neg x_8 \lor x_{10}) \land (\neg x_9 \lor x_{11})$ which extends the previous formula. Assume that the decisions $x_3 = x_6 = x_8 = x_9 = 0$ have been made. A new decision assignment, $x_1 = 0$, causes a conflict which will be avoided in the future by adding clause $(x_1 \lor x_3 \lor x_6)$ to the formula. Assigning $x_1 = 1$ originates a conflict as clause $(\neg x_4 \lor \neg x_5 \lor x_6)$ becomes unsatisfied. Further conflict analysis allows to infer a new shorter clause: $(x_3 \lor x_6)$. This clause requires backtracking non-chronologically to the most recent decision: $x_6 = 0$.

Figure 12.2 illustrates the search tree resulting from learning the two clauses: $(x_1 \lor x_3 \lor x_6)$ and $(x_3 \lor x_6)$. Figure 12.3 illustrates an alternative approach [48] which is more commonly used. After learning clause $(x_1 \lor x_3 \lor x_6)$, instead of flipping the assignment to variable x_1, the search backtracks as much as possible until the learnt clause becomes unit, i.e. to the level where variable x_6 has been assigned. Note that the assignments performed at this level are not undone. However, given that the new clause is unit at this level, unit propagation is applied. After that, the search proceeds as usual.

Another basic technique consists of restarting the search periodically [15, 26]. The search is periodically restarted and randomizing the branching

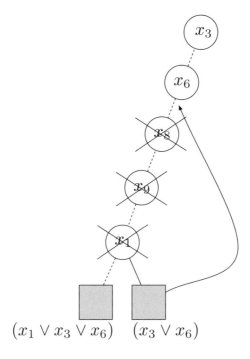

Figure 12.2 Clause learning and non-chronological backtracking

heuristic ensures that a different tree is searched. The motivation for applying this technique comes from the fact that a *bad* decision can have a high impact, specially if such decision is made earlier in the search. It has been shown experimentally that different runs of the same algorithm on the same problem instance can exhibit significant variations if the branching heuristic is randomized.

Data structures are another key issue in modern SAT solvers. Lazy data structures [48] are used for being compact with low maintenance overhead. In each clause only two literals are *watched*. If one of the watched literals is assigned value 0 then another unassigned literal becomes watched instead. This procedure guarantees that unit clauses are identified when there is no literal to replace the watched literal that has just been assigned value 0. As usual, unit propagation is applied to unit clauses. Clearly, conflicting clauses with all literals assigned value 0 are identified as well, and in that case conflict analysis is performed.

Branching heuristics decide, at each level of the search tree, which variable to assign and which value to assign to that variable. Another consequence of learning clauses is to use them in branching heuristics. Actually, modern SAT

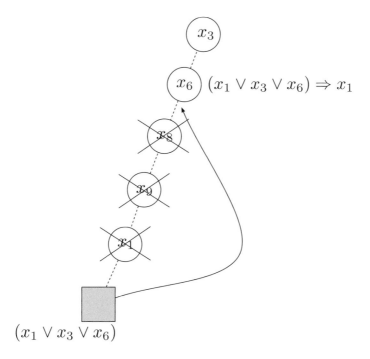

Figure 12.3 Clause learning and non-chronological backtracking: an alternative approach

solvers implement branching guided by conflicts. The first heuristic of this kind was called VSIDS for Variable State Independent Decaying Sum [48]. VSIDS handles one counter for each literal. The literal with the highest score corresponds to the next decision assignment. Whenever a new clause is created, the scores of each literal contained in the clause are incremented. Note, however, that literals scores are only periodically sorted not to affect the solvers performance. Furthermore, all counters are periodically divided by a constant in order to guarantee that literals involved in recent conflicts get higher scores.

Dynamic heuristics such as VSIDS and restarts can be effectively combined as they implement different and complementary strategies [28]. While VSIDS updates the literals scores according to the new clauses being learned, at the time of restarts the VSIDS counters are sorted.

The techniques described above are present in all modern SAT solvers dedicated to solving real world problems. Other additional techniques can also be applied, although with a smaller impact in the performance.

Among the additional techniques, the ones which are considered to be effective will be described as follows. Many of these techniques are related with clause learning, ranging from exploiting extended implication graphs [5] and minimizing learned clauses [59] to discarding learned clauses [25] and identifying *glue* clauses [4]. A more recent approach suggests to *freeze* learned clauses instead of irreversibly deleting them [7]. Other important techniques are formula preprocessing [18], literal progress saving [50] and dynamic restart policies [10].

Other additional techniques are considered not so effective as they are only effective for particular benchmark sets and tend to degrade the performance when applied to other sets of instances. Examples of such techniques are the pure literal rule [16], variable look-ahead [37] and alternative forms of formula preprocessing [13].

12.3.2 Why Does it Work?

The practical success of CDCL SAT solvers has motivated researchers to develop adequate theoretical justifications. These can be organized into proof complexity characterizations and properties of (practical) CNF formulas. These formulas are significantly different from classical random k-CNF formulas in terms of frequency distributions of the variables and the size of the clauses. This explains why these solvers are not effective on solving random formulas.

Proof Complexity Characterizations

A number of researchers have investigated the properties of the CDCL algorithm when formulated as a proof system [9]. The most recent result is that this proof system is as powerful as general resolution [51]. The authors have proved that CDCL SAT solvers, without any extra modifications and given the right heuristics, yield proof systems that p-simulate general resolution, i.e. CDCL SAT solvers generate proofs that are at most polynomially longer than the shortest general resolution proof. Nevertheless, in contrast with the practical effectiveness of the CDCL algorithm, any practical implementation of general resolution is ineffective in practice.

From a more informal perspective, clause learning in CDCL SAT solvers can be explained as a sequence of (trivial) resolution operations [9]. For practical instances of SAT, the clause learning mechanism used by modern SAT solvers [43] identifies the *right* resolution operations to perform, and this is tightly related with the *problem structure* identified by unit propagation.

More recently, researchers have made the key observation that CDCL SAT solvers learn a restricted subset of a formula's implicates [52, 3], which can be exponentially fewer than the set of implicates. For some formulas, the number of these learned implicates can also be exponentially smaller than the set of the formula's prime implicates, provided they are generated in a suitable order [12].

Properties of CNF Formulas

A different approach to justifying the practical effectiveness of SAT solvers consists in characterizing the problem instances for which SAT solvers are effective. Recent work [1] builds on the conjecture that CNF formulas exhibit the properties of scale-free graphs, i.e. graphs for which nodes' arity follows a power law [39]. Preliminary results suggest that although this is true for some classes of instances, it does not hold for some other classes of instances. A more detailed analysis remains an open research topic.

12.4 The (Near) Future

This section provides a tentative glimpse of the future in SAT research, and suggest research directions in SAT and related areas. Several of these research directions are motivated by recent work in areas related with SAT. Concretely, this section outlines a near-term research related with domain extensions, SAT-based problem solving, problem specific solvers, improvements to the core algorithms, and techniques for exploiting tractability.

12.4.1 Domain Extensions

A well-known limitation of SAT is its expressiveness. As a result, there has been extensive research on more expressive problem representations. Recent years have witnessed the development of many new algorithms for different extensions of SAT. Some extensions build on the success of SAT, and include pseudo-Boolean (PB) constraint solving and optimization [55], variants of the Maximum Satisfiability (MaxSAT) problem [38], Quantified Boolean Formulas (QBF) [24], Answer Set Programming (ASP) [23], Satisfiability Modulo Theories (SMT) [8, 56]. Other examples of more expressive formalisms that have built on the success of SAT, thus borrowing some of the techniques used in SAT, include Constraint Programming (CP) [54] and First Order Logic (FOL) [60].

For some extensions of SAT, including PB, MaxSAT, QBF, ASP, and SMT, the most effective algorithms are either build on top of a SAT solver, or implement and extend well-known SAT techniques. Existing solutions for solving and optimizing sets of PB constraints either encode the problem to SAT [20] or extend existing SAT algorithms [41]. Algorithms for

MaxSAT capable of solving large industrial problems consist of iteratively calling a SAT solver [21]. Algorithms for QBF extend the most effective SAT techniques [24], although recent work also proposes iterative calls to a SAT solver, by exploiting the iterative abstracting refinement paradigm. Similarly, recent efficient algorithms for ASP extend the most effective SAT techniques [22]. Finally, the remarkable advances made to SMT solvers build extensively on SAT solver technology. The most often used algorithmic approach for solving SMT is DPLL(T) [49]. This approach enumerates models of the Boolean structure of an SMT formula in a first-order theory T, and incrementally checks the satisfiability of a conjunction of atoms in the background theory T.

In contrast, for other extensions of SAT, including CP and FOL, SAT-based approaches represent a viable alternative, but dedicated solutions are often preferred.

Given the success of SAT technology in supporting the development of algorithms for extensions of SAT, it is expected that this active area of research will continue in the near future. Some recent ideas on how to integrate and exploit SAT technology are highlighted in the next sections.

12.4.2 SAT-Based Problem Solving

The success of SAT is illustrated by the many documented practical applications that either use SAT solvers or solvers for extensions of SAT that build on SAT solvers. Some of these applications were proposed in the recent past, but others have been proposed fairly recently. Hence, one can expect more practical applications of SAT and extensions of SAT to be proposed in the near future. Below we focus on SAT solvers, but the same analysis could be made for solvers for the extensions of SAT indicated earlier.

The general framework for SAT-based problem solving is depicted in Figure 12.4. As described below, this general framework can model a number of existing approaches for problem solving with SAT (or extensions of SAT).

A simple and often used solution is an encoding of a given problem domain to SAT. Concrete examples include test pattern generation, software dependency management [40], haplotype inference and hardware equivalence checking, among many others [44]. Despite the many years of SAT-based problem solving, modeling is often regarded as a less important issue, namely in terms of the CNF encodings used. Indeed, the effectiveness of modern SAT solvers may in part compensate for less adequate modeling solutions. Still, better modeling solutions will certainly help to boost the

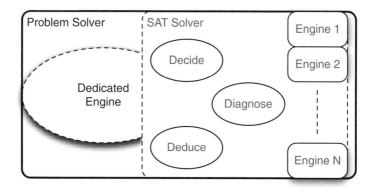

Figure 12.4 SAT-based problem solving

solver's performance [58, 20, 2]. Hence, a common concern in SAT-based problem solving is the choice of suitable modeling solutions.

In addition to SAT-based problem solving of other NP-hard decision problems, recent years have seen more sophisticated uses of SAT technology. Concretely, SAT solvers are often used as NP oracles for solving decision problems in other complexity classes. Well-known examples include artificial intelligence planning [33] and model checking [11]. More recent examples include backbone computation [47], PBO and MaxSAT [42, 29], MUS extraction [45], QBF solving [31], and propositional circumscription [32].

The use of SAT solvers as NP oracles raises a number of practical and algorithmic issues. For example, besides the Yes/No answer of the SAT solver, in most applications one is most often interested in computed models, computed unsatisfiable subformulas, or even generated proof traces and associated resolution proofs. In some settings, it may even be of interest to access the learned clauses, or the final status of the SAT solver's branching heuristic. These requirements motivate considering different ways of integrating SAT solvers in specific problem-solving contexts, that range from pure black box approaches (simply using the Yes/No answer) to white box approaches, where different kinds of information are accessed by the problem solving algorithm. Moreover, in most settings where the SAT solver is iteratively used as an NP-oracle, the preferred integration solution is through incremental SAT. The accepted standard in incremental SAT is through the use of assumption (or indicator) variables that enable activating and deactivating clauses [19]. It should be noted that these same issues are applicable when replacing a SAT solver by a solver to some extension of SAT.

12.4.3 Problem-Specific Solvers

Another promising area of research involves extending SAT solvers with dedicated engines for reasoning about specific sets of constraints, where the number of additional non-clausal constraints is small, and the domains of the variables are Boolean. This work can be related with the DPLL(T) approach used by modern SMT solvers, in that a SAT solver enumerates solutions for the Boolean structure associated with an SMT formula, and the sets of constraints of each theory is handled by a dedicated theory solver. In contrast, problem-specific solvers aim for a tighter integration with the SAT solver. Hence, the SAT solver controls the search process and interacts with the dedicated engines for propagating assignments to the variables and for backtracking purposes. This approach is also depicted in Figure 12.4 by showing the existence of different engines. Examples of algorithms that extend a SAT solver to handle specific kinds of constraints include PBO solvers [41] and, more recently, solvers for handling formulas with parity constraints [35].

12.4.4 Algorithmic Improvements

Analysis of the results from the SAT competitions and associated competitions and evaluations confirm steady improvements in SAT solver technology over the years. Nevertheless, and to the best of our knowledge, CDCL remains the most effective approach for solving SAT in practice. Moreover, the growing number of practical applications and the increasing complexity of practical problem instances motivates considering algorithmic improvements to the basic CDCL algorithm as well as considering new algorithms for SAT.

A number of algorithmic improvements have been considered over the years. Concrete examples include emulating extended resolution [6, 30], as well as different forms of look-ahead reasoning. These include the well-known Dilemma Rule [57], for reasoning about the possible values assigned to each variable, and the recursive learning rule [34, 46], for reasoning about the ways for satisfying clauses. Existing experimental evidence suggests that these techniques are not effective for solving large complex SAT problem instances from practical application domains. However, they remain as promising lines of research for improving the existing CDCL algorithm.

12.4.5 Exploiting Tractability

SAT is well-known for having a number of restrictions that are solvable in polynomial time. These include CNF formulas with 2 literals per clause,

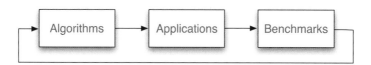

Figure 12.5 SAT development cycle

and CNF formulas with Horn clauses. The same holds true for different extensions of SAT.

One other area of future research is to exploit different forms of tractability in algorithms for SAT and extensions of SAT. One concrete example consists of solving an instance of SAT by enumerating the models of its binary clauses or its Horn clauses (e.g. [36]). Another example, in the area of Boolean-based optimization, consists in solving polynomial sub-problems for computing lower bounds of the complete problem. A related example is to exploit fixed-parameter algorithms [27] for solving sub-problems and computing lower bounds of the complete problem.

12.5 Conclusions

Boolean Satisfiability is a success story in Computer Science. As illustrated by Figure 12.5, SAT research has been able to deliver new and efficient algorithms which have been successfully applied to practical applications thus making available a wide range of benchmarks. Moreover, the development of SAT solvers is benchmark-driven, i.e. new benchmarks are used to evaluate SAT solvers and therefore benchmarks further boost the performance of SAT solvers. The existence of regular competitive events[1] is a significant landmark which has further supported the experimental success of SAT solving.

The SAT field has been the subject of remarkable performance improvements since the mid 90s. Currently, the more competitive solvers implement what can be considered an accepted recipe: clause learning, adaptive branching, lazy data structures and search restarts. Even though, the reasons for performance breakthroughs are still unclear and should be further investigated.

Future research should invest in topics such as extensions of SAT which provide richer modelling languages and allow for optimization, SAT-based problem solving using SAT solvers as NP-oracles, problem-specific solvers

[1] http://www.satcompetition.org

with a tight integration with the SAT solver and new algorithmic techniques to improve the performance of SAT solvers in general.

References

[1] Ansótegui, Carlos, Bonet, Maria Luisa, and Levy, Jordi. 2009. On the Structure of Industrial SAT Instances. Pages 127–141 of: *15th International Conference on Principles and Practice of Constraint Programming*.

[2] Asín, Roberto, Nieuwenhuis, Robert, Oliveras, Albert, and Rodríguez-Carbonell, Enric. 2011. Cardinality Networks: a Theoretical and Empirical Study. *Constraints*, **16**(2), 195–221.

[3] Atserias, Albert, Fichte, Johannes Klaus, and Thurley, Marc. 2011. Clause-Learning Algorithms with Many Restarts and Bounded-Width Resolution. *J. Artif. Intell. Res.*, **40**, 353–373.

[4] Audemard, Gilles, and Simon, Laurent. 2009. Predicting Learnt Clauses Quality in Modern SAT Solvers. Pages 399–404 of: *International Joint Conference on Artificial Intelligence*.

[5] Audemard, Gilles, Bordeaux, Lucas, Hamadi, Youssef, Jabbour, Saïd, and Sais, Lakhdar. 2008. A Generalized Framework for Conflict Analysis. Pages 21–27 of: *International Conference on Theory and Applications of Satisfiability Testing*.

[6] Audemard, Gilles, Katsirelos, George, and Simon, Laurent. 2010. A Restriction of Extended Resolution for Clause Learning SAT Solvers. In: *AAAI Conference on Artificial Intelligence*.

[7] Audemard, Gilles, Lagniez, Jean-Marie, Mazure, Bertrand, and Sais, Lakhdar. 2011. On Freezing and Reactivating Learnt Clauses. Pages 188–200 of: *International Conference on Theory and Applications of Satisfiability Testing*.

[8] Barrett, Clark W., Sebastiani, Roberto, Seshia, Sanjit A., and Tinelli, Cesare. 2009. Satisfiability Modulo Theories. In *Handbook of Satisfiability*. IOS Press.

[9] Beame, Paul, Kautz, Henry A., and Sabharwal, Ashish. 2004. Towards Understanding and Harnessing the Potential of Clause Learning. *J. Artif. Intell. Res.*, **22**, 319–351.

[10] Biere, Armin. 2008. Adaptive Restart Strategies for Conflict Driven SAT Solvers. Pages 28–33 of: *International Conference on Theory and Applications of Satisfiability Testing*.

[11] Biere, Armin, Cimatti, Alessandro, Clarke, Edmund M., and Zhu, Yunshan. 1999. Symbolic Model Checking without BDDs. Pages 193–207 of: *International Conference on Tools and Algorithms for Construction and Analysis of Systems*.

[12] Bordeaux, Lucas, and Marques-Silva, Joao. 2012. Knowledge Compilation with Empowerment. Pages 612–624 of: *Conference on Current Trends in Theory and Practice of Computer Science*.

[13] Brafman, Ronen I. 2004. A Simplifier for Propositional Formulas with Many Binary Clauses. *IEEE Transactions on Systems, Man, and Cybernetics, Part B: Cybernetics*, **24**(1), 52–59.

[14] Cook, S. 1971. The Complexity of Theorem Proving Procedures. Pages 151–158 of: *Proceedings of the Third Annual Symposium on Theory of Computing*.

[15] Crawford, James M., and Baker, Andrew B. 1994. Experimental Results on the Application of Satisfiability Algorithms to Scheduling Problems. Pages 1092–1097 of: *AAAI Conference on Artificial Intelligence*.

[16] Davis, M., and Putnam, H. 1960. A Computing Procedure for Quantification Theory. *J. ACM*, **7** (July), 201–215.

[17] Davis, Martin, Logemann, George, and Loveland, Donald. 1962. A Machine Program for Theorem-Proving. *J. ACM*, **5**(7), 394–397.

[18] Een, Niklas, and Biere, Armin. 2005. Effective Preprocessing in SAT Through Variable and Clause Elimination. Pages 61–75 of: *International Conference on Theory and Applications of Satisfiability Testing*.

[19] Eén, Niklas, and Sörensson, Niklas. 2003. An Extensible SAT-solver. Pages 502–518 of: *International Conference on Theory and Applications of Satisfiability Testing*.

[20] Eén, Niklas, and Sörensson, Niklas. 2006. Translating Pseudo-Boolean Constraints into SAT. *J. SAT*, **2**(1–4), 1–26.

[21] Fu, Zhaohui, and Malik, Sharad. 2006. On Solving the Partial MAX-SAT Problem. Pages 252–265 of: *International Conference on Theory and Applications of Satisfiability Testing*.

[22] Gebser, Martin, Kaufmann, Benjamin, Kaminski, Roland, Ostrowski, Max, Schaub, Torsten, and Schneider, Marius Thomas. 2011. Potassco: The Potsdam Answer Set Solving Collection. *AI Commun.*, **24**(2), 107–124.

[23] Gelfond, Michael. 2007. Answer Sets. In *Handbook of Knowledge Representation*. Elsevier.

[24] Giunchiglia, Enrico, Marin, Paolo, and Narizzano, Massimo. 2009. Reasoning with Quantified Boolean Formulas. In *Handbook of Satisfiability*. IOS Press.

[25] Goldberg, E., and Novikov, Y. 2003. Verification of Proofs of Unsatisfiability for CNF Formulas. Pages 10886–10891 of: *Design and Test in Europe Conference*.

[26] Gomes, C. P., Selman, B., and Kautz, H. 1998. Boosting Combinatorial Search Through Randomization. Pages 431–437 of: *AAAI Conference on Artificial Intelligence*.

[27] Gottlob, Georg, and Szeider, Stefan. 2008. Fixed-Parameter Algorithms For Artificial Intelligence, Constraint Satisfaction and Database Problems. *Comput. J.*, **51**(3), 303–325.

[28] Guo, Long, Hamadi, Youssef, Jabbour, Saïd, and Sais, Lakhdar. 2010. Diversification and Intensification in Parallel SAT Solving. Pages 252–265 of: *CP 2010: Principles and Practice of Constraint Programming*, LNCS **6308**.

[29] Heras, Federico, Morgado, António, and Marques-Silva, Joao. 2011. Core-Guided Binary Search Algorithms for Maximum Satisfiability. Pages 36–42 of: *AAAI Conference on Artificial Intelligence*.

[30] Huang, Jinbo. 2010. Extended clause learning. *Artif. Intell.*, **174**(15), 1277–1284.

[31] Janota, Mikolás, and Marques-Silva, Joao. 2011. Abstraction-Based Algorithm

for 2QBF. Pages 230–244 of: *International Conference on Theory and Applications of Satisfiability Testing*.

[32] Janota, Mikolás, Grigore, Radu, and Marques-Silva, Joao. 2010. Counterexample Guided Abstraction Refinement Algorithm for Propositional Circumscription. Pages 195–207 of: *Logics in Artificial Intelligence*.

[33] Kautz, Henry A., and Selman, Bart. 1992. Planning as Satisfiability. Pages 359–363 of: *European Conference on Artificial Intelligence*.

[34] Kunz, Wolfgang, and Pradhan, Dhiraj K. 1994. Recursive learning: a new implication technique for efficient solutions to CAD problems-test, verification, and optimization. *IEEE Trans. on CAD of Integrated Circuits and Systems*, **13**(9), 1143–1158.

[35] Laitinen, Tero, Junttila, Tommi A., and Niemelä, Ilkka. 2010. Extending Clause Learning DPLL with Parity Reasoning. Pages 21–26 of: *European Conference on Artificial Intelligence*.

[36] Larrabee, Tracy. 1992. Test pattern generation using Boolean satisfiability. *IEEE Trans. on CAD of Integrated Circuits and Systems*, **11**(1), 4–15.

[37] Li, C. M., and Anbulagan. 1997. Look-Ahead Versus Look-Back for Satisfiability Problems. Pages 341–355 of: *International Conference on Principles and Practice of Constraint Programming*.

[38] Li, Chu Min, and Manyá, Felip. 2009. MaxSAT, Hard and Soft Constraints. In *Handbook of Satisfiability*. IOS Press.

[39] Li, Lun, Alderson, David L., Doyle, John, and Willinger, Walter. 2005. Towards a Theory of Scale-Free Graphs: Definition, Properties, and Implications. *Internet Mathematics*, **2**(4).

[40] Mancinelli, Fabio, Boender, Jaap, Cosmo, Roberto Di, Vouillon, Jerome, Durak, Berke, Leroy, Xavier, and Treinen, Ralf. 2006. Managing the Complexity of Large Free and Open Source Package-Based Software Distributions. Pages 199–208 of: *Int. Conf. Automated Software Engineering*.

[41] Manquinho, Vasco M., and Marques-Silva, Joao. 2004. Satisfiability-Based Algorithms for Boolean Optimization. *Ann. Math. Artif. Intell.*, **40**(3–4), 353–372.

[42] Manquinho, Vasco M., Marques-Silva, Joao, and Planes, Jordi. 2009. Algorithms for Weighted Boolean Optimization. Pages 495–508 of: *International Conference on Theory and Applications of Satisfiability Testing*.

[43] Marques-Silva, J., and Sakallah, K. 1999. GRASP: A Search Algorithm for Proposition Satisfiability. *IEEE Transactions on on Computers*, **48(5)**, 506–521.

[44] Marques-Silva, Joao. 2008. Practical Applications of Boolean Satisfiability. Pages 74–78 of: *International Workshop on Discrete Event Systems*.

[45] Marques-Silva, Joao, and Lynce, Inês. 2011. On Improving MUS Extraction Algorithms. Pages 159–173 of: *International Conference on Theory and Applications of Satisfiability Testing*.

[46] Marques-Silva, Joao, and Sakallah, Karem A. 2000. Boolean Satisfiability in Electronic Design Automation. Pages 675–680 of: *Design Automation Conference*.

[47] Marques-Silva, Joao, Janota, Mikolás, and Lynce, Inês. 2010. On Computing Backbones of Propositional Theories. Pages 15–20 of: *European Conference on Artificial Intelligence.*

[48] Moskewicz, M., Madigan, C., Zhao, Y., Zhang, L., and Malik, S. 2001. Engineering an Efficient SAT Solver. Pages 530–535 of: *Design Automation Conference.*

[49] Nieuwenhuis, Robert, Oliveras, Albert, and Tinelli, Cesare. 2006. Solving SAT and SAT Modulo Theories: From an Abstract Davis–Putnam–Logemann–Loveland Procedure to DPLL(T). *J. ACM,* **53**(6), 937–977.

[50] Pipatsrisawat, Knot, and Darwiche, Adnan. 2007. A Lightweight Component Caching Scheme for Satisfiability Solvers. Pages 294–299 of: *International Conference on Theory and Applications of Satisfiability Testing.*

[51] Pipatsrisawat, Knot, and Darwiche, Adnan. 2009. On the Power of Clause-Learning SAT Solvers with Restarts. Pages 654–668 of: *15th International Conference on Principles and Practice of Constraint Programming.*

[52] Pipatsrisawat, Knot, and Darwiche, Adnan. 2011. On the Power of Clause-Learning SAT Solvers as Resolution Engines. *Artif. Intell.,* **175**(2), 512–525.

[53] Robinson, J.A. 1965. A Machine-Oriented Logic Based on the Resolution Principle. *J. ACM,* **12**(1), 23–41.

[54] Rossi, Francesca, van Beek, Peter, and Walsh, Toby (eds). 2006. *Handbook of Constraint Programming.* Elsevier.

[55] Roussel, Olivier, and Manquinho, Vasco M. 2009. Pseudo-Boolean and Cardinality Constraints. In *Handbook of Satisfiability.* IOS Press.

[56] Sebastiani, Roberto. 2007. Lazy Satisability Modulo Theories. *J. SAT,* **3**(3–4), 141–224.

[57] Sheeran, Mary, and Stålmarck, Gunnar. 2000. A Tutorial on Stålmarck's Proof Procedure for Propositional Logic. *Formal Methods in System Design,* **16**(1), 23–58.

[58] Sinz, Carsten. 2005. Towards an Optimal CNF Encoding of Boolean Cardinality Constraints. Pages 827–831 of: *International Conference on Principles and Practice of Constraint Programming.*

[59] Sörensson, Niklas, and Biere, Armin. 2009. Minimizing Learned Clauses. Pages 237–243 of: *International Conference on Theory and Applications of Satisfiability Testing.*

[60] Ternovska, Eugenia, and Mitchell, David G. 2009. Declarative Programming of Search Problems with Built-in Arithmetic. Pages 942–947 of: *International Joint Conference on Artificial Intelligence.*

[61] Tseitin, G.S. 1968. On the Complexity of Derivation in Propositional Calculus. *Studies in Constructive Mathematics and Mathematical Logic,* Part II, 115–125.

13

Tractability and Modern Satisfiability Modulo Theories Solvers

Nikolaj Bjørner and Leonardo de Moura

Satisfiability Modulo Theories (SMT) extends Propositional Satisfiability with logical theories that allow us to express relations over various types of variables, such as arithmetic constraints, or equalities over uninterpreted functions. SMT solvers are widely used in areas such as software verification, where they are able to solve surprisingly efficiently some problems that appear hard, when not undecidable. This chapter presents a general introduction to SMT solving. It then focuses on one important theory, equality, and gives both a detailed understanding of how it is solved, and a theoretical justification of why the procedure is practically effective.

13.1 Introduction

Our starting point is research and experiences in the context of the state-of-the art SMT solver Z3 [13], developed by the authors at Microsoft Research. We first cover a selection of the main challenges and techniques for making SMT solving practical, integrating algorithms for tractable subproblems, and pragmatics and heuristics used in practice. We then take a proof-theoretical perspective on the power and scope of the engines used by SMT solvers. Most modern SMT solvers are built around a tight integration with efficient SAT solving. The framework is commonly referred to as DPLL(T), where T refers to a theory or a combination of theories. The theoretical result we present compares DPLL(T) with unrestricted resolution. A straightforward adaption of DPLL(T) provides a weaker proof system than unrestricted resolution, and we investigate an extension we call *Conflict Directed Theory Resolution* as a candidate method for bridging this gap. Our results apply to the case where T is the theory of equality. Better search methods for other theories and their integration is a very active area of current research.

As a starting point, we will first briefly recall connections between SAT and SMT, connections between the solving methods used for SAT and SMT, and a short survey of some current applications of SMT solvers.

13.1.1 From SAT to SMT

SMT solving extends propositional satisfiability, a.k.a. SAT. The goal of SAT is to decide whether formulas over Boolean variables, formed using logical connectives, are satisfiable by choosing a truth assignment for its variables. SMT solvers allow a much richer vocabulary when creating formulas. Besides Boolean variables, formulas may contain general relations, such as equalities between terms formed from variables, free (un-interpreted) functions, and interpreted functions. The goal of SMT is to decide whether formulas over the richer SMT vocabulary are satisfiable by choosing an interpretation to the free variables and free functions of the formula. The *theories* provide the meaning for the interpreted functions. For example, the theory of arithmetic is commonly used in the context of SMT, and efficient solvers for arithmetic and other theories can be used to solve (arithmetical) constraints.

13.1.2 From DPLL to DPLL(T)

Modern SMT solvers have over the last decade relied on advances in modern SAT solvers. Not only is propositional satisfiability a special case of SMT, but a SAT solver based on the Davis-Putnam-Logeman-Logemann (DPLL) architecture [9] can be extended with theory solvers. Advances in SAT solvers include a better understanding of how to perform case splitting and learning useful lemmas during search using conflict directed clause learning. Section 13.5 recalls the DPLL(T) calculus and contains an abstract account for conflict directed clause learning. As we elaborate on below, one theoretical explanation for the efficiency of DPLL-based SAT solvers with conflict directed clause learning is the fact that it can simulate general resolution using at most a polynomial space overhead. On the other hand, DPLL search is more efficient: unit propagation corresponds to resolution, but unlike resolution, DPLL does not need to construct new clauses during propagation. There is so far no corresponding results in the context of SMT solvers. In fact solvers based on the architecture coined as DPLL(T) are exponentially worse off than resolution, even for the theory T of equality.

The connections between general resolution proofs and modern DPLL solvers have been the subject of several studies. It was shown in [28] that a DPLL calculus could be augmented with lemma learning to polynomially simulate unrestricted resolution [1]. In a quite similar context such clauses have been called *noogood*s in [42]. Modern DPLL-based SAT solvers are based on the conflict learning schemes introduced by the GRASP system [41]. GRASP uses a tight coupling of BCP (Boolean Constraint Propagation) by analyzing an implication graph for generating conflict clauses. The scheme is known as an *asserting clause learning scheme*. More recently it was shown that propositional DPLL with asserting clause learning schemes and restarts p-simulates general resolution proofs [36]. The notion of p-simulation comes from Karp reduction: If a proof in a formal system F_1 can be reduced to a proof in system F_2 using at most a polynomial space increase, then F_2 p-simulates F_1. We write $F_1 \equiv_p F_2$ if F_1 and F_2 can be reduced to each other. Their result strengthens several previous results [2, 7, 24] on connecting modern DPLL search with unrestricted resolution.

The state for SMT solvers is much less advanced. Progress in modern DPLL-based SAT solvers inspired developing efficient and scalable SMT solvers by plugging in theory solvers in a modular way. But it is well known that DPLL(T), and the realization of DPLL(T) in modern SMT solvers can be exponentially worse than general resolution systems, and various ad-hoc solutions, such as extending DPLL(T) [3] and exploring alternatives to DPLL(T) have been examined.

We will later develop an approach that we call *conflict directed theory resolution* to equip DPLL(T) with the ability to compete with general resolution systems. We examine the theory of equality in detail. This theory is fundamental in SMT solvers; formulas from several other theories can be reduced to formulas using only the theory of equality.

13.1.3 Applications

Thanks to technological advances and the ability to directly handle useful theories, SMT solvers are of growing relevance in the context of software and hardware verification, type inference, static program analysis, test-case generation, scheduling, planning and graph problems. Conversely, many features and optimizations in SMT solvers, such as Z3 [13], are based on the needs of applications. We cannot survey all applications here. We refer to [16] for more details. One important use is dynamic symbolic execution tools. They are used for generating inputs to unit tests and they can directly be used to expose bugs in security critical code. There are several tools, including CUTE, Exe/Klee, DART, Pex, SAGE, and Yogi [23]. These tools

---

[1] The terminology *unrestricted* resolution means that there are no ordering requirements or imposed strategies, such as the set of support strategy.

collect explored program paths as formulas and use SMT solvers to identify new test inputs that can steer execution into new branches. SMT solvers are a good fit for symbolic execution because the semantics of most program statements can be easily modeled using theories supported by these solvers. The constraints generated from the tools are mostly conjunctions, but these can in principle still be as intractable as general formulas. Another important area is for static program analysis and verification tools. The ability to handle theories that are used in programming languages is also important here.

13.1.4 Outline

The rest of the chapter is structured into two parts. Sections 13.2-13.4 provide an introduction to tractability and SMT solving. The remainder provides a technical treatment of SMT solving for the theory of equality, which plays a central role in SMT.

Section 13.2 introduces SMT by an example. We then survey theories that are commonly used in SMT solvers in Section 13.3; some theories are tractable for conjunctions of atomic constraints, others are intractable, either NP hard or undecidable. Theoretical limits are not the only factors in SMT solvers. Section 13.4 discusses some practical features in SMT solvers that are useful for dealing with complexity.

Section 13.5 presents the main engine in modern SMT solvers as an abstract transition system. We also present a decision procedure for the theory of equality as an abstract inference system in Section 13.6. Alternatively, one can eliminate the theory of equality entirely as shown in Section 13.7; or adapt a hybrid scheme that applies to equalities under function applications (Section 13.8) and transitivity of equality (Section 13.9). Section 13.10 seeks a theoretical justification for the hybrid scheme: the resulting proof system corresponds closely to a proof system based on unrestricted resolution. We summarize the chapter in the conclusions 13.11.

13.2 SMT – an Appetizer

We will introduce three theories used in SMT solvers using the following example:

$$b + 2 \simeq c \ \wedge \ f(read(write(a, b, 3), c - 2)) \not\simeq f(c - b + 1).$$

The formula uses an un-interpreted function symbol f and the theories of arithmetic and arrays. The theory of arrays was introduced by McCarthy in [31] as part of forming a broader agenda for a calculus of computation. In the theory of arrays, there are two functions *read* and *write*. The term $read(a, i)$ produces the value of array a at index i, while the term $write(a, i, v)$ produces an array, which is equal to a except for possibly index i which maps to v. These properties can be summarized using the axioms:

$$\forall i\, v\, a\, (read(write(a, i, v), i) \simeq v) \tag{13.1}$$

$$\forall i\, j\, v\, a\, (i \not\simeq j \;\rightarrow\; read(write(a, i, v), j) \simeq read(a, j)). \tag{13.2}$$

They state that the result of reading $write(a, i, v)$ at index j is v for $i \simeq j$. Reading the array at any other index produces the same value as $read(a, j)$.

On the other hand, the only thing we know about the un-interpreted function f is that for all t and s, if $t \simeq s$, then $f(t) \simeq f(s)$ (congruence rule). The congruence rule holds for both interpreted and un-interpreted functions and relations. It implies that formulas remain equivalent when replacing equal terms. The example formula is unsatisfiable. That is, there is no assignment to the integers b and c and the array a such that the first equality $b + 2 \simeq c$ holds and at the same time the second disequality also is satisfied. One way of establishing the unsatisfiability is by replacing c by $b + 2$ in the disequality, to obtain the equivalent

$$b + 2 \simeq c \;\wedge\; f(read(write(a, b, 3), b + 2 - 2)) \not\simeq f(b + 2 - b + 1),$$

which after reduction using facts about arithmetic becomes

$$b + 2 \simeq c \;\wedge\; f(read(write(a, b, 3), b)) \not\simeq f(3).$$

The theory of arrays implies that the nested array *read/write* functions reduce to 3 and the formula becomes:

$$b + 2 \simeq c \;\wedge\; f(3) \not\simeq f(3).$$

The congruence property of f entails that the disequality is false. As the example indicates, a main challenge in SMT solvers is to efficiently integrate a collection of theory solvers. The solvers cooperate checking satisfiability of formulas that can mix several theories. Formulas are also in general built from conjunctions, disjunctions, negations and other logical connectives, so the solvers are also required to work efficiently with logical formulas.

Most modern SMT solvers employ theory solvers that work with *conjunctions* of atomic constraints over the theory. So the theory solvers typically do not have to worry about propositional search. The propositional search is taken care of by state-of-the-art methods for propositional satisfiability. Section 13.5 contains a formal presentation of the most widely used integration. Important capabilities of solvers in this context include handling incremental addition and deletion of constraints and to efficiently propagate truth assignments. We here mostly discuss solving quantifier-free formulas, but integrating reasoning for quantified formulas is also of high importance for applications of SMT solvers.

13.3 Tractable and Intractable Theories

As exemplified in the previous section, theories provide the meaning of a collection of functions and relations. Formally, a theory is defined by a *signature* that defines the domains, functions and relations of the theory and a set of interpretations of the relations and functions. We also suggested that theory solvers deal with conjunctions of atomic constraints over the theory. In the following let us examine some common theories and recall the complexity of solving conjunctions of atomic constraints.

13.3.1 Tractable Theories

We first recall the theories of equality and theory of linear real arithmetic that are tractable.

Example 13.1 [*UF* – Equality and Free Functions] *UF* is really best characterized as the *empty* theory. The signature comprises of functions and relations that are un-interpreted. In other words, the functions are not given any interpretation or constrained a priori in any other way. The only properties that hold are that equality $\simeq$ is an equivalence relation and each function f (henceforth for simplicity assumed binary) respects congruences. In other words, if f is applied to equal arguments, then the results are equal. These properties are common to all terms, whether they belong to a proper theory or not. They can be characterized as the set of inference rules:

$$\frac{v \simeq v', u \simeq u'}{f(u,v) \simeq f(u',v')} \qquad \frac{u \simeq v, v \simeq w}{u \simeq w} \qquad \frac{u \simeq v}{v \simeq u} \qquad \overline{v \simeq v} \quad . \quad (13.3)$$

Checking a conjunction of equalities and disequalities for satisfiability is tractable. The Downey-Tarjan-Sethi congruence closure algorithm [18] forms the basis of an $O(n \log n)$ algorithm for checking satisfiability, where n is the number of sub-terms in the conjunction. $\qquad \square$

A theory that is axiomatized using ground *Horn*-clauses is also tractable with respect to satisfiability of conjunctions of equalities and disequalities. An example Horn clause is $f(a,b) \simeq c \wedge f(b,a) \simeq d \rightarrow f(a,a) \simeq f(c,d)$. It has at most one positive equality and other equalities are negated. The polynomial saturation algorithm is obtained by using congruence closure as a sub-routine. Whenever the current set of equalities make all antecedents in a Horn-clause true, then the consequent equality is asserted. Section 13.7 presents an alternative construction, the Ackermann reduction, that shows Horn equalities to be tractable: it reduces Horn clauses with equality to propositional Horn clauses.

The theory of (Horn) equality is also known to be a *convex* theory [34]. Convex theories enjoy the property that if a conjunction of constraints imply a disjunction of equalities, then at least one of the equalities is already implied.

Example 13.2 [LRA – Linear arithmetic over the Reals] The signature of LRA is given by the domain R of reals, relations $\leq, <, \geq, >, \simeq$. The equality relation $\simeq$ is automatically contained in every theory. There is a constant r for every real number R. The operations are addition $+$, subtraction $-$, and multiplication by a constant r.

An example unsatisfiable conjunction of inequality constraints is $x \leq y + 1 \wedge y \leq z + 1 \wedge z < x - \frac{7}{3}$.

Satisfiability of conjunctions of inequalities can be reduced to linear programming feasibility. Thus, convex optimization techniques, such as Simplex and interior point methods, can be used to check for satisfiability of conjunctions of constraints.

Many modern SMT solvers use Dual Simplex [19] with support for efficient backtracking for LRA. A special case is when every constraint is of the form $x - y \leq r$: they contain two variables with unit coefficients 1 and -1. This case, a.k.a. *difference logic*, can be solved using efficient shortest path network algorithms, such as the Floyd-Warshall or the Ford Fulkerson algorithm [38, 39]. □

13.3.2 Intractable Theories

Many useful theories are intractable, even for conjunctions of atomic constraints. These include the theory of arrays, algebraic data-types, arithmetic involving integers and multiplication.

Example 13.3 [A – Arrays] The theory of arrays as formulated with formulas (13.1) and (13.2) is known as the *theory of non-extensional arrays*. Checking conjunctions of equality and inequality constraints for satisfiability in this theory is NP hard. Take for instance a clause C_1: $(a \vee \neg b)$. We will use the array M to encode a propositional model, and for each clause C_i use a corresponding array to encode selecting a literal that evaluates to true in the model. In the context of the single clause, the formula looks as follows:

$$M \simeq write(write(write(write(M', \ell_a, v_a), \ell_b, v_b), \ell_{\bar{a}}, v_{\bar{a}}), \ell_{\bar{b}}, v_{\bar{b}})$$

$$v_a \not\simeq v_{\bar{a}}, \ v_b \not\simeq v_{\bar{b}}, \ \mathtt{distinct}(\ell_a, \ell_b, \ell_{\bar{a}}, \ell_{\bar{b}})$$

$$read(M, sel_1) \simeq 1 \not\simeq read(M', sel_1)$$

$$C_1 \simeq write(write(C_1', \ell_a, v_a), \ell_{\bar{b}}, v_{\bar{b}})$$

$$read(C_1, sel_1) \simeq 1 \not\simeq read(C_1', sel_1) \ .$$

We have used the shorthand $\mathtt{distinct}(t_1, \ldots, t_n)$ for $\bigwedge_{1 \leq i < j \leq n} t_i \neq t_j$. The last line of the encoding ensures that the index sel_1 selects a literal from the clause C_1. Note that the disequality $read(C_1, sel_1) \not\simeq read(C_1', sel_1)$ ensures that sel_1 has to be one of the literals used to update C_1'. The same literal is selected from M, and the value v_ℓ associated with that literal is 1. We can add more clauses to this encoding using a similar style as for C_1. The disequalities on the values v_ℓ associated with literals ensures that clauses are satisfied using the same assignment to the literals.

So what should a solver for the theory of arrays do about this? The approach we take in Z3 is to *reduce* the theory of arrays to the theory UF of uninterpreted functions [14]. The main idea of the reduction is to instantiate the array axioms (13.1) and (13.2) with instances that come from the formula being checked. There is a complete instantiation strategy for the theory of arrays that guarantees that a formula is satisfiable in the theory A of arrays if and only if the instantiation is satisfiable in UF. The size of the instantiated formula grows quadratically with the size of the original formula. Furthermore it introduces disjunctions, so unfortunately the efficient algorithms for checking conjunctions of atoms in UF cannot be applied alone. Heuristics are used to reduce the size of the resulting formula, and reduce the number of instantiations with disjunctions.

The non-extensional theory does not equate arrays that are equal with respect to *read*. The axiom of extensionality can be added and enforces these equalities:

$$\forall a\,b\,((\forall \delta_{ab}\ read(a, \delta_{ab}) \simeq read(b, \delta_{ab})) \rightarrow a \simeq b) \ . \tag{13.4}$$

The practical implications of adding extensionality incur a significant performance penalty in practice: in the limit, a satisfiable model has to determine whether each pair of array terms a, b can be distinguished using some index δ_{ab}. Good heuristics that avoid comparing arrays for equality when it is irrelevant, are therefore critical in this context. $\qquad \square$

The terminology *reduction approach* was used by Kapur and Zarba in [27]. They survey several theories, including some mentioned here, whose decision problems can be reduced to *UF*.

Example 13.4 [CAL] *Combinatory Array Logic* [14] is an extension of the base theory extensional of arrays. Besides *write* and *read*, it admits functions *const* and for every function f there is a function map_f. The term $const(v)$ is an array that evaluates to v on every index, and $map_f(a, b)$ has the same arity as f (in this example f is binary), and maps f on the range of a, b. In other words, we have the axiomatic characterization:

$$\forall i\, v\, (read(const(v), i) \simeq v) \tag{13.5}$$
$$\forall i\, a\, b\, (read(map_f(a, b), i) \simeq f(read(a, i), read(b, i))) . \tag{13.6}$$

CAL is also reducible to *UF* by instantiating the theory axioms. It is tempting to add also an identity array combinator "*id*" with the property $read(id, x) \simeq x$; satisfiability of the resulting decision problem for quantifier free formulas over this theory is highly intractable: it is undecidable. □

Example 13.5 [D – Algebraic Data-types] The quintessential algebraic data-type is the theory of pure LISP S-expressions. There are two constructors cons and nil. Everything that is a pure S-expression is either a cons or the constant nil, but not both. Terms that are cons are uniquely decomposed into a car (head) and a cdr (tail) portion. These are again S-expressions. Inductive data-types furthermore have to be *well-founded*. They correspond to finite trees. The first-order theory of (first-order) algebraic data-types was shown decidable by Malcev [29]. It comes with a non-elementary complexity: the complexity of the decision problem is a tower of exponentials, where the height of the tower is given by the number of alternations of quantifiers. Oppen [35] developed efficient algorithms for ground satisfiability for a theory of S-expressions when it can be assumed that car(nil) = nil = cdr(nil). Without this assumption, the decision complexity of quantifier-free conjunctions of equalities and disequalities of data-type constraints is NP complete. Tractability also gets lost when considering other kinds of data-types than S-expressions.

In Z3, the theory of algebraic data-types is, just like the theory of arrays, also be reduced to *UF* by adding enough instantiations of first-order axioms. To ensure well-foundedness the decision procedure performs unification-style occurs checks and adds axioms whenever the check fails. □

Example 13.6 [LIA – Linear integer arithmetic] Linear arithmetic over the domain of integers is also decidable, but this time satisfiability of conjunctions of inequalities is already well known to be NP complete [22]. □

Example 13.7 [NRA – Non-linear real arithmetic] Non-linear arithmetic over the reals admits multiplication between arbitrary terms, not just multiplication by constants. For example, the formulas $x \cdot x < 0$ is clearly unsatisfiable because every square is non-negative. NRA formulas with quantifiers are decidable using Collin's Cylindric Algebraic Decomposition algorithm [8] or Cohen-Hörmander's sign-based algorithm [25]. The theory is intractable, though still decidable. Designing practically efficient decision procedures, even for quantifier free formulas, is an ongoing challenge. □

Example 13.8 [NIA – Non-linear integer arithmetic] Non-linear arithmetic over the integers is already undecidable for Diophantine equations (Hilbert's tenth problem) [30], and Gödel's celebrated incompleteness result for arithmetic establishes that there is no recursive axiomatization when adding quantifiers. □

There are many other theories of relevance for SMT solvers. These include theories of Boolean algebras (sets), multi-sets, strings and sequences, queues (sequences where you can add and remove elements from both ends), regular languages, bit-vectors and lists and data-structures with reachability predicates. The theoretical complexities for conjunctions range from linear to highly intractable. The theory *UF* of un-interpreted functions is a base theory that many other theories, such as A, CAL and D, can be reduced to.

13.4 Practice and Pragmatics

Theoretical tractability matters, but other factors have an even more significant influence on what makes SMT solving feasible for problems that come from applications. We discuss some here.

13.4.1 Simplification

In many situations, SMT solvers are supplied with formulas that are generated by a tool. The formulas often contain assertions that have nothing to do with the main property. In other cases, assertions are equalities that can be solved, and the solution allows to eliminate variables from the search space. An important component of Z3 therefore comprises of pre-processing simplification routines that reduce the assertions.

13.4.2 Polynomial Factors Matter

Consider the two numbers: 2^{10} and 2^{10^2}. A problem instance of size 10 is solvable even if it is handled by a procedure that takes 2^{10} milliseconds (a second), but it is not solvable for a procedure that takes 2^{10^2} milliseconds (40,196,936,841,331,475,186 years). Of course, even algorithms that are quadratic in time are impractical when applied to inputs of modest size. For example, using insertion sort on an array with 100,000 elements is impractical. When combining two separate theory solvers for disjoint signatures, SMT solvers need to exchange equalities between the two solvers. With potentially one equality for every pair of terms there is a quadratic worst case number of equalities to share. Model-based theory combination [12] uses the fact that most theory solvers build and maintain partial models. Only equalities between terms that are equal in the current partial model are shared. The worst case is still quadratic, but the average case behavior we have observed on applications is far better.

13.4.3 Relevancy Propagation

Z3, similar to the Simplify theorem prover [17] and several other SMT solvers, uses quantifier instantiation to convert formulas with quantifiers into quantifier-free formulas that are handled by ground decision procedures [10]. It uses terms from the quantifier-free assertions to produce new quantifier instances. Each new term may lead to additional instantiations. So terms from sub-formulas that do not contribute to satisfiability can lead to an inhibiting large search space. Relevancy propagation [11] keeps track of which truth assignments are essential for determining satisfiability of a formula. Atoms that are marked as *relevant* have their truth assignment propagated, while atoms that are not marked as relevant do not participate in propagation and do not contribute to quantifier instantiation. We found relevancy filtering useful for quantified formulas, but there is a trade-off: for quantifier-free formulas, it hides potentially useful lemmas.

13.4.4 Reducing Proof and Model Search

Quantified formulas often bind more than one variable. Even if we restrict the set of possible instantiations per quantified variable to a smaller finite set, the number of possible instantiations of a quantifier grows exponentially in the number of different quantified variables. The main method used in SMT solvers for throttling quantifier instantiations is by using *patterns* that control which instantiations are used. The patterns can be used to enforce dependencies between instantiated variables.

A different mechanism with a related aim is to restrict the space of interpretations of relations by using *templates* [15]. The idea is to replace uninterpreted functions and relations by specializations that constrains the set of possible interpretations. For example, we can replace the relation $R(x, y, z)$ by the relation $(R_1(x, y) \wedge y \simeq z) \vee (R_2(x, z) \wedge x \simeq y)$. The resulting formula could become unsatisfiable, but a search for satisfiable instances is on the other hand simpler.

13.5 DPLL(T) – a Framework for Efficient SMT Solvers

As preparation for the theoretical treatment we will now describe the algorithmic underpinnings of modern SMT solvers. Most modern SMT solvers are built around the DPLL(T) architecture that provides a tight integration with efficient SAT solving. Figure 13.1 shows an abstract reconstruction of DPLL(T).

It follows [21], with one difference: we include explicit transitions for conflict resolution. The DPLL(T) procedure is modeled as an abstract transition system. There are two kinds of states. The *search* states are of the form $M \parallel F$, where M is a partial assignment given as a stack of literals, and F is a set of set of clauses. A clause is often referred to as C. It is a disjunction of literals that we refer to as ℓ (which is either an atom p or a negation of an atom $\neg p$). The set $\overline{C}$ is obtained from a clause C by negating all the literals in C. The *conflict resolution* states are of the form $M \parallel F \parallel C$, where C is a conflict clause. We will later make use of these two kinds of states when formulating new rules.

Search starts with the Initialize rule that creates a state $\parallel F$. Search proceeds by a sequence of decision and propagation steps until either reaching a conflict or a satisfiable assignment. Conflicts trigger the conflict resolution rules to be applied. We use two kinds of annotations for the literals in M. Literals annotated as ℓ^d are *decision literals*. They are assigned by the Decide rule. Literals can also be annotated with a clause, so they are of the form $\ell^{(C \vee \ell)}$. The literal ℓ occurs positively in the clause. These literals are added to M as a result of Propagate (or T-Propagate). The clause is later used for conflict resolution. There are two rules that distinguish DPLL(T) from modern DPLL. These are the T-Propagate and T-Conflict rules. The rules describe the main ways for theories to integrate with DPLL. The T-Propagate rule lets theories participate in unit propagation and T-Conflict lets theories determine when a clause is conflicting under the partial assignment M and

Initialize $\implies \parallel F$ F is a set of clauses

Decide $M \parallel F \implies M\ell^d \parallel F$ **if** $\begin{cases} \ell \text{ or } \neg\ell \text{ occurs in } F \\ \ell \text{ unassigned in } M \end{cases}$

Propagate $M \parallel F, C \vee \ell \implies M\ell^{C \vee \ell} \parallel F, C \vee \ell$ **if** $\begin{cases} \ell \text{ unassigned in } M \\ \overline{C} \subseteq M \end{cases}$

Conflict $M \parallel F, C \implies M \parallel F, C \parallel C$ **if** C is false under M

Resolve $M \parallel F \parallel C' \vee \neg\ell \implies M \parallel F \parallel C \vee C'$ **if** $\ell^{C \vee \ell} \in M$

Backjump $M\ell_0^d M' \parallel F \parallel C \vee \ell \implies M\ell^{C \vee \ell} \parallel F, C \vee \ell$ **if** $\overline{C} \subseteq M, \neg\ell \subseteq \ell_0^d M'$

Restart $M \parallel F \implies \parallel F$

Unsat $M \parallel F \parallel \emptyset \implies$ unsat

Sat $M \parallel F \implies M$ **if** $\begin{cases} M \text{ is } T \text{ consistent} \\ \text{and is a model for } F. \end{cases}$

T-Propagate $M \parallel F \implies M\ell^{C \vee \ell} \parallel F$ **if** $\begin{cases} \ell \text{ unassigned in } M \\ \ell \text{ or } \neg\ell \text{ occurs in } F \\ T \vdash C \vee \ell \\ \overline{C} \subseteq M \end{cases}$

T-Conflict $M \parallel F \implies M \parallel F \parallel C$ **if** $\overline{C} \subseteq M, T \models C.$

Figure 13.1 Abstract DPLL(T) Procedure

the theory T. Note that the rules maintain the set of literals from the input F. It is therefore easy to establish that DPLL(T) is terminating (assuming Restart is applied using a back-off).

The condition on Backjump is crucial. It captures how modern DPLL solvers filter which clauses to learn, it is called an *asserting scheme*, and at the same time provides a scheme for backtracking. It states that there is precisely one literal ℓ in the clause $C \vee \ell$, forced false by the last decision literal ℓ_0^d. Some variations of these rules are possible. For example, one can decouple clause learning from back-jumping, and admit garbage collection of learned clauses.

Example 13.9 (A Derivation) To give a feel for DPLL(T), let us prove the following theorem:

$$\underbrace{f^2a \simeq a \wedge f^3b \simeq b \wedge a \not\simeq f(a)}_{M_0} \wedge \underbrace{(a \simeq b \ \vee \ a \simeq c) \wedge (a \not\simeq c \ \vee \ f^4a \simeq b)}_{F}$$

where we used the abbreviation f^2a for $f(f(a))$. We have indicated a state $M_0 \parallel F$ that is obtained by including the unit-literals in the partial model M_0. We continue a derivation by

$M_0 \parallel F$

$\Longrightarrow$ {Decide on $a \simeq b$}

$\quad M_0(a \simeq b)^d \parallel F$

$\Longrightarrow$ {T-Conflict}

$\quad M_0(a \simeq b)^d \parallel F \parallel \underbrace{f^2a \simeq a \wedge f^3b \simeq b \wedge a \simeq b \to a \simeq f(a)}_{C_1}$

$\Longrightarrow$ {Backjump}

$\quad M_0(a \not\simeq b)^{C_1} \parallel F, C_1$

$\Longrightarrow$ {Propagate}

$\quad M_0, (a \not\simeq b)^{C_1}, (a \simeq c)^{(a\simeq b \vee a \simeq c)} \parallel F, C_1$

$\Longrightarrow$ {Propagate}

$\quad \underbrace{M, (a \not\simeq b)^{C_1}, (a \simeq c)^{(a\simeq b \vee a \simeq c)}, (f^4a \simeq b)^{(a\not\simeq c \vee f^4a \simeq b)}}_{M_1} \parallel F, C_1$

$\Longrightarrow$ {T-Conflict}

$\quad M_1 \parallel F, C_1 \parallel f^2a \simeq a \wedge f^3b \simeq b \wedge f^4a \simeq a \to a \simeq f(a)$

$\Longrightarrow$ {Resolve with $(f^4a \simeq b)^{(a\not\simeq c \vee f^4a \simeq b)}$}

$\quad M_1 \parallel F, C_1 \parallel f^2a \simeq a \wedge f^3b \simeq b \wedge a \simeq c \to a \simeq f(a)$

$\Longrightarrow$ {Resolve with $(a \simeq c)^{(a\simeq b \vee a \simeq c)}$}

$\quad M_1 \parallel F, C_1 \parallel f^2a \simeq a \wedge f^3b \simeq b \to a \simeq b \vee a \simeq f(a)$

$\Longrightarrow$ {Resolve with $(a \not\simeq b)^{C_1}$}

$\quad M_1 \parallel F, C_1 \parallel f^2a \simeq a \wedge f^3b \simeq b \to a \simeq f(a)$

$\Longrightarrow$ {Resolve with M_0}

$\quad M_1 \parallel F, C_1 \parallel \emptyset$

$\Longrightarrow$ Unsat

$\square$

$$\text{Assert } \frac{r \equiv (u \simeq v); \quad r}{u \sim v} \qquad \text{Cong } \frac{\begin{array}{c} w \equiv f(u, v), \ w' \equiv f(u', v'); \\ v \sim v', u \sim u' \end{array}}{w \sim w'}$$

$$\text{Trans } \frac{u \sim v, \ v \sim w}{u \sim w} \qquad \text{Sym } \frac{u \sim v}{v \sim u}$$

Figure 13.2 Abstract Congruence Closure

13.6 Abstract Congruence Closure

We introduced the theory *UF* of equality in Example 13.1. Let us here present an abstract decision procedure for it.

Efficient congruence closure algorithms [18, 17, 33] compute the set of all implied equalities from a basis of asserted equalities by maintaining the coarsest equivalence relation $\sim$ that is closed under asserted equalities and the congruence rule. The rule Assert in Figure 13.2 encodes an asserted equality as a state that contains a node definition $r \equiv (u \simeq v)$ and asserted literal r. The congruence rule Cong is triggered whenever there are two nodes labeled by the same function f or relation and whose children are equivalent. Only parents of nodes whose equivalence class are updated need to be processed. Therefore, efficient implementations of this rule index each node by the sets of *parent* nodes where they occur. The other rules Trans and Sym are triggered implicitly by maintaining $\sim$ in a union-find data-structure.

To simplify notation we used a binary function f to represent arbitrary n-ary functions. It is of course possible to literally replace n-ary functions by $n - 1$ binary functions and work entirely with binary functions, but our results do not use any special assumptions about binary functions.

13.7 The Ackermann Reduction

The Ackermann reduction lets us reduce the theory of equality to the theory of purely propositional logic. We describe a basic Ackermann reduction scheme here. The Ackermann reduction can also be seen as a basis of the optimizations we pursue in later sections.

For a fixed set of terms and their sub-terms, $u_1, u_2, \ldots, u_N$ there is a finite number of ways one can apply the congruence closure rules to derived implied equalities. It is therefore straightforward to compile the congruence closure rules into a set of clauses using $\mathcal{O}(N^2)$ auxiliary equality predicates. The procedure ackermannize eliminates the function symbol f from a set of formulas F:

ackermannize(f, F) :
    foreach $f(u, v) \in F$ **where** u, v do not contain f
        create a fresh constant $a_{f(u,v)}$
        replace $f(u, v)$ by $a_{f(u,v)}$ in F
    foreach $a_{f(u,v)}, a_{f(u',v')}$
        add the clause $u \simeq u' \wedge v \simeq v' \;\to\; a_{f(u,v)} \simeq a_{f(u',v')}$ to F

Compilation allows reducing the theory UF for quantifier-free formulas to the theory of pure equalities or all the way to propositional SAT. Many optimizations to the basic Ackermann reduction have been proposed and used over the years, including, [5, 6, 32, 37, 4].

Let us simply note a trivial optimization here: we can avoid the symmetry rule by normalizing all equalities to the form $u_i \simeq u_j$ where $1 \leq i < j \leq N$. The clauses added by the Ackermann reduction are then of the form:

$$u \simeq u' \;\wedge\; v \simeq v' \;\to\; a_{f(u,v)} \simeq a_{f(u',v')} \;\; \mathsf{Cong} \tag{13.7}$$

$$u \simeq v \;\wedge\; v \simeq w \;\to\; u \simeq w \;\; \mathsf{Trans} \,. \tag{13.8}$$

Ackermannization has the disadvantage as the number of additional literals is in the worst case quadratic in the size of the input. It is furthermore a problem to eliminate function symbols using Ackermannization when the same function symbols could be re-introduced to the search space when quantifiers are instantiated incrementally during search.

13.8 Dynamic Ackermann Reduction

Section 13.6 presented an abstract account of a congruence closure based decision procedure for equality. It can be plugged into the DPLL(T) framework as a theory solver. Section 13.7 took a different perspective on the theory of equality; it presented a reduction to pure equalities (without function symbols) or propositional SAT.

Nevertheless, Ackermann reduction has the advantage of admitting exponentially shorter refutations than a DPLL(T) integration of congruence closure. The following formula has a short DPLL refutation after an Ackermann reduction, but does not have a short proof in DPLL(T).

$$\bigwedge_{i=1}^{N} (p_i \vee x_i \simeq v_0) \;\wedge\; (\neg p_i \vee x_i \simeq v_1) \;\wedge\; (p_i \vee y_i \simeq v_0) \;\wedge\; (\neg p_i \vee y_i \simeq v_1)$$
$$\wedge \; f(x_N, \ldots, f(x_2, x_1) \ldots) \not\simeq f(y_N, \ldots, f(y_2, y_1) \ldots) \,. \tag{13.9}$$

In [20], an approach, called *Dynamic Ackermannization*, is proposed to cope with this problem. There, clauses corresponding to Ackermann's reduction are added when a congruence rule participates in a conflict. We can formulate the Dynamic Ackermann reduction as an inference rule that gets applied during conflict resolution.

Dyn. Cong $M \parallel F \parallel C \Longrightarrow$
$$M \parallel F, (u \simeq u' \ \wedge \ v \simeq v' \ \rightarrow \ f(u,v) \simeq f(u',v')) \parallel C$$

subject to a suitable filter that throttles its use.

> (*) **if** the congruence rule is applied – repeatedly – to the premises $u \simeq u' \ \wedge \ v \simeq v'$ and conclusion $f(u,v) \simeq f(u',v')$, such that $f(u,v), f(u',v')$ occur in C.

This filter ensures that no new terms are introduced, but it may still introduce new equalities for either $u \simeq u'$, $v \simeq v'$ or $f(u,v) \simeq f(u',v')$. We will in the following use a stronger filter and call the rule associated with the stronger filter Dyn. Cong$^\sharp$. The stronger filter requires:

Dyn. Cong$^\sharp$ $M \parallel F \parallel C \Longrightarrow$
$$M \parallel F, (u \simeq u' \ \wedge \ v \simeq v' \ \rightarrow \ f(u,v) \simeq f(u',v')) \parallel C$$
$$\textbf{if } (*) \text{ and } \ f(u,v) \simeq f(u',v') \in C \ .$$

Dynamic Ackermannization allows DPLL(T) solvers to find short proofs for formulas, such as (13.9), but are not sufficient for DPLL(T) to find short proofs in cases where full Ackermann reduction applies. In the following, we describe a formula that remains hard, even in the context Dynamic Ackermann reduction.

13.9 The Price of Equality

Dynamic Ackermann reduction has advantages when used on formulas such as (13.9), but there are formulas with equality where DPLL(UF) still suffers from being incapable of generating short proofs. Consider the unsatisfiable formula (13.10) (and illustrated in Figure 13.3) also used in [37].

$$a_1 \not\simeq a_{50} \ \wedge \ \bigwedge_{i=1}^{49} [(a_i \simeq b_i \wedge b_i \simeq a_{i+1}) \ \vee \ (a_i \simeq c_i \wedge c_i \simeq a_{i+1})] \ . \quad (13.10)$$

The formula is unsatisfiable because in every diamond, it is the case that $a_i \simeq a_{i+1}$ because either $a_i \simeq b_i \wedge b_i \simeq a_{i+1}$ or $a_i \simeq c_i \wedge c_i \simeq a_{i+1}$. Therefore, by repeating this argument for every i, we end up with the implied equality $a_1 \simeq a_{50}$. This contradicts the disequality $a_1 \not\simeq a_{50}$. A proof search method directly based on DPLL(UF) is not able to produce a succinct proof like the informal justification just given. Each of the equalities $a_i \simeq b_i$, $b_i \simeq a_{i+1}$,

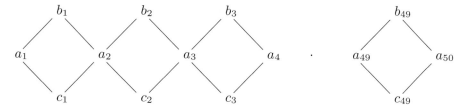

Figure 13.3 Diamond equalities

$a_i \simeq c_i$, $c_i \simeq a_{i+1}$ and $a_1 \simeq a_{50}$ is *treated as an atom*. The atoms $a_i \simeq a_{i+1}$ are not present and DPLL assigns truth values only to the existing atoms. So a decision procedure for equalities detects a contradiction only when for every $i = 1, \ldots, 49$ $a_i \simeq a_{i+1}$ follows from either $a_i \simeq b_i \wedge b_i \simeq a_{i+1}$ or $a_i \simeq c_i \wedge c_i \simeq a_{i+1}$. There are 2^{49} different such equality conflicts, none of which subsumes the other. There is no short unsatisfiability proof that uses only the atoms in the original formula.

Yices and Z3 [3] include a method that uses the Join rule to propagate equalities.

$$\frac{Mp^d \parallel F \Longrightarrow M_1 \parallel F \qquad M\neg p^d \parallel F \Longrightarrow M_2 \parallel F \qquad p \text{ is the only decision variable in } M_1, M_2}{M \parallel F \Longrightarrow M_1 \sqcup M_2 \parallel F} \ \text{Join} \ .$$

The rule Join allows for splitting on a single atom p. The implied consequences of the different cases for p are then combined. We say that this approach uses *one look-ahead*. It bears similarities to the dilemma rule [40] known from SAT. One look-ahead is not always sufficient for learning the right implied facts. The join rule is also applied at the *base level*, that is, when M does not contain any decision variables. The new atoms are then not used in case splits. Consider a simple extension of the diamond problem given in equation (13.11), and illustrated in Figure 13.4.

$$a_1 \not\simeq a_{50} \wedge \bigwedge_{i=1}^{49} \left[\begin{array}{l} (a_i \simeq b_i \wedge b_i \simeq a_{i+1}) \\ \vee \ (a_i \simeq c_i \wedge c_i \simeq a_{i+1}) \\ \vee \ (a_i \simeq d_i \wedge d_i \simeq a_{i+1}) \end{array} \right] \ . \tag{13.11}$$

The Join rule is ineffective at finding short proofs for this and many other cases.

Following the style of dynamic Ackermann reduction we can formulate a rule that does introduce useful lemmas and literals for such cases. We call the rule Dyn. Trans:

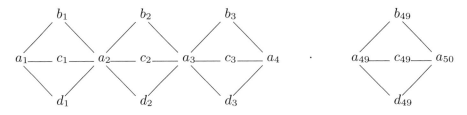

Figure 13.4 Double Diamond equalities

Dyn. Trans $\quad M \parallel F \parallel C \Longrightarrow$
$$M \parallel F, (u \simeq v \wedge v \simeq w \to u \simeq w) \parallel C \qquad u \not\simeq v, v \not\simeq w \in C \ .$$

13.10 Conflict Directed Equality Resolution

We have identified two problems with DPLL(*UF*) where it is unable to find short proofs, and we have presented two rules Dyn. Trans and Dyn. Cong$^\sharp$ that overcome the problems. They introduce new literals, but use a throttle based on conflict resolution to limit the set of new literals. How effective are our additions to DPLL(*UF*)?

To characterize it, we will recall an unrestricted calculus for equality resolution, called E-Res. The purpose of this section is to establish that

$$\text{E-Res} \equiv_p \text{DPLL}(UF) + \text{Dyn. Cong}^\sharp + \text{Dyn. Trans}.$$

In other words, DPLL(*UF*) augmented with the two rules for dynamically adding clauses *p*-simulates resolution style proof systems for quantifier-free equality.

Figure 13.5 shows a ground E-resolution calculus, E-Res. In contrast to super-position calculi for non-ground clauses there are no ordering filters to reduce the set of rule applications. The rules can be applied without ordering filters. This makes the proof system more liberal than ordered super-position calculi, the search space is much bigger, but it admits proofs where the ordered version requires exponential more space [3].

13.10.1 Analysis

Our plan is to simulate E-Res. We first establish that every literal used in an E-Res proof can be produced using a polynomial overhead using the calculus obtained from using congruence closure as a theory solver + Dyn. Cong$^\sharp$ + Dyn. Trans. We call this calculus CDER (for conflict directed equality

$$\text{Sup } \frac{C \ \vee \ a \simeq b \qquad D \ \vee \ \ell[a]}{C \ \vee \ D \ \vee \ \ell[b]} \qquad \text{Res } \frac{C \ \vee \ \ell \qquad D \ \vee \ \bar{\ell}}{C \vee D}$$

$$\text{E-Dis } \frac{C \ \vee \ a \not\simeq a}{C} \qquad \text{Factor } \frac{C \ \vee \ \ell \ \vee \ \ell}{C \ \vee \ \ell} \qquad \text{E-Eqs } \frac{C \ \vee \ a \simeq b \ \vee \ a \simeq c}{C \ \vee \ a \simeq b \ \vee \ b \not\simeq c}$$

Figure 13.5 **E-Res**: Ground E-resolution calculus

resolution). Our results will be established relative to an assumption that is required for our analysis:

Assumption 13.10 *Every derivation in* E-Res *using only unit clauses can be produced as a T-Conflict by CDER.*

In other words, whenever there is an E-Res proof of a conflict using a set of equalities and one disequality, then that same set, and not a subset, is produced by CDER as a conflict clause. Second, we establish that every E-Res proof can be converted into a propositional resolution proof with at most a polynomial overhead. Third, we apply already established results on how DPLL+CL+Restarts p-simulate unrestricted resolution. The relevant propositions are summarized as follows:

Proposition 13.11 Given an E-Res proof Π, then every literal that occurs in Π can be produced from either the input clauses Δ or using a polynomial number of applications of CDER deriving clauses Δ' that imply the additional literals.

Proposition 13.12 Given an E-Res proof Π, there is a proof Π' of size polynomial in Π whose support is $\Delta \cup \Delta'$ that uses only resolution.

Proposition 13.13 ([36]) For any asserting scheme, DPLL+CL+Restarts p-simulates unrestricted resolution.

Let us note that these results rely on heuristics for controlling variable splitting, restarts and when to apply the resolution rules for guiding the proof search. Searching for proofs is still hard in worst case [1].

We will now establish the first two propositions. Let Π be an E-Res proof of the empty clause, then we will establish that every literal that occurs in a clause Π is eventually removed. Let Π' be a sub-tree of Π that introduces the literal ℓ (there could be more than one, but we can consider one at a time). We will first establish that for an inference rule that introduces a fresh literal in Π there is a sequence of theory conflict resolution steps that (1) produce the new literal, (2) allow replacing the inference rule by propositional resolution. In this context consider the rules Res and E-Dis as the ones that are responsible for removing literals. Given an inference with sub-tree Π' we will define a *core* set of literals that can be used to produce the literal introduced by Π'.

Definition 13.14 (Literal core)   Given a sub-tree Π', define:

$$core\,(\pi, \ell, \Pi)_{\Pi'} = \emptyset \quad \text{if } \Pi = \Pi' \,.$$

Otherwise,

$$core\left(\pi, \ell, \ \frac{C \in \Delta}{C}\right)_{\Pi'} = \{\pi\ell\}$$

$$core\left(\pi, \ell[b], \ \frac{C \ \vee \ a \simeq b \quad\quad D \ \vee \ \ell[a]}{C \ \vee \ D \ \vee \ \ell[b]}\right)_{\Pi'} =$$

$$core\left(+, a \simeq b, \ \frac{\Pi_1}{C \ \vee \ a \simeq b}\right)_{\Pi'} \cup \ core\left(\pi, \ell[a], \ \frac{\Pi_2}{D \ \vee \ \ell[a]}\right)_{\Pi'}$$

$$core\left(+, b \not\simeq c, \ \frac{C \ \vee \ a \simeq b \ \vee \ a \simeq c}{C \ \vee \ a \simeq b \ \vee \ b \not\simeq c}\right)_{\Pi'} =$$

$$\begin{aligned}core\left(+, a \simeq b, \ \frac{\Pi}{C \ \vee \ a \simeq b \ \vee \ a \simeq c}\right)_{\Pi'} \cup \\ core\left(-, a \simeq c, \ \frac{\Pi}{C \ \vee \ a \simeq b \ \vee \ a \simeq c}\right)_{\Pi'}\end{aligned}$$

$$core\left(\pi, \ell, \ \frac{\Pi_1 \quad\quad \Pi_2}{\ell \ \vee \ C}\right)_{\Pi'} = \begin{aligned}(core\,(\pi, \ell, \Pi_1)_{\Pi'} \ | \ \ell \in \Pi_1) \\ \cup \ (core\,(\pi, \ell, \Pi_2)_{\Pi'} \ | \ \ell \in \Pi_2)\end{aligned}$$

$$core\left(\pi, \ell, \ \frac{\dfrac{\Pi}{\ell \ \vee \ D}}{\ell \ \vee \ C}\right)_{\Pi'} = core\left(\pi, \ell, \ \frac{\Pi}{\ell \ \vee \ D}\right)_{\Pi'} \,.$$

Finally, let:

$$trail\left(\frac{\dfrac{\Pi_1}{C \vee \ell} \quad\quad \dfrac{\Pi_2}{D \vee \bar\ell}}{C \vee D}\right)_{\Pi'} =$$

$$core\left(+, \ell, \frac{\Pi_1}{C \vee \ell}\right)_{\Pi'} \cup core\left(+, \bar\ell, \frac{\Pi_2}{D \vee \bar\ell}\right)_{\Pi'}$$

$$trail\left(\frac{\dfrac{\Pi}{C \vee a \not\simeq a}}{C}\right)_{\Pi'} = core\left(+, a \not\simeq a, \ \frac{\Pi}{C \vee a \not\simeq a}\right)_{\Pi'} \,.$$

Note that the rules for the ground resolution calculus introduce literals. The rule Sup introduces the literal $\ell[b]$ and rule E-Eqs introduces the literal $b \not\simeq c$. A derivation Π' that ends with Sup introduces the literal $\ell[b]$. A derivation Π' that ends with E-Eqs introduces the literal $b \not\simeq c$.

Lemma 13.15   *Let ℓ be the literal introduced by the rule Π' and let Π be the corresponding descendant of Π' that eliminates ℓ. The computation of* $\mathrm{trail}\,(\Pi)_{\Pi'}$ *consists of recursive calls of the form* $\mathrm{core}\,(\pi, \ell', \Pi'')_{\Pi'}$. *For any such recursive call:*

$$\bigwedge \mathrm{core}\,(\pi, \ell', \Pi'')_{\Pi'} \wedge \ell \to \pi\ell' \ .$$

Proof   The proof proceeds by induction over the calls to *core* with measure $|\Pi|$. Let us illustrate the base cases and one case of induction. The first base case is $\bigwedge \mathrm{core}\,(\pi, \ell, \Pi')_{\Pi'} \wedge \ell \to \ell$, since $\bigwedge \mathrm{core}\,(\pi, \ell, \Pi')_{\Pi'} = \bigwedge \emptyset = \mathit{true}$. The second base case is when $\mathrm{core}\left(\pi, \ell', \dfrac{C \in \Delta}{C}\right)_{\Pi'} = \{\pi\ell'\}$. In this case the implication we need to establish is $\pi\ell' \wedge \ell \to \pi\ell'$. Now consider E-Eqs as an example,

$$\bigwedge \mathrm{core}\left(+, a \simeq b, \ \dfrac{\Pi}{C \vee a \simeq b \vee a \simeq c}\right)_{\Pi'} \wedge \ell \to a \simeq b$$

$$\bigwedge \mathrm{core}\left(-, a \simeq c, \ \dfrac{\Pi}{C \vee a \simeq b \vee a \simeq c}\right)_{\Pi'} \wedge \ell \to a \not\simeq c \ .$$

The conjunction of the two premises imply that $b \not\simeq c$, which is what the lemma requires. $\square$

Lemma 13.16   *For every literal ℓ introduced by the rule Π' there is a descendant Π such that*

$$\ell, \mathrm{trail}\,(\Pi)_{\Pi'} \vdash \mathit{false} \ .$$

Furthermore, if $\ell = \ell[b]$, $\Pi' = \dfrac{\begin{array}{cc} \Pi_1 & \Pi_2 \\ C \vee a \simeq b & D \vee \ell[a] \end{array}}{C \vee D \vee \ell[b]}$, *then*

$$a \simeq b, \ell[a], \mathrm{trail}\,(\Pi)_{\Pi'} \vdash \mathit{false}$$

and if $\ell = b \not\simeq c$, $\Pi' = \dfrac{\begin{array}{c} \Pi_1 \\ C \vee a \simeq b \vee a \simeq c \end{array}}{C \vee a \simeq b \vee b \not\simeq c}$, *then*

$$a \simeq b, \ a \not\simeq c, \mathrm{trail}\,(\Pi)_{\Pi'} \vdash \mathit{false} \ .$$

Proof   We first establish that $\ell \wedge \bigwedge \mathrm{trail}\,(\Pi)_{\Pi'} \to \mathit{false}$, by unfolding the definition of *trail*. Lemma 13.15 implies that

$$\ell \wedge \bigwedge \mathrm{core}\left(+, \ell', \dfrac{\Pi_1}{C \vee \ell'}\right)_{\Pi'} \wedge \bigwedge \mathrm{core}\left(+, \overline{\ell'}, \dfrac{\Pi_2}{D \vee \overline{\ell'}}\right)_{\Pi'} \to \ell' \wedge \neg \ell'$$

and that

$$\ell \wedge \bigwedge \mathrm{core}\left(+, a \not\simeq a, \ \dfrac{\Pi}{C \vee a \not\simeq a}\right)_{\Pi'} \to a \not\simeq a \ .$$

The antecedents are contradictory in both cases. The two other claims in the lemma follow because $\ell[b]$ is implied by $a \simeq b, \ell[b]$ and $b \not\simeq c$ is implied by $a \simeq b, a \not\simeq c$. $\qquad\square$

Lemma 13.16 implies that literals that are introduced by the rules Sup and E-Eqs participate in an E-conflict. Proposition 13.11 is a consequence of lemmas 13.15 and 13.16. We can now prove the next proposition.

Proof of Proposition 13.12 Let us consider the inference rules that introduce new literals and rewrite the inferences to propositional resolution modulo lemmas produced from theory resolution.

Sup rewrites one side of an equality (the literal $\ell[a]$ is of the form $a \simeq c$ for some term c):

$$\frac{C \vee a \simeq b \qquad D \vee a \simeq c}{C \vee D \vee b \simeq c} \longmapsto$$

$$\frac{C \vee a \simeq b \qquad \dfrac{a \simeq b \wedge a \simeq c \rightarrow b \simeq c \qquad D \vee a \simeq c}{D \vee a \not\simeq b \vee b \simeq c}}{C \vee D \vee b \simeq c} \cdot$$

The required lemma $a \simeq b \wedge a \simeq c \rightarrow b \simeq c$ is produced by theory resolution from the conflict that includes the two premises $a \simeq b$ and $a \simeq c$.

Sup rewrites a nested occurrence of a in a term that occurs in an equality or disequality:

$$\frac{C \vee a \simeq b \qquad D \vee t[a] \simeq s}{C \vee D \vee t[b] \simeq s} \longmapsto$$

$$\frac{C \vee a \simeq b \qquad \dfrac{a \simeq b \rightarrow t[a] \simeq t[b] \qquad D \vee t[a] \simeq s}{D \vee a \not\simeq b \vee t[b] \simeq s}}{C \vee D \vee t[b] \simeq s}$$

$$\frac{C \vee a \simeq b \qquad D \vee t[a] \not\simeq s}{C \vee D \vee t[b] \not\simeq s} \longmapsto$$

$$\frac{C \vee a \simeq b \qquad \dfrac{a \simeq b \rightarrow t[a] \simeq t[b] \qquad D \vee t[a] \not\simeq s}{D \vee a \not\simeq b \vee t[b] \not\simeq s}}{C \vee D \vee t[b] \not\simeq s}$$

Suppose $t[a]$ is of the form $f(f(a))$, then we can apply congruence in two stages. First by introducing the clause

$$f(a) \simeq f(b) \rightarrow f(f(a)) \simeq f(f(b))$$

the second time the literal $f(a) \simeq f(b)$ is used in a conflict core, and then we introduce the implication

$$a \simeq b \;\rightarrow\; f(a) \simeq f(b) \;.$$

This restricted way of applying congruence corresponds to the rule Dyn. Cong$^{\sharp}$.

Sup applied to an atomic disequality. The remaining Sup case we have not handled is inferences of the form:

$$\frac{C \;\vee\; a \simeq b \qquad D \;\vee\; a \not\simeq c}{C \;\vee\; D \;\vee\; b \not\simeq c} \;.$$

There is no version of Dyn. Trans that allows learning lemmas of the form

$$a \simeq b \;\wedge\; a \not\simeq c \;\rightarrow\; b \not\simeq c \;.$$

We show that this rule is not necessary, by examining the inference steps that involve $b \not\simeq c$ in the proof tree below. Let us first examine the case where the derivation has the form:

$$\frac{\dfrac{C \;\vee\; a \simeq b \qquad D \;\vee\; a \not\simeq c}{C \;\vee\; D \;\vee\; b \not\simeq c}}{}$$

$$\frac{E \vee b \simeq d \qquad \dfrac{\vdots}{F \vee b \not\simeq c'}}{E \vee F \vee d \not\simeq c'}$$

In this case $a \simeq b \wedge a \not\simeq c \wedge b \simeq d \wedge trail\,(\Pi)_{\Pi'}$ is a theory conflict, where Π' is the derivation snippet given above. Rule Dyn. Trans lets us learn the clause $a \simeq b \wedge b \simeq d \rightarrow a \simeq d$, and we can rewrite the derivation to:

$$\frac{\dfrac{C \;\vee\; a \simeq b \qquad a \simeq b \wedge b \simeq d \rightarrow a \simeq d}{C \vee b \not\simeq d \vee a \simeq d} \qquad D \;\vee\; a \not\simeq c}{C \;\vee\; D \;\vee\; b \not\simeq d \vee d \not\simeq c}$$

$$\frac{E \vee b \simeq d \qquad \dfrac{\vdots}{F \;\vee\; b \not\simeq d \vee d \not\simeq c'}}{E \;\vee\; F \vee d \not\simeq c'}$$

The transformation is similar if the next inference that rewrites b modifies a proper sub-term of it.

E-Eqs also introduces a disequality literal. We can push applications of this rule down in the derivation tree using the following transformation:

$$\frac{C \vee a \simeq b \vee a \simeq c}{C \vee a \simeq b \vee b \not\simeq c}$$

$$\vdots$$

$$\frac{E \vee b \simeq d \qquad \overline{F \vee b \not\simeq c'}}{E \vee F \vee d \not\simeq c'}$$

$\longmapsto$

$$\frac{E \vee b \simeq d \qquad a \simeq d \wedge b \simeq d \rightarrow a \simeq b}{E \vee a \simeq b \vee a \not\simeq d} \qquad \frac{E \vee b \simeq d \qquad C \vee a \simeq b \vee a \simeq c}{\dfrac{E \vee C \vee a \simeq d \vee a \simeq c}{E \vee C \vee a \simeq d \vee d \not\simeq c}}}{E \vee C \vee a \simeq b \vee d \not\simeq c}$$

$$\vdots$$

$$\overline{E \vee F \vee d \not\simeq c'}$$

The transformation requires the clause $b \simeq d \wedge a \simeq d \rightarrow a \simeq b$. It can be learned using Dyn. Trans by first learning $b \simeq d \wedge a \simeq b \rightarrow a \simeq d$, as the original derivation ensures that $b \simeq d \wedge a \simeq b$ participate in a conflict. Then the helpful clause is learned from theory propagation on the assignment $b \simeq d \wedge a \simeq d$.   □

Lemma 13.16 makes use of Assumption 13.10. The derivation below introduces redundant literals $c \simeq d$ and $b \simeq d$.

$$\frac{a \simeq b \quad \dfrac{b \simeq c \quad \dfrac{a \simeq d \quad c \simeq a}{c \simeq d}}{b \simeq d}}{a \simeq d} \qquad f(a) \not\simeq f(d)}{\dfrac{f(d) \not\simeq f(d)}{\bot}}$$

Our proof does not let us disregard such non-minimal derivations. Hence, the working assumption on the theory solver for equalities is that it admits arbitrary equality conflicts, including non-minimal ones. This is in contrast to how efficient congruence closure-based equality solvers work. They seek minimal conflicts. It is an open problem to strengthen the results to equality solvers that perform theory resolution based on a minimal unsatisfiable set of literals. We conjecture that CDER still p-simulates E-Res even when congruence produces only minimal conflicts.

13.11 Conclusions

We exemplified how modern SMT solvers combine algorithms for tractable sub-problems in a framework that addresses intractable problem domains.

An important theme is to harness the size of the problem, since the search space grows exponentially in the problem size. A common trait in many methods was to delay polynomial space increase based on properties of the search and partial models (for model-based theory combination). In this context we examined a method for the *UF* theory that can find short proofs in many cases at the expense of introducing new literals. The new literals are introduced based on an analysis of theory conflicts. We took a proof theoretic perspective and compared the strength of the method relative to general unrestricted resolution proof systems. The main point is that the two proof systems are equally succinct.

Conflict Directed Theory Resolution is a general concept. The high-level point is to integrate theory resolution steps as part of the conflict analysis already performed by the DPLL(T) engine. We analyzed it only in the context of *UF*. With a reduction approach to theory solving, we noticed that A, D, CAL all reduce to *UF*, so an efficient *UF* solver is helpful in all these theories. It is fairly straightforward to use the same ideas for conflict directed theory resolution for difference logic (example 13.2). The situation is more complex for LRA and especially LIA where also proof rules for cutting planes are needed [26].

References

[1] Michael Alekhnovich and Alexander A. Razborov. 2008. Resolution is not automatizable unless w[p] is tractable. *SIAM J. Comput.*, **38**(4), 1347–1363.

[2] Paul Beame, Henry A. Kautz, and Ashish Sabharwal. 2004. Towards understanding and harnessing the potential of clause learning. *J. Artif. Intell. Res.*, **22**, 319–351.

[3] Nikolaj Bjørner, Bruno Dutertre, and Leonardo de Moura. 2008. Accelerating DPLL(T) using joins – DPLL(⊔). Short paper in: *LPAR 08*.

[4] Roberto Bruttomesso, Alessandro Cimatti, Anders Franzén, Alberto Griggio, Alessandro Santuari, and Roberto Sebastiani. 2006. To Ackermann-ize or not to Ackermann-ize? On efficiently handling uninterpreted function symbols in *UF*($\mathcal{E}$). Pages 557–571 of: *LPAR 06*.

[5] Randal E. Bryant, Steven German, and Miroslav N. Velev. 1999. Exploiting positive equality in a logic of equality with uninterpreted functions. Pages 470–482 of: *Computer-Aided Verification*, LNCS **1633**.

[6] Randal E. Bryant, Steven German, and Miroslav N. Velev. 2001. Processor verification using efficient reductions of the logic of uninterpreted functions to propositional logic. *ACM Transactions on Computational Logic*, **2**(1), 1–41.

[7] Samuel R. Buss, Jan Hoffmann, and Jan Johannsen. 2008. Resolution trees with lemmas: Resolution refinements that characterize dll algorithms with clause learning. *CoRR*, abs/0811.1075.

[8] George E. Collins. Quantifier elimination for real closed fields by cylindrical algebraic decomposition. 1975. Pages 134–183 of: *Automata Theory and Formal Languages, 2nd GI Conference*, H. Brakhage (ed). LNCS **33**.

[9] Martin Davis, George Logemann, and Donald Loveland. 1962. A machine program for theorem proving. *Communications of the ACM*, **5**, 394–397.

[10] Leonardo de Moura and Nikolaj Bjørner. 2007. Efficient E-matching for SMT solvers. Pages 183–198 of: *Automated Deduction – CADE-21*, LNCS **4603**.

[11] Leonardo de Moura and Nikolaj Bjørner. 2007. Relevancy propagation. Microsoft Research, Tech. Rep. MSR-TR-2007-140.

[12] Leonardo de Moura and Nikolaj Bjørner. 2008. Model-based theory combination. *Electr. Notes Theor. Comput. Sci.*, **198**(2), 37–49.

[13] Leonardo de Moura and Nikolaj Bjørner. 2008. Z3: An efficient SMT solver. Pages 337–340 of: *TACAS 2008*, LNCS **4963**.

[14] Leonardo de Moura and Nikolaj Bjørner. 2009. Efficient, generalized array decision procedures. Pages 45–52 of: *FMCAD 2009*.

[15] Leonardo de Moura and Nikolaj Bjørner. Bugs, moles and skeletons: symbolic reasoning for software development. 2010. Pages 400–411 of: *Automated Reasoning, IJCAR 2010*, LNCS, **6173**.

[16] Leonardo de Moura and Nikolaj Bjørner. 2011. Satisfiability modulo theories: introduction and applications. *Communications of the ACM*, **54**, 69–77.

[17] David Detlefs, Greg Nelson, and James B. Saxe. 2005. Simplify: a theorem prover for program checking. *J. ACM*, **52**(3), 365–473.

[18] Peter J. Downey, Ravi Sethi, and Robert E. Tarjan. 1980. Variations on the common subexpression problem. *J. ACM*, **27**(4), 758–771.

[19] Bruno Dutertre and Leonardo de Moura. 2006. A fast linear-arithmetic solver for DPLL(T). Pages 81–94 of: *CAV'06*, LNCS **4144**.

[20] Bruno Dutertre and Leonardo de Moura. 2006. The Yices SMT solver. http://yices.csl.sri.com/tool-paper.pdf.

[21] Harald Ganzinger, George Hagen, Robert Nieuwenhuis, Albert Oliveras, and Cesare Tinelli. 2004. DPLL(T): Fast decision procedures. Pages 175–188 of: *CAV'04*, LNCS **3144**.

[22] Michael R. Garey and David S. Johnson. 1979. *Computers and Intractability: A Guide to the Theory of NP-Completeness*. W.H. Freeman.

[23] Patrice Godefroid, Jonathan de Halleux, Aditya V. Nori, Sriram K. Rajamani, Wolfram Schulte, Nikolai Tillmann, and Michael Y. Levin. 2008. Automating software testing using program analysis. *IEEE Software*, **25**(5), 30–37.

[24] Philipp Hertel, Fahiem Bacchus, Toniann Pitassi, and Allen Van Gelder. 2008. Clause learning can effectively P-simulate general propositional resolution. Pages 283–290 of: *AAAI'08: Proceedings of the 23rd National Conference on Artificial Intelligence*, Volume 1.

[25] Lars Hörmander. 1983. *The Analysis of Linear Partial Differential Operators II*. Grundlehren der Mathematischen Wissenschaften, **257**, Springer.

[26] Dejan Jovanovic and Leonardo de Moura. 2011. Cutting to the chase solving linear integer arithmetic. Pages 338–353 of: *Automated Deduction – CADE-23*, LNCS **6803**.

[27] Deepak Kapur and Calogero G. Zarba. 2005. A reduction approach to decision procedures. University of New Mexico Tech. Rep. TR-CS-1005-44.

[28] Karl Lieberherr. 1977. Complexity of superresolution. *Notices of the American Mathematical Society*, **24**, A-433.

[29] Anatoli Ivanovic Malcev. 1971. Axiomatizable classes of locally free algebras of various types. In *Studies in Logic and the Foundations of Mathematics*, **66**, 262–281.

[30] Yuri Matiyashevich. 1996. Hilbert's 10th problem: What can we do with Diophantine equations?
`logic.pdmi.ras.ru/Hilbert10/journal/preprints/H10histe.ps`

[31] John McCarthy. 1962. Towards a mathematical science of computation. Pages 21–28 of: *Proceedings of IFIP Congress 1962*, North-Holland.

[32] Orly Meir and Ofer Strichman. 2005. Yet another decision procedure for equality logic. Pages 307–320 of: *Computer Aided Verification, CAV 2005*, LNCS **3576**.

[33] Robert Nieuwenhuis and Albert Oliveras. 2007. Fast congruence closure and extensions. *Inf. Comput.*, **205**(4), 557–580.

[34] Derek C. Oppen. 1980. Complexity, convexity and combinations of theories. *Theor. Comput. Sci.*, **12**, 291–302.

[35] Derek C. Oppen. 1980. Reasoning about recursively defined data structures. *J. ACM*, **27**(3), 403–411.

[36] Knot Pipatsrisawat and Adnan Darwiche. 2011. On the power of clause-learning sat solvers as resolution engines. *Artif. Intell.*, **175**(2), 512–525.

[37] Mirron Rozanov and Ofer Strichman. 2007. Generating minimum transitivity constraints in P-time for deciding equality logic. *Electr. Notes Theor. Comput. Sci.*, **198**, 3–17.

[38] Alexander Schrijver. 1986. *Theory of Linear and Integer Programming*. Wiley.

[39] Alexander Schrijver. 2003. *Combinatorial Optimization*, volume 24 of *Algorithms and Combinatorics*. Springer-Verlag. In 3 volumes.

[40] Mary Sheeran and Gunnar Stålmarck. 2000. A tutorial on Stålmarck's proof procedure for propositional logic. *Formal Methods in System Design*, **16**(1), 23–58.

[41] João P. Marques Silva and Karem A. Sakallah. 1996. Grasp – a new search algorithm for satisfiability. Pages 220–227 of: *ICCAD '96 Proceedings of the 1996 IEEE/ACM International Conference on Computer-Aided Design*.

[42] Richard M. Stallman and Gerald J. Sussman. 1977. Forward reasoning and dependency-directed backtracking in a system for computer-aided circuit analysis. *Artif. Intell.*, **9**(2), 135–196.